MW00630046

Hungary's Cold War

The New Cold War History

Odd Arne Westad, editor

This series focuses on new interpretations of the Cold War era made possible by the opening of Soviet, East European, Chinese, and other archives. Books in the series based on multilingual and multiarchival research incorporate interdisciplinary insights and new conceptual frameworks that place historical scholarship in a broad, international context.

A complete list of books published in The New Cold War History is available at www.uncpress.org.

Hungary's Cold War

International Relations from the End of World War II to the Fall of the Soviet Union

CSABA BÉKÉS

The University of North Carolina Press
Chapel Hill

© 2022 The University of North Carolina Press
All rights reserved
Set in Minion Pro by Westchester Publishing Services
Manufactured in the United States of America

The University of North Carolina Press has been a member of the
Green Press Initiative since 2003.

Library of Congress Cataloging-in-Publication Data
Names: Békés, Csaba, author.
Title: Hungary's Cold War : international relations from the end of World War II
   to the fall of the Soviet Union / Csaba Békés.
Other titles: New Cold War history.
Description: Chapel Hill : The University of North Carolina Press, [2022] |
   Series: The new Cold War history | Includes bibliographical references and index.
Identifiers: LCCN 2021046315 | ISBN 9781469667478 (cloth) | ISBN 9781469667485
   (paperback) | ISBN 9781469667492 (ebook)
Subjects: LCSH: Cold War. | Hungary—Foreign relations—Communist countries. |
   Communist countries—Foreign relations—Hungary. | Hungary—Foreign
   relations—Europe, Western. | Europe, Western—Foreign relations—Hungary. |
   Hungary—Foreign relations—United States. | United States—Foreign
   relations—Hungary.
Classification: LCC DB956.4 .B44 2022 | DDC 909.82/5—dc23/eng/20211012
LC record available at https://lccn.loc.gov/2021046315

Portions of this book were previously published in a different form and are used here
with permission. Chapter 3 appeared as "East Central Europe, 1953–1956," in *The
Cambridge History of the Cold War*, ed. Melvyn Leffler and Odd Arne Westad, vol. 1,
Origins (Cambridge: Cambridge University Press, 2010), 334–52. Chapter 4 appeared
as "The 1956 Hungarian Revolution and the Declaration of Neutrality," *Cold War
History* 6, no. 4 (November 2006): 477–500. Chapter 6 appeared as "Cold War,
Détente and the Soviet Bloc: The Evolution of Intra-bloc Foreign Policy
Coordination, 1953–1975," in *Imposing, Maintaining, and Tearing Open the Iron
Curtain: The Cold War and East-Central Europe, 1945–1989*, ed. Mark Kramer and
Vit Smetana (Lanham, Md.: Lexington Books, 2014), 247–78. Chapter 8 appeared as
(partly) "The Warsaw Pact and the Helsinki Process, 1965–1970," in *The Making of
Détente: Eastern and Western Europe in the Cold War, 1965–75*, ed. Wilfried Loth and
Georges-Henri Soutou (London: Routledge, 2008), 201–20; and "Hungary, the Soviet
Bloc, the German Question and the CSCE Process, 1965–1975," *Journal of Cold War
Studies* 18, no. 3 (Summer 2016): 95–138. Chapter 9 appeared (partly) as "Détente and
the Soviet Bloc, 1975–1991," in *The "Long 1970s": Human Rights, East–West Détente,
and Transnational Relations*, ed. Rasmus Mariager, Helle Porsdam, and Poul Villaume
(London: Routledge, 2016), 165–83; and "The Long Détente and the Soviet Bloc,
1953–1983," in *The Long Détente: Changing Concepts of Security and Cooperation in
Europe, 1950s–1980s*, ed. Oliver Bange and Poul Villaume (Budapest: Central European
University Press, 2017), 31–49. Chapter 10 and 11 appeared as "Back to Europe:
The International Context of the Political Transition in Hungary, 1988–1990," in *The
Roundtable Talks of 1989: The Genesis of Hungarian Democracy*, ed. András Bozóki
(Budapest: CEU Press, 2002), 237–72.

For my wife Melinda and our son Gáspár

Contents

Abbreviations

ÁVH	Államvédelmi Hatóság (State Protection Authority)
CC	Central Committee
CCP	Chinese Communist Party
CDU/CSU	Christian Democratic Union of Germany (CDU) / Christian Social Union in Bavaria (CSU)
CENTO	Central Treaty Organization
CIA	Central Intelligence Agency
COCOM	Coordinating Committee for Multilateral Export Controls
Comecon	Council of Mutual Economic Assistance
Cominform	Information Bureau of the Communist and Workers' Parties
Comintern	Communist International
CPCz	Communist Party of Czechoslovakia
CPs	Communist parties
CPSU	Communist Party of the Soviet Union
cs.	csoport (group)
CSCE	Conference on Security and Cooperation in Europe
CWIHP	*Cold War International History Project,* Woodrow Wilson International Center for Scholars, Washington D.C.
DDF	Documents Diplomatiques Français
DEM	Deutsche Mark (German mark)
EDC	European Defense Community
EEC	European Economic Community
f.	fond (collection)
FO	Foreign Office
FRG	Federal Republic of Germany
FRUS	Foreign Relations of the United States
GDR	German Democratic Republic
HCP	Hungarian Communist Party

HUF	Hungarian Forint
HWP	Hungarian Workers' Party
IMF	International Monetary Fund
INF	Intermediate-Range Nuclear Forces Treaty
KGB	Komitet gosudarstvennoy bezopasnosti (Committee for State Security)
KÜM	Külügyminisztérium (Ministry of Foreign Affairs, Hungary)
MAORT	Magyar–Amerikai Olajipari RT. (Hungarian–American Oil Company)
MNF	multilateral nuclear force
MNL–OL	Magyar Nemzeti Levéltár—Országos Levéltára (National Archives of Hungary)
Montanunion	European Coal and Steel Community (ECSC)
MSZMP	Magyar Szocialista Munkáspárt (Hungarian Socialist Workers' Party)
NATO	North Atlantic Treaty Organization
NPP	National Peasant Party
NSC	National Security Council
ő. e.	őrzési egység (archival unit)
PC	Political Committee
PCC	Political Consultative Committee
PHP	Parallel History Project on Cooperative Security
PIL	Politikatörténeti Intézet Levéltára (Archives of the Institute for Political History, Budapest)
PRO	Public Records Office, London
RG	Record Group
SDI	Strategic Defense Initiative
SDP	Social Democratic Party
SEATO	Southeast Asia Treaty Organization
SED	Sozialistische Einheitspartei Deutschlands (Socialist Unity Party of Germany)
SHP	Smallholders' Party
SIOP	Single Integrated Operational Plan
TÜK	Titkos ügykezelés (secret document handling)

UN	United Nations Organization
US	United States of America
USSR	Union of Soviet Socialist Republics
WP	Warsaw Pact

Hungary's Cold War

Introduction

This volume is largely the product of the archival revolution that began in 1989 with the collapse of the Communist regimes in East Central Europe. This historic transformation basically coincided with my becoming a full-time researcher in 1991, when I joined the newly founded 1956 Institute in Budapest, dedicated to the research of the history of the Hungarian revolt. Ever since, the focus of my interest has been the role that Hungary and other non-Soviet countries of the Soviet bloc played in shaping East–West relations from the beginning to the end of the Cold War. For me it became gradually obvious, as I had a chance to examine the once top-secret documents of the highest decision-making level on each side of the Cold War divide during the first half of the 1990s, that this role was much more serious than it had been generally assumed at the time.

My career was immensely affected by my becoming one of the first research fellows of the Wilson Center's Cold War International History Project (CWIHP) in Washington, D.C., in the fall of 1992. It was truly a life-changing experience that made me part of the then emerging international group of younger-generation researchers of new Cold War history. At CWIHP and the National Security Archive—another key institution of Cold War research in Washington—I established lifelong cooperation from and friendships with excellent scholars like Tom Blanton, Malcolm Byrne, Jim Hershberg, Christian Ostermann, Svetlana Savranskaya, and Vladislav Zubok. The intensive international cooperation unfolding in the mid-late 1990s, including participation at numerous conferences, was a great impetus for my work, driving me to establish the Cold War History Research Center, Budapest, in December 1998, as the first nongovernmental organization in the former Soviet bloc dedicated to Cold War research.

Another wave of great experiences came from 2001 to 2002, when I spent a whole academic year at New York University's International Center for Advanced Studies as one of the five center fellows of the Project on the Cold War as a Global Conflict. Here the project head, the late Marilyn B. Young, was a wonderful mentor even long after the end of the program, while the extensive and intensive conversations with my co-fellows, especially Odd Arne Westad and Mario del Pero, gave me great professional inspiration. This was followed by my teaching Cold War history at NYU as a Fulbright visiting professor in 2006–7, while from the fall of 2007 I have been a recurring visiting professor teaching East European Cold War history at Columbia University. During the five semesters spent at Columbia so far, I developed an exceptional professional relationship with István Deák, the former head of the East Central European Center, after whom the position is named, who has become a mentor and a friend as well.

This book is a synthesis of my thirty years of research and findings. The most important result was not only a so far little-known history of the Soviet bloc's international relations; my investigations also led to numerous theoretical innovations. Therefore, this unusual introduction will not give the reader a broad overview of the content of the book; rather, it will focus on presenting some twenty theoretical innovations and the same number of novel interpretations and discoveries I have developed so far in the field of Cold War history. Research funding for this book in the past decade as well as support for finalizing its manuscript was provided by the Centre for Social Sciences in Budapest.

––––––––

In the early Cold War era, I find that Churchill's infamous "percentage agreement" with Stalin in October 1944 was nothing more than a game played by Churchill, which had only one real goal: warning Stalin that the Red Army, at that moment already occupying Romania and Bulgaria, should not try to become an occupying power in Greece as well, as that would be done by Britain alone. I have drawn attention to a very important but generally overlooked factor: an armistice agreement was concluded between Hungary and the Allies in Moscow on 11 October 1944, and of course Churchill knew about it. Thus, right at the time of the Stalin-Churchill meeting, it could be realistically expected that the eastern front would very soon be moved abruptly to the middle of Hungary, where the Red Army would fight the Germans supported by the Romanian, Bulgarian, and Hungarian armies. This scenario would imply a fast westward movement of the eastern front, with the Soviets possibly reaching Austria by the end of 1944. Thus, Churchill had to reckon with the fact that basically all the East Central European countries would be liberated and occupied by Soviet troops in a relatively very short period of time. In this light, all the "agreed on" percentages for the countries of the region other than Greece cannot be taken seriously.

Investigating Stalin's expansionist plans in the postwar years, I argue that he looked upon those endeavors as seizing a never-returning opportunity. After the end of World War II, the Soviet Union's position and international prestige increased to an unimagined extent due to the performance of the Soviet Army, and it seemed logical to Stalin to assert his country's interests to the full through the postwar peace settlement. He also assumed that, like the post–World War I settlement, it would be reached in a couple of years, so a lot could be attempted in that time—and what could be attempted, should be. While this rather flexible attitude showed Stalin's actual intentions, in Western perception all these endeavors appeared as real, aggressively intended expansionist efforts, and thus they became major escalating elements in the emerging confrontation, despite Stalin's original intentions. This issue also shows the important role of perception and misperception in the emerging conflict between East and West, as suggested by Robert Jervis.

As for the long-debated issue of the Sovietization of East Central Europe, I argue that this was neither a cause nor a consequence of the emerging Cold War. My research also shows that the Sovietization process started as early as 1944 and the local Communist parties of all the countries of the region were already in a commanding position as early as 1945–46 in the whole region. Therefore, I have proposed to use a novel categorization: *quasi-Sovietized* countries (Albania, Bulgaria, Poland, Romania, and Yugoslavia) and *pre-Sovietized* states (Hungary and Czechoslovakia).

I also interpret the gradual Sovietization of the region as a tacit gesture by Stalin to the Western great powers—especially the United States, with whom he wanted to maintain cooperation for as long as possible. He knew that in Western democracies, public opinion was an important factor in decision-making, so he offered a *tacit deal* to his partners: the Sovietization process would start in the East Central European countries once they were occupied, but it would *look* as democratic as possible. Therefore, I call the process of gradual Sovietization the *stealthy revolution*, for Stalin was determined to realize all this based on cooperation maintained with the Western Allies: it was crucial for him to acquire U.S. economic support for the rebuilding of the Soviet Union and to ensure Western cooperation for the settlement of the German question and other territorial claims, and for concluding peace treaties with Germany's European allies.

Even though a detailed tactical directive bearing Stalin's signature on the manner of assuming power (a sort of "little Red book on how to Sovietize East Central Europe") has not surfaced so far (and likely never will), in a certain sense we may rightly regard Hungarian Communist leader Mátyás Rákosi's speech delivered at the meeting of the Hungarian Communist Party's Central Committee on 17 May 1946 as the missing blueprint for the *stealthy revolution*. Rákosi had traveled on a secret mission to Moscow, where he was trying to achieve better terms for Hungary at the forthcoming peace conference, and he gave a report to his local party leaders about his talks with Stalin and Molotov on 1 April 1946. The most important message from Stalin was that it was now time to speed up the Sovietization process and prepare for full takeover.

That urging came more than a year before the Marshall Plan, so it proves that the U.S. aid program did not alone trigger full Sovietization as assumed by many earlier. Stalin also revealed to Rákosi that the Soviet leadership was already planning to establish a new international Communist organization as early as spring 1946. In other words, the *idea* of forming the Cominform (Information Bureau of the Communist and Workers' Parties) was also not a response to the Marshall Plan, as many believe even today. Finally, Stalin declared that in the next twenty to thirty years there would not be a new world war. It is remarkable that this confidential statement occurred some two months after his infamous election speech on 9 February 1946, which was presented in Western media as proof of the Soviets' break with the Western allies and in which Stalin allegedly forecasted that a new war was inevitable with the West. In fact, he talked about a potential war between capitalist countries, not between East and West.

I interpret the Marshall Plan as a double trap—a trap for both the United States and the Soviet Union. The very idea of the Marshall Plan unintentionally created this trap situation. If the United States had openly decided to limit the aid program to Western Europe, the blame for dividing Europe would have been clearly Washington's, which the Americans obviously wanted to avoid. By eventually offering it to all European states, including the Soviet Union and the East Central European countries, they actually had to cheat, as they knew from the outset that the conditions of the plan would be unacceptable to Moscow, and indeed, it was not meant for them. All of this was seen as a *strategic trap* by Stalin, as well as one by which he could only lose. If he accepted the offer, Western influence would be maintained and perpetuated in his East European sphere of influence, which could not be countenanced. But if by rejecting it he excluded East Central Europe from the program and its potential positive effect, he would have to take responsibility for splitting Europe in two, which he had wished to avoid at all costs so as to maintain cooperation with the West. It is history's irony that, by rejecting the Marshall Plan, Stalin had to publicly reject an "offer" that in reality did not exist (and he knew it). This led to the paradoxical situation that although the *division of Europe* was actually caused by the initiation of the American aid program de facto creating a Western bloc, it was Moscow that had to assume unilateral responsibility for the split by setting up its own Eastern bloc de jure as well as by declaring the theory of the existence of two hostile camps.

Remarkably, the name of the Red Army is usually erroneously used in even the most recent academic works on the Cold War. In reality, the Red Army was renamed the Soviet Army in February 1946 in the framework of a "Westernizing" government reorganization: breaking with the Bolshevik tradition, the peoples' commissariats became ministries, and the peoples' commissars ministers. Remarkably, the change of the name of the army, which was publicly announced at the time, has been totally overlooked by most scholars, and it is still generally mistakenly referred to as the Red Army for the whole Cold War period.

I developed a novel conception for détente: in my view, after 1953 the main characteristic of the relationship between the conflicting superpowers was—despite the ever-increasing competition in the arms race—the continuous *interdependence* and *compelled cooperation* of the United States and the Soviet Union and their respective political-military blocs, while immanent antagonism obviously remained. Competition, conflict, and confrontation remained constant elements of the Cold War structure, but now they were always subordinated to and controlled by the détente elements: interdependence and compelled cooperation with the aim of avoiding a direct military confrontation of the superpowers at all costs. All of this means that détente was not a simple tactical move resulting in the temporary easing of tension in superpower relations, as is usually depicted, but a *new model of East–West compelled coexistence*, characteristic of the second phase of the Cold War from 1953 to 1991, which worked as an automatism controlling and determining the actions of the political leaders on both sides. In other words, it was a system of serious and permanent interdependency based on mutual responsibility for the preservation of human civilization that forced the superpowers to cooperate in order to avoid a direct military conflict between them.

I introduced a new categorization for the international conflicts that occurred during the Cold War by differentiating real crises from pseudo crises; for not every crisis that occurred during the Cold War era was attributable to the Cold War as far as its main character is concerned. Thus, most notably, all the intra-bloc conflicts of the Soviet bloc were not real crises in this sense because, despite what their propaganda said, they did not exceed the cooperation framework of the superpowers; namely, they did not cause a real threat to the interests of the opposing political-military bloc. They did not challenge the post–World War II European status quo and consequently did not disturb the East–West relationship. Such pseudo East–West crises, which had their effect only at the level of public opinion and propaganda, were the uprising in East Germany in 1953, the revolts of 1956 in Poland and Hungary, the invasion of Czechoslovakia in 1968, and the Polish conflict in 1980–81. These were, of course, serious *internal* crises, both in the countries where they occurred and within the Soviet bloc per se. Coupled with this was the 1956 Suez crisis, a serious conflict that happened parallel with the Hungarian Revolution but that did not have an effect on the East–West relationship. Rather, it was an intra-bloc conflict within the Western alliance, as the Soviet leadership assessed the situation realistically and decided not to be involved in it, not willing to directly confront the West in the defense of Egypt. The crises described above were basically different from others that did create a serious clash of interest between East and West, and some of which raised the possibility of a general East–West military confrontation. Such real Cold War crises were the two Berlin crises (1948–49 and 1958–61), the Korean War, the Chinese offshore islands crises in the mid- and late 1950s, and the Cuban missile crisis. The war in Vietnam and the Soviet invasion of Afghanistan were special cases of real crises. These crises represented a real threat to world peace, and they had a long-lasting effect on the East–West relationship both in their own time and in the long run, as opposed to the pseudo crises.

I rediscovered (and turned into doctrine) the policy of "active foreign policy" announced by the Soviet leadership in the spring of 1954, which was meant to increase the fitness of the Soviet bloc states for international society and the maneuvering capability of the entire bloc. From then on, Moscow encouraged its allies to use their international reputation, achieved or to be achieved with Soviet support, as effectively as possible to increase the reputation and influence of the Eastern bloc on the international political scene. Especially from the mid-1960s up to the collapse of the Communist regimes in East Central Europe, this strategy became an effective model for cooperation among the states of the Soviet bloc in the field of foreign policy.

I developed the concept of the emancipation of the Soviet Bloc states. While this term was already used by Brzezinski in a limited sense for depicting the changing relations between Moscow and its allies based on publicly available sources in the mid-1960s, my concept is based on extensive multi-archival research and is about the process of gradual emancipation of these states in three directions: in their relationship with the Soviet Union, with the West, and with the third world. As a result, from the mid-1950s on, the East Central European states could become increasingly more acceptable actors in international politics in order to promote the Soviet bloc's political objectives more successfully in the field of East–West relations and also in the third world.

I pointed out that around 1955–56, Soviet diplomacy—while trying to maintain activity toward the West in general—began to pay special attention to neutral countries, too. In Moscow, there was a general belief that "the neutrality movement" was growing not only in Asia and the Middle East but even in NATO countries like West Germany, Denmark, and Norway. The very category of neutrality was reformulated, too. As distinct from the traditional Western type of neutrality (Sweden, Switzerland), now the Finnish model was turned into a generally applicable model from its hitherto unique status: this was the Eastern type of neutrality. The prime subject of this new policy line became Austria after the conclusion of the state treaty and the declaration of the country's neutrality in 1955. For a while, Soviet leaders seriously believed that there was a good chance that this country would follow the Finnish model in its foreign policy orientation.

I rediscovered an important forgotten doctrinal change that seriously affected the worldview of the Soviet bloc leaders: the introduction of the "two-zones theory" in 1956. It was no secret that the Twentieth Congress of the Communist Party of the Soviet Union (CPSU) replaced Zhdanov's infamous "two-camps theory" of 1947 by the much more flexible new thesis of the two zones; however, this crucial modification in Soviet foreign policy is largely overlooked in international literature on the Cold War. While the Zhdanov doctrine identified two hostile political-military groupings, located in Eurasia and on the North American continent, the new theory divided the whole world into two parts, one of which belonged to the imperialist bloc under the leadership of the United States, which, besides members of NATO, included all U.S. allies from every continent. The other, much greater part was called the "peace zone," embracing not only the Socialist countries but every country in the world pursuing an anti-imperialist policy, thus all the former colonies, now becoming independent nonaligned states in Africa and Asia. What is more, several neutral states were put in this category, like Austria and Sweden, not to mention Finland, which indeed functioned as a "corresponding member" of the Soviet bloc since 1948. This meant the declaration of a fundamental change in the Soviet bloc's alliance policy. "Who is not against us is with us" was the rule from then on. The new policy was designed primarily to win over the third world countries in the fight between the two political-military blocs for acquiring economic and political influence in these areas, emerging in the mid-1950s. Although the two-zones theory itself was soon forgotten in the Soviet bloc, the new strategy itself remained in effect until the end of the Cold War.

As for the establishment of the Warsaw Pact (WP), I emphasize the importance of the multilateralization of the Soviet bloc, for Khrushchev wanted to create a real bloc out of Moscow's dependent states in East Central Europe. Following the organizational model of NATO, the WP served as an excellent framework for promoting the Soviet leadership's new policy of raising the reputation of the satellites in the field of international politics. While earlier in the West they were regarded hardly more than semi-colonies of the Soviet Union, now they formally became equal members of a mighty military-political alliance, led by a nuclear superpower. This marked the beginning of the multilateralization of the Soviet bloc, which led to the gradual emancipation of the East Central European states in three directions, as previously mentioned. All of this will also refute the traditional views that forming the WP served primarily to put tighter control over the allies.

In connection with the Hungarian Revolution in 1956, I established several new theses, the first of which is that present knowledge of the Soviet intentions makes it plain that the fate of the revolution was sealed by 22 October, the day before it actually started. The seed of ultimate catastrophe was sown in the demand for free elections, already one of the sixteen points compiled by students at the Technical University in Budapest and a general demand within a few days.

Another claim is that the first Soviet intervention on 24 October was a mistaken move, since at that moment Moscow leadership was in a real position to decide otherwise. Namely, they could have applied the Polish scenario by refraining from Soviet military intervention. By sending troops to Budapest, however, they achieved exactly the opposite of what they had wanted: not rapid pacification but escalation of sporadic armed actions into an extensive anti-Soviet war of liberation of a kind unparalleled in the history of the Soviet bloc. The second Soviet intervention on 4 November, however, was an unavoidable consequence of the first one.

At the CPSU presidium meeting on 23 October, when the fatal decision was made, this option was presented very plainly by Anastas Mikoyan, a key member of the Soviet leadership and the one who knew the Hungarian situation best. He suggested avoiding the use of Soviet troops and instead making Imre Nagy prime minister, assigning him with the task of restoring order using local forces. From Mikoyan's rational proposal, although it was defeated by his colleagues in the presidium, I have derived the Mikoyan doctrine, which did no less than lay the groundwork for the future Soviet crisis management strategy in case of the emergence of a serious crisis in one of the countries of the Soviet bloc. This meant first trying to find a political solution to restore order (if need be, coupled with using armed forces), executed by local forces only, to avoid Soviet military intervention at any cost. While Mikoyan's proposal to this effect was voted down in 1956, the Soviet leaders learned the lesson well. In their crisis management strategy during later conflicts, they always sought initially and instinctively to use this doctrine—in Czechoslovakia in 1968 for eight months, and in Afghanistan in 1979 for more than a year and a half. While these attempts eventually failed, the first successful application of the Mikoyan doctrine occurred in December 1981, when General Jaruzelski introduced martial law in Poland.

As for the role of the United States, I point out that the famous message by John Foster Dulles on 27 October 1956 caused a change of paradigm in American foreign policy. Even though its role in pacifying the Soviets is usually emphasized, the declaration "We do not look upon these nations as potential military allies" was of historical significance. Prior to this, all the official statements of the Eisenhower administration regarding the Soviet satellite states were based on the supposition that, should these states gain independence, it would mean their joining the Western world, which in the given context automatically meant NATO membership at the same time. Therefore, stating that the United States did not consider these states as potential military allies was in fact the renunciation of their earlier position and the starting point of a process that would determine U.S. policy in the following decades, one that eventually did away with the double-faced character of American foreign policy through cleaning up the remains of its liberation propaganda.

Concerning the role of the United Nations, I point out that the real clash of conflicting viewpoints in the UN, contrary to earlier interpretations, took place not between the Western powers and the Soviet Union during meetings of the Security Council, where what was said on both sides was primarily for public consumption, but behind the scenes, in the course of secret negotiations between the representatives of the United States, Great Britain, and France. Preparing for their military action in the Middle East, the British and the French first tried to block any move on the Hungarian issue. Then, once the emergency session of the UN General Assembly was convened to discuss the Suez crisis on 31 October, they abruptly changed tactics and were pushing for moving the Hungarian question from the Security Council to the emergency session of the assembly, where they hoped that the simultaneous treatment of the two aggressions would lead to a mitigation of the censure they had been receiving. This was successfully blocked by the United States, focusing on resolving the Suez crisis until the second Soviet intervention on 4 November, when the U.S. representative himself arranged the transfer of the Hungarian question to the assembly.

As for the role of the Suez crisis, I argue that it had no impact on the outcome of the Hungarian revolution. The discord among the Western powers made things easier for the Soviets, but it is fairly certain that even without the Suez crisis they would have pursued a similar policy. For the United States, it simply served as a handy excuse to explain why, after years of liberation propaganda, it was not capable of extending even the smallest amount of support to an East European nation that had risen in arms in an attempt to liberate itself from Soviet domination.

On 30 October 1956, the CPSU presidium made the decision that Soviet troops could be withdrawn from Hungary. This surprising information, revealed in the mid-1990s, triggered a scholarly debate about the real meaning of this "offer." While some scholars interpret it as Moscow's willingness to give up on Hungary, my firm position has been that it was just the opposite: full withdrawal of Soviet troops would have been the maximum political concession the Kremlin was willing to make, provided that the Nagy government succeeded in (1) consolidating the situation while maintaining the Communist system, and (2) preserving membership in the Soviet bloc. So the intended result of the Soviet concession on 30 October was not consenting to the restoration of the capitalist system but the consolidation of a situation akin to that in Poland—that is, accepting the creation of a reformed Communist system and displaying more independence internally but remaining loyal to Moscow and within the confines of the Soviet bloc.

I reconstructed the content and the meaning of the most mysterious summit meeting of the Soviet bloc from the available fragmentary sources. The meeting was held in Budapest between 1 and 4 January 1957 with the participation of the leaders of the Bulgarian, Czechoslovak, Hungarian, Romanian, and Soviet parties, and no official minutes of the meeting have been found in any of the archives of the participating countries so far. The Kremlin's main motivation behind the meeting was to discuss the imminent program statement of the Kádár government, which included the possibility of maintaining a special kind of pseudo-multiparty system. The Soviet, Czechoslovak, Bulgarian, and Romanian leaders vetoed this plan and also made a decision on the need to indict the Imre Nagy group, which eventually led to the execution of the former prime minister and several of his associates. This meeting was important because it was the first occasion in the history of the Soviet bloc in which the members of the Warsaw Pact acted *in union* and directly intervened in the internal affairs of one of its member states, paving the way for the policy that was to be called later, after 1968, the Brezhnev doctrine all over the world.

I formulated a novel explanation for why the Hungarian issue was kept on the agenda of the UN General Assembly for such a long time, until December 1962. The heated polemics in the assembly over the years were not supposed to make the Soviet Union change its ways—there was less than a slim chance that the "defendant," pleading guilty, would withdraw its troops from Hungary and leave the country to its own course. Instead, the intent was to convince the "jury"—that is, the nonaligned states that were becoming members of the UN in increasing numbers at that time—about the dangers of becoming allied with Moscow and to cajole them into accepting or preserving Western orientation and political ideology. This became important because, from the mid-1950s on, one of the primary aims of U.S. foreign policy was to arrest the development of Soviet influence in the third world and to correspondingly increase American presence there. The UN General Assembly provided an ideal arena for this; the Americans kept the Hungarian question on the agenda as a device of this political objective.

After Khrushchev's removal from office in October 1964, János Kádár, the leader of the Hungarian party, not only criticized the way of the personnel change but, at a meeting with new leaders Brezhnev and Kosygin, formulated what I call the Kádár doctrine: whether they liked it or not, Moscow's sovereignty was limited, therefore, even when making decisions at home, the Soviet Union's leaders had to take into consideration the interests of the whole Soviet Bloc.

Hungarian foreign policy during the decades following the 1956 revolution is still generally presented as determined solely by the manifest dependency on the Soviet Union. However, my extensive archival research in the field, conducted since 1990, suggests that it can only be properly explained and understood in the framework of a novel theoretical concept: tripartite determinism. While affiliation to the Soviet empire ostensibly implied enforced restrictions (1), the dependence on the West concerning advanced technology, trade contacts, and subsequent loans produced an equally strong bond (2). At the same time, Hungarian foreign policy had to perform a balancing act to pursue specific national objectives in terms of an all East Central European lobby contest (3). While this tripartite determinism of Hungarian foreign policy had always existed in some form and magnitude, the importance of each of the three factors became relatively the same from the mid-1960s on. This theory can also be interpreted in a wider context and, with certain restrictions, applied to the entire Soviet bloc. The three determinations are, in reality, valid for Hungarian, Polish, Romanian, East German, and, to a lesser extent, Czechoslovak and Bulgarian foreign policy as well, especially from the early mid-1960s on.

The German question and the issue of European security became of prime importance for the Soviet bloc by the mid-1960s; however, the bloc was immensely divided on these issues. I identified two sub-blocs within the Soviet bloc with totally opposing attitudes: an economy-oriented sub-bloc (Hungary, Romania, and Bulgaria) and a security-concerned sub-bloc (the GDR, Poland, and Czechoslovakia). The countries in the first group had no serious unsettled issues with West Germany; therefore, they were seriously interested in economic cooperation, increasing trade, and taking over cutting-edge technologies. Thus, they were the primary victims of the lack of diplomatic relations with the Federal Republic of Germany (FRG). Now it was increasingly difficult for them to identify unconditionally with the interests of the security-concerned sub-bloc, which was looking at the FRG as a serious security threat, stemming from the lack of a German peace treaty; thus, its Eastern borders were regarded as insecure until the settlement of the German question.

I introduced the category of "virtual coalition" in the field of analyzing alliance policy based on the functioning of the Soviet bloc. This means the virtual cooperation of a group of states having similar interests in a certain issue without making this collaboration explicit. The members of such a co-alition did not engage in multilateral or even bilateral talks with one another to harmonize their interests; nevertheless, they recognized their joint interests and acted accordingly. In other words, the common interests were represented *individually* during the meetings of the Soviet bloc multilateral forums in their bilateral relations with Moscow and the other Soviet bloc states, as well as vis-à-vis the Western states. Thus, the activity of such virtual coalitions was never formulated in any official form; moreover, their very existence was not even realized during the Cold War.

While different virtual coalitions existed throughout the Cold War era within the Soviet bloc, the most severe clashes occurred between the economy-oriented and the security-concerned sub-blocs during the preparations for the pan-European security conference from the mid-1960s to the mid-1970s. While these internal conflicts and infighting were totally unknown to the public at the time, it is now clear that all this brought temporary victory to the GDR, Poland, and Czechoslovakia (the security-concerned sub-bloc) in 1967, while from 1969 on the economy-oriented coalition took the upper hand.

I also introduced the new category of "constructive loyalty" in the analysis of alliance policy within the Soviet bloc. This refers to the fact that, despite the default dependency of the allied states on Moscow, the constraints could be and in fact were continually tested and gradually loosened; the content of this principle until 1988 implied that "what is not forbidden is (perhaps) allowed." While perhaps Hungary was a role model, the policy of constructive loyalty in Soviet–East European relations can be applied in a certain sense to all non-Soviet members of the Warsaw Pact (except for Romania), although of course the implementation of this policy differed significantly in different states and even in different periods. On the one hand, this generally meant a loyal following of the Soviet line in all public announcements and at the international scene, and avoiding open debates with Moscow at the Soviet bloc's forums, as well as flexibility, adjustment to Soviet demands, and a readiness to cooperate. On the other hand, it meant continuous testing of the boundaries of Soviet tolerance via bilateral channels, lobbying and fighting for one's national interests (as identified by the Communist leaders of the given state), and making confidential initiatives to foster their own goals, which often differed from Soviet interests.

When analyzing the events of the Prague Spring in 1968, to dispel the still surviving myth of "Socialism with a human face" I present my long-held conviction that it would have led to the restoration of parliamentary democracy without foreign intervention, as it eventually did occur in 1990. As for the evaluation of the Soviet decision-making process, I emphasize that the Soviet leadership in reality demonstrated extreme patience and self-restraint during the eight months of the crisis, as a violent solution would not have been irrational from their imperial perspective already in March, following the abolition of censorship in Czechoslovakia. From that time on, there was little hope that the leadership would be able to push the genie of democracy back in the bottle. Yet, learning from the lesson of their fatal mistake of intervening in Budapest too early right at the beginning of the 1956 Hungarian Revolution, they now tried to find a political solution to restore order according to the Kremlin's norms, executed by local forces only, and thus to avoid Soviet military intervention. Thus, during the Czechoslovak crisis, in reality Brezhnev and his comrades wanted to apply the Mikoyan doctrine; initially this meant persuading the Dubček leadership to realize the limits of Moscow's tolerance and then hoping to have the restoration done by the Moscow line "healthy forces." In the end, however, they had no other option than to use the Brezhnev doctrine and stop the dangerous process of political transition by a military invasion. Consequently, the question about a possible alternative course of history is not whether the Prague Spring could have survived under different circumstances but rather this: if János Kádár, the most hated man right after the bloody suppression of the revolution of 1956 in Hungary, was able to develop a rather liberal version of the Communist dictatorship that could generate relative popularity within society and that was also tolerated by the Soviets, why could the same model not be applied to Gustav Husak's Czechoslovakia?

By rejecting the widely held notion that there was a "Second Cold War" from 1979 to 1985, I call these years the *period of standby détente*. Between 1979 and 1985, the new confrontational U.S. policy (both under Carter and in the first term of the Reagan administration) materialized primarily at the propaganda level while the mechanism of compelled cooperation continued to work perfectly. The need to avoid a clash between the superpowers was no less compelling than before. Reagan's policy between 1981 and 1983 can be compared to the Eisenhower administration's dual policy between 1953 and 1956: the real aim of U.S. policy was to find a modus vivendi with the Soviet Union, but this was coupled comfortably with high-sounding rhetoric promising the liberation of the East Central European "captive nations," which, as is now well known, had no real basis at all. Another important feature of this period is that it was the first time that, in a confrontational stage, the European allies of the United States did not follow Washington loyally in a united front, and indeed they sought to keep the East–West dialogue and cooperation alive. Moreover, the alliance system reacted similarly on the Eastern side: the Eastern bloc countries—Hungary, primarily—driven by their special interests, which were by then becoming increasingly independent of Moscow's intentions, sought to do everything they could to preserve the achievements of détente.

I revealed the history of an intra-bloc sub-crisis of the East–West conflict emerging after the Soviet invasion of Afghanistan in December 1979. In late January 1980, shortly after the potential boycott of the Olympic Games to be held in Moscow was announced, the Kremlin took offense and decided to take countermeasures. During this campaign, Hungary, Czechoslovakia, and the GDR were ordered to cancel imminent high-level talks with Western politicians. This unexpected move caused a serious clash of interests between the Soviet Union and the Eastern European Communist states, since by this time these countries were interested in intensely developing their own relations with Western Europe. The Hungarian leadership, while loyally canceling their planned visits to the FRG and the United States, successfully urged Moscow to hold a multilateral consultative meeting on the consequences of the situation in Afghanistan on East–West relations. At the meeting held in Moscow in February, the Hungarian position was adopted as the Soviet bloc's policy line; that in the present situation, the allies must be consulted regularly on the joint policy of the bloc in international politics, and the results of détente must be preserved. This would be possible only by maintaining and strengthening the relations of the East Central European countries with Western Europe, and it would help avoid American influence prevailing in these countries.

While analyzing the drastic changes in East–West relations from 1985 on, I argue that Gorbachev's cooperative attitude toward the West was also highly influenced by Reagan's Strategic Defense Initiative (SDI), which would have started a new, unexpectedly expensive, and qualitatively different phase in the superpower nuclear arms race. In this new phase, the Soviet Union, with its failing economy, had no chance to continue the competition, while from 1945 up to that point, Moscow—true, at the cost of enormous sacrifices by society—was always capable of meeting the new American challenges. Being the prisoner of its superpower status, which meant the desperate need to maintain parity all along, it was vital for Moscow to somehow block the development of SDI. Therefore, once it had become clear to the Soviet leader that the U.S. president was not willing to give up on his "Star Wars" design, the only option left for Gorbachev to block the plan was appealing to the American taxpayers. Why should they spend horrendous sums for a space-based anti-missile system when there was no longer an enemy to fear? The plan worked, and during the unprecedentedly intensive summitry from 1985 to 1988, a real partnership emerged between Reagan and Gorbachev.

As a contribution to the literature on the end of the Cold War, I argue that the exceptional relationship that gradually emerged between Reagan and Gorbachev was based on the continual performance of two excellent actors: Reagan, a professional, was using a nonexistent project (SDI) to push Moscow in the direction of cooperation and disarmament, while Gorbachev could sell the Soviet Union as a potent superpower even when it was on the verge of collapse.

I pointed out that the meeting of the Political Consultative Committee of the Warsaw Pact on 15–16 July 1988 was a real turning point in the history of the Soviet bloc and also the Cold War. Here, at a closed session of the foreign ministers, Eduard Shevardnadze openly admitted that the Soviet Union was "facing a critical situation," and it could no longer afford to run a permanent arms race with the West, given that it exceeded the Eastern bloc "in every possible respect." Therefore, he stressed that the termination of the arms race had to be given absolute priority, and every chance had to be grasped in order to come to an agreement. In fact, this dramatic confession was about nothing less than admitting total defeat in the several decades-long historic competition of the two world systems. Therefore, this moment can be considered the beginning of the end for the Soviet bloc. From then on, the agreements absolutely necessary for the survival of the bloc were not to be achieved in the "normal" way—that is, by mutual compromises based on parity, as in the case of the INF Treaty just a year earlier—but *at any price*. This was the crucial recognition that led to the decisions on the announcement of significant unilateral disarmament measures already in December 1988.

In trying to find an explanation for the enigma of why the Soviet Union agreed to let East Central Europe go so easily in 1989, I introduced the term *Brest-Litovsk syndrome*. The situation of the Soviet Union in 1988–89 might well be called a life-or-death fight. That is, this was the first time since the Russian civil war that the USSR—paradoxically, still one of the two superpowers of the bipolar world order in a military sense—found itself in a situation in which its own survival was at stake. Giving priority to saving the imperial "center" was a logical and necessary step, with respect to which the East Central European periphery gradually but swiftly lost its significance. Back in March 1918, at that critical moment of the civil war, Lenin also argued for a peace treaty to be signed with the Germans that, while requiring the loss of huge territories, would nonetheless ensure the preservation of the Bolshevik state. It is also remarkable that the size of the territory ceded by Soviet Russia in the Brest-Litovsk Treaty was very close to the area of the East Central European region abandoned by Gorbachev.

To explain the complexity of Gorbachev's policy toward East Central Europe in 1988–99 I introduced the theory of the "floating" of the Brezhnev doctrine. As is known, at the 1988 June CPSU party conference, Gorbachev—without any preliminary theoretical elaboration—declared that any nation had the right to choose its own socioeconomic system. This thesis was then repeated by Gorbachev and other leaders several times and in several forms over the course of 1988–89 and was very soon supplemented by the promise to cease the use of military force. The essence of these multifunctional declarations, simultaneously addressed to all interested parties and deliberately meant to be ambiguous, was that although they *implicitly* rejected the possibility of military intervention, they never stated *categorically* that the Soviet Union would not interfere with an ally's domestic affairs should the political transition, horribile dictu, result in the total abandonment of Socialism and the restoration of parliamentary democracy. At the same time, all this was coupled with continual warnings from Moscow to the leaders of the Eastern European countries through secret channels and at confidential bilateral talks. The message was as follows: the limit of the transformation is the safekeeping of Socialism and the assurance of stability. The initially instinctive but later increasingly conscious tactic of floating the Brezhnev doctrine was successful and effective, at least temporarily. In reality, from the middle of 1988, the floating of the Brezhnev doctrine was virtually the only "weapon" left to the Soviet leadership with which it could, at least for a short time, have an influence on the political processes running their course in East Central Europe. It also had a stabilizing effect on the accelerated transition both in East Central Europe and the Soviet Union and contributed to preserving the basically peaceful nature of the changes to a large extent.

I pointed out that the acceptance of internal political changes in East Central Europe in 1989 by no means meant that Gorbachev was ready to give up the Soviet sphere of influence in the region as well; on the contrary, the "regional Finlandization" of East Central Europe was originally regarded as the price of freedom. These efforts were greatly facilitated by the fact that until the end of 1990, the Western powers, while welcoming the internal political transition, did not support the aspirations for independence of the states of the region, not even in the form of neutrality. On the contrary, in this short period NATO and the Warsaw Pact were regarded as the fundamental pillars of the European security system. Consequently, despite what most former Western politicians and diplomats claim in their memoirs, the democratic governments in the region, elected through free elections in the spring of 1990, were urged by Western politicians to maintain membership of the Warsaw Pact and Comecon. In other words, during 1989–90 it was not only Moscow that was interested in the regional Finlandization of East Central Europe; at that crucial historical junction, the Western powers were also willing to accept this option—that is, establishing democratic systems while preserving the Soviet sphere of influence by maintaining the existing integration organizations: the Warsaw Pact and Comecon. The West regarded maintaining the alliance of the Soviet bloc states with the Soviet Union a fair price for the "liberation" of these states as far as their political system was concerned. This position just seemed rather reasonable in view of the Western desire to preserve European stability by supporting the Gorbachev reforms. The ensuing collapse of the Soviet Union, however, eventually gave them a good chance to conveniently forget about this transitional deal for good.

This superpower consensus, paradoxically, opened the way for the countries of the region to play a historic role in the process of the transition. The successful democratic transition in the region—mass movements occurring in some countries notwithstanding—was a result of external conditions, including the favorable development of East–West relations and, above all, the Soviet Union's imminent but not yet visible collapse. In the fight for independence, mainly the Hungarian and Czechoslovak leadership played a prominent role from June 1990 on, joined by the Poles in August, finally achieving their goals by early 1991, when the Soviet leadership, pressed by the ever more chaotic internal situation in the Soviet Union, eventually yielded to the pressure. That is how by 1 April the military structure of the WP ceased to exist, and by the end of June/beginning of July 1991 both the Comecon and the Warsaw Pact were disbanded nearly simultaneously. This was the end of the Soviet bloc, which also meant a collective escape from the Soviet sphere of influence for the East Central European countries.

Chapter 1

The Emerging Cold War

East Central Europe and the Origins of the Cold War

The decades following the Second World War proved undeniably that the postwar European divide determined by the Soviet Union and the United States in 1945 had consigned the countries of East Central Europe to the Soviet sphere of influence without any chance of alteration until the final collapse of the Communist regimes at the end of the 1980s. The superpowers, who together ruled the bipolar international system, considered the arrangement in Europe to be the cornerstone of the East–West relationship throughout the Cold War. For this reason, it is worth providing a brief account of how the Soviet sphere of influence evolved, took firm root, and finally engulfed Hungary and the other countries of the region.[1]

Over the last two years of the war, the Allied leaders negotiated the future of Europe and plans for reconstruction at three summits, held in Tehran, Yalta, and Potsdam. The focus of these meetings, however, was not so much on the division of Europe as it was on how to defeat Germany and Japan. Thus, while there were agreements in Tehran, Yalta, and Potsdam—resulting from Soviet pressure—regarding the new western and eastern borders of Poland, there was no official treaty or agreement ever made that granted the whole region of East Central Europe to the Soviets as a sphere of influence.

Nevertheless, since 1943 there was a series of agreements in which the Western Allies tacitly recognized the Soviets' security interests in the three Baltic states and East Central Europe as acceptable and were prepared to tolerate them. All this was based on the idea that the Soviet Union, suffering enormous losses in the war against the Axis, had legitimate security interests and had a right to have a group of friendly states on its Western border to avoid a future attack by Germany. In reality, all this stemmed from a tacit agreement between Stalin and Roosevelt at the Tehran conference in November–December 1943, when the latter—in spite of Churchill's attempts at planning to open the long-awaited second front in the Balkans—supported Stalin's strongly expressed desire to launch the campaign as far from the eastern front as possible, meaning in Normandy, France, in May 1944.[2] This promise still left the Soviet Union with another six months to fight German forces in Europe basically alone.

Thus, from as early as November 1943 it became rather obvious to the Big Three (the three Allied leaders) that the countries of East Central Europe would be liberated and occupied by the Red Army and would therefore be controlled by Moscow. The decision to enter into this tacit agreement by the American president was not only an appreciation of the huge losses suffered by the Soviets up to that point but also was based on the assumption that while this option would further increase the disproportionate losses to Moscow—a sacrifice Stalin was willing to make[3]—it would save hundreds of thousands of American (and other Western) soldiers' lives, consequently winning the war at a much lower human cost to the United States. Stalin's pledge to enter the war against Japan after the defeat of Germany further strengthened Roosevelt's conviction that he had made a good deal.

Arguably, the postwar fate of East Central Europe was not determined at the Yalta conference in February 1945, as many believe even today, but in Tehran. At that meeting, however, there was no alternative option for Roosevelt and Churchill: the only way of trying to change the course of history would have been presenting Stalin with a joint Western ultimatum demanding his consent to opening the second front in the Balkans. From Stalin's speeches and remarks at the conference, it was only too obvious that he was determined to liberate and occupy all of East Central Europe *at any cost*, which could have been done only by openly risking a breakup of the anti-fascist coalition. This certainly would have led to unpredictable consequences, possibly even a clash between Soviet and Western Allied forces, so such a scenario was just unimaginable for either Roosevelt or Churchill. Not to mention that, even in such an absurd case, the Red Army might have already liberated the greatest part of East Central Europe by the time a successful large-scale landing campaign in the mountainous Balkans, with its harsh geographic conditions, could be launched by the Western great powers.

The only and thus frequently cited negotiations on the postwar future of Europe where ranges of interest and spheres of influence were mentioned in so many words took place in Moscow between Churchill and Stalin on 9 October 1944.[4] This meeting resulted in the infamous "percentage agreement," which seemed to attempt to establish mutually acceptable spheres of influence for the Soviet Union and the Western powers in East Central Europe and the Balkans. Though many have accused Churchill of having callously abandoned those nations to their fate, he in fact most probably wanted to engage in a game with Stalin, trying to test his intentions regarding the future of the region. By the time of this meeting in early October 1944, most of Germany's junior allies had followed Italy's example and capitulated—Romania in August, Finland and Bulgaria in early September—while an armistice with Hungary seemed imminent, as a delegation sent by Admiral Horthy was just negotiating in Moscow, finally signing the preliminary cease-fire agreement on 11 October. Thus, right at the time of the Stalin-Churchill meeting, it could be realistically expected that the eastern front would be very soon moved abruptly to the middle of Hungary, where the Red Army would fight the Germans supported by the Romanian, Bulgarian, and Hungarian armies. This scenario would imply a fast westward movement of the front, with the Soviets possibly reaching Austria by the end of 1944. Thus, Churchill had to reckon with the fact that basically all the East Central European countries would be liberated and occupied by Soviet troops in a relatively short period of time. With this prospect, there was not much hope for any real surviving Western influence in those states. Thus, the relatively high numbers proposed by Churchill and "accepted" by Stalin for the Western Allies (Hungary, 50%; Yugoslavia, 50%; Bulgaria, 25%; Romania, 10%) can be regarded as a "generous" but utterly cynical gesture by the Soviet leader to feed Churchill's assumed desire for self-delusion rather than a real division of spheres of interest. Remarkably, a day later the "Soviet" numbers for Hungary and Bulgaria were modified by Molotov and Eden to 80 percent, a figure that indicated the real intentions of the Kremlin much more realistically. The 5 percent increase for Bulgaria was relatively small, so it could be regarded an adjustment, but a 30 percent successful bargain in favor of Moscow for Hungary is simply incomprehensible if we assume that Stalin and Churchill were serious about 50 percent a day before. While Yugoslavia still seemed to be fifty-fifty, at that moment Stalin could be sure that under Tito's rule, the country would solidly be in the Soviet sphere, whatever the British wishful thinking would assume.

When analyzing the percentage agreement, we must consider a very important factor that is generally overlooked: the impact of a potential Hungarian turnaround. When Churchill initiated the agreement, he in fact had the mistaken notion that the Red Army would penetrate into Hungary much earlier than it actually happened. That is, at that moment his own negotiating position was much weaker than it became a few days later. (As is known, on 16 October the Hungarian turnaround failed and the takeover by the Hungarian fascists, the Arrow Cross Party, made Hungary the last major ally of Germany in Europe, fighting on its side until the end, and in reality, Hungary was liberated only in April 1945.) Thus we can argue that proposing a 50 percent influence for the Western powers in Hungary under such conditions simply cannot be taken seriously. Not surprisingly, while the numbers were modified from 9 October to 10 October in favor of the Soviet Union, they were not changed after Churchill left Moscow, and it turned out on 16 October that the expected Hungarian turnabout failed.

With the benefit of hindsight, it is apparent that the only part of that agreement that retained any "serious" relevance was Churchill's insistence regarding Greece on a 90:10 percent division of interest between Great Britain and the Soviet Union. This was successful in indicating to Stalin the unwillingness of the British to accept any extension of Soviet influence over that country, which had traditionally been of strategic importance to Britain. We now know that, in reality, such an understanding on Greece had already been reached between Stalin and Churchill in May 1944, and Stalin recognized the right of Great Britain to send troops for the liberation of the country in an official note on September 23.[5] Not surprisingly, the British troops indeed started to liberate parts of the Balkan state in late September 1944. Thus, most probably Churchill's only real goal with presenting the percentage agreement was to warn Stalin that the Red Army, at that moment having already occupied Romania and Bulgaria, should not try to become an occupying power in Greece as well—which would have been a rather logical move from a purely military-strategic point of view—as that would be done by Britain alone. Therefore, while Churchill can obviously not be blamed for selling out East Central Europe at this conference, as interpreted in several earlier studies, as well as surviving as one of the Cold War era myths in public memory, by acquiring Stalin's consent for the British military campaign, in reality he deserves some merit for helping save Greece from becoming a member of the emerging Soviet bloc. True, this could be achieved only because of Stalin's original restraint in this issue, as he regarded Greece a country in the British sphere of influence from the beginning of the war. This *oral* agreement had no official status and was thus never referred to in later multilateral negotiations, not to mention the fact that the United States, which had emerged as the real victor of the war and whose viewpoint had begun to become the Western alliance's most important, was not obliged to accept an agreement to which it had not been a party.[6]

By the time of the next summit of the Big Three in Yalta in February 1945, the Red Army occupied most of East Central Europe and the Soviet troops were a mere sixty-five kilometers away from Berlin. At the meeting in the Crimea, another tacit agreement was made about the region; however, now the concession was *formally* made by the Soviets: Roosevelt and Churchill were content with Stalin's signing the Declaration on Liberated Europe, in which the Big Three bound themselves to facilitate free democratic elections throughout East Central Europe after the war, but without any deadline, and the Western partners asked for no guarantees of any kind.[7] Thus they could and did present the joint Allied statement as a great victory to the Western public, worrying about the emerging Soviet dominance in the region, by assuring Stalin's written consent to the democratic development of the region. This act was rather similar to Chamberlain's confident waving of the Munich Agreement at the airport upon his arrival in London in September 1938, by which he allegedly saved the peace. On the Soviet side, Stalin could easily sign the document, as his previous experience prompted him to believe that the United States and Britain would be flexible in handling this issue. In September 1941 he also signed the Atlantic Charter, explicitly claiming that the signatories would not seek territorial gains during and after the war, only to declare to British Foreign Secretary Eden just three months later that Moscow's precondition for a Soviet-British military treaty was the acceptance of the Soviet Union's borders of 1941.[8] These encompassed large territories taken from Finland, Poland, and Romania in 1939–40, as well as the incorporation of the three Baltic states—Estonia, Latvia, and Lithuania—in 1940. While there was much initial resistance concerning these claims by Britain and the United States for a while,[9] by the time of the Yalta conference they accepted all of them, as well as the transfer of the northern part of East Prussia to the Soviet Union.

At the same time, the leaders of the Western great powers were completely aware that if the Soviet leader failed to keep his promise on free elections, they would have no means at all to force him to comply with the declaration—and Stalin knew this too, and they knew that Stalin knew. This understanding was again based on a realistic assessment of the situation; thus, the political fate of the East Central European region was determined by the hard military facts on the ground, not by any secret pacts among the great powers.

In those circumstances, the Western powers were left with a painful dilemma: they could either acknowledge the latest Soviet conquests or, having no alternative solution, attempt to force the Soviets back to within their original borders. The Second World War had not yet finished, and beginning the third one was the last thing the United States and the fatally weakened Britain needed at that time (not to mention France, whose role in great power politics was less than nominal in those years). Thus, we can agree with Mark Kramer's assessment: "Long before the fighting was over, Soviet leaders had many reasons to conclude—accurately, as later events proved—that the Western countries ultimately would not pose a serious challenge to the establishment and consolidation of Soviet military-political hegemony in Eastern Europe."[10]

Therefore, we can argue that the emerging Soviet domination in East Central Europe in 1944–45 caused no real conflict with the Western great powers, their recurring public criticism of the antidemocratic moves in the region notwithstanding. What made it considerably easier for the West to consent to Soviet control over East Central Europe, however, was the fact that the western boundaries of Soviet expansion—excepting the eastern regions of Germany and Austria—largely encompassed the periphery of Europe. The Western European great powers had never held any serious influence in that area—the Ottoman and Habsburg Empires and later partly Russia had occupied or controlled it for hundreds of years, and from the late nineteenth century it had fallen increasingly within the political and economic sway of Germany. In contrast, the British and French colonial empires, though the war had brought the date of their demise significantly forward, were virtually intact in 1945. The foreign offices of these states were thus understandably more concerned with the Mediterranean, North Africa, the Middle East, and the Far East. Even the special relationships that Britain and France had enjoyed with some East Central European countries, such as Poland and Czechoslovakia, were for the most part symbolic and only served to further accentuate their indifference toward the other countries of the region. Washington had followed a policy of declared isolationism between the wars—with a specific emphasis on keeping out of European affairs. With its radically different political role and significance after 1945, the United States, having suddenly become a superpower, was compelled to enter global politics. At that point, it was in the interest of the United States to acknowledge the Soviets' East Central European conquests as an immutable reality, while at the same time making it clear that any further attempts at expansion would not be tolerated and could even lead to military conflict. This turn in U.S. foreign policy in 1946–47 was dubbed the policy of containment.

Thus, the occupation of and emerging Soviet domination in East Central Europe right after the end of the war caused no real conflict with the Western great powers, yet since 1945, relations between the Allies gradually deteriorated in such a way that, in September 1947, the Soviets declared that the world was now divided into two hostile camps. In less than a year, in June 1948, the first serious crisis of the Cold War—as the relationship between the Soviet Union and the Western great powers was then called—started with Stalin's launching of the Berlin Blockade.

Therefore, it is worth examining in more detail how the bipolar world system developed in the postwar years and along what lines of force it did so. In other words, why did the wartime cooperation of the Allies break up, and why did it turn into a hostile relationship in such a short period of time? Even today, almost three decades after the end of the Cold War and the beginning of the "archival revolution" in East Central Europe and the former Soviet Union, most scholars still tend to put much of the blame for starting the Cold War on either the Soviet Union or the United States.

In reality, no such unilateral responsibility can be established, as the Cold War emerged as a consequence of a process stemming from the gradual loss of confidence and escalation of distrust among the Allies in which both sides equally had their share. We can agree with Melvyn Leffler that neither Truman nor Stalin wanted the Cold War[11]—that is, the half-century-long bipolar system was an unintended consequence. But although it was an unwanted result, as we shall see, it was also unavoidable under the circumstances.

About the policy followed by the Soviet Union after World War II, the most important question takes the following form: Did Stalin's policy have *aggressive, expansionist* intentions, or was it marked by *cautious restraint* based on considerations of realpolitik? While this is one of the questions that divide students of the field the most, we can argue that in fact both motives existed side by side in Soviet policy, each with its own major part to play.

The main goal of Soviet foreign policy in the period was to maximize security. The theoretical basis applied was a traditional strategic one: the principle of greater territory equals greater security.[12] Not even Stalin could find anything newer or better than that. This doctrine was part of the czarist heritage, which the Soviets strove to apply to the maximum as justification for their real expansionist endeavors.

We now know for sure that it was not in Stalin's interest before the launching of the Marshall Plan in the summer of 1947 to give up cooperating with the West, and he had absolutely no intention of doing so.[13] As mentioned before, all the Soviets' new acquisitions in the Baltics and in East Central Europe were tacitly recognized by the Western great powers by the end of the war, so there was no reason for Moscow to worry about generating a serious conflict with the West stemming from that region. So the real question is how to explain those expansionist endeavors, which were indeed liable to cause confrontation with the Western Allies by gravely infringing on their potential interests. The best-known examples of this kind were the Soviet ultimatums to Turkey over control of the Turkish Straits, the territorial claims on Turkish Azerbaijan, and attempting to annex northern Iran to the Soviet Union by not complying with the Allied treaty about the withdrawal of all foreign troops from the country within six months after the end of the war.[14] Similar endeavors were the Soviet demand for taking part in the occupation of Japan and a public claim for partial control over Italy's colonial possessions, pushing for the international control of the Ruhr region, as well as the excessive Soviet demands to receive reparations from the Western zones of Germany.

My suggested explanation for this question rests on the compulsion to seize a *never-returning opportunity*. Stalin was well aware of the situation in the aftermath of World War I, when the victors' interests had produced a peace system that redrew the map of Europe. At that time Soviet Russia was a quasi-defeated country, capitulating to Germany, which had itself been defeated a few months later. Regarded as a state non grata, Soviet Russia was not invited to the peace conference, so it had no chance to make territorial gains; on the contrary, it lost huge territories on its Western borders. The Soviet leaders never accepted these losses or the Versailles treaties themselves, but—unlike Hungary and later Germany—did not launch an open revisionist propaganda campaign. Nevertheless, their silent revisionism, waiting patiently for the right opportunity, turned out to be rather effective, first temporarily in 1939–40 and then finally in 1945.

After the end of World War II, the Soviet Union's position and international prestige increased to an unimagined extent due to the performance of the Soviet Army, and it seemed logical to Stalin to assert his country's interests to the full through the postwar peace settlement. He also assumed that, like the post–World War I settlement, it would be reached in a couple of years, so a lot could be attempted in that time, and what could be attempted, should be. For the time being, everything was in such a flexible state that such attempts seemed to incur little risk. It was likewise clear to Stalin that the most durable elements of any peace treaty were the state borders; thus once such a settlement had been made, further territory—the overriding criterion according to the greater territory equals greater security principle—could be gained only through serious conflict, further wars, and even a future world war. Attention has been drawn here by Zubok and Pleshakov to something very important: these attempts that so tried the patience of the Western powers did not really amount to aggressively expansionist efforts or demands.[15] Note how most of them would just disappear later, in a relatively short period of time. Should some attempt run up against stubborn enough resistance, the Soviets would abandon it. Thus, they eventually withdrew from northern Iran in the spring of 1946 and stopped threatening Ankara once Soviet intelligence learned the United States was pondering military moves in Turkey's defense. Similarly, they gave up their claims concerning the occupation of Japan as well as Italian colonies. A minor but strategically very important Soviet acquisition—a mostly forgotten fact by now—was also given up in March 1946: they evacuated the Danish island of Bornholm at the Western edge of the Baltic Sea, which had been occupied by Soviet troops in 1945.[16]

While this rather flexible attitude showed Stalin's actual intentions, in Western perception all these endeavors appeared as real, aggressively intended expansionist efforts, and thus they became major escalating elements in the emerging confrontation, despite Stalin's original intentions.[17]

Therefore it can be argued that Stalin's expansionist efforts displayed a dichotomy:

1. Some were cynically pragmatic ideas, geared to immediate relations of power and alliance and designed to maximize the chances for realpolitik.
2. Others were unrealistic efforts made on a trial-and-error basis, akin in many respects to the later bold foreign-policy endeavors of Khrushchev.

As for the first category, it meant above all that the Soviet sphere of interest looked quite different in 1940, during Molotov's talks in Berlin, when the German alliance was the immediate concern, than it did in the middle or at the end of the war. Back then, the purpose was to control the Turkish Straits, the Persian Gulf, and the Arabian Sea,[18] and to regain northern China. For later, during and after the war, the Persian Gulf and the Arabian Sea were not even suggested as parts of the Soviet sphere of influence. These territories were seen as "obtainable" while Stalin was parleying with Hitler because they belonged to the sphere of interest of a third party, the United Kingdom, which was at war with Germany. It is typical that the Soviet Union's interest in East Central Europe—later the most important region from the expansion point of view—was confined at this stage to Bulgaria, and even this claim was closely connected to the Soviet desire to establish control over the Turkish Straits. This was no accident, as most of East Central Europe then counted as quasi-potential German Lebensraum, implicitly documented in the secret protocol of the Molotov-Ribbentrop Pact concluded in August 1939. The document contains the division "of spheres of influence in East-Central Europe" between Germany and the Soviet Union, but in reality—besides dividing Poland—only the Soviet part of the deal is specified by listing the countries and territories that fall into the Soviet sphere.[19] This apparently meant that *all the other states* of the region belonged to the German sphere. This was also made obvious by the inclusion—at Soviet request—of a special paragraph on calling attention to the Soviet Union's "interest in Bessarabia," then belonging to Romania. It is also an important factor that no Soviet demand was made at that stage for southern Sakhalin or the Kuril Islands—which would later feature large among Soviet expansionist ambitions—as that would have infringed on the interests of Japan, which was allied with Germany.

But it all changed radically once Germany attacked the Soviet Union in June 1941. A new system of alliances meant that the Soviet leadership had to establish new priorities in interest-sphere policy as well. Stalin's attention now swiftly turned to East Central Europe. It was hoped as the war prospects improved that this region, hitherto part of retreating Germany's Lebensraum, would become vacant. It offered a great chance to strengthen security along the Soviet Union's always vulnerable Western borders by inserting a zone of friendly states. By the end of 1941, there are increasingly frequent references in source materials to the idea that would be conceptualized in a plan prepared in January 1944 by the commission headed by Ivan Maisky.[20] This idea envisaged as desirable for Soviet security the creation of a neutral zone in postwar northern Europe, while the desired future relationship with countries along the western border was seen in terms similar to those that would emerge between the Soviet Union and Finland after 1948.[21] All this, Stalin hoped, could be achieved without conflict with the Western Allies, for then, just like in Berlin in 1940, the Soviet Union was intending to expand its sphere of influence at the expense of a third party, that of Germany, the lethal joint enemy just being defeated.

The expansionist aims in Stalin's foreign policy at this time, however, were accompanied also by caution and moderation. Stalin expressly avoided intervening in the West's direct sphere of interest. Well-known examples include the way the Soviet leadership withheld support from the Communist partisans in Greece and eventually from Yugoslavia's territorial claims on Italy and Austria. The Western Communist parties of the time were furnished with a popular-front policy,[22] one of their main tasks being to participate effectively in national reconstruction, not attempting to seize power. Still more important was Stalin's failure to back Mao in the Chinese civil war because he feared that since China belonged to the U.S. sphere of influence, support for the Communists and their accession to power would bring a clash with the United States.[23] Even in 1949, Stalin made explicit references to the Yalta agreement and expressed just such a concern.

Indeed, as we shall see, even the Sovietization process in East Central Europe was influenced by such attempted caution. This can be seen most of all in the way the Soviet Union urged or permitted local Communist parties to assume decisive positions of power before 1947, mainly in places where local conditions were favorable and moves could be made by relatively peaceful means.

About the role and responsibility of the United States in triggering the Cold War, the main question is usually formulated in the following way: Was it the American measures that infringed on Soviet security interests and thus provoked Soviet countermeasures, or was American policy just reacting to Soviet steps tending toward confrontation? No exclusive answer can be given, in my view, as both posited statements are essentially correct.

Indeed, several steps or political measures taken by the United States in that period became unintentional sources of conflict in relations with the Soviet Union due to the irreconcilability and basically different characters of the two political-economic systems and their subsequent strategic interests. One of the most important factors was American ideas on the structure of the postwar world: the "one-world concept," the principle of open markets, and the propagation of liberal democracy. All these were opposed from the outset to Soviet interests and did nothing to increase Moscow's confidence in the United States. According to these American ideas, the newly established World Bank and International Monetary Fund assumed a market economy; therefore, the Soviet Union could not join these institutions and regarded the U.S. plans as part of Washington's worldwide economic expansionism. This in turn increased already existing distrust of the Western partners and raised the prospect of a future collapse of the four-power coalition.

Another important event that eventually and necessarily contributed to raising Cold War confrontation, despite original intentions, was the development and very existence of the atom bomb, for in Stalin's eyes, this superweapon—originally developed against the Axis powers—upset the balance of power that emerged by the end of the war, and this forced the Soviet leaders into countermeasures. This was rightly seen in Moscow as the beginning of the atomic age, so a radical reaction would have been inevitable even if Truman had decided not to drop the bomb on Hiroshima and Nagasaki. Indeed, Moscow's efficient intelligence had brought early news of the bomb, and by 1943 the Soviets were doing experiments of their own. In August 1945, Stalin gave orders to make the country a nuclear superpower and allocated unlimited resources for the project.[24] In the emerging bipolar system based on the opposition of the two superpowers, action triggered reaction, and the ensuing Soviet–American arms race inevitably accelerated the strengthening tendencies toward confrontation.

The sudden and unexpected termination of the lend-lease deliveries to the Soviet Union in April 1945 was not just an unfriendly act toward a fiercely fighting ally, as even the timing of the decision was questionable. While the war in Europe was just about to end, ensuring Soviet participation in the liberation of large territories occupied by Japan in China was still a strong U.S. interest, and the predicted radical impact of the A-bomb could not be calculated until the first test in July. Since the conditions of the booming U.S. economy did in no way justify it, this step was in fact a premature political message about starting to look at the Soviet Union as a future opponent.

It was not too difficult for Moscow to interpret Washington's rejection of the Soviet request for a $3–$6 billion reconstruction loan during 1945–46 as a similar sign of U.S. untrustworthiness.[25] In principle, Stalin could rightly expect that his wealthy partner would support the rebuilding of his country, ruined during the joint fight against Germany, and indeed there had been vague promises to that effect made by U.S. partners. However, the compelled alliance of the United States and Britain with the Soviet dictator lost its original motivation after the defeat of Germany and Japan—that is, they did not need his services of unlimited military losses anymore. By the fall of 1945, the Allies gradually started to turn into opponents; thus, it was rather logical to try to limit providing Western resources to Moscow. All this, then, was portraying the United States as an ungrateful and unreliable partner in the Soviet perception.

The double-faced Western attitude toward East Central Europe also exacerbated the situation. Despite the acknowledgment of the Soviet Union's vital role in the war and the Soviets' right to control East Central Europe,[26] the United States and Britain faced constant pressure from domestic public opinion, which was unaware of the tacit agreement, and therefore time after time, even though half-heartedly, they seemingly attempted to curtail Soviet ambitions in the region. These interventions in diplomatic notes harshly condemning antidemocratic moves and actions by Communists or Soviet authorities in the region usually had the planned positive impact on their own societies, "proving" that the Western great powers would not let down those ill-fated nations beyond the emerging Iron Curtain. At the same time, Moscow was expected to understand the game and not to take these moves at face value. The Kremlin, however, unable to judge the gravity of these moves, often interpreted these Western communications as real intrusions into Soviet internal affairs, violating the tacit agreement about the region, which further raised their suspicion on the Western allies' reliability and willingness to cooperate.

At the same time, there were indeed a number of events and developments in 1946–47 that, in the Western perception, were proof of an aggressive expansionist Soviet policy, which then triggered harsh U.S. reactions. As we have seen before, some of these actions were only misperceived as threats to Western security, while others really involved the danger of a conflict between the allies. Thus, realistic perceptions and misperceptions together shaped U.S. policy toward the Soviet Union.

Stalin's policy toward Iran increased Western distrust considerably. Although in March 1946, following resolute American demands, the Soviets finally withdrew their troops from the northern part of Iran, the mere fact that Stalin had tried to evade the agreement that was supposed to bind all the parties had far-reaching significance, considerably diminishing the credibility of Soviet cooperation. The Soviet pressure on and ultimatums to Turkey in 1945–46 were regarded as further evidence of an expansionist drive aimed at extending the Soviet sphere into areas belonging to the West. Even though Stalin, with the expressed purpose of avoiding confrontation with the West, refrained from supporting the Communist partisans in the Greek civil war, the potential danger that the Greek Communists would win—even without direct Soviet support—and thus bring Greece under Soviet influence, threatened the European status quo of 1945.

All of this resulted in the declaration of the U.S. policy of containment in the form of the Truman Doctrine in March 1947, in which the United States promised to stop any *further* Communist expansion in the world. This can be regarded as an extremely shrewd initiative and an excellent contemporary PR success, as this meant no less than implicitly institutionalizing the tacit agreement on the Eastern and Western spheres of interest while officially not admitting—moreover, denying—its existence.

Perhaps the Chinese civil war did not directly influence the East–West relationship but, in the global perspective, it certainly increased the anxiety of the West. Communist victory in China, if the military situation was anything to go by, was close at hand in 1946–47, even without any substantial Soviet support. This posed the threat that the world's most populous country, which was of definitive strategic value in the increasingly important Far East, would become part of the Soviet empire.[27] When it did occur at the end of the civil war in 1949, it also meant the first and rather spectacular failure of the still quite fresh American containment policy.

Of the factors that aggravated the increasingly acute differences between the Allies—finally bringing about the disintegration of the anti-fascist coalition—the "German question" was the most important. Negotiation between the Soviet Union and the Western great powers on the German question was perhaps the most apparent place where differences approached irreconcilability. The Allied leaders had begun to discuss the future of Germany and its possible partition as soon as the end of the war had appeared on the horizon. Exactly as it had been a century earlier, German national unity became the locus of European politics. This time, as the central element of the young "East–West relationship," the German question had obtained a global importance that it would retain for nearly half a century. Victory, however—or, more precisely, the final geographical position of the Allied armies in their respective occupation zones at the end of the war—did not bring a solution closer but paradoxically created an unsolvable situation.[28]

Peculiarly enough, though officially both the Soviets and their Western allies supported the idea of a united Germany, they could not reach a general agreement. In reality, all the efforts during the postwar settlement to restore German unity were condemned to failure by the sheer fact that one part of Germany was occupied by the Soviet Union.

Stalin was inclined toward reunion because he saw a danger of reviving German revanchism in keeping the country divided for too long, but understandably he was disinclined to release East Germany, his country's westernmost and perhaps most valuable conquest, without adequate compensation. He wanted an economically and militarily weak united Germany, which would pose no further threat to the Soviet Union, and a neutral one, unable to take part in any later anti-Soviet alliance. Moscow also had hopes that neutrality would reduce Western influence. This, and a leavening of postwar economic crisis and penury, would make life much easier for the German Communist Party, through which Soviet influence could spread over the whole country. Stalin probably envisaged as an ultimate goal not a Sovietized Germany but a "Finlandized" one,[29] as that would have suited his security requirements famously. Especially as he could hardly have hoped that the Western great powers, notably the United States, would stand idly by while a Communist system was built there.[30]

The neutrality of a united German state, however, was obviously not acceptable to the West since, besides exposing the country to Soviet influence via the German Communist Party and other covert means, it would have preserved a power vacuum in the very middle of the continent, posing an unpredictable danger to European stability. This scenario was exactly what the Western states wanted to avoid. They eventually concluded that it would be better to accept the partition of Germany so that the Western occupation zones could be rebuilt into a strong, economically viable buffer state, thus the American administration decided to save what it could, working from as early as 1946 toward founding a separate West Germany.[31]

Thus, the main strategic conflict over their German policy was that the United States and Britain planned to rebuild a strong Germany while the Soviets wanted to transform the country into a weak and harmless state. With this radically deferring approach, it was hard to imagine the longtime maintenance of a harmonious joint four-power occupation regime in Germany, established at the Potsdam summit meeting, while the prospects of uniting the country and concluding a peace treaty were already practically nonexistent from the beginning. Under the circumstances, the real clash over Germany was not the country's future but the question of reparations. While the Western powers tacitly accepted Moscow's merciless policy of removing basically all unessential items from the Soviet zone of occupation, the conflict stemmed from Moscow's unrelenting demands for a substantial share from the Western zones. These were not only the much more industrialized parts of Germany but also included the Ruhr region, the center of German heavy industry. It was no wonder that Stalin was fighting for an international trusteeship over the area, yet it was seen as an illegitimate attempt at expanding Soviet influence beyond their tacitly recognized sphere of interest and was rejected by his partners in Potsdam.[32] As he was happy with conquering the eastern part of Germany but at the same time felt very unlucky to have the poorest part of a potentially rich country, he did not give up hope that, by constantly pressuring them, his allies would reward him for the enormous sacrifices the Soviet Union made for winning the war by providing substantial reparations from their own zones. In Potsdam they indeed agreed to a 10 percent share, which was far from Stalin's expectations, but in 1946 even these deliveries were suspended.[33] As previously mentioned, after the defeat of Germany and Japan and especially following the gradual deterioration of relations between the allies, the United States logically tried to limit Western economic support to Moscow. On the other hand, the same reluctance was rightly seen from a Soviet perspective as ungratefulness and, moreover, a violation of existing agreements between the partners. While both sides were right and represented their own interests fiercely, now these interests started to become totally irreconcilable and thus the fight over reparations from West Germany increasingly contributed to the loss of confidence and the escalation of suspicion concerning the reliability of the other party on both sides, especially as all this revealed the differing strategic goals of the allies on Germany's future: consolidation versus neutralization.

The German element was also an important factor in the rejection of the Marshall Plan by Stalin. The plan to rebuild and revitalize German heavy industry with U.S. support clearly meant to the Soviets that the creation of a Western bloc in Europe was in the making, which would include, as a central element, a future West Germany under heavy American influence. This was not just a violation of the Potsdam agreement on the joint four-power administration of Germany as a whole, as it ended all hopes for Stalin to get hold of resources from the Western zones and, in a broader perspective, to spread Soviet influence there. Thus, this prospect forced him to finally give up the idea of a "Finlandized" Germany and, with it, the hope of extending a special version of Soviet influence beyond the demarcation line of 1945—that is, the Iron Curtain—into Western Europe. While Communist parties were strong in France and Italy, it seemed impossible to establish a Communist regime in those countries either through parliamentary means or by a violent takeover without triggering a direct clash with the Western powers, as those states belonged to the Western sphere of interest in toto. No wonder Stalin ordered the Italian Communists to refrain from attempting to seize power in 1948.[34] In divided Germany, however, Stalin had a valuable bargaining chip: the eastern part of the country.[35] Here, at least theoretically, there existed a chance to unite the country as a neutral state, where Soviet influence could work as in Finland throughout the Cold War: while preserving the Western type of parliamentary political system, the foreign policy of the country would be secretly supervised by Moscow. With the inclusion of the Western zones of Germany in the Marshall Plan, all such hopes were doomed for Stalin.

Finally, the East–West relationship was further aggregated in the course of negotiations intended to conclude peace treaties with the smaller Axis allies. The conferences of the Council of Foreign Ministers—established in Potsdam and the meetings of the deputy foreign ministers from September 1945 on—and the Paris Peace Conference held the following year, despite all intentions, failed to achieve their main objective: to prepare the ground for a successful peace treaty with Germany and Japan.[36] While eventually concluding peace treaties with Italy, Finland, Hungary, Romania, and Bulgaria could be regarded as a success story, this was mainly due to the fact that, except for Italy, these former allies of Germany lay in the Soviet sphere, thus any conflicts to be resolved among them were Moscow's sole responsibility. This, however, was also based on a never codified tacit understanding, which prompted the Western participants to occasionally try to change the rigid Soviet attitude in extreme cases, like the issue of the Hungarian-Romanian border.[37] Such interventions, then, were regarded by the Soviets as illegitimate intervention in their "internal affairs." In reality, the only serious fight during the peace settlement emerged over Trieste, an Italian city occupied jointly by Tito's partisans and New Zealand troops in May 1945. As the town was claimed by both Italy and Yugoslavia, this case became a genuine East–West conflict. Remarkably, the Soviets supported Tito only half-heartedly, not risking a clash with the Western allies, and eventually agreed to a compromise. The disputed territory was declared the Free Territory of Trieste by a UN General Assembly resolution in January 1947 and was divided into Zone A—with Trieste under British and U.S. military command—and Zone B under Yugoslav rule. In October 1954, the London Memorandum awarded Zone A to Italy and Zone B to Yugoslavia.

The Sovietization of East Central Europe

While the debate has been going on regarding this issue since the late 1940s, we can argue that the Sovietization of East Central Europe was neither a cause nor a consequence of the emerging Cold War. The Western Allies, as outlined in the previous section, had tacitly accepted the Soviet conquest of East Central Europe from the outset, although they were certainly hoping that Stalin would not necessarily try to Sovietize the region "overnight," as he had the Baltic states, but content himself with the security guarantees of a kind of regional Finlandization. But they could do little but hope, as they had no effective means of influencing events in East Central Europe if they did not want to wage war on the Soviet Union, which was not in the least in their interest. Stalin's team was treating the region as one of prime strategic importance, and we now know that it was prepared to go to war to retain it.[38]

As we still know basically nothing about Stalin's specific plans for the future of the region, experts try to reconstruct them from the Maisky and Litvinov plans, usually concluding that no short-term Sovietization designs can be seen in these materials.[39] But this is an erroneous premise because these are expert materials, and there is no evidence that they would even partially reflect Stalin's point of view. Litvinov's plan contains a strikingly unrealistic desire to classify neutral Sweden as part of the Soviet zone in January 1945, while Maisky's proposal is surprisingly modest in that it presupposes only a Finlandized type of supervision of the area by Moscow in January 1944 in the short run, when it had been clear after the Tehran conference in November–December 1943 that the area would be liberated by the Red Army. Maybe they did not know it, but we now know what Stalin said to Milovan Djilas in April 1945: "This war is not as in the past; whoever occupies a territory also imposes on it his own social system. Everyone imposes his own system as far as his army has power to do so. It cannot be otherwise."[40] And for the Soviet Union, that war started in 1941. (Incidentally, this prophesy was true also for the United States: the former fascist/Nazi states of Italy and West Germany adopted a Western-type democratic model; the former abolished the monarchy and became a republic, while the latter, formally a federation but in fact a strongly centralized state since 1871, directly followed a federal structure, akin to that of the United States.) Consequently, the Maisky and Litvinov plans cannot be taken as evidence that Moscow lacked intentions of Sovietizing the region in the period up to 1947, and therefore there was also no realistic chance behind the postwar Western desire for a "Finlandized" East Central Europe.

The Sovietization of East Central Europe did not affect the development of East–West relations directly and, even if many still claim the opposite, it was not a cause of the Cold War. There is further backing for this argument in the Western reactions to the gradual Communist takeover in the areas liberated and occupied by the Soviet Union. It was not seen as a real casus belli; otherwise, the Truman Doctrine, announced in March 1947 to prevent *further* Communist expansion, would have had to come into force in 1945 or 1946 at the latest. Cutting-edge research shows that irrespective of formal constitutional conditions or the political setup—in most cases a multiparty system and a coalition government—the local Communist parties of all the countries of the region were already in a commanding position as early as 1945–46 in the whole region.[41] Therefore, I use the novel categorizations *quasi-Sovietized* countries (Albania, Bulgaria, Poland, Romania, and Yugoslavia) and *pre-Sovietized* states (Hungary and Czechoslovakia) rather than the terms *democratic interlude* or *limited parliamentary democracy*, as suggested elsewhere.[42]

Yet, in a transposed, indirect sense, the trend in Western policy toward the Soviet Union was influenced to some degree by East Central Europe's deteriorating situation. Western politicians could not admit to their public their tacit acknowledgment that East Central Europe now belonged wholly to the Soviet sphere of influence and that they simply had no effective means to arrest the ongoing Sovietization of the region. Therefore, to satisfy the moral expectations of their societies, they periodically had to utter tough public condemnation of some of the drastic, aggressive steps of the local Communists or the Soviet authorities. The ensuing harsh replies from Moscow then reinforced existing Western suspicions that the Soviet leadership was unreliable, aggressive, and concerned only with its own security—not a force with which it was worth working or cooperating.

On the other hand, we cannot accept the revisionist argument either, still popular in the East and the West, that Sovietization of East Central Europe resulted directly from the breakup of the great-power coalition and announcement of the Truman Doctrine and Marshall Plan—in other words, that before 1947, Stalin had not envisaged imposing the Soviet model on the region's countries. The announcement of the Marshall Plan and the trap it laid for Moscow certainly lay behind the acceleration and completion of the Communist takeover, the herding into one camp of countries often at odds with one another, and the founding of the Cominform to foster the process of establishing the Soviet bloc. The Sovietization process itself, however, as we shall see, began as soon as the Red Army started to liberate and occupy the countries of the region—in the summer of 1944—and it was a most complex phenomenon.[43]

Those denying Moscow's Sovietization plans before 1947 often refer to the paucity of information on Stalin's intentions that local Communist leaders received in the first couple of postwar years, according to the latest research, and to the fact that no blueprint for the regime change has come to light.[44] This may be true, but in fact the local Communist leaders were quite clear about their tasks and acted accordingly. The direct goal was not to take power but to formally retain/establish the system of democratic institutions, thus maintaining the façade of multiparty parliamentary democracy,[45] while building/obtaining a dominant position in the political structure of the given country that would allow the Soviet system to be introduced from a nominally minority position of the local Communist party gradually, peacefully, smoothly, basically imperceptibly, and especially without generating civil war. As accurately formulated by the East German Communist leader Walter Ulbricht, "It's quite clear—it's got to look democratic, but we must have everything in our control."[46]

By modifying the term used by the Soviets to depict the shrewd policies and hard-to-identify activities of the anti-Communist forces during the

Prague Spring in 1968, we can call the Sovietization process the *stealthy revolution*.[47] Stalin was determined to realize all this based on cooperation maintained with the Western Allies; it was crucial for him to acquire U.S. economic support for the rebuilding of the Soviet Union, to ensure Western cooperation for the settlement of the German question and other territorial claims, and for concluding peace treaties with Germany's European allies.[48] Stalin was aware of the functioning of Western democracies in which public opinion was an important factor in decision-making, so he offered a tacit deal to his partners: the Sovietization process would start in the East Central European countries once they were occupied, but it would *look* as democratic as possible. This strategy greatly facilitated playing the game for the United States and Britain, who could thus maintain cooperation with Stalin by constantly portraying the situation in East Central Europe to their own public as not as good as desirable but not as bad as it could be (for example, as that of the Baltic states).[49]

The strategy of gradual Sovietization thus predominantly served the interests of the Western powers and, in reality, was a generous gesture by Stalin, demonstrating his willingness to make serious concessions in exchange for cooperation. Had it not been the case, he could have fully Sovietized the whole region in a few months' time, though perhaps there would have been some local resistance, especially in Poland.[50]

For the political framework of gradual Sovietization, the Soviets recycled a strategy that had proved partly successful in the 1930s in Western Europe in arresting fascist tendencies: the People's Front policy.[51] In a region now occupied by the Soviet Army, this recycled strategy was based on the compelled cooperation of the leftist and centrist political forces forming a broad coalition government, controlled quite openly (or in some cases, in an invisible way) by the Communist Party, and clandestinely but very effectively backed by the Soviet authorities.[52]

The process, the timing, the nature, and the very content of the Sovietization of East Central Europe is still the subject of scholarly debates, with remarkably differing views held by students of the field. Therefore, it is worth examining the main factors that played a key role in ensuring Stalin's double strategic goal: on the one hand, he was determined to maintain cooperation with the Western powers and thus was building regimes with a façade of democracy, but on the other hand, the same systems had to be ready to be turned into the Soviet model at any time, with little difficulty, and especially avoiding civil war. Attaining these irreconcilable-looking aims required a very subtle, complex, and shrewd policy. Building a democratic façade was in fact a rather complicated task, and it required a broad range of means to be applied.

1. *Maintaining the parliamentary system.* Unlike in the Baltic states, where parliaments were eliminated in 1940 when they were annexed to the Soviet Union, parliaments in East Central Europe were formally retained in 1945. This old European constitutional institution was in stark contrast to the Soviet model, with its system of Soviets (councils), so it appeared a promising sign of preserving/creating democratic conditions, especially for an innocent Western public. In reality, however, Parliaments were usually not forums for making important political decisions, and in most cases the governments ruled by issuing decrees. In Romania, Prime Minister Petru Goza completely ignored the otherwise legally existing parliament and in June 1946 simply eliminated the upper house, the Senate, by a government decree. In Poland, the Senate was abolished by a rigged referendum in the same month, while the function of the parliament was exercised by the Communist-dominated National Council up until the elections in January 1947.

2. *Maintaining the multiparty system.* This feature of the new democracies in East Central Europe was strikingly different from the Soviet one-party regime, and this also gave hope to many for the preservation or creating/improving the democratic system. The political spectrum was, however, radically limited from the outset by the Soviets. Traditional right-wing parties were simply not allowed to operate; thus, the existing parties were the Communists, the social democrats, different agrarian parties, and usually smaller liberal parties. Initially this was not necessarily against the wishes of the Western allies, as during the war the Americans and the British themselves were planning to democratize the postwar regimes of the region. A political field limited to leftist and centrist forces was then rather advantageous for the Communists in their efforts to build a dominant position.

3. *Coalition governments.* The Soviets ordered the establishment of broad (and, in several cases, grand) coalitions in every country of the region, which seemed to be a logical step regarding the enormous task of national reconstruction after the war. Indeed, such broad coalitions also existed in Western Europe at the time, where even the Communists were included, as in France, Italy, and Belgium. The Yalta Declaration on Liberated Europe also advocated forming "interim governmental authorities broadly representative of all democratic elements in the population"; thus, this model was supported by the Western allies, too.[53]

The strategy of compelled broad coalition governments, however, was an excellent vehicle for the Soviets to achieve their goals in two different ways.

A. It offered an excellent forum for the Communists to enjoy much greater political influence than their nominal representation and real social support was at the time. This was especially true in the countries where the Soviet Army was present and supported them clandestinely in multiple ways after the end of the war.[54]

B. Conversely, this strategy could be used to create the illusion of a more democratic governance and thus allay Western concerns, when in certain countries the power of the Communist Party was already too strong in the early postwar period. The inclusion of émigré politicians of the London émigré government among the leadership in Yugoslavia and Poland in 1945 were such examples.

Furthermore, the "tradition" (beginning in December 1944) of maintaining a coalition government was a good cover for hiding the unexpected electoral defeat of the Communists in Hungary in November 1945. After the 57 percent landslide victory of the Smallholders' Party, they could—and in normal times should—have governed alone, yet on Soviet orders a coalition government had to be formed with the continued participation of the Hungarian Communist Party (HCP). In general, the model of compelled broad coalition governments, especially in 1945–46, greatly facilitated the Communists' building of dominant positions by using the leverage of continual Soviet support for them and applying pressure on the opponents in a way that was hardly identifiable or perceivable by the outside world.

The system of interparty conferences provided the Communists with additional means to achieve their goals. Many of the key political decisions were not made during sessions of the government but at regular secret meetings of usually two to three delegates of the coalition parties. In Hungary, this model ab ovo gave the HCP a 25 percent representation in a four-party coalition, while they had achieved only 17 percent at the elections in 1945.[55] More importantly, at these sessions the Communists could enforce their agenda by relying on the "requests"—often explicit demands or even threats—of Marshal Voroshilov, the Soviet head of the Allied Control Commission, much more openly than at the sessions of the government, which forced the HCP's opponents to retreat or capitulate in many cases. All of this was greatly facilitated by the Communist-dominated secret police, which gathered information from its agents on the leadership of the other parties and passed it over to the HCP before the interparty meetings.[56]

4. *Elections.* In Yalta, Stalin agreed to hold "free elections" in East Central Europe as soon as possible after the end of the war, and indeed at the end of 1945 elections were held in five countries of the region (out of eight), including Austria. Thanks to the generous attitude of the United States and Britain, no international supervision or deadline was attached to the promise, which greatly facilitated the execution of Stalin's plans. Thus in 1945, elec-

tions were allowed to be organized only in those countries where a positive outcome for the Communists and their allies was expected.[57] "Victory" at these elections did not require an outright Communist success; in fact, it was just the opposite. Due to a Soviet innovation, the parties of the coalition governments were forced to run for the votes jointly as members of an electoral bloc, and the voters could vote only for (or against) this joint list, but not for individual parties within the bloc. This model again offered the double advantage of hiding the relatively weak position of the Communists in Bulgaria, while giving a "democratic" façade to the elections in Yugoslavia and Albania, where the Communists were already in a dominant position at that time, but it was not their parties but a "democratic bloc" that won the polls. The only miscalculation occurred in Hungary in November 1945. Here, the Soviets were originally pushing for an electoral bloc but eventually allowed "real" elections. This fatal concession was due partly to resistance from the United States and Britain, which threatened to not recognize a new government emerging from a bloc-type election in the case of Hungary, and from the leaders of the Smallholders' Party, who expected a good result for themselves. But the main factor convincing Stalin to take the risk was the hyper-optimistic predictions of the Hungarian Communists. In the Provisional National Assembly, set up by the Soviets in December 1944 based on "appointments" rather than election, the HCP had a striking 39 percent overrepresentation. Perhaps this was one of the reasons for their misperception of the situation. For whatever reason, they envisaged a 30 percent share for their party before the elections, which would have been an impressive proof of the great popular support for a party having only a few thousand underground members and starting from scratch in the fall of 1944. While the fact that the Hungarian elections were the only free elections in the Soviet sphere in 1945 is well known, the story of how Stalin secretly intervened to rectify the undesirable result is still hardly known. Stalin ordered Voroshilov to strengthen the Communists' position by initiating the creation of two new deputy prime minister positions in the government, one for the HCP and one for the Social Democratic Party (SDP), to be filled by the leaders of these parties—Rákosi and Árpád Szakasits, respectively. While this move met with relatively little resistance, another demand was more difficult to push through. Stalin was outraged at Voroshilov's lack of vigilance by allowing the position of interior minister to go to the Smallholders' Party, while this post had to be filled everywhere in the Soviet sphere by the Communists. Thus, after a fierce debate, the government had to undo its earlier decision and appoint Imre Nagy of the HCP to this position instead of the strongman of the Smallholders' Party, Béla Kovács.[58]

Stalin learned his lesson from the Hungarian elections and, in future cases, consented to holding elections only when the expected result was certain. The prospects were good from the outset in Czechoslovakia, where the CPCz (Communist Party of Czechoslovakia) had been a legal party in the interwar period and generally achieved about 10 percent in elections.[59] At the elections in May 1946, Stalin's dreams were overfulfilled by the 38 percent result of the party, which made the CPCz by far the strongest party in Czechoslovakia and its leader, Klement Gottwald, prime minister.[60] Remarkably, it was also the highest electoral result for an individual Communist party in the Soviet sphere between 1945 and 1947. The forecasts in Romania, however, were less bright, so Stalin himself had to give detailed instructions (as well as 1 million U.S. dollars, which was multiplied on the black market) to the Romanian Communist leaders on how and when to organize the bloc-type rigged elections to ensure the convincing victory of the government bloc.[61] Proper preparation brought success; to be sure, the elections were first postponed from the spring to November 1946, when eventually the Bloc of Democratic Parties won 70 percent of the votes. Finally, in Poland, the most problematic country of the Soviet sphere, even bloc-type rigged elections had to be put off until January 1947, when the Communist-led government bloc earned an 80 percent victory.

The Stealthy Revolution: The Double-Faced Strategy of the Communist Parties

Under the People's Front strategy, the Communist parties were compelled to compete for political influence with other parties. In reality, in several countries they had been cooperating with mostly these same forces during the war in the framework of the joint anti-German resistance movements encouraged by Moscow from 1941 on, and especially after the dissolution of the Comintern in 1943. Then their task was to fight for national liberation and forget about class struggle and especially taking power. Now their goal was to allay the serious concerns of their societies that their wartime strategy was only a temporary concession and to pretend that Moscow and the Communists had finally given up the goal of establishing the dictatorship of the proletariat in the countries liberated by the Soviet Army. Now they had to pose as one of the democratic parties working for national reconstruction and fight for a set of broad democratic and national goals, thus appearing in a rather constructive role. Therefore, in the mostly backward countries of the region, with a large or even majority agrarian population,[62] they initiated broadly based bourgeois democratic programs, with many popular measures like land reform and land distribution to the poor peasants, democratic electoral law enabling women to vote for the first time, and nationalization of banks and mines. At the same time, Communist parties had to appear as *national* parties, in stark contrast to their interwar image as agents of international Communism directed from Moscow. In several cases, as in Bulgaria, Hungary, and Romania, the parties were renamed from the internationalist model used in the Comintern times to demonstrate their national character; thus, the Communist Party of Romania became the *Romanian* Communist Party. In most cases, these parties were strong supporters and sometimes initiators of even the most radical nationalistic policies of their governments, including ethnic cleansing with the expulsion of altogether ten million Germans from Poland and Czechoslovakia but in smaller numbers from Hungary and Yugoslavia as well.[63]

Among the coalition parties, the Communists were the best organized, most united, and most radical dynamic force. Since their actual political program and activity were limited to implementing the previously mentioned general and, indeed, timely reforms, their popularity grew immensely and rapidly everywhere.

As opposed to this constructive role, the other side of the double-faced strategy of the Communists required them to be prepared for a future takeover whenever the order to that effect came from Moscow. For this they had to build a dominant position in the political life of their countries from the outset. While due to their role in the resistance movement this was no problem in Yugoslavia and Albania, in most other countries the Communist parties (CPs) had to establish themselves from scratch, as they had been marginal and, in most cases, underground political forces until the end of the war. All this required a rather sophisticated and complex strategy, which involved a whole set of political means.

1. The CPs had to acquire strategic positions in the government supporting the attainment of their current and future goals. Thus, the interior ministry, the ministry of justice, and the ministry of agriculture had to be theirs, while traditionally more important posts, like the positions of prime minister or foreign minister, could easily be conceded to their fellow travelers or to other parties. This had the extra advantage of these governments appearing more democratic for the Western public than they actually were, which was an important consideration for Stalin. Thus, until May 1946, out of the seven countries of the Soviet sphere, only Yugoslavia and Albania had Communist prime ministers. Communists got control of the secret police from the beginning in every country, and they had to control the army and key economic positions as well (but not necessarily ministries), like the National Economic Council in Hungary.[64] The secret police directly served the interest

of the Communist parties: they tapped the leaders of the other parties and even the prime minister and passed all relevant information to the CP leaders.[65] From late 1946 on, Hungary played a key role in eliminating the most important political opponent, the Smallholders' Party, by fabricating an anti-Republican conspiracy.

2. Building strong positions for local Communist parties was greatly facilitated by the presence of the Soviet Army in most countries. This, according to Stalin, would give the Communists "such power that even if you say 2 times 2 equals sixteen, your opponents will affirm it."[66] While this extra support was not necessary in Yugoslavia and Albania, the Soviet Army did support the local Communists everywhere, most visibly in Poland but even in Czechoslovakia in the formative period until December 1945, when they were withdrawn from the country. Secret channels to Soviet authorities, and especially to the Soviet-led Allied Control Commissions in Bulgaria, Hungary, and Romania, offered enormous leverage for the CPs.[67]

3. Infiltration into the other parties was another very effective means of undermining the Communists' opponents. There were two main types of this activity: (a) secret CP members joined the other parties and strived for getting into high positions, or (b) leading left-wing politicians of the coalition partners were secretly recruited to work for the Communists. Both were called "crypto-Communists," and while the existence of such "double agents" was common knowledge at the time, it was impossible to prove such collaboration.[68]

4. Organizing left-wing blocs within the government coalition was also used as a powerful vehicle to push through radical measures and to isolate the Communists' political opponents. In Hungary in March 1946, a left-wing bloc was set up with the participation of the HCP, the SDP, the National Peasant Party (NPP), and the trade unions. The bloc demanded the expulsion of twenty-one parliamentary deputies from the Smallholders' Party, labeled "reactionaries" by the Communists. While the Smallholders' Party gained 57 percent of the votes at the elections in November 1945, and both the prime minister and the president of the republic belonged to it, the party eventually yielded to the pressure of the united left and expelled the deputies, thus "voluntarily" starting the self-mutilation of the party, ultimately leading to its total demise by 1948.[69]

5. Utilizing nonparliamentary methods—that is, organizing mass demonstrations against "reactionary forces"—was one of the most absurd means the Communists' used, as these protests were focused directly against the Smallholders' Party, a party the HCP was governing and in coalition with. As the HCP had increasing control over the trade unions, mobilizing the workers was an easy way of intimidating political opponents. At the same

time, the trump card term "reactionary" could be and, indeed, was extended to anyone opposing the politics of the Communists.

6. Applying *salami tactics*—that is, eliminating political opponents one by one, like slicing salami—was perhaps the shrewdest and most effective means of building dominant positions for the Communists. It is generally attributed to Mátyás Rákosi, who indeed coined this term later; however, this tactic was used by all Communist parties in the Soviet sphere.[70] The direction was from the right to the left, starting with the big agrarian parties, which originally had large social support, and ending with the absorbing of the Social Democratic parties through the forced unification of the two workers' parties during 1947–48.

Even though a detailed tactical directive bearing Stalin's signature on the manner of assuming power (a sort of "little Red book on how to Sovietize East Central Europe") has not surfaced so far (and likely never will), in a certain sense we may rightly regard Hungarian Communist leader Mátyás Rákosi's speech delivered at the meeting of the Hungarian Communist Party's Central Committee on 17 May 1946 as the missing blueprint for the *stealthy revolution*.[71] Rákosi had traveled between 28 March and 2 April 1946 on a secret mission to Moscow, where he was trying to achieve better terms for Hungary at the forthcoming peace conference, and he gave a report to his local party leaders about his talks with Stalin and Molotov on 1 April 1946.[72]

In his speech, Rákosi presents in detail the tactics that must be pursued in order to strengthen the position of the Communist Party vis-à-vis the various coalition parties, regarding the trade unions, the peasantry, and so on. In this area, most interesting is the conception according to which the proposal to unite the two workers' parties must be raised now, ignoring the fact that in the short term not even the left wing of the Social Democratic Party supported the merger. It cannot be ruled out that this idea, too, originated from Moscow, and it was part of a general trend: as is known, in the Soviet zone of Germany the unification of the two workers' parties did take place in February 1946, and in 1945 the French Communist Party also attempted the same.

Raising the idea of merging the two workers' parties in the spring of 1946 meant that, at that time, the HCP was experimenting with a model of obtaining power that differed from what would later be realized. As Rákosi clearly explained, a united workers' party with 35 percent of the vote would represent a much greater political force than two parties with 17 percent, and could take more effective action against the overwhelming parliamentary superiority of the Smallholders' Party. Thus, according to this failed plan, the main target and first victim of the HCP's salami tactics would not have been the political opponent positioned on the right of the coalition, the Smallholders' Party, but rather its primary ally, the left-wing Social Democratic Party.

The dominant role of the HCP within the political structure and its strong self-confidence are similarly well illustrated by the way Rákosi spoke of how the Communists must "transform" the internal political relations of their main opponent, the Smallholders' Party: he revealed his plans for how the Smallholders' Party could be turned into a left-wing party instead of a right-wing one with the able services of built-in crypto-Communist members of their leadership. "We will try to force progress to the left from below and from above at once, and thus ensure that the danger, which today is ever stronger, that the right wing of the Smallholders' Party will absorb the center of the Smallholders' Party and with this essentially the bulk of the Smallholders' Party, is reversed so that the left wing of the Smallholders' Party absorbs the center of the Smallholders' Party, and we thereby prevent this largest party from turning to the right."[73]

The speech also contains three extremely important pieces of information on the current priorities of Soviet foreign policy coming straight from Stalin: the Soviet leadership at that time was already planning to establish a new Communist world organization (in other words, the *idea* of forming the Cominform was not a response to the Marshall Plan);[74] in the next twenty to thirty years, there would not be a new world war; and a new situation had arisen in the area of international class struggle.

Thus, we know that in the spring of 1946, Stalin did not expect a new world war in the next twenty to thirty years. It is remarkable that this confidential statement occurred some two months after his infamous election speech on 9 February 1946. Western media presented that speech as proof of the Soviets' break with the Western allies, reporting that Stalin forecasted that a new war was inevitable with the West. Even today, many still regard it as the beginning of the Cold War. Stalin's prediction was also one month after Churchill's "Iron Curtain" speech at Fulton; as can be seen, it did not influence Stalin in the least toward confrontation. Although publicly he reacted harshly to Churchill's speech in a Pravda interview in March 1946, he disclosed his real feelings in a conversation with Romanian Communist leaders a month later: "The peoples and the armies are weary of war. Maybe there will be small skirmishes here and there. The English are screaming, but they would not be able to raise even 100,000 people against us. Churchill wanted to blackmail and intimidate us in his Fulton speech. I answered him so harshly because I wanted to show him that I was not afraid."[75] Indeed, Stalin knew well that Churchill had been speaking only of the actual situation concerning the division of Europe. In other words, in the spring of 1946, Stalin was still determined to maintain cooperation with the Western Allies, and he considered this a realistic possibility.

Because of its outstanding significance, the part of Rákosi's 17 May 1946 speech concerning the new situation in the area of class struggle is worth quoting in its entirety:

> The view will change that was widely spread at the Third International, for example, that we have to wait for the conditions for revolution to appear in at least a number of countries, and that only then can we instigate the revolution will change. . . . One part of this concept is that, in these changed circumstances, whenever a country achieves the conditions for the liberation of the proletariat or for socialism, this will be carried out, with no regard for whether the respective country is in a capitalist environment or not. This is also a new perspective, which simply means that in a country where, as a result of the work of the Communist party, these conditions are present, it has to be realized. This is fresh encouragement for all Communist parties, because now it will principally be dependent on their work whether or not the conditions for the liberation of the proletariat are created in their own country.[76]

All this meant that, in those countries where the Communist Party itself would be able to create favorable internal conditions for a smooth and peaceful takeover, they would now be allowed to do so. However, at this stage Stalin, still eager to maintain cooperation with the Western Allies, did not plan to permit any kind of forceful takeover, relying on direct Soviet support, or implying civil war.

This "encouragement" arriving from Moscow in the spring of 1946 had its effect in Hungary as well: the period of consolidation and gaining strength had come to an end, and it was in fact from this time that we may date the beginning of the complete takeover of power by the Communists in the whole region.[77] So if the green light for finishing the takeover in the Soviet sphere came from Moscow with the founding conference of the Cominform in September 1947, the message in April 1946 can be regarded as the yellow light.

Then, from the summer of 1946 (that is, a year before the Marshall Plan), preparations for political, police, and judicial actions aimed at eliminating political opponents began everywhere, in the spirit of salami tactics. As a result, from late 1946 on, and especially during 1947, a series of anti-government "conspirations" were "revealed" by the Communist-led secret police that resulted in the arrest and imprisonment of many leaders of the non-Communist parties on the right of the political spectrum, the most intransigent opponents of the Communists: the National Peasants' Party in Romania, the Smallholders'

Party in Hungary, and the Polish People's Party. Means applied against the political opponents ranged from intimidating, blackmailing, and corrupting adversaries, to forced emigration, imprisonment, or even execution. This general Communist campaign led in 1947 to the removal of all the top political opponents: Prime Minister Nagy in Hungary was blackmailed into emigration, Deputy Prime Minister Mikołajczyk "voluntarily" left Poland, Iuliu Maniu was imprisoned (and he eventually died in jail) in Romania, and Nikola Petkov, the leader of the opposition, was executed in Bulgaria. As a result, by the end of 1947, all the opposition parties were eliminated or turned into neutralized fellow traveling parties in the Soviet sphere except in Czechoslovakia, where it did not occur until the early months of 1948.

Thus, one part of the Stalinist conception was accomplished almost to the letter: by mid-1948, the Sovietization of East Central Europe was essentially complete—and, moreover, without civil war. In the end, however, this did not happen according to the original plan, since cooperation with the Western Allies could not be maintained simultaneously. As discussed earlier, however, the break was not caused by the Soviet attitude. In reality, during the process of Sovietization, Moscow paid great attention to the special conditions prevailing in the countries of the Soviet sphere all along and demonstrated a great deal of flexibility. Therefore, the Soviets pursued a differentiated policy and played a balancing role in the process: on the one hand a *moderating* role, in order to be able to maintain cooperation with the West, and on the other a *fostering* role, in order to ensure the required level of political leverage over a certain country. When Yugoslav radicalism threatened Moscow's Western relations, Stalin was ready to force even his most loyal ally, Tito, to "slow down" the pace of taking power—that is, to make concessions to the bourgeois forces through the acceptance of Ivan Šubašić of the London émigré government as foreign minister in 1945. When on the other hand, based on their strategic interests, the positions of local Communists had to be strengthened, they did not stay away from the harshest political intervention, as in March 1945, when open threats to the king of Romania eventually led to the appointment of the Moscow-friendly Groza government.

The Marshall Plan, the Cominform, and the Division of Europe

It is now known that the real turning point in Soviet–U.S. relations came with the announcement of the Marshall Plan, not the Truman Doctrine. The Marshall Plan exemplified how U.S. policy was driven by the determination to avert the danger posed by any extension of Soviet influence into the Western half of Europe. The plan was aimed officially at the reconstruction of Europe, but one of its real main tasks was to exclude potential Soviet influence from war-torn Western Europe, notably the Western zones of Germany but also in France and Italy, where Communist parties had great popular support and were very influential. The Marshall Plan in fact was among the first and most effective measures of American containment policy. All this, however, still need not have led to a breach between the two superpowers, as shown by the realistic and reserved acceptance by Moscow of the ban of its expansion in Turkey and Greece declared by the Truman Doctrine. However, the very idea of the Marshall Plan unintentionally created a double-trap situation: a trap for both the United States and the Soviet Union.[78] If the United States had openly decided to limit the aid program to Western Europe, the blame for dividing Europe would have been clearly Washington's, which the Americans obviously wanted to avoid. By eventually offering it to all European states, including the Soviet Union and the East Central European countries, they actually had to cheat, as they knew from the outset that the conditions of the plan would be unacceptable for Moscow, and indeed, it was not meant for them. This was seen as a strategic trap by Stalin as well, one in which he could only lose. If he accepted the offer, Western influence would be maintained and perpetuated in his East European sphere of influence, which could not be countenanced. But if by rejecting it he excluded East Central Europe from the program and its potential positive effects, he himself would have to take responsibility for splitting Europe in two, which he had wished to avoid at all costs so as to maintain cooperation with the West. Since Stalin was unable to escape this great dilemma, he decided, after some hesitation, in favor of making a break, all the while being aware of the consequences.[79]

It has been long debated by scholars when the idea of forming a new international Communist organization after the Second World War was raised. In the absence of relevant sources, the prevailing classical interpretation suggests that this idea was a direct Soviet reaction to the Marshall Plan introduced in the summer of 1947, and after the Soviet Union's refusal of the plan, the formation of the Eastern bloc and its "executive committee"—the Information Bureau of the Communist and Workers' Parties (Cominform)—was a logical next step in breaking off relations with the West. Surprisingly enough, no evidence of any kind has emerged from Russian archives from the time of their partial opening in 1991 pertaining to this important topic. Documents discovered by Russian scholar Leonid Gibiansky in the Tito archives in Belgrade, however, show that the idea of setting up such an organization was already discussed during the talks between Stalin and the Yugoslav leader in Moscow in May–June 1946.[80] Rákosi's account at the session of the HCP Central Committee on 17 May 1946—as mentioned earlier—confirms that a Soviet plan to re-establish an international Communist organization was already in the making as early as March 1946. His account also shows, however, that Stalin took a flexible approach to the question; therefore, the implementation of the plan was postponed in order to avoid its potential negative effects during the forthcoming elections in France, Czechoslovakia, and Romania as well as in the course of the ongoing European peace settlement—especially the conclusion of the peace treaties with Germany's former European allies. All of this proves that the design of setting up the later Cominform, rather than being a simple reaction to the Marshall Plan, was originally part of a wider Soviet scheme aimed at fostering a Communist takeover in East Central Europe gradually and by peaceful means, while preserving Soviet–Western cooperation.

Rákosi gave a detailed account of Stalin's ideas about the new organization. He analyzed in detail how, according to Stalin, the Comintern, established in 1919 and disbanded in 1943 because of its excessive centralization, had in fact not aided but hindered the development and effective activity of the various Communist parties. He stated that now the Soviet leadership—that is, in March 1946 at the latest—was once again planning the formation of an international Communist organization, though it would have to operate on completely different bases: "This will not be an executive body; its task will be to compose, to help in making objections, to communicate the good or bad experiences of one country's Communist party to that of another country, so that they should learn from their neighbors' experiences and losses."[81] In other words, the model described in detail by Rákosi largely corresponded to the Cominform established later, in September 1947, although at this time it was not yet clear—or at least Rákosi's speech did not reveal it—that the new organization, unlike the Comintern, was not striving for the global solidarity of Communist parties but rather would be regional, or an organization primarily of the emergent Soviet bloc.[82]

There were two more important issues in Rákosi's speech concerning the Cominform: first, he mentioned that during recent secret talks between the Hungarian and the Yugoslav Communist leaders, the latter complained about how the Comintern, "unaware of local conditions, sometimes demanded quite the opposite of what they needed." Paradoxically, although Tito and the Yugoslav leaders now became proponents of the new Communist top organization, and indeed Belgrade became the headquarters of the Cominform, their eventual rupture with and expulsion from the Soviet bloc was caused partly by exactly the same Soviet attitude. Second, Rákosi related how, at their recent meeting with the leaders of the Czechoslovak Communist Party, the HCP was advised to publicly attack the Czechoslovak party for its nationalistic policy, while in turn they would attack the Hungarian party. This utterly cynical attitude sheds light on the important role the national issue played in the policy of the Communist parties in East Central Europe aimed at preparing for a future takeover.[83]

Soon after Stalin's final decision to refuse to join the Marshall Plan, Moscow ordered the establishment of the Cominform at a conference in Szklarska Poreba, Poland, in September 1947. Oddly enough, however, the real purpose of the conference—establishing a new Communist international organization—was revealed for the convened participants of the meeting from the countries of the Soviet sphere, including the Polish hosts, as well as representatives of the Italian and French Communist parties, only during the meeting.[84] Setting up the new organization had a double goal: (1) completing the Sovietization process in Moscow's East Central European security zone, and (2) creating a Soviet-dominated unified bloc out of the states of the region that were often in conflict with one another,[85] thus eliminating all elements of uncertainty in order to safeguard against a potential Western attack. In Hungary and Czechoslovakia, where before this point the Communist domination was not yet as visible as in the other countries of the region, this meant a total takeover of power by the Communists.

It is history's irony that, by rejecting the Marshall Plan, Stalin had to publicly reject an "offer" that in reality did not exist—and he knew it. We now know that the Marshall Plan was designed in such a tricky fashion that it was simply impossible for the Soviets to accept it with the given strings attached. This caused the paradoxical situation that although the division of Europe was actually caused by the initiation of the American aid program creating a de facto Western bloc, it was Moscow that had to assume unilateral responsibility for the split by setting up its own Eastern bloc de jure.

By this time, Stalin had realized that the VIP-style American aid for the reconstruction of the devastated Soviet Union he had been expecting since the end of the war would never come, so he decided to declare the strategy of self-reliance. As the Marshall Plan (a good thing) had to be presented to the countries of the Soviet sphere as a bad thing—and, moreover, a dangerous American attempt at subjugating the Western part of Europe—the irrational scheme, declared at the founding conference of the Cominform and later known as the Zhdanov Doctrine, was ready: the world was now divided into two hostile camps: the American-led imperialist camp, which was preparing for a new war, and the camp of the peace-loving East Central European states, led by the even more peace-loving Soviet Union.

Chapter 2

Hungary's Road to the Soviet Bloc

Pax Sovietica: Stalin's Trap and the Hungarian Peace Treaty

In Hungary, the first elections following the end of the Second World War, held in November 1945, resulted in a 57 percent absolute majority victory for the Smallholders' Party, the representative of the bourgeois-democratic political trend. Although Marshal Kliment Voroshilov, the Soviet chair of the Allied Control Commission in Hungary, did his best to influence the results of the elections favorably for the Communists by trying to force a common electoral list, this plan was blocked by the firm opposition of the United States and Great Britain.[1] Thus, the November 1945 elections in Hungary were among those few examples in East Central Europe when the official result of the vote corresponded to the will of the society concerned.

The Hungarian Communist Party obtained 17 percent at the elections, which in fact was a very good result, considering that for the previous twenty-five years they had had to work underground, and the number of party members did not exceed a few thousand during that period. Nevertheless, the leaders of the party had expected a much better outcome, just like the Soviets, who were rather dissatisfied with the performance of the Hungarian Communists. Despite the absolute majority of the Smallholders' Party, the coalition government had to be maintained at Soviet pressure, as this was a key element of their Sovietization strategy. Additionally, under the conditions created by the special needs of reconstruction in a devastated country, it would have been very risky to govern with the workers' parties in the opposition, and the Western great powers also favored the maintenance of the coalition, in which all the major parties participated.

From then on, the principal political aim of the Communist leaders would be *to correct*, as they said, the results of the election—that is, to use every possible means to gain a much greater share of political power than they had been able to obtain in a legitimate way. Analyzing the causes of the electoral failure, they found that one of the greatest mistakes in the party's electoral campaign was to underestimate the importance of the national question, and that is why they were not able to emphasize sufficiently the national character of the Communist Party. As a result, the defense of the national interest was monopolized by the Smallholders' Party, which, it was pointed out, considerably contributed to their victory. Consequently, as early as the end of November 1945, Rákosi, the leader of the Communist Party, proclaimed a new line of policy at a meeting of the Central Committee, which was aimed at strengthening the national character of the party by concentrating on issues considered important in terms of Hungarian public opinion. Such topics included taking a strong line against the persecution of the Hungarian minority in Czechoslovakia, urging the release of Hungarian prisoners of war from the Soviet Union, and demanding the return of the national assets taken to Austrian and German territories at the end of the war.[2]

Realizing this new policy, however, turned out to be rather difficult. On the news of the planned meeting of the American, British, and Soviet foreign ministers in Moscow in December 1945 to discuss the perspectives of the peace treaties with Germany's former European allies, the Smallholders' newspapers began to publish articles urging the formulation of Hungarian peace aims. At the same time they proposed that Hungary's legal claims should expand up to the ethnic borders—that is, the Hungarian government should reclaim territories from Romania, Yugoslavia, and Czechoslovakia, where Hungarian minorities lived in compact blocks along the border.[3] Theoretically, these claims were legal, since those territories had been separated from Hungary as a consequence of disregarding the very basic guiding principle of the peace settlement following the First World War: the principle of self-determination—or, in other words, the ethnic principle. On the other hand, from the point of view of realpolitik, such Hungarian hopes were totally unrealistic, since the peace settlement after the Second World War was not based on the principle of restoring historical justice but directed exclusively by the actual political and strategic interests of the great powers. Paradoxically, while applying the ethnic principle after the First World War served the interests of the peacemakers (in most cases) by supporting the national ambitions of the smaller allies of the victorious entente powers, using the same principle after the Second World War would have favored the very defeated states, especially Germany and Hungary. No wonder, then, that the ethnic principle, originating from President Wilson's Fourteen Points in 1918, was at once discredited in 1945 by the allies, using Hitler's policy vis-à-vis ethnic Germans in Czechoslovakia as a perfect pretext.

From this aspect, considering the country's role in the war, Hungary was definitely in the worst position among the five former German allies preparing for their peace treaties.

The Hungarian Communist leaders were well aware of the realities, and they knew that Hungary had no chance against Yugoslavia and Czechoslovakia, which belonged to the victorious allied powers. Concerning Romania, an ex-satellite of Germany herself, in a peculiar way the political stability of the pro-Soviet Groza government was considered more important by the Hungarian Communists in this early period than trying to regain Hungarian inhabited territories. (Note: At that time, the fate of Groza's *minority* government depended on the possession of northern Transylvania.) They also knew that to raise unrealistic claims concerning the borders would be a very dangerous game for the Communists, since the deciding role of the Soviet Union in disputed issues in East Central Europe had become increasingly obvious by that time, so it was likely that public opinion would eventually blame Moscow's Hungarian exponents for the unfulfilled hopes. That is why the Communists, in spite of the just declared new policy along the national line, took an extremely rigid standpoint in the debate that developed in the press over the potential Hungarian peace aims in December 1945–January 1946.

Thus, the leadership of the HCP undertook another unpopular task, and József Révai, the main ideologue of the party, himself wrote a rather coarse article in the Christmas issue of the HCP's daily, *Szabad Nép*, against the emergence of unnecessary and dangerous illusions concerning the peace goals, in which he described the raising of any territorial claims as "nation-destroying chauvinism."[4] He declared that, by taking part in the war on the side of Germany, Hungary lost the right to reclaim any territory from neighboring states. Therefore, instead of jeopardizing good relations with these countries by raising the border question, the Hungarian government should concentrate on protecting the civil and collective rights of the Hungarian minorities in those countries.

Révai's article triggered a passionate public debate in the still more or less free press among all four coalition parties, in which the Communists were only able to obtain the support of the Social Democratic Party (SDP), and even this just temporarily, leaving the HCP in total isolation with its hyper-realistic position.[5] This was no surprise, as it was extremely unpopular in Hungary in a period when national sentiment penetrated public opinion all over the East Central European region, and at the same time it was obvious that two of the three neighboring countries—Czechoslovakia and Romania—were themselves pursuing strongly nationalistic policies. A public opinion poll from January 1946 showed that the majority of the Hungarian population, obviously not bothering about political realities, was hoping for the restoration of its ethnic borders.[6] Most of the public was expecting from the peace settlement the reparation of the historical injustice committed by the Trianon treaty in 1920; consequently, the realistic position of the HCP was considered as simple indifference to Hungarian national interests. Under such circumstances, the proclamation of this rigid although realistic standpoint resulted in a further fiasco for the Communists in their fight for gaining greater support among Hungarian society. Finally, the press debate had to be banned administratively under Communist pressure, but this did not help the HCP much; this debate meant another political defeat for it. The party lost even from its existing influence, and a considerable part of sympathizers began to turn away from the Communists, and many members, mostly intellectuals, even quit the party.

The leaders of the party soon found the way to manage the crisis: in January 1946, the Communists launched a general attack against the Smallholders' Party, their principal opponent, in order to weaken the strong position it gained at the elections and, at the same time, to expand Communist influence in the country. In cooperation with the Soviet leadership of the Allied Control Commission, they raised economic and political demands against the Smallholders, of which the most important and most dangerous was the pressure that the party exclude twenty-one of its parliamentary representatives, declared reactionaries by the Communists. The Communist Party gave emphasis to these claims by organizing mass demonstrations and eventually, in early March, establishing a so-called leftist bloc with the participation of the parties of the coalition (the HCP, the SDP, and the NPP) and the trade unions, naturally excluding the Smallholders. The general story leading up to the creation of this bloc has been fairly well documented by historians;[7] however, the fact that the Communists used the case of the peace treaty to achieve their political aims in this game was revealed only when formerly top-secret party papers became available for researchers after 1989.

Shortly after their failure in trying to convince public opinion of the realities concerning potential Hungarian peace aims, the Communist leaders showed considerable flexibility and revised their standpoint. They concluded that under the circumstances, it was impossible for the party not to support some kind of territorial claims. Therefore, instead of further holding up such demands, it was rather in their best interest to find out whether there was any hope for gaining Soviet support for such claims, and if so, the Communist Party itself should make capital out of the issue. Consequently, Rákosi initiated exploratory talks with Moscow in late January 1946, which eventually resulted in the following bargain: the Hungarian Communists were authorized to use a potential Soviet promise concerning the peace treaty as a means in their fight against the Smallholders' Party in the ongoing political crisis. According to this promise, if the Smallholders accepted the political and economic demands of the left, the Soviet leaders would be willing to receive a delegation of the Hungarian government in Moscow led by Prime Minister Ferenc Nagy to discuss the issue of peace preparations and other economic matters. It was also indicated that, in such a case, the Soviets would consider favorably Hungary's claim for a minor strip of territory of between four thousand

and ten thousand square kilometers, populated mostly by Hungarians along the Hungarian-Romanian border.[8]

From the available sources, it seems very probable that the offer for this deal was conveyed personally by Rákosi to Ferenc Nagy. The price to pay was big, yet the challenge must have been great for the Smallholders politician. For him, the possibility of leading a delegation to Moscow and to conduct negotiations with Stalin and other leaders, first among the non-Communist East Central European politicians, meant a hope for the fulfillment of the principal aim of his foreign policy; that is, a hope that the Soviets not only legally but practically recognized his government and were willing to accept a non-Communist system in Hungary in the long term.

Indeed, all of this was in line with the foreign policy of the Ferenc Nagy cabinet, which was in fact determined by a clear and pragmatic recognition of the current situation. On the one hand, the politicians belonging to the Smallholders' center entertained hopes that after signing the peace treaty with Hungary, the Soviet troops would be withdrawn from the country, and this would clear the way for freely determining the course of development for the country—that is, using today's terminology, the way toward building and maintaining a market economy and parliamentary democracy. They were also well aware, however, that the Soviet Union, after having suddenly become a world power (and also a new neighbor of Hungary), attached utmost importance to the East Central European region, which played a key role in its security interests. Therefore, from the very beginning, the Smallholders' Party leaders had been making genuine efforts to win Stalin's confidence: they wanted the Soviets to view their party as a trustworthy and reliable partner so that Moscow would base its Hungarian policy on their party, which enjoyed a healthy majority in the Parliament, rather than on the Communist Party, as had been the case in most of the other countries of the Soviet sphere. In doing so, they essentially wanted to convince the Soviets that their long-term security interests could be guaranteed in the future by a non-Communist but friendly government led by the Smallholders' Party just as well as by a Soviet-type regime.[9] This was nothing but an instinctive formulation of the "Finnish model"; therefore, it is not too much to say that if the final Sovietization of Hungary could have been avoided somehow in 1947–48 then, in the decades to come, even a "free Hungary" would most likely have followed a reasonable foreign policy—basically determined by Moscow's proximity—showing much self-restraint, something similar to the quasi-neutrality of Finland during the Cold War.

Anyhow, on 12 March 1946, the Smallholders' Party declared that it had accepted the demands of the left-wing bloc and excluded twenty right-wing parliamentary representatives from the party. On the very same day, only a few hours later, the Political Committee of the Communist Party adopted a resolution to the effect that the Soviet government should be requested to receive a Hungarian delegation headed by Prime Minister Ferenc Nagy in order to discuss the issue of peace preparations. Thus, based on available sources, it is very likely that a deal between Rákosi and Ferenc Nagy significantly contributed, together with other considerations, to the first self-mutilation of the Smallholders' Party—that is, cutting the first slice of the salami (to use Rákosi's infamous terminology)—a move that later proved to have been a fatal step, eventually leading to the disintegration of the party and thus considerably facilitating the Sovietization of the country.

Rákosi did not waste time. At the end of March, he traveled to Moscow on a secret mission to prepare the way for the government delegation. He met Stalin and Molotov on 1 April, all of which shows how the Soviets attached great importance to the matter of supporting the Hungarian Communists in establishing as strong a position as possible.[10] On hearing Rákosi's success story, the Soviet leaders agreed to receive the Hungarian delegation, but there was still another important condition to be fulfilled by the Hungarian government: it had to sign agreements on establishing six joint Hungarian-Soviet companies in the areas of shipping, civil aviation, oil, and bauxite mining in less than two weeks.[11] The negotiations of the experts had been going on for several months, but no settlement acceptable for the Hungarians could be worked out by that time; nevertheless, the agreements on the companies that would lay the foundation for Soviet economic penetration in the country had to be signed before the departure of the delegation.

During the unusually long ten-day visit of the Hungarian delegation to Moscow, from 9 to 18 April, the Soviets did everything to make their guests believe that they were being treated as equals.[12] They were received with ceremony; engaged in exhausting and well-organized sightseeing programs; and met with Stalin, Molotov, and other government officials on several occasions. But since the Hungarians had been "advised" not to take experts to Moscow, the delegation was diplomatically totally unprepared; in fact, the negotiations were far from being genuine diplomatic talks. Concerning the matter of Hungarian prisoners of war and some economic issues, including reparations, minor concessions were made by the Soviets, but in the area of peace preparations they applied very subtle deceptive tactics. When the delegation submitted its alternative proposals for a minimum and a maximum modification of the Hungarian-Romanian border (11800 and 22000 km², respectively), despite the potential promise for Soviet support given to Rákosi earlier, the only reaction was that the Soviet Union recognized the right of the Hungarian government to present this claim at the peace conference. At the same time, it was suggested that Hungary initiate bilateral negotiations with Romania on the issue, although the Soviets were well aware that any loss of territory would lead to the downfall of the Groza government, so it was absolutely hopeless to expect a settlement between the two countries. Moreover, it is very characteristic of the cynicism of Soviet policy that, during the very visit of the Hungarian delegation, Groza was assured that the Soviet government would prevent the existing Romanian-Hungarian border from undergoing any modification.[13]

Stalin and his colleagues played a similar double game concerning the persecution of the Hungarian minority in Czechoslovakia. Stalin declared, to the satisfaction of the Hungarian delegation, that the Hungarians there should have their civil rights; therefore, the Soviet government would raise the question and would try to reach a peaceful settlement. However, in the meantime, during the process of great power peace preparations, the Soviets wholly supported the idea of the forced resettlement of 200,000 Hungarians from Czechoslovakia, and this standpoint was eventually presented publicly by Soviet deputy foreign minister A. J. Vishinsky at the Paris Peace Conference in September 1946, labeling Hungary a bad mother for not being willing to welcome its homecoming children.[14]

To sum up, the Moscow negotiations were rather successful—but only for one of the parties, and it was not the Hungarians. During the talks and meetings, Stalin and his colleagues created an atmosphere that made the inexperienced Hungarian politicians believe that, in return for political and economic concessions and a pro-Soviet foreign policy, the Soviet Union would accept a non-Communist government in Hungary as a long-term partner. Moreover, they made the Hungarians believe, without making any concrete promises, that the Soviets would consider favorably Hungary's peace aims and would even be willing to support minor territorial claims vis-à-vis Romania.

After the return of the delegation, it was not only the Smallholder politicians who cherished great illusions concerning Soviet benevolence. The Communist leaders themselves did not realize for a time that, while performing the role of the pander in this political game, they themselves were used as mere puppets by the Soviets. Just like Prime Minister Ferenc Nagy, Foreign Minister János Gyöngyösi, and other Smallholders, the Communists made rather optimistic declarations—both confidential and public—concerning potential Soviet support for the Hungarian peace aims. Rákosi had so much confidence in Stalin's personal promise to him that on 15 April, even before the return of the government delegation, he informed the British envoy in Budapest that "there is some hope that Hungary will recover part of Northwest Transylvania," as the Soviet Union looks favorably on the question and, according to his information, England and America would not dislike such an adjustment.[15] Moreover, they were so self-confident that even the fact of Rákosi's secret mission and his mediating role was revealed, since now the Communists, too, wanted to have their share in the anticipated success.[16] The HCP not only sought to convince the Hungarian public of its crucial role in resolving this important issue but also wanted to confidentially inform the leaders of the Hungarian minority in Romania about the soon-to-be territorial gains. After the Moscow trip, Miklós Vásárhelyi, a *Szabad Nép* journalist, was sent to Transylvania by Révai with this mission.[17] Moreover, the second man in the HCP, Ernő Gerő, had a secret meeting with Gheorghiu-Dej and other Romanian Communist leaders on the issue in Transylvania, but there the latter firmly rejected even the idea of discussing the territorial question.[18]

The period of great expectations, however, did not last long. The publicly announced decision of the Council of Foreign Ministers in Paris on 7 May 1946 on reestablishing the 1939 borders between Hungary and Romania had the effect of cold water on both the Hungarian public and politicians. Ferenc Nagy tried to explain the situation by stating that it was not the final great power decision on the matter (of course it was) and that it could be changed later through the peace conference.

Rákosi must have been even more surprised at this unexpected turn of events. Nevertheless, owing to his great experience in the Communist movement, he quickly realized that he had no other choice but to comply with the Soviet decision and be ingenious enough to find his own way out of the crisis. From then on, he kept arguing that the Paris decision was due to the Western great powers (which was of course not true) and that it was the Hungarian reactionary forces that should be blamed for the deterioration of the country's international situation.

The Hungarian Communists themselves acted as mere puppets in a game where the only aim of the Soviets was to use both their allies and their enemies to create more favorable conditions for a future takeover. This story is a good example of how the Soviets used not only the Communist parties in these countries but, in fact, every possible means, including non-Communist political forces—that is, the political opponents themselves—to secure their *then* main strategic aim: to create the most advantageous political and economic conditions possible for a future Communist takeover.

Hungary's Incorporation into the Soviet Bloc

The Stalinist "stimulation" of April 1946 accelerated the process of Sovietization not only in Hungary but throughout the Soviet zone. Subsequently, actions aimed at eliminating political opponents became more intense essentially everywhere in the region. In the spirit of salami tactics, the process began with the right-wing forces and ended with the forceful merging of the Social Democratic parties into the Communist Party in 1948.

In Hungary, the left-wing bloc against the Smallholders' Party served as a political framework for the elimination of the opposition, the special feature of which was that the HCP had always governed in coalition with the Smallholders. From the end of 1946, the traditional political struggle increased to a new level, while the unveiling of the "conspiracy against the Republic" provided an excellent platform for the displacement of some of the key Smallholder leaders. In February 1947, the Soviet secret police's arrest of Béla Kovács—secretary-general and strong man of the Smallholders' Party—had already clearly indicated that now the Communists, in cooperation with Moscow if necessary, could use any means against their opponents. The forced resignation of Prime Minister Nagy in June 1947 finally opened the way for the HCP's full takeover: on the basis of a false confession from Kovács, Nagy was suspected to have known about the conspiracy himself; thus, to avoid the expected arrest, he did not return home from vacation in Switzerland and resigned his post.[19] This was the first case in the region where a non-Communist (and openly Western-friendly) prime minister had to be removed by "legal means." In addition, we know about Stalin's personal role in this case, as described in the memoirs of Mátyás Rákosi. According to Rákosi, after he proposed to the Soviet leadership the arrest of Ferenc Nagy, at the instruction of the Soviet envoy to Budapest, he had to travel to Arad, close to the border in Romania, as a matter of urgency. Once in Arad, Ivan Susaikov, the chair of the Allied Control Commission in Romania, handed him a sealed envelope with a message written by Stalin, in which he warned Rákosi that, according to the information of the Soviet authorities, Nagy did not go to Switzerland on holiday but to talk with the "enemy" about the Communists being excluded from the government coalition.[20] Although the credibility of Rákosi's description is questioned by some, it is precisely on the basis of the almost incredibly adventurous circumstances that we can assume that the story describes real events, not to mention the fact that Moscow had often interfered in issues of Hungarian politics with much lesser scope; as such, it is highly unlikely that this major action would have been taken without consulting the Soviets.[21]

The severely weakened state of the Smallholders' Party thus deprived of its intransigent leaders, along with the increasingly unlimited nature of Soviet influence, is well characterized by the fact that the Soviets did not even entrust Rákosi with the election of Nagy's successor; instead, it was V. P. Sviridov, the head of the Hungarian Allied Control Commission, who suggested that the post should be given to Lajos Dinnyés of the Smallholders' Party, who was rightly considered a Communist puppet.[22]

All of this paved the way for the elections in August 1947, in which the new electoral law, various restrictive measures, and electoral fraud made the HCP the largest party, at 22 percent, but the left-wing bloc was able to gather only 45 percent of the votes.[23] So they still needed the Smallholders' Party to have a majority for the government coalition.

At that time, however, it was no longer a serious barrier to the full Communist takeover. In the autumn of 1947, with the intensive use of salami tactics, the opposition parties were either disqualified or eliminated and, in the spring of 1948, the complete neutralization of the Smallholders' Party had occurred. In a peculiar way, according to Stalin's expectations, even in the fall of 1947, "lawful" means had to be applied against the opposition.[24] It is important to note that between April 1946 and September 1947, the deepening of the Sovietization process was still the goal; the acceleration and completion of the process was ordered at the founding meeting of the Cominform. But it was soon made clear that full takeover had to be completed in all countries of the region as soon as possible. In Hungary, this happened in June 1948 with the forceful merger of the two workers' parties: the HCP and the SDP.

The total Communist takeover took place by the summer of 1948 throughout the region. After that, uninterrupted political-military cooperation was secured through a network of bilateral friendship and mutual assistance treaties between Moscow and the Central and East Central European states that had been directly incorporated into the Soviet imperial sphere of interest. The parties committed themselves to providing military assistance in the event that one of them was attacked by Germany or the states allied with it and committed themselves not to participate in an alliance against the party under attack. The Soviets had already concluded such an agreement with Czechoslovakia in 1943 and with Yugoslavia and Poland in 1945, as these states were regarded as allies in the Second World War. With the former enemy states of Bulgaria, Hungary, and Romania, the treaties were signed only in 1948. The member states of the Soviet bloc that had been emerging since 1947 had to conclude similar agreements with one another as well, so a total of fifteen such bilateral agreements formed the specific security system thus established.[25]

The formation of NATO in April 1949 posed a major challenge to the Soviet bloc, but it did not occur in Stalin's life to create a similar military-political multilateral body in the East Central European region. Logically, the question arises why such an organization was not founded in 1949, immediately after the formation of NATO. Cold War logic would have dictated it, and in many other cases the *action-reaction* model was the answer: the Marshall Plan was followed in 1947 by the creation of the Cominform and, in 1949, the Council for Mutual Economic Assistance (Comecon); in 1948 the proclamation of a South Korean state was followed by the creation of the Democratic People's

Republic of Korea; and to the founding of the Federal Republic of Germany in May 1949 came the reply of the German Democratic Republic later that year. In most of these cases, Soviet reaction took no more than a couple of months. In 1949, eight years before Western European economic integration and the creation of the common market, the Comecon—the economic cooperation organization of the Soviet Union and the Central and East Central European countries—was established. In other words, the idea of integration per se was not alien to Stalin's leadership, but the relationship between the center in Moscow and its allies in this classic era of the Cold War was characterized by direct manual control and basically a strictly centralized military economy. A multilateral decision-making mechanism, even in a formal version, would certainly have caused confusion in the operation of the machine. The establishment of a multilateral military-political organization, having meetings regularly and composed of member states that theoretically had an equal status, therefore did not fit into Stalin's political philosophy. Thus, a relationship governed by *bilateral relations* with the allies was more in line with the real hierarchy between the center and the member states of the periphery.

Founded in January 1949, the Comecon was the first integration organization of the Soviet bloc states, but in fact it did not work in Stalin's time. Instead, each country pursued an autarkic economic policy, and the existing insignificant bilateral trade was characterized by barter. Thus, the formation of the Comecon at an early stage was rather a symbolic move, indicating the unification of the Soviet bloc.[26] In a peculiar way, the Cominform also did not play the coordinating role assigned to the organization at its founding conference in September 1947. First of all, it was the organization of the Communist parties, not the states but, more importantly, no meaningful activity was carried out from the end of 1949 until its dissolution in April 1956, and not a single meeting was held during that time. Following the inaugural meeting, only two conferences were convened: the first one in Bucharest in June 1948 was dedicated to the criticism of the Yugoslav Party, and at the last one in November 1949, the task was Tito's and Yugoslavia's final expulsion from the Soviet bloc.[27] True, the secretariat of the Cominform did in principle exist in Moscow, but there is still not much to know about its work. The most prominent appearance of the organization was the journal *For Lasting Peace, for People's Democracy!* This was the official organ of the organization, published in all countries in the bloc in the local language, as well as in English, French and Spanish and it soon became one of the main mouthpieces of international propaganda directed from Moscow.

Until Stalin's death in 1953, even the summit of leaders of the Soviet bloc was summoned only once, but then the stakes were high. The secret meeting in Moscow with the participation of party leaders and defense ministers from 9 to 12 January 1951 was convened by Stalin just over half a year after the Korean War began, to coordinate the bloc countries' military buildup.[28] In his "keynote speech," Stalin gave a dialectic analysis of the state of East–West relations: the United States would like to start a war but is not yet able to launch it; thus, the Soviet bloc states must have powerful armies built by the time the United States could launch the war, in about two to three years' time, thus deterring the aggressor from taking action:

> The opinion arose in recent times that the United States is an invincible power and is prepared to initiate a third world war. As it turns out, however, not only is the U.S. unprepared to initiate a third world war but is unable even to cope with a small war, such as the one in Korea. It is obvious that the U.S. needs several more years for preparation. The U.S. is bogged down in Asia and will remain pinned down there for several years. The fact that the U.S. will be tied down in Asia for the next two or three years constitutes a very favorable circumstance for us, for the world revolutionary movement. These two to three years we must use skillfully. The U.S. has atomic power; we have that too. The U.S. has a large navy; but their navy cannot play the decisive role in a war. The U.S. has a modern air force, but theirs is a weak air force, weaker than ours. Our task consists of using the two-to-three years at our disposal in order to create a modern and powerful military force. This we are capable of doing, we have all the prerequisites for this. China has created a better army than those of the People's Democracies. It is abnormal that you should have weak armies. This situation must be turned around. You in the People's Democracies must, within two to three years, create modern and powerful armies that must be combat-ready by the end of the three-year period.[29]

After Stalin's speech, the defense ministers gave detailed reports about the preparedness of their armed forces. The reports revealed that none of the allies of Moscow in the Soviet bloc were prepared for war. Marshal Rokossovsky, the Polish minister of defense, suggested, that in the case of his country, they could meet these expectations but much later than planned (1953): by the end of 1956. Chervenkov, the Bulgarian party leader, expressed similar concerns.[30] However, Stalin briefly stated that if the Poles (and the Bulgarians) could not ensure that the third world war would not break out before 1953 then they should execute the instruction.[31]

At Stalin's suggestion, a planning committee was set up under the leadership of the Soviet defense minister, Marshal Alexander Vasilyevsky, in which representatives of all participating countries were seated. On 10 and 11

January, the committee drafted detailed development plans for individual states in the building of the Soviet Army's headquarters, according to which the mostly backward countries had to build up an advanced military industry and a capable, modern army with Soviet assistance over three years. The committee also delineated the expected numbers of soldiers in each country:

Poland: 350,000 in peacetime, 900,000 in wartime
Czechoslovakia: 250,000 in peacetime, 700,000 in wartime
Hungary: 150,000 in peacetime, 400,000 in wartime
Romania: 250,000 in peacetime, 600,000 in wartime
Bulgaria: 140,000 in peacetime, 400,000 in wartime
Total: 1,140,000 in peacetime, 3,000,000 in wartime[32]

In a peculiar way, while others found the numbers assigned to their country excessive, Rákosi, who would have liked to be Stalin's best pupil, was dissatisfied with the Hungarian army's number for peacetime. He saw to it that this problem was fixed, so the strength of the Hungarian army became 210,000 by 1952.[33]

In response to a Romanian proposal at the meeting, they agreed on the establishment of a permanent body to coordinate military and army developments. At the plenary sessions, Stalin strongly supported the plan on several occasions, so we can rightly suspect that behind the plan there was a preliminary Soviet-Romanian secret agreement. Nikolai Bulganin was elected chair of the committee, which operated in Moscow with two permanent representatives from each country (one military and one civilian).[34] At the moment, however, we still do not know much about the activities of the committee, which is rather surprising given that, in the majority of the countries of the former Soviet bloc, relevant documents became open for research after 1989. Therefore, this committee cannot be regarded as the predecessor of the Warsaw Treaty Organization established in 1955,[35] especially as Stalin emphasized that this committee should work under strict secrecy.

Although the records of the meeting are seen by many as evidence of Stalin's plans for a war against the West, Stalin did not in fact formulate the Soviet's intentions for war; on the contrary, he proclaimed his strategy one of deterrence. In other words, he declared that the only way to avoid the war that the Americans might launch is to build a strong and powerful army among the Soviet bloc: "Let me remind you that the three years at our disposal are not for sleeping, but for arming, and arming well. Why is this necessary? This is necessary in view of the imperialists' way of thinking: they are in the habit of attacking unarmed or weakly armed countries in order to liquidate them, but they keep away from well-armed countries. This is why you need to arm during this respite, and arm well, in order that the imperialists respect you and keep away from you." That is, at the secret Communist summit in January 1951, Stalin actually revised his earlier thesis on the inevitability of war. This is not even surprising in light of the fact that just a month later, in a Pravda interview, he publicly expressed the thesis that war between East and West can be avoided. All of this can even be seen as the theoretical basis for the détente process that began after 1953: Stalin's message to the West was aimed at ensuring that the Korean War should not be considered as preparation for a Soviet invasion of Western Europe, since the Kremlin was still interested in maintaining the European status quo established in 1945. The same purpose could have been served by the speech of legendary Soviet propagandist Ilya Ehrenburg a few months earlier, in November 1950, in which he proclaimed the importance of peaceful coexistence.[36]

Hungary's integration into the Soviet bloc, formally established in the autumn of 1947, could be realized without any difficulty after the 1947 August elections. Internationally, this meant above all joining a specific virtual military pact consisting of bilateral treaties. Between 1947 and 1949, Hungary concluded bilateral friendship and cooperation agreements with all member states of the Soviet bloc: with Yugoslavia in December 1947, with Romania in January 1948, with the Soviet Union in February 1948, with Poland in June 1948, and with Bulgaria in 1948 July. With Czechoslovakia, the treaty was not signed until April 1949 due to the oppressive policy of the Prague government toward the Hungarian minority there.

In domestic politics, the union of the two working parties in June 1948 cleared the way for the adaptation of the Stalinist political-economic model. The introduction of the one-party system and the planned economy—the full nationalization of industry, the banking sector, and commerce—was completed by 1949. The Sovietization of education, culture, and science was completed by 1950–51.[37] All this transformation was supported by the involvement of a large number of Soviet advisors. It is noteworthy, however, that the countries of Central and East Central Europe did not have to take over the entire Soviet model—that is, parliaments remained and People's Front-type umbrella organizations were operating to simulate the multiparty system. (There were no such things in the USSR.)[38] In addition, in some countries, such as Poland, Czechoslovakia, and the GDR, even some of the so-called fellow traveler parties could continue their activities; they "only" had to accept the leadership of the Communist Party and "the program of building socialism." Similar parties, such as the National Peasant Party and the Smallholders' Party, still participating in the 1949 elections, were not officially banned in Hungary either; however, they simply "passed away" according to contemporary terms.

Hungary's foreign policy room to maneuver was drastically reduced beginning in the autumn of 1947, and from 1948 on, the country's foreign relations were characterized by total Soviet subordination. Parallel to the emerging personal cult of Rákosi, communication with the "Center" in Moscow—that is, with Stalin—became his privilege. The main means of communication was a telegraph connection after 1949, coupled with a special eavesdropping-free secret telephone line.[39] At the same time, Rákosi was lucky to have a chance to personally consult with Stalin on several occasions: between 1949 and 1953 we know of nine such meetings, mostly in Moscow or in other locations in the Soviet Union.[40]

From the available documents, the image of a specifically proactive Rákosi unfolds, as if trying to just prove the contemporary slogan "Rákosi is the best Hungarian pupil of Stalin." In fact, he tried to ignore the adjective "Hungarian," as he really wanted to play a prominent role in the whole Soviet bloc. His ambition was not entirely unfounded; according to "the one-eyed man is the king among the blind" principle, there were not many rivals in the Soviet bloc after 1949. Bulgarian Dimitrov, a hero of the Leipzig trial in 1933, who played a prominent role in the international Communist movement, died in 1948. The Yugoslavian Tito, due to his outstanding role and military success in the Second World War, had been secretly yearning for the position of the region's gauleiter. Now, however, he had become a more hated enemy than the American president, Truman himself. The East German Walter Ulbricht also had a notable workers' movement history but, to his bad luck, in 1949 he became the leader of a Soviet puppet state, the GDR, which was not recognized by anyone outside the Soviet bloc and thus had little international authority. Gheorghe Gheorghiu-Dej in Romania was a "home" Communist, never living in the Soviet Union, which was always seen as a great disadvantage in the Kremlin, especially as he had engaged in constant infighting against the Muscovite faction in his party that only ended in 1952, with the ousting of Ana Pauker. Finally, Bierut in Poland and Chervenkov in Bulgaria were newcomers; both became leaders only in 1948 after replacing Gomułka and Dimitrov, respectively.

At the same time, Rákosi could boast of a well-known international heroic past: he was a member of the leadership in the short-lived 1919 Hungarian Soviet Republic, and from 1920 to 1924 he represented the Comintern in several European countries, serving as one of the secretaries of the organization from 1921. In 1924, he returned illegally to Hungary, where in 1925 he was sentenced to eight years in prison. His last-word speech at his trial made him internationally known, and the slogan "Free Rákosi" became a widely popular demand by the European labor movement. He spent a total of sixteen years in prison in Hungary. Since at that time, after the Molotov-Ribbentrop

Pact of August 1939, the Soviet Union was a quasi-ally of Nazi Germany, Stalin wanted to make a friendly gesture toward the Hungarian government, so in October 1940 Rákosi was freed (together with Zoltán Vass) in return for the banners that had been taken as booty in the 1848–49 War of Independence by the czarist army.[41] After his release, Rákosi was celebrated in Moscow as a hero of the international workers' movement, and at the ceremony on November 7, he had the privilege of standing beside Stalin on the grandstand in Red Square. Though neither Rákosi nor any of his colleagues in the Soviet bloc had a university degree, Rákosi stood out among them, as he spoke four languages, including English. Thus, he was the only member of the Hungarian government delegation visiting Washington in June 1946 who could speak to President Truman without an interpreter. He was also the only Communist leader in the region who had personally talked to the American president and the British and French prime ministers.

All of this probably gave Rákosi political ambition that the others did not have, so he felt responsible for the fate of the Communist system not only in his own country but also in the other states of the bloc. Thus, while trying to follow Stalin's policy in everything, he often tried to play a proactive role in international affairs. Keeping in touch with Stalin was rather one-sided, as the Soviet leader rarely responded to Rákosi's suggestions or plans, or to the actions he had taken or planned. This provided a kind of relative autonomy for Rákosi: he could be enterprising, and as long as there was no clear prohibition or rejection from Moscow, there was no problem. Thus, from 1948, Rákosi provided the Czechoslovak leadership with secret information about the unreliable, "traitorous" elements in their circles. In the summer of 1949, during the preparation of the Rajk trial, he compiled a document concerning six Communist parties on the basis of the confession of Noel Field, an American defendant in the trial, which he presented personally to Stalin in Moscow. General Sándor Nógrádi, a veteran of the Spanish civil war, was sent to Warsaw, while Gábor Péter, head of the ÁVH, the Hungarian secret service, traveled to Bucharest to provide secret information to the local leadership and enlighten them about who he considered their "enemies."[42] Obviously, Rákosi's goal was to deliver enough ammunition for the still hesitating sister parties to organize their own anti-Tito show trials, á la Albania and Hungary. He also made bold incursions into issues with a broader international dimension; thus, in August 1949 he reported to Stalin his suspicions that Louis Weinstock, one of the leaders of the U.S. Communist Party who was visiting Budapest at the time, was a provocateur and was associated with the Rajk trial. In July 1950, shortly after the outbreak of the Korean War, he approached Stalin with the ambitious plan that Hungary would provide medical assistance to the "attacked" North Korea, and immediately proposed the shipping of an entire hospital, for which he got approval.[43] The military hospital—built, financed, and run by Hungarian doctors and staff—was set up in 1950 in the town of Sariwon and was logically named after Mátyás Rákosi.[44]

From the summer of 1948, when Tito's expulsion from the Soviet bloc was to be expected after sharp criticism of Belgrade's policies at the Bucharest meeting of the Cominform, the focus of Rákosi's efforts was on radically changing his own attitude toward Yugoslavia. The Hungarian-Yugoslav relationship had been remarkably good since 1945, especially in light of the serious conflicts with Czechoslovakia. Not only were the interstate relations excellent, but the leaders of the Hungarian Communist Party, including Rákosi himself, often visited secretly for consultations with Tito, who was considered a potential regional leader because of his international authority. In December 1947, Tito made a four-day official visit to Budapest, where he was received with great ceremony. In a conversation with Molotov on 29 April 1947, Rákosi sincerely revealed that Hungary's relationship with Yugoslavia was better than that with the Soviet Union.[45] It was no wonder, then, that Hungary signed the first friendship and cooperation treaty in the Soviet bloc with Yugoslavia in December 1947, during Tito's visit.

Thus, in parallel with the deepening of the Soviet-Yugoslav conflict, from 1949 Rákosi did his best to make his own Yugoslav-friendly past forgotten and, as compensation, tried to play the role of the leader of the anti-Tito campaign throughout the Soviet bloc. This led to the fact that the main "defendant" in the Rajk trial—the first Stalinist show trial in Hungary in September 1949— was actually Tito himself, and the real defendants were responsible for revealing his devilish plans in their fabricated confessions.

The Hungarian leadership also actively participated in the implementation and maintenance of the economic blockade against Yugoslavia. Thus, Rákosi did not shy away from intervening in the internal affairs of a brotherly state for the sake of the sacred purpose; in March 1949 he sent a message—to add emphasis, via Moscow—to Klement Gottwald, stating that he had stopped the Czechoslovak military material shipment to Yugoslavia that was sent through Hungarian territory.[46]

One of the highlights of anti-Tito propaganda was the Cominform's third, and last, conference, in which the only task was to expel Yugoslavia from the Soviet bloc. The meeting was held on 16–19 November 1949 in Hungary, at the resort of Galyatető in the Mátra Mountains. It is possible that the site selection was considered to be Rákosi's "reward game" because of the successful execution of the Rajk trial and his outstanding performance in the anti-Tito propaganda campaign. Typically, the exact location was secret for decades; official documents said only that the meeting was held in Hungary.[47]

The Hungarian-Yugoslav relationship reached an unprecedented nadir between 1949 and 1953. The population was resettled from the frontier zone, a sealed border protection system—similar to the one on the Austrian border—was created with a minefield, and even minor armed incidents were frequent along the border. The Cominform resolution of November 1949 categorized Yugoslavia as an ally of the imperialist powers preparing for a new war, and in fact Belgrade became the primary enemy—not only for Hungary but for the entire Soviet bloc. Rákosi stated that, in this situation, "the danger of war is primarily presented by Yugoslavia."[48] Already at that time the Hungarian army had begun preparations for repelling an attack launched by Yugoslavia and for launching a successful counteroffensive.[49]

It was only a few years ago that researchers discovered that, between 1949 and 1953, a fortress system was built—at huge expense—on the six-hundred-kilometer-long Hungarian-Yugoslav border, which we can rightly call the Hungarian Maginot Line, meaning that a much stronger border protection was established between Hungary and its Communist southern neighbor than between Hungary and its capitalist Western neighbor, Austria. This contradiction, of course, is explained not only by the anti-Yugoslav paranoia of the time but also by the fact that the eastern part of Austria was under Soviet occupation until the autumn of 1955, meaning that Hungary did not have to prepare for an attack from that direction.

Despite all this, diplomatic relations were not broken between the two countries but were reduced to the lowest possible level. True, in 1951, Rákosi took the initiative in this matter and tried to get Stalin's permission to sever diplomatic relations with Yugoslavia. According to Hungarian sources, an attack was carried out in public on the Hungarian chargé d'affaires in Belgrade in March 1951, and the attackers assaulted him and his driver. In the subsequent exchange of diplomatic notes, Rákosi tried to sharpen the situation, even suggesting to Stalin to declare the Yugoslavian chargé d'affaires in Budapest a "hostage" by not only depriving him of diplomatic immunity but also preventing his departure from the country. Stalin, however, who generally suggested restraint toward Belgrade, advised him not to "sharpen the issue with the Yugoslavs." Eventually both diplomats returned home, and diplomatic missions were reduced to a single administrative staff member.[50]

After 1949, Western relations were radically downgraded, and contact between the Budapest legation and the Hungarian government was minimized, with the aim of maintaining only formal diplomatic relations. The U.S. economic embargo applied since 1948 against the countries of the Soviet bloc (from 1949 under the Coordinating Committee for Multilateral Export Controls [COCOM]) did not initially represent a major downturn in the traditionally weak Hungarian–American economic relations. The serious deterioration of relations between 1948 and 1949 was generated by the Hungarian government through organizing show trials in order to achieve the nationalization of U.S.-owned companies, MAORT and Standard Electric, without compensation. Several Hungarian leaders of these companies, as well as American Robert Vogeler and Briton Edgar Sanders, were sentenced to serious prison sentences for espionage in February 1950, and two Hungarian executives were executed. In response, the United States closed the Hungarian consulates in New York and Cleveland, banned its citizens from entering Hungary, and suspended the operation of the Hungarian restitution committee in the U.S. zone in Germany, which was responsible for detecting and returning Hungarian goods.[51] Britain had already terminated the ongoing trade negotiations in December 1949 and introduced an economic embargo against Hungary.

The U.S. legation at that time had 70 U.S. employees (22 of them diplomats, including 7 military officers) and 103 Hungarian employees, or a total of 173 people working on the mission. Compared to the size and importance of the country, this figure was extremely high, so it is not surprising that in 1950—in what was the coldest period of the Cold War—this number had to be reduced by half, at the demand of the Hungarian government.[52] From the end of 1949, the main task of the U.S. legation was to secure the release of Vogeler. During the secret talks between the two governments, the Hungarian side showed serious ambition: for the release of the American "spy," they demanded not only the lifting of the sanctions introduced by Washington but also the return of the Hungarian crown, which had become a "prisoner of war" in the American zone of Germany and had since been guarded in the United States. In addition, they wanted a change in the frequency of the Voice of America, which disturbed domestic broadcasts. The plan was fundamentally successful, as eventually Washington, except for returning the crown, met all Hungarian claims; thus Vogeler could leave the country in April 1951.[53] Rákosi's activist behavior, depicted earlier, was confirmed through his attempts to introduce world political dimensions even in such a bilateral hostage case: he told Moscow that Vogeler's release would have been possible earlier, but he had instead taken into account the interests of the Soviet bloc concerning the development of the Korean War.[54]

In April 1952, in the middle of the Korean War, an international economic conference was held in Moscow, where the main topic was the development of East–West economic relations. In addition to the leaders of the Soviet bloc countries, the meeting was attended by a number of Western economic players who hoped to open up the "Eastern" markets, even though Western governments tried to prevent their participation. The history of this important international forum could hardly be known until recently, when Mikhail Lipkin wrote about it.[55] Although no major breakthrough occurred at that meeting, the Soviet leadership did not give up hope. It was also an important message that in October 1952, in his speech at the Nineteenth Congress of the CPSU, Georgy Malenkov strongly urged the expansion of East–West trade relations. Of particular significance in terms of the development of the East–West relationship is the fact that the thesis of peaceful coexistence had already been included in the official preparatory materials of the conference, although this was not yet included in the final documents.[56] At the same time, as we have seen, this thesis had already appeared in November 1950 in a semi-official version in the speech by Ilya Ehrenburg in Warsaw, which indicated that the Soviet leadership was constantly working on somehow improving East–West relations. Although there was no major breakthrough at the Moscow Economic Conference in April 1952, this meeting also indicated that before Stalin's death in March 1953, processes aimed at reducing the Cold War tension and rebuilding East–West cooperation in some form had already begun.[57]

The Hungarian leadership also became involved in the cautious early process of opening to the West when, beginning in early 1952, it attempted to at least partially restore economic relations with the Western states, which were at a low point after 1949. The most promising was the British relationship. In 1949, Britain suspended trade relations with Hungary due to the incarceration of British businessman Edgar Sanders in Hungary, so the situation seemed relatively simple. As early as February 1950, when the conviction of Sanders took place, the Rákosi leadership initiated secret talks with the British government. In principle, the Hungarian leadership was willing to release the prisoner in exchange for lifting the trade embargo.[58] However, the talks did not succeed, so the Hungarian side changed tactics in November 1952, emphasizing that the Sanders case was not going to be negotiated together with economic issues. In January 1953 it was announced that, in exchange for Sanders, the British should release a Malaysian Communist called Lee Meng, who was sentenced to death on charges of terrorism in her country, then a British colony.[59] In his memoirs, Rákosi writes that the idea came from Molotov, with whom he met in October 1952 at the Nineteenth Congress of the CPSU in Moscow.[60] Thus, the Soviets tried to give the transaction a Cold War dimension, and they wanted to label the deal a "prisoner exchange" for the public, which would also have proved the selfless help of the Soviet bloc toward the colonial peoples struggling for their freedom. It is noteworthy that, in appealing to the "difficult position" of the British, the Hungarian side tried to achieve a partial lifting of the COCOM list as well, which restricted the export of strategic goods to the Communist countries. The British government, which was originally inclined to make a deal for Sanders, refused to accept the idea of exchanging prisoners, so the negotiations were suspended in March 1953.

In August 1953, however, the incoming Imre Nagy government, in one of its first foreign policy decisions, released Sanders unconditionally. In response, the British government immediately lifted the economic embargo, and in the autumn of 1953, the diplomatic preparations for the resumption of Hungarian–British financial and trade negotiations began, eventually leading to a financial agreement in June 1956.[61] This was a significant result under the given circumstances, as a similar treaty between Hungary and the United States was only established in 1973.

Chapter 3

East Central Europe and the First Phase of Long Détente, 1953–1956

Détente Revisited: Interdependence and Compelled Cooperation

There are several interpretations of détente but, in mainstream scholarship, the prevailing idea is that it was the period between 1969 and 1975, when the relaxation of tension in East–West relations produced spectacular results, including the settlement of the German question, U.S.–Soviet agreement on arms limitation, and bilateral cooperation, eventually culminating in the signing of the Helsinki Final Act. There is formidable evidence, however, to argue that in fact détente began in 1953 and was in effect uninterruptedly until the collapse of the Soviet Union in 1991.[1] Proving this thesis, that may be surprising to many, certainly needs a detailed explanation.

The era between 1953 and 1956 is still a controversial issue in terms of its importance in world politics, marked by a range of political events and trends, such as the beginning of détente, a promising attempt at relieving the tension between East and West in the "spirit of Geneva," and the historically important Twentieth Congress of the Soviet Communist Party on the one hand, as well as serious conflicts, such as the 1953 East German uprising, the Indochina War, the Taiwan Straits crisis, the rebellion of Poznan in June 1956, the October 1956 events in Poland, and both the Hungarian Revolution and the Suez crisis in 1956, on the other hand. Since spectacular and palpable results (agreements) were not achieved in the East–West relationship during these years—apart from the end of the Korean War, the settlement in Indochina, and the completion of the Austrian State Treaty—it is generally assumed that this short period was an early failed attempt at improving East–West relations, but the logic of the Cold War prevailed until the following decade, and real détente began only in the mid-or late-1960s.

The analysis of once top-secret documents from the highest levels of decision-making, however, makes it increasingly clear that the most important trend in East–West relations during the formative years between 1953 and 1956 was—despite any disturbing event or propaganda—the mutual and gradual realization and understanding of the fact that the two prevailing political-military blocs and ideologies had to live side by side and tolerate each other in order to avoid a third world war, inevitably waged with thermonuclear weapons, which would certainly lead to the total destruction of human civilization.

The appreciation of this meant such a decisive change in the East–West relationship that it is not too far-fetched to distinguish two fundamentally different phases of the Cold War: before and after 1953. In fact, we could call them Cold War I and Cold War II.[2] I consider the period between 1953 and 1956—despite what many think even today—not only a promising but misfired attempt at realizing the policy of détente but also a major landmark, after which the Cold War meant something other than it did before.

In my view, the main characteristic in the relationship of the conflicting superpowers after 1953 was—despite the ever-increasing competition in the arms race—the continuous *interdependence* and *compelled cooperation* of the United States and the Soviet Union and their respective political-military blocs, although immanent antagonism obviously remained. Competition, conflict, and confrontation remained constant elements of the Cold War structure, but now they were always subordinate to and controlled by the détente elements: interdependence and compelled cooperation with the aim of avoiding a direct military confrontation of the superpowers at all costs.[3] This model began to take shape in 1953, ramped up in 1955–56, then produced more spectacular results beginning in the mid-1960s, developing into a sometimes near-cynical superpower cooperation, which from time to time was disturbed by both real and (more often) pseudo crises, which caused some temporary tension in East–West relations and sometimes not even that.

It could rightly be asked why the year 1953 should be regarded as a watershed. Arguably, even earlier, the leaders of the superpowers, including Stalin, did not actually plan to launch an attack on the other side, although they did not rule out the possibility of their opponent starting a war. Thus, the fundamental change was not due to Stalin's death but to technological developments. The H-bomb was tested by the United States in 1952, followed by a Soviet test in 1953. In reality, the experience of the unprecedented destructive power of the atomic bomb in 1945 did not drastically change strategic thinking on future warfare. Even after the Soviet Union became a nuclear power in 1949, it was assumed that, even in case of the massive use of A-bombs by both sides in an armed conflict, the enemy could be defeated in a third world war.[4] The alarming idea that such a conflict could result in the total annihilation of human civilization by destruction and long-lasting nuclear radiation spreading around the globe emerged only after the invention of the H-bomb. It was the series of H-bomb tests, with an ever-increasing yield between 1952 and 1955, that made it apparent to policy makers that a new war waged by thermonuclear weapons could not be won. Therefore, it is no surprise that the shocking idea of MAD (mutually assured destruction) was "invented" by John von Neumann in the middle of the 1950s, although the term and the doctrine became generally used only a decade later. The recognition of all this led to the early realization that, in such circumstances, the other party simply *cannot want* to launch a war, and soon, as the most important result of the four-power Geneva Summit meeting in July 1955, it was made evident that it really *did not want* to start a war.[5]

Traditional conceptions of détente are based on a linear and exclusive interpretation of the relationship between Cold War and détente. These interpretations basically apply a model according to which—with some simplification—at any given time there was either Cold War *or* détente. That is, when the superpower relationship was bad, one can refer to that period as the Cold War; when it was good, it was détente. In fact, this relationship was not linear at all, and the two categories were certainly not mutually exclusive. They could not and did not replace each other. It is worth noting that the traditional interpretations essentially—and unintentionally—follow the logic of politicians of the Cold War era. After 1953 and especially following the Geneva Summit in July 1955, Moscow and its allies were convinced that the Cold War was over, replaced by peaceful coexistence. That is, they clearly used the two categories in an exclusive way. This is well demonstrated by cases when, in their internal discourse, they identified East–West conflict situations with the Cold War and often argued that the Western powers wanted to bring back the Cold War or Cold War style into the East–West relationship.[6] The same logic was perceivable on the other side as well: in June 1969, when a new wave of Soviet–American rapprochement was unfolding, Henry Kissinger spoke of the Cold War as a category *belonging to the past*, compared to which relations would now enter a constructive phase.[7]

In essence, détente was not a simple tactical move resulting in the temporary easing of tension in superpower relations, as is usually depicted, but rather a *system of serious and permanent interdependency* based on mutual responsibility for the preservation of human civilization, which forced the superpowers to cooperate in order to avoid a direct military conflict. Détente was thus a new model of East–West *compelled coexistence*, characteristic of the second phase of the Cold War after 1953, that worked as an automatism, controlling and determining the actions of the political leaders on both sides. At the same time, détente was an integral part of the Cold War bipolar international structure, which disappeared only after the dissolution of the Warsaw Pact and the Soviet Union in 1991, meaning that the two phenomena are not exclusive. Therefore, we cannot speak about détente "overcoming the Cold War,"[8] as the former did not replace the latter; the two simply coexisted. By the same token, there was no "Second Cold War" between 1979 and 1985, as held by many, since this implies that a *First* Cold War had ended sometime earlier, which was obviously not the case. It must be made clear that the antagonism between the two world systems existed from the Bolshevik revolution in 1917 until the demise of the Soviet Union.[9] Thus, during the whole Cold War era, from the end of the Second World War up to 1991, it was seen as a zero-sum game, based on their mutually exclusive ideologies: both sides regarded the other as an eternal enemy, assuming that, in the long term, peaceful competition between capitalism and Communism, their own system would eventually triumph, and consequently the other one would perish. What made the Cold War so dangerous, however, was not the ideological but the military antagonism, in which field there was no dénouement, not even during the most spectacular period of superpower rapprochement in the first half of the 1970s. On the contrary, from 1945 until 1987, an ever-increasing arsenal of nuclear and conventional weapons was deployed on both sides. NATO and Warsaw Pact military plans alike regarded each other as lethal enemies to be destroyed and annihilated in case of an armed conflict. In both alliances, military exercises and war games were conducted against the other bloc, and more importantly, up until the very end of the Cold War in 1991, an enormous number of intercontinental and medium-range ballistic missiles with a nuclear capacity to make human life impossible on earth were targeted not only at each other's military facilities and infrastructure but also at all the major cities, with the obvious aim to basically eliminate the whole enemy population.[10] This means that, while the leaders of both superpowers did everything they could to successfully avoid a fatal military clash, a third world war could have broken out *by accident* during the signing of the Helsinki Final Act in August 1975, at the very moment of the triumph of détente.

The mechanism of compelled cooperation, however, was not visible to contemporaries. Still, we now know that it is the tacit recognition of the European status quo and spheres of influence that explains American inaction at the time of the Soviet bloc's internal crises, which, consequently, can be regarded as only pseudo crises in the East–West relationship. More importantly, the real crises of the time, especially the second Berlin crisis and the Cuban missile crisis, could be resolved peacefully via secret diplomacy—in the latter case, by totally neglecting the position of their own allies on both sides—which is exactly the mechanism of compelled cooperation, aimed at finding a compromise solution and even directly helping the opponent to save face in order to avoid the escalation of the crisis. While the continuous presence of the elements of cooperation and confrontation during the Cold War has been pointed out by Raymond Garthoff,[11] this novel theory claims that the mechanism of compelled cooperation not only played an important role in periods when the element of cooperation was dominant in East–West relations but was a crucial means of solving the crises exactly at the time of the gravest confrontations, like the Berlin crisis in 1958–61 and the Cuban missile crisis in 1962.[12]

Similar cases of the omnipresent mechanism of compelled superpower cooperation could be mentioned in all stages of the East–West relationship from 1953 to 1991. This new interpretation of détente also explains how it was possible that, just a few years after the alleged "death/demise/fall of détente" at the end of the 1970s, an unprecedented rapprochement between the superpowers occurred just a few years later, with the coming of Gorbachev from 1985 on. While the new wave of the arms race in the second half of the 1970s and the Soviet invasion of Afghanistan resulted in anti-détente rhetoric in the United States, they did not actually change the substance of the superpower relationship that had been determined by the established interdependency.[13]

This also means that despite what the traditional interpretation holds, dating the "classical Cold War" era between 1945/1947 and 1962,[14] I argue that this early stage, based on the idea of total confrontation, lasted only until 1953. Regarding the logic of the relationship, what came after can be called the era of *compelled coexistence*. This term describes this relationship more accurately than the original "peaceful coexistence," used initially by the Soviets from the mid-1950s and later, from the 1960s more generally, especially as the coexistence of the two camps was in reality peaceful only in Europe.[15] In other parts of the world, clashes and military conflicts between the representatives or proxies of the two blocs occurred regularly up until the end of the Cold War era.[16]

The new strategy of peaceful coexistence was introduced by the old-new Soviet collective leadership emerging after Stalin's death, beginning as early as right after the funeral of their former boss, in March 1953. Therefore, it is important to emphasize that this policy was *not* initiated at the Twentieth Congress of the CPSU in February 1956, as most studies on the topic claim. At that forum, it was elevated to the level of a long-term doctrine based on the thesis that war between the socialist and capitalist camps was not inevitable; therefore, the two camps could and indeed should coexist. Most importantly, this doctrine was in force right up until the dissolution of the Soviet Union.[17] This meant a much more flexible foreign policy aimed at radically easing tension in East–West relations and the continuous deepening of political and, especially, economic cooperation with the West, with the obvious aim of reducing the cost of the arms race and thus improving the Soviet Union's chances of surviving the intensifying competition between the two opposing blocs.[18]

For the Soviet bloc leaders, it meant a peaceful competition between the two blocs in which of course, in the long run, the Communist bloc would eventually win. This did not mean giving up the class struggle as such; it only meant that the focus of class struggle was redirected from Europe—the most important territory for advancing Communism so far—to the third world, where supporting mostly indigenous liberation movements created a chance for expanding Soviet influence.[19] Penetration into the third world consequently started as early as 1953—not in the late 1950s or the early 1960s, as assumed by many. Nor did peaceful coexistence mean giving up the arms race, as the main Soviet goal was to achieve and then maintain nuclear parity at any cost with the United States, thus providing the Soviet Union with its long-dreamed-of equal status as a superpower. To be sure, peaceful coexistence was truly peaceful in the meaning that the Soviet bloc leaders wanted to preserve peace by all means and, as far as we can tell from the available sources, they never wanted to start a war against the West.

Therefore, from the middle of the 1950s, Moscow was trying to consolidate the territorial gains of World War II by offering the West a deal on legalizing the European status quo and, in turn, providing a guarantee for Western Europe against a potential Soviet bloc attack while also tacitly denouncing any further aspirations for using the Communist parties in the West to work for a takeover. While the Khrushchev-Molotov plan for a pan-European security pact was presented to the Western powers without any preparations in 1954 and then was not surprisingly turned down as a propaganda means, the idea reemerged just a decade later, eventually leading to the signing of the Helsinki Final Act.[20]

Soviet Foreign Policy after Stalin's Death

After Stalin's death, the new Soviet leadership attempted to make significant changes in both the domestic life and foreign policy of the empire. In the late 1940s, the Soviet Union—whose economy had still not recovered from the trauma of World War II—began spending heavily in order to keep pace with the United States in the arms buildup that had begun with the Cold War. Following the formula that had proved effective in the 1930s, the capital necessary for weapons production was to be generated through an extensive diversion of resources from the agricultural and consumer-goods sectors of the economy. It is for this reason that the new Soviet leadership, especially during Malenkov's premiership from March 1953 to February 1955, attempted to mitigate domestic unrest by establishing a more balanced economic structure marked by reduced emphasis on heavy industry, particularly arms production. However, the Soviet plan to reduce expenditures on arms could only be implemented within the context of a general improvement of East–West relations, which had until then been based on mutual fear of forthcoming direct superpower confrontation.

Accordingly, beginning in March 1953 Soviet foreign policy became much more flexible, and for the first time since the closing stages of World War II, the Soviet Union displayed a serious willingness to negotiate and compromise with the Western powers. This change in Soviet comportment ultimately opened the way for ending the Korean War and reaching a settlement in Indochina as well as in Austria. All of this led to such a significant reduction in East–West tension in a very short period of time that the mid-1950s are referred to as the first period of détente even in traditional mainstream literature.

Soviet foreign policy had four main trends in the years preceding 1956.[21]

1. First of all, it was marked by attempts at a rapprochement with Britain, France, and the rest of Western Europe as well as the United States without seriously considering any change in the European status quo. With the onset of détente, the Soviet Union's relations with the West, based on a growing parity in the balance of power as well as a mutual respect for the post–World War II status quo in Europe, were to receive a new definition. Although Moscow did in fact respect the sanctity of the European spheres of influence throughout even the chilliest years of the Cold War, Western Europeans were nonetheless constantly worried about the possibility of a Soviet attack. The new course in Soviet foreign policy gave rise to a greater sense of security in Western Europe. The increased Soviet inclination toward negotiation was also largely due to the fact that even though they had, with the development of the hydrogen bomb, largely caught up with the United States in the arms race, the differing geopolitical location of the two countries still left the Soviet Union in a vulnerable position, since it was not capable of any direct attack on the American continent until the intercontinental ballistic missile was developed at the end of the 1950s. The Soviet shift to a more conciliatory foreign policy also had another, more concrete motivation: it hoped to prevent the rearmament of West Germany by sowing discord within the Western alliance.

The Soviets nonetheless clearly defined the limits of the compromises they were willing to make throughout the entire course of negotiations with the West, and it soon became obvious that they were only disposed to discuss issues such as the status of Germany and Austria, which the Western great powers had been unable to agree on among themselves. The irreconcilability of Soviet and Western positions regarding the reunification of Germany ultimately prevented the sides from reaching any kind of agreement, and, when West Germany joined NATO in May 1955, the question of German unification as a serious possibility was taken off the agenda until the fall of 1989. The resolution of the Austrian question in 1955 nevertheless demonstrated the willingness of the Soviet leadership to bargain with the West: in exchange for a pledge to withdraw their troops from the country, the Soviets were able to get the Western powers to agree to permanently uphold Austria's strict neutrality and to allow those East Central European countries that were not already members of the United Nations to join the world organization. The Soviets, however, never considered the issue of the satellite countries to be negotiable; in fact, since the Soviet Union's ratification of the Austrian State Treaty in 1955 would remove the legal basis for the continued presence of its troops in Hungary and Romania, the Soviet Union used this as an opportunity to foster integration within its empire by establishing the Communist bloc's military alliance, the Warsaw Pact, one day before the signing of the Austrian State Treaty.[22]

2. Even though the Soviet leadership itself respected the postwar *European* status quo, this did not mean that they had given up on the idea of expanding the Soviet Union's sphere of influence in general. Soviet expansionist ambitions centered now on the new countries born in the wake of the rapid disintegration of the colonial empires after World War II—that is, the third world. Contrary to the strong-arm methods it had used to subjugate East Central Europe after World War II, the Soviet Union was able to peaceably bring many of these primarily Arab and Asian countries into its political orbit. People in these underdeveloped countries, where there was a strong and natural demand for an accelerated modernization, were often allured by the Soviet social and economic model emphasizing equality and centralized planning. Beginning in the mid-1950s, Soviet foreign policy was aimed at exploiting opportunities for ideological expansion into the third world through intensive propaganda and, where necessary, economic aid. By this time, the Soviets had also begun to discreetly provide some of these countries with arms and military advisors. Soviet prudence in this area was proved later, at the time of the Suez crisis in October–November 1956: not only did the Soviets completely exclude the option of providing direct military support to Egypt, but Soviet military specialists and advisors immediately left the country so as not to become embroiled even indirectly in conflict with the Western powers.[23] A few days later, when it became clear that the United States itself would compel Great Britain and France to cease their armed attacks on Egypt, the Soviets resumed their propaganda strategy of portraying themselves as the champion of the independence of the Arab countries and the peoples of the third world in general.

3. One of the major foreign policy aims of the new Soviet leadership was to restore the unity of the socialist camp, broken in 1948 by the aggravation of the Soviet–Yugoslav conflict. Khrushchev and Bulganin sought to conciliate Tito with a visit to Belgrade in May 1955, where the deterioration in relations

between the two countries was blamed on earlier Soviet policy (mentioning initially only the personal role of the since-executed Beria). The Soviets made several other positive gestures in 1955–56 designed to revive friendship, for instance by openly accepting the Yugoslav doctrine that there were other means of building socialism besides the Soviet model. However, this was taken far from seriously by the Soviet leaders, who were still only able to think in terms of military blocs. Their political aim was gradually to reintegrate Yugoslavia fully into the socialist camp by peaceful means, even if that involved concessions, the eventual goal being the country's entering the Warsaw Pact. Only in the spring of 1958 did it become clear to the Soviets that the Yugoslavs were quite opposed to this and indeed were determined to play an ever more intensive role in the nonaligned movement.[24] Consequently, bilateral party relations began to cool again, but connections between the two states were stabilized at a fairly satisfactory level in the coming decades.

4. The main Soviet purpose with the Communist countries of East Central Europe was to maintain political stability at all costs. As this essentially involved deciding the fate of the region's countries, it is worth devoting a separate section to this subject.

Emerging Emancipation: Changing
Soviet–East European Relations

The permissible pace and scope of post-Stalin political reform in East Central Europe depended greatly on which faction happened to have the upper hand in the incessant power struggles within the Soviet leadership, but there was never any question in Moscow that the satellite states should remain inside the Soviet empire.

At the same time, the Soviet leaders were ready to work out and use a more workable, flexible, reliable, and effective model of cooperation that was more predictable for both parties in the "normal" day-to-day relations between Moscow and the East Central European states, so they could maintain political stability. While before this it had generally meant direct contact between Stalin and the top leaders of each East Central European country—the local little Stalins—now the collective Soviet leadership did its best to strengthen the local collective leadership in every country and maintain contacts through them. Another new feature was that the former occasional ad hoc consultations were replaced by regular bilateral and multilateral consultations between top-level leaders, hoping to achieve better results in their cooperation.

As early as June 1953, during talks with the Hungarian leaders in Moscow, the Soviets explicitly stated that they wanted to renew their relations with the allies in a fundamental way. According to Beria, this relationship "was not the proper kind of relationship, and this led to negative consequences. Celebratory meetings and applause constituted the relationship. In the future, we will create a new kind of relationship, a more responsible and serious relationship." Malenkov explicitly stated that "this relationship will be entirely different from that of the past." Beria added that Moscow "will inform the comrades about this," possibly hinting at the preparation of a special document containing directives for the allies on this topic.[25] While such a statute was issued only on 30 October 1956 as part of the Soviet government declaration, there are scattered references in the sources about preparations for such a document between 1953 and 1956, and in June 1956 the British embassy in Moscow had information about a statement on Soviet–East European relations to be published in the near future.[26] Indeed, the practice of Moscow's cooperation with its allies changed remarkably between 1953 and 1955. However, this did not mean any radical change in the state of subordination; it was merely the regulation and rationalization of this relationship, making it more efficient. Whenever the Soviet leaders believed they could only achieve their goal by brutal political intervention, they sharply rebuked the leaders of the East Central European countries in an authoritarian tone that often outdid even Stalin. In January 1955, when Hungarian leaders were again summoned to Moscow for consultations, Khrushchev practically threatened Prime Minister Imre Nagy with execution: "You are not without merits. But then again, Zinoviev and Rykov were not without merits either; perhaps they were more meritorious than you are, and yet we did not hesitate to take firm steps against them when they became a threat to the party."[27] And in a state of emergency, when it was a question of protecting Soviet imperial interests, they would not shrink from using the most drastic means possible. In October 1956 they threatened the local leaders in Poland with military intervention, and at the beginning of November it was a Soviet military invasion that put an end to the revolution in Hungary.

At the same time, in the spirit of a policy of general reconciliation, the Moscow leaders took great pains to make the relationship between the Soviet Union and its allies more flexible and also more regulated. Established in May 1955, the Warsaw Pact was, at that time, seen by many as a means of creating tight unity and strengthening Soviet dominance within the Soviet bloc. However, this political-military alliance itself gradually began to play a catalyst-like role in the new type of Soviet–East Central European relations. To create formal parity, the Warsaw Pact was established based on the organizational framework of NATO;[28] thus, the organization was formally the alliance of sovereign and equal states based on voluntary cooperation. The forming of the Warsaw Pact meant also the institutionalization of multilateral and regular military-political coordination within the Soviet bloc, which in itself meant a *qualitative* change with respect to former conditions. Previously, only bilateral consultations were held on a rather ad hoc basis, usually initiated by the Soviets; multilateral negotiations or Communist summit meetings could only be launched by Moscow. In formal terms, the position of the allies became even more promising: they could participate in shaping the policy of the Soviet bloc as partners enjoying "equal rights" both in the Warsaw Pact and in the Comecon, which was awoken from its slumbers in the spring of 1956.

The doctrine of "active foreign policy" announced in the spring of 1954 was also meant to increase the fitness of the allies for international society and the maneuvering capability of the entire Soviet bloc.[29] From then on, Moscow encouraged its allies to use their international reputation, achieved or to be achieved with Soviet support, as effectively as possible to increase the reputation and influence of the Eastern bloc in the international political scene. During the settlement of the Indochina situation, Poland became the first Soviet ally to acquire an important role in world politics: after the Geneva Accords were concluded in 1954, the country became a member of the International Control Commission set up to oversee the execution of the agreements. As a by-product of the bargain that the superpowers made on the issue of the Austrian State Treaty in 1955, Albania, Bulgaria, Hungary, and Romania were admitted to the United Nations in December of the same year; thus, with the exception of the German Democratic Republic, the European states of the Soviet bloc had achieved a minimum level of fitness for international society.[30] All of these measures gradually and significantly increased the international reputation of the allies, which had before been called simply "Soviet satellite states" in the West. This new development marked the beginning of a process of gradual emancipation in three directions: in their relationship with the Soviet Union, with the West, and with third world states.[31] As a result, the East Central European states could become increasingly more acceptable actors in international politics, enabling them to promote the Soviet bloc's political objectives more successfully in the field of East–West relations and also in the third world.

From this time on, and especially from the mid-1960s up until the collapse of the Communist regimes in East Central Europe, this strategy became an effective model for cooperation among the states of the Soviet bloc in the field of foreign policy. In the spirit of this policy, from 1954 onward Moscow informed its allies intensively and extensively, partly through bilateral channels, of the Soviet position on a given issue of international politics, and often even concerning the steps the Soviets planned to take in shaping East–West relations.

The demand for intensive coordination also brought radical changes in the practice of holding multilateral summit meetings: between the last session of the Cominform in November 1949 in Hungary and Stalin's death, there was only one such meeting that we know of, held in January 1951, while during the period of some two years between November 1954 and January 1957, seven such summit meetings were held.[32] At the conference in Moscow in June 1956, it was explicitly declared that there was no need for the establishment of a new coordinating body for the Communist parties of the socialist countries and, in the future, conferences of these parties could be convened at the initiative of any of the parties.[33]

To conclude, Khrushchev's vision was to furnish new foundations for the relations of the Soviet Union and its allies, essentially by modifying these relations in terms of a dominium, rather than a colony. This was closely connected to another crucial element of Khrushchev's concept: realizing the great potential of a now truly existing Western bloc, he planned to create an Eastern bloc with at least formally equal capabilities out of the group of subordinated states, so that it could successfully take part in the grand historical (and peaceful) competition between the Soviet and the Western models.

Integration in the East: The Establishment of the Warsaw Pact

Beginning in 1948, smooth political-military cooperation was guaranteed by bilateral treaties of friendship and mutual assistance between the Soviet Union and the Central and East Central European states that had become part of its sphere of influence. While the Comecon had been established in January 1949, and NATO had existed since the same year, in Stalin's lifetime, as explained earlier, no plan was ever made to establish a political-military alliance for the Soviet bloc.

After Stalin's death, the old-new Soviet leadership worked out a spectacular new concept for representing Moscow's interest in international politics, and accordingly, a much more flexible approach emerged in the field of East–West relations as well. Apparently, they sought to pacify the conflicts that had stemmed from the ending of the Second World War or from the Cold War system in Southeast Asia, as well as the Far East and Europe. To this end, the Soviets employed a very large amount of diplomacy in the middle and second half of the 1950s. First, they sought to create stable conditions in the rather hot theaters of the Cold War in Asia. They helped to end the Korean War and promoted the settlement of the situation in Indochina, and then started to work for the political stabilization of the most important region, Europe.

In 1954, taking advantage of the favorable international climate created by the peace settlement in Asia, the Soviets proposed the creation of a collective

European security system and agreed to a significant great-power compromise by concluding the Austrian State Treaty, which was followed by the withdrawal of their troops from the eastern part of Austria. The first East-West summit meeting since the Potsdam Conference in 1945, held with the participation of the four great powers in Geneva in July 1955, already clearly indicated the Soviet's determination to achieve the international codification of the European status quo established in 1945, a Soviet dream that would come through two decades later with the signing of the Helsinki Final Act in 1975.[34]

When proposing the establishment of a collective European security system, their main concern was that the Soviet empire's security was not guaranteed by international law due to the lack of a German peace treaty. Therefore, their priority was that Germany's eastern border, established at the Potsdam Conference, should be consolidated by having it recognized by the Western powers and especially by the FRG, even at the price of significant compromises. Ironically, as this was the boundary between the GDR and Poland, they sought to achieve the legalization of a border by the West that lay within the Soviet bloc. The Western powers, however, rejected the Soviet initiative because they were convinced that it only served propaganda purposes, and therefore no attempt was made to test Moscow's real intentions.

After this rejection, Western suspicion seemed to be substantiated by the decision of the Soviet leadership to create a military-political alliance of the Eastern bloc, following the model of NATO. This move raised the question of whether Khrushchev and the other Soviet leaders were seriously interested in the easing of tension in international politics. If so, why did they decide to form the Soviet bloc's military-political organization at a time when many of their initiatives and actions seemed to verify their serious intention and determination to deepen dialogue and cooperation between East and West? Setting up the Warsaw Pact was clearly seen in the West as an aggressive move, as it seemed to be in total contradiction with the current Soviet foreign policy line promoting détente.

Arguably, however, the formation of the new organization eventually benefited the Soviets, both in their negotiations with the Western great powers and in shaping the new federal system within the Soviet bloc. We can identify five main reasons why the Soviet leaders decided on the establishment of the Warsaw Pact in May 1955.

1. In 1954–55, the development of the German question took an unfavorable turn from a Soviet perspective. West Germany's entry into NATO created a new situation for Moscow concerning European security and the question of borders. Up until that time, NATO in fact had not been considered an organization seriously threatening the security of the Soviet Union,

as the Soviet leaders were aware that the Western military alliance had been created to counteract a potential Soviet threat against Western Europe.

Because of their experiences in the Second World War and the unsolved nature of the German question, the Soviets saw the FRG not simply as another NATO member state but as a potential new source of danger, an actor in international politics seeking to change the European status quo hitherto tacitly accepted by both the East and the West. Remarkably, the entry of Turkey and Greece into NATO in 1952,—although the former had a common border with the Soviet Union itself and both were neighbours of Bulgaria, and Albania was bordering on Greece,—did not eventuate any harsh reaction by Moscow.

The FRG was in fact the only European state which openly rejected the boundaries agreed upon by the allies at the Potsdam Conference in 1945, i.e., the border between the GDR and Poland (the Oder-Neisse line) and between the GDR and the FRG, the so-called intra-German border. Theoretically, Bonn even questioned the borders of the Soviet Union proper, as the former German province of East Prussia was divided between Poland and the Soviet Union, thus the northern part of the region, the Kaliningrad (formerly Königsberg) district became a Soviet exclave. This position was conveniently made possible by the lack of a German peace treaty, which would have compelled Germany to recognize these borders. Thus, West German politicians could rightly point out the temporary nature of the Potsdam Agreement, which was originally meant to be made permanent by a peace treaty.

Moreover, Bonn did not regard the Munich agreement invalid from the outset; thus, it potentially questioned the boundary between the FRG and Czechoslovakia as well.[35] All of this was evaluated in Moscow as a serious threat to the security of the Soviet empire's security zone, established in Central and East Central Europe in 1945, which was further aggravated by the rapidly growing economic power of the FRG.

Thus, it was the FRG's joining NATO that changed the status of the Western alliance from annoying to dangerous in the Soviet perception and, to compensate for this situation, the idea logically arose that a military-political organization of the Soviet bloc, including the three "endangered" Central and East Central European countries, should be established to demonstrate unity and power. The German threat was taken seriously by Moscow.

2. The creation of the Warsaw Pact was also apparently part of a diplomatic maneuver, as pointed out by Vojtech Mastny.[36] Khrushchev's original plan was not aimed at setting up a well-functioning powerful military-political organization but to create a device by which he could exert pressure on the Western great powers in order to establish a collective security system in Europe

according to Soviet taste. In this context, the formation of the Warsaw Pact was necessary above all to have an organization of "equal value" to NATO that could be "sacrificed" during bargaining with the West by offering the simultaneous and mutual dissolution of both alliances. Thus, the formation of the Warsaw Pact was primarily motivated by political rather than military considerations.[37]

3. It is also noteworthy that up to this point, bloc policy—political, economic, and military integration—was primarily part of the policy instruments of the West. By 1955 there existed a number of Western or Western-controlled alliances: NATO, Montanunion, the Western European Union, the Balkan Pact, CENTO, and SEATO.[38] However, due to their heavily centralized policies, the Soviets did not even exploit the framework of the two existing joint organizations, the Cominform and the Comecon. The former held only three conferences, in 1947, 1948, and 1949, and then it was dissolved in April 1956, while the Comecon did not function in practice until 1954.[39] Thus, the creation of the Warsaw Pact can be regarded as a logical reaction to the process of continuous block formation in the West.

4. Mostly following the organizational model of NATO, the Warsaw Pact served as an excellent framework for promoting the Soviet leadership's new policy of raising the reputation of the satellites in the field of international politics. While earlier in the West they were regarded as hardly more than colonies of the Soviet Union, now they formally became equal members of a mighty military-political alliance, led by a nuclear superpower. In reality, this marked the beginning of the multilateralization of the Soviet bloc, which led to the gradual emancipation of the East Central European states in three directions: vis-à-vis Moscow, the West, and the countries of the third world.

5. Finally, after the conclusion of the Austrian State Treaty on 15 May 1955, the legal basis for the stationing of Soviet troops in Hungary and Romania ceased to exist.[40] While the statute of the Warsaw Pact published after its founding conference in Warsaw contained no clause that would allow Soviet troops to remain on the territory of other member states, it seems likely that Moscow planned to use the framework of the Warsaw Pact for the satisfactory settlement of this crucial issue. The statement of Warsaw Pact members about the creation of a joint command for their armed forces made a vague reference to the positioning of the Soviet troops on the territory of the member countries: "The deployment of the joint armed forces on the territory of the contracting states will occur by agreement between those states and according to the needs of mutual defense."[41]

Clearly, there was a direct connection between the conclusion of the two treaties: the draft statute of the Warsaw Pact was sent to the prospective member states just a few days after the successful conclusion of Soviet–Austrian negotiations in Moscow in March 1955,[42] while the treaty itself was signed on 14 May in Warsaw, just *one day before* the signing of the Austrian State Treaty. In sum, the formation of the Warsaw Pact was motivated by several concerns; nevertheless, it was the result of a longer process in which the possibility of bargaining with the Western great powers played a central role.

On 23 October 1954, the Western powers signed the so-called Paris Treaties, which included the accession of the Federal Republic of Germany to NATO, set for 5 May 1955. On the same day, Soviet Foreign Minister Vyacheslav Molotov submitted a proposal that the ministers of foreign affairs of the four great powers start preparatory negotiations on convening a pan-European security conference.[43] According to the Soviet idea, such a conference could result in the establishment of a collective European security system that would result in the dissolution of NATO, as the new structure would better guarantee the security of Western Europe. After the West rejected the idea without serious consideration, Moscow threatened to convene such a conference on its own. This is what eventually took place, and the representatives of the European Communist countries, with the exception of Yugoslavia, held a meeting between 29 November and 2 December 1954 in Moscow.[44] As part of the new Soviet doctrine—the so-called doctrine of active foreign policy—aimed at fostering greater formal participation of the East Central European Communist states since early 1954, the official appeal to convene the conference was made public jointly by the Soviet Union, Czechoslovakia, and Hungary at Soviet request.[45] As expected, the resolution made at the conference conveyed a two-fold message: it still urged the establishment of a collective European security system, but it also indicated that if the Paris Treaties were ratified, the Soviet Union and its East Central European allies would take the necessary steps to improve their own security.[46]

Thus, this move could be regarded as the forerunner to NATO's dual-track decision of December 1979 about the deployment of Euromissiles. In reality, the Soviets were using a nonexistent entity as a bargaining chip by making an offer *not to establish* the Warsaw Pact if Germany's entry into NATO was finally avoided. After the forming of the Soviet bloc's political-military organization in May 1955, the offer was altered to proposing the mutual and simultaneous dissolution of NATO and the Warsaw Pact, a proposal that in some form or another resurfaced in Soviet propaganda from time to time up until 1991.

The Western powers rejected the Soviet initiative, however, for they were convinced that it was mere propaganda and therefore did not even attempt to put the genuine intentions of Moscow to the test. This Western suspicion seemed to be supported by the fact that, following the rejection of the Soviet proposal to establish a collective European security system, the leaders of the Soviet Union decided that the Eastern bloc should also establish its own military-political alliance similar to that of NATO.[47]

The Hungarian leadership's response to the situation caused by the creation of the Warsaw Pact and to the predicted consequences of this move is highly instructive. The leadership of Hungarian Workers' Party (HWP) quixotically interpreted the situation, assuming that it did not directly enhance Hungary's security but might even weaken it. The HWP Political Committee discussed the draft treaty of a military alliance received from Moscow on 5 May 1955.[48] The members of the Politburo did not engage in real discussion about the document, and even technical changes of minor importance were not proposed, unlike in East Germany, Poland, and Romania.[49]

Meaningful discussion emerged only about the interpretation of one paragraph of the draft treaty, which rather vaguely hinted at the future deployment of the unified armed forces on the territory of certain countries.[50] The Minister of Defense, István Bata, suggested that the withdrawal of Soviet troops from Austria might be followed by the withdrawal of troops from Romania and Hungary as well. He claimed that the Hungarian armed forces were not sufficient to defend the country; therefore, it must be ensured that at least one Soviet Army corps remained in the country. Ernő Gerő reassured his colleagues that they need not worry about the news circulating in the West, according to which—in spite of the regulations of the Paris Peace Treaty—the Soviet troops would not leave Hungary. He added, "Let them scream themselves hoarse; a sufficient number of troops should still remain here." Rákosi also expressed optimism by explaining that Soviet troops from Austria would not be withdrawn before the end of the year, thus "there are still hundreds of kinds of options to determine what [troops] to ask to stay here."[51] The worry of the Hungarian leadership, obviously having no reliable information about Soviet intentions, turned out to be premature, since Moscow had no intention of pulling its troops out of the region at that time. Similar dilemmas arose in Romania as well, but in a totally different way. The leadership in Bucharest suggested that Soviet troops should be withdrawn from the country in August 1955, but the request was rejected rudely out of hand by Khrushchev.[52]

After the leaders of the East Central European allies had approved the draft treaty, the founding conference of the new military-political organization in mid-May 1955 in Warsaw was held without any substantive discussion.[53] At the meeting, a Political Consultative Committee (PCC) and the High Command of the Unified Armed Forces were set up; however, the real formation of the organization took place only at the PCC's first session, held in Prague on 26–28 January 1956.[54]

Western Policy toward East Central Europe

The international developments of the era between 1953 and 1956 truly had a major impact on what happened in world policy in the forthcoming decades, but one has to remember that the basis of the cooperation of the superpowers, which started in 1953 and significantly increased in 1955–56, was the European status quo, established at the end of World War II—that is, tacitly accepting that the Soviet Union had incorporated East Central Europe into its empire.

The initial Western reaction to the new international situation emerging after Stalin's death was ambiguous, and there was a clear division between the attitude of the United States and its Western European allies. The new American Republican president, Dwight D. Eisenhower, entering office at the beginning of the year, declared a "peace offensive" in April 1953; however, the contents of this message were not much more than a wait-and-see policy. At the same time, the attitude of the British government reflected more pragmatism and initiative. Prime Minister Winston Churchill expressed a profound Western desire for rapprochement with the new Soviet leadership in his speech in the House of Commons as early as May 1953, proposing a summit meeting among the four leaders of the great powers, also giving an explicit nod to the right of the Soviet Union to maintain its East Central European security zone.[55] In this period, the British authorities, just like the French government, continued to make serious efforts to ease tension between East (meaning first and foremost the Soviet Union) and West and to bring about political dé-tente.[56] As early as July 1954, Churchill suggested to Soviet leaders that he would be willing to make an official visit to Moscow. His successor, Anthony Eden, prepared a security plan for the reunification of Germany at the Geneva Summit in July 1955, which basically would have meant the consecration of the existent European status quo—for the rest of the continent—by recognizing mutual security interests.[57] Such a concession, however much in principle, was unimaginable for the Americans at the time. Not to mention that the government of the Federal Republic of Germany also vetoed the idea, so the Eden plan could never be officially presented in Geneva. The suggestion, however, certainly proves that Western European politicians began to realize that the de facto acceptance of the status quo necessarily had to be superseded by its de jure acceptance in order to relieve cold war tension and strengthen the security of Europe as early as the mid-1950s. Not only did these years foster several ideas and suggestions to further develop the East–West relationship, some of which would later be realized in practice (e.g., Eisenhower's Open Skies proposal), but even the roots of the most important result of the policy of détente—the 1975 Helsinki Agreement—go back to the period 1953–56.

The policy of the first Eisenhower administration (1953–56) toward the countries of East Central Europe that had landed in the Soviet sphere of influence after World War II was characterized by a peculiar duality.[58] Eisenhower and his would-be secretary of state, John Foster Dulles, had made the so-called peaceful liberation of the captive nations an integral part of their presidential election campaign platform in 1952; they declared that the Truman administration's policy of mere containment of Communism was not befitting the United States as leader of the free world and that ultimately only a more offensive posture would compel the Soviet Union to surrender its East European domains. This new rhetoric, portraying American self-confidence and promising a more aggressive policy vis-à-vis the Soviet Union, certainly contributed to the Republican victory. Nonetheless, the biggest paradox of this rather controversial thesis was that Eisenhower and Dulles announced this policy at the very end of Cold War I, when the era of open confrontation was about to be replaced by a new era of compelled superpower cooperation. The "peaceful liberation of enslaved nations," as Eisenhower imagined it, in reality meant nothing more than a *moral* obligation that the United States would "fight" by peaceful means—that is, with words or by exerting political pressure at the most. It can be argued that Eisenhower's "dream" about the captive nations did come true, though it was several decades later, at the time of the peaceful self-liberation of East Central Europe that happened without any American involvement and with full Soviet acquiescence in 1989. At the same time, in the favorable international climate after Stalin's death, the new U.S. administration, just like the Soviets, was seriously interested in relieving Cold War paranoia, easing tension, and, more tangibly, keeping down the gallop of the armaments race.

After entering office, however, it was difficult for Eisenhower to simply ignore an extremely ideology-driven but in fact now increasingly inconvenient election promise. The administration eventually found the solution by introducing a dual policy of "rhetoric and reality."[59] Accordingly, the American government devoted considerable sums toward funding subversive radio stations and other such institutions as well as East Central European émigré organizations. Reference to liberation of the captive nations—though exactly how it was to be accomplished was never made clear—was, all the way up until October 1956, a mandatory component of all high-level American political pronouncements, which were subsequently transmitted to East Central Europe through various propaganda organizations, particularly Radio Free Europe and Voice of America.[60] All of this served to create the illusion, not only in East Central Europe and the United States but throughout the world, that the United States, which had in fact never shown any real interest in the region, had made the liberation of these nations the cornerstone of its foreign policy and of East–West relations in general.[61]

In reality, however, American foreign policy of this era was based on thorough pragmatism characterized by the recognition of the post–World War II European status quo and the prevailing balance of power with the Soviet Union, as well as the avoidance at all costs of superpower conflict. The United States, together with the other Western powers, tried to exploit the new disposition of the post-Stalin Soviet leadership in order to open negotiations regarding issues that they found to be vital to their interests, such as ending the Korean War, a settlement in Southeast Asia, disarmament, the reunification of Germany, and the status of Austria.

Thus, particularly after the American government discovered that the Soviets had made unexpectedly rapid progress toward developing an intercontinental ballistic missile, especially from 1955 to 1956, the United States sought to mitigate East–West political tension by finding an acceptable modus vivendi with the Soviet Union.

The Communist countries of East Central Europe initially did not receive a prominent role in this process, since the United States, in its typical "great power" way of thinking, considered the Soviet Union to be its only legitimate negotiating partner. That the United States had no plans at all to liberate the satellite states became apparent from the decision of the National Security Council (NSC 174) as early as December 1953.[62] The next document recording the United States' East European policy was NSC 5608, adopted after the Poznan uprising in July 1956. This policy openly accepted, as a result of the unfolding détente process, that there was no chance of restoring the independence of the satellite states in the foreseeable future, so instead of revolutionary changes, it fostered *evolutionary* developments. Thus, the current task was to promote the Yugoslav road in these countries and the forming of national Communist governments, which were to be supported and assisted by the United States.[63]

During this period of East–West reconciliation and rapprochement, the Western powers occasionally sought to put the issue of the so-called satellite states on the negotiating table with the Soviets—predominantly to soothe their own conscience and satisfy public opinion in their countries.[64] It became quickly apparent, however—especially at the time of the Geneva Summit in July 1955 and in the interval prior to Khrushchev and Bulganin's official visit to Britain in April 1956—that the Soviet Union, which in certain respects had already surpassed the United States in the arms race, was willing to negotiate only from a position of strength. In this way, the Soviets were only prepared to discuss issues that had not yet been settled from their perspective, and any mention of their previous conquests in East Central Europe continued to activate a rejection reflex. Consequently, Western decision-makers tried to find alternative solutions that would make it possible to get rid of this problem and avoid posing a threat to the otherwise promising development of East–West relations while minimizing the loss of prestige.

Therefore, the United States and the other Western powers considered the question of East Central Europe to be of secondary importance to that of overall East–West détente, a position that is quite understandable when viewed from an international political perspective. Though they had not abandoned hope that the peoples of East Central Europe would regain their independence in the distant future, by the autumn of 1956 Western political officials had come to the conclusion that, for the time being, the Yugoslav political model of "national Communism" offered these countries the greatest opportunity for gaining a certain degree of both internal and external autonomy.[65]

The Western countries' reaction to the Soviet bloc's policy of opening after Stalin's death was generally positive. By 1953, bilateral relations between East and West had been reduced to a minimum, although formal diplomatic relations were maintained.[66] This situation was regarded as abnormal by most Western states; therefore, between 1953 and 1956, economic, political, cultural, and other (e.g., sports) connections with East Central Europe began to develop slowly but firmly.

Thus, the Western powers—contrary to what was to become one of the principal elements contained in Communist propaganda for decades thereafter—not only did not help to ignite the Hungarian Revolution or the resistance of Poland to Moscow but did not even remotely expect that an open conflict, let alone an armed uprising, would erupt in one of the Soviet satellite states. The Western powers had no preexisting strategy—except that military intervention was absolutely ruled out under any circumstances—designed to deal with such an unexpected event. Thus, the news of events in Budapest on 23 October 1956 was quite unexpected, by politicians as well as by the general public. In reality, the Hungarian uprising was explicitly inconvenient and embarrassing for the Western powers, as it totally contradicted their policy goals, which were aimed at a compromise with the Soviet Union through the mutual acquiescence of the existing status quo.

Therefore, there is no way that direct Western responsibility for the outbreak of the Hungarian Revolution can be deduced. But there is some *indirect* responsibility attached to the U.S. administration: its two-faced policy over several years helped ensure that the social unrest in Hungary would take the most radical form, armed uprising. The mostly young workers who risked their lives to take up arms against the overwhelmingly superior force of the Soviet Army and the Hungarian state security forces were largely persuaded by massive American liberation propaganda.[67] These workers believed that the United States had to look no further to find a better occasion to fulfill its promises than to support their fight for self-liberation.[68] This also explains why so many think even today that the West, and especially the United States, abandoned and betrayed Hungary in 1956.

The Doctrine of Active Foreign Policy

The doctrine of active foreign policy announced in the spring of 1954—as mentioned earlier—was meant to increase the fitness of Moscow's allies for international society and the maneuvering capability of the entire Soviet bloc. From then on, the Kremlin encouraged its allies to use their international reputation as effectively as possible to increase the reputation and influence of the Eastern bloc in world politics. This was aimed at providing significant new resources for Soviet foreign policy, and the allies had to promote the success of Soviet goals in Europe and even more in the third world, especially in Asia, the Arab states, and Latin America. While in Europe priority was given to the development of economic relations with the Western European states, the primary goal in the third world was to promote economic and political penetration and lasting Soviet influence.[69]

At the beginning of January 1956, less than a month before the Twentieth Congress of the CPSU, the most important summit meeting since Stalin's death was held with the participation of the European Communist states' leaders in Moscow.[70] Since the formation of the Soviet bloc in 1947, this was the first (and at the same time, the last) "global" style Communist summit meeting, where the Soviet leaders, after serious preparations, provided a thorough briefing on current political, economic, foreign policy, and military issues affecting the whole Soviet bloc. In addition, European allies were presented with a profound analysis of the future prospects of Communism and the desired directions of world developments.

At the meeting, Khrushchev emphasized in a very explicit way the importance of the new foreign policy doctrine, known as "active foreign policy":

> All countries of the socialist camp have to make their foreign policy
> efforts more active; they have to strengthen their international relations.
> In this field we do not exploit the possibilities sufficiently. What usually
> happens is that the Soviet Union takes action as the main force of our
> camp and then the countries of peoples' democracies support her. It is
> true that the Soviet Union is the great force of our camp but if we orga-
> nized our work in a more flexible way, the Soviet Union would not always
> have to be the first to take action. In certain situations, one or another
> country of peoples' democracy could take action and then the Soviet

Union would support that country. There are issues in which the countries of peoples' democracies could take action better. It would refute the assertion from our opponents that the people's democratic states do not have independence, for they always have the same opinion as the Soviet Union, and they support only her position. Of course, it is false to give such an interpretation to the unity of the countries in our camp. The reality is that our countries are unified, since they have a common theoretical basis, because they protect identical class positions, and consequently there are no issues that could create conflicts among them. It is right that this is true, and it would be tragic, if it were otherwise. This does not mean that we cannot use our opportunities better, that we should not try to use our forces more wisely so that we can further increase the influence of our camp. This should be taken into account in each country's foreign policy activities.[71]

As is clear from Khrushchev's speech, this did not mean a green light for the allied states to pursue a foreign policy line independent from that of the Soviet Union, but it did encourage them to play a much more active role in world politics. The essence of the new doctrine was that these countries—of course, always in close but confidential cooperation with Moscow—should seek to appear as independent actors in international politics and to be pro-active in international organizations. The aim was to create real and valuable allies out of the satellites, which could act as presentable partners in the international scene so that the Western political-military alliance, NATO, could be faced with a united and well-functioning—or at least one appearing as such—Eastern bloc. From this time on, and especially from the mid-1960s until the collapse of the Communist regimes in East Central Europe, this strategy became an effective model for cooperation among the Soviet bloc states in the field of foreign policy. Paradoxically, by the time the original goal was achieved in the early 1960s, when the "Soviet satellites" began to be called "Soviet allies" in the West as well, the doctrine of active foreign policy disappeared from the vocabulary of the Eastern bloc's diplomacy as it gradually became a practice of daily work.

In sum, Khrushchev's aim was to achieve the Soviet bloc's military, political, and economic integration in the shortest time possible. This is why the reform of the Comecon was initiated in the spring of 1954, and the establishment in May 1955 of the Eastern bloc's military-political organization, the Warsaw Pact, mainly served the same goal. In the second half of the 1950s, Soviet foreign policy was characterized by the dual message of the Moscow conference, proposing a European collective security system in November–December 1954. The combined policy declared that the Soviet bloc would do everything to increase its own security, yet at the same time, Moscow's East Central European allies were encouraged to contribute to neutralizing the German threat peacefully by improving relations not only with Western capitalist countries in general but with West Germany and Austria specifically.

While working for the resolution of the German question seemed to be the exclusive responsibility of the Soviet Union at the time, new research sheds light on the role some of the East Central European states played in this area. One early and special phase of the Soviet policy that urged for an opening toward the West was the attempt to normalize the relations between the FRG and the East Central European countries in some form or another, parallel with the process of establishing diplomatic relations between Moscow and Bonn in September 1955. However, this did not prove to be a simple task, and not only because of the Hallstein Doctrine, according to which the FRG would not establish diplomatic relations with any state that recognized the GDR. Hungary, together with Romania and Bulgaria, were among those Socialist countries that had no significant unresolved issues with the FRG, but they were all the more interested in rebuilding their economic ties, which had been cut after World War II, so for them this new possibility was a rather positive challenge. Making use of the favorable tailwind, the Hungarian foreign minister prepared a proposal as early as the end of June 1955 that Hungary—depending on the outcome of West German chancellor Adenauer's forthcoming negotiations in Moscow—should enter into diplomatic relations with the FRG.[72] Accordingly, in July 1955 the Politburo of the HWP accepted a resolution that, after consultation with countries of the Soviet bloc, this step should be taken. At the same time, Poland, Czechoslovakia, and the GDR had serious conflicts with the FRG, whose government was not willing to recognize the eastern frontiers that had been created after World War II, so they were not in the least happy to see that other members of the camp—following the Soviet Union—were ready to establish diplomatic relations with the FRG *unconditionally*. Therefore, these countries probably lobbied quite intensively against establishing relations, so the planned step could not be taken. It was just these conflicting interests within the camp which showed that, right after the establishment of the Warsaw Pact, cooperation within the organization was not going to be smooth in the future. First of all, they signaled a *qualitatively* new development, reflecting the fact that, in this newly developing model of multilateral political coordination, serious conflicts and lobby fights should be expected among the member states in addition to the opposition and clash of interests between the Soviet Union and its allies.

It was at this time in 1955–56 that Soviet diplomacy—while trying to maintain activity toward the West in general—began to pay special attention to neutral and nonaligned countries.[73] In Moscow, there was a general illusion that "the neutrality movement" was growing not only in Asia and the Middle East but even in NATO countries like West Germany, Denmark, and Norway.[74] The very category of neutrality was reformulated, too; as distinct from the traditional Western type of neutrality (Sweden, Switzerland); now the Finnish model was being turned into a generally applicable model from the hitherto unique status: this was the Eastern type of neutrality. The prime subject of this new policy line became Austria after the conclusion of the state treaty and the declaration of the country's neutrality in 1955. Soviet leaders truly believed that there was a serious chance that this country would follow the Finnish model in its foreign policy orientation.[75] Of course this required a considerable amount of convincing and persuasion, as well as charming prospects for Soviet economic support and beneficial trade relations with the Eastern bloc states. Neighboring Hungary, the former partner in the Austro-Hungarian monarchy, was given a prominent role in this process. Thus, Hungarian–Austrian relations showed a promising development as early as the spring of 1955, so much so that, in the summer of 1956, the invitation of Austrian chancellor Julius Raab to visit Budapest was put on the agenda. Even more significant was the then well-known but by now largely forgotten event of the elimination of the technical barrier, including a minefield— the "iron curtain"—at the Hungarian-Austrian border, which began in the spring of 1956 and was completed by September. It would be hard to overestimate the historical significance of this event, since it is well known that a similar technical opening-up of the border took place at the time when the Communist system collapsed in the summer of 1989, when the "iron curtain" was jointly removed by the Austrian and Hungarian foreign ministers in the form of a symbolic ceremony.[76] It is also of great importance that, as a result of a peculiar turn in history, this seal of the border disappeared just before the Hungarian Revolution broke out in October 1956, so when the uprising failed, some two hundred thousand people could safely flee the country for the West. To stop the flow of refugees, the minefield was reinstated between January and May 1957.[77] Related to political relationships with the capitalist countries, a fundamentally new paradigm was introduced by the Twentieth Congress of the CPSU in February 1956: in the future, the Socialist countries' diplomacy had to regard the host country's governmental circles and other potential governing political forces as partners. This apparently evident statement in fact indicated a radical change: up to that time, embassies and legations operating in Western countries built their local relations on a class basis, meaning that, besides the maintenance of formal diplomatic ties, diplomats of the Communist states had meaningful communication almost exclusively with the leaders of the country's Communist Party and other "progressive social forces." Maintaining good working relations with government officials actually aroused the suspicions of the state security organs, which vigilantly observed any such activity. To fulfill this important task, an estimated 30 to 40 percent of the missions' staff were employed by the state security services. An even more important doctrinal change affected the very worldview of the Soviet bloc leaders. The Twentieth Congress of the CPSU also replaced Zhdanov's infamous two-camps theory of 1947 with the much more flexible thesis of the two-zones theory, although this crucial modification in Soviet foreign policy is largely overlooked in international literature on the Cold War. While the Zhdanov Doctrine identified two hostile political-military groupings, located in Eurasia and on the North American continent, the new theory divided *the whole world* into two parts: one of them belonged to the imperialist bloc under the leadership of the United States, which included—besides members of NATO—all U.S. allies on every continent. The other, much greater part was called the "peace zone," embracing not only the Socialist countries but every country in the world pursuing an anti-imperialist policy, thus all the former colonies, now becoming independent nonaligned states in Africa and Asia. What is more, several neutral states were in this category, like Austria and Sweden, not to mention Finland, which indeed had operated as a "corresponding member" of the Soviet bloc since 1948.[78] This meant the declaration of a crucial change in the Soviet bloc's alliance policy. "Who is not against us is with us" was the rule from then on. (Interestingly, then, this famous slogan generally associated with János Kádár's internal policy from the early 1960s on was indeed an invention by Khrushchev.) The new policy was designed primarily to win over the third world countries in the fight between the two political-military blocs for acquiring economic and political influence in these areas, emerging in the middle of the 1950s. In the process of the transformation of intra-bloc relations, a prominent role can be attributed to the events of 1956. First, the long-term economic cooperation among the member states was based at the Comecon meeting in Berlin in May, which was a real breakthrough, where an agreement was reached on a long-term program of the specialization of industrial production.[79] It was also during 1956 that the five-year plans of the bloc countries began to be coordinated.[80] While the Warsaw Pact was founded in May 1955, creating the organizational structure of the alliance took place only at the first meeting of the PCC in Prague in January 1956. Besides adopting the statute of the unified armed command, a permanent secretariat and a committee for foreign policy coordination were set up, although the decision on the latter two organs was not implemented.[81] The "global" summit in Moscow in January 1956 was soon followed by another important briefing in the Soviet capital in June. This meeting, taking place right after Tito's historic two-week visit to the Soviet Union, is generally presented as dealing with the settlement of relations with Yugoslavia. In reality, while the delegations did receive a detailed account of Tito's visit as well, the conference was predominantly dedicated to discussing the problems of economic cooperation within the bloc and especially cooperation in the field of military industry.[82] At the meeting, the Soviet leaders made it crystal clear for the first time that while these issues had been on the agenda at multilateral forums for a while, now they were to be taken very seriously. As a first spectacular result of such cooperation, the joint nuclear research center of the Socialist countries was established in March 1956 in Dubna, near Moscow. The year 1956 not only brought significant changes in Moscow's relations with its allies but marked the beginning of the transformation and profound improvement of the *horizontal* relationship among the East Central European countries, again at Moscow's initiative. As early as February 1955, a declaration by the Supreme Soviet of the USSR proposed that, in order to foster peaceful coexistence, the states of the world should send delegations of their parliaments to one another's countries. To set a good example, such exchanges were first started among the countries of the Soviet bloc and, especially in 1956, many visits were performed. Bilateral relations between the "fraternal" parties and governments as well as government agencies and social organizations like trade unions were increasingly broadened. Stronger bilateral economic relations also began to emerge among the bloc countries at that time. Bilateral trade on a rather limited scale, based on barter, had existed earlier too, but now the first steps were taken to build industrial cooperation and coordination of the supply of raw materials. In the meantime, the internal system of relations within the Soviet bloc began to be transformed. While after 1949 the people of "brotherly" countries were almost hermetically closed off from one another,[83] beginning in the summer of 1956, several measures made tourism traffic much easier, and the obligatory visa system was abolished—except in the case of the Soviet Union. Thus, one of the most spectacular positive changes affected the travel conditions of the bloc countries' nationals. At Soviet initiative, in June 1956 in Sofia, the Bulgarian, Czechoslovak, Polish, Hungarian, Romanian, and Soviet government representatives concluded an agreement on the introduction of mutual visa-free travel.[84] In principle, this meant that the citizens of these states were now allowed to cross the border of the bloc countries without a passport, by merely using a special card attached to their personal identity card. It was a real breakthrough; previously, travel to neighboring countries was extremely difficult even with a visa, and now suddenly a new policy was introduced that, in principle, surpassed the contemporary liberalism of Western European practices.[85] In reality, however, the situation was more complex: the contracting states of the Sofia agreement had to regulate the conditions of travel in bilateral treaties. Nevertheless, this move made contact and direct communication significantly more dynamic among the societies of East Central Europe, which played an important role in the revolutionary events that broke out in the fall of that year. After the fall of the Hungarian Revolution, this positive trend stalled for several years, and the development of tourism within the Soviet bloc reached the level established in autumn 1956 only by the beginning and middle of the 1960s.

Hungary and the Spirit of Geneva

A unique feature of Hungarian policy in this period was that there were contradictory tendencies emerging in internal and external policies. Between July 1953 and March 1955, Imre Nagy, the new prime minister appointed at Moscow's "advice," introduced significant political and economic changes resulting in a liberalization of the Stalinist regime in the framework of the Hungarian version of the "new course" promoted by the Kremlin. In the field of foreign policy, however, only relatively modest progress was made in that period. This was partly due to following the Soviet policy line effective from March 1953. In the period right after Stalin's death, the Soviet leadership was engaged above all in crisis management in the East Central European states and in seeking to avoid similar situations. Therefore, they did not yet stimulate significant initiatives; nevertheless, Moscow fostered the liquidation of the abnormal situation and restoration of the level of relations with the Western states and Yugoslavia existing prior to 1949. In April 1955, Imre Nagy was demoted, and, in domestic politics, a partial restoration began with Rákosi at the helm,[86] who sought to reverse the process of liberalization and restore previously existing conditions. Paradoxically, in the field of external relations— again, in full compliance with the current Soviet intentions—the most intense opening-up toward the West started during those same months.[87]

In July 1953, the first foreign policy initiatives of the incoming government of Imre Nagy were aimed at urgently settling the explicitly hostile relationship with Yugoslavia and Great Britain.[88] The former was a result of Rákosi's ardent anti-Tito campaign following the Rajk trial in 1949, while relations with Britain deteriorated as a consequence of the arrest of English businessman Edgar Sanders in 1949. Sanders was released unconditionally in August 1953, which was promptly honored by the ending of the economic embargo against Hungary by the British government. In a few weeks' time, diplomatic preparations for starting financial and trade negotiations between the two states were underway. In late 1954, Great Britain and Hungary signed a temporary commercial and financial agreement that enabled the restarting of trade between the two countries, which had been suspended in 1949. Cultural, scientific, and sports relations were gradually improved as well, and the 6–3 victory of the Hungarian football team against England in London in November 1953 left a deep impression in the public memory of both countries. After several years of negotiations, a financial and commercial agreement between Hungary and Britain was finally signed in June 1956. The special significance of the agreement was that the Hungarian government undertook to pay compensation for war damages, pay restitution for expropriated British property during the land reform in 1945, and repay pre–World War II state loans totaling 4.5 million pounds.[89] (With the United States, a similar financial arrangement was signed nearly two decades later, in 1973.)[90] The settlement significantly promoted the development of bilateral relations, especially in the economic field, which was also indicated by the fact that, shortly thereafter, the British government offered technical assistance to Hungary in a number of areas.[91]

In the more relaxed international climate following the four-power summit in Geneva in July 1955, an opportunity arose for some of the East Central European countries to normalize their relationship with the Western states at a faster pace. The Hungarian government also took major initiatives at this time, in particular toward Austria, France, and other countries, which resulted in a gradual improvement of relations with most Western European states. One of the most remarkable achievements was that, in the summer of 1956, diplomatic relations were established between Hungary and Greece, a NATO member.

Paradoxically, in the Hungarian–American relationship, considerable tensions appeared in the same period. Although from 1955, both sides stressed the need to improve relations, the normalization of the situation was aggravated by several factors. Hungary continued to be one of the key targets of the U.S. propaganda campaign aimed at the "liberation of captive nations." Besides the broadcasts of Radio Free Europe in the native languages of the region, the most effective "medium" was sending thousands of unmanned balloons from West Germany over the East Central European countries, dropping millions of leaflets with anti-Communist messages. This campaign reached its peak in 1955–56, resulting in regular protests by the Hungarian government.[92]

On the Hungarian side, normalization of relations was complicated by an emerging conflict among local authorities: during 1955–56, the Foreign Ministry was already determined to normalize relations with the United States as well; however, the Ministry of Interior, in charge of state security issues, sought to sabotage the process of opening, especially by its overzealous activity aimed at "supervising" the U.S. legation. In 1955, two Hungarian employees of the U.S. mission in Budapest were arrested and sentenced for spying.[93] As a result, in September 1955, the U.S. government restricted the information and cultural activities of the Hungarian legation in Washington. In February 1956, two more Hungarian employees of the U.S. mission were arrested. In response, Washington forbade U.S. citizens to travel to Hungary.[94]

Endre Márton and his wife, correspondents of American news agencies UP and AP, were arrested earlier—in 1954 and 1955, respectively—and were sentenced for spying for the United States. The two journalists were Hungarian citizens and had regularly sent reports to the United States about Hungary since the late 1940s. So, regarding their case, the puzzle is why they were not arrested before 1953, when "becoming" an American spy did not need any real evidence, and many were jailed due to such accusations. The Márton couple, on the other hand, had close and very friendly relationships with the diplomats of the U.S. legation in Budapest, including the ministers, and while they were under strict surveillance, watched by and reported on by many of their closest friends as well, they were arrested at a time when the officially proclaimed Hungarian policy sought to normalize relations with Washington.[95] Available documents still do not explain this puzzle, so we can only assume that this was due to Rákosi's desire to effectively block the normalization process while "officially" following the Soviet line of rapprochement.

However, after the Twentieth Congress of the CPSU, held in February 1956, the situation changed considerably. Now, with Moscow's renewed encouragement to all East Central European countries, the promotion of East–West relations became an important priority. At the same time, a gradual process of revaluation took place in Washington's foreign policy as well, the essence of which was that the leadership was increasingly willing to acknowledge realities and sought to work for the settlement of relations with the governments of the Soviet satellite states.[96]

In Hungarian–American relations, a major shift occurred in May 1956, when at the meeting of U.S. minister Ravndal and Lajos Ács, secretary of the HWP Central Committee (CC), the parties agreed to eliminate the obstacles hindering the normalization of relations between the two countries.[97] A policy paper prepared for the meeting of the College of the Foreign Ministry on 4 June 1956 presented a comprehensive program to solve the problem.[98] The document, in order to eliminate the disturbing intelligence oversight of the U.S. legation and the Western missions in general, suggested the establishment of a joint committee of representatives from the Foreign Ministry and the Interior Ministry.

Wishing to avert the main obstacle to the normalization of relations, the proposal also requested the release of all detained U.S. legation employees. More importantly, the document outlined a rather sophisticated model for the development of Hungarian–U.S. relations, one that in reality would characterize the relationship between the two states from the mid-1960s. It was also suggested that, to settle long pending financial and property issues, concluding a trade and financial agreement with the United States, similar to the one recently signed with Great Britain, should be seriously considered. The main obstacle in the development of economic relations was the existence of significant Hungarian debt that arose from war restitution claims and nationalization of U.S. property. Therefore, at that time, due to the great financial obligations involved, the Hungarian leadership could not and in fact did not want to settle these issues with Washington.

The settlement of disputes, including the release of the legation employees, did not take place until October 1956 but, in the summer and autumn, there were many signs on both sides that conditions were now ripe for the normalization of Hungarian–American relations. In August, the abolition of travel restrictions for the employees of the U.S. legation in Budapest was announced. At the same time, an unexpected and rather surprising initiative was made on the other side: the State Department issued an official invitation for Ernő Gerő, Rákosi's successor, to visit Washington in order to study the presidential election due to take place at the beginning of November as an observer.[99] The new leader of the HWP did not accept the invitation, although he could not yet know that, in those very days, he would perform the function of an observer in the capital of the other superpower, where in the Kremlin an extraordinary "prime minister-(s)election" would take place for his own country, Hungary, in utmost secrecy.

In the spring of 1956, as part of the Soviet foreign policy aimed at the pacification of potential enemies in both the West and the East, the issue of normalizing relations with Japan was raised. The great distance between the two states notwithstanding, Hungary played an active role in the rapprochement process for a short while. At that time, Moscow had an illusion that, in Japan, positive internal political developments may eventually lead to the country's turning toward neutrality.[100] Such a lucky turn would have meant Japan's withdrawal from the U.S. sphere of interest, which obviously would have become a major strategic gain for the Kremlin. The Soviet Union, however, had no diplomatic relations with Japan; in fact, an armistice agreement had not been concluded between the two states at the end of the Second World War, meaning that they were still in a state of war by international law. Former Axis ally Hungary, on the other hand, as it was revealed to the great surprise of the Foreign Ministry officials, had never formally, not in 1945 or later, broken off diplomatic relations with Japan; this issue had simply been forgotten at the time.[101] Thus, in this case, the task was not to establish a diplomatic relationship; the official link between the two states had only to be reactivated. Therefore, Moscow tasked the Hungarian leadership in May 1956 with restoring its relationship with Japan as soon as possible. Such a successful move could then be used by the Soviet Union and the other allies as a precedent to normalize relations.

The Hungarian party made the necessary arrangements accordingly, and veteran politician Zoltán Szántó was entrusted with the negotiations.[102] He was to travel first to China and then to Tokyo.[103] He did reach the first station of his mission in September, but the negotiations were suddenly canceled, and as we now know, the Soviet Union directly contacted the Japanese government, and on 19 October 1956 an armistice agreement was signed by the two states, which meant the establishment of diplomatic relations.

Arguably, between January and October 1956, Hungarian foreign policy launched a radical revaluation process and a policy of opening both inside the Soviet bloc and toward the West and the third world, which was all completely in line with contemporary Soviet policy.[104] In reality, this new trend was based on the same principles that would later become the guidelines of the rather pragmatic Hungarian foreign policy pursued from the early 1960s on. This new approach was clearly elaborated in the general foreign policy directives and in the special guidelines for individual countries worked out by the Foreign Ministry in the spring of 1956.[105]

The growing importance of the Foreign Ministry in the field of external affairs, as well as a determination to embark on a partial correction in foreign policy orientation, was indicated by the fact that the most important personal change at the government level following Rákosi's ousting was the appointment of a new foreign minister. In August, János Boldoczki, an uneducated cadre of working-class origin known for his unconditional Soviet friendship, was replaced by professional diplomat Imre Horváth, head of the Hungarian legation in London. In the same month, the Foreign Ministry launched the practice of biweekly press conferences for the foreign media, which meant a qualitative change concerning the government's relations with the public. The conference of "ambassadors and ministers," held for the first time in August 1956 for the leaders of the Hungarian diplomatic missions abroad, was a consultation and orientation forum in which participants were given a thorough and detailed briefing about topical foreign policy issues by leading politicians, including the HWP's new leader, Ernő Gerő.[106]

Due to the new travel regulations introduced within the Soviet bloc in the summer of 1956, Hungary concluded agreements with Poland and Romania about visa-free travel, so that citizens could move with never-before-experienced simplicity with only an ID card. All this had great importance—especially in Romania since, from August to October 1956, large numbers of ethnic Hungarians living in Romania visited Hungary, then returned home with the experience of prerevolutionary ferment and, in October–November, many of them participated in various demonstrations in Transylvania.[107] Travel conditions to Czechoslovakia were considerably improved as well, although to a lesser extent.

For a society completely sealed off from the Western part of Europe since 1949, even more significant was the opening to the West. The only tourist company, IBUSZ, organized the first group tours to England in 1956, and during August–September, several Hungarian tourist groups visited Vienna by cruises on the Danube. This initially slow, then more rapid evolutionary process, however, was soon interrupted by a social explosion, which created radically new challenges for Hungarian foreign policy as well.

Chapter 4

Crisis Year, 1956

Poland, Hungary, Suez

The process of ferment that had begun after the Twentieth Congress of the CPSU led to a social explosion in two countries of the Soviet bloc in October 1956, but the outcome for each was fatefully different: in Poland, the local Communist regime eventually pacified the situation using its own resources and working within the existing frameworks of the Communist system, although at the time of the outbreak, a direct armed conflict between the Soviet Union and Poland seemed like a serious possibility. In Hungary, however, an anti-Soviet revolution and war of independence emerged, spreading all over the country, and in a matter of two weeks a genuine political transformation had taken place, as a result of which a Western-type parliamentary democracy could have developed in the country within a short time, had it not been for outside intervention. Thus, the Communist system, which had been on the verge of extreme peril, could only be saved by the Soviets through the intervention of the Soviet Army.

The Polish October

In Poland, the situation was fluid from the beginning of the year. Bierut, the leader of Polish Stalinism, fell ill while attending the Twentieth Congress of the CPSU and died in March in Moscow. His successor, Edward Ochab, chosen personally by Khrushchev, appeared to be an optimal candidate to implement the Soviet policy of de-Stalinization. In April, in the spirit of controlled liberalization, a general amnesty was declared and several thousand political convicts were released and many rehabilitated, while in the same month, members of Parliament conducted a real discussion on important issues of the country at the parliamentary session.[1] Władysław Gomułka, the former leader of the party, had—unlike several other victims of top Stalinist trials in other countries—survived the cleansing and had been released from prison, so the problem to be resolved was whether he could return to the leadership and, if so, under what conditions. From the beginning of 1955, a process of ferment began to emerge among the party and society, in the course of which barriers were gradually removed, and—mostly as a result of making Khrushchev's secret speech widely public in April 1956—public criticism now began targeting not only extremist manifestations of the Stalinist system in social discourse, such as personal cult or mass terror, but several general issues of even greater importance, like political freedom and the lack of national sovereignty.[2]

Meanwhile, the Soviet leadership began worrying about the course of internal developments in East Central Europe. The concerns were not without foundation, for on 28 June 1956, an armed uprising broke out in the industrial city of Poznan in Poland, in the course of which the workers fought a true battle with Polish military and state security troops. The events unfolded in accordance with the model seen in Plzen and East Berlin before: a mass demonstration that started out with demands for higher wages turned into an anti-Communist uprising within a few hours. The insurgents seized the police headquarters, where they armed themselves, and then broke into the public prosecutor's office, stormed prisons and freed prisoners, and finally made an assault on the headquarters of the security forces. The revolt was put down by Polish military forces, and the fight claimed the life of seventy-three civilians and eight members of the armed forces, while several hundred people were wounded.[3]

Right after the Poznan uprising in June, events picked up speed in Poland. The society had become increasingly more radical, the need for reforms and changes had been expressed by a steadily growing number of people in a very explicit way, and nationalist tendencies had become more intense. Thus, there was a real danger that if the leadership, that was engaged in internal conflicts between various factions, failed to resolve the critical situation, a political explosion might put the whole country in jeopardy. By October 1956, the leadership of the Polish United Workers' Party finally decided to elect the once-discredited Gomułka first secretary and to exclude pro-Soviet officials from the top levels of the party. The radical personal changes were approved by the 8th Plenum of the party, which began on 19 October. This step meant that the reformist forces within the party gained a full victory, which created a possibility to smooth social discontent and pacify the country successfully, for Gomułka's election was received with great enthusiasm all over the country.

The Soviet leaders, however, who had not been consulted about this fundamental change—a rather unprecedented and bold move in the Soviet camp—labeled this step as the beginning of the fall of the Communist system, which was a grave misinterpretation of the situation. In reality, they were alarmed by the possibility of Poland becoming a second Yugoslavia, which eventually might quit the Soviet bloc. For this reason, Khrushchev and a top-level Kremlin delegation made a surprise visit to Warsaw on 19 October to confront the Polish authorities and, if necessary, to order the Soviet Army to intervene. In the meantime, the Soviet troops stationed in Poland, for the moment as a demonstration of power, began to head for Warsaw, which raised a clear possibility that the crisis might lead to an armed conflict between Moscow and its most populous ally, which had assembled the largest army in the Warsaw Pact, second only to the Soviet Army. In a dramatic face-off, however, Gomułka was successful in convincing Khrushchev to make a compromise: the Soviets accepted the new Polish leadership, while Gomułka gave assurances that the political reforms to be introduced in Poland would not threaten either local Communist rule or the unity of the Soviet bloc.[4]

The people of Poland expressed their support for the policy of the new leadership and Gomułka in thousands of mass rallies and demonstrations all over the country, which was a significant success, as the majority of Polish society had a rather anti-Soviet and essentially anti-Communist attitude. One reason for the success was that the people of Poland viewed the protection of the "Polish way of socialism" as a bold anti-Soviet move.[5] It is quite probable that, as a result of this, the majority of Polish society accepted, at least to some degree, the thesis that Communism could have a version that was "fit for good society," which later made it easier for them to gradually become resigned to the unchangeable situation and to create the self-comforting image of the "happiest barracks in the Soviet camp."[6]

At the same time, Gomułka was smart in playing a nationalist card of a different character: although in Poland the withdrawal of Soviet troops was a general demand, just as would make itself known a few days later in Hungary, Gomułka eventually managed to convince the people, referring to "Polish state interests," that the protection of its western borders could only be guaranteed by the Soviet Union and its troops stationed in Poland.[7]

Hopes and Illusions in Hungary

Following the Poznan uprising, the Soviets were eager to avoid further outbreaks of social discontent in the region by applying means of political intervention. This is why in July 1956 Moscow eventually decided to replace Rákosi as the head of the Hungarian party in order to ease the political tension in the country. Mikoyan was sent to Budapest, on whose advice the HWP CC accepted Rákosi's resignation and elected Ernő Gerő as first secretary of the party; Mikoyan also informed the Hungarian leaders, however, that should any unexpected events occur in the country, the Soviet Union would not hesitate to come to the help of the Hungarian party.[8] A similar message was communicated by Khrushchev to Tito through Mićunović, the Yugoslav ambassador in Moscow, informing him that in case of a further deterioration of the situation, the Soviet leadership was prepared to use every possible means to overcome a crisis in Hungary, since the Soviet Union could by no means allow any breach in the front of the camp.[9]

Indeed, the situation in Hungary was extremely tense throughout the summer of 1956, as the leadership was reluctant to make significant concessions to society even after Rákosi's replacement. In early October, the reburial of László Rajk and his companions, who had been executed after a show trial in 1949, was practically a silent demonstration by some one hundred thousand people against the Stalinist system. On 16 October, university students in Szeged established an independent student organization at a mass rally, and on 22 October, their fellow students in Budapest wrote up their claims in sixteen points at a similar assembly. In addition to several elements of the reform program of the party opposition—for example, Imre Nagy's appointment as prime minister and the convention of an extraordinary party congress—these points included several very radical demands, such as the withdrawal of Soviet troops, a free press and freedom of speech, and free multiparty elections.

On 23 October, the university students held a peaceful demonstration in Budapest to support the reforms in Poland, which turned into an armed revolt by evening. The local leadership requested the intervention of the Soviet troops stationed in Hungary to repress the uprising, to which the CPSU presidium, after a lot of hesitation, gave their consent. However, with this move they achieved quite the opposite of what they had intended: instead of rapidly pacifying the situation, the originally sporadic armed incidents had developed into an extensive anti-Soviet freedom fight.

For the historian now, it is clear that the revolution's fate was decided by international politics—above all, by the decisions of the Soviet leadership acting in the context of overall world politics. In order to understand these moves, it is necessary to survey the international implications of all that happened in Hungary after 23 October. If the events of the preceding years were connected to changes in world politics, following the outbreak of the armed uprising and the Soviet intervention, Hungary's fate came to be entirely dependent on the reactions of Moscow. In reality, the Hungarian Revolution was a perfect example of a pseudo crisis in East–West relations, which did not cause a clash of interests between the superpowers. Yet world public opinion—including the Western press and media, in line with the prevailing American liberation rhetoric—nevertheless presented it as one of the most serious Cold War crises up to that time.

The principal foreign political demands of Hungarian society at the time of the revolution were, for the most part, not founded on an awareness of world political realities. This is due partly to the fact that the general public held illusions that hindered, and in some instances even precluded, a clear assessment of Hungary's international circumstances, and partly to the general propensity of people to make unrealistic demands during the upheaval and agitation of revolution.

A significant portion of Hungarian society mistakenly believed (and still believes) that the spheres of influence established in Europe after World War II were just temporary arrangements and that the revolution offered the Western powers an exceptional opportunity to change them. The majority of Hungarians were only able to perceive those world political trends that were encouraging for their aspirations. Although the new orientation of East–West relations was leading to a rapprochement between the two world superpowers, they continued to believe in the unchanged American propaganda emphasizing that the United States would never write off the so-called captive nations. The armed freedom fighters in particular were counting on military intervention; it was precisely these people who harbored the greatest illusions regarding the world political environment, though they were generally aware of the fact that their struggle against the vastly superior Soviet forces would fail without outside support. Consequently, the insurgents commonly appealed both individually to Western journalists or diplomats and en masse before the Budapest legations of the Western powers for political and military intervention as well as arms and ammunition.[10]

It is important to note that the nonbelligerent political entities that sprang up at the time of the uprising, such as the revolutionary and national committees and the workers' councils, just like the reforming political parties,[11] did not make similar requests for direct Western assistance. This was due partly to the general inclination toward self-restraint characteristic of the initial stages of the revolution—for most people were quite aware that exaggerated repudiation of the Soviet Union would certainly provoke immediate Soviet intervention—and partly to the fact that most of these revolutionary organs were directed by intellectuals and workers who tended to advocate an essentially Socialist "third road" for Hungary, which precluded the idea of Western military intervention.

The widespread illusions regarding the will and ability of the United Nations to mediate a settlement of the Hungarian crisis are reflected clearly in the various revolutionary organizations and press. Hungarian expectations regarding UN mediation were nonetheless of a most diverse nature: there was a universal hope among Hungarians that the Security Council or the General Assembly would be able to induce the Soviets to find a peaceful resolution to the Hungarian crisis; others went even further in their expectations, calling for UN observers or immediate intervention by UN military forces. Indeed, in early November, news appeared in the media about the first group of observers arriving in Hungary.[12]

After the second Soviet intervention on 4 November, it became a general hope that the special session, resulting in the resolution of the UN General Assembly condemning the Soviet move, would bring UN observers to mediate between the Kádár government and Hungarian society. Characteristic of those expectations was when, on 16 November, a three-person delegation of the University Revolutionary Committee sought out Imre Nagy at the Yugoslav embassy, where he took asylum, and suggested he "invite the UN into Hungary."[13]

All these hopes were seemingly supported by the fact that the UN (to which Hungary gained membership in 1955) could be regarded as a neutral international crisis management forum, the resolutions of which therefore could be accepted by the Soviet Union itself. On the other hand, it could be argued, the same forum had proved to be an efficient means of containing Communist expansion during the Korean War. This precedent was the basis of the hope of many who believed that UN mediation could result in a "second Korea case" in Hungary. In reality, the UN was able to act effectively only in those cases in which the conflict to be settled was not one between the superpowers or their allies. During the Korean War, the Soviets refused to attend the meetings of the UN Security Council—for the first and last time—unintentionally opening the road to the formation of a Western military coalition against North Korean aggression under the auspices of the UN. The UN intervention in Korea, however, proved to be an exceptional possibility, which was able only to *contain* Communist expansion but was not aimed at rolling it back.

Practically from the very outset of the uprising, the various revolutionary programs gave special prominence to the demand that Soviet troops withdraw from Hungary, a contingency that was commonly regarded as an essential precondition for the general restoration of independence to the country. The only issue that the general public of the revolution unanimously agreed on was the demand for sovereignty; they were less certain about what should happen once they had gained independence. Many imagined their future based on the Yugoslav model: a peculiar Hungarian Socialism, exempt from the political distortions of Stalinism, parallel with a noncommitted foreign policy. This concept was predominantly popular among intellectuals and to some extent among workers at the time. Others, however, thought that only a Western style parliamentary democracy would be the right solution: for them, the bourgeois construction of government and political neutrality of Austria—declared just a year before—were the most attractive examples. Lack of time and the suppression of the revolution, however, made it impossible to find out how popular these concepts actually were.

Hungarian public opinion thus was unanimous concerning the question of sovereignty, and all political programs were based on the wish to remain outside the great power blocs. This desire was reflected in two interrelated demands, which became general by the last days of October: the withdrawal from the Warsaw Pact and the proclamation of Hungary's neutrality. Contributing greatly to the general popularity of the notion of neutrality was the seemingly rational (though, it turned out, erroneous) premise that the Soviet Union would not see any increased security threat in a neutral Hungary. It was also a generally held illusion that, since the Soviets had assented to a negotiated withdrawal from Austria in 1955, they might very well consider doing likewise in Hungary.

The agreement, however, in the case of Austria was the outcome of a genuine *compromise* on the part of the great powers, in which both sides, East and West alike, were satisfied with what they had gained. The Soviets achieved the neutralization of Austria, which could not become a member of NATO. This drove a "neutral wedge" (Switzerland and Austria) between the north and south flanks of NATO, which the Soviets took to be an important geostrategic gain. We now know that the issue of the Austrian State Treaty was handled by Moscow as an integral part of the whole German question, as Austrians were simply German people for the Soviet leadership. Therefore, another major Soviet goal was to achieve the separation of Austria from Germany for good, so that it could not strengthen (West) Germany again.[14] Similarly important to them (and similarly to prove illusory) was the idea that by "working on" Austria, it could be assured that it adopted the "Eastern" (or Finnish) model of neutrality.

The Western great powers, on the other hand, could welcome that Moscow gave up their zone of occupation in eastern Austria and secure the country's development as part of the Western world. Recognizing Hungary's neutrality by the Soviets, a country being 100 percent in the Soviet sphere of influence, however, would have been a huge *unilateral* concession. This, obviously—in view of Hungary's strategically important geographical position— would not at all have befitted the Cold War logic and the rules of the game played by the great powers. An example of how myths can persist is the common assumption even today is that the Western powers were the ones to insist on Austria's neutrality,[15] for this would offer a precedent on which to base hopes that their pressure could achieve Hungary's neutrality as well. In fact the reverse was true. Austria's eternal neutrality was a condition Moscow made for its military withdrawal, and it was the U.S. leaders who accepted it only reluctantly.

Veterans of 1956, journalists, and politicians have written much in the last fifty years about the purpose, substance, and significance of the Hungarian

Revolution: what society did and did not want in 1956. A failed, incomplete, interrupted revolution always provides a good chance for people to assess events and draw conclusions that suit their own view. What a historian must do, so far as is possible, is to apply knowledge of all accessible source materials and powers of thorough analysis to reconstructing the events and historical processes with maximum credibility. But a historian's tasks do not include the practice of "retrospective futurology." Society expects experts to eschew the "what would have happened if" type of question. So, if historians writing about 1956 deal with the question of its possible "outcome" at all, they are usually content to make general and rather vague assessments, saying that the change of system in 1989 essentially accomplished the main aims of the 1956 revolution by establishing democracy and independence.

Yet it is challenging to see how events that did not actually occur might be "forecast" retrospectively. The revolution could not succeed in the world political situation of the time, but that does not prevent us from modeling the processes that were inherently present in 1956. Reliable assessment of an interrupted, incomplete revolutionary process cannot be based simply on views, opinions, or political intentions and motives articulated at the time. The key lies in scrutinizing the immanent, latent tendencies. A historian attempting such a reconstruction must compare the events in Hungary with substantively similar events occurring elsewhere in the world at other times. There were several rebellions in Eastern bloc countries, but it is especially instructive to view the 1989–90 process that broke up the Communist regimes of East Central Europe. Conclusions can be drawn, and a retrospective forecast made—a trend plotted that could not have occurred under the circumstances but that the logic of events suggests as the likeliest model of development had it not been for the outside intervention. The analysis departs from the hardly refutable point that, but for the Soviet intervention of 4 November, Hungary would have soon called free elections. There had been a demand for them from the outset, and revolutionary opinion was united on the matter on 3 November, the last day of "peace." The Imre Nagy government had made no direct promise, but that can be seen partly as caution over Soviet security interests, and the government would not have been able to oppose such a demand if events had been allowed to develop freely. Remember that social backing for the Hungarian Socialist Workers' Party set up on 31 October 1956 on the ruins of the Hungarian Workers' Party was much smaller than it was at the time of the change of system, yet in the latter case, the Hungarian Socialist Workers' Party soon conceded (in May 1989) that free elections would decide the outcome of the transition. Had such elections been held in the fall or winter of 1956, simple statistics suggest the result might well have been a decisive victory for the Smallholders' Party. Most of the active participants in the revolution were workers, students, and intellectuals, but the rules of democracy mean that their merits could not have swayed the elections, where the decisive say would have gone to the relatively passive rural population, for the majority of society consisted of peasant farmers who had been resisting attempts to collectivize them in the Rákosi period. They would certainly have seen the Smallholders' Party (which won 57% of the poll in the free elections of 1945) as the right means of restoring the socioeconomic system based on private ownership that best met their interests. So the elections would have been followed by a process of democratic, constitutional transformation such as occurred after the 1990 elections, or in part during the summer and fall of 1989, as the National Roundtable negotiations were taking place.[16]

So the institutional system of parliamentary democracy would have been installed rapidly. It is less certain how, based on the role played by the various revolutionary bodies, the rebel groups, and above all the workers' councils, such "civil" forces could have institutionalized their political interests during the transformation. It is possible to envisage them in a bicameral system being represented in the upper house—a structure that was discussed in 1988–89—so that the active participants in the revolution could be "pacified" relatively quickly and simply and the transition from revolution to everyday democracy facilitated. But none of this would have had an essential effect on the character of the emerging democratic system. Probably the economic transformation and process of recapitalization would have been influenced more strongly by factors detached from economic criteria than in 1989–90. It would certainly be a mistake to underestimate the decisive opposition to privatization voiced by the working class. For in 1956, the factories would have had to be returned to "capitalists" often known personally to the workers and who had been none-too-popular before the war, which would have run up against strong social opposition. So at least in the short term, the choice would probably have been an economic model with a greater than average role for maintenance of state ownership (nationalization was not rare in postwar Western Europe either) combined with workers' self-management and the use of "coupon" privatization as the tamer, more socially equitable form.

Regarding the country's international status in such a fabulous situation—assuming that the Soviet leaders had accepted the loss of Hungary as a Communist country—the most likely version would have been the emergence of neutrality following the Finnish model. In other words, the Soviet Union, while accepting the bourgeois-democratic character of the new political system and taking note of the country's formal independence, would have treated Hungary as a "corresponding member" of the Soviet bloc, fundamentally determining and limiting the country's room to maneuver by covert means in international politics.

Foreign Policy of the Imre Nagy Government

From the very moment Imre Nagy became prime minister on 24 October, he was faced with increasingly radical demands not only with regard to the internal reorganization of Hungarian society but also concerning the restructuring of the country's international status, namely its position within the Soviet alliance.

Although few people were aware of it at the time of the outbreak of the revolution, Imre Nagy had circulated a theoretical treatise among his friends in January of that year,[17] which expressed support for the Panchseel, or the five basic tenets of the nonaligned movement with regard to peaceful coexistence: mutual respect for national sovereignty and territorial integrity, noninterference in domestic affairs, equality, reciprocal benevolence, and fraternal cooperation. This in itself was not yet a novelty, because at that time, in order to impress the nonaligned states of the third world, these principles were formally accepted by the Soviet leadership as well.

Nagy, however, identified the totality of these principles with the notion of national independence itself. Nagy also expressed his conviction that national independence was not simply a question of achieving international autonomy but had a social dimension as well. In more specific terms, Imre Nagy believed that it was the Yugoslav model—that is, a Socialist domestic order coupled with a nonaligned foreign policy—that offered Hungary the greatest chances for achieving national independence. It is important to note that none of Imre Nagy's thinking was based on Hungary taking any sort of unilateral action; he hoped that the encouraging trends perceptible in international political relations, especially since 1955, would eventually lead to the dissolution of the contentious world power blocs, thus enabling the countries of East Central Europe to continue to build Socialism on a new foundation of national independence and equality and noninterference in internal affairs.

Nagy considered the latter scenario to be all the more possible in light of the Soviet Union's apparently friendly disposition toward the nonaligned movement at that time, accepting the five principles of peaceful coexistence. It was above all the Soviet Union's rapprochement with Yugoslavia that fed the general illusion that the Soviets were prepared to accept the principle that building Socialism could be based on a model other than their own.

It was Imre Nagy's thankless task as prime minister to reconcile his measured vision regarding the restructuring of Hungary's international relations with the increasingly radical demands of the revolution. Nagy was always very aware of the fact that the fate of the revolution was entirely in the hands of the Soviet Union, and from the very outset of negotiations held with a high-ranking

Soviet crisis-management delegation led by Anastas Mikoyan and Mihail Suslov,[18] Nagy attempted to convince the Soviets that, with adequate support, he would be capable of stabilizing the internal situation.

The peaceful resolution of the Polish crisis likely strengthened Nagy's conviction that the Soviets were interested in finding a similar settlement in Hungary, even if they had to grant a certain number of concessions in order to do so. It was for this reason that, as early as 25 October, Nagy suggested that calling for Soviet intervention had been a mistake and that in the interest of calming unrest among the people, it would be wise to announce the government's intentions to initiate negotiations regarding the withdrawal of Soviet troops from Hungary. Later on that day Nagy made this announcement, despite vigorous Soviet objections, in the course of a radio address.[19] On the following day Nagy, playing up the extreme social pressures under which the Hungarian leadership was operating, attempted to convince the Soviet delegation that over and above suppression of armed resistance, the most effective way to bring the prevailing disorder under control would be to place the party at the head of the mass social movement that had materialized with the Revolution.[20]

Similar tactics characterized the behavior of Imre Nagy concerning the declaration of the Hungarian government in the UN Security Council meeting on 28 October. According to a legend born in the days of the revolution but surviving today, the statement read in the Security Council on 28 October by Hungary's permanent UN representative, Péter Kós, saying that the Hungarian government protested against the body debating the Hungarian situation, was nothing other than a forgery, put forward by the "traitor" Péter Kós at the behest of the Soviets. To give credence to that, the revolutionary press immediately discovered that the diplomat's name was actually Lev Konduktorov and that he was a Soviet citizen. This all seemed to be confirmed when on the next day Kós was relieved of his post.[21] The truth of the matter is that Péter Kós had never been a Soviet citizen, although he had borne the name Konduktorov until the early 1950s, when he Hungarianized it on becoming a diplomat. We now know that indeed, the government statement in question had been initiated in Moscow, but it had been preceded through normal channels. On 28 October, the Soviets, through their Budapest ambassador, Yuri Andropov, called on the Hungarian government to issue an immediate statement saying that the events in Hungary were solely a domestic affair and that the government protested against the question being placed on the agenda of the Security Council.[22]

In Moscow it was logically expected that Nagy, having demonstrated willingness to cooperate with them since the beginning of the revolt, would be ready to reject the attempt of the UN for intervention. Nagy, in order to preserve the confidence of the Kremlin, indeed complied with the "request" immediately, however by no means fully. While the detailed Soviet proposal categorically stated that unleashing the events was mainly due to "the machinations of the imperialist states," the declaration of the Hungarian government, endorsed also by Imre Nagy and sent to Kós before the UN Security Council meeting on 28 October, did not contain this reference.[23] It simply stated that the events in Hungary were solely the domestic affairs of the country and therefore the government protested against the discussion of the question by the Security Council. Moreover, according to the original Soviet plan, the declaration should have been published in the press and broadcast over the radio *before* the Security Council meeting, a "request" also neglected by the Nagy government. After the internal political turnaround on 28 October, the political developments of the following days and especially after the telegrams of Nagy to the UN secretary-general on 1 and 2 November, the government's statement at the UN Security Council had become rather uncomfortable. Thus, the legend of Kós the traitor, widely publicized in the revolutionary press, provided an expedient excuse for the leadership to let society place all responsibility on the "Soviet agent" for a declaration that had become inconvenient in light of the radical political changes taking place in the country by the first days of November.[24]

The events of the last days of October seemed to vindicate Imre Nagy's policy toward the Soviets; his pledges to consolidate the situation in Hungary were designed to extract further concessions from them: on 28 October they consented to the reevaluation of the events as a "broad national democratic movement," declaring a cease-fire and, on 29 October, Soviet military units began withdrawing from Budapest.[25] The Soviet government's declaration of 30 October included an explicit promise that it would lay new foundations for relations between the Soviet Union and other Socialist countries based on equality and noninterference in domestic affairs; in addition, it promised to consider a decision to withdraw Soviet troops from Hungary. The same day Nagy announced the reintroduction of the multiparty system and reorganized the inner cabinet of his government on this basis—all of this approved by crisis managers Mikoyan and Suslov.

At nearly the same time, however, signs of the Soviet Union's real intentions began multiplying at an alarming rate: beginning on 31 October came reports that fresh Soviet troops were entering the country, occupying all important strategic locations, including airports, and encircling towns. It was at this point when it became clear that the Soviet invasion, with the obvious aim of overthrowing and abducting the Hungarian government, was imminent, that the cabinet decided to make a heroic last-ditch effort at rescuing the revolution: on 1 November it announced Hungary's withdrawal from the Warsaw Pact and declared the country's intention to be neutral.[26]

Withdrawal from the Warsaw Pact and the Declaration of Neutrality

The withdrawal from the Warsaw Pact and the declaration of Hungarian neutrality have been the most controversial and often criticized measures of the Nagy government; therefore, it is worth examining in detail, after what antecedents this radical foreign policy decision, unprecedented in the history of the Soviet bloc, was made.[27]

The demand for the withdrawal of Soviet troops, which even a few weeks before would have been regarded as utmost heresy, became widespread in the country even in the first few days of the revolt. Since the Warsaw Treaty Organization was regarded by many as the main pretext for the stationing of Soviet troops in Hungary, it was not in the least unexpected that revolutionary public opinion would sooner or later turn toward the need to leave the military alliance.[28] That came about in a very short period of time, and by the end of October it was not only the various revolutionary organizations and the workers' councils but the newly formed political parties that put a lot of pressure on the Imre Nagy cabinet to denounce the Warsaw Pact and declare the neutrality of the country. The demand for neutrality appeared to be a logical next step after having raised the possibility of leaving the military alliance; in this respect, the two factors previously mentioned—the remarkable success of the nonaligned Yugoslavian foreign policy in 1955–56 and the conclusion of the Austrian State Treaty and the declaration of the permanent neutrality of the country—proved to be quite an appealing example.[29] However, as has been seen before, under the current international circumstances these ideas did not have any real bases, since the status of Hungary for the Soviets was very different from that of Yugoslavia, not to speak of Austria, and it did not even occur to the Moscow leaders that they should consider letting any of the satellite countries leave the Soviet bloc, as they formed the Soviet security belt on the Western border of the Soviet empire.

Thus, the demand for the declaration of neutrality and the denouncement of the Warsaw Pact in 1956, however noble the goals that motivated them, were the irrational and unreasonable outcomes of a self-generating revolutionary euphoria that would have enhanced the danger of another Soviet intervention and the destabilization of the situation even if the Imre Nagy government had refused to accept them. At the same time, the demand for neutrality demonstrated a genuine desire by a significant part of society for a policy to be conducted outside the bloc system, but it also showed the instinctively rational, self-restraining nature of an otherwise irrational and radical mass movement. Namely, it was obvious to almost anybody that an open declaration of the intention to join the Western alliance would have resulted in immediate Soviet intervention, but a status of neutrality evoked an illusion in many that a neutral Hungary could be acceptable to the Soviet Union too, for it could provide an equal guarantee for Moscow's security interests. A similar tendency, based on the rational self-limitation of the society, prevailed in Hungary in 1989 during the political transition. In its initial phase in the spring, the emerging opposition uniformly established neutrality as the country's desirable foreign policy orientation among the twelve points declared on 15 March. But by autumn, once it turned out that the Soviets were ready to accept a full and unrestricted democratic transition, it soon became a common goal to work for Euro-Atlantic integration—that is, joining the European Communities (the predecessor of the European Union) and NATO.[30]

The pressure on the government was further increased by the fact that on 31 October, the Transdanubian National Council in Győr, organized on a regional basis and thus representing the whole Western part of the country—and regarded by many to be the center of a potential countergovernment—issued a resolution demanding withdrawal from the Warsaw Pact and the declaration of Hungary's neutrality.[31] Since Imre Nagy's major goal was to consolidate the situation as soon as possible, for this was the only hope that the Soviets would give their consent to the political changes that had already taken place, by the end of October he himself came to the conclusion that society could not be pacified without meeting these demands, which were the most significant in relation to national independence. His view was also shared not only by several leaders of the newly established Hungarian Socialist Workers' Party, among them Géza Losonczy, Ferenc Donáth, and János Kádár, but by the former president of the republic, Zoltán Tildy, a leader of the reorganizing Smallholders' Party, who played a key role in the close cabinet formed on 30 October.[32]

So the Hungarian leadership had fallen into a trap; intent on averting Soviet intervention, they had accepted one of the most important and radical demands of society, but this measure sufficed in itself for the Moscow leaders to decide in favor of an armed solution in order to preserve the unity of the Soviet bloc. The declaration of the Soviet government issued the same day made a significant contribution to turning mere considerations into a programmatic stand, for it admitted the mistakes previously committed in the relationship between the Soviet Union and the East Central European countries, declaring that "the Soviet Government is prepared to enter into the appropriate negotiations with the government of the Hungarian People's

Republic and other members of the Warsaw Treaty on the presence of Soviet troops on the territory of Hungary."[33]

Today we know that the Soviet leadership really meant what they said on 30 October; while this was revealed only in 1996 with the publication of the Malin notes, at the same CPSU presidium meeting, a unanimous decision was made that the Soviet troops should be withdrawn from the country if the Hungarian government requested it.[34] At the same time, there was not even a hint in the Soviet government declaration that the Warsaw Pact as an organization should be reorganized, still less any mention of the possibility of renouncing the treaty by any of the member states.

Imre Nagy, however—together with some others—might have thought that if it had been possible to get the Soviets to accept several significant political changes in a critical situation, which even a few days before would have been considered as the height of heresy, the openly announced flexible attitude of the Moscow leaders might perhaps facilitate the recognition of the planned declaration of neutrality, especially if it resulted in rapid consolidation of the situation in Hungary.

All these considerations had led to the ripening of the decision in the closest cabinet by 31 October, and the same day in the afternoon Nagy delivered a speech to the public who gathered in front of the Parliament, in which he declared that "as of today we have started negotiations on the withdrawal of Soviet troops from the country and the renunciation of obligations incumbent on us as a member of the Warsaw Treaty." However, he also added, "You are all requested to be patient. . . . I believe the results we have achieved deserve some patience on your part." While answering questions put by Western reporters after this speech, Nagy made an even more determined statement: "Hungary has now the chance to leave this alliance on its own, without the general breaking up of the Warsaw Treaty, and we will firmly stand by this position of ours."[35] We do not know what this statement was based on, as the statute of the Warsaw Pact did not in fact contain any options for a unilateral withdrawal from the organization. Most likely this promise was primarily aimed at reassuring the revolutionary public, as now the government—if it had truly accepted to represent these radical demands—had to support its position with some "facts" in order to prove that the pursuit of this goal was not totally unrealistic. Establishing a "legitimate" exit option might have been possible in theory, though, but this would have required modifying the statute of the Warsaw Pact. This option, in light of the Soviet government's declaration of 30 October, including a truly surprising promise to "review the question of Soviet troops stationed on the territory" of Hungary, Romania and Poland,[36] did not seem entirely impossible for the Hungarian leaders.

We also know that in September 1968, Albania—true, after having already severed relations with the Soviet bloc states in 1961—in protest against the Warsaw Pact invasion of Czechoslovakia, unilaterally withdrew from the Warsaw Pact, and although legally this was not possible, the Warsaw Pact member states were forced to take note of the decision.

It is hardly unlikely, however, that at the end of October 1956 the government of Imre Nagy contemplated such a radical option. It is also worth noting that Nagy did not use the term *neutrality* in his speech, while of course, this was an implicit message to the public. We now know that some hours later, in the evening of 31 October, Nagy and János Kádár met with Polish ambassador Adam Willman, who was told that after the hoped-for withdrawal of the Soviet troops from Hungary, the country would leave the Warsaw Pact. Here they also revealed that the government was "investigating Hungarian neutrality of the Austrian or Swiss type or coexistence of the Yugoslav type" and that they were "consulting with Yugoslavia on the latter."[37]

So at this time there was not yet talk of a radical unilateral step that the Hungarian government would have to take the following day in a desperate situation; instead, the discussion concerned the possibly lengthy negotiations to be carried out with the Soviet Union on an independent status as a likely outcome of a bargain agreement. The goal of Nagy's open announcement was clearly to win the support of revolutionary public opinion of that time and to demonstrate that the political leadership endorsed the basic demands of society; however, society, in turn, was now expected to accept the *negotiated* nature of gaining neutrality and to support the government in consolidating the situation in the country without reservation.

By the end of October, however, in view of the political changes that had already taken place in the country (the restoration of a multiparty system, the dissolution of the State Security Police [ÁVH], the disintegration of the party leadership, the passivity of the armed forces, occasional mob violence against ÁVH people and Communists, the increasingly non-Communist shift in the policy of the government, and the existence of a totally free revolutionary press), the Soviet leaders came to the conclusion that "the issue of socialism"— that is, the Soviet type of Communist system—had entered into an ultimate crisis in Hungary; thus, in the 31 October meeting of the CPSU presidium, a decision was made to restore order by military force.[38]

As a result, by 1 November, Soviet–Hungarian relations had undergone a radical change. While by 30 October, as a result of the agreement that had been made between the two sides, the Soviet troops had left Budapest, beginning on 31 October (as mentioned earlier), more and more new Soviet troops were entering the country—occupying the most important strategic points, surrounding the cities, and taking hold of all the airports. The answers given by Andropov to the protest of the Hungarian government made it obvious that a new Soviet intervention, aimed at cracking down on the revolt and overthrowing the Hungarian government, was looming large. It was in this hopeless situation that the Hungarian government took a radical step and unilaterally quit the Warsaw Pact effective immediately and declared the country neutral.

In talks with crisis-management envoys Mikoyan and Suslov in Budapest between 24 and 31 October, Imre Nagy had been trying all along to squeeze significant concessions from the Moscow leaders, relying partly on the pressure coming from the public, but at the same time he made every effort to maintain the confidence of the Soviets. As a politician who knew the Soviet imperial policy all too well, he was very much aware that the fate of the revolution hinged on how long Moscow could tolerate the changes in Hungary and when they would come to the decision that the chances for a political resolution were lost for good and all. So, in a situation like this, it is quite unlikely that Nagy, either on his own account or under the pressure of the public, would have taken such a unilateral and explicitly provocative step if he had seen any chance of coming to an agreement with the Soviets. By the beginning of November, the situation had become so hopeless that no measure of the Hungarian government could have made it any worse. Thus, the views holding that the denouncement of the Warsaw Pact and the declaration of neutrality were inconsiderate and hasty, challenging another Soviet intervention, would prove to be unsound. Quite the contrary, the paradox of the situation is that the decision made by the government on 1 November was just as rational—simply because now there was nothing to lose—as the demand on the part of the public toward the Nagy cabinet to take such a step was irrational and unrealistic.

However, it may be legitimate to ask what Nagy hoped for after this step, unprecedented in the whole history of the Soviet bloc, and in what way he actually tried to prevent complete collapse. Naturally, there was hardly any chance that the Soviet leaders would take Hungarian neutrality seriously and, however unwillingly, resign themselves to the inevitable and withdraw their troops from the country, leaving Hungary to her fate once and for all. Though in his messages sent to the secretary-general of the UN on 1 and 2 November the Hungarian prime minister requested help from the four great powers to protect the neutrality of the country, in reality he did not attach much hope to the support of the West, or of the UN for that matter. Today it is quite clear that Nagy, who had previously often been characterized as an indecisive politician drifting with the current, hit with a good eye upon the only possibility that promised at least a minimal chance of survival: he was trying to put pressure on the Soviets in an indirect way.

In fact, the same attitude characterized his steps on 1 November: on hearing the news of new Soviet troops entering the country, he talked with Ambassador Andropov twice in person and once on the phone in the same morning, trying to persuade him to give some guarantee that the operation would be canceled and further troops would not cross the border.[39] However, since Andropov's attitude made it clear to Nagy that he no longer enjoyed the confidence of the Soviets and that they had tried to mislead him, the same morning he convened the cabinet to discuss the critical situation.[40] They made a unanimous political decision that the government should declare the country's neutrality. Since this paragraph was omitted from the formerly known minutes of the session, the text is worth quoting in its entirety:

> For the sake of both putting an end to the armed fighting and ensuring the full and final independence of the country, the Cabinet discussed the question of neutrality. The cabinet unanimously agreed with the position that the government should declare the country's neutrality. For the time being [the Cabinet] refrains from deciding which form of neutrality should be chosen (Switzerland, Austria or Yugoslavia). This very day, Géza Losonczy will prepare a draft communiqué for public announcement, together with a simultaneous information note for the diplomatic corps, a draft telegram to the General Secretary of the UN, and finally an announcement for the press and radio.[41]

The only concrete decision made by the cabinet, however, was a call to the prime minister that he should immediately protest to Andropov against the most recent intervention of the Soviet troops, and further steps were dependent on the ambassador's response to the protest; in other words, they made a *provisional decision* to the effect that in case the response proved to be unsatisfactory, the protest would be sent to all the diplomatic missions as well as to the UN, and a communiqué on it would be made public.[42]

Right after the cabinet meeting, Nagy summoned Andropov and firmly protested against the intervention of Soviet troops. In his reply sent to Nagy a few hours later, Andropov claimed that the Soviet Union had sent some state security troops to Hungary merely to restore order and discipline among the troops already stationed in the country.[43]

With a view to the emergency situation, Nagy convened the cabinet again in the afternoon on 1 November, to which Andropov was also invited.[44] In doing so, the prime minister most likely wanted the ambassador to see for himself that the government had a uniform assessment of the situation; thus, as a result of the planned intervention the Soviets would have to reckon not only with the resistance of the Hungarian society but with the opposition of a unified leadership. Since the members of the cabinet did not consider

Andropov's explanation for the new intervention of Soviet troops satisfactory, at the motion of Nagy the body made a unanimous decision (including János Kádár) that Hungary should resign membership in the Warsaw Pact, declare the neutrality of the country, and turn to the UN for help, requesting the four great powers to assist in protecting the neutrality of the country and at the same time requesting that the Hungarian issue be put on the agenda in the UN with urgency.[45]

Right after the cabinet meeting, Nagy sent a telegram to UN secretary-general Dag Hammarskjöld requesting that the four great powers help defend Hungary's neutrality and that this question be urgently placed on the agenda of the upcoming General Assembly.[46] The Imre Nagy government had therefore turned to the Western great powers and the United Nations—with the ideal of Austrian-style neutrality in mind—in a last-ditch effort to stave off the increasing threat of a Soviet invasion. Nagy himself was nevertheless quite aware of the extreme improbability of vigorous assistance from either the Western great powers or the UN; he was also quite familiar with Soviet imperial politics and thus recognized that, within the existing international political context, it was likewise very improbable that the Soviet leadership—for whom the suppression of the revolution was never really more than a logistical question—would relinquish one of its strategically important dominions just because the government there had declared its independence.

Thus, Nagy was making every effort to maintain the possibility for negotiations with the Soviets even in the most hopeless situation of all. He had a surprise in store even at this dramatic moment: evaluating the situation very well in that the only nuisance for the Soviets under the given conditions could be the involvement of the United Nations, he told Andropov that, if the Soviet Union stopped the further advance of its troops and withdrew them back to its borders, the Hungarian government would in turn promptly withdraw the request sent to UN, but the country would still maintain its neutrality. After the meeting, Nagy spent another half hour in private trying to convince Andropov that, in spite of the decision of the cabinet, he still believed that "the very serious conflicts that have emerged could be resolved by direct negotiations."[47] He said to Andropov that the Soviet leaders should give him a chance to do so. Although Andropov promised to forward his request, no reply came from Moscow, since the Soviet leaders were already busy setting up a countergovernment to eliminate the revolution.[48]

The same tactical maneuvering can be observed in the wording of his message sent to the UN secretary-general. Though the cabinet decided to request that the Hungarian issue be put on the agenda with urgency, Nagy's 1 November telegram says that the Hungarian government requests the UN to put the issue on the agenda of the next regular meeting of the assembly scheduled for 12 November,[49] whereas the UN Security Council had already started discussing the Hungarian situation as early as 28 October, and the special session of the General Assembly was convened for 1 November to discuss the crisis in the Middle East. Most likely Nagy wanted to give some time to the Soviets to consider his proposal for the bargain agreement sent through Andropov, since the Soviets' consent to it—at least in principle—offered much more promise for the future than any resolution by the UN. For this, however, any prompt UN action had to be prevented, for a speedy resolution condemning the Soviet Union in the Security Council and thus transferring the issue to the special session of the General Assembly—although today we know that there was no danger of anything like that at all—would have demolished the bargain value of Nagy's offer.

This assumption is further supported by the fact that the first draft of the telegram included a paragraph saying that "the Hungarian People's Republic suffered armed aggression" by the Soviet Union, therefore the Hungarian government requests "immediate action by the Security Council of the United Nations Organization."[50] This part was eventually left out of the message sent to the secretary-general with the approval of Nagy, since, according to Nagy's logic, it would have significantly enhanced the possibility of undesirably prompt UN action.[51]

On 2 November, Nagy summoned Andropov again and protested with resolve against the repeated reinforcement of further Soviet troops but at the same time explained that Hungary intended to maintain long-term friendly relations with the Soviet Union. He told the ambassador that the Hungarian government would inform all the diplomatic missions in Budapest and the UN Security Council of the recent developments.[52]

And indeed, on the same day, the prime minister sent another telegram to the secretary-general of the UN, but in it he still did not request "immediate intervention" of the Security Council; rather, he just asked the secretary-general to call on the four great powers to recognize the neutrality of Hungary and the Security Council to order the Hungarian and the Soviet governments to start negotiations on the withdrawal of Soviet troops right away.[53] For Nagy's major goal was not to have the ongoing Soviet intervention condemned by the UN but, using pressure from the Security Council, to persuade the Soviets to negotiate with his government.

On 2 November, the Soviet government sent its reply to the 31 October Hungarian request: it said that the Soviet Union was ready to negotiate, and they requested the Hungarian government to appoint a committee to discuss political issues related to the Warsaw Pact and to set up a military committee to ensure the technical conditions for the withdrawal of the Soviet troops. The memorandum, however, did not say anything about the new troops that had been pouring into the country continuously, and in the meantime, the military situation had changed for the worse; thus, the intention to negotiate on their part was, to put it mildly, dubious. The government, however, did not have much choice. Also, there was some hope—which later turned out to be false—attached to these negotiations that the Soviet intervention would not take place as long as the talks were in progress. Therefore, on the same day, the Hungarian government sent a positive response to the Soviet memorandum, and the negotiations on the withdrawal of troops began in Parliament on 3 November.

On 3 November, the prime minister sent an order by telegram to János Szabó—ad interim leader of the Hungarian UN delegation—to emphatically request the Security Council in its present meeting "to call upon the great powers to recognize the neutrality of Hungary and promptly urge the Soviet and the Hungarian governments to start negotiations."[54] Szabó also had to give an account of the talks between the headquarters of the two armies on the technical conditions of the withdrawal of troops as well as of the fact that the Soviet delegation promised that no more troops would cross the Hungarian border. So, at the last moment, Nagy made another desperate attempt to try to use the UN—through the Hungarian acting UN representative—to prevent the Soviet intervention. Informing the Security Council of the Soviet delegation's promise probably meant to serve the immediate goal of making as much trouble for the Soviets as possible if they decided to breach their promise. If that was so, Nagy's expectations did not stand the test: Szabó, who had presumably consulted with the Soviet UN representative, Arkady Sobolev, on the possible developments anticipated for the next day, deliberately conveyed only the "positive" content of the prime minister's message, related to the start of the negotiations, in the 3 November session of the Security Council, not even mentioning the issue of neutrality.[55] This, then, significantly facilitated the wait-and-see policy of the American and Yugoslav representatives After a brief discussion, the meeting of the council was adjourned to 5 November.

In the first days of November, Nagy summoned the ambassadors of the Socialist countries, first of all Soviet ambassador Yurii Andropov, in order to try to persuade them of the correctness of his policies. Nagy also requested an immediate audience with the highest-level Soviet leadership—a request that the Soviets promptly denied. Finally, in discussions held in Budapest with a Romanian party delegation on 3 November, Nagy attempted to coordinate a plan whereby Gheorghiu-Dej would petition Khrushchev for a Soviet–Hungarian summit meeting.[56] On that very same day, however, the Soviet leadership was holding a summit meeting of a very different nature in Moscow with János Kádár in order to coordinate the violent overthrow of the Hungarian revolutionary government.[57]

On 4 November, a massive invasion of Soviet forces was launched against Hungary, which resulted in the crushing of the revolution in a few days' time. A countergovernment led by János Kádár was installed while Nagy and his associates temporarily took refuge in the Yugoslav embassy.

The Soviet Union and the Eastern Bloc

It is now clear that the outcome of the events in Hungary did not depend (as many have argued) on the West's behavior but on how the Soviet leaders handled the political crisis that erupted on 23 October. Although Tito, in his speech at Pula on 11 November 1956, is known to have called the first Soviet intervention on 24 October a mistaken move, remarkably little heed has been paid in weighing the historical chances to the way the Soviets, and only the Soviets, were in a real position to decide on 23 October 1956—that *then* they could still have decided otherwise.

It contradicts earlier assumptions to find that the Soviet leadership, preoccupied as they were with the Polish crisis that had broken out on 19 October 1956, were expressly reluctant to comply with Ernő Gerő's demand and deploy Soviet forces stationed in Hungary to break up the Budapest demonstration on 23 October. The ultimate decision to intervene followed repeated appeals for help during the evening and above all pressure from Ambassador Andropov, who judged the situation to be very grave.[58]

The CPSU presidium discussed the matter late on the evening of 23 October. By that time, armed clashes had occurred in Budapest, and the situation in Hungary was thought by the Soviet leaders to be far graver than the one in Warsaw. The idea was not even raised of postponing the discussion until the following day, when the Soviet Union's allies could be consulted at the Moscow summit, originally convened to discuss the situation in Poland, and might have decided together whether Soviet troops stationed in Hungary should be deployed, as the country's leadership requested. In the meantime, however, a compromise was reached on the Polish crisis, with Moscow dropping the idea of armed intervention and Gomułka assuring the Soviets that the envisaged reforms would not endanger Communist power or the unity of the Soviet bloc. Indeed, the Polish scenario might have been applied in Hungary, too, in spite of the limited armed conflict that had broken out there.

At the presidium meeting, this was put very plainly by Mikoyan, a key member of the Soviet leadership and the one who knew the Hungarian situation best: "There is no way of mastering the movement without [Imre] Nagy and so this will make it cheaper for us as well. . . . What can we lose? Let the

Hungarians restore order for themselves. Let us try political measures, and only after that send our troops in."[59] In reality, this was the only rational alternative in the given situation, but the presidium stood firm and eventually decided to order the Soviet troops stationed in Hungary to intervene and move into the capital.

Having tackled world political issues pragmatically since 1953, and even in its last-minute solution to the Polish crisis resisted its Cold War reflexes to use armed intervention on ideological and emotional grounds, the Soviet leadership proved incapable of biding its time and exercising such self-restraint in Hungary's case. Khrushchev and his associates thereby took the worst political decision *from their own point of view* and gave rise to a process whose consequences would be just what armed intervention was supposed to spare them. In other words, they achieved exactly the opposite of what they had wanted: not rapid pacification but escalation of the sporadic armed actions into an extensive anti-Soviet war of liberation of a kind unparalleled in the history of the Soviet bloc.[60]

Mikoyan's rational proposal, although defeated by his colleagues in the presidium, deserves special attention, as it might rightly be dubbed the Mikoyan Doctrine.[61] It was no less than laying the ground for a future Soviet crisis-management strategy in case of the emergence of a serious crisis in one of the countries of the Soviet bloc. This meant first trying to find a political solution to restore order (if need be, coupled with using armed forces) executed by local forces only and thus to avoid Soviet military intervention at any cost. While Mikoyan's proposal to this effect was voted down by the CPSU presidium in 1956, in reality the Soviet leaders learned the lesson well. In their crisis-management strategy during later conflicts, they always sought initially and instinctively to use this doctrine: in 1968 in Czechoslovakia for eight months and in Afghanistan in 1979 for more than a year and a half.[62] While these attempts eventually failed, the first successful application of the Mikoyan Doctrine occurred in December 1981, when General Jaruzelski introduced martial law in Poland.[63]

In fact we can argue that, at almost every point in their treatment of the 1956 crisis in Hungary, Khrushchev and his associates were working against their own interests and committed three major mistakes: (1) They paid no attention to the expectations of society for the more tolerable version of Communism promised by the CPSU Twentieth Congress and decided too late to dismiss Rákosi, while they did not hesitate to remove Chervenkov in Bulgaria in April 1956. (2) When they did dismiss Rákosi in mid-July, they did not replace him with János Kádár or some other, lesser known but acceptable leader but with Ernő Gerő, the right-hand man of Rákosi, equally guilty of past Stalinist crimes and thus totally unsuitable for pacifying society. He was also known to have been working for the Soviet NKVD and for being in charge of the bloody elimination of the non-Communist political opponents during the Spanish civil war. On top of that, his character seemed to be even more negative than Rákosi's, as due to his stomach disease he never smiled. Therefore, while his predecessor could occasionally play the role of a jovial dictator and could make an impression on even Western diplomats, Gerő was simply a stern-looking dictator. So, in reality, the Soviets succeeded in finding the worst possible option to replace Rákosi.[64] Indeed, during the revolution, Khrushchev confessed during a meeting of the presidium that "Mikoyan and I made a mistake when we proposed Gerő instead of Kádár. We were taken in by Gerő."[65] (3) Finally, their decision to intervene militarily on 23 October meant that there was only one direction for events to take. Contrary to the Kremlin's expectations, the rapid Soviet intervention radicalized the masses to such a degree that all chance of a political settlement was dispelled. Furthermore, the Soviets unwittingly misled Hungarian society with their method of intervention: they originally intended to pacify the situation through a show of force, but the military force they actually showed was rather limited and ineffective, especially as Soviet troops were ordered to shoot only when they were attacked. This "mild" version of military intervention might have seemed reasonable from a political perspective, but the strategy of intervention with a human face eventually backfired. If Moscow had restored order right away on 24 October with the kind of massive and drastic military action they were to employ on 4 November, thus clearly signaling its unqualified determination to preserve the Communist system at any cost, the revolutionary events of 24 October to 3 November would probably not have ensued.

We can argue therefore that, paradoxically, Moscow could possibly have avoided the revolution in Hungary in two opposite ways: by applying the Mikoyan Doctrine and refraining from using Soviet troops to restore order, or by launching an overwhelming military invasion.

Instead of choosing either of these two rational options, Khrushchev and his associates became trapped by their initial wrong decision. Now they tried out the combination of a military and a political solution, which the revolutionary public interpreted as weakness and uncertainty. This misperception, quite a frequent feature of revolts against dictatorships, only further radicalized society.[66]

The initial successes of the insurgent groups against the poorly organized Soviet units and the continual concessions by the Nagy government and the Kremlin eventually left the general illusion that the revolutionary situation truly had revolutionary possibilities: only persistence was needed to achieve even the ultimate goal of Western-type parliamentary democracy and full independence for the country. Yet present knowledge of the Soviet intentions makes it plain that the fate of the revolution was sealed even before it started, by 22 October. The seed of ultimate catastrophe was sown in the demand for free elections, already one of the sixteen points compiled by students at the Technical University and a general demand within a few days, for thereafter there were only two possibilities: either society would see in good time that the demand was excessive and voluntarily reduce its demands to a tolerable level—this seldom happens during a revolution, which is what makes it a revolution in the first place—or those exercising power in practice, in this case the Soviets, would decide to end the uncertainty and use force to inform the rebels of their error in thinking there was any chance of basic changes.

The presidium of the CPSU, at its meeting on 23 October, had on its agenda not only limited armed intervention in Budapest but some promotion of political development. Learning from the case of Gomułka, the presidium members agreed that Imre Nagy could return to power as prime minister, hoping that his prestige and popularity would make it possible for the Hungarian Workers' Party to consolidate the situation. They also decided to send a four-man delegation to Budapest to promote effective management of the crisis, which was undoubtedly a rational step under the exceptional circumstances. The Soviet delegation that arrived in Budapest on 24 October consisted of presidium members Mikoyan and Suslov, KGB head Ivan Serov, and deputy chief of staff Mikhail Malinin.

For several days after the outbreak of armed conflict, Khrushchev and the rest of the Soviet leadership continued to maintain hope that the newly appointed prime minister, Imre Nagy, would effectively quell the reigning disorder and that the Hungarian crisis could ultimately be resolved within the same framework of compromise and negotiation that had proved successful in Poland. In negotiations conducted with Nagy and the rest of the Hungarian leadership on 26 October, Mikoyan and Suslov defined the outer limits of possible Soviet concessions in their expression of a willingness to allow some politicians who had previously belonged to non-Communist parties into the government (the possibility of a multiparty system was not even considered at that point) and a return of Soviet troops to their garrisons after the restoration of order, similar to what had occurred in Poland. They also warned the Hungarian leadership that further concessions might very well lead to the overthrow of the Communist system, an eventuality that the Soviet delegation quite clearly suggested would evoke a vigorous response from Moscow.[67] The Soviet leadership never entertained the slightest notion of allowing the restoration of a parliamentary system in Hungary, for fear that it would lead to the disintegration of its vitally important East European security zone.

There were also significant ideological factors motivating the Soviets to suppress the Hungarian Revolution. As previously mentioned, during these years, Soviet attempts to expand the influence of the world's Communist empire centered on the third world, and it was exactly at that time when an intensive propaganda campaign coupled with the policy of providing economic aid was unfolding. The Soviet leadership could well imagine the damage that might be done to these expansion efforts if Hungary were to be seen restoring a Western type of multiparty democracy by way of an anti-Soviet uprising less than a decade after the installation of a Communist regime.

The Soviets regarded the following elements to be of paramount importance to the maintenance of the Communist system in the East Central European satellite states: a competent and unified Communist party leadership, a potent and resolute state security apparatus, a loyal and disciplined armed force and military leadership, and strict party control of all media. Any hint of unrest in any of these four institutions immediately set off warning bells within the Soviet decision-making mechanism; the breakdown of all four of them at once, as happened in Hungary in 1956, left the Soviets with only one option: armed intervention.[68]

However, it was in the short-term interests of the Soviet Union to exercise this radical option only if all possible peaceful means of resolving the crisis had been exhausted; the Soviet desire to preserve Communist bloc unity and the process of rapprochement with Yugoslavia, to improve the standing of Communist parties in the West and propaganda efforts in the third world, and to find a peaceful resolution to the Polish crisis all weighed against the option of armed intervention.

Tactical considerations also compelled the Soviets to make further concessions: on 28 October they assented to a cease-fire, agreed to withdraw their military units from Budapest—without having first eradicated the groups of armed rebels—and consented to the reevaluation of the events as a "broad national democratic movement." They did not take official issue with the passage in the new proclamation of the government announcing that it would initiate negotiations over the eventual withdrawal of Soviet troops from Hungary, even though just three days earlier, on 25 October, this idea was harshly rejected by the Soviet emissaries. The Soviet government declaration of 30 October contained further pledges to examine the possibility of troop withdrawals from Hungary.[69]

As many suspected at the time, the Soviet leaders had serious debates about the Hungarian situation from the very beginning. What undoubtedly shows the gravity of the situation is that the presidium held meetings nearly every day between 23 October and 4 November; the main question was to what extent and in what way they should compromise with the government of Imre Nagy, so that the latter would be able to consolidate the crisis in a way that the social system of Hungary and the country's place in the Soviet alliance would remain unchanged. Consequently, they unanimously agreed that Hungary's separation from the Socialist bloc was simply unimaginable and should be prevented at all costs.

Probably the greatest possible compromise was that on 30 October, as mentioned before, it was a matter of consideration whether it would be more advisable for a peaceful reconciliation if Soviet troops were withdrawn from Hungary, provided the Hungarian government could secure the necessary conditions. This decision, however, was by no means meant to give up on Hungary by Moscow as some scholars suggest; in fact, it was just the opposite.[70] Full withdrawal of Soviet troops would have been *the maximum political concession* they were willing to make, provided that the Nagy government succeeded in (1) consolidating the situation while maintaining the Communist system and (2) preserving membership of the Soviet bloc.

More importantly, there is much concrete evidence to be found in the Malin notes to show that the withdrawal would only have been considered on the basis of the satisfaction of those two conditions: the preservation of the Communist system and the unity of the Soviet bloc. For now, it is perhaps enough to mention just the two most strikingly phrased or documented opinions. Foreign Minister Shepilov explained his support for the unanimous decision of the presidium on 30 October as follows: "With the agreement of the government of Hungary, we are ready to withdraw troops. We'll have to keep up a struggle with national Communism for a long time."[71] It is characteristic that it was precisely Mikoyan who set forth the consequences of maintaining the status quo at any price in the most unambiguous terms, someone who otherwise consistently represented the most liberal viewpoint in the leadership regarding Hungary: "We simply cannot let Hungary be removed from our camp," he said at the 1 November session of the presidium, one day after the decision that the intervention was necessary, while in the meantime he tried to convince the others that the possibility of a political solution had not yet completely disappeared and that they should wait another ten to fifteen days before invading.[72]

So, the intended result of the Soviet concession on 30 October was not consenting to the restoration of the capitalist system but consolidating a situation akin to that in Poland—that is, accepting the creation of a reformed Communist system, displaying more independence internally but remaining loyal to Moscow and within the confines of the Soviet bloc.[73]

It is history's irony that while at the beginning of the Hungarian Revolution, on 23 October, Mikoyan was the only member of the Soviet leadership who rationally assessed the situation, advocating a wait-and-see tactic, on 1 November he showed that he was the only one who was unable to understand (or acknowledge) that developments had truly exceeded the limits still tolerable by the Soviet Union. Today it is hardly questioned by anybody that, by the very end of October, an irreversible transition toward democracy was unfolding, which necessarily would have led to the complete elimination of the Communist dictatorship in a short period of time without external intervention. The events between 1 and 3 November only confirmed this evaluation; it was not by chance that at the presidium meeting on 3 November, Mikoyan himself suggested that János Kádár become the head of the countergovernment set up in Moscow.[74]

Thus, we can argue that the Malin notes contain not one fact or piece of information that would indicate that the Soviet leadership, or any one of its members, would have been willing to accept the changes in Hungary that were increasingly demonstrating the abandonment of the Communist regime and the advent of a democratic system. If you think about it, it's not so surprising. Let me refer again to a well-known fact: it has long been known that on the island of Brioni during the night of 2 to 3 November, Tito—negotiating with Khrushchev and Malenkov—agreed with the Soviet plan of intervention to rescue the Communist regime in Hungary, and he later confirmed his position publicly as well. There is little doubt that, in the international field, it was Tito who was the most interested leader in the emergence of a national Communist regime in Hungary, which obviously would have meant supporting the government of Imre Nagy. If, therefore, despite his inherently positive bias and initial support for Nagy, by early November he, too, considered (rightly) that the Communist dictatorship was in mortal danger in Hungary, it would have been very strange if the Soviet leaders, who earlier had accepted much more modest changes within the framework of the system under the weight of a crisis, now demonstrated an attitude more permissive than the Yugoslav's.[75]

The Malin notes also make it clear that the Soviet leaders were not in the least afraid of Western intervention in Hungary, although that cynical argument was blithely advanced in the debates with Hungarian leaders as a way of putting pressure on them,[76] and it became prominent in Soviet propaganda. But there are no signs of any substantive contributions on this to be found in the notes of the presidium meetings.[77] If the Soviet leaders had really considered that there was a risk of Western intervention, they would have had to discuss it not only seriously but almost exclusively. Immediate effective security measures would have been needed, including full mobilization of the army, air force, and naval fleet, for it would have meant nothing less than a direct risk of a third world war breaking out. By contrast, Khrushchev spoke at the 31 October meeting of the expected international repercussions of Soviet intervention in a laconic way that accurately reflected world political realities: "There will be no big war."[78]

The period of optimism in the Soviet leadership closed only one day after the 30 October decision to withdraw the troops, as radicalization of the Hungarian political situation forced the Kremlin to make a further decision. Thorough analysis and rethinking of the events of 28–30 October and the situation that had developed (rating of the events as a revolution, the restoration of a multiparty system, the dissolution of the State Security Police (ÁVH), the disintegration of the party leadership, the passivity of the armed forces, occasional mob violence against ÁVH people and Communists,[79] the increasingly non-Communist shift in the policy of the government, and the existence of a totally free revolutionary press) finally convinced the Soviet leaders that the Leninist-Stalinist type of Communist system in Hungary was in danger and without Soviet armed intervention it could not be saved. It was clear that Imre Nagy, already rated an opportunist and a waverer, was being swept along by the tide of events and no longer able—or, worse still, willing—to contain the processes that threatened to break up the Soviet system. For them, this assessment meant that the chances of a peaceful settlement of the crisis were exhausted, and the presidium meeting of 31 October accordingly took a political decision on the need for armed intervention—that is, to prepare for Operation Whirlwind.[80]

The presidium also decided to inform the Chinese, Czechoslovak, Romanian, and Bulgarian leaders of the plan, and have personal discussions with the Poles and the Yugoslavs. Since this marked a departure from the usual internal decision-making mechanism of the Soviet bloc, it is worth looking in detail at the communications between Moscow and its allies during the Hungarian Revolution.

Having discussed the critical situation in Poland, the 20 October meeting of the presidium of the CPSU CC decided it was urgent to hold a multilateral meeting, for which they would "invite to Moscow the communist party representatives of Czechoslovakia, Hungary, Romania, Bulgaria, and the GDR."[81] Arrangements were also made to brief the Chinese leadership personally by sending a Central Committee representative to Beijing. The fragmentary minutes of the presidium meeting show that hardly a day after the Soviet crisis-management team had returned from its talks in Warsaw, the general view was that the situation in Poland "has to be ended." This is confirmed by the planned measures, which in similar crises had clearly presaged a violent solution or replacement of the leaders of the day by the seemingly legal technique of dismissing them by appointing new ones: "Military exercise. Prepare the document. Assemble a committee."[82]

The Communist summit hastily convened in Moscow on 24 October had been intended originally to prepare and coordinate Soviet military intervention in Poland. It is clear that the political consultative role of the one-and-a-half-year-old Warsaw Pact was still not significant, as it was not even suggested that agreement should be reached by convening its PCC, established in January 1956, though the Warsaw Pact would have provided a requisite legal framework. The crisis management still proceeded in the traditional way of summoning the party leaders to Moscow. The short notice and the extraordinary situation meant that only the Czechoslovaks, the East Germans, and the Bulgarians could send representatives on 24 October. Ernő Gerő was detained by the events in Budapest, while the Romanian leadership, headed by Gheorghe Gheorghiu-Dej, was on a visit of penance to Belgrade on 20–27 October. Meanwhile, the situation was changing radically. The original plan for intervention in Poland came off the agenda, as the new leader of the Polish Communist Party, Władysław Gomułka, had given assurances to Khrushchev on the telephone that Communist dictatorship in Poland was in no danger, and the security interests of the Soviet bloc could be guaranteed.[83] This meant the country would remain a loyal member of the Warsaw Pact and not raise the issue of the withdrawal of Soviet troops. But the situation had reached a critical point in Hungary, where the peaceful 23 October demonstration calling for reforms had escalated by evening into an armed uprising. So Khrushchev presented the 24 October summit with the facts that had occurred.

On the same day, there arrived in Moscow a Chinese delegation headed by Liu Shaoqi, also to discuss the crisis in East Central Europe.[84] The essence of what the Soviets and the Chinese discussed is now more or less known, but there are hardly any sources to say whether agreement was reached with the East Central European allies—and if so, what kind. Sources discovered so far indicate that up to the beginning of November, they mainly had to fall back on what could be gleaned from the Soviet press. Further consultations came only after the 31 October presidium decision to crush the Hungarian Revolution by launching the second Soviet intervention. It was decided at the same time that Khrushchev, Molotov, and Malenkov would meet the next day, 1 November, with the Polish leaders in Brest, after which Khrushchev and Malenkov would travel on to Yugoslavia, where they would discuss that very evening preparations for intervention with Tito.[85] So it had still not been suggested by then that there should be urgent personal consultations with the other leaders, simply that they should be informed.[86] This is also surprising because in Poland's case, as has been seen, Moscow had summoned the allies when Soviet intervention had become a serious possibility but no decision had yet been reached. Now the Soviet leaders clearly decided alone to crush the Hungarian uprising and appoint a countergovernment, despite the unforeseeable consequences this would have for the Soviet bloc as a whole. The urgent tasks were merely to consult the "problematic" Poles and ensure the neutrality of the Yugoslavs.

At the talks in Brest, on the Soviet side of the border with Poland, Gomułka, Czyrankiewicz, and Ochab opposed the intervention, as the Soviets had predicted, emphasizing that the Hungarians had to solve the situation for themselves. The new leadership headed by Gomułka, which had come out of the October crisis, initially gave strong support to Imre Nagy's efforts to consolidate the situation and condemned the first Soviet intervention. This meant that the Polish public, alone in the Soviet bloc, could openly express its solidarity with the Hungarian Revolution in mass demonstrations, statements, and blood-donor and aid campaigns, while the press could report the events impartially. At the end of October, a two-member party delegation left for Budapest with the aim of gaining direct information on the situation from Hungarian leaders, particularly Nagy and Kádár, and trying to convince them that there were realistic chances of attaining something only through the "Polish solution." But the political changes in Hungary in the early days of November were observed by the Polish leadership with growing concern. The withdrawal from the Warsaw Pact and the declaration of neutrality were seen by the Polish leaders as endangering the geopolitical structure erected after 1945, and potentially even the Polish-German border. So Gomułka was obliged to take cognizance of the Soviet decision to intervene to save the Communist regime, probably hoping as Nagy did that it would be avoided by some miracle at the last minute. Thus, the communiqué issued to the Polish people by the Communist Party on 1 November, after the Brest meeting, included the statement that the task of defending Socialism in Hungary was one for the Hungarian people, not outside intervention.[87] Nonetheless, the Soviet leaders were sure that the Poles would accept the realities loyally after the intervention.

The question arises as to why the Romanian, Czechoslovak, and Bulgarian leaders were consulted after all, despite the original plan. Molotov returned from Brest to Moscow as planned, but Khrushchev and Malenkov, instead of going straight to see Tito, flew to Bucharest, where they had discussions with the Romanian and Czechoslovak leaderships, who endorsed the planned intervention, for which the Romanians even offered armed support.[88] The Czechoslovak leaders probably made a similar offer, for on the evening of 2 November, after the return of Novotný and Siroký, the Politburo of the Czechoslovak Communist Party passed a resolution stating that Czechoslovakia would, "if there were a need," cooperate actively in the struggle against the Hungarian "counterrevolution" in defense of the people's democratic system.[89] It is perhaps more surprising still that Khrushchev and Malenkov flew on from Bucharest to Sofia to meet with the Bulgarian leaders, who could not for some reason attend the Bucharest meeting.[90] What has been discovered so far might support the assumption that the Soviets would have considered the Romanian and Czechoslovak offers had there been more time to prepare for the intervention.

This flurried briefing of allies is conspicuous not only because the Soviets had never done anything similar before but also because no such move was envisaged in the presidium resolution of 31 October, as has been seen.[91] One possible explanation is that after the meeting with the Poles, it was concluded that it would be useful to consult the other allies as well, especially as there could be no doubt that the Czechoslovaks, Romanians, and Bulgarians (unlike the Poles) would give the planned measures their decided support. It is also possible that parting advice was given by the Chinese delegation headed by Liu Shaoqi, which left Moscow on 31 October, arguing that consultation would enhance the legitimacy of the Soviet intervention. Finally, there is no way of excluding the possibility that Khrushchev may have recalled the government statement of 30 October, for just a couple of days before, new emphasis had been given to placing relations between the Soviet Union and its allies on a new basis of "partnership." It would hardly have been consistent with that to have an intervention in a Warsaw Pact member-state without consulting the other members.[92] Certainly the incident foreshadowed the slow but inevitable development of a process of multilateral agreement. The two crises in East Central Europe indirectly helped the Warsaw Pact to "define itself," as well as develop its political consultative function and to some extent its policing role.[93]

After Khrushchev and Malenkov had visited Bucharest and Sofia, they arrived totally exhausted in the evening of 2 November on the island of Brioni, where they had talks with Tito, Aleksandar Ranković, Edvard Kardelj, and the Yugoslav ambassador in Moscow, Veljko Mićunović. The Soviets were prepared to implement the plan even if the Yugoslav view was negative, but they held the talks nonetheless, as they knew the strong influence Yugoslav propaganda had had on the radical party opposition in Hungary, especially in 1955–56, and so indirectly on intellectual preparations for the Hungarian Revolution. Furthermore, a letter from Tito to the central leadership of the Hungarian Workers' Party on 29 October had pledged support for the Imre Nagy government and its new policy of reassessing events, although it had sternly warned of the danger of counterrevolution as well.[94] But Tito had been hoping that Hungary would follow the Yugoslav path and been disappointed by events in Hungary in subsequent days. He had found instead that the new system had taken two steps at a time and begun to resemble the Austrian model, which Tito found unacceptable. So it was a great relief to Khrushchev and Malenkov to find that the Yugoslav leaders agreed on the need for intervention and even promised to assist in removing Imre Nagy's group from the political scene.[95]

The Chinese leadership, which was just beginning to reassess its relations with the Soviet Union as the leading force in the Socialist camp, sympathized initially with developments in Poland and Hungary, hoping that they would limit the Soviet Union's influence in East Central Europe and increase China's own. The October events in Poland provided an excellent opportunity for testing this. Moscow, having originally wanted to inform the Chinese Communist Party by sending a representative to Beijing, eventually invited the Chinese comrades for consultation in Moscow, for which a delegation headed by Liu Shaoqi arrived on 23 October. Mao Zedong had already sent a message to the CPSU leaders on 19 October expressly opposing a military solution to the Polish crisis. The original idea had been for the Chinese delegates to play a mediating role in the Polish–Soviet conflict, but the situation had changed completely by the time they arrived. The Soviets had called off the military intervention in Poland but decided to deploy Soviet Army forces to crush the armed rebellion that had broken out in Budapest. The Soviet leadership collated its views with the Beijing delegation on several occasions between 24 and 31 October, and the latter attended several meetings of the CPSU presidium as well.[96] The Chinese delegates did not confine their comments to the crisis of the moment; they strongly criticized the errors that Moscow had committed in relations with its allies in Stalin's time and urged the relations of a new type, based on the Panchseel (five principles). Initially, they agreed fundamentally with the Soviet move in Hungary, even the intervention of 24 October, but on 29 October they opined that Soviet troops should be withdrawn from Hungary to allow consolidation of the situation and thus save the Communist system there. It has been seen that the CPSU presidium also reached this decision at its meeting on 30 October, and our present knowledge suggests that the Chinese view played an important part in this. Yet on that very day, there was a decisive change in the assessment of the situation in Beijing. Hitherto the Chinese had urged for a political solution to the events in Poland and then Hungary, emphasizing in both cases that the changes meant only the renewal of the Communist system. But 30 October brought a new appraisal from Beijing: that the underlying feature of the Polish events was anti-Sovietism, and of the Hungarian events, anti-Communism. So the Chinese leaders were a day ahead of the Soviets in recognizing the real nature of the Hungarian Revolution, at the end of October labeling it a counterrevolution, which it logically was from their point of view, and Imre Nagy's role in it as treachery. Liu Shaoqi accordingly recommended at the presidium meeting on 30 October that the Soviet troops should not be withdrawn from Hungary.

Clearly, the "lost" historical opportunity in 1956 that many still seek today cannot be that the Hungarian Revolution would have triumphed under luckier conditions and democracy and national independence restored. One notable aspect that differs from earlier knowledge is that the Soviet leaders would still have been willing on 30 October 1956 to withdraw their troops from Hungary, if by some miracle the Nagy government had been able to halt the democratization process very rapidly. The historical significance of that decision is that Moscow at that juncture was still willing to make a bigger concession over Hungary than it had made over Poland, where the issue of Soviet troop withdrawal had never seriously been aired. Now the Kremlin was prepared to grant the privilege of relative internal or external self-determination (if the Communist system and the unity of the Soviet bloc were retained, of course) to a specific country: Hungary. Faced with that extraordinary critical situation, Khrushchev and his team would have made a complex concession, something the Soviet leadership would never again be willing to do in the decades to come. Moscow indeed tolerated in the post-1956 decades a type of internal development in Hungary and Poland that was relatively independent and more liberal than in other countries in the Soviet bloc, but the price was loyalty in foreign policy. Romania, on the other hand, was allowed a semblance of foreign political independence, but its internal system remained in many respects more repressive than the post-Stalinist Soviet one. Imperial interests dictated that quasi-independent domestic *and* foreign policies could not be allowed in one and the same allied country. The analysis of the first Soviet intervention on 24 October showed that the historic chances for the revolution were only theoretical, as the Soviet proposal of 30 October was contingent on retaining two basic things: the Communist system and the unity of the Soviet bloc, something that the Imre Nagy government—or any other government or leader—had no chance of doing amidst the sweeping radical revolutionary changes that were triggered by the first Soviet intervention.

The Western World, the Suez Crisis, and the United Nations

The Western public, who felt somewhat guilty about the tragedy of the East European "enslaved nations," received the news of the Polish and, more importantly, Hungarian events of October 1956 with distinctive sympathy from the very beginning. Not only in Europe and North America but, except in the Soviet bloc,[97] nearly all over the world there were smaller or greater events— protests and demonstrations—organized to express sympathy with the Hungarian Revolution. The Hungarian Revolution also became the first great media event of the Cold War beyond the Iron Curtain. The press and the electronic media, through the reports of Western correspondents and camera crews who could work undisturbed in Budapest until the Soviets launched the second military intervention on 4 November, reported firsthand and for the first time on an armed uprising that was happening in a member state of the Soviet bloc. The Western public observed with a mixture of admiration and worry the struggle of revolutionaries, who were fighting the superior numbers of Soviet troops with small arms and Molotov cocktails. As to the government of Imre Nagy, they largely condemned it up until 28 October. Then, however, once the government and the rebels reached an agreement that seemingly the Soviet Union also accepted, the general atmosphere in the West was that of hope and expectation, and many considered the unthinkable suddenly plausible—that a Soviet satellite state could liberate itself without external help.

At the same time, Western governments—unlike their public opinion, which expressed vivid solidarity with the Hungarian uprising from the beginning—were acutely aware of their extremely limited room to maneuver within the existing European status quo and reacted with great caution to the revolt in Hungary from its very beginning and, in most instances, went so far as to give explicit public endorsement of the principle of nonintervention. Behind the Western response to the Hungarian Revolution was the realization that, under the prevailing international political circumstances, any sort of Western military intervention in Hungary contained the implicit threat of war with the Soviet Union, quite possibly to be waged with thermonuclear weapons, which would likely lead first to the obliteration of the very East Central European peoples whom intervention was designed to liberate, and then to that of the rest of the world.

Nevertheless, between armed intervention and total passivity there could have been alternative solutions, especially for the three great powers, with which they could have tried influencing Soviet decision-making in a positive direction. The question is whether the governments of the United States, Great Britain, and France ever considered these possibilities at all, and whether the armed conflict in the Middle East at the end of October, in which Britain and France were heavily involved, influenced the foreign policy of the three great powers toward Hungary and, provided it did, to what extent.

The United States

The events that took place in Poland and, particularly, in Hungary in October 1956 caught the American government completely by surprise, even though it was extremely well informed about the political changes that were taking place in these countries. Secretary of State John Foster Dulles had already publicly distanced the administration from the possibility of armed intervention during the Polish crisis, though this information never did reach those most affected by the crisis. In an appearance on the popular televised political program *Face the Nation* on 21 October, Dulles stated that the United States would not send troops to Poland even in the event of Soviet armed intervention.[98] The American government was exceptionally pleased with what it deemed to be positive developments in the Polish crisis during the following days, for they had come about without any kind of American involvement whatsoever. And moreover, contrary to all the pessimistic predictions, the Soviets had not intervened militarily and had ultimately agreed to accept the new Polish leadership.

The Americans thus found the news of the uprising in Hungary to be all the more disturbing, especially since the American government had no previously prepared strategy for dealing with such an unlikely occurrence. It was at this time that the Eisenhower administration was confronted with the fact that, contrary to one of the predominant themes of the massive liberation propaganda it aimed at East Central Europe since 1953, even the United States, the world's greatest military power, had only extremely limited options regarding any sort of intervention within the Soviet sphere of influence. It was nonetheless very important for the United States to conceal this impotence in order to preserve its international prestige; it was for this reason that on 24 October, Dulles suggested to President Eisenhower that the issue of Soviet intervention should be broached in the Security Council (which indeed happened on 28 October after the three Western great powers requested that the issue be placed on the council's agenda).[99]

On 26 October, the United States' highest-level advisory body, the National Security Council, sat for the first and last time during the period of the Hungarian Revolution in order to evaluate the events taking place in East Central Europe and to plan what kind of official message to communicate regarding U.S. policy on the region. Among the general confusion that reigned during the session, there was one intelligent proposal made by Harold E. Stassen, the president's advisor on disarmament: Stassen suggested that it would be expedient to offer assurances to the Soviets that the United States would not seek to exploit the possible independence of the satellite countries in any way that could threaten the security of the Soviet Union.[100] Although this suggestion was promptly rejected by the National Security Council, the next day proponents of the plan succeeded in getting the president to endorse an expanded version of Stassen's original proposal. According to this plan, the United States, either through Tito or some other diplomatic channel, would attempt to convince the Soviets that a zone of strictly neutral, non-NATO countries, politically akin to Austria, would offer them just as much security as the existing buffer of satellite countries.[101] The essential logic behind the proposal was that during negotiations regarding the Austrian State Treaty, it was precisely the Soviets who had insisted that Austria become strictly neutral and not be allowed to join NATO. Of course, the same possibilities for compromise did not apply to the East European Soviet satellite countries as had applied to Austria, but within the strict confines that circumscribed the United States' room to maneuver, a plan pretending to offer the possibility of mutual concession, such as the plan then being proposed, was preferable to complete passivity. Ultimately Eisenhower instructed Secretary of State Dulles to build the message to the Soviets into the presidential campaign speech Dulles was to deliver in Dallas on 27 October.[102] Dulles, however, who had opposed the proposal from its very inception because he thought it offered the Soviets exaggerated ideological concessions, watered it down—partly with the president's assent and partly on his own initiative—dropping any reference to both neutrality and prohibition on NATO membership. In the end, the American secretary of state's message to the Soviets consisted, in all, of the following celebrated sentence: "We do not look upon these nations as potential military allies."[103]

This fundamentally modified version of Stassen's original proposal did not achieve its original aim of pacifying the Soviets—or, perhaps more precisely, achieved it to an exaggerated degree. Whereas the original idea had been to try to induce concessions from the Soviet Union through explicit recognition of its security interests, the revised version was of a distinctly defensive tenor, which the Soviets logically assumed to mean that the United States was not going to take any action whatsoever on behalf of the independence of East Central Europe. The American leadership nonetheless went to great lengths to make absolutely sure that the message reached its addressee: on 28 October, Henry Cabot Lodge, the U.S. representative to the United Nations, quoted the passages from Dulles's speech that concerned the satellite countries during a session of the Security Council; on 29 October, the American ambassador in Moscow received instructions to confidentially reiterate the germane points of the speech to the Soviet leadership, including Marshal Zhukov; and on 31 October, Eisenhower himself reiterated the previously cited passage in the course of a televised address.[104]

The administration's statement, despite the fact that usually its role in pacifying the Soviets is emphasized, was of historic significance, even in this radically altered version. Prior to this, all the official statements of the Eisenhower administration regarding the satellite states were based on the supposition that, should these states gain independence, it would mean their joining the Western world, which in the given context automatically meant NATO membership. Therefore, stating that the United States did not consider these states as potential military allies was in fact the renunciation of their earlier opinion and the starting point of a process that would determine their politics in the following decades, one that eventually did away with the double-faced character of American foreign policy through cleaning up the remains of their liberation propaganda.

At the end of October, a special National Intelligence Estimate, prepared jointly by the CIA, the State Department, and organizations of military intelligence, determined that the Soviets had only two options: either accede to Hungary's desire for independence and risk unleashing similar forces throughout the satellite countries, or forcibly reinstate their supremacy over the country. The authors of the report nonetheless left no doubt as to which option the Moscow leadership would choose in an emergency.[105] Regarding possible American policy toward the crisis, the report of the National Security Council's advisory committee analyzing the recent events in East Central Europe, completed by 31 October, basically expressed the view that prospects for concrete U.S. action were extremely limited, although it did contain one well-founded proposal for compromise with the Soviet Union, according to which if the Soviets withdrew their troops from Hungary, the Americans would, in exchange, make proportional reductions in the number of their troops stationed in Western Europe.[106]

The agenda for the 1 November meeting of the National Security Council called for deliberation over this document; however, before the meeting got underway, President Eisenhower, at the urging of Dulles, decided to postpone discussion on East Central Europe until a later date so that the council could devote its entire time and energy to examination of the Suez crisis, which had degenerated into armed conflict on 29 October.[107] The American leadership was not again inclined to occupy itself with the events taking place in Hungary until the time of the second Soviet intervention on 4 November. Eisenhower and Dulles had decided—rightly—that since the United States did not have any effective means of exerting its influence inside the Soviet sphere, its energies should be concentrated on resolving the Suez crisis, where it was faced with the task of laying down the law—not with a rival superpower but with its own military and political allies, Britain and France. In spite of its complications, this was a much easier and more feasible undertaking, and within just a few days the resolute actions taken by the United States, particularly its economic arm twisting of Britain, had borne fruit.

NATO, which was gaining more and more significance in the Western European integration during these years, had been concerned since June 1956 with the question of how the West should react to the challenge of the East Central European changes that had taken place after 1953. On 24 October, the NATO council was supposed to have discussed a proposition, which had just been completed after long months of preparations, about its policy toward the satellite states. Due to the Polish and Hungarian events of a few days before, however, there was no possibility for a debate proper, so the startled delegates first of all emphasized that the study had apparently misjudged the role of Titoism as the only evolutionary possibility for East Central European countries to achieve greater independence.[108] The council had more meetings during the Hungarian Revolution, where on the one hand they tried to evaluate the current situation and on the other hand tried to consider possibilities of action. In the end, however, the only point they agreed on was that NATO should not corporately take sides in the question, because it would only provide the Soviet Union with a basis for further intervention.[109]

Thus, the sole international political forum that was apparently willing to give worthy consideration to the Hungarian crisis was the United Nations. However, the previously mentioned conflict of interest that arose among the Western great powers at the time of the simultaneous outbreak of the two international crises began to play itself out in the UN as well, just a few days after the Hungarian question had been placed on its agenda.

Great Britain, France, and the Suez Crisis

The governments of Britain and France, which were already preoccupied with preparations for an attack on Egypt, were likewise caught off guard by the developments in East Central Europe. Indeed, due to their paramount desire for success in the Middle East, the reaction of the British and French to the Soviet intervention in Hungary was even more cautious than the habitually restrained response of Western governments to events in East Central Europe.

Contrary to the renown of the American secretary of state's previously cited Dallas address, it is a little-known fact that representatives of both the British and the French governments delivered similar messages to the Soviet Union, which implied recognition of Soviet security interests in East Central Europe. On 26 October, French foreign minister Christian Pineau, in a speech delivered before a gathering of journalists, stressed that although the Western powers welcomed the developments that were taking place in East Central Europe, it would be ill-advised to try to exploit them for their own military and political profit; Pineau furthermore insisted that raising the issue of relations between the West and East Central Europe was still dangerously premature and that, as for France, it would not intervene in Poland or Hungary under any circumstances.[110] The British were even more adamant about avoiding even an inadvertent provocation of the Soviets and, furthermore, not giving them grounds for accusing the West of having in any way instigated the outbreak of the Hungarian Revolution. According to a memorandum of 27 October, written by Sir John Ward, the deputy under-secretary of state, top-secret sources had informed the British that the Soviets were preparing for

Western intervention in Hungary.[111] Accordingly, on 1 November, the government declared in Parliament: "It is not our slightest intention to try and exploit the events taking place in East-Central Europe in order to undermine the security of the Soviet Union."[112]

The striking simultaneity of the Suez and Hungarian crises inevitably raises the question of whether the outbreak of the Hungarian Revolution had any bearing on the timing of the attack on Egypt, which was planned during secret negotiations between Britain, France, and Israel held at Sévres between 22 and 24 October. Monographs and primary source materials published since 1989 reveal that the date for the Israeli attack on Egypt (29 October) was almost certainly set during the first day of the Sévres talks.[113] When this conditional timetable was established, the foreign ministers of Britain and France immediately made it clear that they would have liked the Israeli attack to be fixed for an even earlier date. The rationale for this was not the presumption that the Soviet Union would be preoccupied with the crisis in Hungary, as is commonly assumed, since the Hungarian Revolution broke out only on the next day. However, the Polish crisis, which erupted a few days earlier on 19 October, may have exercised some influence on the timing of the attack—a suggestion that appears in various Israeli sources. But the most important reason for the haste of the British and French was undoubtedly that their expeditionary forces had been in a state of full preparedness—a condition that could not be maintained indefinitely—for quite some time, simply waiting for the political green light to begin the attack on Egypt.

The official protocol containing the results of the secret Sévres negotiations was finally signed on 24 October. In this protocol, the day of the Israeli attack was concretely fixed for 29 October; thus, the fact of the outbreak of the Hungarian uprising on the previous day did not cause the slightest change to the existing strategy and, contrary to earlier suppositions,[114] did not serve to bring forward the date of the military action in the Middle East. Available sources even raise doubts as to whether the subject of Hungary even came up during the final day of negotiations on 24 October, when news of the Budapest uprising could very well have reached the negotiating partners. According to Israeli prime minister Ben Gurion's diary, he learned of the outbreak of the Hungarian Revolution and the alleged Soviet suppression thereof only after his return to Israel, sometime during midday of 25 October.[115]

The Hungarian Question in the UN Security Council

The American administration, primarily for reasons of prestige, decided on 25 October that, in concert with its allies, it would initiate discussion in the United Nations on the subject of the Hungarian uprising.[116] The British and

French initially expressed reluctance when Dulles proposed on 26 October that the three countries launch a joint initiative to convene a meeting of the Security Council.[117] With the Suez action having already been decided, the British and French leadership was worried that if the question of Soviet intervention in Hungary were put on the agenda and discussed in the UN, it might serve as a precedent for a similar procedure regarding the joint Israeli-British-French attack on Egypt, which was to take place at the end of October. But since they had not informed the United States of their plans, they were forced to accede to American pressure, and on 27 October the United States, Great Britain, and France[118] submitted a joint request that the Security Council be convened to examine the situation in Hungary.

From this date until 3 November, the representatives of the three Western great powers met continually behind the scenes in order to work out a UN strategy that all could agree on; the comportment of the United States, Britain, and France during the three Security Council sessions that dealt with the Hungarian question on 28 October and on 2 and 3 November was completely planned in advance during these secret negotiations.[119]

In the days preceding the Israeli attack on Egypt, the UN representatives of the three Western great powers agreed that it was imperative to voice emphatic public condemnation of the Soviet intervention and that beyond this action, they would employ a wait-and-see policy until the confused situation in Hungary became more transparent. The consequence of this policy was that the three Western powers, which had placed the Hungarian question on the agenda, did not even introduce a draft proposal during the 28 October session of the Security Council. After the widening of the armed conflict in the Middle East with the engagement of Great Britain and France on 31 October, the tenor of the negotiations among the Western great powers regarding Hungary changed completely. Eisenhower and Dulles, who had placed increasing importance on establishing good relations with the Arab world with the aim of expanding American influence in the Middle East, reacted angrily to the actions of its European allies. Not only did they publicly condemn the Suez action, but they also instructed the American UN representative to submit a draft proposal calling for the immediate cessation of all military operations in the Middle East, a motion that brought about a circumstance that had no precedent in the history of the UN, with the representatives of the United States and the Soviet Union voting in concert against Great Britain and France.

As a result of the sudden deterioration in relations between the Western powers, subsequent discussions between them regarding the Hungarian question were conducted in an increasingly icy atmosphere in which the negotiating partners were not really interested in condemning, much less impeding,

Soviet intervention but wanted rather to exploit the Hungarian crisis in the name of their own, in this case drastically conflicting, great power interests. Beginning at this time, the British and French undertook to get the Hungarian question moved from the Security Council to the emergency session of the General Assembly—which had been convened to discuss the Suez crisis on 31 October—where they hoped that the simultaneous treatment of two issues would lead to a mitigation of the censure they had been receiving. Transfer of the Hungarian question to the General Assembly would have been of incidental benefit to the forces of change in Hungary, for in the General Assembly there is no veto power, which left at least the theoretical possibility that the UN would pass a resolution having a positive influence on the outcome of events in Hungary. The sole objective of the American leadership under the existing circumstances was to resolve the Middle Eastern crisis; therefore, they did everything within their powers to frustrate the aforementioned strategy of the British and French: until 4 November, the Americans succeeded in preventing them from submitting a draft proposal concerning the Hungarian question in the Security Council and further blocked them from referring the question to the emergency session of the General Assembly via the "uniting for peace" procedure.

After the second Soviet intervention on 4 November, the American UN representative, Henry Cabot Lodge, unilaterally implemented the former British-French strategy without asking for the cooperation of his Western European allies in the Security Council, with whom he had broken off negotiations regarding Hungary the previous day as a method of punishment for British and French actions in Suez. When the Security Council was subsequently convened upon the arrival of the news regarding renewed Soviet intervention on 4 November, Lodge initiated a "uniting for peace" procedure, which effectively circumvented the Soviet veto and referred the Hungarian question directly to the second emergency session of the General Assembly. On the afternoon of the very same day, a large majority of this body voted to adopt a draft resolution—likewise submitted unilaterally by the U.S. representative— that condemned the intervention of the Soviet Union, called for it to withdraw its troops from Hungary, and recognized the right of the Hungarian people to a government that would represent its national interests.[120]

At the same time, this resolution made not even a reference to the recognition of Hungary's neutrality, for which Imre Nagy had so emphatically appealed in his messages to the UN secretary general on 1 and 2 November, although the British and the French had supported this idea from the outset, hoping that an issue of such importance would help move the Hungarian issue from the Security Council to the General Assembly. This may be due in part to the fact that Hungary's neutrality was unacceptable to the leading personalities of the American leadership. The concept of Hungarian neutrality engendered a good deal of support in the State Department, where it had already surfaced as a topic of discussion days before Nagy launched his appeals to the UN. Dulles, however, who had sharp misgivings regarding the increasingly powerful nonaligned movement and was therefore generally ill-disposed toward the idea of neutrality, not surprisingly came out against the idea with regard to Hungary. Dulles firmly believed that if, perchance, Hungary were to succeed in its struggle to free itself of Soviet domination, the United States should not rest satisfied with the country's neutrality when there existed the real possibility of incorporating it into the Western sphere of influence.[121] President Eisenhower himself sympathized with the idea of establishing a zone of neutral states in East Central Europe, but he hoped to achieve this aim through negotiations with the Soviets in a broad framework of general reconstruction of East–West relationships. It is a paradox of history that although the evolutionary views of Eisenhower and Imre Nagy on neutrality— as we have seen them—were very similar, the Hungarian decision made in an extraordinary situation simply could not be supported by Washington when considering the political implications. Overtly supporting the unilateral radical move of the Hungarian government—that is, recognizing their neutrality— held the possible danger that the American government would take on an international responsibility that would be extremely difficult to cast off after the suppression of the Hungarian uprising, which was seemingly close at hand. However, it was even more important for Eisenhower that such a diplomatic move, due to the probably vehement Soviet reaction, would have seriously jeopardized the well-improving Soviet-American relations and, indirectly, the whole détente process.

In the early hours of the morning of 4 November, the United States nonetheless fervently condemned renewed Soviet intervention in Hungary— Eisenhower even sent a personal message of protest to Bulganin—and in this way succeeded in leading the world to believe that it had, from the very outset, played a constructive role in attempts to settle both the Suez and Hungarian crises.

The real clash of conflicting viewpoints in the United Nations, contrary to earlier interpretations, took place not between the Western powers and the Soviet Union during meetings of the Security Council, where what was said on both sides was primarily for public consumption, but behind the scenes, in the course of secret negotiations among representatives of the United States, Great Britain, and France.

The result of the discord that arose in relations between the Western great powers over the Suez crisis was that the UN was unable to take firm steps toward the resolution of the Hungarian question at a time (from 1 to 3 November) when the circumstances in Hungary, such as Nagy's request for UN mediation, made such steps feasible.

One should not overestimate, however, the potential influence of any UN resolution by the emergency session of the General Assembly condemning Soviet intervention, a measure that remained a distinct possibility right up until 3 November. The Soviet Union, in light of its status as a world superpower and the reassuring pledges it had received from the United States, was by no means disposed to let the moral authority of UN resolutions prevent it from intervening militarily, if necessary, to restore order in a country within its own sphere of influence.

The discord among the Western powers that came about as a result of the Middle Eastern conflict no doubt made things easier for the Soviets, though it is fairly certain that even without the Suez crisis they would have pursued a similar policy. To verify this statement, it is sufficient to examine the circumstances of the 1968 intervention in Czechoslovakia. At that time, when the Western alliance's freedom of movement was not restricted by any internal conflict, the West still responded to the invasion aimed at rescuing the Communist regime with the same passivity as in 1956. Moreover, we now know that U.S. president Lyndon B. Johnson, who, at the end of August 1968, condemned the intervention in Czechoslovakia in a high-sounding declaration for the public, barely a few weeks later (in September) proposed a summit meeting with Brezhnev via diplomatic channels to discuss Vietnam, the situation in the Middle East, and the issue of anti-missile systems.[122]

Therefore, Western passivity in 1956 was not caused by the Suez crisis but by a limitation to its range of options in East Central Europe implicit in the prevailing European status quo and the notion of spheres of influence. The Suez crisis simply served as a handy excuse, especially for the United States, in order to explain why, after years of liberation propaganda, it was not capable of extending even the smallest amount of support to an East European nation that had risen in arms in an attempt to liberate itself from Soviet domination.

Against this background, it must be seen that the United States cannot be held at fault for not providing armed assistance to the Hungarian Revolution. In the given Cold War context, applying a non-interventionist policy was in fact the only possible rational decision, as intervention would have caused a direct danger of triggering the third world war. The potential instruments of political pressure, however, were also fundamentally constrained by the system of spheres of influence established in 1945, because to extort any serious concessions from the Soviet Union could have been possible only through some significant compensation. Charles Gati regards the question of the occupation forces as such, and suggests that Washington should have offered in return for the withdrawal of Soviet troops from Hungary the withdrawal of its troops from one of the Western European states.[123] But in itself the presence of Soviet troops in an allied country could not bear any significance concerning the maintenance of the Communist regime: there were no Soviet troops in Bulgaria from late 1947, in Czechoslovakia between 1945 and 1968, and in Romania from 1958, yet the Communist system did not collapse in any of these countries. And as we have seen, the 30 October decision of the CPSU presidium on pulling Soviet troops out of Hungary was made without any Western pressure, because, for a very brief historical moment, Moscow thought that this concession might facilitate the pacification of the situation and the consolidation of the Communist system that got to the verge of collapse.

To take matters to absurd extremes, if the West had really wanted to ensure that Moscow would "give up on" Hungary, a country belonging to the Soviet empire, it should have proposed compensation of equal value. Then, the exchange value of a concession of this magnitude might have been the "voluntary" Sovietization of a smaller NATO member state—for example, Denmark, the Netherlands, or Greece—and the transfer of that country to the Soviet sphere of influence. It is only too easy to realize that such an option would not have been an attractive alternative for Western policy makers or even the public.

Therefore, after the outbreak of the uprising, the U.S. government had no political means by which it could have affected the events and facilitated the victory of the Hungarian Revolution. Paradoxically, Washington had a historic chance to contribute to *avoiding* the revolution from happening. We now know that the explosion in Hungary occurred basically for internal reasons, as well as because of the serious errors committed by the Soviets in their crisis-management strategy during 1956. The *nature* of the revolt, however, might have been affected by the American liberation propaganda relentlessly pursued between 1953 and 1956—that is, that social unrest took the most radical form possible: armed rebellion and war of independence against the Soviet Army. Instead of conveying this originally well-intentioned but overall tragically irresponsible promise, Washington should have introduced a much more differentiated approach, at least after the crushing of the Poznan uprising in June 1956 that clearly signaled the inherent dangers of U.S. liberation rhetoric. They ought to have encouraged East Central European societies not to engage in active resistance but instead to accept realities and work for the liberalization of their regimes, exactly as it happened later, from the 1960s on.

This undoubtedly defeatist yet realist attitude would have made it clear exactly what for many people was still not at all clear in 1956: that such an uprising in the Soviet empire was doomed to failure, and external help was not to be expected.

Chapter 5

The International Impact of the Polish and Hungarian Revolts

East–West Relations: Confirmation of the Status Quo

A thorough study of the international aftermath of the Hungarian Revolution using multi-archival sources has yet to be done. However, drawing on the sources presently available and the work already accomplished on the subject, it is worth attempting to produce a sketch of the impact of the Hungarian (and Polish) events of October–November 1956 on international politics, especially on the relationship between East and West.

The most obvious outcome of the failed revolution in international political terms was that the Western states' lack of response proved once and for all their unconditional acceptance of the postwar European status quo, despite all earlier propaganda. This was a great consolation for the Soviet leadership: beyond the tacit agreement they had held with the Western states up until that point, the nonresponse of the West in November 1956 gave them full assurance that, should any future conflict occur within the boundaries of their empire, they would have a completely free hand, without any concern of Western interference. In this respect, the Hungarian Revolution was to the advantage of the Soviet state. The uncertainty factor instilled by American psychological warfare—that is, the declared goal of the Eisenhower administration to bring about the "liberation of the enslaved nations," which had seemed to threaten the Soviets' East Central European buffer zone—practically disappeared.

It is also clear that the Hungarian Revolution and its repression did not cause a real crisis in world politics. Simply put, it did not lead to a direct conflict between the two opposing superpowers and their military blocs. The general public, however, believed and still believes that the events represented a serious crisis; the ardent liberation propaganda that the Americans had pursued with such intensity right up until October 1956 had left many with the belief that such an event as the revolution would necessarily result in conflict and political crisis between East and West. The firm public stance of the Eisenhower administration against the Soviet intervention, the debates and resolutions of the emergency session of the UN General Assembly, the concurrent Suez crisis, and the Soviet missile threats suggested to many observers that the Hungarian Revolution was in fact a serious crisis in the relationship between the superpowers.

Consequently, the real significance of the Hungarian Revolution in terms of international politics was never clearly recognized by the public, neither in the Western states nor in the Eastern bloc. On the contrary, the parallel events in Hungary and Poland and the Suez crisis did, and still do, facilitate mythical interpretations of the West's inaction. These explanations, instead of seeing the West's nonresponse as a result of the general acceptance of the post-Yalta European status quo, attempt to portray it as being due to one or another exceptional situation that applied only to the *particular* case of the Hungarian Revolution. Thus, oft-quoted arguments were conjured up: that the crisis in the Middle East prevented the Western states from presenting a united front against the Soviet Union, or that the American leadership was occupied with the upcoming presidential election, or that Secretary of State Dulles was taken to the hospital during the most critical days, or that the American troops were prevented from deploying to Hungary by geography alone.

The Hungarian Revolution and its suppression disturbed for a brief moment the détente process that had been developing since 1953, but by and large it did not halt the process nor even influence its later development. The tensions that the Soviet intervention and its ensuing Western reproaches caused were largely confined to the level of propaganda expressed at the UN General Assembly sessions. All of this had no impact on the United States' (or France's and Britain's) and the Soviets' readiness for negotiation, and so consequently the spring of 1957 brought the revival of a mutual political discourse. By the end of that year, intensive preparations for a Geneva-type four-power summit were underway.

Within these few months, however, the relationship of the two superpowers underwent a radical, unprecedented change that completely redefined world politics.[1] By the summer of 1957, the Soviet Union had developed the first generation of intercontinental ballistic missiles, conducting the first successful test of those missiles in August and then launching its first satellite, Sputnik, in October. The new Soviet missiles posed a threat not only to Western Europe but directly to the territory of the United States, whose strategic invulnerability vanished overnight. In this way, the so far theoretical balance of power had begun to become real and, from then on, the arms race was only a question of which party could threaten its adversary with more missiles. This turn of events increased to an almost irrational extent the self-confidence of Soviet leaders, Khrushchev most of all. Although they were willing to negotiate, and even often initiated talks, they were basically standing on different ground and negotiating from a much stronger position. Between 1955 and

1956, when the Soviet–American relationship had undergone its most spectacular improvement since 1945, the Soviet Union was interested in reaching an agreement with the United States, especially concerning arms control—even if that required significant compromises. From the middle of 1957, on the other hand, the Soviets tried to use the negotiations merely for political gain and to improve their own position. The dramatically changed strategic situation, and most importantly the newly confident position of the Soviets, led to the abandonment of calls often heard in the late 1950s for "total disarmament" and finally to the frenzied arms race of the 1960s and 1970s.

Taking all this into account, perhaps it would not be a completely unsubstantiated hypothesis to say that if the Hungarian Revolution had not disturbed the détente process by halting the negotiations for these crucial few months, the superpowers might have been able to come to an agreement resulting in a lower rate of armament and consequently reduced world tension in the following decades. There is, however, another argument that could be made, similarly based on the question of what might have happened if the détente process had not been temporally interrupted by the events of 1956. According to this line of reasoning, the burdens of the arms race, which were dictated by the Americans, would have been averted or at least lessened and delayed. This arms race, the argument continues, virtually crippled the Soviet economy and eventually led to its utter collapse. Such a political development, therefore, could have lengthened the era of stagnation by decades, and naturally, concludes this line, the fall of the East Central European Communist regimes could not have happened at the end of the 1980s. Both arguments have compelling elements and, as is the case with all historical "what if" questions, there is no way of knowing which scenario would have played out.

The United Nations and the Third World

The only forum of international relations where the suppression of the Hungarian Revolution gained considerable significance was the United Nations. The second emergency session of the General Assembly (the first one was dealing with the Suez crisis) on 4 November 1956, initiated by the United States, and the eleventh session of the General Assembly during November and December, produced several resolutions calling on the Soviet Union to withdraw their troops and the Kádár government to receive the UN secretary-general and UN observers. Since the Hungarian government refused to cooperate, the UN had no chance to investigate the situation on the ground. To get around the problem, the UN set up a special committee in January 1957 to compile a report on the exact course and nature of events in Hungary, based on the accounts of those who had taken part in the revolution and then fled to the West, as well as any other sources available at the time. The report, completed by June 1957, evaluated the uprising as a spontaneous and instinctive expression of the Hungarian nation's striving for freedom.[2] The General Assembly endorsed the report by an overwhelming majority in September. Nevertheless, it repeatedly failed to enforce any decisions regarding Hungary, and the Hungarian question fruitlessly continued to be on the UN agenda year after year until December 1962.[3]

What lay behind the UN policy toward Hungary was first and foremost the intention of American diplomacy to regain some of the prestige it had lost during the revolution because of its inaction. The Eisenhower administration wanted to show the world and the American public that, while it could not risk a direct superpowers conflict to help the cause of the Hungarian Revolution, after its suppression it was willing to commit itself thoroughly to making the aftermath somewhat bearable. But all this had to be done in a subtle way so that the condemnation of the Soviet intervention would not jeopardize the détente process, which had had such promising results by October 1956 and which the U.S. government was determined to develop further. The UN General Assembly provided an ideal playground for this political seesaw game, given that its resolutions were far from being coercive measures, especially not when they condemned a superpower or its allies. Since this was a well-known fact in Moscow, the Americans were hoping that the Soviets, who had earlier not shown much concern about international public opinion, would not be seriously distressed.

Under these circumstances, the Hungarian question should have been on the agenda for a few months, maybe even a few years, but certainly not until the early 1960s. Nevertheless, two important factors in international politics, both reinforcing the strategic position of the Soviet Union, steered the UN in a different direction. One of them, the Suez crisis, was not an actual conflict between the two opposing military blocs, yet its aftermath was to have a significant impact on the superpowers' relationship in the long run. Rectifying the shaky situation in the Middle East, even though the United States had the lion's share of this process, unexpectedly worked in the Soviets' favor in the end. Most of those African and Asian developing countries who had declared their solidarity with Egypt had also condemned the intervention in Hungary, but their real point of interest was to see how certain powers would react to the Western "imperialist aggression" against a vulnerable developing country. The fact that the United States, for the first time in the history of the Western alliance, publicly opposed Britain and France in the UN made a far less significant impact on third world countries than did the Soviet missile threats of 5 November 1956, which were carried out with a brilliant sense of timing. Once it became apparent from the reaction of American leaders that the

Israeli–British–French coalition would be forced to retreat by the United States, the Soviet Union came up with the biggest ever political bluff of the Cold War era: Prime Minister Bulganin sent telegrams to his British and French colleagues demanding a cease-fire without delay, indirectly threatening both states with a missile attack against London and Paris if they did otherwise. At the same time, in a telegram sent to the Israeli government, there was a clear reference to the potential questioning of the very existence of Israel as a state. These missile threats seemed to suggest that the Soviet Union was not afraid of getting involved in a military conflict with the West when the freedom of a third world state was at stake, even though Moscow had only decided to send these telegrams when American political intervention had already made it obvious that the crisis would be solved without much further ado.

The other important factor behind the long duration of the Hungarian issue on the UN agenda was the launch of the Sputnik satellite in October 1957, which demonstrated to the whole world that the Soviet Union had surpassed the United States in a crucially important field of scientific and technological development. The Soviet Union had already been showing its inclination for a peaceful East–West relationship, but this event increased their international prestige to an extent comparable only to the popularity of the Red Army during World War II. These two factors—the missile threats in the Suez crisis and the launch of Sputnik—created such favorable circumstances for increasing their influence in Africa and Asia that the Soviets could not help but take advantage of the situation. The American leadership, on the other hand, was—understandably—deeply worried about this turn of events. As described in chapter 3, the Eisenhower administration had never considered liberating the East Central European countries with force, but they had maintained the Truman administration's overall policy of "containing" the expansion of Communist influence and had several times acted within this framework (e.g., in Guatemala, Taiwan, and Lebanon). In the second half of the 1950s, they found themselves facing the imminent danger that the Soviet Union would exploit its newly improved position and expand its influence peacefully, using the United States' own policy of providing economic and financial aid. This is why, from 1956 on, a primary aim of U.S. foreign policy was to arrest the development of Soviet influence in the third world and to correspondingly increase American presence there. The UN General Assembly provided an ideal arena for this, and the Americans kept the Hungarian question on the agenda as a device of this political objective. The heated polemics in the General Assembly over the years were not supposed to make the Soviet Union change its ways—there was less than a slim chance that the "defendant," pleading guilty, would withdraw its troops from Hungary and leave the country to its own course. Instead, the intent was to convince the "jury"—that is, the nonaligned states—and to cajole them into accepting or preserving Western political ideology. This is a plausible explanation of why the 1968 Czechoslovak intervention—since it would not have aided similar Western designs—never became "the Czechoslovak question" in the UN.

On the basis of official and spontaneous social reaction in the West to the suppression of the revolution, and the commitment of the UN General Assembly to the issue of Hungary, many might have thought that the Kádár regime would not be able to consolidate its relationship with the West for a long time. Indeed, every year until 1962, the "Hungarian issue" was put on the agenda of the UN General Assembly and discussed.[4] During the debates, both the Soviet Union and the Kádár government were condemned for the Soviet intervention in November 1956 and for the subsequent reprisals against the participant of the revolution over and over again.[5]

At the same time, all of this meant the partial and relative diplomatic isolation of Hungary, especially by the Western states. In November 1956, the acceptance of the credentials of the Hungarian delegation to the UN was suspended; however, the country was not excluded from the organization. Furthermore, none of the member states of the Western alliance system—not even the United States, the main coordinator of its events in the UN—broke off diplomatic relations with the Kádár government. In terms of economic indicators among the Western countries, the status quo ante—in other words, the level of turnover before October 1956—had already been restored by the end of 1957.[6] The British also declared their intention to stabilize relations with Hungary as early as the spring of 1957—true enough, it did it only for "internal use" for the time being, given the circumstances. This situation, however, undoubtedly meant Hungary's partial diplomatic isolation, and it also prevented the spectacular development of political relations with the Western countries, which clearly annoyed Kádár—especially as he was aiming for the systematic rehabilitation of the Communist regime beginning right after November 1956.[7] He was trying to establish a system that would get rid of the excesses of the Stalinist past and work effectively, offering much better living conditions for the population—something that in theory should have been more attractive even from a Western perspective. The main problem was that the Kádár regime wanted to accomplish a specifically Hungarian variation of the post-Stalinist system *simultaneously with* the inconceivably brutal and widespread retaliation campaign after the revolution,[8] to which Western politicians responded with morally righteous indignation. Thinking sensibly and considering the security interests of the Soviet Union, they admitted the necessity of pacification and restoring law and order; nonetheless, partly under pressure from public opinion at home, they expected the Hungarian government to forgive the "delinquents" and "deviants" just as magnanimously as it pragmatically intended to win over the majority of the population for its policy.

Such a historical compromise in reality could have been plausible, since the main objective of the Kádár regime in its foreign policy right after 1956 was to break out of almost complete (Western) diplomatic isolation and to prove that even from a Western point of view, the new system, although its conception was far from being immaculate, was no worse, or it was even better than that of other Communist regimes. In Kádár's view, the newly emerging system in Hungary created better and more liberal conditions for the majority of the population than those prevailing in the other countries of the Soviet bloc—except in Poland—and that should have been admitted by the Western powers as well. According to this logic, Hungary would have deserved appreciation and not negative discrimination, putting the country under international isolation.

The main Western demand toward the Kádár regime—besides the unrealistic claim for the withdrawal of Soviet troops—was granting amnesty to those imprisoned after 1956, in exchange for normalizing relations. In theory, this could have been the basis for a compromise; however, both sides proved to be ideologically rigid and inflexible concerning this issue. Considering internal political stability, Kádár deemed the release of the 1956 "criminals" too dangerous until the late 1950s, not to mention that the large-scale retaliation process had not even been completed until 1960. The partial amnesties announced in 1959 and 1960 were both important moves toward internal consolidation and signs of a more flexible attitude aimed at ending the international isolation of the country. The Western bloc, on the other hand, for a long time did not consider that pressurizing the Kádár government in *public forums* would not lead to a solution. Therefore, perhaps we can risk the presumption that had the West, and primarily the United States, exerted pressure on the Hungarian government—to make them moderate the zeal of political retribution—directly, by means of *secret negotiations*, as it happened later in 1960–62, instead of appealing to the widest public, such as the diplomatic forums of the UN, they might have forced more serious compromises from the Hungarian government much earlier. This could have resulted in the retribution campaign itself being significantly influenced, mitigating its harshness and thus directly saving many human lives.

For the United States, however, the recurring issue of Hungary in the UN was so instrumental in the struggle of superpowers for influence over the third world that direct negotiations with the Hungarian authorities only became possible once the UN debate was obviously exhausted by 1960.

American Reactions: From Liberation to Liberalization

In the aftermath of the revolution, the U.S. government found itself under attack by the Western press. The administration was accused of first having urged the Hungarians to revolt and of subsequently having abandoned them in the actual event. By the middle of November 1956, the U.S. leadership had come up with an answer to its media critics, claiming that while government officials had always been deeply concerned about the "enslaved nations"—and had continuously expressed this concern—they had never encouraged suicidal uprisings.[9] This explanation was hardly convincing, yet its significance should not be underestimated. It was no less than a clear and open admission that, should a similar uprising occur in the future, East Central Europe could not expect any help from the United States. At the same time, the administration's explanation also demonstrated that the American propaganda machine could no longer capriciously alternate between the themes of "liberation" and "peaceful liberation." Following the events of the Polish crisis and the Hungarian Revolution, U.S. policy toward East Central Europe was reformulated on a new, more pragmatic and reserved basis.[10] Apparently the basic principles of this new policy—as mentioned in chapter 3—had been in the making as early as the summer of 1956. The Hungarian and Polish events (with their dramatically different outcomes) simply reinforced the fact that the United States was not able to make more than limited tactical moves in the region. Thus, the new U.S. approach toward East Central Europe completely did away with the theory of *liberating* the nations of the region: from then on, the goal was to *liberalize* and "soften" their Communist regimes—a policy that lasted until the late 1980s.[11] Western states exerted political influence and pressure on Eastern governments through economic support, allowances, loans, and cultural and interstate relations—with the aim of encouraging them to pursue more liberal domestic policies and to become independent from the Soviet Union in foreign affairs as much as possible. But all of this happened within an official—not only de facto but increasingly de jure—recognition of the European status quo by the West. Therefore, the "liberation" of the enslaved nations only cropped up in a special limited context after 1956—that is, within the long-term competitive struggle between the two opposing political and economic systems. The idea was that in this contest, the Western democracies would eventually emerge as victors, which would inevitably result in the disintegration of the Soviet Union, which, in turn, would naturally bring about the collapse of the East European regimes and thus ensure their "liberation."

The American leadership was already operating under this new pragmatic policy in the UN when dealing with the Hungarian crisis. Following several years of ineffectual U.S. condemnation of the Soviet intervention in the General Assembly, secret negotiations were initiated between the U.S. government and the Kádár regime in 1960. The direct result of this dialogue was that the U.S. administration allowed the Hungarian question to be removed from the General Assembly's agenda in December 1962, in exchange for which the Hungarian government, in March 1963, granted a general amnesty to the majority of those who had been imprisoned because of their participation in the 1956 revolution.[12]

Lessons of the 1956 Revolts for the Soviet Union

Understandably, the Soviets disapproved of the Hungarian place on the UN agenda and so, in their irony-proof style, they accused the Western states of intervening in Hungarian internal affairs. Moscow had expected the American leadership to show indifference toward the issue in public, just as they had pragmatically acknowledged that the Soviet Union pacified a turbulent situation in a country within her sphere of influence. Following the logical supposition, which later proved to be true enough, that international politics in the future would be determined largely by the opposing two superpowers, the Soviets had hoped that the United States would subordinate comparatively minor issues such as the case of the Hungarian Revolution to the overall U.S.–Soviet relationship.

This effort is manifest in a telegram that Soviet prime minister Bulganin sent to President Eisenhower on 5 November 1956, which pressed for joint military action by the superpowers to solve the Middle Eastern crisis and at the same time answered the American president's missive of the previous day with a dismissal of the issue of Soviet intervention in Hungary as being the exclusively internal affair of the two states concerned. Two days later, the Soviet prime minister telegrammed his congratulations on Eisenhower's reelection. Not only was this something unprecedented in the Cold War up to then, but it had further significance in as much as Soviet propaganda had "supported" Eisenhower's Democratic opponent, Adlai Stevenson, during the presidential campaign. To emphasize their interest in continuing the détente process, Soviet leaders sent a proposition to the American government on 17 November, suggesting substantial reductions in current and future arms levels. The Soviet standpoint seemed to be more flexible on several issues than it had ever been. Naturally, these well-timed political steps were intended to mitigate the international condemnation of Soviet intervention in Hungary, yet it would be a mistake to dismiss them as mere propaganda; in actual fact, the Soviet Union was already preparing for a new type of cooperation between the superpowers.

The conditions of this cooperation, however, were significantly undermined by the debates over the Hungarian issue in the UN General Assembly, where the leading players, especially the United States, were compelled to condemn the Soviet intervention in Hungary. The Soviet leaders, who had never been concerned with international public opinion in the Stalinist era, now found it quite uncomfortable that the "peace-loving Soviet Union" was for months and years being continuously denounced as an aggressor in the United Nations. Again, it did not annoy the Soviet Union with respect to its relations with the Western world; it was worried that keeping the Hungarian issue on the agenda would have an unfavorable impact on its so-far promising relationship with the developing countries. In the battle for influence over the third world, however, the Suez crisis was of substantially larger importance than the Hungarian Revolution. Consequently, the Soviets won this popularity contest, at least in the short term. The Western expectations that the brutal suppression of the revolution would convince the developing countries of the real nature of Soviet power were unfulfilled. On the contrary, Soviet influence in African and Asian countries reached its peak during the 1960s.

What happened to Imre Nagy and his followers after 4 November 1956 undoubtedly damaged the Soviet–Yugoslav relationship. The Yugoslav leadership decided to cooperate with the elimination of this group from the Hungarian political arena only to hasten the consolidation of the jeopardized Communist regime. Nevertheless, Tito considered the political asylum that he had granted Imre Nagy and his colleagues in the Yugoslav embassy in Budapest as a temporary solution to get them out of the way. He hoped that once order could be restored and things returned to normal, they would be readmitted and be allowed to have a stake in Hungarian politics again. The reasoning behind this desire was that should Imre Nagy get back to the leadership, the national Communist, Tito-friendly policy that Nagy had pursued *before* October 1956 would be to some extent integrated into the new political system.

Yet the Kádár–Nagy compromise that the Yugoslavs thought was a historical imperative could not be realized in those circumstances, which meant that the grant of asylum soon landed Belgrade in a political minefield. The joint machinations of the Hungarian and Soviet leaderships—the deportation of Nagy and his colleagues to Romania immediately after their voluntary emergence from the embassy in late November 1956, despite written guarantees to Tito—created a precarious situation for Yugoslavia in the eyes of international public opinion. The Yugoslavs could do nothing but react vehemently to the kidnapping of Imre Nagy and his advocates. There was soon a flurry of sharply worded diplomatic notes between Belgrade and Moscow and between Belgrade and Budapest. In the end, both parties were unavoidably forced onto a track that led to a second deterioration of Soviet–Yugoslav relations. The Imre Nagy case, however, cannot be said to be more than a catalyst in this process, as the worsening of relations was primarily the consequence of the Soviets' realization by early 1958 that Yugoslavia would never return to the Soviet bloc and—even worse from Moscow's point of view—the fact that Belgrade had begun to demand a more and more active role among the nonaligned states.

In the Soviet Union, de-Stalinization halted for a short time after the Hungarian Revolution. Hard-liners in the government, referring to the Hungarian example, were temporarily able to prevent further liberalization. However, following the unsuccessful coup in the summer of 1957, Khrushchev, reinforced in his position, reinitiated the policies begun by the Twentieth Congress of the CPSU. The results of this liberalization campaign were numerous, and long-lasting changes were made in the "building of Socialism"—though the bases of the Stalinist political and economic system were left more or less untouched—up until the first secretary's downfall in 1964. Thus, the failure of the de-Stalinization process commonly associated with Khrushchev and that leader's discharge was not the result of a temporary anti-reform tendency following the Hungarian Revolution. Rather, Khrushchev failed in the end because of his leadership style—that is, his increasingly capricious and unpredictable political moves, which jeopardized the Soviet Union's internal and external stability.

Of course from a moral point of view, the revolution did reveal that the Soviet Union, which had been making a lot of effort during those years to appear as a reliable and civilized actor in international politics, was only able to restore its power in Hungary with cold force reminiscent of the Stalinist era. Despite this obvious black mark on their record, however, the Soviets' international reputation was hardly affected. In fact, the Soviet Union's prestige was much more determined by the process that had started in 1955–56 and reached its peak in the 1960s in which it emerged as a credible superpower rival/partner of the United States. The Americans' overt acknowledgment of the European status quo in 1956 contributed to the new give-and-take relationship between the superpowers. As a consequence of this trend, the intentions of the two superpowers and the state of their relationship increasingly determined the developments of international politics.

Repercussions in the Soviet Bloc

When analyzing the international consequences of the Hungarian Revolution, it is extremely difficult to determine how and to what extent the suppression of the uprising influenced the relationship between the Soviet Union and other

East Central European Communist states. Undoubtedly, a new kind of relationship emerged between the Soviet Union and her allies after 1956, but this cannot be ascribed to the Hungarian Revolution. The practice of this new confederate policy, in keeping with the post-Stalinist model, had been emerging since 1953, and the basic principles were explicitly stated in the Soviet government declaration of 30 October 1956.[13] Thus, the declaration—contrary to previous interpretations—was not merely an improvised gesture to pacify the crises in Poland and Hungary. The document, which had been in preparation for months,[14] was intended to redefine the relationship of the allied states and was only amended to suit the specific situation of that October.

In actuality, the 30 October declaration can roughly be considered as the "constitution" of the post-Stalinist alliance model. It provided a broad outline for the Soviet Union's East Central European allies of their possibilities and limitations and established new equations for political control and economic cooperation. The guidelines for the bloc countries that the Soviets established in October 1956 remained more or less in effect well into the late 1980s. The declaration promised no less than a steadfast policy that realizes Lenin's principle of equal rights of nations. This included respect for the sovereignty of individual states and consideration of the historical past and national characteristics of each country. In Soviet imperial parlance, it was a codification of a political relationship more flexible than that which had existed previously but that was still far from being equitable.

The new relationship between Moscow and its East European allies also included the recall of Soviet advisors. After 1956, the system of direct Soviet control exerted through these locally placed agents was refined into a more sophisticated system of "remote control." The Soviets also replaced the vaguely disguised economic arrangement that had amounted to little more than Soviet exploitation with one that distributed both benefits and liabilities more evenly.

Of course, along with all the elements of the new Soviet flexibility that the 30 October declaration brought, there were clearly set limits defining which changes would be possible and what reforms would be tolerated—provided they maintained the Communist ideology (i.e., the Soviet Bolshevik system) and the confederate structure (i.e., the Soviet empire). This is why the suppression of the Hungarian Revolution was in fact in accordance with the Soviet government declaration—something denied by many at the time. That aspect of the declaration was simply put into practice on 4 November, as indeed by that time the Communist system could be rescued only by Soviet military intervention.

One specific article in the declaration that promised that the Soviet Union would look into the question of Soviet troops stationed in East Central Europe was included in reference to the Polish and Hungarian events of October 1956. The promise was certainly intended as a political tranquilizer, but later the same issue, which was originally adopted more or less as a response to the crises, became a determining factor in Soviet confederate politics. The Western states' unconditional acceptance of the postwar European status quo and the Soviet sphere of influence in East Central Europe at the time of such a critical situation as the Hungarian Revolution significantly increased the Soviet Union's security and, at the same time, altered the reasoning behind the stationing of Soviet troops abroad. This is why Soviet troops could be withdrawn from Romania in 1958: the geopolitical situation of that country ensured that the Soviet political model would be maintained and that Romania would remain a solid member of the Soviet bloc.[15] On the other hand, in Czechoslovakia, where Soviet troops had been absent since the end of 1945, the political crisis that erupted in 1968 was one that the Soviet leadership could resolve only with a military occupation. In order to justify this action, no legal ground was needed; the Soviets had only to declare that the Socialist system in Czechoslovakia was in danger and thus needed "protection."

In the last few years, scholars have established that, at the time of the Hungarian Revolution and directly after its suppression, there were numerous events in nearly all the East European states and in the Soviet Union itself that demonstrated significant public sympathy for the Hungarian cause. These manifestations of political dissent, with the exception of those in Poland, met with varying forms of retaliation: dismissal, expulsion from the party, arrest, detention, imprisonment, and even execution.[16]

The reaction of the increasingly nationalistic regime in Romania provides a conspicuous example of the campaigns conducted throughout East Central Europe against those who had supported—or who were simply accused of having supported—the uprising in Hungary. The government there seized the opportunity to eliminate unreliable or dissatisfied political elements and used the situation to justify further persecution of the Hungarian minority. The Romanian government executed some 50 people, arrested 27,000, and imprisoned 10,000, 170 of whom died in prison. Altogether, the severity of the reprisals was close to the case of Hungary, while all that actually happened in Romania in 1956 was a few isolated demonstrations and occasional manifestations of sympathy with the events in Hungary.[17] In Czechoslovakia, there were no serious demonstrations supporting the Hungarian Revolution; however, isolated actions of expressing solidarity occurred, especially among the members of the ethnic Hungarian community. The reprisals by the authorities were also much milder than in Romania: some 665 people were prosecuted because of some kind of "counterrevolutionary activity."[18]

In the decades following 1956, the Hungarian Revolution had several legacies in East Central Europe: first, the leaders of the various regimes learned from the example of Imre Nagy and party opposition that attempts at radical reform can easily lead to the collapse of the Communist political monopoly; and second, they learned that, in such cases, the Soviets would not hesitate to restore order using the most brutal means. Beyond these basic lessons, the Hungarian Revolution demonstrated that the leadership in East Central Europe could ignore social demands and public opinion only at their own peril. Even though they had seen that any threatened regime could rely on Soviet help in the event of some political crisis, that leadership, which would be held responsible, could also expect to share the fate of the Gerő group in Hungary— that is, to be replaced.

In this way, the Hungarian Revolution, by setting such a drastic example, contributed to a large extent to the success of the attempt—which had begun at the Twentieth Congress of the CPSU in February 1956—to build a post-Stalinist model of Communism in the Soviet Union and throughout East Central Europe. The Polish crisis of October 1956, with its contrasting positive example, also strengthened the same trend; it demonstrated that a limited campaign of moderate reforms, which did not directly threaten the political system or indirectly threaten the security of the Eastern military bloc, could be realized even against the will of the Soviet leadership. More than anything else, this experience motivated the Czechoslovak Communist reformers in 1968. It is another matter that, unlike Gomułka, they were unable to limit social changes to a level that the Soviets could tolerate.

The final legacy of the events of 1956 and shortly after were that they effectively put to rest any ideas that still existed in East Central Europe that the Soviet yoke could be thrown off by active revolt. The inaction of the West, the cruelty of the Soviet intervention, and finally the irrationally broad scale of retaliation all combined to dispel that illusion. Over the decades that followed, this understanding became the basis of all self-regulatory reform activities in Eastern bloc states. While consciously taking the security interests of the Soviet Union into account, those wishing for change worked gradually but effectively to liberalize the Communist system. They no longer aimed to overthrow it.

The Khrushchev Doctrine on Joint Intervention

The Hungarian revolution acted as a significant catalyst to strengthening the multilateralization of the Soviet bloc. While the 1953 uprising in East Germany, the revolt in June 1956 in Poznan, and the Polish crisis in October did not raise the issue of whether the other countries of the region should participate in any way in restoring order and the consolidation process after the crisis, this issue was raised in a different way after November 1956. First, as is well-known today, both the Romanian and the Czechoslovak leaders offered the Soviets their participation in cracking down on the Hungarian Revolution.[19] Based on what is known today, we may take the risk to suppose that if the Soviets had had more time to prepare for the intervention, they might have considered the Romanian and Czechoslovak offers and taken advantage of the benefits inherent in a joint action by the forces of the Warsaw Pact. However, after 4 November, "brotherly" countries, such as Romania, Czechoslovakia, the GDR, and China, all provided significant economic assistance for the Kádár government at the time of the November–December strikes in order to carry out economic consolidation as soon as possible. In return, however, they claimed the right to give specific advice to the "hesitant" Hungarian leadership on restoring order and demanded that the people who actively revolted against the Communist system should be severely punished.

However, the most important turn was at the beginning of January 1957, when the first collective Soviet bloc "tribunal" was held. Both Moscow and Budapest were suggested as a possible venue, but eventually, at a Soviet proposal, it was held in Budapest. What is more, the idea of an incomplete summit of the Soviet bloc, with the participation of the Soviet Union, Hungary, Czechoslovakia, Bulgaria, and Romania, originated from Kádár himself, although it soon turned out that it was not what he bargained for.

The need for a regional meeting in the tense East Central European situation had been maturing for several months, and the initiators, the participants, and the topics to be discussed changed a lot in the meantime. The leaders of the Hungarian Socialist Workers' Party (HSWP) turned to the CPSU as early as 11 November 1956 and proposed to convene a Communist summit meeting to discuss the national issue with the participation of the Chinese and the Yugoslav parties.[20]

The potential chances of negotiations on this, however, might have been significantly influenced by the fact that in the meantime the Hungarian government was going to issue a declaration in late December about its views on the future political and economic structure and functioning of the country. As was characteristic of this transitional situation, at that time the leadership wanted to commission expert committees with the participation of representatives of the workers' councils to work out the economic elements of the government program and the methods of governance.[21] The concept that was taking shape appeared to capture certain elements of the national and left-wing plebeian bloc policy of the coalition period between 1944 and 1948: it envisaged the possibility of including the delegates of only *nominal* parties that were organized into an election alliance in the government, which clearly emphasized national unity.[22] As part of the preparation, the Interim Central Committee of the HSWP discussed the concept on 28 December 1956, which envisaged the possibility of the legal operation of other, non-Communist parties in addition to the Communist party.[23] This concept was especially similar to the Czechoslovak model, in which the partner parties could not have members and functioning organizations, but they were allowed to maintain a national center and run in the elections in a kind of left-wing bloc—the Patriotic National Front in Hungary—together with the leading/dominant Communist Party (i.e., the HSWP). According to the documents that have survived, the Hungarian leaders reckoned with the participation of two parties: the Independent Smallholders' Party and the National Peasant Party.

This version of a simulated multiparty system was far removed from real democratization, and it soon became obvious that even this was way too much for the Soviet leaders. These concepts suggested a continuity of unyielding resistance to Moscow, and the Soviet leaders did not see any convincing evidence for the Kádár government distancing itself from the national reform concepts advocating self-governance, which had been gaining more ground in the previous two years. Moscow was afraid that, under social pressure, the newly established HSWP would want to achieve more of this planned quasi-multiparty system than was desirable, which even the quite large number of Soviet advisors present in the country, would be unable to prevent.

Moscow might also have been concerned because of what Kádár suggested to Andropov in the middle of December: in order to increase the mass base of the party, the leadership was planning to expand the government by non-party members as well as members of other parties.[24] Thus, it may not have been an accident that, at the end of December 1956, Kádár had to face an unexpected challenge: the Romanian leaders informed him that Zoltán Szántó, one of the members of the Imre Nagy group kept in captivity in Romania, would soon return to Hungary.[25] Up to that time, Kádár might have felt his position to be secure, as in the given situation it was quite unlikely that the Soviets would replace him with either of his two rivals, Rákosi or Imre Nagy. Szántó, however, was not only an experienced party leader (his Communist past dated back as far as 1918) but also a Moscow ally and a Muscovite, who worked for the Comintern in the 1930s. Therefore, he may have seemed to be much more trustworthy to the Soviets than the "domestic" Communist Kádár, who, at the age of forty-four, was seen by the Kremlin as too young anyway and who did not speak Russian. In addition, he spent many years in Rákosi's prison, which was a significant black mark on his party data sheet, although it was well known in Moscow that he had been convicted on the basis of false charges. And what was perhaps the most important problem in this context, in November–December 1956, Kádár was seen as a latent Titoist. On the other hand, Szántó did not do much to criticize during the revolution: he was a member of the third Imre Nagy government and was also one of those who escaped to the Yugoslav embassy.[26] Thus, the message sent by the Romanian leadership might have caused a lot of headaches to Kádár, who wondered whether the idea of Szántó's return to Hungary was actually raised by Moscow. Therefore, on December 28 he asked the Soviet leaders through his liaison officer to convene a meeting between the Hungarian, the Soviet, and the Romanian parties, at which they could discuss the issues that had arisen and, on the other hand, work out a joint strategy for addressing the issue of the Imre Nagy group.[27] Although the positive Soviet answer arrived soon, Kádár was not to be satisfied.

Khrushchev also made an unexpected proposal to convene an extraordinary urgent meeting, but his top problem on the agenda was not to clarify the Szántó issue. He was much more concerned with the consolidation program of the Hungarian party leadership that was already taking shape. The Interim Central Committee of the HSWP had decided at its 28 December meeting that a statement would be issued on the government program on 6 January 1957.

The presidium of the CPSU received the draft on 29 December, but Moscow did not like its content, since one of the paragraphs said that the HSWP would like to introduce a special version of a *pseudo-multiparty system*.[28] Although this relevant clause was missing in the draft text sent to Moscow, Kádár, knowing that it was not an insignificant point, sent the missing content to Boris Ponomarev head of the Department of Foreign Communist Parties of the CPSU's CC through his liaison officer.[29]

Moscow was so concerned about this possibility, which had not been negotiated with the Soviets in advance, that on the same day the presidium of the CPSU decided to send Khrushchev and Malenkov to Budapest on 1 January to discuss the issue by means of effective arguments.[30] When Khrushchev called Kádár to inform him about the visit, the leader of the Hungarian party withdrew his proposal for a trilateral meeting and requested that the Czechoslovak and Bulgarian parties should also be invited.

Kádár's intention was probably to extend the range of topics to be covered at the meeting—for example, with a discussion of the practical consequences of the 30 October Soviet government statement. In addition, he wanted to take advantage of this opportunity to seek and find a solution in regard to the fate of the Imre Nagy group together with the other leaders of the Soviet bloc, which would have been beneficial for him from the point of view of sharing responsibility. The meeting turned out to be disappointing for him; one could say he misjudged the situation.

The meeting was held in Budapest between 1 and 4 January 1957, with the participation of the leaders of the Bulgarian, Czechoslovak, Hungarian, Romanian, and Soviet parties.[31] As has been seen, the Kremlin's main motivation behind the meeting was to discuss the imminent program statement of the Kádár government, which also included the possibility of maintaining a special kind of multiparty system. Kádár himself had mixed feelings in connection with this key proposal, which had developed into a significant political issue within the Hungarian party leadership. At its 28 December meeting, the Interim Central Committee of the HSWP was unable to come to a decision because its members had received the text only a few hours before the meeting started. Therefore, they decided to sit down again on 3 January to finalize the text on the basis of the proposals that had arrived in the meantime.[32] However, because of the hastily organized summit meeting, the 3 January meeting was never held, and "obviously" the government did not discuss its own draft statement;[33] thus, the responsibility for the decision was transferred to the international meeting. The Soviets and the leaders of the other parties insisted at the summit meeting that this clause should be excluded from the text of the statement before it was made public on 6 January 1957. After all of this, it is not surprising that the final statement did not even mention the issue of a multiparty system.[34]

The other important issue discussed at the meeting, which was Kádár's main motivation for wanting to convene a meeting at all, was the fate of the Imre Nagy group. Although the available documents do not reveal the position of each participant in detail, it seems obvious that the meeting resulted in a key joint decision, which opened the way for court proceedings and eventually the conviction and execution of Imre Nagy and his associates. In other words, it was no longer treated as a political issue but rather as a criminal case.[35]

This meeting was certainly a significant turn with respect to Hungarian domestic policy. The Soviet, Czechoslovak, Bulgarian, and Romanian leaders vetoed the HSWP's plans targeting a quasi-multiparty system, among other things, at the incomplete summit meeting of the Soviet bloc in Budapest, in addition to making a decision on the need to indict the Imre Nagy group. Despite its intention, the Hungarian leadership served as a catalyst for the Soviet efforts to ensure regional integration by not breaking, despite several warnings, with the Hungarian reform ideas after 1953 in a sufficiently radical way; moreover, they were seeking allies for these ideas in the Soviet camp.

All of this made the Soviet leaders and their allies act against the Hungarian leadership in union and determine the corrective borders and the new principles of cooperation for the long term. Kádár was shaping the Hungarian policy of the first few years after the revolution in this situation. Before the meeting, the HSWP's draft statement envisaged the possibility of creating a special national Soviet system with a bit of real social participation, but the participants of the January consultations in 1957 had the Hungarian delegation adopt a declaration that offered very little room for maneuver.[36] Kádár did not manage to find supporters at the quinquelateral meeting. On the contrary, his negotiating partners raised every issue that may have aroused some suspicion: the plan for granting a right for the parties to operate, the organization of workers' councils on a professional basis, the mistakenly nationalistic interpretation of culture, the autonomy to be granted for universities, and even the plan for setting up a peasants' association, which had already been rejected by the Interim Central Committee.[37] The extremely fragmentary sources suggest that the leaders of the Soviet bloc countries who were present at the meeting found the Hungarian ideas, which were meant to create a special Soviet system, way too much as well as dangerous, even in their tamed form.

On the other hand, as far as the quasi-alliance relationships are concerned, this meeting was important because it was the first occasion in the history of the Soviet bloc on which the members of the Warsaw Pact acted in union and directly intervened in the internal affairs of one of its member states, paving the way for the policy that was to be termed later as the Brezhnev *Doctrine,* all over the world. Thus, the *Khrushchev* Doctrine following the argument of Hungarian historian Melinda Kalmár,[38] emerged as one of the elements of multilateralism, which provided support for a common governing system in both a military and a law enforcement sense: it prompted that the members of the bloc could act in union if the essential elements and the stability of the system were in danger in any of the Soviet bloc's states. In an institutional sense, this was already in place when the Warsaw Pact was established, and in a theoretical sense, it confirmed the Soviet government statement made on 30 October 1956, but the principle of "joint action" was tacitly adopted at the Budapest meeting in January 1957. The responsibility for maintaining power was thereby shared at the super-macro level, too, between the center and the subordinate parts.[39] In this sense, the meeting was a precursor to the global crisis-management process, at the end of which the member states of the Warsaw Pact put an end to the 1968 Prague Spring by means of military intervention. The Soviet leadership, after failing to achieve a political solution, used direct joint intervention in 1968; thus, this approach came to be called the Brezhnev Doctrine after the intervention in Czechoslovakia.

Another remarkable development is that, according to the official statement issued after the meeting, the participants exchanged their ideas on the basic principles related to the relations between the Socialist countries as specified in the Soviet government declaration made on 30 October 1956, and they found these principles entirely in line with the interests of the countries concerned.[40] It is unfortunate that this is all we know about this key meeting. On the other hand, it is important that the Hungarian leaders eventually managed to persuade the Soviets to confirm a Communist "Magna Carta." The 30 October Soviet government statement was seen as a temporary concession after the suppression of the revolution, both in the East and the West, that Moscow undertook in order to pour oil on troubled waters under the duress of the Polish and Hungarian crises. Therefore, the public confirmation of the principles in the declaration that put the relationship between the Soviet Union and its allies on a new foundation, barely three months after the crackdown of the Hungarian Revolution and the first summit meeting of the Soviet bloc after the crisis, represented an extremely important development for the future of the entire alliance system. More importantly, there were significant differences between the two documents. While the Soviet government's statement includes all five of the elevated principles taken formally from the Panchseel (mutual respect for each other's territorial integrity and sovereignty, mutual nonaggression, mutual noninterference in domestic affairs, equality and mutual benefit, and peaceful coexistence), the joint communiqué issued after the Budapest summit includes only the following: respect for the interests and equal rights of nations, noninterference, and the Leninist principles of proletarian internationalism. In addition, the communiqué emphasized that the application of the basic principles set forth in the Soviet government's statement issued on 30 October 1956 would result, in particular, in the strengthening of the unity of the Soviet camp. In other words, the 30 October declaration was the "constitution" of the post-Stalinist alliance system, and, in this respect, the joint January 1957 communiqué was more like an implementing decree of an act that sets out in detail the pragmatic limits of the prevalence of these elevated principles. Another important aspect of this issue is that although the 30 October 1956 Soviet government statement was not frequently used as a reference point in the development of the Soviet–East Central European relationship, it has never been withdrawn formally, so it was actually valid up to 1991.

Public Opinion in the West

The Soviet intervention in Hungary had its strongest effect on those in Western societies who had harbored illusions regarding the Soviet Union—that is, those who lean left. Most of them had seen the Soviet Union as the model for, or supporter of, Socialist society; thus, the Hungarian Revolution provided a test of whether or not it would be possible to realize a Socialist system that managed to incorporate the practice of Western political democracy and the principles of common property and social equality.

This is why the brutal suppression of the Hungarian Revolution had a negative effect, not only on the Western European Communist parties but on the left wings of Socialist and social democratic parties as well. Partly as a consequence of 1956, the New Left of the 1960s and later Euro-Communist movements decisively detached themselves from Soviet influence and sought other models for their ideal of Socialism.

In the Western countries, there were basically two kinds of leftist people: members of the Communist Party and the so-called fellow travelers. In the 1950s, the Communist parties in Western Europe were functioning legally, and especially in France and Italy—although being opposition parties—they were influential and important elements of the political structure, attaining between 20 and 25 percent of the votes at national elections. The Western Communist parties supported the Soviet suppression of the Hungarian Revolution, as they regarded it a counterrevolution. Nevertheless, a lot of people were disillusioned with the Communist parties themselves, and many left. The Communist parties' strength and influence, however, was not reduced in the 1960s.

Fellow travelers were a much broader part of society and consisted of people thinking in leftist terms who had some kind of ideas about a more just society than the Western societies at the time. Many also believed that there was a third road between capitalism and Socialism. The crushing of the Hungarian Revolution came as a big blow to these fellow travelers, and especially the intellectuals, because they came to realize that the Soviet Union, until that time regarded as an unquestionable model to follow for how a Communist system should be built, would not allow a small nation to reform its Communist system and get rid of the excesses of Stalinism. This is how *they* saw the events in Hungary.

Also, there was the general tendency of the de-Stalinization process, which started after 1953 and was intensified after Khrushchev's secret speech at the Twentieth Congress of the CPSU in February 1956. In this speech, Khrushchev unmasked Stalin and presented him as a criminal, which was a great shock—especially for the leftist people in the West. Many people reacted thus: "Stalin was not a god? We were cheering and admiring a criminal? Everything we believed in is now a lie?" There was a huge sense of amazement soon after the secret speech, which became known in the West by the summer. Therefore, the negative perceptions held by the Communist parties and fellow travelers in Western Europe after 1956 were caused by two main factors, the impact of de-Stalinization and the effects of the Hungarian Revolution. It is impossible, however, to tell which one affected them in which way and to what extent.

Aside from those on the Left, most in the West saw the Hungarian Revolution as an oppressed nation's instinctive strike for freedom and democracy, an anti-Soviet and anti-Communist uprising. Accordingly, these people, who took part in often violent demonstrations condemning the Soviet intervention, protested not so much against the Soviet invasion—which after all was the expected reaction from a superpower—as against the passivity of their own governments. The long-running liberation propaganda of the United States—the leading power of the Western world—had led many to believe that the West would naturally help any attempt at freedom behind the Iron Curtain, such as the Hungarian Revolution was. Understandably, then, the Western public was stunned to witness the plight of the Hungarian people, who could never have expected such sympathy because of Hungary's role in the Second World War, as they revolted against the immensely superior power of a world empire, jeopardizing their lives, existence, and families in a heroic, tragic, and—according to political logic and common sense—irrational struggle for freedom, and all the while the governments of the West did next to nothing.

Freedom was the most abstract of ideals in the Western world, and the most important one at the same time, though also something for which the citizens of the consolidated postwar states no longer had to sacrifice their lives. The general public of the West had to face the fact that their governments, by pursuing a passive foreign policy and protecting the interests of their own societies, had failed in their roles as paragons of liberty. It became obvious that the West—with its pragmatic political considerations—would not risk conflict for the ideal of liberty.

The failure of the West to act in 1956 brought to many the disillusioning realization that the self-created sociopolitical image of the Western democracies—that they were the ultimate supporters of universal democratic principles—was not entirely true. This awakening perhaps partially spurred the radicalization in the 1960s of certain elements of Western society—especially within the younger generations. In this way, the Hungarian Revolution, with its brief history of triumph, tragedy, and finally disillusionment, indirectly but with much certainty contributed to the last "anti-capitalist revolt": the student movements of the late 1960s.

Chapter 6

Hungary and the Soviet Bloc in the Khrushchevian Experimental Era, 1956–1964

A Missed Opportunity: The Plan of Withdrawing Soviet Troops from Hungary in 1958

The short period of time between 1956 and 1964 was the most dynamic era in the history of the Soviet Union. The main motivation for the Soviet attitude was the sudden increase in unprecedented confidence—which was due to the fact that, in missile technology, Soviet science was ahead of the Americans temporarily, if only for a few years. Another factor also contributed to the strengthening of the Soviet position: the superpower guarantee, acquired in 1956, basically assured the Soviet Union that in the future, the United States— despite its harsh propaganda—would not interfere in the internal affairs of the Soviet empire, no matter what happened behind the Iron Curtain.

These two significant changes in the late 1950s fundamentally influenced Soviet foreign policy and indirectly helped strengthen two parallel but opposite tendencies. The duality of this policy lay in that it permanently provoked/ tested the opponent and at the same time looked for the possibility of consensus. Thus, the main feature of Khrushchev's foreign policy became launching initiatives persistently in two basically different directions. On the one hand, using their temporary advantage in the field of developing intercontinental missiles, it encouraged risky and clearly destabilizing moves prompted by power politics and entailed a confrontative attitude or even brinkmanship aimed at achieving unilateral concessions. In the case of the Berlin crisis, this meant an attempt to change the European status quo of 1945 by trying to eliminate any Western military presence in West Berlin; while in the case of the Cuban missile crisis, there was an evident effort toward modifying the global strategic balance in favor of Moscow. The second tendency, however, was expressly constructive by nature, and this proved to be a determining factor as far as historical processes were concerned. This entailed the promotion of the policy of compelled coexistence and the search for consensus, which was in harmony all along with the process of détente that had begun after 1953 and spread extensively from 1963. Khrushchev presented radical proposals in the field of disarmament, arms control, and the reduction of nuclear weapons, but most strikingly he made spectacular unilateral concessions—especially regarding troop reductions and withdrawals—while no such or even comparable moves were regarded permissible by his successors up until the end of the 1980s. Thus, in the long run, the enormous increase in confidence after 1956 strengthened an emancipation process, during which the Soviet Union became an equivalent superpower to the United States from a military-strategic point of view by the late 1960s. This, however, indirectly helped the emergence of a cooperative tendency that resulted in the deepening of a new wave of the détente policy from the mid-1960s, eventually leading to the signing of the Helsinki Final Act in 1975. That act not only meant the de jure recognition of the European status quo of 1945 but could also be regarded as the "constitution" of the praxis of compelled coexistence that had by then been accepted not only in the East but also in the West.

The rather constructive policy of introducing unilateral concessions was to prove the expressly peaceful intentions of the Soviet Union and the whole Warsaw Pact.[1] The plan to announce the withdrawal of all Soviet troops from Hungary and Romania served exactly that purpose in 1958. Such a spectacular move was to have a great impact not only on Western policy makers but also on the public, as no similar concession was expected on the opposite side in return. Just three years earlier, the conclusion of the Austrian State Treaty and the subsequent withdrawal of the allied troops from that country were a result of a classical great power compromise. This time, the Soviet Army planned to leave two East European countries occupied during the Second World War, without any quid pro quo on the Western side. Moreover, we now know that this initiative was not preceded by any request or pressure like that which occurred in 1955 and in 1956 either, during the Hungarian Revolution, when the Romanian leadership requested the withdrawal of Soviet troops.[2] Therefore, it is clear that it was Khrushchev's own initiative, and it was part of his greater plan aimed at creating favorable conditions for his rapprochement policy with the West. It is also very likely that he expected this move to be an important card to use at the forthcoming—but never held—Geneva-type four-power summit meeting in the summer of 1958, for which busy preparations were underway in the spring.

Totally withdrawing Soviet troops from Hungary and Romania would have also raised the prestige of the Soviet Union as a law-abiding power from the perspective of international law because, after such a move, Soviet troops would be stationed only in countries (GDR, Poland) where, in the absence of a German peace treaty, the legal basis was granted by the still valid Potsdam Agreement of the three allied powers. This is because the legal basis for stationing troops in Hungary and Romania expired after the signing of the Austrian State Treaty in May 1955 and the withdrawal of the Soviet troops from the eastern part of Austria. These troops were originally in place to secure the communication lines between the Soviet-occupied zone in Austria and the Soviet Union, as was stipulated in the Paris Peace Treaties signed with Hungary and Romania in February 1947. However, according to the provision of the treaties, ninety days after the Soviet troops are withdrawn from Austria following the conclusion of the peace treaty, they must leave Hungary and Romania as well. According to this, the withdrawal of the troops should have taken place in the autumn of 1955. However, on 14 May 1955, one day before the signing of the Austrian State Treaty, the Soviet bloc's military-political alliance—the Warsaw Pact (WP)—was established in the Polish capital. While the Warsaw Pact's founding statute that was made public at the time did not contain any passages that would have enabled the stationing of Soviet troops in the territory of other member states, it seems possible that later, as mentioned in chapter 2, they may have wanted to use the WP's organizational framework to create a legal basis for the further stationing of Soviet troops in Hungary and Romania.[3] This solution, however, would have proved to be a unilateral step and a serious violation of the international responsibilities taken by the Soviet government previously in the peace treaties. Thus, the decision by Khrushchev in reality was aimed to make a virtue of necessity, namely to make the withdrawal of the troops from two East Central European countries, which were strategically less important anyway, seem like a unilateral concession and a confidence-building act aimed at the radical improvement of the East–West relationship.

In general, the Hungarian leadership enthusiastically supported Khrushchev's initiatives for disarmament because Kádár—as a leader of a small and not too developed country—actually deemed the army as a necessary evil and tried to spend as little as possible on defense. He knew very well that increasing military expenditure would seriously jeopardize his standard-of-living policy, which aimed to pacify society after 1956. In reality, he was expecting the Soviet Union to ensure the protection of Hungary, because Moscow's allies even collectively did not represent a significant force against NATO. Therefore, during the years following 1956, the Hungarian leadership was constantly referring to the extra burden of a massive economic reconstruction following the "counterrevolution" as well as to the need to permanently raise the standard of living of the population in order to restore the people's confidence in the new leadership and thus ensure political stability in the country. By doing so, they could achieve a temporary special status whereby Hungary would be allowed to have a significantly lower defense budget than the other WP member states.[4]

In all likelihood, this is the main reason for Kádár rejecting the proposal of Khrushchev in the spring of 1958, when the First Secretary of the Soviet Communist Party suggested that, just like in Romania, all Soviet troops could be withdrawn from Hungary. This crucial offer, which was kept top secret until the end of the Kádár era, was made at the time of the visit of the Soviet party and government delegation to Budapest on 2–10 April 1958.[5] At that time, the Soviet leadership made a similar offer to Romania as well and, as is well known, the Soviet troops were completely withdrawn from the country in June 1958.[6] A few months later, Khrushchev interpreted the events in a similar manner during a talk with Mao Zedong, which confirms that his offer was serious: "When I was in Hungary I offered to Kádár to withdraw the troops. He disagreed and only consented to the reduction of one division. They deployed our troops along the Austrian border, but the Austrians do not threaten us. I believe that the situation in Hungary is very good. Kádár is a good man."[7]

Based on the currently known documents, Kádár himself, without consulting the HSWP leadership, rejected this proposal, arguing that while the internal situation of the country was stable, the Hungarian army alone would be incapable of guaranteeing the security of the country if there were an external threat.[8] While the first part of the argument was simply not true in the spring of 1958, the second part in reality applied to any other non-Soviet member of the Eastern bloc as well; this very weak excuse must have been the result of improvisation by Kádár when he had to react to the unexpected offer. The really big puzzle is why Khrushchev accepted this explanation and let Kádár thwart the great plan of withdrawing Soviet troops from all the countries where there was no legitimate basis for their stationing, in one spectacular move. Paradoxically, the main reason for this may be the exceptionally close personal relationship between the two leaders, and it is rather likely that no such concession would have been given by Khrushchev to any other leader in the Soviet bloc in a similar situation. Another motivation could be that this was clearly a temporary agreement, so the troop withdrawal from Hungary could have taken place some years later, creating another confidence-building measure to be used at a later stage of the unfolding détente process. This is all the more likely as, at the 1960 February meeting of the WP PCC, Khrushchev raised the issue again—probably at that time only in a theoretical sense—of the withdrawal of Soviet troops from Hungary and even from Poland.[9]

Since the available sources confirm that this was a serious offer by the Soviets, we can state that János Kádár, and indirectly the whole Hungarian party leadership, made a decision on this crucial issue in total contradiction to the national interests of the country, based solely on short-term interests, and for this conduct Kádár bears serious historical responsibility. It can also be argued that this was Kádár's most irresponsible foreign policy decision during his long reign.

True, the troop withdrawal for Romanian society was far from producing clearly positive results; in fact, the local leadership used the somewhat increased room for maneuvering to strengthen the repressive function of the Communist dictatorship over the next decades. The question, however, arises quite differently in the case of Hungary. If the withdrawal of the Soviet troops had happened in 1958, it would have had undoubtedly great importance for Hungarian society. First of all, in moral terms, the continuing Soviet occupation—especially during the years right after the revolution—was one of the greatest moral offenses people felt, particularly because it did not follow in an a priori manner from the fact that one had to live in a Communist dictatorship: in the middle of the 1950s there were no Soviet troops in Czechoslovakia or in Bulgaria. The withdrawal of Soviet troops would not by itself have been a deciding factor in increasing the standard of living, and the independence of the country would not have been restored by it either. But in Hungary, such a move would have greatly improved the psychological state of the population and, indirectly, the quality of life in a Communist country where, just two years before, most of the citizens had unequivocally demanded the withdrawal of Soviet troops and where the Communist leadership deemed the feeling of material satisfaction of the population a central issue anyway. I believe that this potential and long-term profit cannot be compared to the short-term and rather limited material advantage that came from the fact that, between 1956 and 1961, Hungary had to spend considerably less on military developments than the other members of the bloc.[10]

So whereas no full withdrawal of Soviet troops took place in Hungary, with the withdrawal from Romania in June 1958, the contingent in Hungary was eventually reduced by one division. This was because, after Khrushchev had left the country, Kádár partly changed his mind, and he suggested that one division be withdrawn from Hungary as well. Most likely he was worried about the reaction of the public, which surely would have been unable to understand why, with a total Soviet withdrawal from Romania, not even a reduction was possible in Hungary. It was originally planned for September; in the end, however, it occurred along with the withdrawal of the Soviet troops from Romania for the sake of a greater international impact.[11] All of this was made part of an immense unilateral disarmament initiative, aimed to prove the peaceful intentions of the Soviet bloc, which was formally approved by the WP's PCC at its Moscow meeting in May 1958.[12] At that time, the member states of the WP made a promise for the curtailment of 119,000 troops. Romania reduced the numbers of its army by 55,000, and even Albania symbolically reduced its armed forces by 1,000 personnel. Directly before the meeting, the Soviet Union announced a 300,000 troop reduction. It is typical of the state of the Hungarian army in the period, destabilized in 1956, that Hungary was the only WP member state who did not announce any curtailment at this conference.

In some sense, this was the moment when the Warsaw Pact became an adult, because, since the foundation of the organization, this was the first time that important decisions affecting international politics were not made by the Soviet Union, or some of its allies, but by the collective members of the military-political organization of the Soviet bloc, which was made public as such after the meeting of the PCC. It is true that the meeting itself was called together as the result of a typical Khrushchevian improvisation, because the leaders of the allied countries originally came to Moscow for the meeting of the Comecon. At the meeting, the invited were told that, since they were together anyway, the WP PCC should hold a meeting as well. Beyond the formal approval of the reduction of the armies, the Soviet draft was approved, which suggested signing a nonaggression pact between the WP and NATO.

During these years, Khrushchev—clearly trying to find the proper function of the Warsaw Pact concerning the role of the allied armies—proved to be extremely imaginative regarding how they could enhance general Soviet political goals. In March 1957, he raised the possibility that Warsaw Pact states, "including Hungary, could send their troops to the Soviet Union, perhaps to the Far East, to guard the socialist camp from the Japanese. Perhaps some units could be brought to Moscow too. This would not weaken the unity between our countries. We raise our people in the spirit of this unity."[13] He advertised his bold idea to Kádár.

The extemporization that exhibits Khrushchev's noble intentions was not kept in consideration in the future; however, another similar idea was almost executed in the same year. He proposed to Kádár that to demonstrate the unity of the Socialist camp, the Socialist countries' selected military units should take part in the ceremonies on Red Square in Moscow to honor the fortieth anniversary of the 1917 October Revolution on 7 November. In line with the doctrine of active foreign policy, fostered by Khrushchev during these years, they agreed that this suggestion would be introduced by the HSWP as a Hungarian initiative to the other sister parties.[14] This did happen in July 1957, but prior to that, for the sake of orderliness, the HSWP Provisional Executive Committee (as the Political Committee/Politburo was called until June 1957) passed a resolution about it at its 2 April meeting. Then, in his letter to the CPSU CC, Kádár officially brought up the suggestion, and "surprisingly," he got a positive response about it from Moscow. However, the evolution of world politics was not favorable to the realization of the plan: in October 1957, the Soviet leadership, which was increasingly interested in continuing the policy of détente, eventually refused the suggestion, saying that the enemy would consider it a demonstration of strength, which would impede the normalization of the East–West relationship.[15]

The Berlin Crisis and the Soviet Bloc

However surprising, the mechanism of compelled cooperation of the superpowers can be pointed out clearly when investigating the history of the two most serious East–West conflicts of the era, the Berlin crisis and the Cuban missile crisis; moreover, the peaceful resolution of these crises was exactly the result of such cooperation.

The model of both crises was similar: the Soviet leadership started an offensive to change the status quo in their favor, which caused a severe conflict of the superpowers, and to avoid the escalation of the crisis, Moscow was forced to retreat. The U.S. administration, however, also highly interested in avoiding an armed conflict at all costs, assisted its opponent in the successful retreat. Eventually a compromise was reached, which not only meant a return to the status quo ante as far as the interests of the parties were concerned but also made the recognition of rational Soviet interests possible, which enabled Khrushchev to present the Soviet capitulation as a partial victory in his own bloc.

After the attempts at a Geneva-type four-power summit failed by the summer of 1958, Khrushchev, eventually yielding to the longtime pressure of the East German leadership, decided to try to resolve the problem of Berlin through unilateral action. A decade earlier, in 1948, Stalin ordered the blockade of Berlin primarily for prestige, not because of being compelled to do so by pressing external factors. Having realized that the German peace treaty that was to end the allied occupation of the city would not be concluded in the foreseeable future, his plan was to force the Western powers to leave the Western zones of the city. Thus, Stalin was hoping to get rid of the capitalist enclave that was originally meant to be a temporary measure, in place for just a short armistice period, but that had wedged itself as a malignant cancer into the Soviet-occupied zone of East Germany. From the early 1950s on, however, a new factor increasingly urged the Soviet leadership to find a solution to the issue of Berlin as soon as possible, even at the cost of taking some risks. By the end of the decade, about two hundred thousand people a year were fleeing the country to the FRG via the basically open border between the eastern and western sectors of Berlin. This created a grave political and economic crisis in the GDR, especially as most of the refugees were highly trained professionals, intellectuals, and skilled workers.[16]

Endeavors to settle the situation were significantly motivated by the fact that, by that time, the Soviet leadership had given up the idea of German unification and envisaged the solution of the German question based on the existence of two German states. Thus, it became a key issue not only for the

Soviet Union but for the whole Soviet bloc to enhance the political and economic stability of the GDR. In November 1958, Khrushchev issued a note to the three Western powers, proposing to start negotiations about declaring West Berlin a free city. He also stated that if an agreement was not reached within six months, the Soviet Union would bestow its occupying rights regarding Berlin on the GDR authorities. The suggestion became known to the public as well as in Cold War historiography as Khrushchev's "ultimatum" on Berlin, although today it is clear that the Soviet leadership actually endeavored to solve the issue through negotiations. Despite the threatening rhetoric, Khrushchev made unilateral steps only after years of unsuccessful trials. As for the negotiation tactics, which were elaborated by Soviet diplomacy before the conference of the foreign ministers of the four great powers in May 1959, any one of three versions would have been acceptable for the Soviet bloc: (1) the Western occupying powers withdraw their troops from West Berlin, and the UN guarantees the special status of that part of the city; (2) control is taken over by troops of neutral states; or (3) the current occupying powers maintain a military of symbolic value in West Berlin. In any case, the Soviets wanted to give inspection of the roads leading to the city from the FRG to Berlin to the authorities of the GDR.[17]

During the Berlin crisis, the matter of the German peace treaty was resumed, but only as an important tool in the struggle for the international recognition of the GDR. According to the new Soviet idea, the allied powers should sign a peace treaty with the two German states. A successful realization of this plan would have brought positive results for the Soviet bloc in two ways: it would have meant the recognition of the Oder-Neisse Line as the eastern "German" border and the "legalization" of the GDR as a state.

In reality, the Soviets had no hope regarding the acceptance of the proposition; rather, they deemed the issue of the peace treaty significant from the aspect of propaganda. This is why, from 1958 up until the middle of the 1960s, also due to pressure from the GDR's leadership, they constantly floated the possibility that if no agreement was reached, the Soviet Union and the countries of the Eastern bloc would sign a separate peace treaty with the GDR. In fact, they did not seriously consider that option either, for that would have meant a grave breach of the four-power agreements on Germany following World War II, greatly endangering the shaping of East–West relations. Consequently, this step was never taken despite Khrushchev's threatening rhetoric.

Between 1959 and 1961, the Soviet leadership tried to get the aforementioned program approved by the representatives of the Western powers, primarily the United States, at various high-level talks, such as during Khrushchev's visit to America in September 1959, as well as at the superpower summit with Kennedy in Vienna in June 1961. The member states of the Warsaw Pact unanimously supported both the general Soviet campaign and the independent moves of the GDR leadership. The West, however, rejected the plan from the outset because it was interpreted—and rightly so—as a change in the European status quo that was created in 1945 and, moreover, without any sort of reciprocity. In addition, West Berlin had a symbolic importance from the aspect of the protection and propagation of the Western way of life, which is why the West regarded the maintenance of current positions especially important. In accordance with this, Kennedy publicly stated in July 1961 that the United States would protect West Berlin with the use of arms if necessary.[18]

A fundamental change, resulting in an immense increase in the number of East German refugees, occurred in 1961, which clearly led to the emergence of a critical economic situation in the country: in the first half of the year, more than two hundred thousand people escaped to the FRG; thus, an annual 100 percent increase could be envisaged.[19] This also meant that, prospectively in 1961 alone, some four hundred thousand people would have left the GDR.[20] The primary aim of the WP PCC meeting in March 1961 was to prepare the member states for a situation arising in consequence of unilateral moves by Moscow or the East German leadership. Consequently, the body made a resolution about the significant increase of the defense budget and the intensive development of the cooperation of the military industry within the Soviet bloc.[21] The participants of the meeting also discussed the issue of the German peace treaty. The Soviet representatives issued a warning: one must prepare now, for in a "certain period of time" the FRG and the West in general would advocate an economic boycott against the Socialist countries. The suggested countermeasures included tightening economic cooperation within the bloc on the one hand and reshaping the bloc countries' Western economic relations in a way that would end the dominant role of the FRG on the other.[22]

The crisis was at its peak when, on 13 August 1961, the East German authorities—keeping the preparations for the action a topmost secret—blocked the border between the eastern and western sectors of Berlin with a wire fence and then, a few days later, began building the Berlin Wall. The GDR leadership had been asking for Khrushchev's approval for this move for a long while, but that was only possible after it became evident in a summit with Kennedy in Vienna in June that the United States would under no circumstances agree to the creation of a peace treaty to be signed with two German states.

In the case of the Berlin crisis, the main motive of the unilateral, "offensive" move by the GDR was stopping the flow of the East German refugees, because its current scale gravely threatened the economic and political stability of the GDR.[23] The solution, suggested by the Soviets—making Berlin a free city—was not acceptable to the West, for there was no guarantee that, after the withdrawal of the Western occupying forces, the GDR would not annex West Berlin, which would have caused a radical change in the European status quo. In the end, the only rational solution seemed to be the building of the Berlin Wall. It is not a coincidence that, by early August 1961, Kennedy himself also deemed this the most efficient solution. "He [Khrushchev] must do something to stop the flow of refugees—perhaps a wall?"—he rhetorically asked his advisor, Walt Rostow.[24] On hearing about the closing of the sector border in Berlin, he reacted with great relief and said that it was "not a very nice solution but a wall is a hell of a lot better than a war."[25]

In reality, his public statement made at the end of July was exactly aimed at facilitating such an option. In his speech, he basically limited American political goals to the protection of West Berlin only, implicitly waiving the right of the West to control *all* of Berlin.[26] Khrushchev understood the message and acted accordingly. In turn, the West paid a serious price from a moral point of view, because, while saving West Berlin, it had let down the East Germans, who up until then had enjoyed a special "most-favored nation" position: in the Soviet bloc, sealed off hermetically from the West by the Iron Curtain since 1949, they alone could freely emigrate to the FRG. Now the bizarre phenomenon of a prison state with an open border to the West was over; the GDR was turned into a "normal" Soviet bloc state. Thus, while the West in general and the United States in particular was not responsible for "selling out" East Central Europe in Yalta, as is believed by many even today, and similarly was not betraying Hungary by not intervening at the time of the 1956 revolution, in reality it was now betraying most of the East Germans. The tacit deal, offered by Kennedy to Khrushchev, led to saving the freedom of 2.5 million West Berliners, who, we should not forget, had originally been *East* Germans. The price of this freedom, however, was to collaborate with the Soviets in installing the Iron Curtain in the middle of Berlin and thus stopping the free emigration of seventeen million "real" East Germans to the West. But did Kennedy have another option besides this historic deal? We can argue that, in reality, this was the best available compromise under the circumstances. The erection of the Berlin Wall was also the most acceptable solution as far as realpolitik was concerned because it did not fundamentally violate the European status quo, so the interests of the Western powers were not hurt substantively. Although formally this was also a violation of the agreement on Berlin concluded at the Potsdam Conference in 1945, as the city was to be administered jointly by the four occupying powers, in reality joint administration had already ceased at the time of the Berlin blockade in 1948. Symbolic Western control of the Soviet zone of Berlin was also not hampered, and Western military patrols indeed continued to make regular visits into the eastern part of the city.

The Western powers could have rightfully implemented retaliations due to the *unilateral* nature of the solution, as was expected by many at the time, among them the leaders of the Soviet bloc themselves, who anticipated a Western economic embargo. Instead, the American leadership rationally acknowledged the security interests of the Soviet bloc, knowing that in a similar case they would have acted in the same way. Their goal was not the deepening of the conflict but just the opposite: to facilitate a peaceful solution to the crisis and to maintain the possibility of East–West cooperation. Because of this, while in Western propaganda the Berlin Wall quickly became the symbol of a divided Europe, in reality this step was valued in Washington as the best possible solution of the problem.[27]

Between 3 and 6 August 1961, barely a few months after the meeting of the WP PCC in March, the leaders of the WP countries were again convened in Moscow to discuss the German issue. It is now clear that Khrushchev and East German leader Walter Ulbricht had agreed before the meeting on the closing of certain sectors of the border in Berlin, but it is still not evident from the available documents whether the participants were informed about the actual decision to build a wall in Berlin.[28] At the talks, the Soviet proposition was discussed and accepted, which stated that by the end of the year the German peace treaty must be signed, if possible, with both German states, and if it is not, then with the GDR separately. This resolution, which became part of the communiqué issued at the meeting, can be regarded as a gesture to the leaders of the GDR because, after the building of the Berlin Wall, the Soviets did not actually want to create new sources of conflict. In the given situation, even the propaganda value of the issue was not the same as it had been before. The main goal of the meeting was primarily the preparation of the WP member states for the handling of the new international situation arising from the forthcoming unilateral move by the GDR authorities. This mainly meant that the Soviet bloc had to prepare for serious countermeasures in the field of economic relations, because it was known from Soviet intelligence sources that, despite a unilateral action, the West was not planning any military move.[29] At the conference, however, the WP states, at Soviet initiative, decided on a considerable increase in their defense budget. The basis for this decision was the principle that "unified actions and adequate military preparedness are the necessary conditions to avoid a war."[30]

Thus, the states of the Eastern bloc knew that there was no need to prepare for a military confrontation. The nature of the measures to enhance combat readiness in Hungary during the Berlin crisis also confirms that the Warsaw Pact states did not expect the development of a war situation. General mobilization was not ordered, and, on the basis of the directive from the WP Unified Armed Forces on 17 August 1961—in addition to other regulations—only furlough was suspended in the army and a mere 3,092 reservists, including 258 officers, were called up.[31]

At the same time, they were convinced that they must prepare for not only a "simple" Western economic blockade but for an East–West "economic war" as retaliation. To direct and control the joint "economic warfare," a special committee was set up within the Comecon, and it was also decided that special committees be created to coordinate the work of several related fields.[32] As it later became clear, the overly pessimistic prognosis that had predicted an economic war was based on the bad conscience of the leaders of the Soviet bloc rather than on the realistic analysis of the probable reaction of the West. At this meeting of the WP PCC, the Hungarian delegation also contributed "constructively" to the enhancement of the extraordinary situation: they suggested that every party should appoint a member of its Political Committee as a liaison officer and thus create a virtual ad hoc committee in charge of securing quick and effective multilateral consultation on the German issue.[33]

To conclude, the building of the Berlin Wall—however negative its effects from a moral point of view—turned out to be the most rational manner of solving the problem. What actually happened in Berlin was that the harsh rules of the Cold War were being put into effect, according to which a Communist police state should have no open borders. In reality, the situation did not become abnormal *after* the erection of the Berlin Wall but rather *before*. Under the circumstances, the GDR, having already lost 20 percent of its population between 1948 and 1961, simply could not afford to have open borders with the West any longer; otherwise, they would have had to reckon with the gradual emptying of the country.

At the same time, the Western powers' occupational rights and interests in Berlin were not violated. The securing of the connecting routes had not fallen into the hands of the East German authorities; the social system and the autonomy of West Berlin had not changed. This is exactly why, against all previous warnings and threats, the West basically accepted the new situation quickly and easily. At the level of rhetoric, they naturally condemned both the GDR and the Soviet Union for this unilateral and unlawful step, but retaliation basically finished with that.

Hungary was mainly affected in three areas by the Berlin crisis and the WP decisions about it: (1) accelerated military developments, (2) preparation for a Western economic embargo, and (3) governmental centralization in preparation for a period of enduring international tension. From the military development and modernization campaign issued at the meeting of the WP PCC in March 1961 and reinforced by the conference of the East Central European countries' party leaders held in Moscow between 3 and 6 August, the Hungarian army was not an exception anymore: the country had to eliminate its backlog—and do it at an accelerated pace. So, it was finally the end of the exceptional status of Hungary, in which the country, referring to the economic hardship of the reconstruction period after 1956, spent considerably less on defense than the other WP member states.[34]

The army headcount was increased from the 78,000 approved in March 1961 to 85,000, then a further increase was decided in September 1962. The targeted headcount was 88,000–90,000 after the fall of 1965, and 92,000–95,000 by 1970.[35] The key directions of army development were also identified: primarily anti-aircraft defense and armored forces. It turned out that the weaponry of the Hungarian army as well as its organizational structure was extremely obsolete; therefore, a new army command had to be established by dividing and reallocating the functions of the Ministry of Defense in order to increase military efficiency. In addition, referring to the tense international situation, all these steps were to be executed in a short period of time; thus, the new organizational structure of the army was in place by 3 August 1961.[36] Marshal Grechko, the supreme commander of the Warsaw Pact Unified Armed Forces, also indicated that the Hungarian army might potentially be equipped with missiles carrying nuclear warheads in the foreseeable future.[37]

In addition to the restructuring of the army, the Hungarian party leadership was concerned about the future development of economic relations. The possibility of an "economic war" projected by the Berlin crisis seemed to gravely endanger the favorable development of the economic relations maintained with the Federal Republic of Germany. At the HSWP CC session on 1 August 1961, János Kádár stated that approximately 30 percent of the country's foreign trade was conducted with Western countries, and one-quarter of that volume involved the FRG. In other words, the FRG was Hungary's most important Western economic partner.[38] "Of course, this is what the German issue means for us," pointed out János Kádár when addressing the core of the problem in a CC session two months before.[39]

The Hungarian leadership expected that the Berlin crisis would lead to the development of persistent tension in international politics, and especially in the East–West relationship, and that reacting to the new situation would be a more complex task than it was previously. They believed that the forecasted East–West "economic war" would encumber the development of Hungary's key Western economic relations, and the envisaged loss of foreign trade with the FRG would be especially difficult to replace. In order to be able to conduct a Hungarian foreign policy that would also meet the requirements of this new international situation, government centralization was implemented. In the new government formed on 12 September 1961, János Kádár took over the post of prime minister from the aging Ferenc Münnich, thus reuniting party leader and premier functions and bringing back the model applied between

1956 and 1958, which had seemed temporary at the time. Another motivation for Kádár could have been to follow the example of his mentor, as Khrushchev himself had held these two positions since 1958. The post of the foreign minister was assigned to a person whose career was rather unique in a Communist state. János Péter was educated in the West, in Paris and Glasgow, and became a Protestant pastor in 1935. In 1945 he joined the Foreign Ministry, working in the department responsible for the preparations for the peace treaty, and he was a member of the Hungarian delegation at the Paris Peace Conference in 1946. From 1949 to 1956, he was a Protestant bishop, and beginning in 1950 he was one of Hungary's representatives in the World Peace Council. He became first deputy foreign minister in February 1958 and was appointed foreign minister on 13 September 1961. He had much more wide-ranging international (especially Western) connections than did his predecessor, and during his time in the ministry (1961–73), he proved to be the most ambitious and imaginative Hungarian foreign affairs leader of the Cold War era.

The Challenge of Early *Ostpolitik*, 1962–1963

As is well known, no "economic war," not even a general Western embargo, followed the construction of the Berlin Wall. On the contrary, the economic relations of the WP members with West Germany even gained significance in the following years. This was mainly due to a slowly changing attitude among the FRG leadership. The first step on the road to a new approach to dealing with the Soviet bloc, later dubbed *Ostpolitik*, was the exchange of commercial missions with Bulgaria, Hungary, Poland, and Romania in the fall of 1963, resulting in a noticeable improvement in economic relations in the following years.

By the early 1960s, the Soviet bloc was clearly divided into an *economy-oriented* (Hungary, Romania, and Bulgaria) and a *security-concerned* sub-bloc (the GDR, Poland, and Czechoslovakia) as far as the German question was concerned.[40] Hungary, together with Bulgaria and Romania, had no serious unsettled issues with the FRG; therefore, they were seriously interested in economic cooperation, increasing trade, and taking over cutting-edge technologies. In the case of Hungary, the FRG was the country's most important Western economic partner since the middle of the 1950s, and it kept this position until 1989. Therefore, the FRG played a crucial and special role in Hungary rebuilding her economic ties with the Western countries. This relationship was motivated by a number of important factors, such as geographic proximity, existing traditional economic links, the dominance of the German language among Hungarian economic experts, and even the similarity of the standardization system that had been established on a German sample at the time.[41] On the other hand, this was the same West Germany that, in the Soviet bloc's propaganda of the early and mid-1960s, appeared as the most dangerous European "satellite" of American imperialism, aiming at acquiring nuclear weapons, and as a "revanchist" power, aiming at a revision of the 1945 European status quo. Thus, the Hungarian leadership followed a dual policy: as to the German question, they loyally followed the general political line of the Soviet bloc, while, in the field of economic relations, they tried to exploit the favorable situation that evolved by the emerging of détente since 1953 and especially 1955.[42]

In this drive, the year 1963 was a clear caesura for Hungarian foreign policy, in both a symbolic and a practical sense. After the removal of the Hungarian issue from the agenda of the UN General Assembly, the period of Hungary's international isolation following the 1956 Hungarian Revolution finally ended. That is how Hungary could become part of the spectacular result of the first *Ostpolitik* in the fall of 1963, when—as a result of secret negotiations initiated by the FRG in April 1962—commercial missions were mutually established with Bulgaria, Hungary, Poland, and Romania. In the case of Hungary and Poland, a Polish and a Hungarian commercial bureau had been operating in Frankfurt since 1946, so an agreement in 1963 allowed the FRG to open similar missions in Budapest and Warsaw, and the missions were mutually given diplomatic status. That move clearly opened a new chapter in Hungarian–West German relations.[43]

The Lessons of the Cuban Missile Crisis in the Soviet Bloc

Hardly a year after the Berlin crisis peaked, a major East–West conflict erupted due to the installation of Soviet nuclear missiles in Cuba, bringing the world the closest it had come to a direct superpower clash during the Cold War era. The unique feature of the Cuban missile crisis of October 1962 was that, in this case, originally the idea of changing the status quo by exporting revolution to Cuba had never occurred to the Soviet leadership, yet it still arose, in an indigenous way, thanks to the victory of the revolution led by Fidel Castro.

We now know that, during the crisis management, both parties showed great responsibility and flexibility and an ability for working out a compromise solution, although at the time this could be publicly perceivable only on the Soviet side. At the categorical American response, Khrushchev quickly retreated as soon as it became apparent to him that, otherwise, there was a serious threat of a direct superpower clash. In his message on 28 October, Khrushchev promised to withdraw the missiles, and this did happen relatively soon (at least the medium-range and intermediate-range missiles, as opposed to the tactical nuclear weapons, still essentially undetected), in early November.

We now know that the Soviets would have retreated without conditions, but the American leadership, being unaware of this and also extremely worried about the potential escalation of the crisis, facilitated the Soviet retreat even further: Kennedy, besides making a public announcement promising that the United States would not attack Cuba, made another, secret concession as well: he promised the withdrawal, within four to five months, of American Jupiter missiles from Turkey.[44] This meant nothing less than that the American administration made a secret pact with the Soviets behind the back of its NATO allies. It is no wonder that, in exchange, Kennedy asked that there be no written traces of this deal on the American side. So now it was the Soviet's turn: Ambassador Dobrynin, after some hesitation, was eventually willing to withdraw the Soviet letter that contained the American promise.[45]

We can argue that the peaceful solution of the crisis was at the same time a victory and a fiasco for both superpowers. The United States successfully barred the construction of a Soviet nuclear striking force on the American continent, but it had to give up on invading Cuba and thus had to tolerate the existence of a Communist bridgehead in the vicinity of the United States. For the Soviets, it had caused a significant loss of prestige from the perspective of international politics, as they had to withdraw their missiles from Cuba; nevertheless, they had achieved one of their main aims: securing the survival of the Cuban Communist regime. Thus, their maximum goal was not achieved but their minimum project succeeded.

Based on all of this, it can be said that during the resolution of the Berlin and Cuban crises, which are still deemed to be the most dangerous ones from the aspect of world peace, the threat of starting a third world war was in reality not as immense as it was regarded in world public opinion at the time. And this was exactly because, while solving the crises, the leaders of the superpowers showed a great sense of responsibility and moderation. The lesson of these two grave crises was clear for both parties: in the future, the emergence of such dangerous conflicts that could result in a direct superpower clash and thus threaten to destroy human civilization must be avoided at all costs, primarily through the perfection of the cooperation between Washington and Moscow. Arguably, the peaceful solution of the Berlin and Cuban crises became further successful test cases of the mechanism of compelled cooperation between the superpowers. All of this significantly contributed to the creation of new, more effective institutionalized forms of superpower cooperation and to the success of the new wave of the détente process unfolding from the early 1960s. The first spectacular results of this understanding were the establishment of the hot line between the White House and the Kremlin and the conclusion of the partial nuclear test ban treaty in July and August 1963, respectively.[46]

During the conduct of the Cuban missile crisis, Moscow's policy toward its allies was exactly the opposite of the one it had followed while solving the problem of Berlin. At that time, the Soviet leadership consulted continuously and frequently with the WP member states, and with the most concerned GDR, the coordination was downright intensive.[47] This time, however, the Soviet action was prepared in the topmost secrecy; moreover, during the crisis, they did not inform even the Cubans about the possible course of events.[48] This is why news of the evolving crisis—which they heard from the media—caught the countries of East Central Europe totally by surprise and unprepared.

In Budapest, it was not only the danger of a direct East–West military conflict and the fear of a new world war that caused worries. It was also alarming that even in the event of a peaceful resolution of the crisis, war hysteria could develop in society, which would be hard for the leadership to control. Such a turn could then seriously disturb the progress of internal pacification that had been going on successfully since the upheavals (i.e., the revolution and Soviet invasion) of 1956.

Based on the currently available sources, a precise picture still cannot be drawn about the Hungarian leadership's actions, or of what information it possessed and when, during the crisis. At 10 A.M. on 23 October, the Hungarian minister of defense received the following telegram via military channels from Marshal Andrei Grechko, commander in chief of the Supreme Command of the Unified Armed Forces of the Warsaw Pact: "Considering US President D. Kennedy's [sic] provocative announcement on 23 October 1962 and the increased danger of the outbreak of war caused by the Western aggressors, I hereby propose:

1. To introduce increased combat readiness for all troops of the services of the armed forces subordinated to the Supreme Command [of the Unified Armed Forces].
2. Please report on the arrangements made by you on 24 October."

The "proposal" was put into effect on the same day, and in Hungary mostly the air force and air defense units were put into combat readiness.[49] The same day, the HSWP PC held a regular meeting but, according to the transcript of the session, the situation in Cuba was not even mentioned.[50] The session was probably over by the time the news of Grechko's telegram reached the political leadership.

Sometime later, however, after the news about a lengthy Soviet government declaration arrived in Budapest,[51] an ad hoc group of top leaders under the direction of János Kádár, and including the deputy prime ministers and the foreign minister, worded a short declaration on behalf of the Hungarian government in which it condemned the aggressive moves of the United States, threatening the independence of Cuba.[52] The government itself, however, was convened only two days later, on 25 October, when the cabinet members had to retroactively approve the announcement. However, there must have been considerable hesitation among the leadership—perhaps they were hoping to get more information from Moscow via diplomatic or party channels—so the declaration was not published the next day, on 24 October, but on the 25th in the HSWP's daily, *Népszabadság*. At the meeting of the Council of Ministers on 25 October, Kádár, who since September 1961 had held the positions of both prime minister and first secretary of the HSWP, enlightened the cabinet members about the Cuban situation, probably based on the information gathered from Marshal Grechko.[53] His report, however, as we now know, was very deficient. Kádár said, after reviewing the American moves, that combat readiness was ordered in the Soviet Union, but reserves were not called in. A significant number of new Soviet forces were transported to the territory of the GDR, while Poland made troop reinforcements on the Oder-Neisse border, and Bulgaria did the same at its borders with Turkey and Greece. Besides these measures, in every member state of the Warsaw Pact, the militaries were put on combat readiness. Kádár also told the government that, at the "request" of Marshal Grechko, the Hungarian military leadership had introduced the necessary measures; thus in Hungary, mostly the air force and air defense units were put into readiness. This was a clear admission of the fact that the Hungarian army was actually mobilized directly by Moscow, without the knowledge of the local party leadership. That was why the Council of Ministers now had to retroactively approve the move of the "extraordinary cabinet"—as the improvised emergency session of a few top leaders on 24 October was now called euphemistically.[54]

Although the Hungarian leadership obviously did not possess adequate information about the situation, Kádár rightly evaluated the crisis as the gravest international conflict since the Second World War. While he evidently had no firsthand information from Moscow, as a pragmatist and one who knew Khrushchev's thinking rather well, he concluded that the conflict would very likely be solved peacefully. This conclusion rested mainly on two factors: there was no clash between Soviet and U.S. ships "when the blockade and the ships should have clashed," and the Soviet Union in the meantime had announced that Moscow was ready to participate in a summit meeting. This convinced Kádár that "the most critical danger [wa]s over and diplomacy ha[d] come to the fore."

In accordance with this, the government authorized the "extraordinary cabinet"—now complemented by the minister of defense—to take the necessary measures in connection with the crisis. During the following days, most probably this ad hoc crisis management body handled the problems resulting from the crisis, although no documents of any kind have been found pertaining to its activity. The official organs of the Hungarian party did not deal with the situation connected to the Cuban crisis, according to the minutes of the PC and secretariat meetings held on 2 November.[55] Prior to that, on 25 October, the secretariat had decided by instant voting to send an MTI (Hungarian News Agency) reporter to Havana. This also suggests that the leadership had already ruled out the possibility of a superpower clash at that stage. It seems the idea of convening an extraordinary session of the Central Committee, which would have been a logical move in such a grave situation, had also not arisen; at any rate, no such meeting took place. In the given situation, the Hungarian leadership could not do much, because they could have no impact of any kind on the course of events, although the potential result of the crisis, if disadvantageous, would have crucially affected Hungary's fate as well. That is why the only field for activity became that of propaganda: state and party authorities tried to strengthen the population's empathy for Cuba and organized solidarity meetings in factories and plants.

The most spectacular and largest mass rally was held in the Sports Hall in Budapest on 26 October, where the main speakers were Deputy Prime Minister Gyula Kállai and Cuban ambassador Quintín Pino Machado. At the rally, a message was adopted to be sent to UN acting secretary-general U Thant, asking for his mediation to solve the crisis.[56] In another important gesture of solidarity, János Kádár received the Cuban ambassador along with two journalists from the Cuban paper *Revolution*, and their conversation was published on the front page of *Népszabadság* next to the Hungarian government declaration on 25 October. Nevertheless, it is striking that when on 31 October Kádár addressed the party conference in Budapest, in preparation for the Eighth Congress of the HSWP held in late November, his speech contained not one word about Cuba or any other international issue.[57] According to the confidential reports on the mood of the people at the time of the crisis, there was no war panic in the country; the population trusted that the Soviet Union would avert the danger of a violent conflagration successfully.[58] All of this is quite plausible, especially as the leadership did everything it could to make the people understand as little as possible about the true nature of the crisis.

Significant firsthand Soviet information was not given to the Hungarian leadership until the beginning of November. At a special closed meeting of the HSWP PC on 5 November, János Kádár reported that, during a phone call with Khrushchev that morning, they had agreed that Kádár would immediately travel to Moscow.[59] In the first days of November, many Soviet bloc leaders had visited the Soviet capital,[60] so Kádár's explanation seems logical, according to which the meeting was requested by him, because the "people could misunderstand" if the Hungarians did not participate in such a consultation. However, another explanation is possible: on 2 November, British citizen Greville Wynne was arrested on charges of espionage in Budapest while visiting the Budapest International Fair.[61] On the 14th he was transferred to the Soviet authorities with the explanation that most of his crimes were committed against the Soviet Union. Indeed, Wynne was a British entrepreneur and frequent visitor to Moscow, acting as an intermediary for the famous Soviet spy Oleg Penkovsky, who was selling military secrets to British intelligence. Wynne was sentenced for spying to eight years in prison in May 1963. He was released in exchange for Soviet spy Gordon Lonsdale, serving a twenty-five-year prison term in Great Britain, in 1964. We know nothing of any similar case, neither from previous nor from later times, so it is not impossible that this important international issue was at least one of the main reasons for Kádár's visit to the Soviet capital on 7–10 November. The information about the Cuban crisis acquired in Moscow was not much more extensive than what was already known by the Hungarian leaders: the Soviet Union reached its goal, for basically it had managed to acquire an American guarantee that the existence of the Cuban Communist regime would be tolerated.[62]

The leaders of the Warsaw Pact member states learned a serious lesson from the Cuban missile crisis, as they suddenly realized the extent of their defenselessness and vulnerability. It was especially hard for them to understand that if the Soviet leaders had considered the Berlin crisis, which had generated significantly lower international tension, important enough to hold regular consultations with the allies, then how could it have happened that a third world war had nearly broken out while the members of the Eastern military bloc just had to stand by and wait for the denouement without any substantial information?[63] Had they known that, contrary to the claims of Khrushchev's propaganda, it was not the Soviet Union but the United States that had a significant superiority with respect to intercontinental missiles at the time of the crisis! It was the Romanian leadership that drew the most radical conclusion from the case: in October 1963, the Romanian foreign minister, requesting utmost secrecy, informed his American counterpart that Romania would remain neutral in the case of a nuclear world war. On the grounds of this standpoint, he requested that the Americans not set Romania as a target for a nuclear strike.[64] Thus, the Romanian "trend" of conducting a deviant policy, which had appeared in the economic area as early as 1958 and was officially declared in 1964, can be attributed, at least to a significant extent, to the impact of the Cuban missile crisis.

The Polish leadership was equally indignant at the events; furthermore, it considered that the Soviet leaders did not understand the significance of the affair and that the Kremlin would continue to regard preliminary consultations with the allies as unimportant. Among other things, the Polish leaders objected to Moscow's lack of consultation with Warsaw Pact member states concerning the nuclear test ban treaty, especially since they had to sign it well after the contract had been concluded. During his negotiations in Budapest in November 1963, Gomułka stated that Cuba intended to join the Warsaw Pact, which would pose a significant threat to the security of the Eastern bloc as well as world peace.[65] Therefore, he firmly stated that, should the request be officially submitted, Poland would veto Cuba's admission. A similar negative Polish stand prevented another Soviet bloc ally, Mongolia, from joining the Warsaw Pact during the same year. This plan was seen in Warsaw as a clearly anti-Chinese move that was to seriously exacerbate the Soviet bloc's relations with Beijing and make the Sino–Soviet split irreversible. The Polish position was based on the legal argument that the Warsaw Pact was a European defense alliance; therefore, extending it to Asia would be a violation of the statute of the organization.[66] To avoid similar unexpected challenges, the Polish leaders proposed intensifying preliminary consultation within the Warsaw Pact, and significantly boosting the political role of individual member states.

The East German leaders were also critical of Soviet behavior during the Cuban missile crisis. Years later, Walter Ulbricht complained to the Romanian leaders: "It goes without saying that we must make improvements since we do not want things to happen as in 1962, during the crisis in the Caribbean Sea. If we are a pact intended for defense and fight in common, the steps that are to be taken must be the result of everybody's will."[67]

Although the Hungarian leadership was much more cautious in criticizing the Soviet behavior than the Poles were, it basically agreed with the Polish views pertaining to the nature of future cooperation within the Warsaw Pact. It was clearly indicated by the fact that Kádár, during his visit to Moscow in July 1963, proposed the establishment of a Committee of Foreign Ministers long before the plans to reform the Warsaw Pact were officially placed on the agenda in 1965–66.[68] The clear objective of the initiative was to place the Soviet leadership under the pressure of necessity for consultation and information provision as well as to enforce the multilateral nature of the decision-making process. Kádár clearly stated to Khrushchev that "the question is that there must not be a case when the Soviet government publishes various statements and the other governments read them in the newspaper. . . .

I thought of a preliminary consultation. I have also told [Khrushchev] that experience showed it is better to argue sooner rather than later."[69] The proposal was rejected by the Soviet leaders—who themselves came forward with the same idea two years later—on the pretext that at a time when a "sovereignty disease" had broken out (referring to Romania), the reaction of the member states would be wrong, and they would only misunderstand the intention.[70]

It is interesting that the Soviet leaders, who had actually suggested the idea at the cradle of the Warsaw Pact in January 1956 and then supported it from 1965 on, flatly rejected the proposal. Khrushchev's argument was based on the pretext that Romanian opposition blocked this plan; Romania, however, opposed only the *institutionalization* of foreign policy coordination and in fact was herself pressing for preliminary consultations, as was clearly presented at the meeting of deputy foreign ministers in Berlin in February 1966.[71]

Cold War Conflicts Revisited: Real and Apparent Crises

After World War II, and especially until the mid-1960s, both Eastern and Western public opinion was determined by an ideological and a strategic East–West opposition, thus automatically labeling all major internal crises within the Eastern bloc as well as other conflicts of the East–West relationship without differentiation as East–West (i.e., Cold War) crises. More importantly, this pattern has been applied by scholars as well, incorporating all these conflicts into the general history of the East–West relationship. The multinational archival evidence now available for scholars, however, proves convincingly that not every crisis that occurred during the Cold War era was attributable to the Cold War as far as its character is concerned. Therefore, we should divide the international conflicts of the Cold War era into two distinct categories: *real* and *pseudo crises*. Thus, most notably, all the intra-bloc conflicts of the Soviet bloc were not real crises in this sense, because they did not exceed the earlier outlined cooperation framework of the superpowers, in spite of what their propaganda said; namely, they did not cause a real threat to the interests of the opposing political-military bloc. They did not challenge the post–World War II European status quo and consequently did not disturb the East–West relationship. Such *pseudo East–West crises* that had their effect only at the level of public opinion and propaganda were the 1953 Berlin uprising, the events of 1956 in Poland and Hungary, the invasion of Czechoslovakia in 1968, and the Polish conflict in 1980–81. These were, of course, serious *internal* crises both in the countries where they occurred and within the Soviet bloc per se. Although these conflicts were rooted in the domestic situation, they were not isolated from international impacts. In fact, they happened in a Cold War constellation, and thus their initiation and course were partly affected while their outcome was basically determined by the Cold War. They were also perceived as real conflicts between East and West by contemporary public opinion (but not by policy makers) both in the East and the West, and this evaluation has survived in public memory even after the end of the Cold War. In this limited sense (and only in this sense) they could be called Cold War crises, but they were not crises of the East–West relationship.

The Suez crisis in 1956 must also be mentioned here, a serious conflict that happened simultaneously with the Hungarian Revolution but did not have an effect on the East–West relationship. Rather, it was an intra-bloc conflict within the Western alliance, as the Soviet leadership assessed the situation realistically and decided not to be involved in it, as they were not willing to directly confront the West in the defense of Egypt.[72]

Fundamentally different from these conflicts were those crises that did create a serious clash of interest between the East and the West, and some of which raised the possibility of a general East–West military confrontation. Such real Cold War crises were the two Berlin crises (in 1948–49 and then between 1958 and 1961), the Korean War, the Chinese offshore islands crises in the mid- and late 1950s,[73] and the Cuban missile crisis. The war in Vietnam and the Soviet invasion of Afghanistan were special cases of real crises. These crises represented a real threat to world peace, and they had a long-lasting effect on the East–West relationship, both in their own time and in the long run, as opposed to the previously mentioned pseudo crises.

Similarly, this new interpretation of the essence of Cold War could explain a contradiction that is seemingly difficult to unravel: why the most outspoken and direct military threat of the whole era (the "missile notes" of Soviet prime minister Bulganin) happened during the Middle East pseudo crisis in 1956, while recent sources reveal how restrained in fact the leaders of the superpowers were, showing a strong sense of responsibility and well-meaning when it came to rectifying the Cuban crisis, the largest ever threat to global peace to date.[74]

The Kádár Doctrine: Transition from the Khrushchev to the Brezhnev Era

On 14 October 1964, the plenum of the CPSU CC relieved Khrushchev of his posts as leader of the Communist Party and head of the government by replacing him with Leonid Brezhnev as first secretary, and elected Alexei Kosygin as prime minister. János Kádár, the leader of the HSWP and also prime minister since 1961, who was on an official visit to Poland at the time, was shocked by the news, as the decision was completely unexpected.

For Kádár, the deposed Soviet leader was not simply his current "boss" in Moscow; during the years since 1956, a genuine friendly relationship had evolved between the two men, although the Hungarian leader was eighteen years younger than his mentor. One of the rare sources illuminating the nature of this relationship is a "love letter" from Kádár dated 21 June 1961 addressed to Khrushchev, from which the following statement is quoted: "I also have enough things to do and concerns. That is why your last call filled me with warm feelings, but at the same time it confused me as well. I was surprised that you, with immeasurably more things to do, in addition to your other concerns, could also take the attention and time to congratulate me on my birthday. Your thoughtfulness fills me with profound gratitude, for which I hereby thank you. I cannot and do not want to flatter you, but even without beautiful words you must know and feel what my attitude towards your person is."[75] Kádár, indeed, was not a flattering type, and no similar letter was ever written by him to any of his mentor's successors, including Gorbachev.

As Kádár's "special relationship" with Khrushchev was generally known, the "best pupil" now rightly feared that a change in Soviet politics, the start of a possible process of re-Stalinization, could jeopardize all the policy he had made in his own country thus far. He later honestly revealed his own state of mind to Brezhnev at that moment by saying that "some Hungarian intellectuals even raised the question for themselves: who will come home first, Kádár or Rákosi?"[76]

Thus, Khrushchev's removal created the first grave crisis in the relationship of the CPSU and the HSWP since the 1956 Hungarian Revolution, which became also public. Information about the developments in Moscow appeared in the 17 October 1964 issue of the party daily *Népszabadság* with the title "Tovább a lenini úton" (Forward on Lenin's path), and Khrushchev's merits were mentioned in it, even if only in a half sentence. It was also unprecedented that, in the immediate period after Khrushchev's removal, both the HSWP and the CPSU mutually censored each other's press communiqués. The Soviets omitted from the communiqué those parts of the HSWP's announcement that contained Khrushchev's merits, while the Hungarians deleted from the Soviet announcement what they considered an exaggeration of Khrushchev's mistakes.

Therefore, in order to secure political backing for his standpoint, Kádár summoned a meeting of the HSWP CC on 23 October; then, referring to the discussion that took place there, he turned to Brezhnev by letter the next day. In the letter, Kádár stated that the HSWP leadership accepted the decision made by the CPSU based on the information received from Moscow but did not approve of the way Khrushchev was removed because his merits were not mentioned.[77] Via other channels, he also indicated that he would like to go to

Moscow in the middle of November for two to three days to consult with the new Soviet leadership about "issues that concern the two sister parties."[78]

On 29 October 1964, however, the Chinese Communist Party (CCP), interpreting the dismissal of their greatest opponent, the "revisionist" Khrushchev, as a great opportunity to lead the new Soviet leadership back to the "right path," unexpectedly informed the CPSU that, for the forty-seventh anniversary of the October Revolution, they would like to send a party and government delegation under the leadership of Prime Minister Zhou Enlai to Moscow. The CCP also suggested that, for the occasion, the CPSU CC invite all the Socialist countries' party and governmental delegations. The new Soviet leadership, after having consulted with the parties of the European Socialist countries, including the HSWP, announced that they supported the Chinese suggestion, hoping that this unexpected opportunity would contribute to the improvement of the Soviet bloc's relations with China.[79] Thus, Kádár's first clarifying meeting with the new Soviet leaders took place during this visit in Moscow, on 9 and 10 November.

Kádár was aware that the discussions with the new Soviet leaders would be crucial for the future of Soviet–Hungarian relations, and he felt that, for the first time, he could negotiate from a relatively strong position. While he had a close personal relationship with Khrushchev, that did not mean that he ever had the chance to talk with him as an equal partner, due to his outstanding international stature as the leader of a superpower as well as the world's Communist movement. Brezhnev and Kosygin, on the other hand, as the former himself openly admitted during the talks, "compared to Khrushchev, are still young men; they do not have this kind of prestige."[80]

Kádár, on the other hand, while he was still only fifty-two, was the only leader in the Soviet bloc who had successfully managed political and economic consolidation after a "counterrevolution" in his country. By 1964, just eight years after political stability had been restored, most political prisoners had been released, agriculture was not only entirely collectivized but also efficient, the standard of living of the population was steadily rising, and after long years of Western boycott, the international reputation of the country had been elevated to the level of that of the other Soviet bloc countries. All of this resulted in changing Hungary's position from the "weakest link" to a success story in a relatively short period of time, which consequently made Kádár, besides Gomułka, the most successful leader of the Soviet bloc by the mid-1960s.

Therefore, Kádár, sensing his relatively strong and his partners' relatively weak positions, did not limit the agenda to complaining about the way Khrushchev was removed, but he wanted to create a tabula rasa and to base Soviet–Hungarian relations—and indirectly Soviet–East European relations—

on a new foundation. According to this, while the leading and dominant role of the Soviet Union would remain unquestionable, the Soviet bloc member states should be given a limited partnership position, and their interests and position should be taken much more seriously by Moscow than they had been earlier. In the future, the results and lessons of building Socialism should be mutually exchanged among the countries of the camp and should not be limited to following the Soviet experience, as in the past.

To make their position look more serious, the Hungarian delegation led by Kádár prepared a written memorandum containing fourteen points on the topics they wanted to discuss, which was presented to the CPSU CC on 9 November 1964.[81] These points were actually phrased as short theses, representing the HSWP's position on a number of important issues.

However, while the Hungarians expected to have a meeting with Brezhnev on the following day, they were unexpectedly invited to start talks at thirty minutes' notice. Thus, at the meeting, Kádár put emphasis on pointing out that the Hungarian delegation's position was based on the 23 October resolution of the HSWP CC, which discussed the reactions to the 14 October resolution of the CPSU CC in Hungary. It is hard to decide whether the numerology, including two important elements referring to the Hungarian revolution in 1956, was a mere coincidence or if it was a direct or an unconscious reference by Kádár: 23 October was the anniversary of the outbreak of the revolution, while the uprising itself was preceded by a big students' rally in Budapest, compiling their political demand in sixteen points (in one circulated version, fourteen points). In any event, at previous meetings with the CPSU leaders, the Hungarian delegation never submitted their points prior to the negotiations in writing. Since the Hungarian memorandum was handed over just a few hours earlier, no substantive negotiations were possible on this occasion, and another appointment was made for the next day.

At the second meeting on 10 November, Brezhnev informed the Hungarian delegation that he had discussed the memorandum the night before with Mikoyan, Kosygin, Podgorny, Suslov, Andropov, and Ponormarev, and all of them thought that Kádár's letter was written in the spirit of friendship, brotherhood, and respect.[82]

Brezhnev agreed that friendship between the Soviet Union and Hungary should be strengthened in the future regarding its content and form. There are so many issues in the world that the spectacular party and government delegation meetings every three years cannot be considered the only and most suitable mode of contact, he continued, and the leaders of the two states must meet more often informally. Trying to show considerable openness and a cooperative attitude, he stated that the leaders of the CPSU were aware that they alone could not solve every issue; thus, they required the help and initiative of the sister parties.[83]

Brezhnev agreed concerning the second point of the memorandum, with the explanations concerning the main line of the parties' activity. They invariably stand in the line of the Twentieth Congress of the CPSU. At the two-day presidium meeting, they underlined Khrushchev's merits on the development of the Twentieth, Twenty-First, and Twenty-Second Congresses. Brezhnev then explained that Khrushchev's error was that he spoke too much about the Twentieth Congress's resolutions, but he did not do enough to make them reality. For example, Khrushchev claimed that Stalin was responsible for the shortage of potatoes, but Stalin had been dead for twelve years. Speaking less and doing more to make the resolutions of the Twentieth Congress a reality—that is the party's main task right now.

The Soviet leader stated that, in the bilateral relations between the two countries, the best comradely cooperation had prevailed, and Brezhnev declared that he was certain that this friendship would strengthen in the future. The Soviet leaders' relationship, behavior, and feelings toward Hungary had not changed—and would not change. Regarding the Hungarian observations about the way Khrushchev was dismissed and about his mistakes, Brezhnev stated that he understood the situation of the HSWP, but he asked that the Hungarians understand the CPSU's situation as well. If he had been in the place of Novotny or Kádár, he would also have been surprised at first.[84] Khrushchev had a lot of prestige around the world, and the sequence of events increased his popularity. The sympathy manifested around the world for Khrushchev, however, was not solely for his personal character; it was the recognition of the Soviet Union's and the Soviet party's strength and the people's greatness, as well as proof of the rightness of the collectively developed policies.

Brezhnev went on to say that Khrushchev was doubtlessly popular among the Hungarian people because he supported the Hungarian government's policies. The help given in the suppression of the "counterrevolution," however, was not only the personal merit of Khrushchev; he also carried out the resolution of the presidium. The outside world viewed him differently; they did not know about a lot of things inside the Soviet Union. Khrushchev's dismissal was solely due to internal matters, though he did make mistakes in foreign policy as well, but neither the presidium nor the Central Committee debated that.

Brezhnev said that Khrushchev departed from the principle of collective leadership. He rudely rejected or suppressed the opinions of other members. He forced his will onto the presidium and the Central Committee. He mocked the comrades who voiced their disagreements and humiliated them. Such an atmosphere developed in the presidium that its members were forced to vote without their own conviction for bewildering experiments and ideas. There had not been a real Central Committee meeting in eleven years; they resembled congresses instead, Brezhnev complained. In six years, agricultural production grew only by 1.6 percent. Khrushchev suffered from a need to reorganize; with his violently forced steps, he disorganized the Soviet Union's national economy. Brezhnev stated that the issue of Khrushchev's dismissal was solely the CPSU's internal matter. The settlement of his issue happened in accordance with Leninist principles and on the basis of democracy. They notified Khrushchev in advance that they would like to discuss his methods of leadership at the next presidium meeting. Khrushchev agreed to this. At the two-day presidium meeting, he was the one who presided till the end; he controlled who spoke. The members of the presidium and the secretariat all criticized Khrushchev according to the party line. The critique was free from individual personal assaults and did not hurt Khrushchev's dignity either in its content or its form. Every speaker praised Khrushchev's past activity and merits.

At the end of the two-day session, according to Brezhnev, Khrushchev realized that he was no longer capable of changing himself or his developed stance for resolving the questions; his age did not permit it either, which is why he asked for his dismissal. Brezhnev added that, in the past few years, Khrushchev had mentioned several times that he was preoccupied with the thought of resigning. In the recent past, he said that after two hours of work he felt tired.

Brezhnev said that he had known Khrushchev since 1938, and he personally had much for which to thank him. He was promoted to the position of county secretary by Khrushchev. Brezhnev never wavered in following that political line in the development of which Khrushchev had a significant role. That is how it was during the time of the Twentieth Congress as well.

Brezhnev then revealed his personal role in the ousting of the "anti-party group" in the summer of 1957. He related that just three days before the crucial Central Committee meeting, he had a cardiac thrombosis. On Khrushchev's wishes, and against his doctors' orders, he went to the CC meeting. He was the second to speak during the discussion, and although he could not see anything in front of him, he spoke for more than an hour and passionately defended Khrushchev and his proper policies against the opposition. According to Brezhnev, however, Khrushchev later committed mistakes that led to his release from his positions of party head and prime minister, but this happened in a democratic way. Brezhnev tried to neutralize the main criticism of the Hungarians by emphasizing that while in the public communication there was no talk about Khrushchev's merits, in fact these were dealt with extensively at the presidium meeting. In his report at the CC meeting, Suslov also lengthily praised these. The fact that Khrushchev remained a Central Committee member also meant that his merits were recognized.[85] Brezhnev also tried to convince the Hungarian delegation that this part of the story could not be made public because of the anti-Khrushchev atmosphere that had developed at the CC meeting that formally relieved him of his positions. There, if the presidium had not mitigated the Central Committee members' actions, a much harsher resolution would have been reached. Brezhnev explained that, in such an atmosphere, there could be no public mention of Khrushchev's merits, although he admitted that if they had been listed, the resolution would have undoubtedly been received much better abroad. He added that it was possible that, in the future, they may find a way of mentioning Khrushchev's merits.

Brezhnev concluded that the majority of the sister parties also interpreted Khrushchev's dismissal in the right way. Lack of consensus regarding the method could be found only in certain sister parties. For the CPSU, the Khrushchev question was a closed case; they did not wish to revisit it, and he promised that they would not begin a campaign against Khrushchev.

In his long reply, Kádár—elaborating on the fourteen points of the memorandum of 9 November one by one—stressed that no similar situation has occurred in the relationship of the two countries for many years; therefore, it was important that the Soviet comrades understand the Hungarian position properly. The Hungarian party acknowledged the necessity of Khrushchev's dismissal and now fully understood it. He admitted that the dismissal was the CPSU's internal matter; nevertheless, he drew Brezhnev's attention to the global responsibility of the CPSU. "There is no Comintern today, but we still handle our movement as a united worldwide party, thus we cannot be indifferent about what happens in another sister party. This applies in particular to the CPSU. The Soviet Union holds such a position in the world that, whatever it does, there are reverberations around the world and the Soviet leaders can never forget about this. Regarding its form, Khrushchev's dismissal is only an internal matter; however, it concerns everyone politically, morally and emotionally, and therefore it concerns the Hungarians as well." This was no less than formulating the Kádár Doctrine whether they like it or not, Moscow's sovereignty is also limited; therefore, even when making decisions at home, the Soviet Union's leaders have to take into consideration the interests of the whole Soviet bloc.

Kádár related that after the HSWP received the CPSU's directive, they had to explain Khrushchev's dismissal while keeping in mind the thoughts of the Hungarian people. Khrushchev did not offend the HSWP PC, did not break up the party organizations, and did not reorganize Hungarian agriculture. Hungarians knew the other side of his actions. They were familiar with his role in developing the line of the Twentieth Congress, providing help during the 1956 Hungarian events, and developing the cooperation between the two countries. His visits to Hungary strengthened the friendships of the two peoples and the prestige of the Soviet Union and the CPSU. The HSWP could not find drawbacks in these things.

Kádár pointed out that, from a political standpoint, Khrushchev's dismissal had serious consequences in Hungary. There was uncertainty. The people raised the question; will Hungarian or Soviet policy change? The HSWP explained that there would be no change. Using the directive from the CPSU, it internally shed light on the reason for the dismissal. It also told the public that Khrushchev did have merits.

Kádár then began to further educate the new Soviet leaders by saying that—contrary to their criticism to this effect—it did not cast a shadow on Khrushchev at all when he appeared at some of his foreign visits accompanied by his wife or one of his family members. On the contrary, "The simple people living in the capitalist countries sympathize more with those politicians of whom they see their human side, their human features. People believe those politicians who speak of the necessity for peace more when they know that they have children and grandchildren."[86]

Reacting to Brezhnev's talking about Khrushchev's mistakes at length, Kádár faced Brezhnev with the problem that all that had happened in the Soviet Union was seen as the collective responsibility of the leadership by the Soviet bloc countries. "We were not familiar with a part of Comrade Khrushchev's mistakes, or rather, we did not know to what extent the certain decisions reflected his personal standpoint or the opinion of the CC of the CPSU. We always read in the newspapers that the resolutions were adopted by the CPSU CC."[87] By saying this, he openly implied that, in fact, all the mistakes now blamed on Khrushchev alone were the responsibility of the *whole Soviet leadership*.[88]

Kádár told Brezhnev that Khrushchev's dismissal sparked a huge surprise and shock in Hungary, where he was very popular, and people felt sorry for him. They thought he had been fighting for the cause of Socialism and probably committed some mistakes; but the CPSU should have at least said that he did some good things as well. Hardly concealing that he regarded the mode of the removal uncivilized, he explained that "in our country, where societal relations are in a transitional state, in order to popularize the system, it is necessary to deal with human issues in a humane way." Then he brought up the example of the Western states, saying that "the bourgeois dispose of their elderly leaders in a more elegant way." Churchill and Eisenhower were once the imperialists' leaders.[89] Churchill also got old, he had many obsessions, and he certainly committed many errors. Yet they still bade farewell to him nicely, retired him, and even the Queen received him.[90]

He went on to explain that the mode by which Khrushchev was dismissed presented problems from a human point of view because the non-Communists critically evaluate the Communists. "They know, too, that the communists work day and night, working even with cardiac thrombosis, putting their personal lives completely aside, for as long as they are able to do so. If we throw these people away like a squeezed lemon when they cannot give maximum potential, or they make mistakes, it is bad because the people, the ordinary people cannot understand it."

Then he warned Brezhnev that denouncing Khrushchev's activity could easily backfire: "We cannot deny that he was our man, our system's leader. We can say what we want, but the ordinary people put their mistakes on the bill of our system."

Kádár then elaborated on the problem of the personality cult, arguing that the present Soviet position gave rise to misunderstandings. One cannot call Khrushchev's mistakes a personality cult. Stalin's cult was foreign to the Communist system, and it caused great damage to it. After eliminating Stalin's personality cult, it would be a mistake to announce that after this came Khrushchev's personality cult. People would think that the personality cult is truly inherent in the system. He explained that the Hungarian party is respected by the masses because it stood up against both the counterrevolution and the personality cult. "Our people are *calm* [emphasis added] because they see that there is a guarantee against the return of a personality cult." This was a barely hidden reference to the 1956 revolution, when people revolted against the Stalinist system and were not calm at all.

Kádár then put forward a scenario that, in his opinion, would have been the proper solution to the problem: it would have been very good if the first resolution about the dismissal had suggested that while Khrushchev had always worked for the cause of Soviet power, he had grown old, picked up bad habits, and made mistakes, and thus was no longer capable of properly working for the benefit of the common cause. It could have also been suggested that he himself admitted to this and asked for a dismissal considering his age and state of health. It could have also been stated that the CPSU was invariably following the lines of the Twentieth, Twenty-First, and Twenty-Second Congresses, and the spirit of the 1957 and 1960 resolutions, and was fighting for peace with undiminished energy. A resolution of this kind would have had a better reception.

Kádár concluded that, the CPSU's position notwithstanding, the HSWP judged the work of Khrushchev's whole life as positive. He had devoted his entire life to the common cause. "We respect him for this. If we saw him on the street, we would not turn away from him. We cannot go from one day to the next and spit on a person like him who always fought with us. The exception is the person who went from one side to the other, who became a traitor. In Imre Nagy's case we did not hesitate, and we dealt with him in a proper manner."

Finally, Kádár once again repeated the Hungarian party's "dialectic" standpoint: "We say that we consider Comrade Khrushchev's entire work to be positive. We see different sides of Comrade Khrushchev's work. We will never again revisit this question. We understand the CPSU's justification for their decision, and we agree with it."

While Brezhnev was hardly satisfied with the Hungarian position, he thanked Kádár for his detailed explanation and evaluation, as well as for his openness and honesty. He said that, with Kádár's account, he better understood how the issue appeared in Hungary. The CPSU accepted the resolution of the HSWP with satisfaction; they considered it to be an honest, friendly position. He expressed his conviction that the relations of the two sister parties and of the two countries' leaders would be more intense and friendlier in the future.

Besides Khrushchev's dismissal, several other pressing issues were also discussed at the meeting, among them the most important being the case of the possible return of former Stalinist leader Mátyás Rákosi to Hungary, now living in exile in the Soviet Union since his removal from office in July 1956. This was a convenient yet temporary solution for the Hungarian party, which was made evident when, at the news of Khrushchev's fall, Rákosi immediately approached both the Hungarian and the Soviet parties, pushing for his release from exile and for his return to Hungary. This eventuality had Kádár extremely worried, and he wanted to solve this problem once and for all by acquiring an absolute guarantee from the new Soviet leaders that Rákosi would never be allowed to leave the Soviet Union. First, he reminded Brezhnev that, since the fall of 1957, there had been no difference in opinion on Rákosi's person and role between the two leaderships.[91] He then introduced a shrewd argument, claiming that if it was a burden for the Soviets to keep him there, the HSWP was ready to agree to his return. Kádár stated that they were not scared of Rákosi, and they could arrange for him to live in peace in some quiet area. Knowing only too well that he would not stay passive, Kádár added that if he decided to fight against the party, they would publicly expose him, and eventually he would be put on trial. The plan worked, and Brezhnev declared that the CPSU's opinion of the assessment of Rákosi's abilities and position had not changed at all since November 1957. He assured Kádár that Rákosi's exile in the Soviet Union would now be a permanent solution. Thus, Kádár's greatest opponent died there in 1971, just a few months before the death of Kádár's former mentor, Khrushchev.

Finally, Brezhnev and Kádár discussed the new situation concerning China. Kádár tried to play a mediating role by emphasizing that it would be wise to use the unexpected positive attitude of the CCP and to put an end to the open polemics between China and the Soviet bloc. While admitting that it would not be easy to coexist with the Chinese after 14 October either, and one could expect a long debate, he stressed that it was in the collective interest of the Soviet bloc that the debate proceed in a different way than it had up until then. Kádár advised Brezhnev that, if the Chinese wanted to make their positions more reasonable, "let's not make it harder for them to do so. We should maintain the de facto truce for a while."

To facilitate a successful rapprochement between the CPSU and the CCP, Kádár also tried to convince Brezhnev that they should postpone the meeting of the preparatory committee for the big meeting of the Communist and workers' parties planned for December 15, as it was clear that the Chinese would not take part.[92] Finally, he called on Brezhnev to reciprocate the CCP visit by sending a CPSU delegation to Beijing.[93]

Brezhnev gave a detailed account of the three meetings of the CPSU with the Chinese delegation.[94] His conclusion was that the CCP leaders' trip to Moscow was of an exploratory nature and that there emerged not much hope from the talks for undoing the split between China and the Soviet bloc. The Chinese had expected that, with Khrushchev's removal, the CPSU would change its political line, and they wanted to find out in what direction and to what extent it would happen. They regretted to see that there was no new situation because the CPSU had not altered its previous policy. They even openly threatened the new Soviet leaders that if they followed the old line of politics, then "they will also be relieved." In the CCP's opinion, unity could be strengthened only if the CPSU changed its political positions.

Kádár was consistent in his policy of fighting a two-front battle at all times: while he persuaded the Soviets to grab the opportunity for rapprochement with the Chinese leadership, he was also keen on preventing the Chinese, who were hoping for a change in Soviet politics in what they believed to be "the right direction," from turning the event of the 7 November ceremonies into an anti-Khrushchev demonstration. According to the original Chinese as well as Soviet idea, the leaders of the guest nations present at the event would have also given speeches, but Kádár, referring to the resolution adopted at the 30 October meeting of the HSWP PC in a letter written to Brezhnev on the same day, expressly suggested that such speeches should not be delivered. As an explanation, he said, "Touching on the well-known theoretical-political matters of debate even in a hidden way would make the trip useless, since the goal of it will be to demonstrate the willingness to strive for unity." And then referring to the Chinese, he mentioned, "In light of Comrade Khrushchev's recent removal, it would be extraordinarily harmful for our common cause if anyone insinuated 'as winners' that they 'now' have better conditions." Regardless of the aforementioned causes, there was probably a third, unspoken motive as well: if the sister nations' leaders had to speak, they obviously could not have avoided expressing in some form their approval of the decision to remove Khrushchev, and naturally swearing their loyalty to the new leadership, which would have been a very difficult thing for Kádár to do after such a short period of time since the shocking events. In the end, the Hungarians' recommendation was accepted, and sister party speeches were not delivered at the celebrations.

Kádár's attitude toward Khrushchev was well demonstrated by the fact that the Hungarian delegation had brought gifts to Khrushchev, among other Soviet leaders, although it is true that, for the sake of peace, they named Khrushchev's wife as the official addressee. Nevertheless, this caused a great stir, and the administrative clerk in charge said that he would have to report this. "We said that he could feel free to report it."[95]

Kádár did not disown his former mentor even later, either. In his 8 December 1967 letter to the leader of the Hungarian party (forwarded via regular post), Khrushchev expressed his condolences on the occasion of former prime minister Ferenc Münnich's death. Kádár, although surprised by the initiative, responded to the letter, but for the sake of order, the response and the request to forward two gift boxes was sent to Brezhnev. However, the Soviet party's leader, referring to the fact that the CPSU "CC and the apparatus have no direct link to Khrushchev," suggested that the Hungarian embassy in Moscow send the shipment to its addressee. That did actually happen on 4 February 1968.[96]

By having lectured the new Soviet leaders about their responsibility for the Soviet bloc states, Kádár did not become Brezhnev's favorite, and the relationship between the two leaders never came close to the one between Kádár and Khrushchev. Paradoxically, Hungary's room to maneuver did not diminish in the Brezhnev era, just the opposite: it gradually expanded in both the country's internal policy and its international relations from the mid-1960s on. This development was clearly not dependent on personal feelings; rather, it was the result of the emancipation process of the Soviet bloc countries, which began in the mid-1950s and was more or less completed by the end of the 1960s.

Chapter 7

The Main Features of Kádárist Foreign Policy

Foreign Policy and National Interests

On a closer look at the Hungarian Communist model to determine whether this regime included attributes organic to "traditional" democracy, it would soon transpire that such attributes are absent from this regime, and thus parliamentary democracy and the post-1948 Communist dictatorship are simply not compatible. Consequently, it is understandable that today, in-depth historical research and analysis as regards the mode of operation of the regime in the given situation primarily focus on the characteristics of the domestic dictatorship model.

By contrast, such comparative consensus among researchers does not exist in respect to the evaluation of foreign policy. In my view, the categories of foreign policy, independent foreign policy, and sovereignty, as well as the concept of national interest, can be assessed only within the framework of the given regime and not in relation to the tradition and condition of a democratic state. Taking into consideration this assertion, it would not be too difficult to prove that the countries of the Soviet bloc could not conduct independent foreign policy and, consequently, it would be a waste of energy to offer an academic corroboration thereof. Hence, the question should be phrased thus: taking the lack of freedom and independence as given attributes and in view of the apparent Soviet dependency and determinacy, what options did respective leaderships have to exploit the available foreign political space for maneuver, and to what extent did they want or were they able to pursue national interests within the given frame of constraints? It is probably even more important to establish the extent to which each country could separately and jointly influence and shape the attitude of successive Soviet leaderships as regards international politics and especially East–West relations. In order to provide authentic answers to these questions, more rigorous research would be needed in all the former Soviet bloc countries, since the results obtained so far from this type of research are emerging only now in the form of academic publications. While comparative research would carry more weight in assessing the performance of particular countries as regards the history of foreign policy, this is still in its infancy. Consequently, mostly stereotypes dominate public opinion and even academic approaches. When speaking of the Soviet bloc's international relations, Romania's deviant foreign political conduct comes to everyone's mind. This was spectacular indeed, and hence the logical conclusion was that this kind of conduct was the only or at least the most effective method for pursuing self-interest within the bloc. Taking into account the findings of international research, however, it seems more and more likely that this was only one of the options. Furthermore, if we discount the expression of deviance as a value per se, then the advantages gained by Romanian society through this "independent" foreign policy are highly questionable. By contrast, the complicated but in many ways undeniably positive role Romania had played in the Warsaw Pact, the Comecon, and common policy-making, particularly during the 1970s and 1980s, is just beginning to emerge.[1]

Hence, I am confident that the exploration of other quasi models, such as East German, Polish, Hungarian, or even Bulgarian conduct, might yield an equally striking result. The specific role played by the GDR is subjected to thorough investigation in the West and is providing evidence that warrants the upgrading of the significance of the GDR's policies as regards its decisive influence on everyday Soviet politics. In other words, a series of events, construed earlier as occurrences initiated by the Soviet leadership, were in reality extorted by the GDR leadership; notably, the crucial role played by the East German leadership during the Berlin crisis is a proven fact. Hence, it is safe to assert today that the GDR leadership's ability to assert its self-interests was—in its entirety—considerably more effective than that of the Romanian leaders.[2]

One of the most important lessons yielded by the scrutiny of Hungarian foreign policy entails, first and foremost, the establishment of an international environment for the attainment of the top priorities of this foreign policy: the maintenance of political stability at all costs and the realization of a relatively autonomous domestic and economic policy. Regarding the composition of the Kádár government, gaining power on 4 November 1956, a distinct continuity is apparent with the leadership that had been reorganized after the dismissal of Rákosi in July 1956. It soon became obvious, however, that the undertaking of the bestowed task—namely the renewal of the Communist dictatorship for long-term functioning—could only be achieved efficiently by applying new methods after the revolution. The primary means of creating political stability and pacifying society was Kádár's newly introduced special quality-of-life-policy, which provided a much better and tolerable life almost instantly for the great majority who were willing to distinguish themselves from the revolution, while those who were found "guilty" or resisted were severely punished.[3] However, a constantly increasing standard of living could only be guaranteed by a well-functioning economy, so it soon became clear that the long-term development of the Hungarian economy—which very much depended on external sources and foreign trade—could only be achieved if the leadership was able to exploit both Eastern and Western relations effectively. In regard to the Soviet Union, this above all meant the stable supplying of the Hungarian economy with raw materials and energy resources at a "friendly" price (i.e., well below world market prices), and, in relations with the West, the at least partial (re)joining into the world economic processes by adopting advanced technologies that were necessary for modernization and more efficient functioning.

The lessons gained from the experience of the revolution, the circumstances of the birth of the Kádár regime, and the political views of the Hungarian leaders together made clear that the main principle of Hungarian foreign policy became a middle of the road line.[4] On the one hand, this policy constantly declared loyalty to the Soviet Union, while on the other hand it aspired for more effectively using its room for maneuvering, and for the fulfillment of national interests (naturally, as defined by the leadership), on condition that it did not openly oppose the interests of the Soviet Union.

The international environment for implementing this circumspect but pragmatic foreign policy was favorable not only in the 1960s but, in a sense, during the years following 1956. Although the partial international isolation of Hungary prevailing between 1956 and 1963 seem to contradict this, the determinative and long-term factors affected the leadership's room for maneuvering positively. In this regard, the most important event was that, in the Soviet Union—especially after the aborted coup against Khrushchev in June 1957—the de-Stalinization process and the construction of the post-Stalinist system continued and even accelerated with the leadership of Khrushchev. In addition, the policy of peaceful coexistence in international politics was confirmed at the Moscow conference of the Communist and workers' parties in 1960, and at the Twenty-First and Twenty-Second Congresses of the CPSU in 1959 and 1961, respectively. Beyond declaring anew the preventability of a third world war, this meant the peaceful competition of the two camps, the meeting of politicians, negotiations, and the development of economic and cultural relations between the two blocs.[5] All of this resulted in the gradual emergence of an almost normal relationship compared to the antagonistic differences between the two ideologies. During this period, the eminent increase in the international prestige of the Soviet Union, predominantly enhanced by the "Sputnik shock," greatly assisted in the following of this policy.

All of this made it possible for the Soviet leadership to continue to transform its relationship with its allies, a process that began in 1953. The theoretical basis for this move was the Soviet government's declaration of 30

October 1956, and although the equality and not-interfering-in-internal-affairs policy contained in that document never came into effect in reality, this relationship went through significant changes in the post-Stalinist era. Decisions regarding the strategic questions remained in Soviet hands; however, concerning tactics—within certain boundaries also including the formation of internal development—the allies gained more considerable independence than before. Thus, by the early 1960s, they had acquired a sort of limited partnership status. The process of gradual emancipation of the Soviet bloc states that began in 1953 continued and accelerated in the early to mid-1960s in three directions: in their relationship with the Soviet Union, with the Western countries, and with non-allied states. Soviet advisors were withdrawn, the previous hand control was replaced by a sophisticated system of remote control. No Communist world organization, not even a regional one as the Cominform used to be, was set up; the current issues were discussed at the regular summit meetings of the leaders of the Socialist countries and at the sessions of the Warsaw Pact and the Council for Mutual Economic Assistance. There, the representatives of the member states often took the initiative in generating serious debates, the stakes of which were the representation of the specific interests of each country. In economic relations, the previous barely concealed Soviet exploitation was replaced by the well-known but of course differently named principle and practice of mutual advantages and disadvantages.[6] After the Hungarian Revolution, the most important set of goals for Moscow was the maintenance of political stability, thus consolidating Soviet control over the Eastern bloc countries. For this, not only allowances were given but also, from time to time, economic aid was granted to the allies stricken by serious internal problems. For the same reason, the Soviet leadership—however unhappily—accepted the less than advantageous situation that, in most of the East Central European countries, the standard of living of the population would be considerably higher than that in the Soviet Union. This clearly meant the emergence of a new model: a reversed imperium–colony relationship. Besides better living conditions in the dependent states, the structure of economic relations also showed an absurd turn: the Soviet Union supplied its allies with subsidized raw materials and energy resources, for which they delivered mostly manufactured goods.

Thus, following the Soviet standard became more and more voluntary for the allies, and it was based on the admission that, since there was no chance of breaking free from the Soviet sphere of interest (see the example of the Hungarian Revolution), the most that could be done was to use the granted room for maneuvering in the most effective way. The appearance of a separate Chinese political line after 1956, followed by a public debate from 1960, and finally by a break with the Soviet Union, only valorized the importance of the more flexible opportunities granted by the post-Stalinist Soviet alliance model. This also contributed to the fact that, apart from Albania,[7] Beijing could not manage to seduce any other state from the Soviet bloc.

It depended on the composition and temperament of the party leadership of each member of the Soviet bloc how they maneuvered and according to what priorities they conducted their policies. In this regard, from the perspective of finding an efficient strategy, Kádár and his team began quite well, for the experiences of the Hungarian Revolution had given an enormous impulse to the construction of a unique Hungarian post-Stalinist model. As a consequence, the new policy, for most of the population—along with the widespread retaliations—granted significantly better living conditions from as early as 1957.[8] Hungarian historian Melinda Kalmár applied the term *reconstruction* (*szanálás*) for the early Kádárist period, which is clearly a better phrase to meet the requirements of scholarly analysis than the previously used *restoration* and *consolidation* concepts, which unintentionally had opposing political connotations.[9]

In the period from 1956 to the mid-1960s, the serenity of Soviet–Hungarian political relations—in addition to the Hungarian leadership's constantly loyal behavior—was assured above all by the especially close friendship between Nikita Khrushchev and Hungarian leader János Kádár. In spite of their quite different personalities and the great age gap between the two men, their ideas concerning the modernization of the functioning of the Communist dictatorship were so similar that, of all Soviet bloc leaders, Kádár was the most capable of identifying himself with Khrushchev's policy.[10] At the time, Rákosi only wished to be able to become the best student of Stalin. Kádár, however, successfully turned Hungary into a Khrushchevian model state by the middle of the 1960s, something the Soviet leader was never able to achieve in his own country.[11]

Thus, Khrushchev was able to present Hungary as a model country that had accomplished the most progress in terms of de-Stalinization in the Soviet bloc, where, only a few years after 1956, political stability was total, while living standards were continuously rising.[12] It is perhaps even more remarkable that Hungary's number one position concerning the achievements in de-Stalinization was also admitted in a White House memorandum in April 1964.[13]

Following Khrushchev's replacement in October 1964, Kádár clarified and acknowledged to his satisfaction that there would not be any negative changes in the relations between the Soviet Union and Hungary. In exchange for her loyalty, the country could expect to maintain her relative internal independence, and further Soviet economic assistance could also be provided on an individual case basis.

Toward Emancipation

The year 1963 was a clear caesura for Hungary: in December 1962, the Hungarian issue was finally removed from the agenda of the UN General Assembly following a secret deal between the United States and Hungary,[14] which was followed by the visit of UN Secretary-General U Thant to Budapest in July 1963, a symbolic action that in effect terminated the period of Hungary's diplomatic isolation after the 1956 Hungarian Revolution.

That historical compromise created favorable conditions for normalizing Hungary's relationship with the Western countries. And this came exactly at a time when major demand arose for developing connections with the East Central European countries, not only by Great Britain, France, and the United States but also by the Federal Republic of Germany, which earlier had kept aloof from this as a question of principle. Based on the achievements in internal political developments, Hungary started off with especially great chances in this competition, since a U.S. memorandum, prepared in April 1964 for President Johnson on fostering the development of bilateral relations, claimed that "Hungary has perhaps gone farther than any other satellite in de-Stalinizing the Communist system and the movement in that direction continues."[15]

The spectacular series of diplomatic successes following Hungary's release from international isolation opened with the two-day visit of UN Secretary-General U Thant in July 1963. At the end of the year, the process started, by which Hungary's relationship with the Western countries with whom diplomatic ties had existed was upgraded to ambassador level: Great Britain, France, and Greece (1963); Austria, Sweden, Italy, Canada, Denmark, and Japan (1964); the Netherlands and Norway (1965); Iceland, Luxembourg, and the United States (1966); and Belgium and Turkey (1967).[16]

During 1963 and 1964, Hungary—first in the Soviet bloc—started intensive negotiations with the Vatican about pending ecclesiastical matters and, above all, about the settlement of the Mindszenty case.[17] The changed conditions are demonstrated by the fact that Hungarian diplomacy asked for mediation by the United States to help convince the Holy See to reach an agreement. Foremost because of the rigidity of Cardinal Mindszenty's position, an agreement was reached only in 1971, by which he was eventually able to leave the building of the American embassy in Budapest and travel abroad. Finally, the negotiations with the Vatican were successfully concluded. Thus, from the Soviet bloc, Hungary was the first to sign an agreement in September 1964, which, although it left a series of questions open, played an important role in improving the operating conditions of the Hungarian Catholic Church.[18]

Although Hungary did not establish diplomatic relations with the FRG, the country's most important Western trade partner, until December 1973, after the general settlement of the German issue, with the commercial agreement concluded in the fall of 1963—as mentioned in chapter 6—the two countries established intergovernmental relations and mutually agreed on setting up trading agencies in each other's countries, which resulted in the rapid development of economic relations in the following years.[19]

Diplomatic relations picked up significantly; ministers, government delegations, and the representatives of various social organizations paid regular visits on a mutual basis, and Western journalists, public figures, scholars, and artists regularly came to Hungary. There was a breakthrough in tourism as well: beginning in 1964, the number of tourists from the West increased significantly, and traveling by Hungarian people to the West was regulated into law that year. From then on, Hungarian citizens were allowed to travel to the West once every three years, while they could travel to East Central European Socialist countries—except to the Soviet Union—without a visa.[20] On the basis of the American assessment mentioned previously, the process of normalizing relations with the United States also began in 1964. On the one hand, this made it easier for President Johnson to carry on with his "bridge-building" policy announced in July 1966; on the other hand, the agreement between the two countries was made difficult by problems such as the Mindszenty issue, property law questions on the basis of which the United States claimed a significant amount in damages for the property of its citizens as well as for the destruction caused during World War II, and the loss caused by nationalization. After the escalation of the Vietnam War in February 1965, the conditions of the negotiations further deteriorated as the Hungarian government, along with the countries of the Soviet bloc, sharply condemned the bombarding of North Vietnam. The evaluation of the Vietnam conflict by the Socialist countries was, however, much less based on ideology than one would have thought based on the insensitivity of contemporary propaganda. This explains why, although there were several economic issues left open in Hungarian–American relations, in December 1966, right in the middle of the American bombing campaign, diplomatic relations between the two countries were raised to the level of ambassadorship, although the American ambassador was not inaugurated until October 1967, and the Hungarian ambassador in August 1968.[21]

All of this meant that between 1963 and 1968, Hungary accomplished double emancipation. First, the Western isolation stemming from the suppression of the Hungarian revolution was totally over and the country was again regarded as simply one of the members of the Soviet bloc. At the same time, the emancipation of the Soviet bloc states (except for the GDR) had basically been completed by this time—in their relationships with the West, with the third world states, and with the Soviet Union. As for the latter, of course, this did not mean an equal status but a special position of relative partnership.

The Tripartite Determinism of Hungarian Foreign Policy

Hungarian foreign policy during the decades following the 1956 revolution is still generally presented as being determined solely by its dependency on the Soviet Union. The extensive archival research in the field conducted by me since 1990, however, suggests that it can only be properly explained and understood in the framework of a novel theoretical concept: "tripartite determinism."[22] While (1) affiliation with the Soviet empire ostensibly implied enforced restrictions, (2) the dependence on the West concerning advanced technology, trade contacts, and subsequent loans produced an equally strong bond. At the same time, (3) Hungarian foreign policy had to perform a balancing act to pursue specific national objectives in terms of an all-East-Central-European-lobby contest.[23] While this tripartite determinism of Hungarian foreign policy had always existed in some form and magnitude, the import of the three factors became relatively the same from the mid-1960s. This theory can also be interpreted in a wider context and, with certain restrictions, applied to the entire Soviet bloc. These three determinations are valid for Hungarian, Polish, Romanian, East German, and, to a lesser extent, Czechoslovak and Bulgarian foreign policy as well,[24] especially from the early mid-1960s on.

1. In its relationship with the Soviet Union, Hungary—even after the sudden replacement of János Kádár's patron, Nikita Khrushchev, in October 1964 and even until 1989—played the role of a loyal, dependable, and predictable partner. Two main factors justified Kádár's conviction that the maintenance of this political line was most advantageous. One of these involved the exigency with regard to bolstering Western economic relations, which were pivotal to the modernization of Hungarian economy. During the 1960s, this process demanded verification of Hungary's unswerving loyalty, as well as the indivisibility of the bloc, since Leonid Brezhnev purposefully emphasized at the WP PCC meeting in Warsaw in January 1965 that "the imperialists are trying to extend their contacts to the Socialist countries to influence their domestic lives in a direction favorable to them and to undermine their unity by offering economic, technological and scientific incentives. Hence, it is of the utmost importance to prevent their ideological penetration and subversive endeavors."[25] A second and equally important factor entailed the preparations for reforming the economic mechanism. Plans to reform the Hungarian econ-

omy proved to be the most significant structural change in the Soviet bloc since the establishment of the Communist system of the Stalinist-Leninist-type, and thus it was essential to reassure the Soviet leadership that the reforms applied solely to the sphere of *economy*. Hence, Hungarian foreign policy vis-à-vis Hungarian–Soviet relations aimed to apply the policy of "constructive loyalty."[26] The main features of this conduct entailed conflict prevention—primarily with regard to political issues—credibility, predictability, flexibility, and adjustment to Soviet requirements, as well as a willingness to cooperate. In this context, Hungary throughout this period played a mediating role in the Warsaw Pact, in the Comecon, and in multilateral negotiations in order to support perpetual Soviet goals. However, *constructive* loyalty implied that, despite all these factors, the constraints could be and in fact were continually tested and gradually loosened. The content of this principle until 1988 implied that "what is not forbidden is (perhaps) allowed." Another important aspect of this policy implied that the Hungarian leadership—taking advantage of the credibility status acquired through loyalty—constantly tried to influence the Soviet leadership and get concessions within the framework of bilateral relations, which served the concrete interests of Hungary as well as the other East Central European countries in most cases. Whereas this endeavor did not always yield results, in several instances it was possible to exercise positive influence on the Moscow leadership with respect to fundamental issues affecting the improvement of East–West relations. Constructive loyalty yielded another result, too. Since the fundamental and perpetual aims of the Hungarian leadership following 1956 entailed the preservation of the conditions of a relatively independent domestic development, Soviet–Hungarian economic relations and, first and foremost, the guarantee of an uninterrupted supply of Soviet raw materials and energy carriers for a "friendly" price to sustain the domestic economy were of primary importance. In exchange for overtly preventing conflicts in political matters by the Hungarian leadership, in most cases the Soviets turned a blind eye to the fact that the specialists negotiating more favorable conditions were extremely hard bargaining partners during bilateral economic talks and, on the whole, managed to extort economic concessions in return for political cooperation.

While perhaps Hungary was a role model, the policy of constructive loyalty in Soviet–East European relations can be applied in a certain sense to all non-Soviet members of the Warsaw Pact (except for Romania), although of course the implementation of this policy differed significantly in each state and even in different periods. On the one hand, this generally meant a loyal following of the Soviet line in all public announcements and at the international scene, usually avoiding open debates with Moscow at the Soviet bloc's *multilateral* forums (except in the Comecon), as well as flexibility, ceaseless adjustment to Soviet demands, and a readiness to cooperate. On the other hand, it meant continuous testing of the boundaries of Soviet tolerance, mostly via *bilateral* channels, lobbying and fighting for one's national interests (as identified by the Communist leaders of the given state), and making initiatives to confidentially foster their own goals, which often substantially differed from Soviet interests.[27]

2. From the beginning of the 1960s, Hungary's economic needs dictated the continual fostering of relations with the West. The basis of this drive was the realization of the fact that only a functioning and gradually growing economy would secure political stability and a constant rise in the standard of living, as set out by the Kadárist political concept. The rapidly advancing modern technology gained an ever-growing role in the emerging global economic environment. However, the country indisputably depended on Western relations in this respect, since—except for military equipment and space research—Soviet technology lagged behind the West, at least as much as it had at the beginning of the 1950s, and the gap was progressively widening.[28] Owing to the peculiarities of a shortage economy, even those products that met the required standards were not always available, and so the Soviet Union simply could not deliver.[29]

Since Hungary had no substantial amounts of raw materials and energy resources, the country's economy was one of the most open in the Soviet bloc, and therefore it was relying on foreign trade to a great extent. While the bulk of the commercial trade was conducted with Comecon countries, from the early 1960s on the ever-growing need for hard currency (needed to counter imports from the West) as well as loans became a driving force behind Hungary's endeavors to develop economic and trade relations with the capitalist states, especially in Western Europe.

The policy of selective Western economic embargo (COCOM) applied against the countries of the Eastern bloc also became an incentive for fostering relations with the West, since the Hungarian leadership could expect the lifting of the restrictions only from a radical, positive change in East–West relations. Consequently, from the mid-1960s on, Hungary—within the prevailing threshold of Soviet tolerance—intensively broadened relations with West European countries and became one of the main proponents of rapprochement politics.

3. Analyzing Hungary's participation in the all-East-Central-European-lobby contest is a more difficult task than analyzing its relations with the West and the Soviet Union.[30] Beginning in the early 1960s, an extremely complex and alternating system of relationships developed among the Soviet Union's European allies. The various countries strove to realize their economic, political, and strategic interests in a struggle, not just against Moscow

but also against one another. As a consequence of the constant lobbying and infighting—manifest to the international community only in Romania's deviant path—several permanent and numerous ad hoc virtual coalitions formed within the Soviet bloc. This means the virtual cooperation of a group of states having similar interests in a certain issue without making this collaboration explicit. The members of such a coalition did not engage in multilateral or even bilateral talks with one another to harmonize their interests, as any such activity could be regarded as dangerous fractionalizing by Moscow. Nevertheless, they *recognized* their joint interests and acted accordingly. In other words, the common interests were represented *individually* during the meetings of the Soviet bloc multilateral forums, in their bilateral relations with Moscow and the other Soviet bloc states, as well as vis-à-vis the Western states. Thus, the activity of such virtual coalitions was never formulated or articulated in any official form; moreover, their very existence was not even realized during the Cold War.

Two particularly important and durable groupings were formed on the basis of economic and social development: the more developed group comprised Czechoslovakia, Poland, Hungary, and the GDR, while Bulgaria and Romania constituted the less developed group. But even this division was not quite so simple. Within the more developed group, the relatively undeveloped Poland and Hungary tended to side with others in the group on matters concerning the direction of development of the Comecon and on integration, but these two countries often sided with the less developed countries when this was necessary to protect their own economic interests.

From the early 1960s, a crucial issue for the Soviet bloc was the settlement of the German question. As discussed in chapter 6, by the early 1960s the Soviet bloc was clearly divided into an economy-oriented (Hungary, Romania, and Bulgaria) and a security-concerned sub-bloc (the GDR, Poland, and Czechoslovakia) as far as the German question was concerned.[31] Hungary, together with Bulgaria and Romania, had no serious unsettled issues with the FRG; therefore, they were seriously interested in economic cooperation, increasing trade, and taking over cutting-edge technologies. On the issue of European security, opinions were divided on similar lines, reflecting the fact that settlement of the German question was a central element of this issue. Hence, within the Soviet bloc, Hungary conducted a coalition-building policy based on pragmatism and driven by its interests as they arose. The rather complex system of relationships can be illustrated with several noteworthy examples in the period under investigation.

Polish–Hungarian bilateral relations were excellent throughout the period, and the two leaderships tended to share the same opinion on international politics and on the issue of East–West relations. In numerous instances, however, their positions differed substantially. Indeed, on occasion—for instance, during the early phase of preparations for the European security conference—Hungarian diplomacy joined forces with the Soviets to scupper over-ambitious Polish efforts.

In the case of Romania, the equation was the reverse: bilateral relations were afflicted by severe problems throughout the period—above all, the grave discrimination suffered by the 1.7 -million-large Hungarian ethnic minority in Romania—as a consequence of which the Hungarian leadership exhibited an antipathy toward Romania that bordered on nationalist indignation, though only in the closed circle of the Politburo.[32] Still, in the field of East–West relations and on the issue of European security—and, from time to time, in many areas of political and economic cooperation within the Soviet bloc— the interests of the two leaderships coincided or were similar. Although the Hungarian leadership refrained from overtly supporting Romania's customary position during multilateral negotiations, Hungary nevertheless often employed the tactic of benevolent neutrality disguised as passivity to facilitate Romania's efforts. Within the framework of Hungarian–Soviet bilateral relations, the Hungarian negotiating partners frequently gave their support to proposals that served to promote such shared interests.

Relations between Hungary and the GDR were also of a unique character. Regarding the progression of Hungary's economic and domestic policy, throughout the period the harshest criticism tended to come from the GDR, alongside the Soviet Union. At the same time, however, Hungary's relations with the GDR in the economic field were fairly balanced. Indeed, within the Eastern bloc, it was this relationship that proved the most valuable to Hungary in terms of obtaining (relatively) advanced technology.[33]

Foreign Policy Coordination in the Warsaw Pact and Attempts at Reform

As is well known, no structure of any kind was set up for the military-political alliance of the Soviet bloc—except for formally establishing a Political Consultative Committee—when the treaty establishing the Warsaw Pact was signed in May 1955.[34] While the future function of the new organization was to be clarified for the Soviet leaders themselves during the years to come, in the course of the year of the "spirit of Geneva" it became obvious that a more effective model of foreign policy coordination had to be established in the bloc.

It was thus not by chance that, at the first session of the Warsaw Pact PCC held in Prague on 28 January 1956, just a few weeks following the Soviet bloc summit in Moscow in early January, a decision was made that the Council of

Foreign Ministers and a permanent secretariat should be established as a subsidiary organ of the PCC. As is well known, no such bodies were formed within the Warsaw Pact in 1956, or indeed, not up until exactly twenty years later, in 1976. While it is clear that, from the mid-1960s, the opposition of Romania blocked such plans, further research is needed to show why the Soviet leadership did not implement these resolutions in the period between 1956 and 1961, when they were still "plenipotentiary" masters of the Soviet bloc. This is all the more interesting in that we now know that, during this same period, an intensive process of policy coordination, never seen before, was taking place in the Soviet bloc.

Following the year of crises in 1956, concerning foreign policy coordination in the Soviet bloc there was a shift from the multilateral model of the years 1953–56 to a mixed model of bilateral and multilateral consultations. After the failed coup of June 1957, Khrushchev solidified his power and from 1958 filled both the post of prime minister and CPSU first secretary.[35] Unlike Stalin, he loved to travel, and, until his fall in October 1964, he made numerous visits to the countries of the Eastern bloc as well. Foreign policy coordination at the multilateral level became increasingly intensive between 1957 and 1964; during these eight years, five summit meetings, five WP PCC meetings,[36] five Comecon summits (attended by the top leaders), one meeting of the foreign misters, and three meetings of the defense ministers were held—fifteen summits plus four high-level consultations all told.[37]

At these meetings, no serious debates occurred—except for in the Comecon. Mainly what happened was that Khrushchev gave detailed information on the international situation and the position of the Soviet Union. The practice during these years, however, set the model for Soviet bloc policy coordination, which became more intensive, including serious internal debates starting right after the fall of Khrushchev. This period of intensive policy coordination within the Soviet bloc during the years 1956–61, and especially during the second Berlin crisis from 1958 to 1961, created the illusion that the East Central European leaders were now important—even if not equal— partners of Moscow. Therefore, the Soviet policy of providing zero information to the allies concerning the Cuban missile crisis in 1962 caused a real shock in the Soviet bloc.

By the middle of the 1960s, it became obvious that the operational efficiency of the Warsaw Pact was satisfactory neither for the Soviet leaders nor for the member states; therefore—especially after the Cuban missile crisis—the efforts to reform the organization appeared more and more resolutely.[38] Thus, those member states of the Warsaw Pact that were ready for modernizing the organization and strengthening cooperation—especially Hungary and Poland—were interested in the development of a more effective and democratic structure, in which the member states would obtain a significantly more serious role. These countries were thinking along the lines of semi-democratic reforms for which the Soviets showed at least some willingness. The idea of forming a Council of Foreign Ministers in the Warsaw Pact now offered Moscow's loyal allies a chance for regular preliminary consultation on foreign policy issues—exactly the practice they had been lobbying for.

The pressure for regular consultation by the allies eventually turned out to be stronger than expected, so hardly half a year after Kádár's intervention, on 2 January 1964—referring to such demands for consultation from "individual sister parties," meaning those of the Hungarian and Polish parties—Khrushchev himself made a proposal for the organization of regular meetings of the Warsaw Pact foreign ministers or their deputies.[39] This was the first reference to the possibility of establishing foreign policy coordination in the Warsaw Pact at a level lower than the originally designated Council of Foreign Ministers—that is, at the level of deputy foreign ministers. The first meeting of deputy foreign ministers took place in Warsaw in December 1964, and, from that time on, they held sessions more and more regularly, often several times a year. These meetings gradually became the most important working forum of foreign policy coordination within the Warsaw Pact until the dissolution of the alliance in 1991.[40]

Other forums of consultation developed gradually, and eventually a more-or-less well-working mechanism of Moscow regularly informing its East Central European allies on important international issues had developed at the meetings of the WP PCC (since 1956), the Council of Defense Ministers (since 1969), and the Council of Foreign Ministers (since 1976). Also, there were consultations for the ruling parties' Central Committee secretaries for foreign affairs beginning at the close of the 1960s.

The organizational transformation and institutionalization of the Warsaw Pact had been on the agenda from the very beginning. As early as the first PCC session in Prague in January 1956, a decision was made that a Committee of Foreign Ministers and a permanent secretariat should be established as a subsidiary organ of the PCC.[41] Nevertheless, it took the Soviet leaders a long time to discover what they could use this organization for, as Khrushchev's original plan to use the Warsaw Pact for negotiation and bargaining with the West failed. Although the Romanian deviant tendencies did not bolster the intensification of cooperation, the Warsaw Pact, by the mid- to late 1960s—even within the given organizational framework—became a multilateral consulting, decision-support, and decision-making organization of the Eastern bloc countries.

The issue of the organizational transformation of the Warsaw Pact, however, was placed on the agenda in official form only at the PCC session of January 1965 in Warsaw.[42] As a result of the resistance of the Romanian leaders opposing the transformation without any consideration, besides the discussion of the issue, no real decision was made at that time, although all parties but the Romanians supported the Soviet proposal to form the Committee of Foreign Ministers. They also discussed the work of the Supreme Command of the Unified Armed Forces and, in spite of the fact that the majority of the member states had been insisting on making important organizational changes in this field for a long time, no decision was made in this matter due to the Romanian opposition. The main strategic aim—that is, the demonstration of a unified Warsaw Pact standpoint against NATO's plan to establish a multilateral nuclear force—created a favorable situation for the deviant Romanian policies, and the Soviets eventually gave up trying to enforce the organizational changes in return for Romanian approval.

The session of the PCC held in Warsaw can, however, be considered a milestone in the history of the organization. This was the first time that the body pursued a real exchange of views about the most important current matters, and the decisions were not made the same old way—that is, according to the agenda proposed by the Soviets, as had been the custom before. The fact that this was the first session of the PCC after the replacement of Khrushchev in October 1964 also played a significant role in this development. The representatives of the member states presumed that the new and "young" Soviet leadership, having amassed considerably less respect, would be essentially more flexible to the member states' efforts to obtain a greater influence in the organization. Therefore, following the session of the PCC in Warsaw, the member states continued to enforce the organizational changes, especially concerning the military organization.

Daily cooperation, however, was hampered by the fact that important issues concerning authority and organization had not been clarified, and the current coordination practice—manual control from Moscow—did not enable the leadership of national armies to execute any complex tasks. Not to mention the fact that, in the event of war, practically no cooperation model or regulation existed, and this situation—especially after the crises of Berlin and Cuba—did not seem reassuring. Thus, those WP members that were ready for the modernization of the organization were in favor of limited reforms, which seemed to be acceptable to Moscow as well. The Romanians, however—on an all-or-nothing basis—insisted on the full "democratization" of the Warsaw Pact. As there was not too much chance of achieving that goal, the Romanians were interested in maintaining the existing rather unregulated structure, since it was much more suitable for the justification of their particular policy.

Military Reform

The Hungarian leadership insisted on the transformation of the military organization of the Warsaw Pact, and the Hungarian delegation put forward a proposal for it at the PCC session in July 1963. Minister of Defense Lajos Czinege reported to the HSWP PC in November 1964 that he had attempted to raise the problem directly at the Supreme Command without success.[43] After the question had been officially put on the agenda at the session of the PCC in Warsaw in January 1965, the HSWP PC discussed the matter on 27 April 1965.[44] The HSWP PC accepted the report and the proposals of the minister of defense concerning the organizational changes. The main articles of the report are as follows:

1. It is unacceptable that the commander in chief of the Supreme Command is the deputy minister of defense of the Soviet Union at the same time and that the deputies of the commander in chief are the ministers of defense of the member states—that is, they are subordinated to the deputy minister of another state. For that reason, a Soviet general, having no post in his own country, is to be assigned as commander in chief. The deputies of the commander in chief are to be assigned from generals, having no other post at home, delegated from the member states.
2. The Military Council of the armies of the member states shall be established as a joint leading organization, the members of which may be the ministers of defense of the member states, perhaps also their chiefs of the general staff, as well as the deputies and the headman of the commander in chief.
3. To assist the commander in chief, a properly organized and composed staff is to be set up.
4. The organizational regulation of the Military Council and staff of the Supreme Command is to be worked out in order to fix their duties and sphere of authority.

János Kádár made these proposals known before the Soviet leadership, and they accepted a significant part of the suggestions. In this way, the Hungarian reform draft concerning the military organization of the Warsaw Pact served as a base for the development of a common standpoint of the closely cooperating parties; therefore, its main paragraphs were included in the draft resolution elaborated for the session of the PCC to be held in July 1966 in Bucharest.[45] The question of the political reform of the Warsaw Pact, however, fell victim to a further separate bargain of the Soviets with Romania, as Moscow's priority was to unanimously adopt a proposal for the convocation of a European security conference. Thus, the discussion about the organizational reform, prepared at the cost of hard work but opposed by the Romanians, had been taken off the agenda of the PCC session just before the meeting started.

Political Reform

The transformation of the political organization of the Warsaw Pact was discussed again in the session of the deputy foreign ministers in February 1966 in Berlin, held after the session of the PCC in January 1965.[46] At a subsequent summit meeting of the party's first secretaries held on 7 April, during the Twenty-Third Congress of the CPSU in Moscow, it was decided that the issue should be submitted to the next session of the PCC. After the meeting, the GDR leadership summarized the proposals of the member states, and the summary was sent to the sister parties in June. Based on this letter, the meeting of the foreign ministers held in Moscow in June was charged with agreeing on the definitive proposals. The closely cooperating parties proposed holding the sessions of the PCC at regular intervals and establishing a Committee of Foreign Ministers as well as a permanent secretariat with headquarters in Moscow. These proposals were all rejected by the Romanians, and agreement was only reached in a few issues of lesser importance: (1) the sessions of the PCC would subsequently be held in the capitals of the Warsaw Pact; (2) on the basis of a prior agreement, representatives of states not belonging to the organization may be invited as observers; and (3) the preliminary agenda of the PCC session and concerning matters would be sent to the member states in due time.[47]

The HSWP PC discussed the matter of the transformation of the Warsaw Pact during its sessions of 21 and 28 June 1966. On the basis of the experiences acquired during the meeting of foreign ministers in Moscow, János Péter announced that, as far as the session of the PCC to be held in Bucharest in July was concerned, no result could be expected, since a stalemate situation had developed concerning the reform.[48] The planned changes could not be realized because of the Romanian opposition. In addition to this, the problem was caused partly by the fact that the statute of the Warsaw Pact, signed in 1955, did not meet the current requirements, since it identified the PCC as a consultative body and not as a decision-making organ. Thus, concluded the foreign minister, the Romanians had a formal right to insist on the original interpretation. The PC members forecasted that the Soviets would probably make efforts to reach a compromise with the Romanians in Bucharest so that the PCC could accept the declaration concerning the European security conference on the basis of the Soviet proposal.

The members of the HSWP PC perceived correctly that a new situation had developed in the Warsaw Pact. The Romanians formerly hindered and encumbered the work of the organization several times but, in order to maintain unity, both factions refrained from open disagreement, even at the closed forums of the Warsaw Pact. Now several PC members considered conflict as inevitable, and it was suggested that the Romanians should be provoked to openly express their standpoint at the beginning of the meeting during a closed session. Others proposed to postpone the meeting. Gyula Kállai objected to the fact that the Soviet Union granted too many concessions to Romania, and there was an opinion that it would not really matter if Romania did not sign the declaration. In spite of these facts, the HSWP PC made a decision, based on János Kádár's proposal, that the most important goal in the given circumstances was to further maintain the *appearance* of unity—that is, the Warsaw Pact should not issue a declaration without Romania.

The events were developed as forecasted by the HSWP PC—in order to obtain a compromise, the question of the organizational transformation was taken off the agenda of the PCC's Bucharest session at the last minute. We can state that, from that time on, the effort to reform and make the organization operational remained ever-present and suffered acute problems until the dissolution of the Warsaw Pact in 1991. Essential changes were effected only in 1969 and 1976 by the establishment of the Committee of Defense Ministers and the Committee of Foreign Ministers, respectively.[49]

Hungarian Secret Mediation during the Vietnam War

It is well known that U.S.–Soviet and Soviet–West German back-channel diplomacy played a crucial role in the settlement of the German question and the success of the process in the golden years of détente between 1969 and 1975, leading up to the signing of the Helsinki Final Act, but the same willingness for cooperation was already perceivable during the escalation of the Vietnam War in 1965–66. In public, the Soviets and their allies harshly condemned the American aggression; therefore, official Soviet–American relations were rather strained. The Kremlin, however, interested in a rapprochement with the United States, was aware of the sincerity of the Johnson administration's wish to find a peaceful solution to the crisis. Therefore, Moscow tasked some of the Soviet bloc countries, notably Poland and Hungary, with a mission to conduct secret negotiations with the leaders of North Vietnam and to urge them to enter into negotiations with Washington and eventually accept the division of Vietnam.[50] These mediation attempts failed because of the Chinese leaders, who, by that time, had a predominant influence over Hanoi and who urged the North Vietnamese to fight until a final victory over the Americans. Beijing's impact on Hanoi was especially decisive during the crucial period of 1965–66, when the escalation of the military conflict could have been stopped by negotiations, at least in principle.[51] At a meeting with Hungarian leader Kádár in May 1965, Brezhnev himself expressed his belief that the Chinese wanted to use the conflict in Indochina to cause a direct military conflict between the Soviet Union and the United States, and he added that Moscow would do everything possible to thwart that evil plan.[52] "It seems to be that using the war in Vietnam the Chinese want to force the Soviet Union and the United States into a direct conflict. This provocation will be rejected by the Soviets. . . . The Soviet Union will give all support to Vietnam, but it will prevent the conflict from developing into a World war."[53] Brezhnev also confessed that

> since the existence of the Soviet Union they have never been engaged in a fight where they did not know the tactics, the strategy and the goal. For the first time, they have no idea about the plans of the Vietnamese and indeed the Chinese, and this has a very bad effect. It must be added that they do not blame the Vietnamese for this. In spite of this, they will help wherever they can. . . . They have the impression that the bombing pause was not just a tactical move on the side of the Americans, but it shows that they themselves do not know how they would get out of this situation. Their intention to negotiate should be taken as serious.[54]

Ironically, the Chinese position voiced by Deng Xiaoping at his meeting with Ceaușescu in the same period, in July 1965, basically confirms the Soviet view.

> We have recently received precise information from which it results that the USA is still wondering whether they should bomb Hanoi and Haiphong, because this would mean bombing the guided-missile bases of the Soviet Union. However, through diplomatic contacts between the Soviet Union and the United States of America, the latter were officially informed about the locations of the Soviet guided-missile bases. That is what these common actions mean! To act jointly with them?! The Soviets wanted us to act jointly with them under the aegis of solving the Vietnamese issue on the basis of the collaboration between the United States of America and the Soviet Union. This is their real purpose.[55]

Deng Xiaoping was right: by 1965, the Soviet leadership was determined to start a campaign for legalizing the post–World War II European status quo, and they were fully aware that it would be impossible without a rapprochement with the other superpower, the United States.

This entails nothing less than the necessity of reconsidering the assessment of the nature of the Vietnam War still dominant in the mainstream literature—namely, that it should be seen as a conflict between two superpowers, the Soviet Union and the United States, in the form of a local war that is similar to the Korean War. As shown in the sources, the Chinese, who took control of the Vietnamese party as early as the beginning of the 1960s, wanted to prevent any Soviet–American rapprochement in world policy by escalating the conflict and trying to trigger a presumably real superpower conflict. This means that the real main actor in the Vietnamese conflict was *China*, and the world did not suspect a thing about Beijing's destructive role.[56] Moreover, it was not in the interest of the Soviet leadership to reveal everything, because in that case it would have had to admit publicly that the North Vietnamese regime only accepted economic and military support from Moscow, while the political orders came from Beijing.

Thus, the Soviets had caught themselves in a trap. On the one hand, they saw support for their ally—the Vietnamese Communist state, attacked by the "American imperialists"—as their internationalist obligation while, on the other hand, they made every effort to ensure that the clash would not turn into a direct conflict with the United States.

It was under these circumstances that Brezhnev, the first secretary of the Soviet party, asked the Hungarian leaders in May 1965 to send a delegation to Vietnam to try to persuade Ho Chi Minh and his company to negotiate a peaceful settlement.[57] Kádár and the Hungarians offered their services, but they also immediately overfulfilled their mission. At its meeting on 22 June 1965, the Politburo not only made a decision on sending this delegation but also provided guidance for Foreign Minister János Péter before his visit to London on discussing with his partner the peaceful settlement of the conflict through negotiations.[58] Thus, there were several attempts made both in the East and in the West, and in the second half of the year, the negotiations were continued directly with the leadership of the United States. The Hungarian and the Soviet leaders (as well as the Polish leaders, who were conducting similar mediation)[59] were surprised to see that the Americans were ready for peaceful settlement and, with this aim in mind, they suspended bombardment from the end of December to the end of January. At the same time, the Vietnamese leaders, programmed by China, did not really seem willing to negotiate—although they sent several signs of willingness for negotiation—because, in accordance with the Chinese orders, this would only become possible when the United States had suffered a crushing defeat. The attempts of Hungary and Poland at mediation had thus run aground in January 1966 because of the firm position taken by the brotherly ally in Asia.[60] The Hungarian leaders made another attempt at mediation in the fall of 1966: in September, Foreign Minister János Péter paid a secret visit to Hanoi, where he talked with the Vietnamese leaders, including Ho Chi Minh. In October, during the time of the UN General Assembly, he conducted negotiations with American secretary of state Dean Rusk, but this attempt also failed because of the uncompromising approach of the Vietnamese leaders.[61]

However, the Hungarian attempts did have some positive yields: both Poland and Hungary were selected to represent the Soviet bloc in the international supervisory committee set up under the peace talks that began in Paris in 1968 and that was responsible for supervising the cease-fire in Vietnam between 1973 and 1975.[62]

Kádár's Mediation during the Prague Spring in 1968

The reform movement in the Czechoslovak Socialist Republic that began in January 1968 coincided with the introduction of the "new economic mechanism" in Hungary.[63] The Hungarian leadership saw three possible scenarios on which to base a prognosis regarding the potential consequences of the events in Prague on Hungary. In the best-case scenario, the Czechoslovak reforms would remain moderate; they would, if reluctantly, be accepted by the Soviets in a development that was analogous to that in Poland in October 1956. In this case, Hungary and Czechoslovakia, the two leading reformist countries within the Soviet bloc, would be able to support each other and serve as an example to the other countries. This would echo the first half of the 1960s, when Hungary and Poland had played a leading role in de-Stalinization. In the second scenario, the far-reaching political reforms in Prague might prove unacceptable to Moscow, which could lead to Hungary's course of moderate restructuring, which did not threaten political destabilization, being given a green light as the lesser of two evils. A comparison of the two processes, which differed in their objectives, might even awaken a certain amount of sympathy on the part of the Soviet leadership for the downright moderate Hungarian reforms, which officially aimed at improving economic efficiency and indirectly served Soviet interests. It was, in fact, this scenario that was turned into reality in 1968 and the ensuing years. The Soviet leadership, after being rather tolerant at the beginning, exerted substantial pressure on the Hungarian leadership in the early 1970s to prevent the reforms from leading to the country's destabilization, and they made sure that the leading reformists were removed during those years; the most important measures of the Hungarian economic reform, however, were allowed to remain in place. In the worst-case scenario, which seemed rather probable at the time, the Czechoslovak reforms, which were above all political in nature, would sooner or later—perhaps even contrary to the original intentions of their initiators—move beyond the limits set by the Soviet leadership. This would ultimately lead to an armed intervention on the pattern of Hungary in 1956 and at the same time could seriously discredit and jeopardize all initiatives and reforms in the Soviet bloc that deviated from the Soviet model, including the Hungarian economic reforms.

Since the beginning of 1968, the primary objective for Kádár and the Hungarian leadership was to do everything in their power to make the first scenario come true. Failing that, the next one in order of preference was the second one; the third one, discrediting and banning all reforms, was to be avoided at all costs. This determination was the driving force behind Kádár's resolve to engage in intensive mediation efforts between Prague and Moscow and the other Soviet bloc states as well from January to September 1968. Thus, he tried to persuade the Czechoslovak leaders to be cautious, to slow down the pace of reform, to acknowledge realities, and to respect Moscow's level of tolerance while he worked hard up to the middle of July and even after that, to convince the Kremlin and the other Soviet bloc leaders to muster more understanding and patience because the cause of Socialism was not yet critically endangered in Czechoslovakia.

Remarkably, during their intensive interaction, Dubček, a "soft" type of Communist leader, was forging an alliance with Kádár, a Communist of the "hard" type, even if, as leader of Hungary's "soft" dictatorship he was generally regarded as a liberal Communist in the West by the end of the 1960s. The main difference between these two types was that a soft Communist leader was neither willing nor capable of using brute force against society in a crisis to suppress the process of democratization, whereas a hard Communist would not hesitate to do so. Besides Dubček, Hungary's Imre Nagy or Poland's Stanisław Kania in 1980–81 belonged to the soft type, and the most well-known soft Communist is clearly Gorbachev. On the basis of this categorization, hard Communists with a proven record were Novotny, Ulbricht, Ochab, Cyrankiewicz, Gerő, Khrushchev, Kádár, Tito, Castro, Mao, Brezhnev, Gomułka, Pol Pot, Jaruzelski, Zhao Ziyang, and Ceaușescu.[64]

Kádár's mediating role stemmed from his own convictions, but it was also an assignment from Brezhnev, who saw from the outset that the only leader in the camp who could successfully influence Dubček was Kádár. Kádár's mediation was fulfilled in the course of a great number of bilateral and multilateral meetings. Between January and August 1968, Kádár met Dubček nine times, five times bilaterally (on three occasions in secret) and four times at multilateral meetings.[65] The bilateral talks were the following: Topol'čianky, 20–21 January; Komárno, 4 February; Budapest, 13–15 June; Komárom, 13 July; and Komárno, 17 August. The two leaders also met at the following multilateral meetings: celebrations of the twentieth anniversary of the Communist takeover in Czechoslovakia, Prague, 22–24 February; the meeting of the WP

PCC, Sofia, 6–7 March; the meeting of the Six (the WP members without Romania), Dresden, 23 March; and the meeting of the Six, Bratislava, 3 August. Brezhnev, besides meeting the leaders of the five other countries of the Six at the summit meetings, was also in regular telephone contact with them, and he very often called Kádár for purposes of sharing information and consultation. On average, he spoke to Kádár at least once a week, with occasional peaks of twice a day.

The difference of opinion between Kádár and the Soviets or the other Socialist leaders did not concern the question of whether the Soviet Union and the member states of the Warsaw Pact were entitled to intervene if a restoration of capitalism was to be attempted in Czechoslovakia. Thus, the difference was not in the degree of loyalty to the Communist system but in the assessment of the situation—that is, in choosing the right moment once it became obvious that there was no longer the chance for a political settlement and that Czechoslovakia could only be kept within the Socialist camp through a military invasion. Yet, in this question, he stubbornly clung to the formula that was for him a tried and proven one on the basis of his own experience: armed intervention was the method of choice only once the counterrevolution had already gained the upper hand. If this undesirable development did indeed come to pass then the Soviet Union was in a position to restore the Communist system in a matter of a few days. This was why, at the beginning, the official Hungarian position on developments in Czechoslovakia emphasized that, despite negative tendencies, there was as yet no counterrevolutionary danger; the goal was merely the correction of earlier mistakes.

By early May 1968, Kádár, too, saw the danger of a counterrevolution and the seriousness of the situation, and he modified his position accordingly. From that point on, he underlined that at least the counterrevolution had not yet been victorious. At the Warsaw meeting of the five in July, Kádár endorsed the plan of a joint invasion *in principle* and declared Hungary to be prepared to participate,[66] but he continued to do everything to prevent a drastic solution from happening. In the end, he bowed to the inevitable, and Hungary took part in the military action on 21 August by "officially" sending one division.[67] Even then, Kádár maintained his position that Czechoslovakia, as opposed to Hungary in 1956, had not yet reached the counterrevolutionary phase in August 1968, so the intervention had been premature.[68] In this case, however, Kádár's assessment of the situation was mistaken. For we have to dispel the still surviving myth of "Socialism with a human face": indeed, from a historical perspective, it is now clear that the Prague Spring would have led to the restoration of parliamentary democracy without foreign intervention, as it eventually did in 1990.[69] The Soviet leadership in reality demonstrated extreme patience and self-restraint during the eight months of the crisis, as a violent solution would not have been irrational from their imperial perspective already in March, following the abolition of censorship in Czechoslovakia. From that time on, there was little hope that the local leadership would be able to push the genie of democracy back into the bottle. Yet, learning from the lesson of their fatal mistake to intervene in Budapest too early, right at the beginning of the 1956 Hungarian Revolution, they now tried to find a political solution to restore order according to the Kremlin's norms, executed by local forces only, and thus to avoid Soviet military intervention. Hence, during the Czechoslovak crisis, in the first phase this meant persuading the Dubček leadership to realize the limits of Moscow's tolerance and then hoping to have the restoration done by the Soviet line's "healthy forces." In the end, however, they had no other option but to use the Brezhnev Doctrine and stop the dangerous process of political transition by a military invasion.

Consequently, the question about a possible alternative course of history is not whether the Prague Spring could have survived under different circumstances but rather this: if János Kádár, the most hated man right after the bloody suppression of the revolution of 1956 in Hungary, was able to develop a rather liberal version of the Communist dictatorship that could generate even relative popularity within society, and which was also tolerated by the Soviets all along, why could the same model not be applied to Gustáv Husák's Czechoslovakia?

The general public both at home and abroad rightly raised the question, which is timely even today: what would have happened if Hungary had not joined the invasion coalition? From a moral viewpoint, this political step had incalculable consequences. Although everybody knew, including the people in Czechoslovakia, that the decision was not made voluntarily by a legitimate Hungarian government, the fall into sin was evident. Hungary's participation in the occupation of Czechoslovakia was a serious historic crime, which cannot be remedied by any later apology. Moreover, one of the member states of the Soviet bloc, Romania, did not take part in the invasion—although it is true that it was not invited to. What is more, Ceaușescu openly condemned the action, but it had no perceivable negative consequence for Romania. Indeed, the Hungarian leadership could also have decided not to participate in the invasion despite Soviet pressure. Today we also know that, despite the initial plans, the GDR army did not take part in the intervention, not because Ulbricht did not want to, but, on the contrary, at the request of collaborating Czechoslovak leaders, who reminded the Soviets of the historical precedents, so the Soviet leaders withdrew permission for East German participation at the last moment.[70] However, in the Socialist propaganda, the entire Warsaw Pact, with the GDR in the lead, was proud to proclaim for decades that GDR troops had also been there. Since Romania's absence was an obvious fact, a negative decision on participation by Kádár would have automatically placed him in the same camp as Ceaușescu. This would not have been an attractive alternative, not only because Kádár was on bad terms with the Romanian leader but also because the main principle of Hungarian foreign policy was totally contrary to that of Romania. In their "deviant" policy, the Romanians were seeking as much publicity as possible in every case, so they were able to "sell" more deviation to the West than what the real difference was. For Kádár, however, the most important criterion was predictability and trustworthy partnership in international relations—with both the East and the West. This trustworthy status, which Kádár had been building since 1956, would have been severely jeopardized if Hungary had opted out of the invasion. He was afraid that losing the confidence of the Soviet leadership would have a strong negative impact on the political and economic development of Hungary. The first victim would have been the economic reform being introduced at that time, which a few years later still earned the disapproval of Moscow and, as a result, had to be restrained significantly. The removal of Kádár could also have been a logical option, as Dubček was replaced by Soviet persuasion in April 1969, Ulbricht in May 1971, and Stanislaw Kania a decade later, in October 1981, for much less deviance, whereas Gomułka had to resign, especially for internal reasons, in December 1970.

All in all, we can say that Kádár might have tried to stay out of the invasion, but he as a leader, for his mental constitution, was unsuitable for taking such a radical step against the Soviet Union. If he had done so, it probably would not have been possible for Hungary to achieve the relative independence the Hungarian leaders had managed to secure in the 1970s and 1980s in the Soviet camp, precisely based on reliability. In other words, Hungary, the "happiest barrack in the Soviet camp," would have been less happy and by no means the happiest one. Most likely Hungary would have ended up with a "neither meat, nor fish" kind of political line, which would have been similar to the period of "normalization" in Czechoslovakia. Thus, in a moral sense, Hungary paid a high price for the invasion but, in a material sense, she was probably better off.

Chapter 8

The German Question and the CSCE Process

*Foreign Policy Coordination and Lobby Fights
in the Soviet Bloc, 1964–1975*

The Issue of European Security

The results of new Cold War history research, unfolding following the archival revolutions in East Central Europe in the post-1989 period, make it increasingly clear that the key objective of Soviet *Westpolitik* was the creation of European security according to the interests of the Soviet bloc already from the mid-1960s. This primarily meant the settlement of the post–World War II international situation—that is, codifying the European status quo established in 1945, at the end of the war. At the center of the problem was the German question, and among the tasks to be resolved were insurmountable issues like the recognition of the Oder-Neisse border and the GDR, the status of West Berlin, the relations between the two German states, and the establishment of diplomatic relations with the Federal Republic of Germany by the Soviet bloc states.[1]

As discussed in chapter 3, the Soviet leaders proposed the establishment of a collective European security system as early as 1954. Although the Western powers rejected the Soviet initiative, which they considered a propaganda ploy, Moscow did not give up on the idea in the long run. The period following the establishment of the Warsaw Pact in May 1955, however, was full of turbulent events in world politics that did not favor such endeavors.[2] Nevertheless, in 1959, at the initiative of the GDR leadership a "Permanent Committee for studying the questions pertaining to European security" was established, with the participation of the relevant academic institutes of the Soviet Union, the GDR, Czechoslovakia, and Poland. The committee organized conferences in Prague in 1961 and in East Berlin in 1964 and 1965. Hungary joined the committee in September 1965.[3]

The idea of starting a campaign for holding a pan-European security conference reemerged just a decade after the abortive initiative of Khrushchev and Molotov in 1954. This time, it began as a project of the Polish leadership, which raised the issue at the end of 1964. In his speech at the UN General Assembly on 14 December, Adam Rapacki, the Polish foreign minister, proposed convening a European security conference with the participation of the United States and Canada.

The proposal was then officially put forward at the session of the WP PCC held in the Polish capital in January 1965, but without any special preparation or previous consultation with the member states. Although the issue was originally not even on the agenda of the meeting, the participants supported the improvised proposal unanimously. Thus, in the declaration published at the end of the session, a special paragraph was included to the effect that the member states of the Warsaw Pact considered it necessary to convene "a conference of European states to discuss measures to ensure collective security in Europe."[4]

Yet this message—although it may be considered to be the starting point of the process that eventually led to the signing of the Helsinki Final Act—was presented in a rather marginal way in the document. This was due to the chaotic nature of the PCC session, held just a few months after the fall of Khrushchev and the first such meeting since 1956 in which real debates took place among the representatives of the member states. At the gathering, numerous issues, more important at the time but historically less relevant, had to be discussed. In the first place, there was the East bloc's reaction to the Western plan for the establishment of a multilateral nuclear force (MNF).[5] Consequently, the declaration—besides stating that, in the event the MNF plan was implemented, the Warsaw Pact "would be forced to carry out the necessary defense measures"—put forward a series of previously suggested confidence-building proposals, such as the establishment of a nuclear-free zone in Central Europe, the conclusion of a nonaggression pact with the NATO countries, and a commitment on the nuclear-free status of the two Germanys.[6]

In the second half of 1965, the management of the issue of a potential European security conference was taken over by Soviet diplomacy. From that time on, this question—in close correlation with Moscow's endeavors to settle the German question—became the central problem of the period lasting until the middle of the 1970s.

Consequently, the next session of the WP PCC, held in Bucharest in July 1966, was wholly devoted to the issue of the security conference. As opposed to the improvisational character of several previous and many later PCC meetings, this session was preceded by a very lengthy process of intensive multilateral coordination, including the longest foreign ministers' session in the history of the alliance, lasting some two weeks.[7] The Soviets had an ambitious plan for the PCC meeting: on the one hand, they wanted to carry out the organizational transformation of the alliance that had been urged by several member states, such as Poland and Hungary, for a long time, and at the same time they wanted to issue a powerful declaration, now focusing exclusively on the European security conference. Moscow's priority was the latter, and this was clearly shown by the last-minute special deal made with Romania, who strongly opposed the reforms. Because of that arrangement, the reform of the political and military organization was taken off the agenda just before the meeting.[8] In turn, the Warsaw Pact's Bucharest Declaration was accepted unanimously. The extremely lengthy seven-page document called on the leaders of the states of the continent to start preliminary talks on the staging of a conference on European security.

At the same time, however, the East bloc's preconditions were also established: the West was to accept the existence of the two German states, and the FRG was to give up the claim of sole representation of the German people and recognize the existing eastern borders. In addition to this, the document—due to Romanian pressure—urged the withdrawal of foreign troops from the territory of the European states and the elimination of foreign military bases and called for the simultaneous dissolution of the two military-political alliance:, NATO and the Warsaw Pact. This appeal from the Bucharest session of the WP PCC constituted the East bloc's first serious initiative concerning the institutional settlement of East–West relations and, at the same time, represented the first important step on the road leading to the signing of the Helsinki Final Act in 1975.

Reactions to the declaration were not totally unfavorable in the West either, but the preconditions concerning the convening of the conference could not yet, at that time, be accepted by most states concerned. Nevertheless, these were basically demands of a *defensive* character, and in fact they were far from irrational. This was clearly illustrated by the fact that, just a few years later, during the general settlement of the German question between 1970 and 1973, the FRG and the West in general accepted all preconditions set down in Bucharest. At the same time, the Bucharest Declaration had a very harsh anti-American and anti-FRG tone, the text quite overtly calling on the Western European countries to rid themselves of U.S. influence.[9] Although this idea might have coincided with the wishful thinking of many in the societies and even in the governmental circles of a number of Western European countries, such tactical advice coming from, as it were, the "other side of the moon" could hardly contribute to the success of the Soviet bloc's initiative. In reality, as we will see, it was exactly the case that acquiring the cooperation of these two states—that is, the United States and the FRG—was the key factor in the eventual success of the process leading up to the signing of the Helsinki Final Act.

Thus, the Bucharest Declaration of the Warsaw Pact states calling for the summoning of a pan-European security conference seemed to be a premature initiative that did not give rise to the actual preparation process for such a gathering—at least as far as the public reactions were concerned. The Bucharest Declaration promptly triggered a serious but of course confidential multilateral reevaluation process in NATO, which resulted in the adoption of the Harmel Report in 1967. This new policy guideline established the dual goal of security by strength on the one hand and détente and cooperation on the other in the Western alliance's dealings with the Soviet bloc. The general cooperative tone of the report, prepared with the active participation of several smaller NATO countries, hinted that, on the Western side too, there was by now a genuine willingness for recognition of the post–World War II geopolitical realities in Europe. Thus, a settlement between East and West based on a historic compromise looked much more likely in 1967 than how it appeared in the public policies of the Western side.

Considering the positive, or at least neutral, response to the Bucharest Declaration in several Western countries and also having thoroughly analyzed the reaction of the West to the East bloc's initiative, the Soviets concluded that a grand and comprehensive political campaign had to be launched in order to convince Western Europe of its position, both at a governmental level and at the level of society.

As far as working on the public was concerned, they could reckon primarily with the assistance of the Communist parties in Western Europe. During this period, these parties were already much less willing to follow obediently the orders of Moscow than before the Second World War or in the 1950s. The de-Stalinization process under Khrushchev had already been a serious test for most of them, and in the 1960s, they had to face various challenges and influences, such as Maoism and other new left-wing ideologies, the polycentrism theory, convergence, and the nonallied movement, as well as some proto-Eurocommunist tendencies. Thus, as far as the Western European Communist parties were concerned, unity in the old sense was already a thing of the past, and Soviets had every reason to be concerned about whether they would be able to line up these parties again on the "battlefield," this time with the aim of codifying the European status quo. Eventually, all the participants attending the conference of the European Communist and workers' parties held in April 1967 at Karlovy Vary in Czechoslovakia accepted the Soviet proposal, and the declaration issued after the conference unanimously endorsed the convening of a pan-European security conference.

From then until March 1969, the Bucharest appeal of the Warsaw Pact and the Karlovy Vary Declaration were jointly used by the countries of the East bloc as the principal basis for further steps concerning the security conference.

As for convincing the political and governmental circles in Western Europe, the Soviets again resorted to the tools of a decentralization policy. After the WP's Bucharest appeal, Moscow began very firmly urging the member states of the alliance to engage in bilateral negotiations with the Western European countries to convince them how significant this initiative was with respect to the development of East–West relations. The main goal of this campaign was to promote the Soviets' most important strategic goal—that is, convening the European security conference in order to confirm the European status quo that had been established after the Second World War. Yet, as a by-product of this process not to be underestimated, the East Central European states had a chance to strengthen their Western relations "legally." While carrying out the task set by the Soviets, they gained extensive knowledge and experience during the intensive bilateral talks, as a result of which they could quickly emancipate themselves within the structure of East–West relations. Up to the early 1960s, they were regarded simply as "Soviet satellite states" in common parlance as well as in the internal confidential political documents in the West, but by the end of the decade—with the exception of the GDR—they could present themselves as legitimate partners in international politics. This was not simply an additional consequence of the unfolding détente process that had radically transformed East–West relations but a qualitatively new status acquired by these countries in their own right, made possible through a series of bilateral negotiations with the Western states aimed at paving the way for the European security conference.

Naturally, the Socialist countries of East Central Europe had conducted one-on-one negotiations with Western countries earlier, especially from the beginning of the 1960s, but these were primarily bilateral talks in the classical sense of the term, focused mostly on the development of economic relations. Up to that time, however, the Soviet Union had basically had the privilege of representing the Eastern bloc on the most important issues of world politics. Now, from this time on, the Soviet leadership tried to give more maneuvering room to its allies in the arena of world politics, and, subsequently, it had no alternative but to regard them as partners, although only in a limited sense.

This development resulted in the active participation of some of the East Central European countries on an unprecedented level—especially Poland, Hungary, and Romania—in international politics, which promoted their accelerated emancipation, both within their own alliance and in the East–West relationship overall.

These negotiations contributed to easing international tensions, gradually increasing confidence between the representatives of the two sides and promoting the development of a common European conscience in the long run. The active and intensive participation in the unfolding East–West dialogue—mainly concerning general issues up to this point—prepared these countries for the role that they would later play in the process initiated by the WP PCC's Budapest Declaration, issued in March 1969. As a result, the European allies of the Soviet Union participated in the preparatory negotiations for the Helsinki Conference, not simply as the mere executors of Soviet policy but, in several cases—and in many areas—as independent entities, often playing an important role in shaping the overall process.

As discussed in chapter 6, by the middle of the 1960s, the Soviet bloc was divided into an economy-oriented (Hungary, Romania, and Bulgaria) and a security-concerned (the GDR, Poland and Czechoslovakia) sub-bloc as far as the German question was concerned.[10] The countries in the first group had no serious unsettled issues with the FRG; therefore, they were seriously interested in economic cooperation, increasing trade, and taking over cutting-edge technologies. Thus, they were the primary victims of the lack of diplomatic relations with West Germany. Now it was increasingly difficult for them to identify unconditionally with the interests of the security-concerned sub-bloc, looking at the FRG as a security threat, since the public in their countries had difficulty accepting the fact that their country could not establish diplomatic relations with its most important Western economic partner.

The existence of the two sub-blocs, however, was not visible to the public; they were not separated within the Soviet bloc, and the members did not engage in multilateral talks with each other to harmonize their interests. The sub-blocs actually functioned as a virtual coalition: their recognized common interests were represented individually during the meetings of the Soviet bloc's multilateral forums, in their bilateral relations with Moscow and the other Soviet bloc states, and vis-à-vis the Western states.[11]

In the case of Hungary, by the beginning of the 1960s, about 30 percent of the country's foreign trade was being conducted with Western countries, and one-quarter of that volume involved the FRG.[12] In reality, the FRG had been Hungary's most important Western economic partner since the middle of the 1950s, and it kept this position until 1989. Thus, the FRG played a crucial role in Hungary's rebuilding of her economic ties with the Western countries.[13] In contemporary Soviet bloc propaganda, however, West Germany was presented as a dangerous revanchist power, aiming at a revision of the 1945 European status quo. Thus, the Hungarian leadership had to follow a dual policy: vis-à-vis Bonn, they loyally followed the general line of the Soviet bloc, while in the field of economic relations, they tried to exploit the favorable situation emerging, especially from the early 1960s on.[14]

Regarding the question of European security—the central issue being the settlement of the German question—the positions in the Soviet bloc were roughly the same as those concerning the previous equation. Hence, Hungary conducted a specific type of pragmatic politics within the Soviet bloc, which was determined by the country's perpetual interests. Consequently, working for détente became an important priority for the Hungarian leadership from the mid-1960s onward, and one of the prime foreign policy goals became fighting for making the détente process irreversible.

The first policy paper on Hungary's international relations reflecting this determination was prepared just half a year after the WP PCC's Bucharest Declaration.[15] In January 1967, Foreign Minister János Péter submitted a comprehensive concept to the HSWP PC, proposing an important role for Hungary in the intensification of the détente process and the radical improvement of East–West relations.[16] In order to actively work for the convening of a European security conference, he proposed to establish intensive official and personal relations primarily with Austria, Great Britain, and France, as well as with other smaller Western European countries, such as Belgium, Denmark, the Netherlands, and Norway. The most radical thesis of the concept was the proposal for establishing a framework for close cooperation among "the countries of the Danube Valley and the Central European states"[17] (Hungary, Czechoslovakia, Yugoslavia, and Austria).

In all probability, János Péter was the only Hungarian foreign minister of the whole post-1945 era who did not consider his post to have simply a political function but rather a profession independent of the circumstances and who therefore could rightly be called the Hungarian Rapacki.[18] His "Danube valley" idea was almost expressively aimed at virtually rebuilding the regional unity of the former Austro-Hungarian monarchy, which had once proved to be a rational and effective model of cooperation in many respects. All of this indicated that, already at the beginning of 1967, he could give a prognosis of such radical transformation of East–West relations that would make a close cooperation possible, spanning over different social systems. János Péter, who probably considered lobbying for this idea his personal matter, had made numerous attempts at convincing the Soviet leadership up until the early 1970s, among others using the refined reasoning that neutral Austria could be drawn closer to the Eastern bloc.[19] Although in the following years détente resulted in a rapprochement between the two camps as had never been seen before, the "Danube Valley" idea did not become acceptable, either at that time or later for Moscow, since the Soviet leadership instinctively worried about the potential negative consequences of any specific East Central European regional coordination. Péter's intransigence concerning his pet project might very well have contributed to his being relieved from the position of foreign minister in December 1973.

The plan of January 1967, however, unambiguously signaled the endeavor of Hungarian foreign policy makers to participate actively and in a rather innovative way in the process of the transformation of East–West relations.

Consequently, following the WP PCC's declaration in Bucharest in July 1966, Hungarian diplomacy, also encouraged by the Soviet leadership, launched a large-scale campaign for conducting bilateral negotiations with West European partners, promoting the idea of a European security conference. In the period between 1966 and 1969, talks were conducted with numerous states at the level of foreign ministers, deputy foreign ministers, and foreign policy experts. It was during this period, in March 1968, that the Hungarian prime minister's first visit to Western Europe since 1946 took place: Jenő Fock conducted talks with President de Gaulle and Prime Minister Georges Pompidou in Paris.

Thus, the Soviet drive for improving East–West relations emerging in the mid-1960s fully coincided with the interests of the Hungarian leadership. The explicit purpose of the Soviet bloc's campaign involved an all-encompassing effort to set in motion one of the most important strategic targets of the period, namely the staging of the European security conference and thus sanctioning of the post–World War II European status quo. Meanwhile, in the course of intensive bilateral negotiations, the East Central European states, including Hungary, could "legally" augment their ties with the West and had acquired a negotiating competence they never had before. From then on, as the Soviet leadership tried to advance the role of their allies in world politics, Moscow itself had come to regard them as partners, albeit only in a limited sense. This development resulted in unprecedented international activities by some of the East Central European countries—especially Poland, Hungary, and Romania—which in turn promoted their emancipation both within their own alliance and in East–West relations in general.

This development also upgraded Hungary's role in the Eastern bloc. While Hungary had started out with a serious disadvantage due to the events of 1956, this gap had virtually disappeared by the mid-1960s, and the country became a model state for the West in the context of de-Stalinization and relative internal liberalism in a Communist country. Apart from the Soviet Union, Poland, and Romania, Hungarian diplomacy also assumed an important role in international politics, and this position was strengthened further when Hungary became a nonpermanent member of the UN Security Council for two years beginning in January 1968. Despite Hungary's participation in the invasion of Czechoslovakia, the West judged it according to its pre-August 1968 performance. Hence, Hungary gradually assumed an important position alongside Romania and Poland in the context of developing East–West relations and promoting the cause of the European security conference—and moreover, by this time, with some advantage: the Hungarian economic reform, launched in January 1968, was perceived in the West as a shift toward market economy and was therefore assessed positively. At the same time, the anti-Semitic campaign that emerged in Poland after the 1967 war in the Middle East indisputably damaged the international standing of the Warsaw leadership, while the security concerns of the country vis-à-vis West Germany also seriously limited its international room to maneuver.

A Missed Opportunity: The Challenge of Establishing Diplomatic Relations with the FRG, 1966–1967

When the issue of solving the German question emerged at the Warsaw Pact PCC meetings in January 1965 and July 1966, the Hungarian leadership loyally adopted the Soviet position, and they also fully supported the fight initiated for the international recognition of the GDR. The joint WP position, however, worked out at the Bucharest PCC conference, was interpreted in Budapest as an incentive for fighting against the Hallstein Doctrine that would eventually strengthen the position of the GDR as well; therefore, it was supported by the East Germans at the time.

Consequently, when the new West German government of the Grand Coalition, now including the Social Democrats, initiated secret preliminary talks with Czechoslovakia, Hungary, Romania, and Bulgaria in December 1966 in order to establish diplomatic relations with these states,[20] the Hungarian leadership was eager to respond positively to this challenge. This step indicated a radical turning point in the foreign policy of the FRG, since it would clearly have meant voluntarily giving up the Hallstein Doctrine, which would have been considered a victory in the Soviet bloc. In return for this significant concession, they asked to consider the "Moscow model" as the basis of the settlement of the relations,[21] meaning that none of the parties could set preconditions. Thus, the East Central European partners had to tacitly accept the long represented FRG position concerning the German question. With this, it seemed high time to convene a consultative meeting, as it was suggested by Gomułka in October in Moscow,[22] but Romanian opposition prevented it. Thus, the countries concerned—harmonizing their standpoints with Moscow—made their decisions independently. Besides the Soviets, Hungary informed all the other WP member states about the negotiations as well, but she received ambiguous responses, if any. Nevertheless, no rejection was received from any of the parties. The Hungarian leadership considered this an approval, and thus the HSWP PC session on 10 January 1967 accepted a resolution to start official negotiations with the FRG.[23] On the basis of this authorization, Rolf Lahr, a leading official of the West German foreign ministry, conducted negotiations in Hungary on 23–26 January 1967. As a result, the Hungarian leadership was ready to establish diplomatic relations.

At that time, the Soviet leadership also deemed it desirable to settle the relations on the basis of the Moscow model. The East German and Polish leadership, however, reacted hysterically to this opportunity and immediately began to lobby with the Soviet leaders to block the plan.[24] At the end of January 1967, at their meeting in eastern Poland, Gomułka tried to blackmail Brezhnev by threatening that such a move would lead to the disintegration of the Warsaw Pact. Moreover, he called on the Soviet leader to convene a meeting of the Warsaw Pact PCC if Moscow was unable to prevent the planned steps of the allies. Brezhnev finally gave in and promised that within a few days, a meeting of the Warsaw Pact foreign ministers would be summoned.[25]

At that point, a totally unexpected move upset the ongoing crisis-management process: on 31 January 1967, without any consultation with the WP member states, it was suddenly publicly announced that Romania had agreed with the FRG to establish diplomatic relations. To make things worse, the Romanian decision was openly criticized in the GDR press, which generated a public dispute between East Berlin and Bucharest—an unprecedented action within the Warsaw Pact. Therefore, to handle the emerging grave intra-bloc crisis, an extraordinary meeting of foreign ministers was summoned in Warsaw.[26] János Péter, the Hungarian foreign minister, took part in the conference with the mandate that, for tactical reasons, establishing diplomatic relations with the FRG might be postponed temporarily as a consequence of Romania's unilateral step, but that at the same time the WP members should reach an agreement on how the other member states could enter into diplomatic relations at a later date, perhaps in a few months' time. Instead of adopting this flexible tactical proposal, under hard pressure from the GDR and Poland (with Soviet assistance), and with no previous information—the participants were presented with an ultimatum, forcing them to accept a secret protocol that could be called the "Warsaw diktat."

This protocol stated that, in the case of the East Central European countries that still had no diplomatic relations with the FRG, the conditions were not suitable for establishing such relations. The preconditions for the FRG were summarized in six points:

1. Renunciation of the principle of sole representation of the German nation
2. Recognition of the GDR
3. Recognition of existing borders—including the Oder-Neisse Line
4. Recognition of West Berlin's special status and that it did not belong to the FRG
5. Renunciation of the possession of nuclear weapons

6. Recognition of the invalidity of the Munich agreement from the beginning[27]

According to the East German and Polish standpoint, with due persistence, the FRG could be forced to recognize the GDR within a few years, to renounce the claim to the sole representation of the German people, and to accept the European borders settled after World War II.[28]

The Hungarian leadership was shocked when they realized that their plans had been thwarted by their allies. During the HSWP PC session of 13 February 1967, a vehement debate developed over the Warsaw diktat and possible reactions to this humiliating situation.[29] They had been accustomed to being compelled to follow certain steps of the Soviet leadership even if they did not agree with them, but this was the first time when such a serious sacrifice was the result of pressure not from the Kremlin but from allies that were subject to Moscow's power in the same way that Hungary was.[30] It is not an exaggeration to say that this represented the gravest crisis for the Hungarian leadership since 1956 with regard to the alliance.[31] In the ensuing debate in the Politburo, it became obvious that none of the members regarded the six points of the Warsaw diktat as realistic. Eventually the HSWP PC decided that, in order to maintain the unity of the Warsaw Pact, the parties concerned should be informed about the special Hungarian position: they would loyally carry out the joint resolution accepted in Warsaw, but the HSWP did not agree with the main thesis of the protocol, because consultation on the issue of establishing diplomatic relations with the FRG should have been left open. In any case, none of this changed the situation significantly, so the Hungarian plan to normalize relations with Bonn was sacrificed for the common interests of the Soviet bloc.

In a paradoxical way, however, from a historical perspective, we can conclude that in this case the rigid and persistent standpoint of the GDR and Poland was eventually justified by the course of history, as the results they had been hoping for were achieved in what turned out to be a relatively short period of time. If the FRG had opened relations with these three countries along the lines described, it is more than likely that such a development would have significantly affected the budding process of the general settlement of the German question. Even the very outcome of the West German elections in September 1969—that is, the victory of the Social Democratic Party—could have been called into question; indeed, it could have rightly been argued that if it had been possible to achieve such an important diplomatic victory in the field of *Ostpolitik* by applying a flexible policy but without making basic concessions, this could have been a model for a successful FRG strategy in the future as well. This, in turn, might well have influenced the entire process of détente.

The preconditions set forth in the Warsaw protocol were publicly reinforced in the declaration of the conference of the European Communist and workers' parties in April 1967 in Karlovy Vary, Czechoslovakia; thus, there seemed to be not much hope for the Hungarian leadership to change the joint Soviet bloc position in the short run. Yet, in the following few years, from time to time the HSWP leaders tried to speed up the process by putting forward proposals to this effect at multilateral and bilateral talks but, in the end, they were loyally keeping to the obligatory bloc timetable. Eventually, on 21 December 1973, Hungary became the last WP member state to establish diplomatic relations with the FRG. Thus, an important and hitherto unknown initiative by FRG chancellor Willy Brandt was also turned down: before the early general elections in 1972, Brandt confidentially approached the Hungarian leadership and asked for a meeting with János Kádár to ask him to support the victory of the Social Democratic Party by swiftly establishing diplomatic relations. At the same time, during these years, both sides had the opinion that bilateral economic relations could not be any better, even in the case of having diplomatic relations.[32]

The Breakthrough: The Making of the Budapest Appeal

At this juncture, another fine opportunity emerged for Hungary through the unexpected acceleration of the CSCE process, in which Budapest played an important role. It is a well-known fact that the Budapest appeal of the Warsaw Pact, issued at the PCC session on 17 March 1969, became a milestone in the history of East–West relations, since this initiative of the Soviet bloc commenced the process that led to the signing of the Helsinki Final Act in 1975. This was both a novelty and a success, since—contrary to the Bucharest Declaration in 1966—it called on the European countries to hold a security conference without setting any preconditions.

The declaration of the Warsaw Pact member states that finally did initiate the preparatory process for the European security conference was issued in the glorious neo-Gothic building of the Hungarian Parliament on the Danube, modeled after the Houses of Parliament in London. The official signing ceremony of the declaration on 17 March 1969 was open to the press as an unprecedented media event in the history of the Warsaw Pact. Thus, the active role played by Hungarian diplomacy in supporting the Soviet project was rewarded by the fact that Budapest could become the venue of the most important WP PCC meeting since the establishment of the alliance—or at least this is how it was perceived in retrospect.

We now know that the Budapest call was in fact not the result of a well-conceived and prepared synchronized action, as it seemed to the public, based on unprecedented on-the-spot media coverage at the time. In truth, it was a document published by the WP member states at the end of a surprisingly short political coordination process comprising numerous improvised elements as a result of unprecedented fierce debates among the participants.[33]

Documents pertaining to the multilateral preparations for the session shed new light on the genesis of this historically important declaration.[34] First, with the exception of Berlin, Budapest was the only capital where there had been no PCC meeting up to that time so, on the basis of the rotation system that had been in effect since 1965, it was quite logical to have the next one there. Second, on the agenda of the session, which was originally to take place in December 1968, there was, up to the last moment, *only one issue*: the establishment of the legal military structure of the WP for peacetime.[35] In early February 1969, Soviet leader Leonid Brezhnev mentioned to Kádár in Moscow that it would be a great achievement if, in addition to the required changes in the military structure, a general political declaration on the main issues of international politics could be unanimously adopted in Budapest (the first PCC meeting to follow the WP's military intervention in Czechoslovakia, publicly condemned by Romania at the time).[36]

Based on currently accessible sources, we still do not know much about the circumstances under which the Soviet leadership made the decision on issuing a call for a European security conference at the Budapest meeting. Several important developments had taken place since the beginning of 1969, and especially prior to the meeting of the PCC, each of which might have made its own contribution to the decision. Richard Nixon, the newly elected president of the United States, took office in January 1969. During his election campaign, Nixon had already indicated that he was ready to take significant steps to improve Soviet–American relations, and in February, a back channel was established at his initiative between the two governments as a result of secret negotiations led by the president's national security advisor, Henry Kissinger.[37] Since the Americans were willing to include European affairs in the negotiations, there was now some hope among the Soviets that the United States would also endorse the issue of a European security conference, which had been advocated by the Soviet Union for so many years within the general framework of improving East–West relations.[38]

On 2 March 1969, little more than two weeks before the Budapest meeting, there was an armed incident at the Ussuri River on the Soviet-Chinese border that evoked the danger of an open military conflict between the two countries, which had severed relations at the beginning of the 1960s.[39] Since the eastern borders of the Soviet Union now seemed to be severely threatened, it was quite logical that the Soviets should make new efforts to secure the final borders of the empire in the West—that is, to codify the status quo established after the Second World War. The main opponent of this endeavor had, up to that time, been the West German government. On 5 March 1969, however, the social democrat Gustav Heinemann was elected president of the FRG. Although his post was not comparable to that of the American or the French president, the fact that he was elected half a year before the forthcoming general elections in September 1969 boded well for the Social Democratic Party and its chancellor candidate, Willy Brandt. As minister of foreign affairs in the Grand Coalition government that had taken office in 1966, Brandt had already provided ample evidence that he was ready to take even radical steps to improve relations with the East Central European states if he were to come to power. As seen before, the Soviet leadership had long been preparing to promote the issue of a European security conference, and, at the beginning of March 1969, they faced immediate pressure in the East and a great opportunity in the West. These factors may have strengthened the recognition by Soviet leaders that the forthcoming conference of the WP PCC in Budapest would be a great opportunity for them to see whether conditions for the European security conference had really improved as a result of the efforts made since the Bucharest Declaration and the most recent developments in international politics. This also required the approval of their allies, who could be persuaded by the notion that this "Easter gift package" had something for all parties involved. The Romanians' share was the repeated announcement of the Bucharest Declaration of July 1966 calling for a security conference—this time *without any conditions*, which was welcomed by the Hungarian hosts as well. The Poles and the East Germans understood that the resolution of the German question, so important for them, could only be achieved by a *unified* Warsaw Pact bargaining with the West, and this unity could only be maintained by making concessions to Romania.

The idea of issuing a declaration on European security at the Budapest meeting was raised in a letter from the Soviet leadership dated 7 March 1969 to János Kádár. Even at that point, just ten days before the session, it was clear that the declaration was meant to be a secondary issue on the agenda, as the Soviets were planning to issue a general document evaluating the most important issues of world policy.

Thereafter, events gathered considerable speed. On 9 March, Soviet deputy foreign minister Nikolay Firyubin sent two documents to the Hungarian leadership. One was the draft of a general political statement evaluating the main issues on the international scene in accordance with the old tried and tested practice. It formulated the position of the Soviet bloc concerning NATO, the FRG, the situation in the Middle East, the war in Vietnam, and the Chinese violations of the Soviet frontier. The other document was the draft of an appeal for convening a pan-European security conference; the text proposed setting up an operative preparatory committee. Apart from the military documents to be signed at the PCC meeting, these were the two official drafts that were submitted *as Hungarian proposals* to the member states.[40] This was all the more interesting given that the Hungarian leadership had fundamental objections to the first document, which was regarded as a rather confrontational draft.[41]

On 13 March, Firyubin arrived in Budapest for preparatory talks with the Hungarian leaders about the forthcoming meeting. János Kádár strongly argued for seeking the simultaneous acceptance of the military documents and the declaration on European security. He warned Moscow, however, that this was possible only if serious concessions were made to the Romanians concerning delicate issues such as China, the FRG, and Israel, as otherwise Bucharest would not sign the general foreign policy document.[42] The Hungarian proposal was accepted by Moscow, and thus a *virtual* Soviet–Hungarian–Romanian joint position was in the making. As a new development in the decision-making process within the alliance, however, all of this was not enough for a unified decision: it was now the turn of the Polish and East German leaders, who were fighting fiercely for their special interests. During the discussions of the deputy foreign ministers and the party leaders preceding the PCC meeting, the Poles and the East Germans urged stronger wording on the condemnation of the FRG especially, whereas the Romanians were keen on producing a shorter and less bellicose text.[43]

The Hungarian tactical proposal therefore eventually became the basis of a compromise that made it possible to accomplish two tasks: the concurrent signing of the military documents and the appeal urging a European security conference. This was accomplished by finally giving up on a general foreign policy statement regarding current political issues. This result was achieved in a very intensive process of negotiations that could be characterized as dramatic rather than routine.

The deputy foreign ministers of the WP states started preparatory negotiations on 15 March, in the course of which they discussed the content of the planned document on world policy.[44] The Polish party submitted a proposal that was even sharper in tone than the original Soviet draft but soon withdrew it. In the course of lengthy negotiations that lasted until the early morning hours of 17 March, the Poles and the East Germans energetically insisted on making the text longer and using much harsher language—especially concerning the FRG—but the Romanians advocated a more conciliatory tone and a shorter version. On the morning of 16 March, after the delegations had arrived, the Hungarian negotiators—János Kádár, Jenő Fock, Béla Biszku, and Zoltán Komócsin—sat down to talk with the Soviet leaders. The views of the two parties were in perfect harmony. This was especially because Brezhnev had in the meantime fully accepted the Hungarian position mediated by Firyubin and stated that in the interest of unity, the focus should be on the signing of the military documents. As for the political statement and the call for European security, concessions should be made, if necessary. After sounding out the delegations before the meeting, Brezhnev also predicted that the major problem would be convincing the East German and Polish leaders.[45] Kádár suggested that in the worst case—if there was no way to achieve a compromise—they should simply abandon the idea of a joint political declaration in the interest of unity and instead issue a brief general communiqué. Brezhnev endorsed the proposal and stated, "It is feasible that a short communiqué and the appeal should be accepted eventually."[46] As we will see, this is exactly what happened.

The worst was still to come for the Soviet delegation. On 16 March, Brezhnev spent the whole evening and much of the night visiting the various delegations in their rooms at the Grand Hotel on Margaret Island in an attempt to achieve a compromise, but his efforts met with little success.[47] During these encounters, he met with the Romanians and the Bulgarians twice and once each with the Czechoslovak, Polish, and East German leaders. Between two and half past three in the morning, the Soviet leaders shared with Kádár and Komócsin the information they had gathered during their night patrol. They said that, as had been expected, the Poles and East Germans insisted on sharpening the tone of the political declaration and condemning the FRG, Israel, and the Chinese border violations, while the Romanians adopted a much more flexible position on these issues. The middle-of-the-road stance of the Soviet–Hungarian duo was loyally supported only by Czechoslovakia and Bulgaria. In view of the extraordinary situation, Kádár and Brezhnev eventually agreed to move the time of the forthcoming meeting from ten in the morning to three in the afternoon so that the Soviets could have another chance to talk with the leaders of the delegations. On the morning of 17 March, the Soviets sat down to talk again with the Czechoslovak, Bulgarian, and Polish delegations. Since the negotiations with the Poles were drawn out, there was a danger that the PCC would not be able to meet at the newly set time in the afternoon, which justifiably caused the host delegation to fear for the success of the meeting. "It was close to half past twelve, and we were still waiting for the results. Then we decided to take action," recalled János Kádár of the dramatic events taking place at the 24 March meeting of the HSWP Politburo. "The Soviet comrades were still negotiating with the Polish delegation, and we said that Comrade Károly Erdélyi should make his way into the negotiating room and tell them we propose that the first secretaries and the prime ministers come together at two o'clock to discuss how we could start the negotiations at three. The proposal was then accepted."[48] Eventually, the crisis could only be resolved by cutting the Gordian knot: the party leaders and the prime ministers made a decision at the extraordinary meeting that the planned foreign policy document would not be issued at all. This was a serious concession on the Soviet side, since Brezhnev was under strong domestic pressure to have the recent Chinese moves harshly condemned at the Budapest meeting, and now the WP PCC session would say nothing about the issue.[49]

After all this, there was no more excitement for the participants at the merely two-hour meeting of the PCC. The session was chaired by Alexander Dubček, and only two comments were made on the speech delivered by Marshal Yakubovskii, one by Kádár and one by Brezhnev. Then the five military documents were signed. The short communiqué and the text of the appeal for the European security conference were unanimously accepted by all the parties without any comments, as had been previously agreed. The cooperative and civilized tone of the appeal was primarily due to the efforts of the Romanian leaders, who had made several motions for an amendment along those lines. It was also the Romanian leaders who persuaded the Poles at the meeting between Gomułka and Ceaușescu in the morning to accept a more conciliatory evaluation of the FRG.[50]

Thus, the visible and rather spectacular outcome of the meeting—that is, executing the first reform in the military structure of the Warsaw Pact[51] *and* issuing a promising appeal for convening a conference on European security—was based on a virtual coalition of the Soviet Union, Hungary, and Romania.[52]

The main achievement of the meeting was that the Soviet- and Hungarian-sponsored proposal stipulating that there be no precondition of any kind for the convening of a European security conference was eventually accepted by all parties, although originally the Polish and East German leaders heavily objected to this option. The inclusion of this standpoint in the appeal of the Warsaw Pact states would later become a crucial factor in successfully initiating the CSCE process.

The Hungarian leaders, who played a crucially important mediating role in bringing about this historical compromise, nevertheless originally failed to recognize the real significance of the Budapest Declaration in shaping world politics, even after assessing its success. They recognized the inherent potentials of the initiative only some time after the session, particularly when the Soviets launched a new campaign pertaining to the security conference at the end of March. At this juncture, the Hungarians realized that the declaration—in a favorable environment—could in fact become the basis for launching a process that would lead to the staging of a pan-European security conference.

Consequently, in July 1969 the HSWP Politburo made a resolution about Hungary's relations with the FRG, admitting that the road toward normalization with West Germany led through the general settlement of the German question.[53] At the same time, encouraged by the success of the Budapest call, Hungarian foreign policy began to focus on fostering the issue of the all-European security conference. It was evident that there was a serious inter-relationship between the CSCE project and the German issue, so they were hoping that progress on the security conference would enhance Hungary's chances to normalize relations with the FRG.

Following the Budapest session of the WP, the Soviet leadership conducted an intensive campaign from the end of March to propagate the cause of the European security conference.[54] While the signing of the final document took place only in 1975, on the basis of the available source materials, we can assert that the foundations of the process were laid during the one-and-a-half-year period between two Budapest sessions: the WP PCC and the June 1970 WP foreign ministers' meeting.

The issue of the security conference occupied an exceptional position as a result of a prolonged period of preparatory work at the conference held a few months later in Moscow in June 1969 by the Communist and workers' parties and also as a feature in the final document of the conference. However, it was the positive changes on the other side (the West) that made it possible to implement the plan. Following the accession to office in January 1969, Richard Nixon, as mentioned earlier, established a back channel with Moscow via Henry Kissinger, and not much later he spoke positively of a new opportunity for an East–West rapprochement at the NATO Council session in April.[55] An equally important development followed when the Social Democratic Party together with the liberal Free Democratic Party formed a government following the September 1969 elections in the FRG and announced a new *Ostpolitik* shortly after. Thus, the two key players that determined the conduct of the West, namely the United States and West Germany, shifted considerably in comparison to their earlier stance, thus enhancing the chances of the Eastern bloc's initiatives.[56]

In the Soviet bloc campaign for the intensive promotion of the idea of a pan-European security conference, unfolding after the Budapest call, the Hungarians became one of the closest collaborators of Soviet diplomacy, as their interests basically coincided with those of the Soviets in fostering a radical rapprochement in East–West relations. The Hungarian leaders had no preconditions concerning a European settlement—unlike Poland, Czechoslovakia, and the GDR—and therefore could only gain by the success of the process. By that point, they had developed contacts with the Western part of

Europe and acquired a certain level of prestige as promoters of détente. The Hungarians were innovative and ready to take the initiative, but they were also much more loyal, reliable, flexible, and obedient partners in accommodating perpetual Soviet tactical requirements to the maximum than the much less manageable East Germans and Poles, who often stuck rigidly to their own ideas concerning the potential agenda of the security conference, not to mention the Romanians.

The Soviet Bloc's CSCE Agenda: Foreign Policy Coordination and Lobby Fights

At the end of September 1969, the Soviets indicated to their allies that they were to hold a conference of the WP foreign ministers in October, the main task of which was going to be the forming of a reconciled position concerning the Conference on European Security. From 1964 up until 1972, this had been the Soviet bloc's planned name for the conference, clearly indicating that their priority was European *security*—that is, the legalizing of the European status quo. "Cooperation," advocated by the Western states, was added only in January 1972 at the WP PCC meeting in Prague.

For the purpose of the preliminary testing of the opinions of the individual states, several Soviet deputy foreign ministers made simultaneous visits to the member states, and, on 26 September, Leonid Ilyichev had talks with Hungarian foreign minister János Péter in Budapest. According to the Soviet suggestion, the two main items on the agenda were to be the renunciation of the use of force and a declaration urging the development of economic, trade, and technological-scientific cooperation between the European states.[57] Following this, the session of 7 October of the HSWP PC commissioned the Ministry of Foreign Affairs to elaborate the Hungarian position. The memorandum, which was ready by the middle of October, contained a remarkable number of independent suggestions, which, in the opinion of the ministry, served the purpose of "presenting the ... ideas of the European socialist countries in a more attractive and meaningful way" and of making the persuasion of uncertain states easier.[58] The document suggested that, as an addition to the first item on the agenda; there should be a debate on the European security system and its institutions, dealing with the following topics:

- the signing of bilateral and regional agreements (e.g., between the countries of the Danube Valley)
- the preparation of the agreement on European security suggested by the Poles
- the establishment of a series of conferences on European security

- the establishment of a European Security Council responsible for European security issues, linking the European Economic Council to the European Security Council

Regarding the second item on the agenda, as an addition to the document the proposal suggested the following:

- the elaboration of the system of European economic cooperation (which would concern the linking of the European systems of electricity, gas, and oil; postal service and telecommunication; the harmonized improvement of European transportation networks; the promotion of industrial cooperation; the harmonization of standards; the abolition of trade barriers; and the encouragement of tourism)
- the setting up of a Committee for European Economic Cooperation or ensuring that the UN European Economic Committee functioned in accordance with the guiding principles of the conference on European security
- the convening of a conference of the mayors of European capitals in Budapest to debate issues of better cooperation between the capitals and of common municipal problems

Finally, for the purpose of consolidating foreign policy coordination, the plan suggested that, after the Prague session of the WP foreign ministers, a meeting of the competent central committee secretaries of the member states should be organized concerning the conference on European security.

The Hungarian suggestions formulated rather ambitious and far-reaching ideas concerning European cooperation. Numerous points were aimed at such ways of cooperation that were to be realized only after the change in the political system in 1989–90 or even following Hungary's accession to the European Union in 2004. As we have seen, the Hungarian draft indeed comprised a medium and long-term "package" rather than a limited program to satisfy the tactical requirements of the initial phase.

Another point that deserves attention is that while the Polish, Romanian, and East German proposals were all aimed at strengthening European *security*, the Hungarian proposals almost exclusively intended to develop European *cooperation*; in other words, Hungarian diplomacy—only in formal accord with Soviet intentions—essentially followed the Western strategy of emphasizing cooperation.

It was (naturally) not specified in the proposals, but it is easy to see that perhaps the most important "relation" in which these ambitious plans would have been implemented was the Hungarian–FRG relationship, based on the number one status of the FRG among Hungary's Western economic partners at that time.

However, in the meantime, as a result of preliminary bilateral consultations, it became obvious to the Soviets that it would not be so easy to achieve a unified position at the nearing meeting of WP foreign ministers, and this did not only refer to the expected Romanian attitude this time either. Therefore, on 17 October, Soviet deputy foreign minister Semyonov requested the Hungarian party to make personal consultation possible urgently and, the following day, Deputy Minister Károly Erdélyi had talks with his partner in Moscow.[59] The Soviets had serious worries that, owing to the Polish, Romanian, and East German suggestions—qualified as excessive—they would not reach consensus, which could result in the Warsaw Pact failing to control the initiative concerning the security conference in spite of the favorable international circumstances. Therefore, in the framework of the "special relationship" evolving at this time, the Soviets asked the Hungarian leadership to act as moderators in neutralizing the excessive Polish, East German, and Romanian proposals at the forthcoming meeting of the WP foreign ministers in Prague on 30–31 October 1969, which was convened to reconsider the Warsaw Pact's policy in light of the victory of the Social Democratic Party in West Germany in September.[60] The Polish proposals were aiming at the recognition of the territorial status quo and the existing European borders, as well as the de jure recognition of the GDR.[61] The Romanians wanted to include in the joint documents an appeal for the dissolution of the military blocs, the withdrawal of foreign troops from Europe, the elimination of foreign military bases, and the renunciation of the demonstration of force.[62] The East German proposals were aiming at recognizing the GDR by the security conference.[63]

In addition, to facilitate the talks, the Hungarians were advised not to present their own proposals, although they were encouraged to resubmit them at a later point in the preparatory process. According to the Moscow leadership, the key to success lay in gradualism, and consequently the negotiations would have to focus on the previously mentioned two points, since these issues had been favorably received by the West.

As a result of the Soviet request for Hungarian mediation on 21 October, the HSWP PC simultaneously discussed the finalized foreign ministerial proposal and the outcome of Deputy Foreign Minister Károly Erdélyi's recent consultations in Moscow.[64] János Kádár was rather indignant about the procedure and insisted that, instead of formulating a final position at the foreign ministerial meeting, proposals raised there should be presented to the respective party leaderships for debate and endorsement. Finally, after some debate, the HSWP PC—as so often before—accepted the situation and authorized the foreign minister to assume a "constructive" position at the foreign ministers' meeting to comply with the Soviet requests. Consequently, the "friendly request" was listened to and the Hungarian delegation played an important mediating role at the session of the foreign ministers in Prague on 30–31 October 1969.

At the meeting, a vigorous debate erupted once again. At the preceding deputy foreign ministers' meeting, discussing the various options pertaining to the security conference, the Polish, Romanian, and East German delegates staunchly defended their own special interests.[65] Finally, however, the preprepared Soviet–Hungarian gambit triumphed, and at the end of the meeting, consensus was reached along the lines of the Soviet–Hungarian position.[66] Two documents were endorsed at the session: (1) an open declaration and (2) a memorandum, which were handed to the respective Western governments. The latter also contained the draft of the one-and-a-half-page final document of the planned security conference, which mirrored considerable optimism; however, today we may argue that it was only a misguided naivety.[67] The leaders of the Eastern bloc were similarly optimistic in regard to the possible timing of the conference: thereafter, at practically every meeting, they insisted that the conference could be convened within a period of six months or one year later at the most.[68]

In return for its cooperation in Prague, however, Hungarian diplomacy succeeded in presenting several important proposals at this early stage, which would later become crucial elements of the joint WP policy concerning the CSCE process. Thus, the idea was accepted by the foreign ministers in Prague that there should be a *series* of security conferences and that a *permanent organ* should be set up to coordinate the preparation work.[69] It was also agreed that a group of experts dealing with European economic cooperation should be established within the WP, and its work should be coordinated by the Hungarian foreign ministry. This showed a clear interest on the side of the Hungarian leadership in being the driving force of promoting East–West economic relations, but this assignment showed the country's growing international status as well.

The main result of the foreign ministers' meeting was the declaration that the WP states propose to discuss two basic topics at the security conference:

1. the issues of European security and the renunciation of violence in the relationship of states
2. the widening of trade, economic, and technological relations based on equality, serving political cooperation among the European states[70]

A major achievement of the Prague conference of the WP foreign ministers in October 1969 included the subsequent launching of a series of intensive bilateral East–West dialogues, with the active participation of the East Central European countries. Until June 1970, Hungary held consultations at the foreign ministerial level with Belgium, Sweden, the Netherlands, Norway, and Italy, as well as at the deputy foreign ministerial and head of departmental levels with the British, French, West German, Austrian, and Turkish foreign ministries regarding the security conference.[71]

The CSCE process entered its intensive phase at this time, which became a milestone not only in regard to specific developments in Hungary's Western political relations but also in regard to the impact it had on Hungarian–Soviet relations. Namely, as of 1969, a special Soviet–Hungarian partnership mechanism had evolved, and, as previously mentioned, the Hungarian leadership proved to be an ideal partner for the Soviets in this extremely complex process, since convincing the allies was often ostensibly more difficult than persuading the other side.

Subsequently, a qualitative shift occurred in the transformation of Hungarian foreign policy. The old model remained formally unchanged—notably, every important issue at the decision-making level remained in the hands of the HSWP PC. However, major qualitative changes were introduced in the sphere of preliminary decision-making, implementation, initiation, proposals, and auxiliary diplomatic work: the role of the foreign ministry apparatus increased significantly; the intensity of multifaceted and multidirectional negotiations simply escaped the stronghold of the Political Committee and, concerning some aspects, assumed an independent role. To raise the professional level of diplomatic activity, the Institute for Foreign Affairs was established in 1971 as the first Hungarian think tank, and the academic journal *Külpolitika* [Foreign policy] started publishing in 1974. Ostensibly, this became the starting point for the emancipation process in the realm of Hungarian foreign political activity. While it did have a narrative between 1963 and 1969, the real qualitative change for Hungarian diplomacy was manifested in the active and intensive role it assumed during the CSCE process.

From this time on, the fate of the European security conference became a burning issue for the Hungarian leadership, intensely pursuing economic opportunities vis-à-vis the West since the mid-1960s. For besides Romania and perhaps Poland, Hungary could expect the most from the successful outcome of the process due to its positive effects on the evolution of East–West relations. The Hungarian leadership assumed correctly that these objectives must be pursued within the framework of a rather divided Warsaw Pact. Hence, they deduced that for the sake of success, more than before, a more effective and more systematic coordination of foreign policy was necessary within the Soviet bloc. In this respect, the establishment of the Council of Foreign Ministers—proposed by the Hungarian leadership on several occasions since

1958[72]—might have served as a suitable platform. Clearly, there was an aware-ness that Romania opposed the establishment of this body; nevertheless, they hoped that "Leninist gradualism" would prevail in this respect, mean-ing that one of the two proposed versions would be "light"—not an official body, namely the Council of Foreign Ministers, but a regular platform of for-eign ministers. During a visit to Moscow in December 1969, Foreign Minis-ter János Péter put forward this proposal to Andrei Gromyko, which was promptly adopted by the Soviets, who authorized the Hungarians to start preparations for the required bilateral consultative negotiations.[73] In Janu-ary 1970, Deputy Foreign Minister Frigyes Puja paid a visit to Bucharest to discuss the plan, but the mission failed. The Romanians consented to the cre-ation of the Council of Foreign Ministers only in 1974 and under different conditions, and the body was finally established in 1976.[74]

By the end of 1969, it transpired that the formation of the Brandt govern-ment in Bonn produced a real breakthrough regarding the question of Euro-pean security. The radical change in the West German position produced a qualitative change in comparison to the previous situation and foreshadowed the possibility of the all-important (from the point of view of European se-curity) settlement of the German question. Soviet–FRG negotiations com-menced on 8 December and resulted in an agreement to hold consultations before long between the FRG and Poland over the recognition of the Oder-Neisse border.[75]

At the initiative of a rather confused GDR leadership, a summit meeting with the participation of the WP member states' party leaders was held in Moscow on 3–4 December to coordinate the Warsaw Pact's policy vis-à-vis the FRG.[76] The GDR leaders wanted to thwart the signing of an agreement with the FRG behind their back, and moreover, they also vehemently op-posed the planned Polish–West-German negotiations.[77] However, a virtual Polish–Hungarian–Romanian coalition emerged during the meeting to ex-plore the situation, which the Soviets also supported in essence; thus, accord-ing to majority opinion, the significant changes in the FRG's policies offered good hope for settling the German question in concordance with the inter-ests of the Soviet bloc. The summit resulted in working out a compromise: no drastic changes were allowed in the WP member states' relations with West Germany, but they could start negotiations on bilateral relations with Bonn. However, diplomatic relations could not be established until the FRG recog-nized the GDR in terms of international law.

Thus, the way to direct negotiations with the FRG was reopened after the Soviet bloc summit in Moscow in December 1969. This was in some sense a move away from the still valid Warsaw protocol of February 1967, stating that the necessary conditions for entering into diplomatic relations with the FRG were not ripe for those East Central European countries that did not yet have such relations with West Germany.

At the beginning of 1970, new favorable developments in international politics signaled that the chances of staging a security conference had improved significantly. In a speech to the U.S. Congress on 18 February, President Nixon declared that the United States recognized the Soviet Union's legitimate security interests in East Central Europe and stressed the willingness of the American government to negotiate in the interest of reducing international tension and promoting rapprochement. While the resolution adopted by NATO at the 26–27 May 1970 meeting in Rome also contained numerous new and positive elements, the declaration notably mentioned the security conference in concrete terms and considered the staging of multilateral negotiations under certain conditions. It was also a promising sign that the issue of troop reduction in Europe was not linked to the question of the CSCE.

Following these developments, the real turning point concerning the plans for a European security conference came about at the June 1970 meeting of the WP foreign ministers in Budapest, convened on a Hungarian initiative. This event marked the end of exploratory negotiations and the beginning of the period of direct East–West dialogue over the staging of a European security conference. A dynamic debate ensued among the participants at the meeting, as well as at the preceding deputy foreign ministers' session, and the Hungarian hosts played an at least as intensive mediating role, as they did during the formulation of the Budapest Appeal.[78]

The conference became the second major turning point in the CSCE process within the WP (the first being the Budapest Appeal), primarily because the countries of the Soviet bloc adopted two conditions demanded by the Western side, without which the minimum consensus needed for the commencement of preparatory negotiations would not have been achieved: (1) the conference recognized the right of the United States and Canada to participate in the conference as full members, and (2) apart from the two points on the agenda proposed by the WP, a third point was included: the issue of cultural relations and the investigation of the human environment. While earlier the Soviets and the WP member states were well aware of the fact that the staging of the conference would not be possible without the United States and Canada, for tactical reasons they floated this eventuality until they managed to secure the participation of the GDR in exchange. The topic of cultural relations was adopted on a Hungarian initiative, which meant no less than the tacit incorporation of this "third basket"—as it was named in a later phase of the East–West dialogue—in the structure of the multilateral talks. It is well known that the question of the third basket played a key role at a later stage, since this basket contained those components that mirrored basic Western interests during the great European settlement. This factor served as a foundation for the evolution of the human rights campaign of the post-Helsinki period, which would play a limited role in the disintegration of the East Central European Communist systems at the end of the 1980s.

A decision was also reached at the foreign ministers' meeting in Budapest regarding the establishment of a permanent body that would assume responsibility for issues related to European security and cooperation, with the principal task of assessing various options for the reduction of the armed forces. The Soviet Union agreed to hold talks on the reduction of European armed forces parallel with the negotiations on European security, which was an explicitly confidence-building step, though it primarily aimed to deflate the significance of a NATO proposal of similar content formulated at the time. Furthermore, the foreign ministers sent a draft document to Western governments outlining economic, technological-scientific, and cultural cooperation. Helsinki was accepted as the venue for the conference, and thereafter the procedure empowering accredited ambassadors to carry out preparatory work in the Finnish capital became an official proposition.

Last but not least, the WP foreign ministers reiterated at their meeting in Budapest that the convening of a European security conference *had no preconditions.* This was highly significant, since the Polish, East German, and Czechoslovak sides—as we have seen before—unswervingly insisted during the post–Budapest Appeal period that the Soviet bloc would stress that the settlement of the German question should be a specific precondition. In other words, the WP theoretically could have backtracked tactically as a result of internal pressure, which would have seriously hindered and delayed the process. However, the specific close cooperation between Soviet and Hungarian diplomacy, coupled with the virtual support of the Romanian side, succeeded in circumventing this eventuality.

After the WP PCC conference in Prague in January 1972, the preparatory work in the Warsaw Pact regarding the Conference on Security and Cooperation in Europe gathered considerable speed. From the very beginning, the Hungarian leaders attached a distinguished role to the issue of European economic cooperation since, in this field, Hungary could expect the most from a successful conference. Accordingly, as early as April 1970, economic experts held an expert conference in Budapest; and in October 1971, a detailed summary was prepared based on previous consultations and sent to all member states of the WP. And in February 1972, a twenty-six-page guideline was prepared under the title "The Potentials of Economic Cooperation at a Pan-European Level." In addition to several remarkable proposals, one of the most important suggestions was to make the European Economic Committee the body responsible for European economic cooperation after its proper transformation.[79] What made this proposal something special was that the authors of the document were fully aware that the Soviets were against giving this body a key role after the conference.

Between 27 November and 1 December 1972, a Soviet state and party delegation conducted negotiations in Hungary. In his talks with Brezhnev, Kádár again raised the issue of diplomatic relations with the FRG, showing considerable "flexibility" by now saying that he believed it was the right decision for Poland to establish diplomatic relations with Bonn.[80] With a view to the Czechoslovakia–FRG talks, he again tried to push the notion that Hungary should not have to wait until the end of this process: "It is not a good idea to drag out the establishment of Hungarian–West German diplomatic relations too much, because such a step might produce just the contrary effect."[81]

Brezhnev did not respond to the suggestion but caught his hosts by surprise when he gave a general analysis of the international situation, emphatically stating that, despite the results achieved in détente, "great attention should be devoted to increasing the defensive power of the Warsaw Treaty. The defensive capability of the national military forces of the European Socialist countries must be increased and provided with modern military technology, since there is a clear shortfall in this respect. The defense of the homeland is a number one issue in the Soviet Union, and accordingly it has priority over anything else when deciding on the allocation of financial resources."[82] Although the talks on reducing troops in Central Europe, to begin in Vienna a month later, were mentioned only in a general context at the meeting, after these comments Kádár had no doubts whatsoever that the Soviet party would not take any real steps to reduce armament. Brezhnev also promised that the WP PCC would be convened soon to discuss the international situation, which had been urged by Kádár since the beginning of the year, but the session did not take place until April 1974.[83]

During the preparatory talks in Helsinki, Hungary—using the key principle of Hungarian foreign policy, *constructive loyalty*—actively participated in the work, constantly negotiating with the Soviets and the other WP member states. Using a policy quite contrary to that of the Romanians, the Hungarians did by no means aim for any spectacular action but instead tried to mediate between the two camps, mostly in a quiet but flexible and effective way. They made efforts to popularize the position of the WP at the talks conducted with the Western countries, while within the Eastern bloc they tried their best to "sell" any rational Western proposal that seemed acceptable.

Of all the speeches delivered at the summit meeting held on 30 July–1 August 1975 on signing the Helsinki Final Act, János Kádár's speech was certainly one of the most remarkable contributions. Among the Socialist countries, Kádár spoke in detail about the issues in the third basket, in addition to the topic of European cooperation, which was greatly appreciated and cited by the contemporary Western press. He devoted some one-third of his speech to cultural cooperation and the exchange of information, and he did so in quite a positive sense. He demonstrated the interest of Hungary in facilitating foreign travel and relations between the people with data that sounded quite convincing in the given context: he said that every year, eight million visitors came to Hungary, and over three million Hungarians traveled abroad, out of a country of ten million inhabitants. Mentioning these really spectacular data clearly served a double purpose: on the one hand, Kádár fulfilled an assignment by presenting the best available figures of all the Soviet bloc countries, thus offering the misleading image of a rather "open" Warsaw Pact, while in reality, except for Poland, all the other WP members were much less flexible in promoting tourism even within the bloc, not to mention traveling to the West. On the other hand, Kádár sent a motivating message to his own colleagues that maintaining large-scale contacts between people within the Soviet bloc and even with the West *was* compatible with running a Communist regime.

As another striking aspect of his speech, Kádár strongly emphasized the attachment of the Hungarian nation to Europe, and what was really unprecedented was that a Hungarian Communist leader openly spoke about the Trianon syndrome as he did, explaining that Hungary had lost two-thirds of its territory after World War I.[84] The significance of this statement was that everybody knew that most of the territories cut off from Hungary had been taken by four neighboring (currently Socialist) countries—and three of them were members of the Warsaw Pact.

In Helsinki, Kádár was content with presenting the simple historical facts, which were rather impressive anyhow, to the general public. Three year earlier, in February 1972, he had explained to Brezhnev in detail that the economic situation in Hungary, the openness of its economy, and its extreme dependence on foreign trade were closely related to the severe land loss suffered by Hungary at Trianon. Thus, supporting the Soviet policy aiming to legalize the European status quo and finalize the existing borders meant a major sacrifice and jettisoning any historic rights for a territorial revision for good on the side of the Hungarian leadership. In return, Kádár was expecting greater generosity from the Soviet leadership in promoting Hungary's economic needs.[85]

The Hungarian leadership did not remain inactive after signing the Helsinki Final Act, either. The HSWP PC made a detailed resolution at its session on 15 August 1975 on performing the obligations deriving from the signing of the Final Act as soon as possible.[86] The resolution started out from the fact that Hungary was in a good position as far as the application of the provisions contained in the Final Act was concerned, so the Hungarian government could "actively and assertively" act in the field of bilateral relations. In accordance with the resolution, state authorities had to be instructed to work out proposals for the development of economic and cultural relations with the Western states, and preparations had to begin promptly for the series of talks to be held in Belgrade in June 1977. Shortly afterward, 100,000 copies of the full text of the Helsinki Final Act, together with Kádár's speech, were published by the party.[87]

Chapter 9

Standby Détente

Hungary as the Promoter of East–West Relations

The Impact of the Helsinki Process on East–West Relations

The German question was finally settled according to the wishes of the Soviet bloc by the end of 1973 in what was clearly regarded a great success victory in the East. Similarly, the Helsinki Final Act was seen as a long-awaited
legal guarantee for the legalization of the European status quo. The price for
the compromise was accepting the third basket with a promise that the freer
movement of people, information, and ideas would be made possible within
the Soviet bloc as well. It should be remembered, however, that in Yalta in February 1945, Stalin signed the Declaration on Liberated Europe, explicitly
promising to hold free elections in Soviet occupied East Central Europe. The
result of that promise is only too well-known. Indeed, the Soviet bloc leaders,
while aware of the problem, were confident that their authoritarian regimes
and closed societies would effectively block Western and internal opposition
attempts at using the third basket to undermine their regimes.[1] The principle of noninterference in the internal affairs of other states, also included in
the Decalogue of the Helsinki Final Act, gave them a convenient legal basis
for rejecting any unwanted intervention. While it is widely believed that the
third basket and the human rights campaign launched by U.S. president
Jimmy Carter in the second half of the 1970s crucially contributed to the eventual collapse of the Communist regimes in East Central Europe,[2] in reality
this role was marginal. On the other hand, the role of the second basket is
generally underestimated, although the ever-broadening economic cooperation between the eastern and western parts of Europe eventually led to serious economic and financial dependency on and indebtedness to the West in
most Soviet bloc states. We can argue that economic cooperation, originally
seen in the East as a vehicle for consolidating Soviet bloc economies, especially by transfer of developed technologies, became a catalyst in the process
of the destabilization of the Communist systems by the end of the 1980s.[3] The
collapse itself, however, was due neither to the economic nor the human rights
factor but rather occurred as a consequence of the collapse of the Soviet Union
itself, which had been underway since the middle of 1988. To be sure, the economic factor was by far the more important of the two.[4] This also means that

while credit is generally given to U.S. policy for ending the Cold War on the Western side, the role of the FRG is generally underestimated. As the number one Western economic partner of most Soviet bloc states, the role of the FRG in destabilizing the East Central European countries was much greater than previously assumed. History's irony, however, is that none of this was intentional; on the contrary, Bonn was interested in reforming and stabilizing the Communist regimes as late as the summer of 1989.[5]

For the Soviets, the Helsinki process was explicitly a *European* project. This is important to emphasize, as the involvement of the United States in the CSCE led to a general misperception in the West that stabilizing the status quo between the superpowers was a deal effective worldwide, not just in Europe. For the Soviets, however, détente was absolutely compatible with their penetration into the third world, especially as in most cases, their military and economic support was provided for indigenous revolutionary movements. In reality, Moscow did not expect the harsh resistance and criticism it had to face from the United States, since the countries involved were among the poorest in the world (e.g., Afghanistan and Ethiopia), and their geopolitical location was mostly peripheral in the nuclear age. We can add that in retrospect, the U.S. leaders should have been pleased to see how the Kremlin was wasting its limited resources without any sensible reward. Indeed, the Soviet leaders maneuvered themselves into a strategic trap by not being able to resist the temptation to expand their influence on a global scale when they should have concentrated all their efforts on saving their failing "internal empire"— including East Central Europe. Such decisions were made partly because of the absurd secrecy about the real state of the declining Soviet economy. We know from Gorbachev—not from his memoirs but from a document prepared in 1989—that even in the early 1980s under Andropov, the state budget of the Soviet Union with real figures was unavailable even to key Politburo members like Ryzhkov and Gorbachev. "Some time ago, when I was already a Politburo member, I basically did not know our budget," Gorbachev told Egon Krenz, the newly appointed East German party leader on 1 November 1989. "Once we were working with Nikolay Ryzhkov on some request of Andropov's that had to do with budgetary issues, and we naturally decided that we should learn about them. But Yurii V. Andropov said: 'Do not go there, it is not your business.' Now we know why he said so. It was not a budget, but the devil knows what."[6] (Just a few years later, in 1985, Gorbachev assumed the post of general-secretary of the CPSU, while Ryzhkov became prime minister.)

This truly sensational information demonstrates the utmost absurdity of the Soviet system better than anything else, and it also reminds us that the real question is not why the Soviet Union collapsed but rather how it could have lasted so long.[7] Thus, eventually Moscow had to pay a high price for the unprofitable expansion of the Soviet empire from the 1970s onward (later including the war in Afghanistan), as it became an important factor in the subsequent fall of the Soviet Union—together with the enormous costs of the arms race, which used up the reserves of the state,[8] and the expenses of subsidizing Moscow's allies in East Central Europe.

The conclusion of the Helsinki Final Act in 1975 further boosted Hungary's international prestige, primarily because the fulfillment of the obligations concerning human rights, undertaken by the Eastern countries with little enthusiasm, caused the least amount of trouble for the Hungarian leadership. After Helsinki, it became increasingly obvious that Hungary benefited most from the Helsinki conference in the Soviet bloc, as well as from the period of rapprochement that had evolved in the meantime. The success of the CSCE process provided an excellent opportunity for the country to pursue the uninterrupted development of relations with the West, which became one of the most burning issues in terms of the country's economic survival. By contrast, the post-Helsinki human rights campaign initiated by the Carter administration affected Hungary the least among the Warsaw Pact states, and moreover, the continual appraisal by the West led to an upgrading of conditions in Hungary. Western expectations, especially in the beginning, were in fact rather limited: the release of political prisoners, a liberal policy of family reunification, and Jewish emigration. Still, these demands created serious problems for the Soviets and most East Central European Communist leaderships. For the Hungarian government, however, it was relatively easy to fulfill them.

Hungarian diplomacy was quick to take advantage of the situation. In 1976, Hungary—alone among the countries of the Soviet bloc—dispatched a package of proposals to nineteen Western countries, including the United States, proposing the intensive development of bilateral, political, economic, and cultural cooperation in the given relationship.[9] Consequently, the country's Western relations evolved dynamically.

From the second half of the 1970s, a series of visits at the highest level took place: János Kádár visited Bonn and Rome in 1977 and went to Paris in 1978, French prime minister Raymond Barre paid a visit to Hungary in 1977, and West German chancellor Helmut Schmidt visited Hungary in 1979. In addition, many visits at the prime ministerial and ministerial levels were realized as well.

By the end of the 1970s, Hungarian–American relations were substantially improved, too. In 1972, U.S. secretary of state William P. Rogers visited Hungary, and the next year a financial treaty was signed, finally settling the long-established debates between the two states. The real breakthrough occurred in 1978, when President Carter, in appreciation of the decent human rights record of the country compared to other Soviet bloc states, decided to return the Holy Crown to the "Hungarian nation." In the same year, the long hoped for most-favored-nation status was also given to Hungary.[10]

The culmination of the Helsinki process meant nothing less than the possibility for a virtual unification of Europe, in which, on the basis of the long-term recognition of the European status quo, the goal was to create civilized relations between the eastern and western parts of Europe. From then on, this recognition became the leitmotif of Hungarian foreign policy, which fundamentally determined the country's international relations up to the political transition in 1989. After Helsinki, a gradually evolving process began to emerge, indicating the formation of a common European consciousness; and in the ever more-intensifying East–West dialogue, Hungary played an important role.

Since the end of the 1970s, Hungarian foreign policy had enjoyed a kind of special, relatively independent status. One important aspect of this special status was that, due to a new wave of opening to the West, based on the adoption of a new foreign economic strategy in 1977, it enabled Hungary to develop intensive economic and political relations with Western states precisely during those years when, due in part to the gradual alienation in the late 1970s and the Soviet invasion of Afghanistan, superpower relations were at a low unprecedented since the Cuban missile crisis. The Hungarian leadership, however, did not achieve this status in opposition to Moscow's wishes but rather with their knowledge and consent. Kádár managed repeatedly to persuade Brezhnev and his successors—and this was no easy task—that, in view of the worsening economic situation, Hungary's political stability could only be maintained by such means. Hungary's increasing use of Western credit temporarily appeared advantageous to the Soviet Union as well, since it indirectly removed the burden from the Soviet economy, while Kádár himself guaranteed unquestionable political loyalty to Moscow.

The East–East Crisis Following the Soviet Invasion of Afghanistan

Interdependence and compelled cooperation, as discussed in chapter 3, were not only working on the superpower level, but they affected the relations between the two alliances as well. The Warsaw Pact states were not involved in the invasion of Afghanistan, unlike in the case of Czechoslovakia in 1968. The ensuing East-West crisis, however, affected Moscow's East Central European allies in a peculiar way. A fine example of this is the history and the outcome of the crisis following the Soviet invasion of Afghanistan in December 1979. In late January 1980, shortly after the potential boycott of the forthcoming

Moscow Olympics was announced, the Soviet leadership took offense and ordered the Warsaw Pact states to freeze their Western contacts immediately.[11] During this campaign, Hungary, Czechoslovakia, and the GDR were ordered to cancel imminent high-level talks with Western politicians.[12] This unexpected move caused a serious clash of interests between the Soviet Union and the East European Communist states, since by this time they were all interested—to varying degrees and in different ways—in developing relations with Western Europe. All of this, then, resulted in an internal rebellion within the Soviet bloc, which demonstrated the functioning of the strategy of constructive loyalty in an excellent way.

As Hungary was a solid member of the group of "closely cooperating socialist countries" (the WP members minus Romania), there was nothing much to do other than accept the Soviet explanation and follow the general line of the bloc in the field of propaganda. Initially, this did not seem to cause too much trouble, as Hungary's main concern was to maintain its good political and, above all, economic relations with the West, especially Western Europe, which had been developing in a dynamic way since the mid-1970s. This time, as opposed to the case of the Warsaw Pact's intervention in Czechoslovakia in August 1968, Hungary was not directly involved as an aggressor in the international crisis concerning Afghanistan. According to the official Hungarian position developed during the first weeks following the intervention, Soviet support of the Afghan revolutionary forces did not constitute an internal affair of the Warsaw Pact but exclusively that of the Soviet Union and Afghanistan.[13]

Although the American reaction against the invasion made many people worry for the future of East–West relations, for the Hungarian leaders it was reassuring that both the Soviet leaders—per Brezhnev's speech on 16 January—and most key politicians in Western Europe, including West German chancellor Helmut Schmidt, made it clear that there was a strong joint interest in maintaining the results of détente. This Hungarian hope was conveyed to the U.S. State Department during the special mission of Gyula Horn, deputy head of the HSWP CC International Department in early January.[14] Horn visited the United States and Canada on 7–20 January 1980 officially as a "diplomatic courier" of the Hungarian embassies in Washington and Ottawa to visit the party organizations in preparation for the impending HSWP congress. However, the diplomatic services were also informed about the presence of the Hungarian official, so Horn was invited to have talks with deputy foreign ministers in both countries.[15] In New York, his partners warned that the Soviet Union had to "prepare for an extremely hard fight" and indicated that the intervention in Afghanistan meant the removal of the last barriers on the road that would lead to an increase in the defensive powers of the United States and her allies.[16] With regard to bilateral relations, the leaders of the State Department emphasized that the United States was still using a distinguishing approach in her policy concerning the East Central European countries. They stressed that, in the coming hard period, when a lasting deterioration of Soviet–American relations was expected, these states would acquire an important role and could ensure continuity in keeping up the policy of détente. They called attention to the fact that U.S.–Hungarian economic relations and, particularly, the most-favored-nation status achieved just two years earlier, in 1978, as a result of the hard work of several years, would now depend on Hungary's behavior toward the United States.[17] They requested the Hungarian side not to take a step backward in the field of bilateral relations, and in this respect they attributed great importance to the upcoming visit to the United States of the parliamentary delegation headed by speaker of the parliament and HSWP PC member Antal Apró.

The Horn mission also confirmed the Hungarian leadership's belief that the estrangement of the superpowers would not necessarily lead to the narrowing of the country's Western relations. On the contrary, it seemed that, under the given circumstances, besides Poland, Hungary had the greatest chance for using the situation to her advantage. Thus, it was a real shock when in late January 1980, Moscow "requested" that Hungary freeze its high-level contacts with the West immediately.

American countermeasures announced at the beginning of 1980 (including restrictions on the sale of fodder grain to the Soviet Union, a freezing of cultural and economic relations, and a ban on transferring advanced technologies) had not yet caused too great a trauma for the Soviet leaders. Similarly, the fact that the UN Security Council had put the Afghan question on the agenda on 5 January 1980 and that the Soviet step was condemned at a special General Assembly session did not cause any change in Moscow's foreign policy. Although the possibility of the UN keeping the "Afghan question" permanently on the agenda could later have contributed to the reinforcement of the confrontational trend within the Soviet leadership, Brezhnev's speech of 16 January still unambiguously emphasized the need for the maintenance of East–West cooperation. At the same time, however, U.S. president Jimmy Carter called on the whole world to boycott the Olympic Games to be held in Moscow in the summer of the same year if Soviet troops were not withdrawn within a month. Since this was the first time that the Olympics were to be held in a Socialist country, this event had been viewed as an important prop in gaining international prestige for the Eastern camp.

Thus, in late January 1980, Moscow became offended and decided to take countermeasures. During this campaign, Hungary, Czechoslovakia, and the

GDR were ordered to cancel imminent high-level talks with Western politicians. As a result, two visits of West German politicians were canceled: Foreign Minister Hans Dietrich Genscher was to visit Prague, and Chancellor Helmut Schmidt was to have talks with Erich Honecker in Berlin. Although the Bulgarians did not have upcoming meetings with Western politicians, they, too, were warned against planning such steps.

This caused a serious clash of interest between the Soviet Union and the East European Communist states increasingly interested in developing relations with Western Europe. Further research will show how exactly this conflict affected the relations of the individual countries with Moscow. To be sure, for Hungary, this Soviet move caused one of the most serious crises since 1956, both within the Hungarian leadership and in the field of Hungarian–Soviet relations. The Soviets "requested" that the visit of Hungarian foreign minister Frigyes Puja to Bonn, which was due to take place in less than a week, be canceled and, similarly, the visit of a delegation of the parliament to the United States be put off. At the January 29 meeting of the HSWP PC, one of the most dramatic meetings in the history of this body, the Hungarian leadership got the closest to making the political decision to openly defy Soviet will. During a heated debate, several Politburo members—including hard-liners like Antal Apró, Dezső Nemes, and Károly Németh—proposed that, regarding the extremely short notice and considering the country's economic interests, the Soviet request should be disregarded, and there seemed to be a clear majority for this position.[18]

It was then, perhaps for the first time since 1956, that János Kádár, the first secretary of the HSWP, got into a situation involving relations with the Soviet Union, which had been considered determinant from the beginning, in which his position completely contradicted the position of the main operative body of the party. Moreover, this time, in the particular circumstances evolving during the debate, Kádár, who had always striven to play a centrist role, was forced to defend the policy considered to be the only possible reality as basically a "leftist" deviator. The routine of carefully listening to the members of the body, then at the end of the session summing up the essence in his own speech and declaring the resolution, which had worked well for decades, now brought its own punishment. In his rather confused speech, full of curses that revealed his state of great agitation, Kádár argued that "we are again in a situation when we have the choice of two evils."

As an anticipated conclusion, he announced immediately that the high-level visits to Bonn and Washington had to be canceled. He considered that Hungary could not lose anything by obeying Moscow; at the worst, he, Kádár, would be called "a Soviet satellite" in the West. "Some presumed advantage may only be hoped for, [but] the negative effect is immediate," warned the experienced party leader to the members of the PC, referring to the fact that, by forfeiting the trust of the leaders of the Kremlin, the country might lose a lot.

In order to enlighten those who might have still had illusions concerning the nature of the Soviet request, he added, "What do you think, how long will they be polite to us? Why with us, . . . excuse me for the phrase, with our little lousy life and country. . . . How long will they behave politely towards us?" This desperate declaration of the veteran Hungarian party leader was perhaps the most blunt and drastic manifestation concerning the true nature of Hungary's relations with the Soviet Union in the whole Kádár era.

After Kádár's dramatic speech, the PC finally passed a resolution on the cancellation of both visits. At the same time—as a confidence-building measure toward the West—they requested that the Soviets postpone the joint Soviet–Hungarian military exercise that was to be held in the Western part of the country between 11–16 February.[19]

In some sense, this Political Committee session meant the starting point of the process leading up to Kádár's political fall. Although at that point the veteran party leader was still successful in imposing his will on his comrades, it is safe to say that he had won the battle but lost the war. Some years later, due to the increasingly difficult economic situation of the country, this conflict significantly contributed to the evolving situation, when even his closest colleagues did not want him to lead the party anymore.

The two visits were canceled but, paradoxically, the humiliation Kádár had to suffer in this case eventually contributed to the development of positive processes for his country.[20] This was due to a series of diplomatic maneuvers that were aimed at exerting pressure on the Soviets to change their position on the one hand and at explaining Hungary's difficult situation to the Western partners on the other. At the same Politburo session, it was also decided that Moscow should be asked to urgently hold a multilateral consultative meeting on the consequences of the situation in Afghanistan on East–West relations. A special envoy, András Gyenes, CC secretary for foreign affairs, was immediately sent to Moscow for personal consultation, and Kádár himself sent a letter to Brezhnev. In the letter, he put forward a firm Hungarian position: in the present situation, the allies must be consulted regularly on the joint policy of the Soviet bloc in international politics, and the results of détente must be preserved. This was possible only by maintaining and strengthening the relations of the East European countries with Western Europe. Only this—Kádár concluded—would prevent American influence in those countries to prevail.

Brezhnev was continuously ill at that time; therefore, internal fights intensified between the lobbies within the Soviet leadership. It was under such circumstances that the Hungarian request concerning an urgent need for consultation arrived in Moscow. Foreign Minister Gromyko replied to the suggestion nervously, as he did not understand what the Hungarians wanted to conduct talks about.[21] The Hungarian proposal for consultation, however, was soon accepted, and a meeting of the CC secretaries for foreign affairs of the "closely cooperating socialist countries" was scheduled in Moscow for 26 February 1980.

At the meeting, Boris Ponomarev, CPSU CC secretary for international affairs, not only adopted the rather shrewd Hungarian position but he put forward Kádár's thesis *as the current CPSU line*, emphasizing that "the socialist countries should make the maximum use of the possibilities contained in existing relations with the Western-European countries to counter-balance the United States' foreign policy line."[22]

This was a great victory for Hungarian diplomacy.[23] Not only did they get a green light for further developing their Western relations, which were beyond crucial for the country's economy by that time, but freezing those relations in 1980 would have blocked Hungary from acquiring a crucial $1.7 billion Western loan in that year, and this—we now know—would have led to the country's insolvency.[24]

From a historical perspective, it is even more important that Kádár's firm personal intervention and the effective Hungarian diplomatic initiatives eventually helped the "liberal" forces in the Soviet leadership—mostly key members of the Central Committee apparatus who were interested in maintaining détente—to overcome their adversaries, led by Gromyko, who represented a more belligerent attitude toward the West. As Vadim Zagladin, first deputy head of the International Department of the CPSU CC, told Gyula Horn on 16 July 1980, "For several months in the CPSU Politburo, there had been heated debates about the Soviet Union's specific foreign policy steps, the general evaluation of the international situation and the situation of the communist movement."[25] He emphasized that, in this debate, "Comrade János Kádár's message to the Soviet leadership played an important role."[26] The Kádár Doctrine had worked.

Parallel with the letter sent to Brezhnev, Kádár sent explanatory messages to Social Democratic Party chair Willy Brandt and West German chancellor Helmut Schmidt. In these, he apologized for the cancellation of the visit of the Hungarian foreign minister at such short notice and subtly explained the difficult situation of the Hungarian leadership. He also stressed, however, that his country was strongly committed to maintaining the results of détente and to fostering East–West cooperation. In his reply, Helmut Schmidt, who was the first German chancellor to visit Hungary a year before, formulated the historical challenge facing the European states in the following way: now it depends on these states "whether they let themselves be drawn into the Cold War, instigated by the two superpowers or not! Neither the FRG, nor any other West or East European country can keep out of this [cold war] alone. This is possible only by the collaboration of all states concerned."[27]

No question, by the beginning of the 1980s, Hungary, while remaining a loyal member of the Warsaw Pact all along, was compelled by its economic interests to get ever closer to this virtual European community. Therefore, the resolution of this internal crisis can be regarded as an important lesson concerning the limits of small state diplomacy in the Warsaw Pact—or, more generally, the chances of a small state, belonging to the "closely cooperating" group, exerting pressure on Moscow to achieve certain political goals. While it turned out to be impossible for Hungary to openly defy the Soviet will, the subsequent diplomatic maneuvers and Kádár's personal intervention could play an important role in the internal fighting in the Kremlin and thus influence the outcome of the events according to the crucial interests of the country and in fact of the whole international community.

Standby Détente, 1979–1985

The new interpretation of détente (outlined in chapter 3), emphasizing the role of compelled cooperation and interdependence, also explains how it was possible that, just a few years after the alleged death/fall/failure/demise of détente at the end of the 1970s, an unprecedented rapprochement between the superpowers occurred with the coming of Gorbachev in 1985. In spite of the view held by many, there was not (and could not have been) a "Second Cold War" between 1979 and 1985, as this term implies that a *First* Cold War *had ended* sometime earlier.[28] Such widely accepted but flawed interpretations assume that, with the "victory" of détente between 1969 and 1975, the Cold War disappeared, and then, at the end of the decade, it resurfaced again until it completely melted away under Gorbachev. Such explanations can be attributed—as explained in chapter 3—to a widely accepted linear and exclusive interpretation of the relationship between Cold War and détente. These interpretations basically apply a model according to which—with some simplification—at a certain time there was either Cold War or détente. That is, when the superpower relationship was bad, one can refer to this period as the Cold War; when it was good, it was détente. In fact, this relationship was not linear at all, and the two categories were certainly not mutually exclusive. They could not and did not replace each other; rather, they simply coexisted.[29] It is therefore difficult in the conventional sense to evaluate the period 1979–85, as it was both preceded and followed by détente. It has often been described as a period when the element of confrontation was dominant again and has been "logically" named the "second Cold War," "little Cold War," or "mini-Cold War" using old reflexes, since this logic links a cold war to a time when the superpower relationship was struggling. In reality, however, this was not the case. First, previously, in periods of confrontation, confrontational intentions (at least at the propaganda level) were *mutual*—that is, they prevailed on both sides. Now, however, they appeared only on the American side, while the Soviet leadership strongly insisted on the preservation of the fruits of détente. Second, it was the first time that, in a confrontational stage, the European allies of the United States did not follow Washington loyally in a united front, and indeed they sought to keep the East–West dialogue and cooperation alive.[30] Moreover, the alliance system reacted similarly on the Eastern side as well: the Eastern bloc countries—Hungary, primarily—driven by their special interests, which were by that time becoming increasingly independent of Moscow's intentions, sought to do everything they could to preserve the achievements of détente.

This is why Moscow was so desperately trying to apply the Mikoyan doctrine[31]—namely, using local forces and avoiding Soviet military intervention—during the resolution of the crisis in Afghanistan. While Mikoyan's proposal to this effect was voted down by the CPSU presidium in 1956, the Soviet leaders learned the lesson well. In their crisis management strategy during later conflicts, they always sought initially and instinctively to use this doctrine—for example, in Czechoslovakia for eight months in 1968 and in Afghanistan for more than a year and a half as of 1979. The leaders of the Afghan Communist regime, established in April 1978, urged Soviet military intervention to support the government against Islamist insurgents no less than fourteen times before December 1979. The Soviets, however, did everything they could to consolidate the political situation through the use of local forces, providing economic, military, and logistical support but categorically ruling out sending fighting Soviet troops into the neighboring state.[32] So, while Vietnamization became the U.S. goal in the final stage of the Indochina war, the Kremlin arguably tried to apply the policy of "Afghanization" at the initial stage of the Afghan conflict. According to the Western interpretation, however, Moscow had breached the tacit agreement based on European status quo policy since the end of the Second World War by invading Afghanistan. Up to that point, the Soviets had not expanded their military presence to any state that did not belong to the tacitly recognized Soviet sphere of influence. On the contrary, the Soviet Union had withdrawn its military from several formerly occupied countries and military bases (Czechoslovakia in 1945, Iran and Denmark in 1946, Bulgaria in 1947, Korea in 1948, Austria in 1955, Finland in 1956, and Romania in 1958) and had not sent troops to fight in the Korean or the Vietnam War.[33] The invasion of Afghanistan was thus seen as an alarming move by the West, the beginning of a new Soviet policy aimed at expanding Soviet influence in the world by sending troops to the allied states if need be, wherever their location might be. In reality, however, this was nothing more than the application of the (limited) Brezhnev Doctrine that is, saving a Communist system in an allied state through the use of Soviet forces as an ultimate solution.[34] It is also important to realize that Afghanistan effectually became part of the Soviet empire as early as April 1978, following the Communist takeover, and triggered no Western protest; thus, the Soviet military occupation of that country itself did not change the East–West status quo.

Between 1979 and 1985, the new confrontational U.S. policy (both under Carter and in the first term of the Reagan administration) materialized primarily at the propaganda level, while the mechanism of compelled cooperation continued to work perfectly. The need to avoid a clash between the superpowers was no less compelling than before. Reagan's policy between 1981 and 1983 can be compared to the Eisenhower administration's dual policy between 1953 and 1956, when the real aim of U.S. policy was to find a modus vivendi with the Soviet Union, but this was coupled comfortably with high-sounding rhetoric promising the liberation of the East Central European "captive nations," which, as is now well known, had no real basis. At the time, and even for several decades, this secret could not be documented from primary sources. Documents gradually becoming available from Reagan's first term will in all likelihood reveal an American foreign policy line following the main direction of realism: a traditional policy based on the strategy of containment, which realized the need for compelled superpower cooperation in the same way as its predecessors did. Available sources together with indirect evidence strongly support this hypothesis while, from 1983 on, it is clear that the Reagan administration was seeking the resumption of superpower cooperation.[35]

A deterioration of the Soviet–U.S. superpower relationship certainly occurred following NATO's double-track decision and the Soviet invasion of Afghanistan in December 1979. However, for the first time in the Cold War era, this was not followed by an automatic worsening of East–West relations in general.[36] Mutually interested in preserving the results of détente, the two parts of Europe began to gravitate toward each other rather than obediently follow the superpowers' confrontational line. The Soviet leaders themselves— with a short period of hesitation in the first half of 1980—were keen on preserving those results as well.

With the invasion of Afghanistan, the Soviets had assumed a certain level of criticism from the West but had expected that, after a short period of time, it would be accepted as a fait accompli, similarly to the case of Czechoslovakia in 1968. They also believed that the West would soon forget the problem of Afghanistan, assuming that keeping up the results of détente was a priority that would overshadow it. However, the West—especially the United States—reacted differently this time, because they correctly evaluated the situation as the first time since 1945 that the Soviet Union had militarily occupied a country that did not belong to the Soviet sphere of interest tacitly recognized by the West. While at the time of the East Central European crises of 1953, 1956, and 1968 the West rationally recognized the Soviet Union's right to restore order within her empire, they considered the invasion of Afghanistan to be a unilateral and aggressive expansion of the Soviet sphere of interest. According to Western interpretation, Moscow had breached the tacit agreement based on the European status quo policy, which had functioned well since the end of the Second World War. Considering Afghanistan's geostrategic position, however, the acquisition of that territory violated only *potential* Western interests; this is why the intensity of the international crisis, brought on by Soviet aggression, in spite of the excessive official American rhetoric,[37] did not ever reach the level of the Berlin and Cuban crises at the beginning of the 1960s.

Thus, the invasion of Afghanistan, in which the non-Soviet Warsaw Pact states were not involved, in fact helped amplify the notion of an East Central Europe pursuing its own interests and having a special identity significantly different from that of the Soviet Union. All of this paradoxically contributed to the gradual establishment of a common European consciousness that had been formulating since the late 1960s: this slowly emerging virtually united Europe would surely include East Central Europe, but not necessarily the Soviet Union.

Soviet crisis management during the Polish crisis of 1980–81 also demonstrated that Moscow was keen on avoiding another Soviet invasion in order to keep détente alive and preserve the chance for a continued East–West dialogue. From the outset, they sought to apply the Mikoyan Doctrine—that is, first trying to find a political solution and then executing a military solution carried out by local forces in order to avoid the use of Soviet troops—just like initially in 1968 in Czechoslovakia and 1978–79 in Afghanistan. The first successful application of the doctrine occurred in December 1981, when General Jaruzelski introduced martial law in Poland.[38] During the Polish crisis of 1980–81, the Soviet leaders applied a different negotiating strategy than they had in 1968, at the time of the Prague Spring. Rather than using the Warsaw Pact as a forum and organizing multilateral summits, now Moscow wanted to resolve the situation according to Soviet wishes through bilateral talks with the Polish leadership. While their efforts were eventually successful, it is important to make clear that there existed a plan B as well: if the introduction of martial law had failed, Soviet troops would have been used to restore order.[39]

The Soviet leaders learned other lessons as well. During the Euromissile crisis in December 1983, Moscow did not repeat their mistake of 1980 after the boycott of the Olympics, namely applying a general line of retaliation against the West. According to a guideline sent from Moscow to the Soviet bloc leaders: "Under the new circumstances it is important to approach the development of relations with the different western countries in subtle ways. The countries that agreed to the deployment of the missiles should experience the political consequences of this move. Naturally, priority should be given to countries in which no such missiles will be deployed. It seems to be useful to intensify our relations and contacts with the neutral countries of capitalist Europe in every respect and area."[40] The Soviet policy of differentiation was now clearly aimed at maintaining dialogue with as many partners as possible in the West.[41]

This same commitment by the Soviet bloc states to continue the policy of détente and indeed improve East–West cooperation was demonstrated by their attitude toward the CSCE follow-up conference in Madrid from September 1980 to September 1983. As the meeting was convened in the rather strained international climate following the Soviet invasion of Afghanistan, it was to be expected that the harsh attacks launched at the Eastern states for their human rights violations at the first follow-up conference in Belgrade in 1977–78 would now be multiplied and supplemented by the charge of Soviet aggression. From a publicity perspective, it appeared a lost cause for the Soviet bloc. In such a situation, it would have been logical to try to postpone or even boycott the conference to avoid a serious loss of prestige. Yet the Soviet leadership decided to follow the original agenda and enter the fight. During the conference, the introduction of martial law in Poland in December 1981 further exacerbated the situation. However, by September 1983, the conference had produced tangible results, with agreements on issues such as religious freedom and family unification. Most importantly, the participants agreed on convening three important meetings: a human rights conference in Ottawa in 1985, a cultural forum in Budapest the same year, and a human contacts conference in Bern in 1986.

In the second half of the 1970s, three of the Warsaw Pact states were the most important proponents of détente in the Soviet bloc; Poland, Hungary, and Romania. By the beginning of the 1980s, however, two of them, Poland and Romania, were disqualified. Poland lost the sympathy of the Western states after the introduction of martial law in 1981, while Romania ceased to be the favorite of the West and especially the U.S. administration due to its increasingly repressive internal policy. Thus, Hungary became the number one favorite in the eyes of the West as the most presentable country of the Eastern bloc. One important aspect of this special status was that it enabled Hungary to develop intensive economic and political relations with Western states precisely during the years of the standby stage of superpower détente from 1979 to 1985.

In this period, from the invasion of Afghanistan to the rise of Gorbachev in 1985, Hungary served as a model case by showing how a small state, driven by its economic interests, could—while being a "closely cooperating" member of the Warsaw Pact—maintain and intensify the policy of détente as if nothing had happened between the United States and the Soviet Union.[42] In fact, these years brought a dynamic and prosperous era in developing the country's economic and political relations with the West: while Hungary had signed the General Agreement on Tariffs and Trade in 1973, the country was finally able to join the International Monetary Fund (IMF) and the World Bank in 1982. (Hungary had tried to join the IMF and the World Bank as early as 1967, but at that time, as well as several times later in the 1970s, this plan was blocked by Moscow.)[43] Moreover, as early as 1981, exploratory talks were already underway concerning a potential agreement with the European Economic Community. This was later prevented not by Moscow but by Chancellor Helmut Schmidt, who was worried about the potential negative effect of such a step on his own country's relations with the Soviet Union. Therefore, he explicitly talked Kádár out of this plan on his visit to Bonn in April 1982.[44] During this period, high-level contacts with Western countries became very intensive. Kádár paid visits to Bonn and Rome in 1977, to Paris in 1978, to Bonn again in 1982, and to London in 1985. Hungary, in turn, was visited by French prime minister Raymond Barre in 1977, Chancellor Helmut Schmidt in 1979, French president François Mitterrand in 1982, and U.S. vice president George Bush in 1983. During these visits, it was becoming increasingly obvious that there was no alternative to maintaining and enhancing dialogue and cooperation between the two parts of Europe.

Hungary played a moderating role during the Polish crisis of 1980–81 as well. Seriously concerned about the potential spillover effect of the events, the Hungarian leadership communicated constantly with Polish officials at several levels, including the trade unions. János Kádár played a mediating role, similar to the one in 1968, although the intensity of the interaction was considerably lower.[45] While the East German, Bulgarian, and Czechoslovak leaders demanded the restoration of order in Poland by military means beginning in the fall of 1980 and were ready to participate in such an invasion, Hungary, together with Romania, advocated a political solution, both publicly and in confidential bilateral and multilateral meetings up until November 1981. Even then, only the use of Polish forces was regarded acceptable to "save socialism," and the Hungarian army was not expected to take part in any potential joint maneuver. At a meeting of the WP ministers of defense in Moscow just two weeks before the introduction of martial law on 13 December 1981, it was the Hungarian minister who—at Kádár's instruction—blocked the adoption of the inclusion of a sentence in the final communiqué about a potential Warsaw Pact move.[46]

The most spectacular demonstration of Hungarian mediation in the East–West relationship occurred during the height of the Euromissile crisis in 1984, when three prime ministers—Helmut Kohl, Margaret Thatcher, and Bettino Craxi—visited Hungary. Remarkably, all three states (the FRG, Great Britain, and Italy) were on the Soviets' blacklist, as they had consented to the deployment of U.S. Euromissiles on their territory the previous year.[47] What makes this move by Hungary even more interesting is that this was not achieved through a Romanian-type deviant foreign policy action but by convincing the Soviet leaders about the crucial nature of these visits for the stabilization of Hungary's economy, since by that time the country was increasingly dependent on Western loans.[48] Maintaining high-level contacts with key leaders of the NATO bloc via a small state mediator was in reality beneficial for Moscow as well, since this channel enabled the Soviet leaders to play the double game of "punishing" the Euromissile-deploying states and keeping the door open for the resumption of negotiations at the same time.

At the CSCE follow-up conferences in Belgrade, Madrid, and Vienna, Hungarian diplomacy played an increasingly proactive role; thus, it was not by coincidence that the only follow-up conference taking place in a WP state was the European Cultural Forum, held in Budapest in 1985.[49]

Chapter 10

The Soviet Union and East Central Europe, 1985–1990

At the end of the 1980s, as had been the case over the last few centuries, the fate of East Central Europe was determined by the great powers and the realities of world politics. This was not always disadvantageous for the countries of the region; the peace treaties after World War I, for instance, explicitly favored the interests of most of these nations by establishing nation-states and by satisfying territorial demands at the expense of the defeated countries. After World War II, however, the states of the region were all incorporated into the Soviet empire and, with the exception of Yugoslavia and Albania, remained part of it for more than four decades, without any hope of regaining their independence. Thus, not only did the political changes of 1989–91 result in the establishment of democracy and the restoration of sovereignty, but after a long period, East Central Europeans could enjoy a social experience that proved that the rivalry between the superpowers and the changing conditions of world politics could exert a positive effect on the enforcement of their national interests.[1]

Imperial Status Quo, Imperial Armament

When Mikhail Gorbachev was elected as secretary-general of the CPSU in March 1985, he undertook a task no less formidable than that of breathing new life into a Socialist economic-political model that had already fallen into serious crisis at both the center of the Soviet empire and at its East European periphery. It would have been interesting to find out whether the reforms Gorbachev introduced or just envisioned could have proven to be effective a few decades *earlier*. By the middle of the 1980s, however, it was too late. The arms race with the United States, the need to maintain parity in nuclear strategy, and the expenses of an irrationally oversized imperial periphery (Cuba, Nicaragua, Afghanistan, Ethiopia, Angola, and so on) that brought no real profit, as well as subsidizing the East Central European allies, had eaten up the economic reserves of the Soviet Union to such an extent that the chances for consolidation were rather slim in a Socialist economic system that was in any event extremely inefficient.

In addition, Gorbachev and his reformer associates did not adequately assess the severity of the upcoming crisis, even though they were aware of its inevitability. Thus, up until 1988, the reforms, initially formulated with much caution in terms of perestroika and glasnost, did not significantly improve either the political conditions or the efficiency of the economy. Although the new leadership had emphasized from the beginning its commitment to establishing a new international order that would replace the old Cold War opposition, it failed to make the best of this possibility by reducing the armament costs of the Soviet Union radically and promptly. While the Soviet–American disarmament talks, which became increasingly intensive beginning in the middle of the 1980s, brought a remarkable result in December 1987 with the signing of the Intermediate-Range Nuclear Forces (INF) Treaty on eliminating medium-range and short-range nuclear missiles in Europe, up until the summer of 1988, the Soviet leadership refused to concede any unilateral steps in disarmament. As basically all the other Warsaw Pact member states were in a state of permanent economic crisis by the middle of the 1980s, they would have badly needed some relief measures. However, up until mid-1988, they were not allowed to ease the situation by cutting their military budgets. Only Romania—the openly deviating black sheep of the bloc, which had been urging for unilateral reductions for years—in spite of a definite Soviet "request" to the contrary, reduced its armed forces by 5 percent in 1986.

The Soviet leadership failed to make any concessions in spite of the fact that the considerable Soviet advantage, especially in conventional armament, would have given them a great chance to reduce military expenses significantly at an early stage. Moreover, this would have had a positive effect on building security and trust between East and West, which Gorbachev regarded as especially important. It should also be remembered that a much less amicable Khrushchev did in fact use the "weapon" of unilateral cuts and troop withdrawals very effectively as confidence-building measures in promoting East–West rapprochement at the end of the 1950s.[2] Because of the resistance of the Soviet military lobby and the conservative members of the leadership, as well as the traditional imperial attitude that also characterized the views of even the reformers to quite a large extent, a real turn could only take place at the Warsaw meeting of the WP PCC on 15–16 July 1988. In his address, a still ex officio optimistic Gorbachev assessed the role of the Socialist camp in shaping world politics and its chances for the future as definitely positive. On the other hand, at a closed session of the foreign ministers, Eduard Shevardnadze openly admitted that the Soviet Union was "facing a critical situation," and it could no longer afford to run a permanent arms race with the West, given that it exceeded the Eastern bloc "in every possible respect." Therefore, he stressed that the termination of the arms race had to be given absolute priority, and every chance had to be grasped in order to come to an agreement.[3]

In fact, this dramatic confession was about nothing less than admitting total defeat in the several decades-long competition between the two world systems. Therefore, this moment can be considered the beginning of the end for the Soviet bloc. From then on, the agreements absolutely necessary for the survival of the bloc were not to be achieved in a "normal" way—that is, by mutual compromises based on parity, as in the case of the INF Treaty just a year earlier—but *at any price*. This was the crucial recognition that led to the decision on the announcement of significant unilateral disarmament measures. Thus, the WP PCC meeting of July 1988 in Warsaw can be considered an important turning point in the history of the Cold War as well; from this moment on, the Soviet bloc's attitude toward rapprochement with the West was no longer limited by the obligatory search for parity.

With a view to this, the WP PCC decided to speed up preparations for the upcoming East–West negotiations on conventional armament, to transform the structure and deployment of the armed forces of the WP (now exclusively for meeting defensive needs), to develop a more flexible negotiating strategy, and, in particular—after changing its former position—to take unilateral steps in disarmament. The Committee of the Defense Ministers was then commissioned to consider how the real data on the armies and the armament of the Warsaw Pact states could be made public. At its special meeting in Prague in the middle of October 1988, however, the non-Soviet members of the committee were shocked to learn that the vast numerical superiority of the Warsaw Pact in conventional armaments was in fact not the invention of Western propaganda—as they themselves truly believed—but a fact. Thus, the committee concluded that admitting the advantage of the WP in a number of fields before the negotiations started would have an unfavorable effect on the position of the alliance. Therefore, this step, which was originally intended to strengthen security and confidence, was postponed till March 1989, when the so-called CFE (conventional armed forces in Europe) talks commenced in Vienna.[4]

The unilateral steps for disarmament, however, had been announced by Gorbachev well before that time, when he delivered his speech at the UN General Assembly on 7 December 1988. On this occasion, the secretary-general of the CPSU announced that the Soviet Union would reduce its armed forces by five hundred thousand troops and that this would partly be accomplished by pulling out some of the forces stationed in the GDR, Czechoslovakia, and Hungary. Altogether, he planned to withdraw some fifty thousand Soviet troops from these three countries. The worsening of the political-economic situation in the Soviet Union by this time and the significantly more flexible attitude of the Soviet leadership resulting from this are reflected by the fact that half a year earlier, at the July 1988 Warsaw meeting of the WP PCC, Gorbachev had maintained that the *total* Soviet reduction could concern only some seventy thousand troops and their armament.[5]

The decision to unilaterally disarm half a million troops seemed quite radical at the time to a public that did not know that this was just some 10 percent of the total headcount of the Soviet armed forces. More importantly, it was a rather late move in terms of consolidating the Soviet economy, and it was not free from inconsistency. The reduction of the armed forces by no means signified a cut in military spending by the Soviet leaders. Quite the contrary: however surprising it might seem, in the summer of 1988 the Moscow leaders intended to *increase* the defense budget by 43 percent, including the use of the state reserves as well.[6] The imminent comprehensive modernization program of NATO had caught the Soviets—who still wanted to maintain strategic parity by all means—in a trap out of which the only escape was to accomplish the unavoidable reduction simultaneously with or right after the Soviet Army's accelerated modernization, which would involve extremely large short-term costs. It is quite likely that it was primarily this challenge (or the failure to meet this challenge), rather than the American SDI "Star Wars" program that eventually brought the Soviet Union to its knees in the arms race, and thus led to the fall of the Communist system itself.

One of the most remarkable results of the Gorbachev reforms was undoubtedly the introduction of pragmatic policy making and the reduced emphasis on Communist ideology in both foreign and home policy. Despite this strategic change, almost nothing was achieved in the area that could otherwise match what could have offered the Soviet Union the most profit for the least investment: cutting down on the imperial periphery. Gorbachev was ready to replace the Soviet expansionist policy based on supporting the "liberation movements" of the third world with a more up-to-date strategy of exporting the revolution via the appeal of the new Socialist model, which, he hoped, had in the meantime been reformed and made functional. Due to the resistance of the conservative members of the leadership and the need to consider the prestige of the Soviet Union as a world superpower, however, very few concrete steps were taken in this direction before 1988.[7] Although the pullout of troops from Afghanistan began at the beginning of that year, to be followed by the exit of Cuban volunteers from Angola in January 1989, these happened too late. Even in 1989, financing the imperial periphery inherited mostly from the Brezhnev era consumed huge sums (keeping Cuba alive alone cost 27 billion rubles annually), pushing the economy to the brink of total collapse.[8]

This inflexible imperial policy, predetermined by ideological considerations that prohibited the timely elimination of most earlier obligations, eventually led to the loss of Soviet influence over the East Central European region. Furthermore, as a result of constant overexpansion, or exhausting the "action radius"—a problem under which several empires had previously collapsed in the course of history—the Soviet Union could eradicate the intolerable economic burden of supporting its allies only through its own dissolution.[9]

The Soviet Union and East Central Europe

Up to the present, the most important question to have engaged the greatest attention is how the Soviet leadership could have eventually tolerated losing the region previously considered to be of utmost importance, and for which their predecessors had made great sacrifices for more than four decades. At the time when Gorbachev rose to power, Soviet policy continued to give the preservation of East Central Europe as a security zone for the Soviet Union the absolute priority it had uninterruptedly enjoyed since 1945. Initially, the primary goal of the transitional policy announced by the new secretary-general was to make the economic system more efficient and the political system more democratic in a limited sense—in other words, modernizing the Socialist model inherited from the Stalinist era. Gorbachev believed not only that this program could be successfully accomplished in the Soviet Union but also that the modernization of the system was an "objective necessity" deriving from the essential conditions of the age.[10] Sooner or later, he maintained, the countries of East Central Europe would follow this good example of their own accord, for it represented the only possible means of avoiding imminent crisis—or surviving it once it developed.

In similar situations, Gorbachev's forefathers—especially the father of the de-Stalinization campaign, Khrushchev—never bothered relying on the principle of voluntarism when urging partners to follow the Soviet Union's good example. Gorbachev, however, had good reasons not to try to impose the reforms on his allies. He regarded political stability as a key factor in accomplishing a successful transition in both the Soviet Union and East Central Europe. At the same time, the situation was rather confused in this respect. In Hungary and Poland, where commitment to reforms was quite alive even without the Soviet influence, dire economic conditions, indebtedness to Western creditors, and growing social dissatisfaction gave cause for serious alarm as early as the mid-1980s. In the GDR, Romania, Czechoslovakia, and Bulgaria, however, each of which had a more conservative leadership, the political situation seemed much sounder, despite the apparent stagnation. Thus, imposing the new Soviet policy on these countries would not only not have been in accord with the new Gorbachev style but also have involved the risk of *destabilizing* those countries in which this problem, at least, had not existed before. Therefore, in the second half of the decade, Gorbachev followed the policy of patient persuasion and attempted to achieve his goals via frequent bilateral and multilateral talks, personal visits, and public appearances.

At these meetings, Gorbachev tried to make it very clear from the beginning that he wanted to establish relations with the East Central European allies on new foundations, although the principles of such a new policy were not codified in any particular document for the public. As regards the principles or promises of this policy, not much new had to or could be offered, given that the Soviet government's 30 October 1956 declaration—the force of which had never been canceled—stated that the Socialist countries could "build their mutual relations only on the principles of complete equality, of respect for territorial integrity, state independence and sovereignty, and of noninterference in one another's internal affairs."[11] This is not to say that Gorbachev, contrary to his predecessors, took these high principles seriously, or that he was ready to give up the leading role of the Soviet Union within the Socialist camp. It is obvious, however, that—contrary to any other former leader—he seriously believed that a new relationship must be built that was *more* equal than it had been in the past: one that could put an end to the Soviet guardianship,[12] that could achieve real mutuality in the exchange of ideas and experiences, that acknowledged the right of finding one's own way within the Socialist model—in practice as well as in principle—and that could offer the chance for relatively independent policy making, provided the alliance system was still respected. One could even say that, between 1985 and 1989, Gorbachev offered the entire Eastern camp an alliance system for lasting use, which the Khrushchev leadership, confused by the events in Poland and Hungary, had regarded as tenable for only a single day (30 October 1956), and even then only for Hungary.[13]

All of this did not mean, however, the abandonment of the Brezhnev doctrine—that is, acknowledgment that the East Central European nations were entitled to a truly free choice, including the elimination of the Socialist system and the restoration of a Western type of parliamentary democracy. This must be emphasized because some of Gorbachev's former associates suggested that the rejection of the Brezhnev doctrine took place essentially in 1985–86, or even, as some argue, in 1981, when the Soviet military intervention in Poland did not take place.[14] Based on currently available sources, however, it can be clearly established that no significant change in Soviet attitude occurred before the summer of 1988. Even then, when the thesis came to be adopted that, in the case of potential crisis in the Socialist countries, the possibility of Soviet military intervention must be excluded, this was formulated in the hope that the outcome of even radical changes would be a new model of Socialism.

All of this was closely related to the radical changes that took place in the Soviet Union in the summer and fall of 1988. The national CPSU conference held in June gave new momentum to perestroika and, from this time on, the major direction of the reforms was increasingly aimed at restructuring the system of political institutions, since the measures that had already been introduced in the field of economy had brought very poor results. At the end of September, Gorbachev strengthened his position in the leadership,[15] and from this time on he enjoyed the unquestionable authority that every secretary-general of the CPSU was entitled to have in times of peace. During these few months, qualitative changes took place in Soviet policy in several respects. The program of modernizing the Stalinist model came to be replaced by an effort to develop a new model of Socialism that could possibly blend the most advantageous features of both the Communist and the capitalist systems—a new model that, thanks to its capacity for renewal and thus its popularity among the public, could ensure a dominant role for the Communist Party in political life even after free elections. This "rubber" concept—heavily influenced by the theory of convergence—went through a number of transitions in 1989–90. Nobody knew what it really involved until it turned out that it was nothing other than capitalism.

It was at this time that the Gorbachev–Shevardnadze duet could start accomplishing their own initiatives, this time without any significant obstacles. This resulted in a real breakthrough in the most important field, that of Soviet–American relations, and a new relationship between the leaders of the two superpowers began to be established, which could not have been conceivable even a few years earlier.

Given Gorbachev's ardent urgings to build a new world order based on trust, mutual security, peaceful coexistence, cooperation, and the elimination of the division of Europe, normalization of the relations with the leading powers of Western Europe became extremely important. Although only in the summer of 1989 did the secretary-general pay his crucial visits to London, Paris, and Bonn, the intensive exchange of ideas had begun earlier, and serious reservations were replaced by qualitative changes in the attitude of the Soviet government, especially with regard to the FRG. This latter development was to a large extent due to the intervention of the Hungarian leadership, which had for some time cultivated excellent relations with the West Germans and was negotiated by Károly Grósz during his Moscow visit in July 1988 at the request of Chancellor Kohl.[16]

Gorbachev's Last Weapon: "Floating" the Brezhnev Doctrine

As far as East Central Europe is concerned, there were two fundamental changes in the Soviet policy at this time that considerably determined the fate of the region: the adoption of the principle of "socialist pluralism" and the introduction of a new strategy in the alliance—the "floating" of the Brezhnev Doctrine,[17] a term coined by this author. At the CPSU conference in June 1988, Gorbachev—without any preliminary theoretical elaboration—declared that any nation had the right to choose its own socioeconomic system.[18] Canadian political scientist Jacques Lévesque raises three reasons for the announcement of this very important (albeit far from unambiguous) thesis. In his view, Gorbachev's major goal was to win the confidence of the West, since in addition to his position on Afghanistan, Gorbachev's willingness to tolerate changes in East Central Europe was the main basis the West used to judge his true intentions. Another aim was to prepare the Soviet nomenclature and the party apparatus for the changes so that they could eliminate their old reflexes. A third goal was possibly to warn the Communist leaders of East Central Europe that in the future event of a domestic crisis, they should not expect automatic Soviet aid. This could be conceptualized as a kind of political pressure, aiming to nudge the unwilling allies toward adopting reforms.[19]

Based on currently available sources, it seems quite likely that in June 1988, these factors had only an instinctive rather than a conscious influence on Gorbachev's intentions. The most important goal might have been the introduction of a new type of discourse on the increasingly critical topic of the Soviet Union's relations with the East Central European states—a discourse that could provide the leaders of the Soviet reforms greater room and possibility to maneuver than they had possessed before, thus giving them the chance to respond flexibly to the ever-changing situation. This thesis was repeated by Gorbachev and other leaders several times and in several forms over the course of 1988–89 and was very soon supplemented by the public promise to cease the use of military force. Moreover, especially during 1989, it was from time to time stated explicitly that the Brezhnev Doctrine was not valid anymore, which in principle could not be interpreted otherwise than that Moscow would no longer intervene militarily in an allied state in cases of internal crisis. But was this really so? We now know that, as of the summer of 1988, the Soviet leadership had given up on the idea of a military option. So, the trick was in the fact that from this time on, Gorbachev wanted to enjoy the positive international effect of this benevolent public promise but at the same time do everything he could to mislead the East Central European Communist leaders into believing that this offer was valid *only* if they could keep the reforms within the limits of the Socialist system. This is what we can call the floating of the Brezhnev Doctrine. Consequently, the essence of these multifunctional declarations, simultaneously addressed to all interested parties and deliberately meant to be ambiguous, was that although they *implicitly* rejected the possibility of military intervention, they never stated *categorically* that the Soviet Union would not interfere with an ally's domestic affairs should the political transition go beyond a new model of Socialism and, horribile dictu, result in the total abandonment of Socialism and the restoration of a Western type of parliamentary democracy.[20] In other words, this thesis concerning the free choice of individual countries could be conveniently interpreted in harmony with one's own interests and desires, while at the same time, given the turbulent circumstances, it could also be interpreted in precisely the opposite way.

More importantly, all of this was coupled with continuous warnings from Moscow to the leaders of the East Central European countries through secret channels and at confidential bilateral talks. The message was as follows: the limit of the transformation is *the preservation of socialism*.[21] Sometimes this dialectical approach manifested itself in a very concrete form. During Károly Grósz's visit to Moscow at the end of March 1989, for example, Gorbachev stated that "today the possibility of repeating the interference into the domestic affairs of other socialist countries must be excluded once and for all" but, on the other hand, he also emphasized that "we clearly have to draw the boundaries, thinking about ourselves and others at the same time. Democracy is much needed, and the interests have to be harmonized. *The limit, however, is the safekeeping of socialism* [emphasis added] and assurance of stability."[22] As for how to interpret "the boundaries," no one in the Eastern bloc had more experience in this than the Hungarians, as the official explanation of the Soviet invasion on 4 November 1956 was based on the same logic: "safekeeping of socialism" was not possible without Soviet intervention.

The initially instinctive but later increasingly conscious tactic of floating the Brezhnev Doctrine was successful and effective, at least temporarily.[23] It also had a definite stabilizing effect on the accelerated transition, both in East Central Europe and in the Soviet Union, and contributed to preserving the peaceful nature of the changes to a large extent. One can imagine what would have happened to the position of the Soviet reformers, within both the leadership and society, if a categorical declaration had been made overnight that East Central Europe, for which the Soviet Army had shed so much blood, could now determine its fate freely—including the possibility of capitalist restoration. At the same time, floating the Brezhnev Doctrine had the advantage of enabling the Soviet leadership to accustom society, and themselves as well, gradually to the idea that the Soviet Union might have to accept heretofore unheard-of radical changes in East Central Europe.

This tactic had a similar stabilizing effect on the transition in the region, and it probably played a key role in ensuring that, apart from the Romanians, the Communist leaders were too unclear concerning Soviet intentions to dare to engage in any kind of repression against the mass movements that emerged in the fall of 1989. The same blocking effect deriving from uncertainty can be generally observed in the policy of the opposition forces, although it manifested itself in different forms in the two leading reform countries: Poland and Hungary.[24]

The deviation from the Polish model and the special nature of the Hungarian transition are well reflected by the fact that, at the beginning of 1989, the Hungarian leadership was just as interested in eliminating the Brezhnev Doctrine as was the opposition, since they hoped to transform the basis of their legitimacy from Soviet support to the potentially positive outcome of the upcoming elections.[25] Strangely enough, the opposition expected its political rival, the HSWP, to provide the external conditions for a peaceful transition and to give them a guarantee that the Brezhnev doctrine was no longer in force. The representatives of the Opposition Roundtable posed an explicit question on this issue to Hungary's defense minister, Ferenc Kárpáti, on 30 August 1989, when he gave them confidential information on current military-political issues.[26]

Beyond all this, from the middle of 1988, the floating of the Brezhnev Doctrine was virtually the only weapon left to the Soviet leadership with which it could, at least for a short time, have an influence on the political processes running their course in East Central Europe. After all, by that point Gorbachev and his associates had given up on the possibility of military intervention. Unlike their predecessors, who possessed much more modest goals, the Soviet reformers, striving for a radical reformation of East–West relations and a new world order based on cooperation, could simply not afford any kind of armed intervention aimed at restoring order and the old system without jeopardizing the progress that had already been achieved.[27] Doing so not only would have been a danger to world politics but also would have caused the West to lose its confidence in Gorbachev.[28] In the end, this would have meant the fall of perestroika, the program of transformation, which was Gorbachev's first priority.[29]

It was at this time that the fate of East Central Europe was subordinated to two factors of a different order: the highly ambitious goals of the Gorbachev leadership in world politics on the one hand, and the success of the Soviet transition on the other.[30] The latter—based on the available sources and with knowledge of the later events—might well be called a life-or-death fight for the survival of the Soviet Union. Thus, I believe that the main reason that the Soviet Union agreed to let East Central Europe go so easily was that this was the first time since the Russian civil war that the Soviet state—paradoxically, still one of the two superpowers of the bipolar world order in a military sense—found itself in a situation in which its own survival was at stake. Giving priority to saving the imperial center was a logical and necessary step, with respect to which the East Central European periphery gradually lost its significance. If one tries to find a historical parallel, this could be described as an instance of Brest-Litovsk syndrome. At that critical moment of the civil war in March 1918, Lenin had argued for a peace treaty to be signed with the Germans that, while requiring the loss of huge territories, would nonetheless ensure the preservation of the Soviet state. Lenin proved to be right about this, but like the Soviet Union itself, his later successor, Gorbachev, was to be surpassed by history.[31]

This Leninist tradition meant that, in a critical situation to protect the integrity of the imperial center, Moscow could temporarily make even serious territorial concessions. But, as Melinda Kalmár points out, it could not plan these retreats forever; the imperial radius could be retracted for some time, only to extend again.[32] It is a remarkable fact that the territory given up by Gorbachev in 1989 (the GDR, Poland, Czechoslovakia, Hungary, Romania, and Bulgaria) was of the same order as what the Bolsheviks handed over to Germany and the Austro-Hungarian monarchy in the Brest-Litovsk peace treaty and, in connection with it, to Turkey. It is also an interesting coincidence that twenty-two years passed between 1918 and 1939/1940, when Moscow regained most of its territories lost between 1918 and 1921, and the annexation of the Crimea by Russia took place about twenty-two years after the breakup of the Soviet Union.

Western Reactions to the Changes in East Central Europe

Gorbachev's rise to power, along with his reforms and initiatives in the field of international politics and domestic relations, posed great challenges to the Reagan administration, which had led the United States since 1981. In his first two years, Reagan's new confrontative rhetoric claimed that America's historical mission was to end the Cold War in such a way that the new round of the arms race, which had resumed in the second half of the 1970s, would bankrupt the Soviet Union. The primary means of executing this new strategy would have been the Star Wars (SDI) program initiated in 1983. In reality, as we saw in chapter 9, this propaganda was meant mostly for internal consumption, demonstrating the need for "making America great again," while internationally this was aimed at persuading the Soviet Union to engage in serious negotiations on arms control.

After Gorbachev entered the scene, it became increasingly obvious, especially over the course of 1987–88, that Gorbachev's dynamic personality made him more than just another Khrushchev and that his initiatives aimed at eliminating confrontation should be taken seriously. At that time, a new, rather tempting alternative began to unfold. This alternative envisioned the possibility of agreement and long-lasting cooperation, which would have made possible a radical reduction in armaments as well as international tensions. Due to its budget deficit, the United States also had an interest in reducing military spending, although it is quite likely that, if needed, it would have been able to find the necessary resources to finance the SDI program, albeit at the cost of great sacrifice. Such a pact between the superpowers would have also had the advantage of strengthening the leading position of the United States in relation to Western Europe, just on the brink of unifying into a potential third power. The October 1986 summit meeting in Reykjavík between Gorbachev and Reagan can be regarded as a step in this direction, which provoked heated criticism from the United States' Western allies. The Malta summit between Bush and Gorbachev three years later belongs to this same category of meetings.[33] No significant change can be discerned in the United States' East Central European policy before 1989. This policy involved a different approach for each of the countries of the region, and the goal, realistic under the given circumstances, was to soften and liberalize the Communist systems by several means: exerting economic pressure, continuously calling these countries to account for their human rights records, and supporting the opposition movements. Strangely enough, during the period between 1985 and the end of 1988, American and Soviet views concerning the desired transition of the region had gradually become closer. For the Soviets, more and more elements could be regarded as being part of the democratization process and a new Socialist model, while, for the Americans, there was still not much hope for a truly radical change in the situation—that is, the restoration of parliamentary democracy.

The first important change took place in the spring of 1989, after President Bush took office in January. This was not due, however, to the new leadership taking a completely new approach to the question but rather to the fact that, in the meantime, a turn of historical importance was beginning to emerge in East Central Europe. At the beginning of February, roundtable talks between the government and the legally acknowledged Solidarity trade union began in Poland. By April they came to an agreement, and the first "semi-free" elections could be held in June, resulting in a sweeping victory for the opposition, which won most of the seats under competition. In Hungary, the HSWP CC accepted at its 10–11 February meeting the introduction of a multiparty system, and it also adopted the position that the 1956 events in Hungary constituted a popular uprising and not a counterrevolution. In June, roundtable negotiations began between the state party and the members of the Opposition Roundtable, and the reburial of former prime minister Imre Nagy and his associates, executed after the 1956 Hungarian Revolution, also took place. Although the position and the social legitimacy of the Hungarian opposition was much weaker than that of the Polish, what was at stake was no less than the total demolition of the party state, the restoration of the constitutional state, and the preparation for free elections.[34]

Assessing this from the American viewpoint, the most important factor was that these events, which would have seemed unbelievable just a year before, took place without any Soviet retribution, or even any sign of disapproval. In the spring of 1989, the Bush administration began to accustom itself to the idea that the old American dream originated by President Eisenhower was about to come true: the peaceful *self-liberation* of East Central Europe under Soviet approval. All that was needed for success was for the United States, and Western Europe in general, to give the Soviet Union—as far as it was possible—the opportunity for a dignified withdrawal from the region.[35] When visiting Budapest after a trip to Warsaw in July 1989, President Bush explicitly stressed at the negotiations with the leaders of the Hungarian government and the HSWP that the United States would show a neutral attitude concerning the Hungarian transition.[36] Essentially the same position was communicated at the meeting with the leaders of the opposition, a meeting that left President Bush with a rather poor impression. He explained to his associates that "these really aren't the right guys to be running this place. At least not yet."[37]

At the December 1989 summit in Malta, Bush outlined the essence of his policy to Gorbachev in very clear terms:

> I hope you noticed that while the changes in Eastern Europe have
> been going on, the United States has not engaged in condescending
> declarations aimed at damaging [the prestige of] the Soviet Union.
> There are people in the United States who accuse me of being too
> cautious. It is true, I am a prudent man, but I am not a coward, and my
> administration will seek to avoid doing anything that would damage your
> position in the world. But I was insistently advised to do something
> of that sort—to climb the Berlin Wall and to make broad declarations.
> My administration, however, is avoiding these steps, [as] we are in favor
> of reserved behavior.[38]

In reality, in 1989–90, U.S. policy vis-à-vis the transition in East Central Europe was not just neutral, as from time to time Washington explicitly urged the leaders of especially Poland and Hungary through confidential channels to be moderate and slow down the process of political transition. All of this was meant to be supportive of Gorbachev's reforms and his position in the Soviet Union by not exacerbating his situation in the Warsaw Pact states.[39]

Gorbachev's entrance onto the scene posed a great challenge not only to the United States but also to Western Europe in at least two respects. The most important issue was the security of the Western part of Europe—that is, the problem of the potential Soviet threat, which since 1945 had been a cardinal issue for Western politicians and societies. The new Soviet policy, promising the elimination of confrontation and truly peaceful coexistence of the two systems, as well as ardent urgings to build a new world order based on trust, mutual security, cooperation, and overcoming the division of Europe, thus normalizing relations with the leading powers of Western Europe, seemed to offer a chance for a lasting solution in this respect.[40] Western European hopes for a new model of coexistence with the East began to flourish, especially after the signing of the INF Treaty, eliminating the short- and medium-range missiles in Europe in 1987; the beginning of the unilateral reduction in the armed forces of the Soviet Union and the Warsaw Pact in December 1988; and the start of promising talks in Vienna concerning the radical reduction of conventional armaments in Europe in March 1989.

Gorbachev's vision of a "common European home" implied that a unified Europe could play a more significant role in the bipolar world order than previously, creating a potential "third force."[41] Therefore, many politicians and a large part of the societies in Western Europe received the Soviet initiatives with great sympathy, especially over the course of 1988–89. All of this was facilitated by the fact that Gorbachev's "common European home" idea was an extremely vague conception, conveniently allowing varying interpretations and making it easy to see it as the implementation of the post-Helsinki dream of many in Western Europe: a virtually united Europe, where the capitalist West and the states of the Communist East, with radically reformed and liberalized (but still Communist) political systems, could live side by side and cooperate in a civilized manner as "normal" partners until the end of time.[42] It is a historical irony that, in the Soviet assessment, the most positive reactions came from the Soviet Union's two main enemies during World War II: the FRG and Italy.[43]

It is important to stress that Gorbachev's cooperative attitude toward the West was also highly influenced by Reagan's SDI project, which would have started a new and unexpectedly expensive qualitatively different phase in the superpower nuclear arms race. In this new phase, the Soviet Union, with its failing economy, had no chance to continue the competition, whereas from 1945 up to that point, Moscow—though at the cost of enormous sacrifices by its people—was always capable of meeting the new American challenges. Being the prisoner of its superpower status meant the desperate need to maintain parity all along, thus it was vital for Moscow to somehow block the development of SDI.[44] Once it had become clear to the Soviet leader that the U.S. president was not willing to give up on his Star Wars plan, hypocritically calling it a purely "defensive project,"[45] the only option left for Gorbachev was to appeal to the American taxpayers. Why should they spend horrendous sums for a space-based anti-missile system when there was no longer an enemy to fear? The plan worked, and during the unprecedentedly intensive summitry from 1985 to 1988, a real partnership emerged between Reagan and Gorbachev. It is history's irony that by the end of his second term in 1988, when the Soviet Union was on the verge of collapse, Reagan—who had originally promised to drive the Soviets bankrupt via a new wave of the arms race—went out of his way to stabilize the power of his opponent, Gorbachev. It is also worth noting that this exceptional relationship was based on the continual performance of two excellent actors: Reagan, a professional, was using a nonexistent project to push Moscow in the direction of cooperation and disarmament, while Gorbachev could "sell" the Soviet Union as a potent superpower even when it was on the verge of collapse.

Up until 1989, no one in Western Europe had expected that the developments in East Central Europe could lead to the total collapse of Communism, much less the fall of the Soviet Union;[46] thus, the fate of the region—as had always been the case over the previous decades—was logically subordinated to the interests of Western–Soviet relations, which were becoming better and increasingly more promising. The main consideration for politicians interested in the success of perestroika was ensuring the security interests of the Soviet Union, and they viewed the maintenance of the East Central European status quo as its primary guarantee. Although, on moral grounds, they did support developments pointing toward a democratic transition in these countries and the opposition movement fighting for this course, maintaining stability at any cost was of primary importance. This position was not only motivated by concern about the potential Soviet reaction but also by the worry that the total collapse of the East Central European countries on the verge of economic bankruptcy might result in social explosions, ethnic conflicts, and so on, which would have a negative influence on Western Europe as well. Such conflicts would endanger the process of integration and, more importantly, would jeopardize the stability of the entire continent.

Therefore, the leaders of the Western European countries did not simply want to stay neutral; rather, they intended to exercise a blocking and moderating effect on the process of East Central European transition. They envisioned this transition as a slow process that would last for years, much as the Communist reformers had originally envisaged. Thus, when in the first half of 1989 developments in Hungary and Poland accelerated—partly as a result of the initiations of the reformers—most Western European leaders judged the pace of transition to be too rapid. Therefore, they intended to exert a moderating influence in two different directions: on the one hand, they periodically assured the Soviet leadership and Gorbachev himself that the West would not interfere with the events in East Central Europe and would not do anything that would cause destabilization in these countries. On the other hand, they sought to convince both the Communist and opposition leaders in Hungary and Poland that they should slow down the pace of change in order to maintain stability. At his meeting with Gorbachev on 12 June 1989 in Bonn, Chancellor Helmut Kohl explicitly stated, "I am not doing anything to destabilize the situation. This applies to Hungary and Poland, as well. To interfere with anybody's internal political development now would mean to take a destructive line which would throw Europe back to the times of caution and mistrust."[47]

At her 6 April 1989 meeting with Gorbachev in London, British prime minister Margaret Thatcher not only expressed her conviction that Jaruzelski was "a prominent and honest politician" who "does everything he can for his country at a very difficult stage in its development" but also declared that she had warned the leaders of Solidarity "to seek a dialogue, not limit themselves to confrontation. I said to them that you can never leave the negotiating chair empty, it would not lead to anything, and I can see that they have listened to my advice."[48]

This moderating role was taken so seriously by the FRG leadership that, even in the summer of 1989, they believed the desired stability could only be maintained by avoiding the change of the whole system—that is, the political transition itself. At his meeting with Gorbachev on 14 June 1989, Helmut Kohl outlined his position on the Hungarian transition as follows: "We have rather good relations with the Hungarians. However, we also do not want destabilization there. That is why when I meet with the Hungarians, I tell them: we consider the reforms that are underway in your country your internal affair, we are sympathetic. However, if you would like to hear our advice, we recommend that you do not accelerate too much, because you might lose control over your mechanism, and it will start to work *to destroy itself* [emphasis added]."[49]

Chapter 11

The International Context of the Political Transition in Hungary

The Political Transition and the Foreign Policy of Hungary

Since the end of the 1970s, Hungarian foreign policy had enjoyed a special, relatively independent status. One important aspect of this special status was that it enabled Hungary to develop intensive economic and political relations with Western states precisely during those years when superpower relations were at a low not seen since the Cuban missile crisis (see chapter 9). After Gorbachev entered the scene, the situation changed in as much as the Soviet leadership took over the role as the primary promoter of dialogue between East and West. The initiating and moderating nature of Hungarian foreign policy was preserved all along, now only as second fiddle.

The first qualitative turn in foreign policy—just as in the transition within the country—took place in 1988.[1] This turn had nothing to do with the removal of Kádár or with the party conference in May but rather with the significant positive changes taking place that could possibly give Hungary the role of a sort of bridge in East–West relations based on a new world order of cooperation. This concept still assumed the preservation of the given alliance frameworks (Warsaw Pact, Comecon), but it also expected that these organizations would undergo necessary democratic changes and, as a result, no longer hinder Hungary in establishing relations with other countries or organizations that would satisfy her own national interests.

The old foreign policy deriving from the 1970s was built on a relative autonomy, which in simple terms meant that *whatever is not forbidden is (perhaps) allowed*. In turn, the new concept meant—to borrow the terms of the rules of the road—that if a police officer tells you to stop, rather than lose heart, try to convince the officer to let you through. Indeed, if you feel it to be justified, you can even run the risk of later admonition by ignoring the officer and simply driving through the intersection. This new, dynamic, and proactive foreign policy was, in practice, aimed at accomplishing a kind of quasi neutrality, although this thesis was never articulated in explicit form for either public or confidential use. Today, however, we can establish that this characterized the Hungarian endeavors between 1988 and the 1990 general elections.

The question is how this new approach exerted its influence in six important areas: (1) Hungarian–Soviet relations, (2) conflicts with the countries of the Soviet bloc, (3) reorganization of the Warsaw Pact and the issue of neutrality, (4) reduction of military spending and the pullout of Soviet troops, (5) transformation of the Comecon, and (6) opening to the West and joining the European integration processes.[2]

The Moscow–Warsaw–Budapest Virtual Coalition

Hungarian–Soviet relations were characterized by a particular dichotomy concerning the questions of perestroika, glasnost, and the reforms in general. Hungary simultaneously played the part of best student and teacher. It was no accident that Gorbachev's policy was received most favorably in Hungary, for the Hungarians considered it to be subsequent justification of the reforms that had been going on since the 1960s amid adverse Eastern winds. After carefully considering the Hungarian experience, the Soviets introduced several changes and innovations, such as reorganizing agriculture, accepting the role of the market in a limited sense, and accepting more than one candidate in the general elections. Moreover, in the fall of 1988, after studying what the Hungarians had accomplished a few months before, different special committees of the CPSU CC were formed, among them the new International Committee headed by Yakovlev.[3]

Over the course of 1988–89, an informal Moscow–Warsaw–Budapest virtual coalition was formed, which was referred to in contemporary Hungarian documents as "those in close cooperation."[4] The leaders of the three countries tried to harmonize their views on economic and political reforms during *bilateral* negotiations, and since they were in the numerical minority in the Warsaw Pact and the Comecon, they attempted to establish a unified position within both organizations so that they could exercise pressure on the countries with a conservative leadership. This special relationship most likely made a significant contribution to the positive Soviet attitude and the Soviets' tolerance of the transition in Hungary and the pioneering efforts of the country's foreign policy.

Close cooperation had its drawbacks too, however. Coordinated action very often meant that the Soviet leadership requested support for a position that, although more progressive than the position of the conservative camp, did not fully, or even partially, represent the interests of Hungary, which was well ahead of its partners in the transition process. A significant compromise was imposed on Hungary with respect to the handling of the Hungarian–Romanian conflict, which became public by 1988. In July 1988, Gorbachev explained to Károly Grósz, the new leader of the HSWP, on his visit to Moscow that the Soviet leadership definitely took Hungary's side in the debate, but that they could not represent this position officially, because such a move—with respect to the separatist movements and the ethnic conflicts within the country—could have unforeseeable consequences in terms of the inner stability of the Soviet Union. While Gorbachev was absolutely right about this, he was wrong in persuading the explicitly unwilling secretary-general to take a step—meeting with Romanian leader Ceaușescu in Arad—that not only destroyed Grósz's prestige as a leader but also undermined the position of the HSWP.[5] This is because the meeting, which public opinion viewed as a betrayal of Hungarian national interests, "naturally" had to be sold as an autonomous Hungarian decision. The only possible explanation for Gorbachev's aggressive intervention in Hungarian politics is that the Soviet leader was not merely worried about the possible outcome of an open endorsement of the Hungarian position but regarded the mere fact of a Romanian–Hungarian conflict as a source of danger that could further erode the already weak inner cohesion of the Warsaw Pact and—even worse—strengthen centrifugal forces in the multinational Soviet Union itself. It is only in this context that we can understand what made Gorbachev request his close ally to make such an unfortunate compromise with a Romanian leadership that had already accused the Soviet Union of betraying Socialism and of which the Soviet secretary-general himself had a very low opinion.[6] In fact, what was at stake here was no less than the survival of the imperial center, which, as has been seen, was given utmost priority.

At the same time, in the spring of 1988, the reformers of the HSWP believed they could rightly expect direct Soviet support for the removal of János Kádár, who now stood in the way of radical changes. However, Kádár—after Gorbachev—was still the most respected and presentable leader of the Eastern camp in the West. Considering his competition, this was not a remarkable achievement in itself, but it was viewed as such by the Soviet leaders, for whom attempting to improve East–West relations was an important factor. In addition, despite the stagnation under Kádár, the Hungarian transition was still well ahead of the Soviet reforms. Gorbachev thus originally had no interest in speeding up the reform process in Hungary. Yet we now know that, by the spring of 1988, he became convinced that Kádár's continued leadership could soon become a destabilizing factor, therefore before the HSWP national party conference in May, Gorbachev sent KGB head V. A. Kryuchkov to Budapest to meet with Kádár. While nothing of their discussion has become public to date, from other documents it is clear that his task was to convince the aging Hungarian leader to leave.[7]

The first important development in the course of the Hungarian transition for which there was no Soviet consent was the 28 January 1989 interview with Imre Pozsgay—or, more precisely, his assessment of the 1956 October events as a popular uprising. This announcement is even more significant when we consider that it was also the first "anti-Soviet" move by the Hungarian leadership, since the new interpretation of events meant that, on 4 November 1956, the Soviet Union had cracked down on a democratic national movement and not a counterrevolutionary uprising. This thesis was so far removed from current Soviet views that although the 1968 Czechoslovak invasion was denounced in December 1989, a similar step was never to be taken during the existence of the Soviet Union. Therefore, it would have been a logical step to reprove the Hungarian leadership. Today we know that a draft letter was written, but—by the explicit order of Gorbachev—it was never sent to Budapest.[8] Gorbachev must have understood very well that this genie could never again be ordered back into the bottle, while at the same time he might have hoped that the HSWP's position could be greatly strengthened if the party itself dealt with the matter rather than letting the opposition capitalize on it politically. Moreover, the proper dialectical nature of handling the problem made it possible to avoid having to address the direct historical responsibility of the Soviet Union. From a formal aspect, this need was basically met by the text of an announcement issued after the 10–11 February meeting of the HSWP CC, declaring that on 23 October 1956 a *popular uprising* broke out, but that, in reference to the inevitable outcome, by the end of October *counterrevolutionary* developments had begun to unfold.

All of this coincided with a radical turn in the previously outlined East Central European policy of the Soviet Union, as a result of which four decades of firm control was replaced by an automatic process whose central element was floating the Brezhnev Doctrine and deliberately maintaining the uncertainty deriving from it. This turn was not perceived, even by those involved, for some time, which was exactly how it was intended. We have already discussed Károly Grósz's experiences in this respect during his visit to Moscow in March 1989.[9] The best example of the almost unsolvable dilemma it brought to the Hungarian leaders can be found by comparing two contemporary statements made by Gyula Horn. As undersecretary of state at the Foreign Ministry, Horn said the following in his speech on the second day of the 20–21 February 1989 meeting of the HSWP CC: "Today there is no question at all of an intervention within the Warsaw Pact—we have long surpassed the Brezhnev Doctrine as is well exemplified by the decision on a multiparty system which was our own sovereign decision."[10] Four months later at the end of June, however, Horn, already in the role of foreign minister, cautioned the members of the Central Committee against any illusions: "Our situation should not be confused with that of any other democratic country. In Hungary there is no rotation in politics. . . . If the HSWP falls as a governing party, this would be equivalent to a political transition, a different political system. I wonder whether it will be tolerated by the alliance system. I do not think so."[11] That was what a Hungarian politician, who very likely had the most information concerning the intentions of the Soviet leadership, predicted *after* the victory of Solidarity in the general elections in Poland in June. In a confidential analysis made a few weeks before, it was explicitly stated that "the present guarantees do not exclude the possibility that, in case of a retreat to the old system [in the Soviet Union,] a unilateral or multilateral military action should take place in the name of defending socialism [in Hungary]."[12] The success of the Soviet tactic is well reflected by the fact that ten years after the events, Rezső Nyers marked July 1989 and Imre Pozsgay November of the same year as the point in time when it looked sure to them that the Soviets would not intervene in Hungary, even if the transition was to lead to a total abandonment of Socialism.[13]

Conflicts with the Countries of the Soviet Bloc

The structure of the conflicts within the Warsaw Pact had changed radically by 1988–89. From the early 1960s up until the late 1970s, the main division was between the security-concerned sub-bloc and the economy-oriented sub-bloc.[14] From the mid-1960s on, there was another dividing line, between the loyal majority and deviant Romania. Now they were replaced by an opposition between the reformers (the Soviet Union, Poland, and Hungary) and the conservatives (the GDR, Czechoslovakia, Romania, and Bulgaria). Even in the summer of 1989, however, the public had very little knowledge of these conflicts, thanks to the great efforts of the Soviet leaders, who all along tried to maintain at least the façade of bloc unity by all possible means. Paradoxically, Hungary—known earlier for its loyalty to Soviet interests—simultaneously assumed the double role of leading reformer and primary troublemaker in the Eastern Bloc. This is not only because Hungary fell into serious conflict with three of the four conservative countries—Romania, Czechoslovakia, and the GDR—but, even worse, because these conflicts took place openly before the public.

Since 1956, and especially after Nicolae Ceaușescu came into power in 1965, the human and collective rights of the 1.6 million Hungarian ethnic minority had been drastically restricted in Romania. The situation became especially serious with the 1972 announcement of the national homogenization program—aimed at the total elimination of national minorities—and the establishment of a Romanian nation-state. By the end of the 1970s, this resulted in serious tension in the relations of the two countries.[15] Since Hungarian attempts to resolve the problem on the basis of bilateral negotiations all met with failure, Hungarian foreign policy tried to achieve the international denunciation of the Romanian policy through international forums by placing the issue of human rights into the limelight.

This tactic was motivated by two different but related factors: on the one hand, it took place at a time when the Western states placed great emphasis on human rights issues and human rights records in the Eastern bloc countries. On the other hand, the Hungarian leadership could take advantage of its special position as the country whose internal situation most closely fitted Western expectations during those years. The first open step was taken in March 1987 at the Vienna follow-up meeting to the Conference on Security and Cooperation in Europe, when Hungary joined the Canadian proposal, which was formally aimed at strengthening the rights of European minorities but was essentially a call to the participating nations to denounce Romania. The situation got even worse at the beginning of 1988, when Romania launched its so-called systematization project, whereby it intended to destroy several thousand villages, while at the same time masses of Hungarians began fleeing from Romania to Hungary because of increasing discrimination. The 28 August 1988 meeting of the secretary-generals of the two parties in Arad was held under Soviet pressure and initiative—Ceauşescu gave the Hungarian leaders two days to consider accepting his offer for negotiations—and did not bring any improvement in the relations of the two countries.

This unsuccessful action had fatal consequences for the HSWP, in spite of the fact that afterward, in the second half of 1988 and in 1989, Hungarian officials took a firm stand on defending the interests of Hungarians living in Romania and openly admitted their conflict with the Romanian leadership. The meeting in Arad cast a long shadow on these attempts. It was therefore the opposition rather than the ruling party that was able to capitalize on the rehabilitation of national feelings and sentiment.

The last attempt of the Hungarian leadership to resolve the conflict through bilateral negotiations was made at the session of the WP PCC at the beginning of July 1989 in Bucharest. This time, Ceauşescu invited chairman of the HSWP Rezső Nyers, Prime Minister Miklós Németh, and Foreign Minister Gyula Horn to an on-the-spot, unofficial meeting, which the Hungarian delegation—possibly following Soviet advice again—accepted.[16] Although at the Arad meeting Károly Grósz had been forced to retreat into a defensive position against the Romanian leader, this time the Hungarians were able to negotiate from a different position. They imposed conditions on regulating the relations between the two countries: the Romanian side should cease its discrimination against the Hungarian minority as well as the propaganda and the military threats against Hungary, it should abort the fulfillment of the systematization project in the regions inhabited by Hungarians, it should allow

Hungarian cultural products into the country, and it should stop the humiliating harassment of masses of Hungarian tourists at the Hungarian–Romanian border. In addition, Gyula Horn indicated that, if necessary, Hungary would propose international supervision of the situation of the national minorities and the systematization plan.[17] Although under the given circumstances there seemed little hope that the Hungarian demands would be fulfilled, in order to continue with the tug-of-war, the negotiating parties agreed to have a meeting of the prime ministers. Furthermore, they agreed to exchange a parliamentary-local council delegation with the proviso that the Hungarian delegation should have a chance to visit areas inhabited by Hungarians when studying the accomplishment of the systematization plan. None of this materialized, however, because of the events of the fall and winter of 1989. Thus, the renewal of Hungarian–Romanian relations took place only after the radical turn in December 1989.

In Hungarian–Czechoslovak relations, three fundamental questions caused serious tension in 1989: the Gabcikovo–Nagymaros dams, the situation of Hungarians in Czechoslovakia, and the reassessment of the 1968 intervention. In May 1989, the Hungarian government, partly for economic reasons and partly as a result of social pressure that had been intensifying for years, unilaterally stopped the process of building dams on the river Danube based on a treaty made between the two countries in 1977. Since the Czechoslovak government—also referring to social pressure—insisted that the dams should be built as planned, a long-lasting conflict on this issue emerged between the two countries.

The Hungarian minority in Czechoslovakia did not have to endure a drastic policy of discrimination similar to that in Romania, but this by no means signifies that the Hungarians were able to exercise their collective minority and human rights without any restriction. The Hungarian media, which became increasingly independent and outspoken beginning in 1989, discussed this issue quite frequently, thus provoking resentment in the Czechoslovak leadership. Fearing the establishment of a Czechoslovak–Romanian axis, the official Hungarian leadership explicitly refrained from addressing this issue and stressed at the bilateral meetings that its conflict was essentially with Romania.[18]

The greatest tension between the two countries, however, was caused by Hungarian developments concerning the Prague Spring and the military intervention in Czechoslovakia. Since their own legitimacy was at stake, the Czechoslovak leadership had every reason to be worried. First, they expressed their resentment concerning an interview with Alexander Dubček aired on Hungarian television.[19] Then, at the beginning of August, they indignantly objected to an interview in which the head of the Foreign Affairs

Department of the HSWP CC envisaged the reassessment of the 1968 events.[20] The Czechoslovak ambassador to Budapest commissioned to mediate in this matter, however, also stated as his private opinion that the leadership in Prague would accept a scenario in which Hungary had initially supported a political settlement of the problem and later, only under international circumstances, decided to participate in the intervention. The official communiqué issued by the Hungarian party leadership on 17 August did take this proposal into consideration. While the declaration was meant to be cautious, the fact that a member state of the WP, which had also taken part in the intervention, said that it "does not identify with" the intervention doubtlessly contributed to the destabilization of the Czechoslovak situation a few months later.

Inarguably, the decision that had the greatest impact on the collapse of the East Central European Communist systems was the one that made it possible for GDR citizens staying in Hungary to leave for the FRG through Austria on 11 September 1989. Paradoxically enough, this German refugee situation was the only one in which the Hungarian leadership considered itself absolutely innocent, since it had no interest whatsoever in destroying relations with the GDR that were fairly balanced under the given circumstances. Indirectly, however, this conflict was initiated by the Hungarian side when, at the beginning of May 1989, in accord with the policy of opening up to the West, Hungary decided to remove its electronic signaling system and barbed wire—the "iron curtain"—from the Austrian-Hungarian border.[21]

This move, which became a historic one in perspective, was preceded by a longer process of preparation. To compensate the population for the ever-worsening economic situation on 19 May 1987, the HSWP Politburo passed a resolution on introducing the so-called world passport, which allowed any Hungarian citizen to travel freely to any country of the world any number of times from 1 January 1988.[22] Thus, the sealing of the borders lost its significance. Therefore, as early as the summer of 1987, the removal of the technical closing system was proposed; and on 28 February 1989, the HSWP Politburo decided to remove the closing systems on the Hungarian-Austrian and Hungarian-Yugoslavian borders by 1991. In reality, the work was completed much earlier, by the end of June 1989. On 2 May 1989, the decision was publicly announced, and on 27 June, the Austrian and Hungarian foreign ministers made front-page news in Western media by ceremonially cutting the barbed wire fence on the border of the two countries.

As a consequence, tens of thousands of East German tourists traveled to Hungary in the hopes that they would be able to flee through Austria to the FRG via the now open "green border."[23] Some six hundred people did succeed, most of them at the time of the Pan-European Picnic—a friendly meeting of two villages on different sides of the border, organized by civic groups near the town of Sopron on 19 August 1989. However, following an accident in which the gun of a border guard shot an East German refugee dead in hand-to-hand combat, it became clear that the settlement of the problem required political means. The leadership of the GDR demanded that Hungary comply with the 1969 secret bilateral treaty, based on which the trespassers should have been deported back to their own country. Hungary, however, in the meantime—as the first and only state in the Soviet bloc—had joined the UN Refugee Convention in March 1989 in order to create a legal basis for not returning the Hungarians escaping from Romania. Now they could argue that the UN convention, an international treaty, was a stronger legal agreement than the secret bilateral treaty between Hungary and Romania, and it obliged Hungary to respect the rights of the refugees; therefore they could not be sent back to their home country. As an unintended consequence, this obligation was now binding Hungary vis-à-vis the East German refugees as well. The leadership, having built a very solid relationship with the FRG by now, was not willing to return the East German "tourists" anyhow, for they had been hoping for some time that the two German states would reach an agreement in order to resolve the crisis. After they failed to do so, and the Hungarian–East German secret bilateral talks also met with failure, Prime Minister Miklós Németh and Foreign Minister Gyula Horn discussed the issue on 25 August 1989 with Chancellor Helmut Kohl and Foreign Minister Hans-Dietrich Genscher in the Gymnich castle near Bonn, where they presented a Hungarian plan according to which the Hungarian government would make it possible for the GDR citizens to freely leave the country.[24] In some sense, this step meant crossing the Rubicon, for an internal issue of the Eastern bloc was at stake, and, according to the practice of the past couple of decades, the Soviet Union should have been consulted in advance on an issue of such import.

By the summer of 1989, it had become characteristic of the radical changes in international politics that, while the Hungarians agreed on the settlement of an issue with a NATO member without consulting the Soviets, Chancellor Kohl, despite his promise to the Hungarians, called Gorbachev to learn what Soviet reaction should be expected concerning the planned Hungarian move. "Miklós Németh, the Hungarian prime minister, is a good man" was the obscure answer,[25] and as it turned out later, it meant Soviet approval of the situation.

It still begs the question why Gorbachev reacted so weakly to this rather significant challenge. Now, not only the question of East Central Europe in general was at stake, but the German question as well, which since 1945 had always been regarded as the cornerstone of the foreign policy of any Soviet leadership. Most likely they—like the other players of the game—did not estimate the potential consequences of such a decision and hoped that if disillusioned people left the GDR, it would have a pacifying rather than a destabilizing effect and could even facilitate the acceleration of the transition in the country in a controlled manner. By now we know that exactly the opposite took place, and the mass movements emerging in the fall of 1989 led not only to the opening of the Berlin Wall and the collapse of the GDR but also to the accomplishment of German unification without significant restrictions—including NATO membership, something that in the summer of 1989 would have been called illusory by most people, even in the FRG.[26] Hungary's opening of the border on 11 September 1989 was simply meant to solve a serious internal problem; however, this unintentionally historic step contributed to the fall of the Communist system in the GDR and finally to German reunification.

As has been seen, Hungary's engagement in such open conflicts was not motivated by an intention to raise tension in any of these situations. On the contrary, in all three cases the Hungarian leadership acted only after lengthy agony and under the influence of external forces and pressure. All in all, each of these steps in Hungarian foreign policy represented new milestones on the road toward true autonomy; these were the first cases in which the leadership decided to prioritize national interests over those interests of the alliance system (and also of the Soviet Union). All of this, however, had another dimension as well: beyond indirectly contributing to exporting counterrevolution through her own example as a leading fighter on behalf of reform, Hungary *directly* facilitated the fermentation process and the destabilization of the Communist systems in three states of the Soviet bloc.

Restructuring the Warsaw Pact and the Issue of Neutrality

After rising to power, Gorbachev not only promised a new relationship with the East Central European allies but, from the very beginning, urged that the mechanism of cooperation within the Warsaw Pact be modernized. To this effect, as early as October 1985, he proposed establishing a permanent political body whose task would be the improvement of coordination among the member states.[27] No significant change was accomplished in the structure of the WP, however, until it was dissolved in 1991. The outcome of spontaneous democratization under the influence of the new Soviet policy of emphasizing the importance of partnership was, among others, that in addition to the traditional dissenter Romania, the other member states began to enforce their own special interests much more effectively than they had previously. Thus, for example, Gorbachev's proposal, which could have become the means of not only coordination but centralization as well, was not accepted by the Hungarian leadership—which had been in close cooperation with the Soviet Union all along—until July 1988.[28]

Strangely enough, a real debate over the reformation of the Warsaw Pact was initiated by a Romanian motion submitted at approximately the same time. Basically, it suggested that the WP PCC should be dissolved and the organization turned into an exclusively military alliance, totally abandoning its political functions.[29] At the Warsaw session of the WP PCC in July 1988, an expert committee was formed to study the questions related to reforming the organization and, based on this work, the Hungarian leadership framed its position by March 1989.[30]

By this time, however, thanks to the political changes in the country, the issues concerning Hungarian relations with the alliance system were no longer under the exclusive jurisdiction of the HSWP. By the spring of 1989, Hungary already had a de facto multiparty system; moreover, after the Assembly Act was passed in January, the opposition parties mushrooming all over Hungary could function legally. At the beginning of that year, the Alliance of Free Democrats suggested that Hungary should request a special status in the Warsaw Pact and that, following the "French model," it should not participate in the military cooperation of the organization. Then, on 16 April, the governing board of the Alliance of Free Democrats proposed in its statement that the government should declare Hungary's neutrality.[31]

The tradition of the 1956 revolution, at least in political rhetoric, served as the starting point for nearly all the opposition organizations, and in addition, the 1 November 1956 declaration of neutrality (which was in force for three days) had an impact on the foreign policy ideas of several parties for some time. Moreover, the only joint declaration concerning the country's foreign orientation that was endorsed by all the opposition organizations over the course of the political transition was point 9 of the declaration titled "What Does the Hungarian Nation Demand?" which was read out by a prominent actor at a huge demonstration on the national holiday of 15 March 1989 and set the goal of achieving neutrality. Remarkably, in the same point, the opposition jointly demanded the withdrawal of Soviet troops from Hungary; thus, this "brave" public move was not made for the first time by Victor Orbán on 16 June at the reburial of Imre Nagy and his associates, as is commonly believed today. Although the demand for neutrality could be regarded as more of a symbolic position based on an emotional approach than a mature and coordinated plan by the opposition, the leadership of the HSWP had every reason to be worried, especially because the declaration was also signed by those historical parties with whom they intended to form a coalition after the general elections.[32] While the Hungarian leadership considered neutrality to be a possibility in the long term—*after* the dissolution of the two political-military blocs—in the short term, it did not believe it to be a realistic goal but rather a factor jeopardizing the peaceful transition in the country.[33] This was not a groundless view, for at this stage the Soviet Union— and, more importantly, the Western partners, which otherwise supported the Hungarian transition—consistently sent signals warning Hungary that such an endeavor should not expect endorsement in international politics. During Károly Grósz's visit to Moscow at the end of March 1989, Gorbachev stressed that "under the present conditions it is the modernization of the WP that should be the main target, and not neutrality."[34] In April 1989, Volker Rühe, deputy leader of the CDU/CSU parliamentary group, also declared to his Hungarian negotiating partners that on a number of issues, "the Hungarians entertain illusions, such as the issue of neutrality, Hungary's rapid withdrawal from the Warsaw Pact, and instant integration with the West." Egon Bahr, member of the presidency of the Social Democratic Party, warned that "today the Soviet Union recognizes the sovereignty of its allies and allows them to choose their own course of internal development. The line for the Soviet Union is drawn so that this course of development should not endanger the unity of the Warsaw Pact. It is very important that all the Hungarian parties reach a consensus on not going beyond this line."[35] In July 1989, Giovanni Jannuzzi, secretary-general of the EEC in charge of political cooperation, told his Hungarian negotiating partner that "it would be fine with the EEC if Hungary had a government led by the Communist Party and also, if Budapest became a member of the WP with a special status, similar to the one France had in NATO. He also warned the Hungarian leaders that it is 'not only a possibility but a task for Hungary to remain a member of the Warsaw Pact,' as this is a requirement needed to maintain European stability."[36]

Taking these signals into consideration, the Hungarian leadership essentially took a pragmatic position on the issue of the Warsaw Pact. They reckoned that, on the one hand, the WP—or, more precisely, the Soviet nuclear umbrella—would continue to ensure the security of the country, and on the other hand, the positive Soviet attitude would enable the country to fulfill its peaceful transition. Thus, the main goal of Hungarian diplomacy should be to ensure the highest possible degree of national sovereignty that is achievable *under the given conditions*. As a result, the Hungarian position on the status of the Warsaw Pact gave priority to the benevolent attitude of the Soviet Union, and although in any event Soviet ideas were largely in harmony with Hungarian proposals, Hungarian tactics were aimed at ensuring that the three "reformers" could effectively represent their position against the four "conservatives." Therefore, they endorsed not only those proposals that were meant to change the political nature of the organization, to improve its efficiency, to strengthen the democratic process of its decision-making, and to eliminate the principle of mandatory consensus but—against their better judgment—also those that sought the establishment of a permanent political body or the deepening of cooperation between the parliaments of the member states.

At the same time, the Foreign Ministry and the Ministry of Defense worked out several Hungarian proposals aimed at reforming the Warsaw Pact in the spring of 1989: (1) The Soviet WP communication officers stationed in each of the member states must be withdrawn. Instead, the permanent delegates of the member states staying in Moscow must be given more responsibility in matters of coordination. (2) The passage enforcing the Brezhnev Doctrine must be removed from the text of the peace and war resolutions of the Unified Armed Forces of the WP. (3) The Military Council must be dissolved.[37]

From time to time, this compromise-seeking policy also claimed some sacrifices. In June 1988, the Hungarian side submitted a proposal at the Warsaw meeting of the WP PCC suggesting the creation of a permanent committee of deputy ministers responsible for humanitarian issues and human rights, which would also facilitate the constant supervision and discussion of the situation of national minorities. When it turned out, however, that the Soviet Union was ready to obstruct the Romanian plan proposing devoting a separate session at the 1989 July meeting in Bucharest to the issue of endangering the cause of Socialism in Hungary and Poland, but Moscow would not support the motion concerning the human rights committee, the Hungarian leadership decided to give up on this idea, even though it had been regarded as extremely important all along.[38]

Reduction of Armament and the Withdrawal of Soviet Troops

From the very beginning, the new leadership that rose to power in May 1988 in Hungary considered a reduction in military spending to be the primary means of surviving the economic crisis. This intention luckily coincided with the July 1988 Soviet decision that made it possible to take unilateral steps in the reduction of armament. This explains why, upon Károly Grósz's visit to Moscow, Gorbachev simply acknowledged his declaration that, for economic reasons, Hungary was not able to comply with the agreement on the military cooperation of the WP in force until 1990, and at the same time was compelled to reduce its military production by half a billion rubles.[39] As a result, without making this fact public, military spending was reduced by some HUF 10 billion by the end of 1988.[40] Then, at the end of that year, it was officially announced that Hungary's 1989 military budget would be reduced by 17 percent in real value as compared to the previous year.

Since these modest results in the field of reducing military spending could liberate significant financial resources, in August 1988 the Hungarian leadership indicated to the Soviets that they would gladly play an initiative and coordinating role in the armament reduction of the WP member states.[41] A month before, they had already managed to win Gorbachev's support for a very promising concrete initiative. Hungarian diplomacy, after having consulted with the Italian government, a member of NATO, suggested that the Soviet Union should offer to pull out their air regiments stationed in Hungary if the F-16 fighter planes to be withdrawn from Spain were not deployed in Italy. Eventually Soviet support for this intricate political game was acquired; however, it proved to be insufficient, and this proposal was to meet with failure because of the position of the United States.[42]

Another especially important step for Hungarian diplomacy was its August 1988 public declaration that the forthcoming international agreement on the reduction of conventional armed forces in Europe should extend to the troops stationed in Hungary already in the first phase. This opportunity, however, was only possible if Hungary were to be grouped into the Central European theater, which could by no means be taken for granted. Because the Warsaw Pact had a decisive advantage in this region, it was in the interest of the organization to keep Hungary in the Southern European theater, so as to improve the ratio figures where NATO had the upper hand. In that region, however, it was the Western allies that needed to make significant reductions, so the Hungarian endeavors would have met with utter failure. Although the Hungarians managed to win the Soviet leadership's support for their position, the differing interests of the other member states proved to be a significant factor of uncertainty, even in the spring of 1989.[43]

It was characteristic of Soviet behavior that Gorbachev reacted positively to Prime Minister Miklós Németh's announcement during his March 1989 visit to Moscow that the Hungarian government had decided to reduce its army by 30 to 35 percent by 1995. He "merely" requested that this be kept secret, since publicizing it would greatly weaken the position of the Warsaw Pact at the negotiations on armament reduction in Vienna.[44]

While the reduction of national military spending was motivated primarily by economic considerations, the call for the withdrawal of the Soviet troops stationed in Hungary mostly served a political cause. The issue was raised based on the 1988 Soviet announcement that the Soviet Union would pull out all its forces from foreign land by 2000. Therefore, as early as August and September 1988, Hungarian foreign policy experts tried to convince their Soviet partners that the speedy withdrawal of Soviet troops would have a very positive political, moral, and economic impact on Hungary.[45]

The need for a *partial* unilateral reduction had already been proposed by the Soviets as well, as a result of which in December 1988 it was announced that some ten thousand Soviet troops and their technical equipment would be pulled out of Hungary, which indeed occurred in April–May 1989. A similar partial withdrawal had already taken place before, in 1958, but it had not resulted in any significant change.[46] Thus, the real question was whether the Hungarian leadership could end the Soviet occupation of the country, which had been a major grievance for most of the population for the past four decades. The other important question was whether the HSWP could capitalize on this sufficiently during the political transition.

As a result of the persistent activity of Hungarian foreign-policy makers, who consistently attempted to strengthen elements of national sovereignty while adjusting their course of action according to Soviet interests, Moscow sent a signal in the middle of May 1989 that, at the next meeting of the WP PCC to be held in Bucharest, Gorbachev would be ready to start negotiations with the Hungarian delegation on the complete withdrawal of Soviet troops.[47] Real negotiations finally took place when Károly Grósz and Rezső Nyers, the general-secretary and the chair of the HSWP, respectively, visited Moscow at the end of July, and Gorbachev agreed to issue a memorandum stating that, under the appropriate international conditions, the pullout of forces already underway might lead to the full withdrawal of Soviet troops.[48] Further negotiations began between the two governments in August and, as a result, an agreement was signed by the last Hungarian Communist government in Moscow on 10 March 1990 on the withdrawal of the approximately fifty thousand Soviet troops by 30 June 1991. (In the meantime, in November 1989, at the request of Prime Minister Miklós Németh, the Soviet nuclear warheads stationed in Hungary by the Soviet Army since the late 1960s were withdrawn from the country in total secrecy.) The process of the pullout was not free from disputes, but the Soviets met the deadline: the last Soviet soldier left the country on 19 June 1991. Thus, one year after the inauguration of its first freely elected government, Hungary regained its sovereignty in full.[49]

Transformation of the Comecon

As early as the spring of 1988, the Soviet leadership had a very critical opinion about the operation of the Comecon. Gorbachev characterized the situation at the 10 March 1988 meeting of the Politburo of the CPSU as follows: "In the Comecon we almost have no trade. Only primitive exchange.... It has become excessively hard for us to conduct business as we have been doing for the last decades. The program [of socialist integration] is dead."[50]

Soviet reformers thought the resolution of the Comecon crisis should breathe fresh life into the organization in such a way that it would be capable of responding collectively to the challenges presented by the Western European integration set to be accomplished in 1992. This did not appear to be an easy task, since very different views existed among the member states concerning the future of the organization. In addition to the three reform countries, Bulgaria and Czechoslovakia both supported the transformation, but apart from the Hungarian leadership, everybody wanted to accomplish this goal via a top-down process—using political rather than economic means.

By the beginning of 1989, the Hungarian transition in the economy was so much ahead of all the others that a compromise would seriously have jeopardized the success of the Hungarian changes. As the Hungarian leadership was not willing to do so, the 14 March 1989 meeting of the Politburo of the HSWP accepted a resolution that gave priority to fully opening the country to world economy and trading.[51] One week later, another basic principle was adopted on the Comecon integration, stating that Hungary was interested in developing cooperation within the Comecon inasmuch as it facilitated opening the country to the world. As for the concrete Hungarian position, the following principles were laid down by the Politburo: (1) the mechanism of cooperation within the Comecon must be transformed radically, and in this framework, cooperation among the member states must be built on bilateral and multilateral relations instead of seeking consensus; (2) the development of economic integration is a task to be performed by the member states, meaning that any ideas, endeavors, and institutions over and above the participating nations must be rejected; (3) a unified Socialist market is a reality only when the national markets are already established, meaning that the goal is not realistic at the moment; and (4) the Comecon must adopt the principle that "the most important prerequisite for the transformation of socialist economic cooperation is the modernization of internal market forces building on the conditions of goods and finances."[52]

The Hungarian leadership firmly represented this position throughout the internal disputes concerning the transformation of the Comecon; moreover, at the last real summit of the organization on 9 January 1990 in Sofia, Prime Minister Miklós Németh made a prophecy in the name of the—by then totally autonomous—Hungarian government that in case the Comecon was not capable of total transformation to its foundations, it was doomed to extinction.

At that time, Hungary had a $20 billion debt to Western creditors, which earned the country the dubious title of the most indebted state in the world per capita. Since the end of the 1970s, Hungary was in a constant state of insecurity concerning the country's capacity to pay the interest on its loans, and it occurred on more than one occasion that a deadline was just a few weeks away when eventually a new loan helped solve the problem. A telling example of this situation was when in 1982 Hungary had to pay its entrance fee to the International Monetary Fund and the missing $100 million could only be covered by an emergency loan from the Chinese government. All in all, the country was always one step ahead of insolvency, although just at the time of the political transition in the early spring of 1989 a similar hot situation had to be resolved.

Opening to the West—toward European Integration

The likely integration of Western Europe expected by 1992 presented a serious challenge to Hungarian foreign policy as well, for what was at stake was no less than the question of whether it was possible to preserve the extraordinarily good position that it had acquired with respect to Western relations. If not, then Hungary, too—like all the other nations of the Eastern bloc—would have to face the danger of separating from the Western world. Therefore, it was viewed as a significant achievement that, thanks to the persistent work of several years—and most of all to the efficient support of the FRG[53]—Hungary was the first in the Socialist camp to make an agreement concerning economic cooperation and to enter into diplomatic relations with the European Economic Community in September 1988. The particularly close and fruitful relationship between the Hungarian and the West German leadership was a positive development, with much promise and good prospects for the future, and as a result, Hungary received altogether DEM 2 billion credit in 1987–88 to transform and modernize its economy. In July 1989, the Bundestag, in a symbolic act unique in the Western world, accepted a declaration endorsing the Hungarian democratic transition.[54]

In the spirit of preparing for the situation after Western European integration, in as early as January 1989 the Hungarian leadership elaborated a detailed analysis and plan concerning the necessary steps to be taken, and at the 14 March meeting of the HSWP Politburo, priority was given to opening to the world economy, which essentially marked the beginning of a shift in economic reorientation.[55]

This opening to the West was well served by two successful pioneering initiatives of Hungarian foreign policy, as a result of which, in February 1989, Hungary entered into diplomatic relations with South Korea by exchanging ambassadors, and in September, diplomatic relations broken off in 1967 were restored with Israel. Both steps had been preceded by lengthy preparatory work, over the course of which Hungary gradually managed to win the approval of the Soviets.[56] Even in July 1988, Gorbachev was still stressing to Károly Grósz that, as far as the relations with Israel were concerned, "the clocks" must be synchronized; whereas in the case of South Korea, he explicitly warned against establishing diplomatic relations at the level of embassies.[57] In both cases, the Hungarian leadership expected significant economic advantages from these unprecedented steps of high import. A precondition with South Korea was the deposit into the Hungarian National Bank of $1–$1.5 billion, which was meant to lessen the liquidity problems of the country.[58] In the case of Israel, above all it was hoped that this "historic" act would exert a positive influence on U.S. policy toward Hungary and in general on Western financial circles, especially the World Bank.

Based on the relations developed in the 1980s, Hungarian diplomacy also made intensive attempts to play a mediating role in promoting East–West rapprochement in 1988–89. With this knowledge, in the spring of 1988, the Soviets requested the Hungarian leadership to host a conference to be attended by European political parties and which, according to the original idea, would have paved the way for the "second Helsinki" conference proposed by the Soviet Union. The conference, titled "Europe and the Future of European Cooperation on the Eve of the 1990s," was held in Budapest on 11–13 May 1989 and attended by twenty-three different parties. The outstanding significance of this conference was that, for the first time, the representatives of every major political trend of the parliaments of the states participating in the European security and cooperation process had a chance to exchange their ideas and views in an informal manner: Communists, Social Democrats, centrists, liberals, Christian Democrats, and conservatives.[59] The dialogue between East and West was further intensified by the Warsaw Pact's adoption of the Hungarian proposal that the representatives of the thirty-five states who had signed the Helsinki Final Act should hold regular summit meetings in the future.

In the spring of 1989, Hungary took steps to pave the way for establishing official relations between the Warsaw Pact and NATO after the undersecretary of state for foreign affairs Gyula Horn—as the first representative of the Eastern bloc—participated and delivered a speech at the session of the Political Committee of the North Atlantic Assembly in Hamburg in November 1988. In addition, the Hungarian leadership undertook some rather confidential missions from time to time: Károly Grósz not only lobbied Gorbachev on behalf of West German interests but, when he was prime minister, played an important role in facilitating the improvement of relations between Poland and the FRG at the request of Chancellor Helmut Kohl.[60]

Like the physical removal of the Iron Curtain, there was symbolic as well as political significance in the Council of Europe giving Hungary—together with Yugoslavia, Poland, and the Soviet Union—special observer status on 8 June 1989. A few months later, in November 1989, the Hungarian government submitted its application for membership in the council. Following the free general elections the following spring, the council recognized the democratic transition of historical importance in the country, and on 6 November 1990, Hungary was admitted as a member state. Symbolically speaking, for Hungary this represented the end to the era of four decades of exclusion.

Epilogue

The End of the Soviet Bloc

During the first free elections held in the spring of 1990, Hungarian society had regained political freedom of movement, but the restoration of sovereignty, the withdrawal of Soviet troops, and regaining the choice of foreign policy orientation were all tasks of the period following the transition.

From a historical perspective, the period from the spring of 1990 to the end of 1991 can be regarded a success story for the Central and East Central European states because, during this short period, radical changes occurred in regard to the international situation in the region, which fundamentally changed the fate of these countries. Germany was (re)united, the Comecon and the Warsaw Pact were disbanded by mutual consent, Soviet troops were withdrawn from Hungary and Czechoslovakia, and in December 1991, the Soviet Union—the hegemon of the Soviet bloc itself—ceased to exist as well.[1]

At the time, however, all of this was far from predictable; moreover, today we know that such a turn of events not only was not in the interest of the Soviet leadership but was not supported by the Western powers, either. The United States and the Western European States were first and foremost interested in maintaining European stability; therefore, keeping Gorbachev in power for as long as possible was a top priority for them. As the price for stability seemed to be the preservation of the existing status quo, Western policy toward East Central Europe was once again—understandably—subordinated to the relations of the West with the Soviet Union.

The acceptance of internal political changes in East Central Europe by no means meant that Gorbachev was ready to give up the Soviet sphere of influence in the region as well. These efforts were greatly facilitated by the fact that, until the end of 1990, the Western powers, while welcoming the internal political transition, did not support the aspirations for independence of the states of the region, not even in the form of neutrality. On the contrary, in this short period, NATO and the Warsaw Pact were regarded as the fundamental pillars of the European security system. Consequently, in spite of what many former Western politicians and diplomats claim in their memoirs, the democratic governments in the region, elected through free elections in the spring of 1990, were urged by Western politicians to maintain membership in the Warsaw Pact and the Comecon.[2] In other words, during 1989–90, it was not only Moscow that was interested in the regional Finlandization of East Central Europe; at that crucial historical junction, the Western powers were also willing to accept this option—that is, establishing democratic systems while preserving the Soviet sphere of influence by maintaining the existing integration organizations: the Warsaw Pact and the Comecon. The West regarded maintaining the alliance of the Soviet bloc states with the Soviet Union a fair price for the "liberation" of these states as far as their political system was concerned. This position seemed rather reasonable in view of the Western desire to preserve European stability by supporting the Gorbachev reforms. The ensuing collapse of the Soviet Union, however, eventually gave them a chance to conveniently forget about this transitional deal for good.

This superpower consensus paradoxically opened the way for the countries of the region to play a historic role in the process of the transition. The successful democratic transition in the region—mass movements occurring in some countries notwithstanding—was a result of external conditions, including the favorable development of East–West relations and, above all, the Soviet Union's imminent, although in 1989 not yet visible, collapse. In the struggle for independence, mainly the Hungarian and Czechoslovak leadership played a prominent role from June 1990 and—joined by the Poles in August—achieved their goals by early 1991, when the Soviet leadership, pressed by the ever more chaotic internal situation in the Soviet Union, eventually yielded to the pressure.

This explains how, by the end of June–beginning of July 1991, both the Comecon and the Warsaw Pact were disbanded nearly simultaneously. This was the end of the Soviet bloc, which also meant a collective escape from the Soviet sphere of influence for the East Central European countries. This process, however, started as a rather difficult endeavor. The most radical approach was taken by the Antall government in Hungary, which took office in May 1990. The desire to leave the Warsaw Pact was already included in the government program, although in a not too categorical form. This goal, however, remembering the lesson of 1956, was to be achieved not by unilateral steps but gradually and through a negotiated settlement, whereby the first step would be following the French model—that is, withdrawal from the Warsaw Pact military structure.

At the WP PCC meeting in Moscow in June 1990, Hungarian prime minister József Antall proposed a radical restructuring of the organization; he argued that because the WP's military organization was not needed anymore in the new international situation, it should be disbanded by the end of 1991.[3] The transformation of the WP had been initiated by Gorbachev himself in his opening speech, while the Czechoslovak representatives put forward specific written proposals for the radical democratic transformation of the military structure, including the abolition of the staff of the Unified Armed Forces, at this session.[4]

Paradoxically, the very idea of totally eliminating the WP was raised by the Soviet leader himself, though just as a rhetorical question: "To what extent are the structures and forms of our alliance appropriate to current challenges, and in what sense should they be restructured? Perhaps it is time to unilaterally declare the dissolution of the Warsaw Treaty, or at least of its military organization, altogether. These are questions for which we must find answers or about which we should at least exchange views."[5] Gorbachev immediately responded emphatically to his own rhetorical question, stressing that in the talks with the West during the transition period, the preservation of the WP would play a key role. And to convince those who might have different views, referring to his personal negotiations, he added that all leaders of the Western powers themselves had exactly the same opinion. In this context, however, it was of great importance that the prime minister of one of the member states had made a proposal for the elimination of the military organization of the WP, with a concrete deadline in the not-so-distant future. To demonstrate the seriousness of the Hungarian position, in late June 1990 the Parliament adopted a resolution calling on the government to start negotiations on the country's withdrawal from the WP.[6]

Plans for transforming the organization were to be worked out by an interim Committee of Government Representatives, set up following a Hungarian proposal at the PCC meeting in Moscow. While at the first meeting of the committee, held in Prague in July 1990, the plans for the transformation looked rather moderate, at the second session, held in Sofia in September, a real breakthrough occurred.[7] This was due to a Hungarian initiative: in August, a secret Hungarian–Czechoslovak–Polish negotiation took place in Budapest at the ambassadorial level, at which the parties agreed on a radical transformation plan. This was a minor coup, as the Soviet delegation in Sofia was totally unprepared for the coordinated action of "the Three" and was even more surprised by its direction. They had been prepared to discuss the rather moderate plans outlined in Prague, only to be faced with the fact that the Czechoslovak representatives now withdrew all their previous proposals.

Moreover, it turned out that, in Moscow, there was no unified position on the future of the WP, so the Soviets found themselves in a difficult negotiating position. Finally, they were compelled to make concessions, and a decision was made that the military organization of the WP should be abolished by 1 July 1991. Following a Hungarian proposal, it was decided to keep this decision secret. As it turned out, the secret was so well managed that it is still the common view that it was at the WP foreign and defense ministers' meeting in Budapest in February 1991 when a decision was made on the dissolution of the military structure. In Sofia in September 1990, the Hungarian representative stressed the importance of eliminating the Warsaw Pact as a whole; however, this position was not supported by anyone at the time. Informally, the Polish and Czechoslovak experts told their Hungarian colleague that they still considered the survival of a modified, "weak" Warsaw Pact important.[8]

In the subsequent months, the main purpose of the Three was to codify the decision in Sofia, which originally should have happened at the WP PCC meeting planned in Budapest in November. The Soviets, however, tried to sabotage the implementation of the decision and so the PCC meeting was postponed. In the meantime, the Hungarian government made further efforts to persuade its two partners about pushing for dissolving the WP military structure, which is how the initiative for the Visegrád cooperation was born at the CSCE meeting in Paris in November 1990. (A similar abortive attempt had been made on 8 April 1990, when, on a Czechoslovak initiative, Polish president Wojciech Jaruzelski, Czechoslovak president Václav Havel, and interim Hungarian president Mátyás Szűrös held a meeting in Bratislava.)

The breakthrough occurred as a consequence of the developments in the Baltic in early 1991: the Hungarian, Czechoslovak, and Polish foreign ministers held a meeting in Budapest on 21 January, where it was decided to swiftly enforce the convening of the long-overdue PCC meeting. This time the pressure group of the Three was successful, and on 25 February 1991 in Budapest, the foreign and defense ministers of the Warsaw Pact member states made a decision on the liquidation of the WP military organization by 31 March 1991—three months before the original date established in Sofia in September 1990. However, this did not mean the dissolution of the Warsaw Pact itself, as in principle it still would have been possible to reform the political alliance by putting it on a democratic footing, at least as a temporary solution. But now it was too late. At that point, the majority of the member states wanted to terminate the WP and, due to the ever-growing number of crisis phenomena indicating the approaching dissolution of the Soviet Union, even Gorbachev did not see the point in continuing the struggle. Although the precise reconstruction of events needs more research, it is well known that the disintegration process sped up in the first half of 1991: on 28 June in Budapest, the Soviet bloc's economic organization, the Comecon, was dissolved. Three days later, on 1 July, the dissolution of the Warsaw Pact was announced in Prague, and on 26 December, the Soviet Union itself ceased to exist. Many believe that the Cold War ended at the Malta Summit between Gorbachev and Bush in December 1989, when the general-secretary declared that Moscow did not regard the United States as an enemy anymore.[9] In reality, the Cold War as an international system ceased to exist only when one of its main protagonists, the Soviet bloc, and its main architect, the Soviet Union, vanished in 1991.

Some countries in the region—above all Hungary and Czechoslovakia, as well as Poland—undoubtedly played a historic role in this process. It should be added that it was in actuality a *relatively* historic role that accelerated the course of history by half a year, but this does not detract anything from the performance of the actors. At the time, in 1990–91, they could not know what we now know—that in December 1991 the Soviet Union itself would break up, and that along with it, both the Warsaw Pact and the Comecon would cease to exist as well.

Notes

Chapter 1

1. On the establishment of spheres of influence and on the role of East Central Europe in the early Cold War, see Fejtő, *History of the Peoples Democracies*; Lundestad, *American Non-policy toward Eastern Europe*; Kertesz, *Fate of East Central Europe*; Kovrig, *Myth of Liberation*; Gati, *Caging the Bear*; Hook and Spanier, *American Foreign Policy*; Campbell, *American Policy toward Communist Eastern Europe*; Mark, "American Policy toward Eastern Europe"; Leffler and Painter, *Origins of the Cold War*; Gaddis, *Strategies of Containment*; Gati, *Hungary and the Soviet Bloc*; Kovrig, *Of Walls and Bridges*; Holloway, *Stalin and the Bomb*; Zubok and Pleshakov, *Inside the Kremlin's Cold War*; Gori and Pons, *Soviet Union and Europe*; Gaddis, *We Now Know*; Zubok, *Failed Empire*; Leffler, *For the Soul of Mankind*; Tismaneanu, *Stalinism Revisited*; Pechatnov, "Soviet Union and the World"; Naimark, "Sovietization of Eastern Europe"; Plokhi, *Yalta*; Applebaum, *Iron Curtain*; Rieber, *Salami Tactics Revisited*; Békés, Borhi, Ruggenthaler and Trasca, *Soviet Occupation of Romania, Hungary, and Austria*; Rieber, *Stalin and the Struggle for Supremacy*; Borhi, *Dealing with Dictators*; Westad, *Cold War*. For the most recent study on the topic, see Naimark, *Stalin and the Fate of Europe*.

2. Roberts, "Stalin at the Tehran, Yalta, and Potsdam Conferences."

3. In August 1942 in Moscow, Stalin told Churchill that "ten thousand men a day were being sacrificed on the Russian front.... The Russians did not complain of the sacrifices they were making, but the extent of them should be recognized." Westad, *Cold War*, 49.

4. Resis, "Churchill-Stalin 'Percentages' Agreement."

5. Rieber, *Stalin and the Struggle for Supremacy*, 372.

6. The only written "document" prepared at the meeting and containing the percentages was a small slip of paper on which Churchill wrote the countries' names and the percentages. According to Churchill's account, it was ticked off by Stalin.

7. On the declaration, see Westad, *Cold War*, 51–52.

8. Rieber, *Stalin and the Struggle for Supremacy*, 322–23.

9. Churchill accepted it in a letter to Roosevelt as early as March 1942. Zubok and Pleshakov, *Inside the Kremlin's Cold War*, 19. See also Hopkins, "United States and Eastern Europe," 43.

10. Kramer, "Stalin, Soviet Policy," 15.

11. Leffler, *For the Soul of Mankind*, 57.

12. Zubok and Pleshakov, *Inside the Kremlin's Cold War*, 16–18, 37–38.

13. Rieber, *Stalin and the Struggle for Supremacy*, 286–92. See also Pechatnov, "Soviet Union and the World, 94.

14. Iran was temporarily occupied by British and Soviet forces during the war.

15. Zubok and Pleshakov, *Inside the Kremlin's Cold War*, 94.

16. Failing to evacuate the island was one of the "proofs" of the unreliability of the Soviets in George Kennan's long telegram just a month earlier, in February 1946.

17. On the role of misperceptions in international politics, see Jervis, *Perceptions and Misperceptions*.

18. The latter two new spheres were offered by Hitler as the Soviet share of the planned joint elimination of the British colonial empire. While Molotov did not give an answer to this offer on the spot, in the reply of the Soviet government to the German draft proposal on Moscow's joining the Tripartite Pact on 16 November 1940, the offer was accepted.

19. For the text of the secret annex of the pact, see Sontag and Beddie, *Nazi–Soviet Relations*, 69–78.

20. Rieber, *Stalin and the Struggle for Supremacy*, 322–23; Juhász, *Magyar–brit titkos tárgyalások*, 180.

21. Pechatnov, *Big Three after World War II*.

22. Mark, *Revolution by Degrees*.

23. On the American aspects of Soviet–Chinese relations, see Westad, "Sino–Soviet Alliance."

24. Zubok and Pleshakov, *Inside the Kremlin's Cold War*, 43.

25. Rieber, *Stalin and the Struggle for Supremacy*, 293.

26. Kramer, "Stalin, Soviet Policy."

27. On China, see Westad, *Cold War*, 139–47.

28. Judt, *Postwar*, 100–128. On Germany, see Schwartz, "Division of Germany."

29. The term *Finlandization* was, of course, emerging only after 1948, when the country could retain its Western-type internal political and economic structure, but its foreign policy became clandestinely controlled by Moscow.

30. We now know that in 1948, before the Italian elections, the United States ensured the victory of the Christian Democrats over the Communists by providing them with huge financial and logistical support.

31. Eisenberg, *Drawing the Line*. See also Schwartz, "Division of Germany."

32. Petchatnov, "Soviet Union and the World," 96.

33. Rieber, *Stalin and the Struggle for Supremacy*, 296.

34. Zubok, *Failed Empire*, 76.

35. For a recent monograph on the role of East Germany in the early Cold War period, see Ostermann, *Between Containment and Rollback*.

36. For the history of the European peace settlement following the Second World War, see Kertesz, *Last European Peace Conference*. See also Fülöp, *Unfinished Peace*.

37. For the history of the debate over the Hungarian-Romanian border at the London meeting of the Council of Foreign Ministers in September 1945, see Fülöp, *Unfinished Peace*, 79–84.

38. Zubok and Pleshakov, *Inside the Kremlin's Cold War*, 37.

39. For an analysis of these sources, see Pechatnov, *Big Three after World War II*.

40. Djilas, *Conversations with Stalin*, 114; quoted recently in Westad, *Cold War*, 53–54.

41. Békés, *Európából Európába*, 49.

42. Békés, *Európából Európába*, 49. The Soviet-occupied zone of Germany was also in the quasi-Sovietized category. The overwhelming (57%) victory of the Smallholders' Party in the 1945 general elections in Hungary and the traditionally strong position of President Beneš and the non-Communist political forces in Czechoslovakia made it possible to establish and

maintain a provisional regime, where the façade of democracy was prevailing more visibly than in the other countries of the region, until mid-1947 and early 1948, respectively. For recent collections of essays on the Sovietization of the countries in the region, see Creuzberger and Görtemaker, *Gleichschaltung unter Stalin?*; Tismaneanu, *Stalinism Revisted*. See also Gati, *Hungary and the Soviet Bloc*; Kenez, *Hungary from the Nazis to the Soviets*.

43. This author has been arguing for this position since the beginning of the 1990s, when Hungarian archives became open for research. Recent scholarship has confirmed this theory; see, especially, Kramer, "Stalin, Soviet Policy."

44. See Murashko and Noskova, "Stalin and the National-Territorial Controversies." See also Naimark, "Sovietization of Eastern Europe."

45. Pechatnov, "Soviet Union and the World," 94.

46. Cited in Judt, *Postwar*, 131.

47. The term *stealthy counterrevolution*—a rather appropriate term indeed—was dubbed by Soviet propagandists during and following the suppression of the Prague Spring in Czechoslovakia in 1968. For the first use of *stealthy revolution*, see Békés, "A lopakodó forradalom."

48. This topic is covered in detail in Rieber, *Stalin and the Struggle for Supremacy.*

49. One striking example of this attitude was when both the U.S. and the British governments publicly dissociated themselves at once from the content of Churchill's "Iron Curtain" speech in Fulton on the situation in East Central Europe in March 1946.

50. Remarkably, Anne Applebaum originates Sovietization from the Molotov-Ribbentrop pact in 1939. Applebaum, *Iron Curtain*. In her magnum opus on the Soviet system in Hungary, historian Melinda Kalmár goes as far as finding the roots of the fatal Soviet affection for the region, as well as the formation of the Sovietization designs and techniques, in Lenin's works in 1919–20. Kalmár, *Történelmi galaxisok vonzásában*. Roosevelt told Harriman in May 1944 that "he didn't care whether the countries bordering Russia became communized." Quoted in Hopkins, "United States and Eastern Europe, 44. This newly found evidence proves that the United States would not have tried to block even a swift Baltic-style Sovietization of the region.

51. Mark, *Revolution by Degrees.*

52. On the role of the Soviet Army and Soviet authorities, see Békés, Borhi, Ruggenthaler, and Trasca, *Soviet Occupation of Romania, Hungary, and Austria.*

53. For the text of the declaration, see https://digitalarchive.wilsoncenter.org/document/116176.

54. This includes Czechoslovakia, where this support could strengthen the CPCz in the formative period before December 1945, when the Red Army was withdrawn from the country. It is important to emphasize that the Red Army became the Soviet Army in February 1946 in the framework of a "Westernizing" government reorganization: breaking with the Bolshevik tradition, the peoples' commissariats became ministries, and the peoples' commissars ministers. And this occurred exactly at the time of Stalin's now infamous election speech, which is still presented by many authors as a bold anti-Western turn in Soviet policy. Remarkably, the change of the name of the army, which was no secret at the time, has been totally overlooked by most scholars, and it is still generally mistakenly referred to as the Red Army for the whole Cold War period.

55. The minutes of the interparty conferences in Hungary are published in Horváth, Szabó Szűcs, and Zalai, *Pártközi értekezletek 1944–1948.*

56. Péter Gábor to Korotkevics, 5 April 1947, in Izsák and Kun, *Moszkvának jelentjük*, 170–71. For the Russian version, see Murashko et al., *Vostochnaja Evropa*, 1:606.

57. Austria was a special case, as it was under four-power occupation; thus, the Soviets did not have a dominant position in deciding on the elections there. Still, they were expecting a much better result for the Austrian Communists, who got a mere 5.5 percent of the votes.

58. Vida, *Iratok a magyar–szovjet kapcsolatok történetéhez*, cited in Borhi, *Hungary in the Cold War, 1945–1956*, 77.

59. The Communist Party of Czechoslovakia was the second strongest party at the elections in 1925 and was the fourth strongest in 1929 and 1935.

60. Remarkably, this was by far the best election result for any party in Czechoslovakia since 1920, as before the war, no more than 25 percent was won by the victors.

61. "Report of the Meeting between Stalin and the Romanian Communist Party Leaders on the Situation in Romania, 2–3 April 1946, Moscow," in Békés, Borhi, Ruggenthaler, and Trasca, *Soviet Occupation of Romania, Hungary, and Austria*, 102–18.

62. Czechoslovakia is not included in this group.

63. Békés, "Communist Parties and the National Issue."

64. While officially the chair of the National Economic Council was the prime minister, Ferenc Nagy, the actual work of the council was directed by its energetic secretary-general, the Communist Zoltán Vass.

65. Péter Gábor to Korotkevics, 5 April 1947, in Izsák and Kun, *Moszkvának jelentjük*, 170. For the Russian version, see Murashko et al., *Vostochnaja Evropa*, 1:606.

66. Kramer, "Stalin, Soviet Policy," 15.

67. A full collection of Allied Control Commission documents for Hungary are published in Cseh, "Documents."

68. The Hungarian Communists proudly reported to Moscow in April 1947, "We have our men in every party.... We have succeeded in recruiting functionaries of other parties.... We have our men in every ministry, moreover, among the dignitaries of the churches." Péter Gábor to Korotkevics, 5 April 1947, in Izsák and Kun, *Moszkvának jelentjük*, 170. For the Russian version, see Murashko et al., *Vostochnaja Evropa*, 1:606. In March 1948, Stalin advised the SED leaders in East Germany to plant agents in the West German Social Democratic Party, "just as the Polish and Hungarian Communists had done to their opposition parties." Quoted in Zubok, *Failed Empire*, 74.

69. For a detailed analysis of this political crisis, see chapter 2.

70. For a recent study, see Rieber, *Salami Tactics Revisited*.

71. This speech was discovered by the author in 1991. PIL, 274. f. 2/34. The thirty-three-page speech is published in English in toto in Békés, Borhi, Ruggenthaler, and Trasca, *Soviet Occupation of Romania, Hungary, and Austria*, 188–221.

72. No minutes of that meeting have been found on either side to date. After returning from Moscow, Rákosi reported on his visit at the 3 April HCP Politburo meeting, but according to the then prevailing practice, no minutes were taken. However, on 18 April he gave a speech at the meeting of party secretaries of factories and plants in Budapest, where he briefly summarized the Soviet ideas on setting up a new Communist international organization (PIL 274. f. 8/14). For the story of this Hungarian Communist initiative, see Békés, "Dokumentumok a magyar kormánydelegáció 1946. áprilisi moszkvai tárgyalásairól"; for an English version, see Békés, "The Communist Parties and the National Issue."

73. Békés, Borhi, Ruggenthaler and Trasca, *Soviet ccupation of Romania, Hungary, and Austria*, 211–12.

74. I first presented this finding at the international conference "Internal Factors Facilitating Communist Takeover in East Central Europe, 1944–1948," Opocno, Czech Republic, 9–11 September 1993. See Békés, "Mad'arsk politick krize na jare 1946." For an English version, see Békés, "Soviet Plans to Establish Cominform."

75. Romanian minutes on the meeting between Ernő Gerő and Gheorhghe Gheorghiu-Dej, (undated), ca. end of April–early May 1946, copy on file in the Cold War International History Project Archive (Woodrow Wilson Center), Washington, D.C.

76. Rákosi's speech at the 17 May 1946 meeting of the HCP Central Committee is published in toto in Békés, Borhi, Ruggenthaler, and Trasca, *Soviet Occupation of Romania, Hungary, and Austria*, 188–221. This quote is from pp. 219–20. For the first presentation of this finding, see Békés, "Dokumentumok a magyar kormánydelegáció 1946. áprilisi moszkvai tárgyalásairól." For an English version, see Békés, "Soviet Plans to Establish Cominform."

77. Most recently, Vit Smetana found another important document demonstrating that the Czechoslovak Communists were also planning to take power in the forseeable future as early as February 1946. Smetana, "Consessions or Conviction?," 65.

78. See Westad, *Cold War*, 94.

79. On Soviet policy toward the Marshall Plan, see Parrish and Narinsky, *New Evidence on the Soviet Rejection of the Marshall Plan*.

80. Gibiansky, "Kak voznik Kominfom," 135–36, quoted in Tucker, "Cold War in Stalin's Time," 275.

81. Békés, "Soviet Plans to Establish Cominform." The full text of Rákosi's speech is published in Békés, Borhi, Ruggenthaler, and Trasca, *Soviet Occupation of Romania, Hungary, and Austria*, 188–221.

82. According to a recently found document, it is not impossible that the plan of establishing the Cominform originated not from Stalin but from Rákosi himself. According to the Romanian minutes on the meeting between Ernő Gerő and Gheorghe Gheorghiu-Dej in late April–early May 1946 (cited earlier), Gerő briefly informed Dej about Rákosi's meeting with Stalin on 1 April 1946. The document contains this sentence at the beginning: "Comrade Rákosi suggested the creation of an international organisation." It would have been rather risky to claim this if the author was in fact Stalin, as he could have been informed about Rákosi's "plagiarism" by the Romanian Communists.

83. Békés, "Communist Parties and the National Issue in Central and Eastern Europe."

84. Procacci, *Cominform*. At the conference, Albania was represented by the Yugoslav party.

85. Remarkably, even at the very founding conference of the Cominform, the Hungarian representatives harshly attacked the Czechoslovak party because of the persecution of the Hungarian ethnic minority in their country.

Chapter 2

1. On Soviet-Hungarian relations in this period, see Vida, *Iratok a magyar-szovjet kapcsolatok történetéhez*. Numerous Soviet documents on Hungary are published in Murashko et al., *Vostochnaja Evropa*.

2. PIA, 274. f. 2/33. ő. e.

3. Dessewffy, "A békekötés előkészítése"; Rubleczky, "Készüljünk a békére."

4. Révai, "Nemzetrontó sovinizmus."

5. The articles of the debate are discussed in Balogh, *Magyarország külpolitikája, 1945–1950*, 135–37. See also Békés, *Kísérletek a külföld felvilágosítására*, 99–107.

6. According to the reports of the Hungarian Public Opinion Service of 24 January 1946 and 12 February, more than 50 percent of the respondents hoped that the peace treaty would set boundaries for Hungary based on the ethnic principle. Magyar Távirati Iroda Magyar Közvéleménykutató Szolgálat.

7. Balogh, *Parlamenti és pártharcok 1945–1947*; Vida, *A Független Kisgazdapárt politikája 1944–1947*.

8. Rákosi's information about a potential 4,000–10,000 km² territorial adjustment is mentioned in the memoirs of Ferenc Nagy. See Nagy, *Struggle behind the Iron Curtain*.

9. On the foreign policy of the Smallholders' Party, see Vida, *A Független Kisgazdapárt politikája 1944–1947*, chapter 2; Nagy, *Struggle behind the Iron Curtain*, chapter 3. On the foreign policy of the Hungarian Communist Party, see Békés, *Európából Európába*, 37–52.

10. "Posetiteli kremlevskava kabineta J.V. Stalina," 121.

11. On the joint companies, see Borhi, *Hungary in the Cold War, 1945–1956*; Békés, Borhi, Ruggenthaler, and Trasca, *Soviet Occupation of Romania, Hungary, and Austria*.

12. The minutes taken during the Hungarian delegation's talks in Moscow are published in Békés, "Dokumentumok a magyar kormánydelegáció 1946." Some of these records were published in English in Kertesz, *Last European Peace Conference*. Two Russian documents on the Hungarians' talks with Molotov and Stalin are published in Murashko et al., *Vostochnaja Evropa*, 1:140, 141.

13. Fülöp, *Unfinished Peace*, 174.

14. Pető, "A. J. Visinszkij: A magyar–csehszlovák lakosságcseréről." When facing resistance to this plan from the British and the Americans, Moscow eventually withdrew its support, and the Czechoslovak demand was not adopted at the peace conference.

15. Public Record Office, London, Kew Gardens, Foreign Office General Correspondence, FO 371 59005, R 6151/256/21; cited in Fülöp, "A Sebestyén-misszó."

16. "Speech by József Révai on the 'Hungarian Peace.'"

17. The author's interview with Miklós Vásárhelyi on 3 October 1987. See Békés, *Kísérletek a külföld felvilágosítására*, 126.

18. PIA, 274. f. 7/314. ő. e.

19. The story of Nagy's resignation is discussed in detail in Borhi, *Hungary in the Cold War, 1945–1956*, 117–18.

20. Rákosi, *Visszaemlékezések 1940–1956*, Vol. 1., 377.

21. On the intervention of the Soviet authorities in the region, including Hungary, see Murasko et al., *Vostochnaja Evropa*; Volokitina T. V. et al., *Sovietskij faktor v Vostochnoj Evrope*.

22. Borhi, *Hungary in the Cold War, 1945–1956*, 118.

23. On the elections of 1947, see Szerencsés, *A kékcédulás hadművelet*.

24. Zubok, *Failed Empire*, 73.

25. The GDR, established in October 1949, was not considered a sovereign state until 1954, even by the Soviet bloc countries. Although diplomatic relationships were immediately established, and it also became a member of the Warsaw Treaty of 1955, bilateral

friendship and mutual assistance treaties were signed only in 1968 with the East German government.

26. Feitl, *Talányos játszmák.*

27. Procacci, *Cominform*; Agyibekov, *Kominform i poszlevoennaja Jevropa.* On Yugoslavia's relations with the Soviet bloc, see Rajak, "Cold War in the Balkans"; Rajak, *Yugoslavia and the Soviet Union.*

28. Detailed minutes taken at the conference by the Romanian defense minister are published in Cristescu, "Ianuarie 1951." An English translation is available on CWIHP's Digitarchive: "Stalin's Conference with East European Delegates," January 1951. All quotations are from the CWIHP translation. The developments at the conference are covered in detail in Kramer, "Stalin, Soviet Policy," 105–7.

29. Cristescu, "Ianuarie 1951."

30. According to Rákosi's memoirs, all non-Soviet participants shared this view.

31. On the conference, see also Rákosi, *Visszaemlékezések*, 860–61.

32. The original numbers for wartime were modified at the meeting on January 11. For Romania, it was reduced from 700,000 to 600,000; for Bulgaria and Hungary, it increased from 350,000 to 400,000.

33. Borhi, *Hungary in the Cold War, 1945–1956*, 226.

34. The Hungarian members of the committee were Ernő Gerő, member of the leading troika in charge of the economy, and Defense Minister Mihály Farkas. See Rainer, "Sztálin és Rákosi."

35. See Rainer, "Sztálin és Rákosi."

36. Hegedüs, *Magyar–angol kapcsolatok, 1944–1956.*

37. Kalmár, "Socialist or Realist."

38. Regarding the theory of the "peoples' democratic twist," see Kalmár, "A sztálinizmus kelet-közép-európai esélyei."

39. The text of the known thirty telegrams between Rákosi and Stalin from 1949 to 1952 are published in Rainer, "Távirat 'Filippov' elvtársnak." No documents have emerged so far about the content of the messages of the high-frequency telephone connections before 1953.

40. Rainer, "Távirat 'Filippov' elvtársnak."

41. As the background of the story is not yet clear in all respects, it is an interesting datum that in 1959 Khrushchev interpreted the question for Mao as exchanging Rákosi for a Hungarian spy imprisoned in the Soviet Union. Zubok, "Khrushchev–Mao Conversations."

42. Rainer, "Sztálin és Rákosi."

43. Rainer, "Távirat 'Filippov' elvtársnak."

44. The hospital was turned into a civilian one after the end of the Korean War in 1953, and Hungarian doctors continued to work there until 1957. On the history of the Hungarian hospital in Korea, see Kocsis, "Magyar orvosok Koreában."

45. Izsák and Kun, *Moszkvának jelentjük*, 200.

46. Rainer, "Távirat 'Filippov' elvtársnak."

47. Gibiansky, "Last Conference of the Cominform."

48. Okváth, *Bástya a béke frontján*, 110.

49. Okváth, *Bástya a béke frontján*, 110. Documents on offensive plans against Yugoslavia have not been found in the Hungarian archives, so such previous claims have not

been verified by research. See Király, *Honvédségből néphadsereg.* For another study denying the existence of the Yugoslav offensive plans, see Ritter, Nuenlist, and Locher, *War on Tito's Yugoslavia?*

50. Rainer, "Távirat 'Filippov' elvtársnak."

51. Borhi, *Hungary in the Cold War, 1945–1956*, 183–84.

52. Rainer, "Távirat 'Filippov' elvtársnak." See also Szörényi, "Adalékok a Vogeler-ügy diplomáciatörténetéhez."

53. Borhi, *Hungary in the Cold War: 1945–1956*, 184.

54. Rainer, "Távirat 'Filippov' elvtársnak."

55. On the preparations for and the history of the conference, see Lipkin, "Soviet Snowdrops in the Ice Age?"

56. Lipkin, "Soviet Snowdrops in the Ice Age?"62.

57. The attention to the caesural importance of the year 1952 was first drawn to by Melinda Kalmár in connection with the analysis of Hungarian literary politics. See Kalmár, "A politika poétikája." The emerging crisis of the economy from 1952 was pointed out in Urbán, *Sztálin halálától a forradalom kitöréséig.* The same issue, in a less categorical form, was already dealt with in the report of the so-called Fact-Finding Committee of the HSWP set up in 1989. See "Történelmi utunk."

58. MNL–OL, KÜM TÜK Nagy-Britannia XIX-J-1-j, 00183/13/1953; Békés, "Nagy-Britannia." On the Sanders case and the Hungarian–British secret talks, see Szörényi, "A brit–magyar diplomáciai kapcsolatok és a Sanders-ügy"; Hegedüs, *Magyar–angol kapcsolatok, 1944–1956.*

59. The death sentence was eventually changed to life imprisonment by the British authorities.

60. Rákosi, *Visszaemlékezések, 1940–1956.*

61. Békés, "Nagy-Britannia."

Chapter 3

1. I first published this thesis in Hungarian in 1997 (Békés, "Hidegháború, enyhülés és az 1956-os magyar forradalom") and later in English (Békés, *Cold War, Détente and the 1956 Hungarian Revolution*) and then in several other English language publications (e.g., Békés, "Cold War, Détente and the 1956 Hungarian Revolution").

2. Günter Bischof used the term "first Cold War" in his 1999 book, arguing that the resolution of the Austrian question by signing the state treaty in 1955 was a "major turning point in the overall history of the Cold War." Nevertheless, he did not contrast the features of the two different stages of the Cold War, focusing only on the early period. My conception differs from his also in that I regard not 1955 but 1953 as a caesura, and, most importantly, not because of Stalin's death but because of the beginning of the thermonuclear age. Bischof, *Austria in the First Cold War,* 3.

3. Békés, "Cold War, Détente and the 1956 Hungarian Revolution."

4. Holloway, "Nuclear Weapons and the Escalation of the Cold War."

5. For an edited volume on the Geneva Summit of 1955, see Bischof and Dockrill, *Cold War Respite.*

6. At the Soviet bloc states' summit meeting on 31 July 1972 in the Crimea, Brezhnev argued that if the opposition won the early elections to be held in the FRG in the fall, it

would mean a return to the Cold War. Report by János Kádár at the meeting of the HSWP PC 2 August 1972. MNL–OL, M-KS, 288. f. 5. cs. 587. ő. e.

7. Memorandum of conversation (Kissinger–Dobrinin), Washington, 12 June 1969, in Keefer, Geyer, and Selvage, *Soviet–American Relations*, 64.

8. Loth, *Overcoming the Cold War*.

9. See Engerman, "Ideology and the Origins of the Cold War."

10. Burr, *Creation of SIOP-62*. While in later decades, nuclear strategists worked out plans for a limited nuclear war on both sides, a "full-scale retaliation" following the unwanted but possible escalation of the conflict remained a final option in the scenarios. In a U.S. analysis prepared in 1983, this option "would totally destroy the Soviet Union even though the Soviet Union could still retaliate in similar fashion against the United States." Carnesale et al., *Living with Nuclear Weapons*, 139.

11. Garthoff, *Détente and Confrontation*.

12. For an analysis of the Berlin and Cuban crises from this perspective, see chapter 6.

13. For a recent edited volume supporting the author's long-held position, see Bange and Villaume, *Long Détente*.

14. This chronology is generally used in international historiography.

15. The term "peaceful coexistance" was originally used by Lenin and then reinvented by the old-new Soviet leadership right after Stalin's death. For a long time, however, it remained a *Soviet* category, since the Western powers, especially the United States, were unwilling to accept this concept, regarding it an intolerable ideological concession. This happened only gradually from the mid-1960s on.

While the view that the Suez crisis was basically a conflict within the Western alliance is quite generally accepted in Western scholarship, interestingly enough, in the former Soviet bloc countries it is still widely regarded as a serious East–West conflict. This contradiction itself suggests that the further examination of the nature and the contemporary and retrospective perception of the crises during the Cold War era would be beneficial not only for history writing but for other disciplines like international relations, political science, sociology, and anthropology as well.

16. On the military conflicts during the Cold War, see Westad, *Global Cold War*.

17. Békés, "East Central Europe, 1953–1956."

18. For a recent survey of Soviet policy after Stalin's death, see Mastny, "Soviet Foreign Policy, 1953–1962." See also Békés, "East Central Europe, 1953–1960." Another important collective work on the topic is Larres and Osgood, *Cold War after Stalin's Death*.

19. On Soviet policy toward the third world, see Westad, *Global Cold War*.

20. On the Soviet bloc's policy concerning European security, see chapter 8.

21. For a classical survey of Soviet foreign policy, see Ulam, *Expansion and Coexistence*. For accounts on the topic based on the use of new Soviet archival sources, see Chubarian, *Sovjetskaja vesnaja politika v retrospective, 1917–1991*; Nezhinskij, *Sovjetskaja vesnaja politika v godi holodnoj vojni*; *Politicheskie krisy i konflikty 50–60.h godov*. For other recent studies, see Roberts, *Chance for Peace?*; Zubok, *Failed Empire*; Mastny, "Soviet Foreign Policy, 1953–1962."

22. The Warsaw Pact was established on 14 May 1955, and the Austrian State Treaty was signed on 15 May. On the establishment of the Warsaw Pact, see the section in chapter 3: "Integration in the East: The establishment of the Warsaw Pact."

23. McCauley, "Hungary and Suez 1956," 786. For a recent study, see Even, *Two Squadrons and Their Pilots.*

24. On Soviet–Yugoslav relations, see Gibiansky "Soviet–Yugoslav Relations and the Hungarian Revolution."

25. Békés, Byrne, and Rainer, *1956 Hungarian Revolution*, 22.

26. Békés, Byrne, and Rainer, *1956 Hungarian Revolution*, 114–15. For an analysis of the Soviet government declaration, see chapter 5.

27. Békés, Byrne, and Rainer, *1956 Hungarian Revolution*, 63. It is also remarkable that Khrushchev, though he denounces Stalin's crimes just a year later in his secret speech at the Twentieth Congress of the CPSU, here seems to be explicitly defending Stalin's role in the great purges of the 1930s.

28. Mastny and Byrne, *Cardboard Castle?*

29. On this doctrine, see the section in chapter 3: "The Doctrine of Active Foreign Policy."

30. Poland and Czechoslovakia were founding members of the UN.

31. The term "emancipation" was already being used by Zbigniew Brzezinski but only for depicting the changing relations between Moscow and its allies in his masterpiece of Kremlinology, based on publicly available sources at the time. see Brzezinski, *Soviet Bloc, Unity and Conflict*, 442. This author, however, introduced the term in international literature as a new approach to analyzing the international relations of the Soviet bloc based on extensive multiarchival research. In this concept, emancipation in *all three directions* (Moscow, the West and the third world) had an increasingly important role in the policies of the East European allies of the Soviet Union. For the author's novel concept of the emancipation of the Soviet bloc member states, see Békés, "Warsaw Pact and the Helsinki Process"; Békés, "East Central Europe, 1953–1956." On the process of emancipation, see also chapter 7. Laurien Crump has recently used this author's thesis to develop an analytical concept to explain the multilateralization of the Warsaw Pact in her book *The Warsaw Pact Reconsidered.* Yet sadly this author is not mentioned in the book's introduction among the numerous scholars having had an impact on her work, although it is clear from several references as well as from her earlier publications that she was fully aware of my works (cited above).

32. The meeting was held in Galyatető, a health resort in the Mátra mountains.

33. Minutes of the Communist summit meeting in Moscow on 22–23 June 1956, 27 June 1956. MNL–OL, 276. f. 53. cs. 293. ő. e. The Cominform, established in September 1947, was disbanded after the Twentieth Congress of the CPSU in April 1956.

34. On the Soviet position at the Geneva Summit, see Zubok, "Soviet Policy Aims at the Geneva Conference of 1955."

35. In the Munich agreement in September 1938, the four great powers—Great Britain, France, Germany, and Italy—agreed on the annexation of the Sudetenland in Western Czechoslovakia, predominantly populated by Germans, by Nazi Germany.

36. See Mastny, "Learning from the Enemy."

37. Mastny, "Learning from the Enemy." See also Fejtő, *History of the Peoples' Democracies.*

38. Creating the EDC (the European Defense Community) was also a probability until it was vetoed by the French parliament in 1954.

39. For a recent archive-based study, see Feitl, *Talányos játszmák.*

40. According to the first paragraph of Article 22 of the peace treaty signed between Hungary and the Allies in Paris on 10 February 1947, Moscow was allowed to station troops in Hungary in order to secure communication lines between the Soviet Union and the Soviet zone of occupation in Austria until the conclusion of a peace treaty with Austria. Halmosy, *Nemzetközi szerződések, 1945–1982*, 84.

41. Agreement on the Creation of a Unified Command of the Armed Forces of the Member States of the Treaty on Friendship, Cooperation, and Mutual Assistance, 14 May 1955, www.php.isn.ethz.ch/kms2.isn.ethz.ch/serviceengine/Files/PHP/17542/ipublicationdocument _singledocument/bea8e1d7-b93e-46be-bba7-c843a015628e/de/Agreement550514.pdf.

42. See Bischoff, *Austria in the First Cold War.*

43. Mastny, "The Soviet Union and the Origins of the Warsaw Pact." www.php.isn.ethz .ch/. For the general history of the Warsaw Pact, see Mastny and Byrne, *A Cardboard Castle?*

44. Békés, "Titkos válságkezeléstől a politikai koordinációig."

45. Urbán, "Magyarország és a Varsói Szerződés létrejötte."

46. Urbán, *Sztálin haláltól a forradalom kitöréséig*, 77.

47. For the history of the establishment of the Warsaw Pact, see Mastny, "Soviet Union and the Origins of the Warsaw Pact." www.isn.ethz.ch/php. See also Békés, "Titkos válságkezeléstől a politikai koordinációig."

48. MNL–OL, 276. f. 53/229. ő. e. Minutes of the HWP PC, 5 May 1955.

49. Mastny and Byrne, *Cardboard Castle?*

50. As pointed out earlier, this paragraph did not appear in the final text of the treaty.

51. MNL–OL, 276. f. 53/229. ő. e. Minutes of the HWP PC, 5 May 1955.

52. Mastny and Byrne, *Cardboard Castle?* On Romanian policy, see Tismaneanu, *Stalinism for All Seasons.*

53. Mastny and Byrne, *Cardboard Castle?*

54. The documents of the WP Political Consultative Committee (1956–90) are published on the PHP website: www.php.isn.ethz.ch/lory1.ethz.ch/collections/colltopic3bcf.html ?lng=en&id=14465.

55. White, *Britain, Détente and Changing East–West Relations*, 55–56.

56. On French policy toward the Hungarian Revolution, see "Kecskés, French Foreign Policy and the 1956 Hungarian Revolution."

57. On the Eden Plan, see Dockrill, "The Eden Plan."

58. On U.S. policy toward East-Central Europe in the 1950s, see Kovrig, *Myth of Liberation*; Immerman, *John Foster Dulles and the Diplomacy of the Cold War*; Kovrig, *Of Walls and Bridges*; Marchio, *Rhetoric and Reality*; Békés, "1956 Hungarian Revolution and World Politics"; Borhi, "Rollback, Liberation, Containment or Inaction?"; Tudda, *Truth Is Our Weapon.*

59. Marchio, *Rhetoric and Reality.*

60. For a recent monograph on Radio Free Europe and Radio Liberty, see Johnson, *Radio Free Europe and Radio Liberty.*

61. Marchio, *Rhetoric and Reality*; Kovrig, *Of Walls and Bridges*; Békés, "1956 Hungarian Revolution and World Politics"; Borhi, *Dealing with Dictators.*

62. Békés, Byrne, and Rainer, *1956 Hungarian Revolution*, 34–53.

63. In 1990, *Foreign Relations of the United States* published only a heavily sanitized copy of the document. See NSC 5608 and NSC 5608/1 in *FRUS*, 25:190–194 and 25:216–221,

respectively. The full text of the document is published in Békés, Byrne, and Rainer, *1956 Hungarian Revolution*, 119–28.

64. For surveys on British and French policy toward the region, see Frankel, *British Foreign Policy, 1945–1973*; Hanrieder and Auton, *Foreign Policies of West Germany, France and Britain*; White, *Britain, Détente, and Changing East–West Relations.*

65. In the United States, a new policy paper on East Central Europe, replacing NSC 174, was adopted by the National Security Council in July 1956. See NSC 5608 and NSC 5608/1, *FRUS*, 25:190–94 and 25:216–21, respectively. For the changed attitude of NATO countries, see Public Record Office, London, Kew, Foreign Office General Correspondence FO 371 (hereafter PRO FO 371), 122081 N 1059/9. The British NATO delegation to the Foreign Office on the 24 October meeting of the NATO Council, 24 October 1956. See also Kecskés, "North Atlantic Treaty Organization and the Hungarian Revolution."

66. Formal diplomatic relations were maintained for all but Bulgaria.

67. For the transcripts of two Radio Free Europe broadcasts to Hungary during the revolution, see Békés, Byrne, and Rainer, "1956 Hungarian Revolution," 286–89. The full text of RFE's Hungarian program during the revolt is published in Vámos, *A Szabad Európa Rádió és a magyar forradalom*. The documents of RFE's research section are available in the Open Society Archive in Budapest.

68. According to a public opinion poll among Hungarian refugees in Austria, the great majority (96%) of the interviewed persons had expected some kind of U.S. support, and of these, 77 percent believed that it would be military support. International Research Associates, Inc. "Hungary and the 1956 Uprising: Personal Interviews with 1,000 Hungarian Refugees in Austria," February 1957, as cited in Marchio, *Rhetoric and Reality*, 417.

69. For the text of a complex policy paper on the future role of the Soviet bloc in world policy, prepared by the Soviet Foreign Ministry for the summit meeting of European Communist leaders in Moscow in early January 1956, see "A szovjet külügyminisztérium feljegyzése a külpolitika kérdéseiről, 1956. január 4," MNL–OL M-KS, 267. f. 62. cs. 75. ő. e., in Kiss, Ripp, and Vida, *Top Secret*, 33–40. For the English text of the document, see Soviet Foreign Ministry notes on current issues in Soviet global policy, 4 January 1956, in Békés, Byrne, and Rainer, *1956 Hungarian Revolution*, 106–13.

70. China was also represented at the summit meeting as an observer, similar to the session where the Warsaw Pact was established in May 1955. Speech of N. S. Khrushchev at the meeting of the European Socialist countries' leaders, Moscow, January 4, 1956, MNL–OL, M-KS-276. f. 62/84. ő. e.

71. Speech of N. S. Khrushchev at the meeting of the European Socialist countries' leaders, Moscow, January 4, 1956, MNL–OL, M-KS-276. f. 62/84. ő. e., quoted in Békés, "Warsaw Pact and the CSCE process, 1965–1970," 216.

72. As Soviet Ambassador Yuri Andropov himself assured the Hungarian leaders of the Soviet support, explicitly encouraging them to take this step in September 1956, it is very likely that the initiative in July 1955 was preceded by a similar positive message from Moscow. See Borhi, *Magyarország a hidegháborúban*, 98.

73. Soviet Foreign Ministry notes on current issues in Soviet global policy, 4 January 1956, in Békés, Byrne, and Rainer, *1956 Hungarian Revolution*, 106–13.

74. Békés, Byrne, and Rainer, *1956 Hungarian Revolution*, 113.

75. Békés, Byrne, and Rainer, *1956 Hungarian Revolution*, 111, 113.

76. On the international context of the political transition, see Békés, "Back to Europe." On the opening of the border and the issue of the East German refugees, see Horváth and Németh, *És a falak leomlanak*, 350–75; Oplatka, *Egy döntés története*. (For the German edition, see Oplatka, *Der erste Riss in der Mauer*.)

77. Gecsényi, "Ausztria."

78. Soviet Foreign Ministry notes on current issues in Soviet global policy, 4 January 1956, in Békés, Byrne, and Rainer, *1956 Hungarian Revolution*, 106–13.

79. For a recent study on Hungary's relations with the Comecon, see Feitl, *Talányos játszmák*.

80. Pető, Szakács, *A hazai gazdaság négy évtizedének története*.

81. Mastny, "Warsaw Pact as History," 6–7.

82. The minutes on the summit meeting prepared by the Hungarian leaders is published in Urbán and Vida, "Jegyzőkönyv a Politikai Bizottság 1956. június 28-i üléséről." The conference discussed the following three issues: (1) the resolutions of the seventh session of the Comecon in Berlin and the coordination of the economic plans of the member states, (2) the plans of the member states' military industry and the mutual delivery of "special materials" (the code name used for armaments and military equipment even in top secret documents), and (3) the form of the cooperation of the Communist and workers' parties of the Socialist countries.

83. It is remarkable that between the two world wars, when the relationship was rather hostile between Hungary and its neighbors belonging to the Little Entente (Czechoslovakia, Romania, and Yugoslavia), travel to and communication with these states was much freer than it was between 1949 and 1956.

84. Nagy, *A magyar külpolitika, 1956–1989*, 12.

85. On the planned measures concerning the alleviation of travel before the revolution, see also Bencsik and Nagy, *A magyar úti okmányok története, 1945–1989*, 26–27.

86. As Rákosi was allowed to keep his post of the head of the HWP in 1953, this did not mean his "return" to power, as is often claimed; he simply got rid of his main opponent. Nagy was ultimately replaced as prime minister by András Hegedűs, a thirty-three-year-old protégé of Rákosi.

87. For an archive-based edited volume of twelve essays on Hungary's bilateral relations with the most important Western and Eastern states between ca. 1953 and 1958, see Békés, *Evolúció és revolúció*.

88. On Hungarian relations with Yugoslavia, see Ripp, "Jugoszlávia."

89. The annual installment was 6.5 percent of the value of Hungarian exports to the UK. MNL–OL KÜM TÜK Nagy-Britannia XIX-J-1-j, 1. d. 26/1959.

90. Borhi, *Magyar–amerikai kapcsolatok, 1945–1989*, 916–17.

91. A követi konferencia anyaga, undated [August, 1956], MNL–OL. KÜM TÜK XIX-J-1-j, 4/fb 27. d. 4956/1956.

92. For a U.S. report on the balloon missions to Hungary from 1955, see Békés, Byrne, and Rainer, *1956 Hungarian Revolution*, 66–68.

93. Borhi, *Magyar–amerikai kapcsolatok 1945–1989*, 47. Seven other employees of the U.S. legation had been arrested earlier, and there was no information available about their fate.

94. Amerikai beavatkozás magyar ügyekbe, undated, MNL–OL, KÜM TÜK USA XIX-J-1-j, 26/a 6.d. On U.S.–Hungarian relations, see Borhi, *Hungary in the Cold War, 1945–1956*.

95. For a fascinating story of the Márton case by the couple's daughter, see Marton, *Enemies of the People*.

96. "A magyar–amerikai viszony," MNL–OL KÜM TÜK USA XIX-J-1-j, 17/1 002388/1957.

97. Borhi, *Hungary in the Cold War, 1945–1956*, 294–95.

98. "Kollégiumi előterjesztés: A magyar–amerikai viszony alakulása 1945-től 1955-ig," MNL–OL, KÜM TÜK USA XIX-J-1-j, 26/a 6. d. 00800/8/1956.

99. Borhi, *Magyarország a hidegháborúban*, 302. While the East Central European Communist states did not send observers to the U.S. elections, the Soviet Union did. See *Foreign Relations of the United States, 1955–1957*, 2 November 1956. Ernő Gerő replaced Rákosi in July 1956 as the first secretary of the HWP.

100. See Soviet Foreign Ministry notes on current issues in Soviet global policy, 4 January 1956, in Békés, Byrne, and Rainer, *1956 Hungarian Revolution*, 111.

101. While the Provisional National Government of Hungary declared war on Germany at Soviet request on 28 December 1944, no such move was deemed necessary toward Japan. Nota bene, the Soviet Union itself did not enter the war against Japan until August 1945.

102. Minutes of the HWP PC, 17 May 1956, MNL–OL, M-KS, 276. f. 5. cs. 287. ő. e.

103. For a recent archive-based study on reestablishing diplomatic relations between Hungary and Japan in 1959, see Wintermantel, "A magyar–japán diplomáciai kapcsolatok."

104. For the reports of the Soviet ambassadors from 1953 to 1956, see Baráth, *Szovjet nagyköveti iratok Magyarországról 1953–1956*.

105. Guidelines for the work of the Foreign Ministry and the diplomatic missions for the second and third quarters of 1956, 7 April 1956, MNL–OL M-KS 276. f. 71. cs. 29. ő. e.

106. Material of the mission heads' conference, undated [August 1956], MNL–OL, KÜM TÜK XIX-J-1-j, 4/fb 27.d. 4956/1956.

107. Bottoni, "Románia."

Chapter 4

1. Machcewicz, "Social Protest and Political Crisis in 1956," 107.

2. Machcewicz, 103–6.

3. Paczkowski, *Spring Will Be Ours*, 202.

4. For contemporary Polish accounts on the talks with the Soviet delegation, see Gluchowsky, "Poland, 1956," 40–43.

5. Machcewicz, "Social Protest and Political Crisis," 116–18.

6. It is history's irony that in the forthcoming decades, independent from each other, Polish and Hungarian societies both developed the self-delusory notion of living in the "happiest barracks in the Soviet camp."

7. In the absence of a German peace treaty after World War II, West Germany did not recognize the Oder-Neisse Line, established at the Potsdam summit meeting in 1945, until 1970.

8. Mikoyan's report to the CPSU CC, 14 July 1956, in Szereda and Sztikalin, *Hiányzó lapok 1956 történetéből*, 40.

9. Mićunović, *Moscow Diary, 1956–1958* [Note on 15 July 1956], 86.

10. Minutes by Thomas Brimelow, Head of the Northern Department, 25 October 1956, National Archives, London, FO 371 122378 NH 10110/175; transcript of a teletype conversation between the U.S. legation in Budapest and the Department of State, 25 October 1956,

National Archives, Washington, D.C., Department of State, Central Files, 764.00/10-2556, in *FRUS* 25:280–86;

11. Izsák, "Az 1956-os forradalom pártjai és programjaik."

12. See the 3 November 1956 issues of *Magyar Ifjúság, Népszabadság* and *Új Magyarország*. The history of this news is presented in Nagy, *A Bang-Jensen ügy*, 33–34.

13. Contribution by Dr. Gisele Friedrichs at the international conference titled "A Crack in the Iron Curtain or a Mortal Wound for Communism? The Impact of the Hungarian Revolution of 1956" (Washington, D.C., 25 October 2001) and her personal communication to the author on that day.

14. See Ruggenthaler, *Concept of Neutrality in Stalin's Foreign Policy*, 366; Ruggenthaler, "On the Significance of Austrian Neutrality," 329–48.

15. On the links between Austrian neutrality and the Hungarian Revolution, see Nielsen, "Neutrality vs. Neutralism"; Adair, "Austrian State Treaty"; Gémes, *Austria and the 1956 Hungarian Revolution*.

16. On Hungarian Socialist Workers' Party strategy during the change of system, see Kalmár, "From 'Model Change' to Regime Change."

17. Nagy, *On Communism*. This treatise was a result of discussions and debates with two members of the Imre Nagy circle, journalists Miklós Gimes and Miklós Vásárhelyi. While Nagy sent most of his memoranda written in 1955–56 aimed at the reformation of the Communist system to the party center as well, this writing was not among them, most probably because of the rather delicate nature of the topic. Author's interview with Miklós Vásárhelyi, 2 December 1996.

18. The Soviet delegation that arrived in Budapest on 24 October consisted of presidium members A. I. Mikoyan and M. A. Suslov, KGB head I. Serov, and deputy chief of staff M. S. Malinin. While Mikoyan and Suslov conducted talks with the Hungarian leaders, Serov and Malinin were staying in the country incognito, so the fact of their presence in Hungary during the revolution was confirmed only by the Soviet archival sources declassified in 1992.

19. Telegram of Mikoyan and Suslov to the CPSU CC, 25 October 1956, in Gál et al., *A "Jelcin dosszié,"* 51. On Imre Nagy's activity during the revolution, see Rainer, *Nagy Imre 1953–1958*, 235–336.

20. Telegram of Mikoyan and Suslov to the CPSU CC, 26 October 1956, in Szereda and Sztikalin, *Hiányzó lapok 1956 történetéből*, 111.

21. For the most recent "academic" version of this legend, see Varga, "Az ENSZ és a magyar forradalom."

22. Gál et al., *A "Jelcin dosszié,"* 57–60. Article 2 (7) of the UN Charter states that none of the provisions of the charter entitles the organization to intervene in issues that "fall within the internal jurisdiction" of a state.

23. Both the English language draft prepared in the Foreign Ministry and the statement sent to the UN mentioned 22 October as the starting date of the extraordinary events in Hungary. It is unlikely that this was due to a clerical error; rather, it may be the case that the officials drafting the text regarded the student rally at the technical university on that day the beginning of the revolution rather than the demonstration in Budapest on 23 October. Due to this mistake, however, based on the Hungarian government declaration that has become an official UN document, the date of the outbreak of the uprising is often erroneously mentioned as 22 October in Western literature.

24. The clarification of the case took place in the early 1990s, although many people today probably still know only the original story, especially since that undoubtedly more exciting version pops up in articles on 1956 from time to time. On the role of Péter Kós, see the 1990 interview with him by Gábor Murányi (1956 Institute Oral History Archive, No. 239) and Murányi, "A Konduktorov-ügy."

25. On the debates within the HWP leadership and the political turn on October 28, see Ripp, "A pártvezetés végnapjai"; Rainer, *Nagy Imre 1953–1958*, 270–90.

26. For the text of the declaration of neutrality, see Békés, Byrne, and Rainer, *1956 Hungarian Revolution*, 334.

27. For a detailed account on the declaration of neutrality, see Békés, "1956 Hungarian Revolution and the Declaration of Neutrality."

28. The demand for neutrality in fact already appeared right before the revolution: such suggestions were raised at student rallies in Sopron and Miskolc on 22 October. See Szakolczai, "Győr-Sopron megye," 149.

29. On Austrian neutrality, see Bischoff, *Austria in the First Cold War*.

30. On the international context of the political transition, see Békés, "Back to Europe."

31. *Magyar Honvéd*, október 31 1956.

32. "The Trial of Imre Nagy and His Associates," MNL–OL, XX-5-h, Investigations reports, vol. 1/1, Imre Nagy's interrogation, 29 June 1957, 169.

33. For the English text of the Soviet government declaration, see Békés, Byrne, and Rainer, *1956 Hungarian Revolution*, 300–302.

34. Békés, Byrne, and Rainer, *1956 Hungarian Revolution*, 295–99. For the full text of the English translation of the Malin notes on the debates in the CPSU presidium, see Kramer, "The 'Malin Notes.'"

35. *Magyar Nemzet*, 1 November 1956.

36. Békés, Byrne, and Rainer, *1956 Hungarian Revolution*, 301.

37. Békés, Byrne, and Rainer, *1956 Hungarian Revolution*, 326.

38. Békés, Byrne, and Rainer, *1956 Hungarian Revolution*, 307–10.

39. *Az igazság a Nagy Imre ügyben*, 86–87.

40. Important new evidence concerning Imre Nagy's position can be found in the report presented by János Kádár on 2 November 1956 at the meeting of the CPSU presidium. According to the report, right before the decision was made on the declaration of neutrality, Nagy "was convinced that a strike against Budapest was being prepared." Equally telling is Kádár's report about the other members of the cabinet: "The whole cabinet, other than Kádár[,] declared that the Sov. gov't is deceiving the Hungarian gov't." Békés, Byrne, and Rainer, *1956 Hungarian Revolution*, 338.

41. The official minutes of the meeting published first in 1989 did not contain point 12, including the quote cited above. (See Glatz, "A kormány és a párt vezető szerveinek dokumentumaiból.") Thus, up to the late 1990s, we had only indirect evidence that there was a discussion of the issue at the morning session of the cabinet on 1 November and a political decision was made on the declaration of neutrality. However, the present author discovered a one-page fragment in the documents of the Imre Nagy trial to be found in Géza Losonczy's contemporary records, which basically corresponds to the text of the second part of point 11 of the official minutes, but it also contains a point 12 on the issue of neutrality. "The Trial of Imre Nagy and His Associates," MNL–OL, XX-5-h, Investigations

reports, vol. 12, Géza Losonczy's records. For the English text of the minutes, see Békés, Byrne, and Rainer, *1956 Hungarian Revolution*, 321–23.

42. Békés, Byrne, and Rainer, *1956 Hungarian Revolution*, 322.

43. *Az igazság a Nagy Imre ügyben*, 87–88. According to János Kádár's report presented in Moscow on 2 November, Andropov first stated that "these are railroad workers," later he said it was merely a redeployment of troops, then he explained the surrounding of airports by saying that they were transporting the injured. Békés, Byrne, and Rainer, *1956 Hungarian Revolution*, 338.

44. Andropov's report on the cabinet meeting is published in English in Békés, Byrne, and Rainer, *1956 Hungarian Revolution*, 330–31.

45. For the text of the declaration of neutrality, see Békés, Byrne, and Rainer, *1956 Hungarian Revolution*, 334.

46. For the text of Nagy's telegram to Hammarskjöld, see Békés, Byrne, and Rainer, *1956 Hungarian Revolution*, 333.

47. "The Trial of Imre Nagy and His Associates," MNL–OL XX-5-h, Investigations records, vol. 1/1, Imre Nagy's interrogation July 1, 1957, 172.

48. "The Trial of Imre Nagy and His Associates," MNL–OL XX-5-h, Investigations records, vol. 1/1, Imre Nagy's interrogation July 1, 1957, 172.

49. The telegram is published in Békés, Byrne, and Rainer, *1956 Hungarian Revolution*, 333.

50. The Hungarian version of the telegram, including the omitted paragraph, is published in Kiss, Ripp, and Vida, "Források a Nagy Imre-kormány külpolitikájának történetéhez," 86.

51. "The Trial of Imre Nagy and His Associates," MNL–OL, XX-5-h, Investigations records, vol. 3, records of the hearing of witness Pál Felix on 3 July 1957, 263.

52. Andropov's report on the meeting is published in Gál, et al., *A "Jelcin dosszié,"* 81.

53. Nagy's telegram of 2 November is published in Békés, Byrne, and Rainer, *1956 Hungarian Revolution*, 346.

54. Order issued by Prime Minister Imre Nagy to János Szabó, acting Hungarian UN representative on 3 November 1956, MNL–OL XIX-J-1-j, Foreign Ministry, documents of the ministry secretariat, box no. 66. The telegram is published in English in Békés, Byrne, and Rainer, *1956 Hungarian Revolution*, 362. János Szabó, assistant secretary of the Hungarian UN delegation, was put in charge of leading the Hungarian mission on 29 October to replace Péter Kós, who was relieved.

55. Statement by János Szabó at the Security Council meeting on 3 November 1956, MNL–OL XIX-J-1-j, Foreign Ministry, documents of the ministry secretariat, box no. 66. Szabó similarly sabotaged an instruction from the foreign ministry on 2 November—which was probably not discussed with Imre Nagy—to request in writing that the issue of Hungarian neutrality be put on the agenda of the special General Assembly convened to discuss the Suez crisis. He reported that he had not had a chance to deliver the speech received from Budapest because, following a previous order, he did not take part in the Middle East debate. Békés, Byrne, and Rainer, *1956 Hungarian Revolution*, 362.

56. Rainer, *Nagy Imre 1953–1958*; Szereda and Rainer, *Döntés a Kremlben, 1956*, 91.

57. For the discussion of the Soviet presidium with Kádár and Münnich on 2 and 3 November, see Békés, Byrne, and Rainer, *1956 Hungarian Revolution*, 336–40, 356–61. These Soviet sources reveal, however, that it was not János Kádár's original intention to form a

countergovernment when he left together with Ferenc Münnich for the Soviet Union on 1 November. On their first meeting with the members of the presidium on 2 November, Kádár was trying to convince the Soviet leaders that there was still a chance for the peaceful consolidation of the situation in Hungary. However, by the next day, when they met again—this time the presidium was supplemented by Khrushchev and Malenkov—he recognized that the decision had already been taken in Moscow and the alternative for him remained only whether he was willing to collaborate or not.

58. Szereda and Rainer, *Döntés a Kremlben, 1956*, 26–27. On the first Soviet intervention of 24 October 1956, see Hajdu, "Az 1956. október 24-i moszkvai értekezlet."

59. Szereda and Rainer, *Döntés a Kremlben, 1956*, 26.

60. This excepts the Afghan partisan war precipitated by the Soviet intervention in December 1979, where the circumstances were rather different.

61. For the first publication of this doctrine, see Békés, *Cold War, Détente and the 1956 Hungarian Revolution.*

62. See chapters 7 and 9.

63. On the Polish crisis, see Paczkowski and Byrne, *From Solidarity to Martial Law.*

64. Khrushchev was much more skillful in finding a proper candidate when he handpicked Edward Ochab to succeed the Polish little-Stalin, Bierut, who died in Moscow at the time of the Twentieth Congress of the CPSU.

65. Working notes of Imre Horváth from the session of the CPSU CC presidium, 3 November 3 1956, in Békés, Byrne, and Rainer, *1956 Hungarian Revolution*, 359.

66. Recently, another fundamental mistake of the Soviet leadership in handling the crises in Hungary after 1953 was presented by Melinda Kalmár. According to this theory, Moscow mistakenly chose Imre Nagy as prime minister to consolidate the situation in Hungary in June 1953, since Nagy's political persona was incompatible with the Soviet expectations. See Kalmár, *Történelmi galaxisok vonzásában*, 98–99.

67. "Mikojan és Szuszlov távirata az SZKP KB-nak, 1956. október 26," in Szereda and Sztikalin, *Hiányzó lapok*, 112.

68. The importance of the first three factors is emphasized in Rainer, "Yeltsin Dossier," 25.

69. For the English text of the Soviet government's declaration of 30 October 1956, see Zinner, *National Communism and Popular Revolt*, 485–89. Reprinted in Békés, Byrne, and Rainer, *1956 Hungarian Revolution*, 300–302. The declaration is analyzed in chapter 5.

70. This position has been taken most firmly by Kramer, "New Evidence on Soviet Decision-Making."

71. Kramer, "The 'Malin Notes,'" 392.

72. Kramer, "The 'Malin Notes,'" 394.

73. For a detailed elaboration of this interpretation, see Békés, *Cold War, Détente and the 1956 Hungarian Revolution.*

74. Kramer, "The 'Malin Notes,'" 397.

75. According to these, in November–December 1956, Yugoslav leaders, including Tito, made statements during negotiations with Soviet counterparts that if the Soviet Union had not intervened to crush the Hungarian uprising on 4 November, the Yugoslav troops would have done so. Szereda and Sztikalin, *Hiányzó lapok 1956 történetéből*, 249; Kiss, Ripp, and Vida, *Top Secret*, 99. This surprising claim, still unconfirmed by Yugoslav sources, was published for the first time by Swiss historian Pierre Maurer. Maurer, *La réconciliation sovéto–yougoslave 1954–1958.*

76. Mikoyan and Suslov told Ernő Gerő on 26 October that it had been a grave mistake for Imre Nagy to state in his radio broadcast of the previous day that the government would initiate talks on the withdrawal of Soviet troops, as their withdrawal would "inevitably lead to the arrival of American troops." It has been seen that the CPSU presidium reached a decision only four days later to (potentially) withdraw the troops, and this absurd eventuality was not even mentioned.

77. In the presidium on 31 October, Khrushchev argued for crushing the revolution by the following argument: the imperialists would see Soviet troop withdrawal from Hungary as a sign of weakness and "will go onto the offensive." It becomes clear from the wider context, however, that this was none too logical an argument, serving only to push for a reversal of the previous day's decision. Kramer, "The 'Malin Notes,'" 393.

78. Kramer, "The 'Malin Notes,'" 63. "Big war" in Soviet party jargon meant direct armed conflict between East and West. In other words, it was code for a third world war.

79. While this topic does not appear at all in the Malin notes before 3 November as an argument in support of intervention, it seems likely that this was also a great concern for the Soviet leaders.

80. On the second Soviet military intervention, launched on 4 November 1956, see Györkei, Horváth, *Soviet Military Intervention in Hungary, 1956.*

81. Kramer, "The 'Malin Notes,'" 388.

82. Kramer, "The 'Malin Notes,'" 388.

83. Hajdu, "Az 1956. október 24-i moszkvai értekezlet," 151.

84. On China's role, see Jian, *Mao's China and the Cold War*; Szobolevszki and Vida, *Magyar–kínai kapcsolatok, 1956–1959*; Vámos, *Sino–Hungarian Relations and the 1956 Revolution*; Vámos, *Kína melletünk?*

85. Kramer, "The 'Malin Notes,'" 394.

86. Kramer, "The 'Malin Notes,'" 394.

87. For the reactions of Polish leaders to events in Hungary, see Tischler, *"Hogy megcsendüljön minden gyáva fül."*

88. Mićunović, *Moscow Diary*, 130.

89. Békés, Byrne, and Rainer, *1956 Hungarian Revolution*, 347.

90. Mićunović, *Moscow Diary*, 129. Interestingly, several recent accounts still state wrongly that the Bulgarian leaders were also briefed in Bucharest.

91. Also odd is the absence of any reference to the Bucharest or Sofia visits in the next presidium minutes after 31 October 1956.

92. Another question might be why the East German leaders were left out. In the mid-1950s, even the Soviet Union hardly saw the German Democratic Republic as a sovereign state, treating it in many ways as an occupied country, and this appeared in its status as an ally. The leaders of the German Socialist Unity Party had been invited to the 24 October consultation in Moscow, perhaps because the Polish crisis was on the original agenda and they were directly affected as a neighboring country, all the more in view of the controversy over the Oder-Neisse Line. In Albania's case, the country was seen as of little importance, and the idea of briefing its leadership was not mentioned. On the other hand, it cannot be ignored that this omission, too, may have contributed to the steady worsening of Soviet–Albanian relations from the end of the 1950s.

93. For reactions to the Hungarian Revolution in other Soviet bloc countries, see Békés, *Evolúció és revolúció*. The meeting minutes of the Soviet, Polish, Romanian, and

Czechoslovak party leaders during the revolution appear in English in Békés, Byrne, and Rainer, *1956 Hungarian Revolution*, 489–93.

94. *Magyar Nemzet*, 30 October 1956.

95. On the role of the Yugoslavs, see Ripp, *Belgrád és Moszkva között*; Mićunović, *Moscow Diary*; Maurer, *La réconciliation sovéto-yougoslave*; Kiss, Ripp, and Vida, *Top Secret*; Gibiansky "Soviet-Yugoslav Relations and the Hungarian Revolution of 1956."

96. It is clear from the Malin notes that the Chinese party delegation, apart from having other important talks with Soviet party leaders, attended the presidium meetings on 24, 26, and 30 October. For China's role in detail, see Jian, *Mao's China and the Cold War*; Vámos, *Sino–Hungarian Relations and the 1956 Revolution*.

97. Polish society could freely express its solidarity for the Hungarian Revolution due to the revolt taking place in Poland at the same time.

98. *FRUS*, 25:274.

99. Memorandum of a telephone conversation between the Secretary of State in Washington and the Representative at the United Nations (Lodge) in New York, 24 October 1956. *FRUS*, 25:273.

100. Minutes of the 301st meeting of the National Security Council, 26 October 1956, Eisenhower Library, White House Office, National Security Council, Staff Papers, in *FRUS*, 25:295–99.

101. Harold E. Stassen to Eisenhower, 26 October 1956, Eisenhower Library, Whitman File, Administrative Series, in *FRUS*, 25:305.

102. Memorandum of Conversation between Eisenhower and Dulles, 26 October 1956, Eisenhower Library, Dulles Papers, White House Telephone Conversations Series, in *FRUS*, 25:305–6.

103. For the full text of the speech, see Seeley G. Mudd Manuscript Library, Princeton University, Princeton, New Jersey, J. F. Dulles Papers, in Department of State, Bulletin 5, November 1956; selected parts of the speech printed in *FRUS*, 25:317–18.

104. UN Security Council, Official Records, 734th–755th meetings, New York, 1956; *FRUS*, 25:328; *FRUS*, 25:351.

105. Special National Intelligence Estimate SNIE 12-2-56 Washington, 30 October 1956. *FRUS*, 25:330–35.

106. "U.S. Policy toward Developments in Poland and Hungary," 31 October 1956, NSC 5616. An unsanitized copy of this document is now available at the National Security Archive, Washington, D.C. This compromise proposal on U.S. troop withdrawal was omitted along with several other points from the published text of the memorandum in the *Foreign Relations of the United States* series. From the comment on the report prepared by the Committee of the Joint Chiefs of Staff, however, it was clear even earlier that point 20 contained a troop withdrawal proposal. (National Archives, Washington D.C., Joint Chief of Staff, Central Decimal File RG218, box 28.) A slightly modified version of the document ("U.S. Policy toward Developments in Poland and Hungary," NSC5616/2), adopted on 19 November 1956 is published in: Békés, Byrne, and Rainer, *1956 Hungarian Revolution*, 437–42. The idea of mutual troop withdrawal was very likely included in the document on Harold E. Stassen's initiative; he prepared a statement on 29 October proposing exactly the same plan. (Eisenhower Library, White House Office, NSC Staff, OCB Central Files.) Stassen's proposal was published in Békés, "Demokratikus eszmék és nagyhatalmi érdekek," 1402–8.

107. Minutes of the 302nd meeting of the National Security Council, 1 November 1956, Eisenhower Library, Whitman File, NSC Series, in *FRUS*, 25:358–59.

108. The British NATO delegation to the Foreign Office on the 24 October meeting of the NATO Council, 24 October 1956, PRO FO 371 122081 N 1059/9.

109. Telegram No. 180 of the British NATO delegation to the Foreign Office on the 27 October meeting of the NATO Council, 27 October 1956, PRO FO 371 122380. On the debates in NATO during the Hungarian Revolution, see Kecskés, "North Atlantic Treaty Organization and the Hungarian Revolution."

110. British Embassy, Paris, to the Foreign Office, No. 392, 27 October 1956, PRO FO 371 122063 NH 1012/26. No archival sources have confirmed this British information so far.

111. Minutes by Sir John Ward, 27 October 1956, PRO FO 371 122379 NH 10110/221.

112. Foreign Office minutes, 1 November 1956, PRO FO 371 122808 NS 1051/96.

113. The most important publications on the Suez crisis based on declassified archival sources are Lamb, *Failure of the Eden Government*; Louis and Owen, *Suez 1956*; Kyle, *Suez*; Troen and Shemesh, *Suez–Sinai Crisis 1956*; Bar-on, *Etgar Ve'tigra*. The 22 October date is mentioned in the contemporary diary of the Israeli prime minister in Troen and Shemesh, *Suez-Sinai Crisis 1956*, 308.

114. Molnár, *Budapest 1956*, 203.

115. "Diary of Ben Gurion," 315. On the Hungarian and the Middle East crises, see Kecskés, "Suez Crisis and the 1956 Hungarian Revolution."

116. Memorandum of a telephone conversation between the President in New York and the Secretary of State in Washington, 25 October 1956. *FRUS*, 25:290–91.

117. Foreign Office minutes, 26 October 1956, PRO FO 371 122378 NH 10110/188, DDF 1956 Tome III, 19.

118. On British policy toward the Hungarian crisis, see Békés, "A brit kormány és az 1956-os magyar forradalom." On French policy toward the Hungarian Revolution, see Kecskés, "French Foreign Policy and the 1956 Hungarian Revolution."

119. For the story of the secret talks of the three Western great powers on the Hungarian situation, see Békés, "A brit kormány és az 1956-os magyar forradalom"; Békés, "A magyar kérdés az ENSZ-ben és a nyugati nagyhatalmak titkos tárgyalásai."

120. UN General Assembly, Official Records, First and Second Emergency Special Sessions, 1–10 November 1956, Plenary Meetings and Annexes, New York, 1956, Minutes of the plenary meeting on November 4, 1956, A/3286.

121. Minutes of discussion between Harold E. Stassen and John Foster Dulles, 26 October 1956, Eisenhower Library, Dulles Papers, General Memoranda of Conversations Series in *FRUS*, 25:305.

122. Békés, *Európából Európába*, 236; Dobrynin, *In confidence*, 189–95.

123. Gati, *Failed Illusions*, 206.

Chapter 5

1. On the developments in East–West relations in this period, see Trachtenberg, *Constructed Peace*; Loth, *Overcoming the Cold War*.

2. UN General Assembly, "Report of the Special Committee on the Problem of Hungary."

3. The mandate of the Hungarian UN delegation was suspended in November 1956, but Hungary's expulsion from the UN was never seriously considered. The treatment of

the Hungarian issue in the UN is thoroughly analyzed in Radványi, *Hungary and the Superpowers*; Borhi, *Dealing with Dictators*.

4. On the Hungarian issue in the United Nations, see Nagy, *A Bang-Jensen ügy*; Lidegaard, *A legmagasabb ár*.

5. Békés, "1956 Hungarian Revolution and World Politics."

6. Report by János Kádár at the session of the HSWP Central Committee on 1 November 1957, MNL-OL, M-KS-288 f. 4/13. ő. e.

7. Instead of the commonly used terms "restoration" and "consolidation"—with opposite political bias—for describing the reconstruction period following 1956, in recent scholarship Melinda Kalmár introduced a term much more appropriate for an academic analysis: *rehabilitation* (szanálás). See Kalmár, *Ennivaló és hozomány*, 277–81.

8. After the second Soviet invasion, some 190,000 people emigrated to the West. The communist reprisals and terror led to 13,000 people being interned and over 20,000 imprisoned. The number of those sentenced to death because of their participation in the revolution was incredibly high: altogether, 230 people were executed, including Prime Minister Imre Nagy and several of his closest associates. On the reprisals following the 1956 Hungarian Revolution, see Szakolczai, "A forradalmat követő megtorlás során kivégzettekről."

9. Marchio, *Rhetoric and Reality*, 417–18.

10. For the presentation of the changes in the Eisenhower administration's policy toward East Central Europe, see Marchio, chapter 9.

11. This new policy was explicitly recognized in NSC 5811 (Policy toward the Soviet-dominated nations in Eastern Europe), adopted on 9 May 1958. Published in Békés, Byrne, and Rainer, *1956 Hungarian Revolution*, 543–51. On U.S. policy toward East Central Europe, see Kovrig, *Of Walls and Bridges*; Borhi, *Dealing with Dictators*.

12. For the story of the Hungarian–American secret talks, see Radványi, *Hungary and the Superpowers*. From March 1962, Kádár was chargé d'affaires of the Hungarian legation in Washington and was personally involved in the negotiations. See also Borhi, *Dealing with Dictators*, 168–83.

13. Békés, Byrne, and Rainer, *1956 Hungarian Revolution*, 300–302. See discussion in chapter 3 on the transformation of Soviet–East European relations.

14. Békés, Byrne, Rainer, *1956 Hungarian Revolution*, 114–15.

15. According to Khrushchev's original plan, Soviet troops would have been withdrawn from both Romania and Hungary. See chapter 6.

16. For the history of repercussions in the Soviet bloc, see Rainer,and Somlai, *1956 Hungarian Revolution and the Soviet Bloc*.

17. For the findings of recent research on the reprisals in Romania following the Hungarian Revolution, see Bottoni, "Kényszerből stratégia." For a recent collection of documents on Romania, see Sinitar, "Echoes of the 1956 Hungarian Revolt in Romania."

18. On Czechoslovakia, see Janek, "Csehszlovákia."

19. Békés, *Az 1956-os magyar forradalom a világpolitikában*, 94.

20. Némethné and Sipos, *A Magyar Szocialista Munkáspárt ideiglenes vezető testületeinek jegyzőkönyvei*.

21. Eleven committees were set up with fifteen to thirty members as well as two coordinating supercommittees, one for industrial organization and one for economics. One of them was headed by György Péter, the other one by István Varga and István Antos. Berend, *Gazdasági útkeresés. 1956–1965*, 33–62.

22. Speech by János Kádár at the 28 December 1956 meeting of the HSWP Central Committee, in Némethné and Sipos, *A Magyar Szocialista Munkáspárt ideiglenes vezető testületeinek jegyzőkönyvei*, 282–83.

23. Némethné and Sipos, *A Magyar Szocialista Munkáspárt ideiglenes vezető testületeinek jegyzőkönyvei*, 282–83. Currently known documents on the preparation and organization of the Budapest summit, which reveal more on the planned multiparty coalition than do the contemporary records of the HSWP, are published in Békés, Byrne, and Rainer, *1956 Hungarian Revolution*, 485–95. The Soviet documents were made available for the editors by Vyacheslav Sereda, the Czechoslovak documents by Tibor Hajdú, and the Romanian documents by Mihail Retegan.

24. Szereda and Sztikalin, *Hiányzó lapok 1956 történetéből*, 184–87.

25. The way this information reached its target was remarkable. State minister György Marosán, the strong man of the Kádár cabinet, spent the Christmas holidays at his relatives in Transylvania, Romania. Georghiu-Dej, the leader of the Romanian party, joined by other leaders, made an unexpected visit (at Christmastime!) to tell Marosán in person that Szántó would soon be sent home. (The Romanian party leader also told Marosán that he wanted to host György Lukács and his wife, who had also been deported to Romania in November 1956, for a dinner on New Year's Eve.) Békés, Byrne, and Rainer, *1956 Hungarian Revolution*, 485.

26. Although Szántó served as minister of state in the cabinet formed on 3 November, Moscow did not regard this fact on its own as a reason for exclusion. Between 1 and 4 November, even Imre Nagy was an option for a second-ranking leader if he were willing to resign and support the new government.

27. Békés, Byrne, and Rainer, *1956 Hungarian Revolution*, 485–86.

28. This clause of the draft, if it had ever been completed, has not been found to date. It is only known from Kádár's speech delivered at the 28 December 1956 meeting of the Interim Central Committee of the HSWP, as well as from some Romanian and Czechoslovak document fragments cited previously. Kádár said the following about this: "One chapter of the text, the last one is missing. I should have done it yesterday, but I didn't have the time. What would the last chapter include? It would be about the parties and we would say in it that we want to work together with those parties that are ready to work with the HSWP in a bloc. This is the essence of the issue. By a bloc I mean acting together with the party in the elections and on other occasions rather than separately. This chapter would also talk about national cooperation and the like, according to the plan." Némethné and Sipos, *A Magyar Szocialista Munkáspárt ideiglenes vezető testületeinek jegyzőkönyvei*, 282–83.

29. Békés, Byrne, and Rainer, *1956 Hungarian Revolution*, 487.

30. Békés, Byrne, and Rainer, *1956 Hungarian Revolution*, 487.

31. Strangely enough (or perhaps not), no record or note on this crucial meeting has ever been found in the Hungarian or the Russian archives. However, there is a Czechoslovak memorandum as well as an abridged note made in 1960 available for researchers, which is based on a more detailed contemporary Romanian document. However fragmentary they may be, these documents make it possible for us to reconstruct most of the issues discussed at the summit meeting.

32. Némethné and Sipos, *A Magyar Szocialista Munkáspárt ideiglenes vezető testületeinek jegyzőkönyvei*, 298.

33. Baráth, *Kádár János első kormányának jegyzőkönyvei*, 146. Although the government made a decision at its 28 December 1956 meeting about "an extraordinary meeting to be held on a date to be announced later, which will discuss the government program," this meeting was never held. The next meeting of the government was on 18 January 1957. Baráth, *Kádár János első kormányának jegyzőkönyvei*, 146–47.

34. *Népszabadság*, 7 January 1957.

35. On the Imre Nagy case, see Litván, "A Nagy Imre-per politika háttere"; Rainer, *Nagy Imre 1953–1958*.

36. Statement of the Revolutionary Workers' and Peasants' Party on the most important tasks, *Népszabadság*, 6 January 1957.

37. Békés, Byrne, and Rainer, *1956 Hungarian Revolution*, 491.

38. Kalmár, *Történelmi galaxisok vonzásában*, 179.

39. For the integration levels, see Kalmár, *Történelmi galaxisok vonzásában*, 224, 326, 345.

40. *Népszabadság*, 7 January 1957.

Chapter 6

1. On Soviet troop reductions in this period, see Evangelista, *"Why Keep Such an Army?"*

2. Moscow's response was negative in both cases.

3. The statement of the WP members about the creation of a joint command for the WP military forces made a vague reference to positioning the Soviet troops on the territory of the member countries: "The deployment of the joint armed forces on the territory of the contracting states will occur by agreement between those states and according to the needs of mutual defense." "Agreement on the Creation of a Unified Command of the Armed Forces of the Member States of the Treaty on Friendship, Cooperation, and Mutual Assistance, 14 May 1955," PHP website, Party leaders. www.php.isn.ethz.ch/kms2.isn.ethz.ch /serviceengine/Files/PHP/17542/ipublicationdocument_singledocument/bea8e1d7-b93e-46be -bba7-c843a015628e/de/Agreement550514.pdf.

4. On the integration of the Hungarian army into the Warsaw Pact, see Okváth, "Initial Phase of Hungary's Integration." On the development of the Hungarian military industry, see Germuska, *Unified Military Industries of the Soviet Bloc*.

5. Even though they never negotiated this question in public, the issue of the Soviet troops' withdrawal appeared from time to time in public opinion, beginning as early as 1959. See Esterházy, *Javított kiadás*, 89. On the plan, see Sipos, "Miért ragaszkodott Kádár a szovjet csapatokhoz?"; Rainer, "Hruscsov Budapesten, 1958. április"; Békés and Kalmár, "Hruscsov és Kádár."

6. Munteanu, *Romania and the Warsaw Pact*, vol. 1, doc. 6.

7. Zubok, "Khrushchev–Mao Conversations."

8. For the report of János Kádár about the meeting of the WP PCC, see Soós, *A Magyar Szocialista Munkáspárt Központi Bizottságának 1957–1958*, 336–41. For the visit of the Soviet delegation, see Rainer, "Hruscsov Budapesten, 1958. április."

9. Mastny, "Third Meeting of the PCC." At the 12 February 1960 meeting of the HSWP CC, Kádár interpreted this initiative as Khrushchev having claimed that the "occupying army's role is decreased, not increased, decreased" in Hungary and Poland.

10. In his report on the 10 June 1961 HSWP CC meeting, Kádár said that there had been a year (1957) when Hungary devoted only 2.7 percent of its national income to defense ex-

penditures. This "intolerable" situation will now change, he said, and in 1961 7.7 percent, and during the second five-year plan an annual 9–10 percent share will be for defense. MNL–OL, M-KS-288. f/4./41. ő. e.

11. Soós, *A Magyar Szocialista Munkáspárt Központi Bizottságának 1957–1958*, 338.

12. For the documents of the meeting of the WP PCC in May 1958, see PHP website, www.isn.ethz.ch/php. For the report of Kádár about the meeting of the WP PCC, see Soós, *A Magyar Szocialista Munkáspárt Központi Bizottságának 1957–1958*, 336–41.

13. Békés, "Magyar–szovjet csúcstalálkozók, 1957–1965," doc 1.

14. Békés, "Magyar–szovjet csúcstalálkozók, 1957–1965," doc. 1.

15. Békés, "Magyar–szovjet csúcstalálkozók, 1957–1965," doc. 1.

16. Between 1949 and August 1961, some three million East Germans fled to the West.

17. Report on the 5 May 1959 HSWP PC meeting, and Deputy foreign minister János Péter's report on the conference of the WP Foreign Ministers held in Warsaw on 28–29 April 1959, both in MNL–OL, M-KS-288. f. 5/129. ő. e.

18. Loth, *Overcoming the Cold War*, 61.

19. Fischer, *A kétpólusú világ, 1945–1989*, 207.

20. For a fascinating conversation between Ulbricht and Khrushchev just before the erection of the wall, see "Notes on the Conversation of Comrade N. S. Khrushchev."

21. On 8 July 1961, the Soviet Union announced that due to the international crisis that had developed because of the German issue and the status of Berlin, it would cease the previously decided reduction in military forces and increase the defense budget by 25 percent. On the Hungarian situation, see Germuska, "A magyar hadiipar a hatvanas évek elején."

22. János Kádár's report about the meeting of HSWP CC on 10 June 1961, MNL–OL, M-KS-288. f/4./41. ő. e.

23. On the Berlin crisis, see M. Zubok, *Khrushchev and the Berlin Crisis*; Zubok and Pleshakov, *Inside the Kremlin's Cold War*, 236–58; Loth, *Overcoming the Cold War*, 57–67; Harrison, *Driving the Soviets up the Wall*.

24. Loth, *Overcoming the Cold War*, 63.

25. Catudal, *Kennedy and the Berlin Wall Crisis*, 38. Quoted in Symser, *Kennedy and the Berlin Wall*, 106.

26. Loth, *Overcoming the Cold War*, 61.

27. Loth, *Overcoming the Cold War*, 63.

28. Harrison, *Driving the Soviets up the Wall*; Zubok, *Khrushchev and the Berlin Crisis*. János Kádár's report about the meeting of the HSWP CC on 10 August 1961, MNL–OL, M-KS-288. f. 4/42. ő. e.

29. Zubok, *Khrushchev and the Berlin Crisis*, 24. On the Berlin crisis, see the website of the PHP, www.isn.ethz.ch/php.

30. János Kádár's report about the meeting of the HSWP CC on 10 August 1961, MNL–OL, M-KS-288. f. 4/42. ő. e. The details were worked out at the meeting of the WP ministers of defense on 8–9 September 1961 in Warsaw, MNL–OL, M-KS-288. f. 11/914. ő. e. See also Germuska, "A magyar hadiipar a hatvanas évek elején." For the text of the Joint Declaration of the Warsaw Treaty States on the Berlin Wall on 13 August 1961, see Mastny and Byrne, *Cardboard Castle?*, 126–28.

31. Summary of Minister of Defense Lajos Czinege on the meeting of WP Defense Ministers in Warsaw on 3–6 September 1961, MNL–OL M-KS-288. f. 11/914. ő. e.

32. János Kádár's report at the meeting of the HSWP CC on 10 August 1961, MNL–OL, M-KS-288. f. 4/42. ő. e.

33. János Kádár's report at the meeting of the HSWP CC on 10 August 1961, MNL–OL, M-KS-288. f. 4/42. ő. e.

34. János Kádár's report at the meeting of the HSWP CC on 10 June 1961, MNL–OL, M-KS-288. f/4./41. ő. e.

35. Report of Minister of Defense Lajos Czinege on the consultations held at the headquarters of the (WP) Unified Armed Forces to the HSWP PC, 6 September 1962, MNL–OL, M-KS-288. f. 5/278. ő. e.

36. Account by János Kádár at the meeting of the HSWP CC on 10 August 1961, MNL–OL, M-KS-288. f. 4/42.

37. Account by János Kádár at the meeting of the HSWP CC on 10 June 1961, MNL–OL, M-KS-288. f 4/41. ő. e. In reality, this never happened, but the Soviet military units stationed in Hungary were supplied with nuclear missiles from the late 1960s.

38. Account by János Kádár at the meeting of the HSWP CC on 10 August 1961, MNL–OL, M-KS-288. f 4/42.

39. Account by János Kádár at the meeting of the HSWP CC on 10 June 1961, MNL–OL, M-KS-288. f 4/41. ő. e.

40. Békés, "Warsaw Pact, the German Question and the Making of the CSCE Process," 113–14.

41. For a survey of Hungarian–FRG relations, see Kiss, "Az első államközi megállapodástól a diplomáciai kapcsolatok felvételéig."

42. For a detailed study on the author's novel concept of détente, see chapter 3.

43. On the talks between the FRG and Hungary in the early 1960s, see Ruff, "A magyar–NSZK kapcsolatok 1960–1963. See also Kiss, "Az első államközi megállapodástól a diplomáciai kapcsolatok felvételéig."

44. Since for this move, the formal approval of NATO was needed, it did not happen until April 1963. Among the U.S. administration, only the president's brother, Robert Kennedy, and Secretary of State Dean Rusk knew about this secret Soviet–American deal. Fursenko and Naftali, "One Hell of a Gamble," 281–83.

45. Telegram from Soviet ambassador to the U.S. Dobrynin to the USSR Foreign Ministry, 30 October 1962, CWIHP Digital Archive, https://digitalarchive.wilsoncenter.org /document/112633.

46. Contrary to public belief, initially it was not a telephone connection but a duplex wire telegraph system, which was changed to a telephone line in 1971.

47. See Békés, "Titkos válságkezeléstől a politikai koordinációig," 26–30.

48. See Mikoyan and Savranskaya, Soviet Cuban Missile Crisis.

49. The alert was ended on 22 November 1962. After the Cuban crisis, the tendency that began in the spring of 1961 continued; therefore, the defense expenditure was further increased. In the Ministry of Defense's 1962 proposal, the number of soldiers was projected to be 85,000 by 1964, and between 92,000 and 95,000 by 1970. The process was sped up, however, and by August 1963, the real headcount was already 106,400, and for 1970, the planned number was 120,000–122,000. Report of Lajos Fehér to the Political Committee on 30 August 1963, MNL–OL, M-KS-288. f. 5/312. ő. e.

50. Report from the Session of the HSWP PC on 23 October 1962, MNL–OL, M-KS-288. f. 5./280. ő. e.

51. The news was published in the HSWP's daily, *Népszabadság*, on 24 October 1962.

52. Minutes of the meeting of the Council of Ministers, 25 October 1962, MNL–OL, XIX-A-83-a-245/1962 ő. e.

53. No written records have been found on Grechko informing the Hungarians about the situation concerning the crisis at that stage; only a vague reference is available about his "oral instruction," obviously by telephone (see Békés and Kalmár, "Hungary and the Cuban Missile Crisis," 429). It is also possible that Moscow's ambassador in Budapest provided some information to the Hungarian leaders, since according to the minutes of the CPSU presidium meeting discussing the Cuban situation on 22 October, "the Ministry of Foreign Affairs should inform Ambassadors representing the countries in the Warsaw Treaty." Fursenko, *Prezidium TsK KPSS 1954–1964*. Nevertheless, no record of such information has yet been found in the Hungarian archives.

54. For a collection of documents on the reaction of the Hungarian leadership to the crisis, see Békés and Kalmár, "Hungary and the Cuban Missile Crisis."

55. Minutes of the HSWP PC, 2 November 1962, MNL–OL, M-KS-288. f. 5/281. ő. e.; Minutes of the HSWP Secretariat, 2 November 1962, MNL–OL, M-KS-288. f. 7/146. ő. e.

56. *Népszabadság*, 26 October 1962.

57. Speech of János Kádár at the party conference in Budapest, 31 October 1962, MNL–OL, M-KS-288. f. 11/1048. ő. e.

58. Information report about the reactions to the American provocation against Cuba, 24 October 1962, MNL–OL, M-KS-288. f. 11/1038. ő. e.; Note about the reactions to the American provocation against Cuba, 26 October 1962, MNL–OL, M-KS-288. f. 11/1041. ő. e.

59. Report from the special closed session of the HSWP PC on 5 November 1962, MNL–OL, M-KS-288. f. 5/281/1. ő. e.

60. For the minutes of a meeting of Novotny and Khrushchev, see "We Were Truly on the Verge of War."

61. Greville Maynard Wynne (1919–90) published his memoirs quite soon after his release. See Wynne, *The Man from Moscow*.

62. János Kádár's account at the session of the HSWP CC on 12 November 1962, MNL–OL, M-KS-288. f. 4/60. ő. e.

63. On the reaction of the Soviet bloc states and Yugoslavia to the crisis, see the essays and document publications by James G. Hershberg, Oldřich Tůma, Csaba Békés and Melinda Kalmár, Petre Opriş, Jordan Baev, Svetozar Rajak, and Mark Kramer in the *CWIHP Bulletin*, no. 17–18, 349–621.

64. Garthoff, "When and Why Romania Distanced Itself from the Warsaw Pact," 111.

65. Minutes of the HSWP PC session on 26 November 1963, MNL–OL, M-KS-288. f. 5/320. ő. e.

66. On Poland, see Jarzabek, *Hope and Reality*; Selvage, "Warsaw Pact and the German Question."

67. Transcript of Ceauşescu-Deng conversation, 26 July 1965, in Deletant, Ionescu, and Locher, *Romania and the Warsaw Pact*.

68. The Hungarian leadership first proposed the establishment of the Committee of Foreign Ministers as early as 1958, but the Soviets did not even reply to the suggestion at the time. (See Baráth, "Magyarország a szovjet diplomáciai iratokban," 79.) The forming of this body was originally decided on at the first meeting of the WP PCC in January

1956 in Prague, but no action followed that decision. As is known, it was eventually established in 1976.

69. Account by János Kádár on the visit of a party and government delegation to the Soviet Union, Minutes of the HSWP PC session on 31 July 1963, MNL–OL, M-KS-288. f. 5/309. ő. e.

70. See the introduction by Békés in Békés, Locher, and Nuenlist, *Records of the Meetings of the Warsaw Pact Deputy Foreign Ministers*.

71. For the English translation of the WP deputy foreign ministers' documents, see Békés, Locher, and Nuenlist, *Records of the Meetings of the Warsaw Pact Deputy Foreign Ministers*. The summary of the Polish record on the meeting is published in Mastny and Byrne, *Cardboard Castle?*, 212–14.

72. A fine example of this pragmatic Soviet opinion is Khrushchev's announcement at the meeting of the CPSU presidium on 31 October 1956, hastening an armed intervention in Hungary: "If we depart from Hungary, it will give a great boost to the Americans, English and French—the imperialists. They will perceive it as weaknesses on our part and will go onto the offensive. . . . To Egypt they will then add Hungary." Namely, the possibility of backing president Nasser was not even considered; the Soviet leaders gave up on Egypt at the very moment of the Israeli–British–French attack. See Kramer, "The 'Malin Notes,'" 393.

73. Communist China started to shell the offshore islands of Quemou and Matsou, occupied by the Chinese Nationalist government in Taiwan, in 1954. Although it never became clear what the real motives of the Beijing leadership were (as eventually they did not invade the islands), these attempts potentially posed a continuous danger of "hot war" between the two military alliances in the mid- and late 1950s because of a U.S. security guarantee defending the territorial integrity of Taiwan. The historical importance of this crisis, however, has been generally and unduly underestimated in public memory both in the East and the West. For a recent account on this crisis, see Jian, *Mao's China and the Cold War*, 163–204. For the fascinating minutes of conversations between Mao and Khrushchev discussing this issue in 1958 and 1959, see Zubok, "The Khrushchev–Mao Conversations."

74. For the latest research on the Cuban crisis, see *CWIHP Bulletin*, nos. 1 (Spring 1992), 3 (Fall 1993), 5 (Spring 1995), and especially 17–18 (Fall 2012) published at the 50th anniversary, presenting some five hundred documents. See also *Cuban Missile Crisis, 1962*.

75. Kádár's letter to Khrushchev, June 21, 1961. MNL–OL, M-KS-288. f. 47. cs. 731. ő. e.

76. Békés, "Magyar–szovjet csúcstalálkozók, 1957–1965." Rákosi was in exile in the Soviet Unon from July 1956 until his death in 1971. See Feitl, *A bukott Rákosi*.

77. Baráth, "Kis októberi forradalom," 209–12.

78. Békés, "Magyar–szovjet csúcstalálkozók, 1957–1965.

79. Békés, "Magyar–szovjet csúcstalálkozók, 1957–1965," doc. 5.

80. Békés, "Magyar–szovjet csúcstalálkozók," doc 5. "Young" by Soviet standards meant that Brezhnev was fifty-eight and Kosygin was sixty in 1964.

81. Békés, "Magyar–szovjet csúcstalálkozók," doc. 4.

82. The Hungarian memorandum was a letter formally addressed to Brezhnev and signed by Kádár as the head of the delegation. The text of the minutes of the Soviet–Hungarian talks on 10 November 1964 is published in Békés, "Magyar–szovjet csúcstalálkozók, 1957–1965," doc. 5. Anastas Ivanovich Mikoyan was a Soviet politician, the government's deputy chair and then first deputy chair from 1937 to 1964, member of the

PC from 1935 to 1966; Mikhail Andreyevich Suslov was a Soviet politician, secretary of the CPSU CC from 1949, member of the presidium and the party's main ideologist from 1955; Yuri Vladimirovich Andropov was a Soviet diplomat, politician, Soviet ambassador to Hungary from 1954 to 1957, later head of the CPSU CC department that dealt with the parties of the Socialist countries, secretary of the CC from 1962 to 1967, head of the KGB from 1967, and general-secretary of the CPSU from 1982 to 1984; Boris Nikolayevich Ponomarev was a Soviet politician, member of the CC from 1956 to 1986, secretary of the CC from 1961.

83. On Soviet–Hungarian relations in this era, see Földes, "Kötélhúzás felsőfokon."

84. Antonin Novotny, a Czechoslovak politician, was first secretary of the CPCz from 1953 to 1968. According to a HSWP report, the leaders of the Soviet bloc parties had similar observations regarding the mode of Khrushchev's dismissal. Békés, "Magyar–szovjet csúcstalálkozók, 1957–1965," doc. 5.

85. This concession did not last long, as Khrushchev was soon ousted from the Central Committee as well.

86. See the recurring line in the famous song by Sting, "Russians": "I hope the Russians love their children too."

87. Békés, "Magyar–szovjet csúcstalálkozók, 1957–1965," doc. 5.

88. This claim was presented even more openly during the talks of Béla Biszku and Dezső Nemes with Suslov and Kirilenko, Ponomarev, and Tolkunov on 20 October in Moscow. The two HSWP Politburo members were sent there to acquire firsthand information on Khrushchev's dismissal on the spot. At the talks, a rather defensive Suslov admitted that responsibility by saying, "All this led to the adoption of the resolutions becoming formal. For this the collective is responsible too. For this, we are responsible too." Baráth, "Kis októberi forradalom."

89. Winston Churchill was a British Conservative Party politician, serving as prime minister in 1940–45 and in 1951–55. He resigned from his post in April 1955.

90. Biszku used an illuminating example of another kind of extreme case at their meeting with Suslov: he argued that in Hungary, if a factory doorman retired, he was offered a nice farewell party and was invited to visit the factory in the future as well, and he would be received kindly. Baráth, "Kis októberi forradalom."

91. Kádár was likely referring to the fact that during the course of the meetings, the Soviet leaders stated that they considered Rákosi to be dead politically but, as a criticism, added that the dead cannot be reburied over and over again, meaning that they found the constant mention of Rákosi's mistakes and crimes too much. For more on Rákosi's emigration after 1956, see Feitl, *A bukott Rákosi.*

92. By 1964, preparations for the "great meeting" of the Communist and workers' parties, like the one in Moscow from November to December 1960, had been going on for years. According to the original plan, the representatives of the participating countries should have met at the preliminary discussions in Moscow on 15 December 1964; however, the Soviets finally postponed the preliminary meeting, a move Kádár strongly supported. The "great" conference was eventually held in June 1969 in Moscow.

93. Kádár learned in Moscow that Gomułka had also told the Soviet leaders that "they have to confer with the Chinese, because it does, after all, concern a nation of 650 million people, and the Chinese leaders will surely have different opinions on certain issues in 10 years."

94. Békés, "Magyar–szovjet csúcstalálkozók, 1957–1965," doc. 5.

95. János Kádár's account at the session of the HSWP PC, 17 November, 1964. MNL–OL, M-KS-288. f. 5. cs. 351. ő. e.

96. Békés, "Magyar–szovjet csúcstalálkozók, 1957–1965," 173.

Chapter 7

1. On Romania, see Tismaneanu, *Stalinism for All Seasons*; Deletant, "New Evidence on Romania and the Warsaw Pact."

2. On the GDR, see Harrison, *Driving the Soviets Up the Wall*; Sarotte, *Dealing with the Devil*; Bange, "Onto the Slippery Slope."

3. The thesis that Kádár's dual policy of stick and carrot started right after the revolution and not in the early 1960s as historians previously thought was introduced by Kalmár, *Ennivaló és hozomány*.

4. While the study of Hungarian foreign policy after 1956 based on archival research began at the time of the political transition in 1989, the first comprehensive monograph on the topic was published only in 2015. See Földes, *Kádár János külpolitikája*. For the present author's recent synthesis, see Békés, *Enyhülés és emancipáció*. Another volume focuses on Hungary's conflicts in the postwar era: Békés, *Európából Európába*. For a few existing monographs on Hungary's bilateral relations (e.g., with the United States and France) as well as for documents on Hungarian foreign policy, see the bibliography. There are also a great number of journal articles and book chapters on the topic; the relevant publications are referred to in the endnotes of this book.

5. For an edited volume on the development of world Communism in this period, see Naimark, Pons, and Quinn-Judge, *Cambridge History of Communism*.

6. At the session of the Political Committee on 28 June 1966, János Kádár almost word for word formulated this principle thusly: "We must say: the cooperation of the countries allied in the Comecon . . . and if we must, we shall say two principles, namely mutual advantage and mutual assistance. Or we can say the adequate development of national interests, but then we must write there that and the universal progress of the socialist world order too. But let us remain with mutual advantage and mutual assistance."

7. Albania had not taken part in the work of the Warsaw Pact since 1961 and left the organization in September 1968.

8. Kalmár, *Ennivaló és hozomány*.

9. Kalmár, *Ennivaló és hozomány*.

10. On the Khrushchev–Kádár relationship, see Békés, "Magyar–szovjet csúcstalálkozók, 1957–1965." On Soviet–Hungarian diplomatic relations in this era, see Baráth, "Magyarország a szovjet diplomáciai iratokban, 1957–1964"; Baráth, *Szovjet Diplomáciai Jelentések Magyarországról a Hruscsov-Korszakban*.

11. Hungary as a Khrushchevian model state was first described by Hungarian historian Ferenc Fehér in "A hruscsovista mintaállam."

12. On Soviet–Hungarian relations in this period, see Földes, *Kádár János külpolitikája és nemzetközi tárgyalásai*, 1:36–65.

13. Memorandum from the President's Special Assistant for National Security (Bundy) to President Johnson, 14 April 1964, in *FRUS*, 17:301.

14. On the secret U.S.–Hungarian talks, see Radványi, *Hungary and the Superpowers*; Borhi, *Iratok a magyar–amerikai kapcsolatok történetéhez. 1957–1967*; Borhi: *Dealing with Dictators*, 168–83.

15. Memorandum from the President's Special Assistant for National Security (Bundy) to President Johnson, 14 April 1964, in *FRUS*, 17:301.

16. *A szocializmus útján*, 603–30.

17. Cardinal József Mindszenty, Archbishop of Esztergom, found asylum in the building of the U.S. legation in Budapest on 4 November 1956 at the time of the second Soviet intervention.

18. On Hungarian–Vatican relations and the Mindszenty case, see Ólmosi, *Mindszenty és a hatalom*; Gyarmati, "A Mindszenty–ügy 'diplomáciai' rendezésének kudarca."

19. Note of Regional Department 5 of the Ministry of Foreign Affairs on Hungarian–German relations, 18 March 1967, MNL–OL, XIX-J-1-j, 70. doboz.

20. Bencsik, Nagy, *A magyar úti okmányok története*.

21. On Hungarian–American relations, see Magyarics, "Az Egyesült Államok és Magyarország, 1957–1967"; Borhi, *Magyar–amerikai kapcsolatok, 1945–1989*; Borhi, *Dealing with Dictators*.

22. For the first use of this novel concept, see Békés, "Hungarian Foreign Policy in the Soviet Alliance System."

23. For an archive-based study on Hungary's foreign policy, see Békés, "Hungarian Foreign Policy in the Soviet Alliance System."

24. For the GDR, the Western relationship meant, above all, their unique and highly controversial relationship with the FRG.

25. Minutes of the session of the HSWP PC, 26 January 1965, MNL–OL, M-KS. 288. f. 5/237. ő. e.

26. On this concept, introduced by this author, see Békés, "Hungarian Foreign Policy in the Soviet Alliance System," 89.

27. While no synthesis on such foreign policy lobby activity by the non-Soviet WP members has emerged so far, a number of important works have been published since the mid-1990s in the field of economic cooperation within the Comecon and between the Soviet bloc countries and the West. These publications provide convincing evidence on how from the 1960s on, Moscow's omnipotence was considerably challenged and restricted by the WP member states' constant lobbying for their own specific economic interests. See Stone, *Satellites and Commissars*; Poznanski, *Poland's Protracted Transition*; Godard, "Shaping the Eastern Bloc through the Economy"; Steiner, *Plans That Failed*; Kansikas, *Socialist Countries Face the European Community*; Pula, *Globalization under and after Socialism*.

28. The importance of the Western relations has been raised by economic historians, whereas this is still neglected by most scholars dealing with political history. See, for example, Csaba, "Változó erőtérben—változó egyensúlyozás." Csaba goes as far as claiming that by the 1980s, Hungary's dependency on the West was stronger than the Soviet bind. For a recent archive-based monograph on the functioning and the transformation of the Soviet system in Hungary, see Kalmár, *Történelmi galaxisok vonzásában*.

29. Perhaps the best-known example is the Soviet passenger car LADA (or Zhiguli), which was manufactured on the basis of a license of the FIAT 124 and soon became a favorite in

Hungary, too. Buyers, however, had to wait for five to six years after they had paid half of the price of the car until they could actually drive it.

30. This lobby contest will be demonstrated in detail in chapter 8 through the presentation and analysis of the Soviet bloc's internal debates preceding the conclusion of the Helsinki Final Act in 1975.

31. Békés, "Warsaw Pact, the German Question," 113–14. On the emerging conflict and occasional clash between the two sub-blocs, see chapter 8.

32. On Hungarian–Romanian relations, see Földes, *Magyarország, Románia és a nemzeti kérdés.*

33. Kádár Béla, "Magyarország gazdasági kapcsolatai az NDK-val és az NSZK-val."

34. For the history of the establishment of the Warsaw Pact, see Mastny, "Soviet Union and the Origins of the Warsaw Pact." See also Békés, "Titkos válságkezeléstől a politikai koordinációig"; Baev, "Organizational and Doctrinal Evolution of the Warsaw Pact."

35. On Khrushchev, see Taubman, *Khrushchev.*

36. An extensive multi-archival collection of the Warsaw Pact's records is available on the Parallel History Project on Cooperative Security website: www.php.isn.ethz.ch.

37. For a chronology of the Soviet bloc's multilateral meetings (1947–91), visit the website of the Cold War History Research Center, Budapest, www.coldwar.hu.

38. On early reform plans of the Warsaw Pact, see Mastny, "Warsaw Pact as History."

39. Nikita Khrushchev's letter to János Kádár, 2 January 1964, MNL–OL, M-KS-288. f. 5/325. ő. e.

40. For an English language collection of the meetings of the WP deputy foreign ministers, see Békés, Locher, and Nuenlist, *Records of the Warsaw Pact Deputy Foreign Ministers.*

41. Mastny, "The Warsaw Pact as History," 6.

42. For a multi-archival collection of the records of the WP PCC sessions, with introductions by Vojtech Mastny, see the PHP website: Party leaders, www.php.isn.ethz.ch. For the Hungarian record on the meeting, see Account by János Kádár at the HSWP PC session on 26 January 1965, MNL–OL, M-KS-288. f 5/357. ő. e.

43. Report of Lajos Czinege to the HSWP PC, 6 November 1964, MNL–OL, M-KS-288. f. 5/388. ő. e.

44. Minutes of the HSWP PC session on 27 April 1965, MNL–OL, M-KS-288. f. 5/364. ő. e.

45. Proposal by Lajos Czinege for the HSWP PC on the Hungarian position concerning the development of the Supreme Command to be represented at the meeting in Bucharest, 18 June 1966, MNL–OL, M-KS-288. f. 5/398. ő. e.

46. Report on the meeting of the Warsaw Pact deputy foreign ministers and ministers of defense in Berlin and Moscow, respectively, 22 February 1966, MNL–OL, M-KS-288. f. 5/388. ő. e.

47. Report by János Péter for the HSWP PC on the meeting of the Warsaw Pact foreign ministers held from 6–17 June in Moscow, 20 June 1966, MNL–OL, M-KS-288. f. 5/398. ő. e. On the reform plans within the Warsaw Pact, see Crump, *Warsaw Pact Reconsidered,* 133–69.

48. Minutes of the HSWP PC session on 21 June 1966, MNL–OL, M-KS-288. f. 5/398. ő. e.

49. Locher, *Records of the Warsaw Pact Committee of the Ministers of Foreign Affairs.* For the records of the Committee of Foreign Ministers and the Committee of Defense Ministers, see the PHP website.

50. Békés, "Magyar–szovjet csúcstalálkozók, 1957–1965," doc. 6.

51. Békés, *Európából Európába*, 249–51. On Soviet policy, see Gaiduk, *Soviet Union and the Vietnam War*. On the Chinese role see Zhai, *Beijing and the Vietnam Peace Talks*. See also Hershberg, "Peace Probes and the Bombing Pause." For a study relying on recently released Vietnamese sources, see Asselin, *Vietnam's American War*.

52. Békés, "Magyar–szovjet csúcstalálkozók, 1957–1965," doc. 6.

53. Memorandum on the visit of HSWP PC members János Kádár, Antal Apró, and Béla Biszku in Moscow on 23–29 May 1965, MNL–OL, M-KS-288. f. 5. cs. 367. ő. e.

54. Memorandum on the visit of HSWP PC members János Kádár, Antal Apró, and Béla Biszku in Moscow on 23–29 May 1965, MNL–OL, M-KS-288. f. 5. cs. 367. ő. e.

55. Stenographic Transcript of Ceauşescu-Deng Conversation 26 July 1965, in Deletant, Ionescu, and Locher, *Romania and the Warsaw Pact*.

56. This view was first substantiated by the research carried out by the Russian historian Ilya Gaiduk. See Gaiduk, *Soviet Union and the Vietnam War*. Since then, it has been confirmed by the research carried out in East Central European archives. See Békés, "A kádári külpolitika 1956–1968"; Békés, "Magyar–szovjet csúcstalálkozók, 1957–1965"; Hershberg, "Peace Probes and the Bombing Pause"; Szőke, "Delusion or Reality?"; Hershberg, *Marigold*.

57. Békés, "Magyar–szovjet csúcstalálkozók, 1957–1965," 179.

58. Minutes of the meeting of the HSWP PC on June 22 1965, MNL–OL, M-KS—288.f /5. 368. ő. e.

59. See Hershberg, "Peace Probes and the Bombing Pause."

60. The history of the Hungarian attempt at mediation has been studied most recently by Zoltán Szőke on the basis of some previous research of this author and through a comprehensive exploration of Hungarian archival sources. See Szőke, "Delusion or Reality?" For a very special approach, see Radványi, *Delusion and Reality*. János Radványi was a chargé d'affaires at the Hungarian legation in Washington, who defected in 1966 and settled down in the United States. In his book, he presents the attempt at mediation on the basis of his own experiences and recollections in which he himself played a key role because he forwarded the messages of the Hungarian foreign minister to Secretary of State Dean Rusk. The essence of Radványi's concept is that Foreign Minister János Péter's activity was totally unfounded, which essentially means that he was merely feeding the American politicians hopes, driven by his own political ambitions, in that he was able to persuade the Vietnamese leaders to enter into negotiations under the given circumstances. Based on Hungarian archival sources (and the comprehensive research carried out by Zoltán Szőke), however, it is clear that János Péter was acting as a mediator all along with authorization from the top Hungarian leadership. For more on the Hungarian and Polish attempts at mediation during 1965 and 1966, see Hershberg, "Peace Probes and the Bombing Pause"; Hershberg, *Marigold*.

61. For the history of a later similar Romanian mediation attempt, see Munteanu, "Over the Hills and Far Away"; Watts, *Mediating the Vietnam War*.

62. The activity of the Hungarian section of the Control Committee was presented by Zoltán Szőke in "Magyar békefenntartók Vietnamban."

63. For recent works on the Prague Spring, see Navrátil et al., *Prague Spring 1968*; Williams, *Prague Spring and Its Aftermath*; Karner et al., *Prager Frühling*; Bischof, Karner, and Ruggenthaler, *Prague Spring and the Warsaw Pact Invasion of Czechoslovakia in 1968*;

Stolarik, *Prague Spring and the Warsaw Pact Invasion of Czechoslovakia, 1968*; McDermott and Stibbe, *Eastern Europe in 1968*. On Hungary's economic reform in 1968, see Berend, *Hungarian Economic Reforms, 1953–1988*.

64. Tito's independent foreign policy line was highly appreciated in the West, while the Yugoslav political and economic model was the most serious deviation from the Leninist–Stalinist Communist model. Moreover, he was also lucky for not having had to face and suppress a serious internal crisis during his reign. Nevertheless, when Nikita Khrushchev and Georgy Malenkov secretly visited him before the Soviet intervention to crush the Hungarian Revolution in November 1956, Tito not only agreed that intervention was necessary to save the Communist system there but also promised to help eliminate his virtual allies—Prime Minister Imre Nagy and his adherents—from political life. Gomułka's true attitude was not tested in October 1956, but in December 1970 he ordered Polish troops to fire on the demonstrating workers.

65. For the author's detailed account on Kádár's mediating role, see Békés, "Hungary and the Prague Spring"; Békés, "Hungary 1968: Reform and the Challenge of the Prague Spring."

66. For a monographic work on Hungary's role in 1968, see Huszár, *1968: Prága, Budapest, Moszkva*.

67. In reality, the Soviets outmaneuvered the Hungarians by constantly changing the conditions during the invasion. In late August, the latter were eventually forced to "voluntarily" double their contribution and mobilize army units, equaling approximately two full divisions with some 20,000 troops, 155 tanks, 200 cannons and 99 fighter planes. With benevolent Soviet acquiescence, however, what survived in the public memory was that the reluctant ally took part in the invasion with only the smallest possible units. For the role of the Hungarian army in the invasion of Czechoslovakia, see Pataky, *A vonakodó szövetséges*.

68. Minutes of the meeting of the HSWP CC, 20 August 1968, MNL–OL, M-KS-288, f. 5/467. ő. e.

69. For the author's detailed arguments about the evaluation of the Prague Spring, see Békés, "Hungary and the Prague Spring."

70. Two GDR divisions were on high alert, waiting for the order to move in. Wentzke, "Role and Activities of the SED," 151.

Chapter 8

1. For recent studies on the general framework of European security, see Niedhart, "Introduction: CSCE, the German Question, and the Eastern Bloc"; Niedhart, "Ostpolitik: Transformation through Communication," 14–59.

2. It is revealing that, in the complex policy paper on the future role of the Soviet bloc in world policy, prepared by the Soviet Foreign Ministry for the summit meeting of European Communist leaders in Moscow in early January 1956, there is no mention of any plans for the establishment of a European security system. The document is published in English in Békés, Byrne, and Rainer, *1956 Hungarian Revolution*, 106–15.

3. Minutes of the HSWP PC, 12 October 1965, MNL–OL, M-KS-288. f. 5/377. ő. e.

4. Jain, *Documentary Study of the Warsaw Pact*, 409. The potential participation of the United States, however, was not mentioned in this declaration.

5. On the meeting, see Mastny, "Seventh Meeting of the PCC." See also Békés, "Titkos válságkezeléstől a politikai koordinációig," 37–38. On MNF, see Selvage, "Warsaw Pact and Nuclear Nonproliferation."

6. Jain, *Documentary Study of the Warsaw Pact*, 408; Békés, introduction to *Hungary and the Warsaw Pact*; Békés, "Titkos válságkezeléstől a politikai koordinációig."

7. For the records of the conference, see Locher, *Records of the Committee of the Ministers of Foreign Affairs*. See also Locher, "Shaping the Policies of the Alliance."

8. On the meeting, see Mastny, "Eighth Meeting of the PCC." See also Békés, "Titkos válságkezeléstől a politikai koordinációig," 42–43.

9. For the text of the declaration, see Mastny, "Eighth Meeting of the PCC."

10. Békés, "Warsaw Pact, the German Question," 113–14.

11. On the functioning of virtual coalitions within the Soviet bloc see chapter 7.

12. Report by János Kádár at the HSWP CC session, 10 August 1961, MNL–OL, M-KS-288. f. 4/42. ő. e.

13. On the evolution of Hungarian–West German relations, see "The Challenge of Early Ostpolitik, 1962–1963" in chapter 6.

14. For a detailed analysis of the author's novel concept of détente, see chapter 3.

15. For a detailed account of the Soviet bloc's policy concerning the issue of European security, see Békés, "Warsaw Pact and the Helsinki Process."

16. Memorandum by János Péter for the HSWP PC on issues of European peace, security, and cooperation, 17 January 1967, MNL–OL, M-KS-288. f. 5/415. ő. e. The document is published in Békés and Locher, *Hungary and the Warsaw Pact*.

17. Memorandum by János Péter for the HSWP PC on issues of European peace, security, and cooperation, 17 January 1967, MNL–OL, M-KS-288. f. 5/415. ő. e.

18. Adam Rapacki was Polish foreign minister from 1956–68. He presented a proposal for a nuclear-free zone in Central Europe in 1957 in the United Nations, later called the Rapacki plan.

19. Report to the HSWP PC and to the government on the visit of János Péter, Foreign Minister, to the Soviet Union (22–29 December 1969), 6 January 1970, MNL–OL, KÜM, XIX.-J-1-j-Szu–00949-1/1970.

20. For a detailed account of the WP's policy concerning the German question, see Békés, "Warsaw Pact and the Helsinki Process"; Selvage, "Warsaw Pact and the German Question"; Békés, "Warsaw Pact, the German Question and the Making of the CSCE Process"; Békés, "Hungary, the Soviet Bloc, the German Question."

21. In September 1955, the Soviet Union established diplomatic relations with the FRG without any preconditions during the visit of Chancellor Adenauer to Moscow.

22. The resolution made at the HSWP PC session on 27 October 1966 agreed to this proposal. MNL–OL, M-KS-288. f. 5/ 408. ő. e.

23. Minutes of the HSWP PC, 10 January 1967, MNL–OL, M-KS-288. f. 5/414. ő. e.

24. Bange, *Ostpolitik und Détente*, 73–78, 136, 257.

25. Selvage, "Warsaw Pact and the German Question," 183–84.

26. Under the circumstances, the original venue of East Berlin was not acceptable for Romania.

27. Guidelines for the forthcoming negotiations with the FRG, 17 March 1967, in MNL–OL, KÜM, XIX-J-1-j, box 70. On the Polish position, see Jarzabek, "Hope and Reality."

28. Minutes of the HSWP PC session, 13 February 1967, MNL–OL, M-KS-288. f. 5/417. ő. e.

29. Minutes of the HSWP PC session, 13 February 1967, MNL–OL, M-KS-288. f. 5/417. ő. e.

30. On the Polish and East German role, see Selvage, "Warsaw Pact and the German Question," 184.

31. The collective decision at the summit meeting of five WP members in early January 1957 in Budapest was regarded as an exceptional case triggered by the very weak position of the new Hungarian leadership emerging after the 1956 Hungarian Revolution. (See chapter 5.)

32. Foreign Ministry proposal on Hungarian–FRG political talks, 31 March 1972, in MNL–OL, KÜM, XIX. J-1-j, box 78. On bilateral relations between Hungary and the FRG, see Békés, "Hungary, the Soviet Bloc, the German Question."

33. For a detailed account of the secret talks preceding the WP PCC session, see Békés, "Warsaw Pact and the Helsinki Process."

34. On the Hungarian role, see Békés, "Warsaw Pact and the Helsinki Process." For a detailed account, see Békés, "Magyarország és az európai biztonsági értekezlet."

35. For the innovations concerning the Warsaw Pact's military structure agreed on at the PCC meeting in Budapest, see Mastny, "Tenth Meeting of the PCC."

36. Account by János Kádár of his visit to the Soviet Union on 5–10 February 1969 at the HSWP PC session on 18 February 1969, MNL–OL, M-KS-288. f. 5/484. ő. e.

37. Dobrynin, *In Confidence*, 204. The determination of the U.S. leadership to start top-level negotiations with the Soviet Union was expressed as early as the last months of the Johnson administration. Surprisingly, soon after the Warsaw Pact's intervention in Czechoslovakia, while first harshly condemning Moscow's move to the public, in September 1968 Johnson made a secret proposal to Brezhnev to hold a Soviet–American summit on Vietnam, the Middle East, and anti-missile systems (but not on Czechoslovakia). The Soviets agreed to the idea, and the summit was planned for Leningrad in October 1968, but it was eventually canceled. Békés, *Európából Európába*, 236. See also Dobrynin, *In Confidence*, 189–95.

38. On American policies vis-à-vis the CSCE process, see Kieninger, *Dynamic Détente*. See also Hanhimäki, *Rise and Fall of Détente*. On Soviet foreign policy during this period, see Zubok, *Failed Empire*, chapter 7.

39. While incidents on the Chinese–Soviet border became widely publicized at the time, Hungarian archival documents prove that at the very same time a similar raid occurred on the Chinese–North Korean border as well. On 15 March 1969, along the boundary river Anmokan (Yalu), a formation of fifty Chinese soldiers entered Korean territory, but Korean border guards and Red Guards managed to push the group back to the Chinese bank of the river. Report of the Hungarian Embassy in Pyongyang to the Foreign Minister, 17 April 1969, MNL–OL XIX-J-1-j-Korea-1-002216-1969. Document obtained by Balázs Szalontai.

40. Memorandum by Deputy Foreign Minister Károly Erdélyi for János Kádár on the WP PCC meeting in Budapest on 17 March 1969 (19 March 1969), MNL–OL M-KS-288. f. 5/486. ő. e.

41. Account by János Kádár at the HSWP PC session on 24 March 1969, MNL–OL M-KS-288. f. 5/486. ő. e.

42. Memorandum by Deputy Foreign Minister Károly Erdélyi for János Kádár on the WP PCC meeting in Budapest on 17 March 1969 (19 March 1969), MNL–OL M-KS-288.

f. 5/486. ő. e., and Account by János Kádár at the HSWP PC session on 24 March 1969, MNL–OL M-KS-288. f. 5/486. ő. e. For an English translation of the document, see Békés and Locher, *Hungary and the Warsaw Pact*.

43. On Romanian policy in this period, see Munteanu, *Romania and the Warsaw Pact*; Deletant, Ionescu, and Locher, *Romania and the Warsaw Pact*; Deletant, *New Evidence on Romania and the Warsaw Pact*; Deletant and Ionescu, "Romania and the Warsaw Pact, 1955–1989."

44. Record of the meeting of the WP deputy foreign ministers on 15 March 1969 (16 March 1969), MNL–OL, XIX-J-1-j-VSZ-VI-1-001547/63/2/1969, 106. d.

45. On East German policy vis-à-vis the CSCE process, see Bange and Kieninger, "Negotiating One's Own Demise?"; on Poland, see Jarzabek, "Hope and Reality."

46. Memorandum by Deputy Foreign Minister Károly Erdélyi for János Kádár on the WP PCC meeting in Budapest on 17 March 1969 (19 March 1969), MNL–OL M-KS-288. f. 5/486. ő. e.

47. Account by János Kádár at the HSWP PC session on 24 March 1969, MNL–OL M-KS-288. f. 5/486. ő. e. For an English translation of the document, see Békés and Locher, *Hungary and the Warsaw Pact*.

48. Account by János Kádár at the HSWP PC session on 24 March 1969, MNL–OL M-KS-288. f. 5/486. ő. e. For an English translation of the document, see Békés, and Locher, *Hungary and the Warsaw Pact*. Károly Erdélyi was a Hungarian deputy foreign minister and a confidant of Kádár at the time.

49. According to Ceaușescu, Brezhnev presented the China issue during their talk in a rather dramatic way: "How can we go home and tell our Political Bureau that we came here and did not speak about this issue, that we receive information every two hours that the situation is changing, that (so and so) took over the command of the troops, that [the Chinese] mobilize their agricultural divisions, etc. Why do we keep discussing the FRG.... I can spit on the FRG, but China is the main danger." For Ceaușescu's account of the talks in Budapest, see transcript of the meeting of the Executive Committee of the Central Committee of the Romanian Communist Party, 18 March 1969, in Deletant, Ionescu, and Locher, *Romania and the Warsaw Pact*.

50. Memorandum by Deputy Foreign Minister Károly Erdélyi for János Kádár on the WP PCC meeting in Budapest on 17 March 1969 (19 March 1969), MNL–OL M-KS-288. f. 5/486. ő. e. On the behind-the-scenes talks during the conference, see also Crump, *Warsaw Pact Reconsidered*, 268–83.

51. At the meeting the following organizational reforms were adopted: the establishment of the committee of defense ministers, a military council and a committee on technology. The PCC also adopted the statute for the unified command for peacetime.

52. For the position of the Romanian leadership at the Budapest meeting of the WP PCC, see transcript of the meeting of the Executive Committee of the Central Committee of the Romanian Communist Party, 18 March 1969, in Mastny and Byrne, *Cardboard Castle?*, 332–38.

53. Minutes of the HSWP PC, 1 July 1969, MNL–OL, M-KS.-288. f. 5/493. ő. e.

54. Soviet information about the Soviet foreign ministry's activities regarding the European security conference, 1 April 1969, MNL–OL, KÜM, XIX. J-1-j-VSZ-VI-1-001547/3/1969, box 106.

55. On U.S. policy, see Keefer, Geyer, and Selvage, *Soviet–American Relations*.

56. On the Helsinki process, see three excellent edited volumes: Bange and Niedhart, *Helsinki 1975 and the Transformation of Europe*; Loth and Soutou, *Making of Détente*; Wenger, Mastny, and Nuenlist, *Origins of the European Security System*.

57. Notes on the discussion with Soviet deputy foreign minister L. F. Ilyichev, 27 September 1969, MNL–OL, KÜM, XIX. J-1-j-Szu-1-00358-20/1969, box 85.

58. Foreign Ministry memorandum on the European Security conference for the HSWP PC, 13 October 1969, MNL–OL, M-KS. 288. f. 5/501. ő. e.

59. Notes by deputy foreign minister Károly Erdélyi for the HSWP PC, 18 October 1969, MNL–OL M-KS-288. f. 5/501. ő. e., in Békés and Locher, *Hungary and the Warsaw Pact*.

60. Memorandum of conversation between Hungarian deputy foreign minister Károly Erdélyi and Soviet deputy foreign minister Semyonov on 17 October 1969 in Moscow, 18 October 1969, MNL–OL, M-KS. 288. f. 5/501 ő. e.

61. On Polish policies, see Jarząbek, "The Impact of the German Question," 139–57.

62. On Romanian policies, see Ionescu, "Romania, *Ostpolitik* and the CSCE, 1967–1975."

63. On the lobby fights within the Soviet bloc, see Békés, "Warsaw Pact and the Helsinki Process"; Békés, "Hungary, the Soviet Bloc, the German Question and the CSCE Process."

64. Minutes of the HSWP PC, 21 October 1969, MNL–OL, M-KS-288. f./5. 501 ő. e.

65. On Poland, see Jarzabek, "Hope and Reality." On the GDR's policies, see Bange, "Onto the Slippery Slope."

66. Report to the Revolutionary Workers–Peasants Government on the meeting on 30–31 October 1969 in Prague by the representatives of the foreign ministries of the seven Socialist countries, MNL–OL, KÜM, XIX-J-1-j- VSZ-VI-003272/1969, box 105.

67. Remarkably, the text of the Helsinki Final Act, signed on 1 August 1975, was over one hundred pages!

68. Finally, multilateral preparatory talks began only in November 1972, and the conference itself opened in July 1973.

69. The proposal for a series of security conferences originally came from the Soviet side: it was raised during deputy foreign minister Semyonov's talks with János Péter in Budapest on 24 September 1969. The idea became a "Hungarian" initiative in the framework of the Soviet–Hungarian diplomatic game preceding the WP foreign ministers' meeting in Prague in October.

70. Foreign Ministry memorandum for the HSWP PC on the European security conference, MNL–OL, M-KS-288. f. 5/ 501. ő. e.

71. Daft proposal for comrade Frigyes Puja's speech to be presented to the conference of the deputy foreign ministers of the Warsaw Pact, 19 June 1970, MNL–OL, KÜM, XIX. J-1-VSZ-1-SZU-003272/1969, box 105.

72. See Békés, "Titkos válságkezeléstől a politikai koordinációig."

73. Report to the HSWP CC and the government on the foreign minister's official visit to the Soviet Union (22–29 December 1969), 6 January 1970, MNL–OL, KÜM, XIX. J-1-j-SU-00949-1/1970, box 80.

74. On the WP Committee of Foreign Ministers, see Locher, *Shaping the Policies of the Alliance*.

75. The Soviet–FRG treaty on sanctifying the Oder-Neisse border was signed on 12 August 1970, and a similar Polish–FRG treaty was signed on 7 December 1970.

76. Report to the Central Committee and the Government on the session of the party and state leaders of the European Socialist countries in Moscow on 3–4 December 1969 (8 December 1969), MNL–OL, M-KS-288. f./5. 507. ő. e.

77. On the GDR's foreign policy in this period, see Sarotte, *Dealing with the Devil*.

78. Report to the Revolutionary Workers-Peasants Government on the 21–22 June 1970 conference of WP foreign ministers in Budapest, 29 June 1970, MNL–OL, KÜM, XIX. J-1-j-EU-2008-00482/20/1970, box 93.

79. "The Prospects of Pan-European Economic Cooperation: Proposal for the Committee of International Economic Relations," 24 February 1972, MNL–OL, KÜM. XIX-J-1-j-EU-208-IX-00709/1-1972, box 12.

80. Report by János Kádár at the HSWP Political Committe meeting, 5 December 1972, MNL–OL, M-KS-288. f. 5. cs. 599. ő. e.

81. Report by János Kádár at the HSWP Political Committe meeting, 5 December 1972, MNL–OL, M-KS-288. f. 5. cs. 599. ő. e.

82. Report by János Kádár at the HSWP Political Committe meeting, 5 December 1972, MNL–OL, M-KS-288. f. 5. cs. 599. ő. e.

83. For a recently published monograph on the Warsaw Pact's activity from 1969 to 1985 see Bílý, *Warsaw Pact, 1969-1985*.

84. After World War I, the peace treaty by which Hungary lost two-thirds of its territory and one-third of its ethnic Hungarian population was signed in the Grand Trianon Palace in Versailles in June 1920. Territories were ceded to Austria, Czechoslovakia, Romania, and Yugoslavia. Subcarpathian Ruthenia was originally given to Czechoslovakia, but in 1945 it was "voluntarily" ceded to the Soviet Union.

85. Kalmár, *Történelmi galaxisok vonzásában*.

86. Minutes of the HSWP PC, 12 August 1975, MNL–OL, M-KS-288. f. 5. cs. 670. ő. e.

87. *Az Európai Biztonsági és Együttműködési Értekezlet záróokmánya* [The Final Act of the Conference on European Security and Cooperation].

Chapter 9

1. For the Soviet bloc's policy vis-à-vis the Helsinki process, see the following works: Savranskaya, "Logic of 1989"; Savranskaya and Taubman, "Soviet Foreign Policy, 1962–1975; Zubok, "Soviet Foreign Policy from Détente to Gorbachev"; Niedhart, "Introduction: CSCE, the German Question, and the Eastern Bloc"; Békés, "Hungary, the Soviet Bloc, the German Question." On the policies of the individual Soviet bloc countries, see Grozev and Baev, "Bulgaria: Balkan Diplomacy and the Road to Helsinki"; Jarzabek, "Hope and Reality"; Ionescu, "Romania, *Ostpolitik* and the CSCE, 1967–1975"; Bange, "Onto the Slippery Slope."

2. See Thomas, *Helsinki Effect*; Snyder, *Human Rights, Activism and the End of the Cold War.*

3. I fully support the argument recently put forward by Juhana Aunesluoma to this effect. See Aunesluoma, "Finlandisation in Reverse."

4. For two important collective works presenting the initial results of studying East-West cooperation in Europe, see Autio-Sarasmo and Miklóssy, *Reassessing Cold War Europe*; Romano and Romero, "European Socialist Regimes Facing Globalization."

5. Record of third conversation between Mikhail Gorbachev and Helmut Kohl, 14 June 1989. In Blanton, Savranskaya, Zubok, *Masterpieces of History, 477*. On Soviet interventions

in the third world, see Westad, *The Global Cold War*. On Bonn's reactions to the political changes in East-Central Europe at the end of the 1980s, see chapter 10.

6. Record of conversation between Mikhail Gorbachev and Egon Krenz, 1 November 1989. In Savranskaya, Blanton, and Zubok, *Masterpieces of History*, 570.

7. See Brown, *Rise and Fall of Communism*, chapter 28.

8. We should keep in mind that, according to the author's estimate, during the Cold War, the United States spent approximately 5 to 6 percent of its GDP on military costs, while the Soviet Union spent around 25 percent.

9. The proposals are in MNL–OL, M-KS-288. f. 32/1985, box 15. For the English translation of the document, see Békés and Locher, *Hungary and the Warsaw Pact*.

10. The Hungarian Holy Crown was taken by the withdrawing Hungarian army to Germany in 1945, where it was captured by U.S. troops and transported to Fort Knox. On the history of the crown's return, see Glant, *A Szent Korona amerikai kalandja*. On U.S.-Hungarian relations, see Borhi, *Dealing with Dictators*.

11. Békés, "Why Was There No 'Second Cold War'?"

12. For a detailed account of this crisis, see Békés, "Why Was There No 'Second Cold War'?"

13. Bulletin for the members of the Political Committee and the Secretariat on the talks of the deputy head of the HSWP CC International Department in the United States and Canada. 23 January 1980, MNL–OL M-KS-288 f. 5/ 791. ő. e.

14. Horn's report on his mission, as part of a collection of documents on Hungarian archival sources on the Soviet intervention in Afghanistan, was published in Békés, "Why Was There No 'Second Cold War'?" Later, Gyula Horn served as foreign minister (1989–90) and then prime minister (1994–98).

15. Bulletin for the members of the Political Committee and the Secretariat on the talks of the deputy head of the International Department in the United States and Canada, 23 January 1980, MNL–OL M-KS 288 f. 5/ 791. ő. e.

16. At the elections on 4 November 1980, Republican candidate Ronald Reagan was elected president.

17. The status of most favored nation was granted to Hungary in a way that it had to be renewed by the U.S. Congress annually.

18. Minutes of the session of the HSWP PC on 29 January 1980, MNL–OL, M-KS-288. f. 5/791. ő. e. The full text of the verbatim minutes pertaining to this topic, as part of a collection of documents on Hungary and the East–West crisis following the Soviet intervention in Afghanistan, was published in Békés, "Miért nem lett második hidegháború?"

19. The Soviets approved the suggestion and postponed the military exercise to July 1980.

20. Hungarian foreign minister Frigyes Puja eventually visited Bonn on 10–12 September 1980.

21. Memorandum of conversation between János Kádár and Leonid Brezhnev, 4 July 1980, MNL–OL, M-KS-288. f. 47/764. ő. e.

22. Memorandum of conversation between Vadim Zagladin, first deputy head of the International Department of the CPSU CC, and Gyula Horn, deputy head of the HSWP CC Department of Foreign Affairs, on debates inside the Soviet leadership on issues of international politics [16 July 1980], MNL–OL M-KS-288 f. 47/ 764. ő. e.

23. On the history of Hungarian foreign policy in this period, see Békés, *Európából Európába*; Békés, "Hungarian Foreign Policy in the Soviet Alliance System." See also Kiss, "A kádárizmustól az EU tagságig."

24. Minutes of the session of the HSWP PC on 29 January 1980, MNL–OL, M-KS-288. f. 5/791. ő. e., in Békés, "Miért nem lett második hidegháború?"

25. For the substance of these debates, see Memorandum of conversation between Vadim Zagladin, first deputy head of the International Department of the CPSU CC, and Gyula Horn, deputy head of the HSWP CC Department of Foreign Affairs, on debates inside the Soviet leadership on issues of international politics [16 July 1980], MNL–OL M-KS-288 f. 47/ 764. ő. e. The English translation of the document was published as part of a collection of Hungarian archival sources on the Soviet intervention in Afghanistan in Békés, "Why Was There No 'Second Cold War'?"

26. Békés, "Why Was There No 'Second Cold War'?"

27. Bulletin for the Political Committee and the Secretariat concerning the oral reply of Chancellor Helmut Schmidt to the message of János Kádár, 14 February 1980, MNL–OL, M-KS-288. f. 11./4512. ő. e.

28. Békés, "Why Was There No 'Second Cold War'?"

29. For the author's most recent publications on this topic, see Békés, "Détente and the Soviet Bloc, 1975–1991" and "Long Détente and the Soviet Bloc, 1953–1983."

30. For a recent edited volume challenging the interpretation of mainstream literature and including several papers supporting this author's long-held conception, see Bange and Villaume, *Long Détente*.

31. See chapter 4.

32. Westad, *Global Cold War*, 299–330.

33. In March 1946, Soviet troops were withdrawn from the Danish island of Bornholm, the westernmost conquest of the Soviet Union, which was occupied in the spring of 1945. In April 1958, Khrushchev planned to withdraw all Soviet troops from both Romania and Hungary. However, at the request of Hungarian leader János Kádár, he agreed to the continued presence of the Soviet Army in Hungary. For details, see chapter 6.

34. The Brezhnev doctrine, introduced after four Warsaw Pact states' invasion of Czechoslovakia, meant that it was the *joint* responsibility of the Soviet bloc to prevent the fall of the Communist system in any of the countries belonging to the alliance. The invasion of Afghanistan, however, was the sole responsibility of the Soviet Union.

35. For a recent archive-based monograph supporting this position, see Miles, *Engaging the Evil Empire*.

36. For two recently edited volumes on this period, see Villaume and Westad, *Perforating the Iron Curtain*; Mariager, Porsdam, and Villaume, *"Long 1970s."*

37. In a televised speech on 23 January 1980, President Carter called the Soviet invasion of Afghanistan "the most serious threat to the peace since the Second World War," a surprising statement that could be easily challenged by anyone having heard of the second Berlin crisis or especially the Cuban missile crisis.

38. On the Polish crisis, see Paczkowski and Byrne, *From Solidarity to Martial Law*.

39. While this can be proved only by indirect evidence until the full opening of Soviet documents, it is clear that the Soviets did not plan to give up on Poland in 1980–81. Suffice it to say that at the Warsaw Pact summit meeting in Moscow in December 1980, there already

existed a fully prepared plan for a Warsaw Pact joint invasion. Mastny, "Warsaw Pact as History," 50. On the Polish crisis, see Paczkowski and Werblan, "On the Decision to Introduce Martial Law"; Mastny, " Soviet Non-invasion of Poland"; Kramer, *Kuklinski Files and the Polish Crisis of 1980–1981.*

40. Records of the HSWP PC session on December 6 1983. MNL–OL, M-KS-288. f. 5/897. ő. e.

41. On the Soviet bloc's policy during the Euromissile crisis, see Byrne, "Warsaw Pact and the Euromissile Crisis, 1977–1983."

42. For a recently edited volume supporting the present author's long-held position on the important role of small states in shaping East–West relations, see Crump and Erlandsson, *Margins for Manoeuvre in Cold War Europe.*

43. For the history of Hungarian accession, see Földes, *Kádár János külpolitikája és nemzetközi tárgyalásai,* 1:321–33; Mong, *Kádár hitele*; Kalmár, *Történelmi galaxisok vonzásában.*

44. Horváth, Németh, . . . *És a falak leomlanak,* 173–76. See also Földes, *Kádár János külpolitikája és nemzetközi tárgyalásai,* 1:348–50. Eventually the treaty was signed in September 1988, when official relations between Hungary and the EEC were established.

45. On the Hungarian reaction to the Polish crisis, see Tischler, *Hogy megcsendüljön minden gyáva fül.* See also Mitrovits, *A remény hónapjai.* The Hungarian documents pertaining to Hungarian–Polish relations during the crisis and its aftermath are published in Mitrovits, *Lengyel–magyar "két jóbarát,"* 589–765.

46. The minutes of the meeting of the WP Ministers of Defense on 1–4 December 1981 are published in Paczkowski and Werblan, *On the Decision to Introduce Martial Law in Poland,* 37–43. Reprinted in Mastny and Byrne, *Cardboard Castle?,* 451–55.

47. This was Prime Minister Margaret Thatcher's first visit to a Soviet bloc country. On her talks in Budapest on 2–4 February 1984, see Földes, *Kádár János külpolitikája és nemzetközi tárgyalásai,* 1:422–24. The minutes of the talks are published in Földes, 2:622–29. For the British Foreign Office documents on the trip, see www.margaretthatcher.org/archive /1984hungary.asp (accessed 20 January 2017).

48. For a detailed analysis of Hungarian foreign policy in this period, see Békés, *Enyhülés és emancipáció.* See also Földes, *Kádár János külpolitikája és nemzetközi tárgyalásai.*

49. On the CSCE follow-up conferences, see Dunay and Gazdag, *A Helsinki folyamat.*

Chapter 10

1. Archival documents on the international politics of the period became available beginning in the late 1990s. Thanks to the pioneering international research project founded in 1997 by the National Security Archive in Washington, D.C. (Project on Openness in Eastern Europe and the Former Soviet Union), significant results have been achieved in this field. Thus, much has become known about the state of contemporary American policy and even more about the opinion of the Soviet leaders, especially that of Gorbachev and his immediate circle; see *The End of the Cold War in Europe, 1989.* The documents, together with the minutes of the Musgrove conference in 1998, are published in Savranskaya, Blanton, and Zubok, *Masterpieces of History.* For selected records of the Warsaw Pact's activity in the 1980s, see Mastny and Byrne, *Cardboard Castle?* The full collection of the Warsaw Pact leading bodies is available on the website of the Parallel History Project on

Cooperative Security (http://www.php.isn.ethz.ch). For a recent volume of all the minutes of the Gorbachev-era Soviet–American summits, see Savranskaya and Blanton, *Last Superpower Summits*. For scholarly analyses on the changing dynamics of East–West relations in this period, see Garthoff, *Great Transition*; Lévesque, *Enigma of 1989*; Zubok, *Failed Empire*, 303–35; Savranskaya, "Logic of 1989"; Blanton, "US Policy and the Revolutions of 1989"; Brown, "Gorbachev Revolution and the End of the Cold War"; Fischer, "US Foreign Policy under Reagan and Bush"; Service, *End of the Cold War*. For the author's analysis of the topic, see Békés, "Back to Europe." For an edited volume on the development of world Communism in this period, see Fürst, Pons, and Selden, *Endgames?*

2. On Khrushchev's foreign policy, see Taubman, *Khrushchev*; Zubok, *Failed Empire*, 94–153.

3. Report to the PC and the Council of Ministers on the Warsaw meeting of the Political Consultative Committee of the Warsaw Treaty Member States, 18 July 1988, MNL–OL, M-KS-288. f. 11/4453 ő. e.

4. Comment made by Ferenc Kárpáti, Minister of Defense, at the 22 November 1988 meeting of the HSWP Central Committee, MNL–OL, M-KS-288. f. 4/246. ő. e.

5. Report to the PC and the Council of Ministers on the Warsaw meeting of the WP PCC, 18 July 1988, MNL–OL, 288. f. 11/4453 ő. e. For the records of the WP PCC meeting in Warsaw in July 1988, visit the PHP website: www.php.isn.ethz.ch/collections/colltopic.cfm ?lng=en&id=17113&navinfo=14465.

6. Comment by Károly Grósz at the 22 July 1988 meeting of the HSWP CC, MNL–OL, M-KS- 288. f. 5/1031. ő. e.

7. For Gorbachev's endeavors to reduce Soviet activities in the third world, see Kalinovsky, and Radchenko, *End of the Cold War and the Third World*.

8. Notes taken by Anatoly Chernyaev at the meeting of the CPSU Politburo on 10 March 1988, in *End of the Cold War in Europe, 1989*, doc. no. 4.

9. One proof of the survival of this imperial approach is the fact that although the ten-year occupation of Afghanistan cost the Soviet Union $5 billion per year for the sake of maintaining Soviet influence, even after the pullout the leadership reckoned with an annual cost of $3 billion. Károly Grósz's comment made at the 12 July 1988 meeting of the HSWP PC, MNL–OL, M-KS-233. f. 5/1031 ő. e. On a recent study of the economic factor in the Soviet collapse, see Miller, *Struggle to Save the Soviet Economy*.

10. Károly Grósz's comment made at the 12 July 1988 meeting of the HSWP PC, MNL–OL, M-KS-233. f. 5/1031 ő. e.

11. *Pravda*, 31 October 1956. For a recent English translation of the declaration, see Békés, Byrne, and Rainer, *1956 Hungarian Revolution*, 300–302.

12. At the November 1986 Moscow Communist summit meeting, Gorbachev explicitly emphasized the need to abandon the policy of "guardianship." Comment by János Kádár at the 18 November 1986 meeting of the HSWP PC, MNL–OL, M-KS-288-5/983 ő. e.

13. See chapter 5. For Soviet policy concerning the 1956 Hungarian Revolution, see Szereda and Rainer, *Döntés a Kremlben, 1956*; Kramer, "'Malin Notes'"; Kramer, "New Evidence on Soviet Decision-Making"; Békés, "1956 Hungarian Revolution and World Politics."

14. See the minutes of the Musgrove conference in 1998, published in Savranskaya, Blanton, and Zubok, *Masterpieces of History*, 99–214. For the same position held by a historian, see Ouimet, *Rise and Fall of the Brezhnev Doctrine*, 3–5.

15. Lévesque, *Enigma of 1989*, 76–77.

16. Károly Grósz's comment made at the 12 July 1988 meeting of the HSWP PC, MNL–OL, M-KS-233. f. 5/1031 ő. e

17. On the theory of the floating of the Brezhnev doctrine, see Békés, "Back to Europe," 242–45.

18. Lévesque, *Enigma of 1989*, 80–81. For the analysis of Soviet policy toward East Central Europe in this period, see also Gati, *Bloc That Failed*.

19. Lévesque, *Enigma of 1989*, 80–81.

20. One rather characteristic example of this attitude is that, at the 14 June 1989 talks between Gorbachev and Helmut Kohl, the Soviet leader stated that the Brezhnev doctrine was no longer in force, only later to maintain that only a new model of *socialism* would satisfy the interests of the Soviet Union in East-Central Europe. See *End of the Cold War in Europe*, doc. no. 42.

21. "Report for the members of the PC on the visit of Károly Grósz to the Soviet Union on 23–24 March 1989," in Békés et al., *Political Transition in Hungary*, doc. no. 16.

22. "Report for the members of the PC on the visit of Károly Grósz to the Soviet Union on 23–24 March 1989," in Békés et al., *Political Transition in Hungary*, doc. no. 16.

23. From all this, we can gather that the doctrine linked to the name of Brezhnev after the 1968 intervention in Czechoslovakia might just as well be called the Khrushchev doctrine, after the crackdown on the 1956 revolution in Hungary. In reality, this thesis is nothing but an organic part of the Stalinist tradition. It is merely history's irony that Stalin himself never had to resort to it.

24. For a detailed analysis of this issue, see Békés, "Back to Europe," 242–45.

25. According to polls, in the summer of 1989 the HSWP had reason to expect to win 36 to 40 percent of the votes.

26. Kalmár and Révész, *A rendszerváltás forgatókönyve*, doc. no. 3.

27. For an interesting and novel interpretation of Gorbachev's policies toward the political transformation in East Central Europe, see Kalmár, *Történelmi galaxisok vonzásában*, 515–93.

28. On Soviet foreign policy in the Gorbachev era, see Zubok, *Failed Empire*, 303–35.

29. For an archive-based recent analysis of this process, see Savranskaya, "Logic of 1989."

30. Savranskaya, "Logic of 1989."

31. It is noteworthy that at a top-level meeting on 26 January 1990, Gorbachev himself used this analogy, albeit in a somewhat different context. "There was a Brest peace No. 1 and now we are in the position of a 'Brest peace' No. 2. If we do not cope with it, half of our country will be taken away from us." The present author first used the term "Brest-Litovsk syndrome" in 1999 to explain the serious situation in the Soviet Union, without yet having access to the Soviet materials, which were not researchable at the time. Gorbchev's reference to the Brest-Litovsk Peace Treaty was discovered in 2019 by Tsotne Tchanturia, a PhD student at Corvinus University in Budapest, who is working on a comparative analysis of Gorbachev's East Central European and Baltic policies for his dissertation.

32. Kalmár, *Történelmi galaxisok vonzásában*, 548.

33. Kalmár, *Történelmi galaxisok vonzásában*, doc. no. 69.

34. On the HSWP's policy concerning the transition, see Tőkés, *Hungary's Negotiated Revolution*; Kalmár, "From 'Model Change' to Regime Change."

35. On U.S. policy toward East Central Europe, see Beschloss and Talbott, *At the Highest Levels*; Hutchings, *American Diplomacy and the End of the Cold War*; Bush and Scowcroft,

World Transformed. On the U.S. position concerning the Hungarian political transition, see Borhi, *Dealing with Dictators*, 323–433.

36. "Report on President Bush's visit to Hungary, 15 July 1989," in Békés et al., *Political Transition in Hungary 1989–1990*, doc. no. 81; report by Rezső Nyers at the 28 July meeting of the HSWP CC, in Kosztricz et al., *A Magyar Szocialista Munkáspárt Központi Bizottságának 1989*, 2:1294–95.

37. Beschloss and Talbott, *At the Highest Levels*, 91, cited in Lévesque, *Enigma of 1989*, 138.

38. "Records made by Anatoly Chernyaev on the summit in Malta, 2 and 3 December 1989," in *End of the Cold War in Europe*, doc. no. 69.

39. See also the epilogue.

40. For recent archive-based analyses of Gorbachev's foreign policy, see Savranskaya, "Logic of 1989"; Zubok, *Failed Empire*, 303–35. For the author's analysis of the topic, see Békés, "Back to Europe."

41. On Gorbachev's "common European home" concept, see Savranskaya, "Logic of 1989," 18–22; Rey, "Europe Is Our Common Home."

42. While in mainstream literature the general notion is still that the West wanted to change the political systems of the East Central European states in the 1970s and 1980s, this author's long-held position to the contrary is recently confirmed by the analysis of the EEC's policy toward the region. See Romano, "Untying Cold War Knots."

43. Report by Rezső Nyers at the 28 July 1989 meeting of the HSWP CC, in Kosztricz et al., *A Magyar Szocialista Munkáspárt Központi Bizottságának 1989. évi jegyzőkönyvei*, 2:1293.

44. Gorbachev desperately tried to convince Reagan to abandon the plan at their summit meetings, especially those in Geneva and Reykjavík.

45. Reagan even offered Gorbachev the "license" of SDI for free once it was developed, knowing that the Soviet Union was not capable of building it due to the exorbitant cost of the project.

46. For an edited volume on different interpretations of the end of the Cold War, see Pons and Romero, *Reinterpreting the End of the Cold War*.

47. "Private talk between Gorbachev and Helmut Kohl, Chancellor of the FRG, on 12 June 1989," in *End of the Cold War in Europe*, doc. no. 40. The same was confirmed by French President Francois Mitterrand during his conversation with Gorbachev on 4 July 1989 in Paris, in *End of the Cold War in Europe*, doc. no. 43.

48. "Margaret Thatcher's talks with Mikhail Gorbachev on 6 April 1989," in *End of the Cold War in Europe*, doc. no. 33.

49. "Private talk between Mikhail Gorbachev and Helmut Kohl, Chancellor of the FRG, on 14 July 1989," in *End of the Cold War in Europe*, doc. no. 42. Many other documents confirm that this was not merely intended to reassure Gorbachev. See, for example, Proposal submitted to the Political Executive Committee of the HSWP [Western views on the policy of the HSWP], 30 August 1989, in Békés et al., *Political Transition in Hungary, 1989–1990*, doc. no. 104.

Chapter 11

1. Since the late 1990s, a huge number of archival documents have been published on the Hungarian political transition and its international context. See Kosztricz et al., *A Magyar Szocialista Munkáspárt Központi Bizottságának 1989*; Bozóki et al., *A rendszerváltás*

forgatókönyve; Békés et al., *Rendszerváltozás Magyarországon 1989–1990*; Békés et al., *Political Transition in Hungary, 1989–1990*. For Hungarian and Russian sources on Gorbachev's policy toward Hungary, see Baráth and Rainer, *Gorbacsov tárgyalásai magyar vezetőkkel*. For a synthesis of the international context of the Hungarian transition, see Békés, "Back to Europe." Lévesque's *Enigma of 1989* devotes chapter 7 to the role Soviet policy played in the Hungarian transition. On the U.S. position concerning the Hungarian political transition, see Borhi, *Dealing with Dictators*, 323–433.

2. In 1998, a research project was initiated to investigate the international background of the Hungarian transition. This project was supported by the Hungarian Program of the Project on Openness in Eastern Europe and the Former Soviet Union at the National Security Archives in Washington, D.C.

3. Károly Grósz's comment made at the 12 July 1988 meeting of the HSWP PC, MNL–OL, M-KS-233. f. 5/1031. ő. e.

4. See, for example, the Report to the PC and the Council of Ministers on the Warsaw session of the WP PCC, 18 July 1988, MNL–OL, M-KS-288 f. 11/4453. ő. e.

5. Although the Hungarian leadership had already made it clear that they were ready to negotiate with Romania, by July 1988 they declared that only a meeting between the *prime ministers* would be possible. (In this way, Károly Grósz could have avoided negotiating personally with Ceauşescu, given that Grósz held the positions of both party general secretary and prime minister at that time.) Károly Grósz's comment at the 12 July 1988 meeting of the HSWP PC, MNL–OL, M-KS-233. f. 5/1031 ő. e.

6. Károly Grósz's comment at the 12 July 1988 meeting of the HSWP PC, MNL–OL, M-KS-233. f. 5/1031 ő. e.

7. Evidence for this can be produced only by the further opening of Russian archives. See Baráth and Rainer, *Gorbacsov tárgyalásai magyar vezetőkkel*, 25.

8. Lévesque, *Enigma of 1989*, 130.

9. See epilogue.

10. "Gyula Horn's comment at the meeting of the HSWP CC on 21 February 1989," in Kosztricz et al., *A Magyar Szocialista Munkáspárt Központi Bizottságának 1989*, 1:362.

11. "Gyula Horn's comment at the meeting of the HSWP CC, 23–24 July 1989," in Kosztricz et al., *A Magyar Szocialista Munkáspárt Központi Bizottságának 1989*, 2:1174.

12. Document of the meeting of the International, Legal and Public Administration Committee of the HSPW CC held on 9 July 1989, MNL–OL, M-KS-288. f. 62/5 ő. e

13. Reply given by Rezső Nyers and Imre Pozsgay to a question posed by the present author at the international conference "Political Transition in Hungary 1989–1990," held in Budapest in 1999.

14. On this division, see chapter 8.

15. On Hungarian–Romanian relations, see Földes, *Magyarország, Románia és a nemzeti kérdés 1956–1989*.

16. According to the report given by Rezső Nyers to the HSWP CC on 28 July 1989, during the visit of the Hungarian leaders to Moscow on 24–25 July 1989, Gorbachev stressed that "you must negotiate." In Kosztricz et al., *A Magyar Szocialista Munkáspárt Központi Bizottságának 1989*, 2:1298.

17. Not much earlier, in March 1989, Hungarian diplomacy officially supported the resolution of the Human Rights Committee of the UN—accepted at the initiation of Western countries—which ordered the investigation of human rights in Romania.

18. "Report given by Rezső Nyers to the HSWP CC on 28 July 1989," in Kosztricz et al., *A Magyar Szocialista Munkáspárt Központi Bizottságának 1989*, 2:1300.

19. "Talks between Rezső Nyers and Miloš Jakeš at the Bucharest meeting of the PC of the WTO, memorandum, 12 July 1989," in Békés et al., *Political Transition in Hungary 1989–1990*, doc. no. 80.

20. "Memorandum for the Presidency of the HSWP [Czechoslovak objections concerning Imre Szokai's interview], 14 August 1989," in Békés et al., doc. no. 92.

21. For a detailed history of the opening of the Iron Curtain in 1989, see Oplatka, *Egy döntés története*. See also Horváth and Németh, . . . *És a falak leomlanak*, 329–32.

22. Minutes of the 19 May 1987 meeting of the HSWP PC, MNL–OL, M-KS-288. f. 5/997. ő.e.

23. Before the opening of the Berlin Wall (9 November 1989), some fifty thousand GDR citizens left for the West through Hungary. Oplatka, *Egy döntés története*, 55.

24. The two German records made on the meeting can be found in Békés et al., *Political Transition in Hungary 1989–1990*, doc. nos. 99 and 100.

25. Oplatka, *Egy döntés története*, 216.

26. On the history of German reunification, see Sarotte, *1989*.

27. On the history of the Warsaw Pact in the Gorbachev era, see Mastny, "Warsaw Pact as History."

28. Current questions related to the development of the Warsaw Pact (joint proposal of the Foreign Ministry and the Ministry of Defense), 6 March 1989, Document of the 13 March 1989 meeting of the International, Legal and Public Administration Committee of the HSWP CC, MNL–OL, M-KS-288 f.—62/3. ő. e.

29. Proposals of the RCP on the improvement and democratization of the activities of the Warsaw Treaty bodies, 8 July 1989, MNL–OL, M-KS-288 f.—62/3. ő. e.

30. Proposals of the RCP on the improvement and democratization of the activities of the Warsaw Treaty bodies, 8 July 1989, MNL–OL, M-KS-288 f.—62/3. ő. e.

31. Szabó, "From Big Elephant to Paper Tiger."

32. On the strategy of the HSWP during the transition, see Kalmár, *Történelmi galaxisok vonzásában*, 556–93.

33. "Comment by Gyula Horn at the meeting of the HSWP CC on 20–21, February 1989," in Kosztricz et al., *A Magyar Szocialista Munkáspárt Központi Bizottságának 1989*, 1:362.

34. "Report to the PC on Károly Grósz's negotiations with Mikhail Gorbachev," in Békés et al., *Political Transition in Hungary 1989–1990*, doc. no. 16.

35. Information issued for internal use by the Department of International Relations of the HSWP CC, MNL–OL, M-KS-288–11/4508. ő. e.

36. Borhi, "'Magyarország kötelessége a Varsói Szerződésben maradni,'" 265. In his study, extending the argument put forward by the present author in 2000, Borhi cites several reports on similar warnings by Western European and American politicians and diplomats, based on Hungarian Foreign Ministry reports in this period. See also Békés, "Back to Europe."

37. Current questions related to the development of the Warsaw Pact (joint proposal of the Foreign Ministry and the Ministry of Defense), 6 March 1989, Document of the 13 March 1989 meeting of the International, Legal and Public Administration Committee of the HSWP CC, MNL–OL, M-KS-288 f. 62/3. ő. e.

38. Minutes of the 16 May 1989 meeting of the HSWP PC, MNL–OL, M-KS-288-5. 1065. ő. e.

39. On the highest-level Soviet–Hungarian relations, see Baráth, "A 'csúcsról' szemlélve: a Szovjetunió és a magyarországi átmenet." See also Baráth and Rainer, *Gorbacsov tárgyalásai magyar vezetőkkel.*

40. Károly Grósz's comment made at the 27 September 1988 meeting of the HSWP CC, MNL–OL, M-KS-288. f. 4/242. ő. e.

41. Baráth, "A 'csúcsról' szemlélve."

42. Károly Grósz's comment made at the 12 July 1988 meeting of the HSWP PC, MNL–OL, M-KS-288. f. 5/1031. ő. e.

43. The security situation of the Hungarian People's Republic and some military objectives. Memorandum by István Földes, advisor of the secretary-general of the HSWP, 7 March 1989, Document of the 13 March 1989 meeting of the International, Legal, and Public Administration Committee of the HSWP CC, MNL–OL, M-KS-288 f. 62/3. ő. e.

44. "Records of the negotiations between Miklós Németh and Mikhail Gorbachev, Moscow, 3 March 1989," in Békés et al., *Political Transition in Hungary 1989–1990*, doc. no. 22.

45. Baráth, "A 'csúcsról' szemlélve."

46. According to an agreement between the Soviet and Hungarian governments signed in March 1957, the cost of the stationing of Soviet troops in Hungary was covered by the Soviet Union.

47. Minutes of the 16 May 1989 meeting of the HSWP PC, MNL–OL M-KS-288-5/1065. ő. e.

48. "Rezső Nyers and Károly Grósz's negotiations with Mikhail Gorbachev. Report to the Political Executive Committee of HSWP, 30 July," in Békés et al., *Political Transition in Hungary 1989–1990*, doc. no. 84.

49. On the process of pulling out the troops and the Hungarian–Soviet disputes over the withdrawal, see Keleti, "Szovjet csapatkivonások."

50. "Notes by Anatoly Chernyaev on the meeting of the Politburo of CPSU, 10 March 1988," in *End of the Cold War in Europe, 1989*, doc. no. 4.

51. Minutes of the 14 March 1989 meeting of the HSWP PC, MNL–OL, M-KS-288 f.-5/1057. ő. e.

52. Minutes of the 12 March 1989 meeting of the HSWP PC, MNL–OL, M-KS-288 f.-5/1059. ő. e.

53. On the role of the FRG in supporting the Hungarian transition, see Horváth and Németh, . . . *És a falak leomlanak*, chaps. 8, 9, and 10.

54. Horváth and Németh, . . . *És a falak leomlanak*, 336–42.

55. Proposal submitted to the HSWP CC on the political strategy concerning European political and economic development and the issues of integration, January 1989, MNL–OL, M-KS-288. f. 5/1051. ő. e.; minutes of the 14 March 1989 meeting of the HSWP PC, MNL–OL, M-KS-288. f. 5/1051. ő.e.

56. Károly Grósz's comment at the 12 July 1988 meeting of the HSWP PC, MNL–OL, M-KS-288 f. /5 1031. ő. e.

57. Károly Grósz's comment at the 12 July 1988 meeting of the HSWP PC, MNL–OL, M-KS-288 f. /5 1031. ő. e.

58. Károly Grósz's comment at the 12 July 1988 meeting of the HSWP PC, MNL–OL, M-KS-288 f. /5 1031. ő. e.

59. "Report to the HSWP PC, 15 May 1989," in Békés et al., *Political Transition in Hungary 1989–1990*, doc. no. 45.

60. Károly Grósz's comment made at the 12 July 1988 meeting of the HSWP PC, MNL–OL, M-KS-288. f. 5/1031. ő. e.

Epilogue

1. For the analysis of the changes in the Soviet Union, see Kramer, "Collapse of East European Communism," pts. 2 and 3.

2. Békés, Enyhülés és emancipáció, 356. See also footnote 36 for chapter 11.

3. Békés, Enyhülés és emancipáció, 356.

4. See Mastny and Byrne, *Cardboard Castle?*, 674–77.

5. Gorbachev's speech at the meeting of the WP PCC in Moscow on 7 June 1990 is available on the PHP website: www.php.isn.ethz.ch/collections/colltopic.cfm?lng=en&id=19001 &navinfo=14465. The quote is from page 10.

6. Gazdag, "Szövetségtől szövetségig," 200.

7. Report on the second meeting of the interim Committee of Government Representatives in charge of the revision of the Warsaw Treaty Organization, 27 September 1990, MNL–OL, Külügyminisztérium. 002686/1/1990.

8. Report on the second meeting of the interim Committee of Government Representatives in charge of the revision of the Warsaw Treaty Organization, 27 September 1990, MNL–OL, Külügyminisztérium. 002686/1/1990.

9. Soviet transcript of the Malta summit, in Savranskaya, Blanton, and Zubok, *Masterpieces of History*, 636.

Bibliography

Archival Sources

Archives of the Institute for Military History, Budapest
Archives of the Institute for Political History, Budapest
Archives of the Ministry of Foreign Affairs, Budapest
Dwight D. Eisenhower Presidential Library and Museum, Abilene, Kansas
    Dulles, John Foster: Papers, 1951–59
    Eisenhower, Dwight D.: Papers as President of the United States, 1953–61
        (Ann Whitman File)
    Eisenhower, Dwight D.: Records as President, White House Central Files,
        1953–61, Confidential File
    Jackson, C. D.: Papers, 1953–67
    White House Office, National Security Council Staff: Papers, 1948–61
    White House Office, Office of the Staff Secretary: Records of Paul T. Carroll,
        Andrew J. Goodpaster, L. Arthur Minnich, and Christopher H. Russell, 1952–61
Historical Archives of the State Security Services, Budapest
Hungarian National Archives, Budapest
    Council of Ministers
    Hungarian Socialist Workers' Party
    Hungarian Workers' Party
    Ministry of Foreign Affairs
Lyndon Baines Johnson Presidential Library and Museum, Austin, Texas
The National Archives, London, Kew
    Cabinet meetings, Prime Minister A. Eden papers
    Foreign Secretary S. Lloyd papers
    Foreign Office, General Correspondence
National Security Archive, Washington, D.C.
Seeley G. Mudd Manuscript Library, Princeton University,
    Princeton, New Jersey
    Allen W. Dulles Papers, 1945–1971
    John Foster Dulles Papers, 1860–1988
United Nations Archives, New York, New York
    PSCA Confidential Notes, Chronological Summary regarding Hungary,
        Andrew Cordier File
United States National Archives and Records Administration,
    College Park, Maryland
    Department of State, Central Decimal Files, RG 59
    National Security Council Reports, RG 273

Papers of Admiral Radford, RG 218
Records of the Joint Chiefs of Staff, RG 330
Records of U.S. Department of State, Office of Public Opinion Studies, RG 59

Published Documents

Allinson, Mark, Peter Brugge, Csaba Békés, Melissa Feinberg, Hope M. Harrison, Matthew Jones, Pawel Machewicz, Kristin Roth-Ey, Balázs Szalontai, and Stephen Twigge, eds. *Cold War East-Central Europe*. London: Routledge, 2017. [Online database of the British National Archives documents on East Central Europe, 1953–75.]

Bange, Oliver, and Stephan Kieninger, eds. "Negotiating One's Own Demise? The GDR's Foreign Ministry and the CSCE Negotiations." E-dossier No. 17, Cold War International History Project, Woodrow Wilson International Center for Scholars, Washington, D.C., 2011.

Baráth, Magdolna, ed. *Kádár János első kormányának jegyzőkönyvei: 1956. november 7–1958. január 25.* Budapest: Magyar Országos Levéltár, 2009.

———, ed. *Szovjet diplomáciai jelentések Magyarországról a Hruscsov-korszakban.* Budapest: Napvilág Kiadó–Politikatörténeti Intézet, 2012.

Baráth, Magdolna, and János M. Rainer, ed. *Gorbacsov tárgyalásai magyar vezetőkkel. Dokumentumok az egykori SZKP és MSZMP archívumaiból, 1985–1991.* Budapest: 1956-os Intézet, 2000.

Békés, Csaba. "Demokratikus eszmék és nagyhatalmi érdekek. Egy megvalósulatlan amerikai javaslat az 1956-os magyar forradalom megsegítésére." *Holmi* 10 (1993): 1402–8.

———. "Dokumentumok a magyar kormánydelegáció 1946. áprilisi moszkvai tárgyalásairól." *Régió* 3 (1992): 161–94.

———. "Kádár János és az 1968-as csehszlovákiai válság." In *Évkönyv*, vol. 15, *2008*, edited by Pál Germuska and János M. Rainer, 190–228. Budapest: 1956-os Intézet, 2008.

———. "Közread. A magyar kérdés az ENSZ-ben és a nyugati nagyhatalmak titkos tárgyalásai 1956. október 28.—november 4 (Brit külügyi dokumentumok)." In *Évkönyv*, vol. 2, *1993*, edited by András B. Hegedűs, Péter Kende, György Litván, János M. Rainer, and Katalin S. Varga, 39–71. Budapest: 1956-os Intézet, 1993.

———. "Magyar–szovjet csúcstalálkozók, 1957–1965." In *Évkönyv*, vol. 6, *1998*, edited by György Litván, 143–83. Budapest: 1956-os Intézet, 1998.

———. "Miért nem lett második hidegháború Európában? A magyar pártvezetés és az 1979. évi afganisztáni szovjet intervenció. Dokumentumok." In *Évkönyv*, vol. 11, *2003*, edited by Éva Standeisky and János M. Rainer, 223–56. Budapest: 1956-os Intézet, 2003.

———. "Why Was There No 'Second Cold War' in Europe? Hungary and the Soviet Invasion of Afghanistan in 1979: Documents from Hungarian Archives." *Cold War International History Project Bulletin*, no. 14/15 (Winter 2003–Spring 2004): 204–19.

Békés, Csaba, Malcolm Byrne, Melinda Kalmár, Zoltán Ripp, and Miklós Vörös, eds. *Political Transition in Hungary, 1989–1990: A Compendium of Declassified Documents and Chronology of Events.* Budapest: National Security Archive, Cold War History Research Center, 1956 Institute, 1999.

———, eds. *Rendszerváltozás Magyarországon 1989–1990.* Budapest: Hidegháború-történeti Kutatóközpont, 1956-os Intézet, National Security Archive, 1999.

Békés, Csaba, Malcolm Byrne, and János M. Rainer, eds. *The 1956 Hungarian Revolution: A History in Documents*. Budapest: Central European University Press, 2002.

Békés, Csaba, James G. Hershberg, János Kemény, and Zoltán Szőke, eds. "Documentary Evidence on the Hungarian Mediation Efforts between the US and the Democratic Republic of Vietnam (1965–1967), Volume 2: December 1965–January,1966." E-dossier Series No. 3, Cold War History Research Center, Budapest, 2018.

———, eds. "Documentary Evidence on the Hungarian Mediation Efforts between the US and the Democratic Republic of Vietnam (1965–1967), Volume 3: January–February 1966." E-dossier Series No. 4, Cold War History Research Center, Budapest, 2018.

Békés, Csaba, and Anna Locher, eds. *Hungary and the Warsaw Pact, 1954–1989: Documents on the Impact of a Small State within the Eastern Bloc*. Washington D.C.–Zurich: Parallel History Project on NATO and the Warsaw Pact, 2003.

Békés, Csaba, and Melinda Kalmár, eds. "Hungary and the Cuban Missile Crisis: Selected Documents, 1961–1963." *Cold War International History Project Bulletin*, no. 17–18 (Fall 2012): 410–62.

Békés, Csaba, and Gusztáv D. Kecskés, ed. *Az Egyesült Nemzetek Szervezete és a magyar forradalom, 1956–1963. Tanulmányok, dokumentumok és kronológia*. Budapest: Magyar ENSZ Társaság, 2006.

Békés, Csaba, and János Kemény, eds. "Documentary Evidence on the Hungarian Mediation Efforts between the US and the Democratic Republic of Vietnam (1965–1967), Volume I: The Early Stages of the Mediation (1965)." E-dossier Series No. 1, Cold War History Research Center, Budapest, 2017.

Békés, Csaba, Anna Locher, and Christian Nuenlist, eds. *Records of the Warsaw Pact Deputy Foreign Ministers*. Washington: Parallel History Project on NATO and the Warsaw Pact, 2005. www.files.ethz.ch/isn/108639/11_WP_Dep_Foreign_Ministers.pdf.

Békés, Csaba, László J. Nagy, and Dániel Vékony, eds. "Bittersweet Friendships: Relations between Hungary and the Middle East, 1953–1988." E-dossier No. 67, Cold War International History Project, Woodrow Wilson International Center for Scholars, Washington, D.C., 2015.

Borhi, László. *Iratok a magyar–amerikai kapcsolatok történetéhez. 1957–1967. Dokumentumgyűjtemény*. Budapest: Ister, 2002.

———. *Magyar–amerikai kapcsolatok 1945–1989. Források*. Budapest: MTA TTI, 2009.

Bozóki, András, Márta Elbert, Melinda Kalmár, Béla Révész, Erzsébet Ripp, and Zoltán Ripp, eds. *A rendszerváltás forgatókönyve. Kerekasztal tárgyalások 1989-ben*. Vols. 1–4. Budapest: Magvető, 1999.

———, eds. *A rendszerváltás forgatókönyve. Kerekasztal tárgyalások 1989-ben*. Vols. 5–9. kötet, Budapest: Új Mandátum, 2000.

Byrne, Malcom, and Andrzej Paczkowski, eds. *From Solidarity to Martial Law*. Budapest: Central European University Press, 2007.

"Czechoslovakia and Cuba, 1963 (Introduced by James G. Hershberg)." *Cold War International History Project Bulletin*, no. 17–18 (Fall 2012): 404.

The Cuban Missile Crisis, 1962: A National Security Archive Documents Reader. Washington D.C.: National Security Archive, 1999.

Deletant, Dennis. "New Evidence on Romania and the Warsaw Pact, 1955–1989." E-dossier No. 6, Cold War International History Project, Woodrow Wilson International Center for Scholars, Washington, D.C., 2011.

Deletant, Dennis, Mihail E. Ionescu, and Anna Locher, eds. *Romania and the Warsaw Pact: Documents Highlighting Romania's Gradual Emancipation from the Warsaw Pact, 1956–1989.* Parallel History Project on NATO and the Warsaw Pact, March 2004. www .php.isn.ethz.ch.

Documents diplomatiques français 1956. Tome III (24 octobre–31 décembre). Paris: Ministére des Affaires Étrangéres, 1990.

Ehrenberger, Róbert, Erika Laczovics, József Solymosi, and Imre Okváth, eds. *A dolgozó népet szolgálom!" Forráskiadvány a Magyar Néphadsereg Hadtörténelmi Levéltárban őrzött irataiból, 1957–1972.* Budapest: Tonyo–Gráf Nyomdai és Grafikai Stúdió, 2006.

The End of the Cold War in Europe, 1989: New Thinking and New Evidence. Washington D.C.: National Security Archive, 1998.

Az Európai Biztonsági és Együttműködési Értekezlet záróokmánya. Budapest: Kossuth, 1975.

Földes, György. *Kádár János külpolitikája és nemzetközi tárgyalásai.* 2 vols. Budapest: Napvilág Kiadó, 2015.

Foreign Relations of the United States, 1955–1957. Vol. 25, *East-Central Europe.* Washington D.C.: Government Printing Office, 1990.

Foreign Relations of the United States, 1964–1968. Vol. 17, *Eastern Europe.* Washington D.C.: Government Printing Office, 1996.

Fursenko, A. A., ed. *Prezidium TsK KPSS 1954–1964.* Vol. 1, *Chernovye protokol'nye zapisi zasedanii, stenogrammy, postanovleniya.* Moskva: Rosspen, 2003.

Gál, Éva, András B. Hegedűs, György Litván, and János M. Rainer, ed. *A "Jelcin dosszié."* *Szovjet dokumentumok 1956-ról.* Budapest: Századvég Kiadó–1956-os Intézet, 1993.

Garadnai, Zoltán, ed. *Iratok a magyar–francia kapcsolatok történetéhez, 1963–1968.* Budapest: Gondolat, 2008.

Gecsényi, Lajos. *Iratok Magyarország és Ausztria kapcsolatainak történetéhez. 1956–1964.* Budapest: Magyar Országos Levéltár, 2000.

———. *Iratok Magyarország és Ausztria kapcsolatainak történetéhez. 1945–1956.* Budapest: Magyar Országos Levéltár, 2007.

Glatz, Ferenc, ed. A kormány és a párt vezető szerveinek dokumentumaiból 1956. október 23–november 4. *História* 11 (1989): 4–5.

Gluchowsky, Leszek, W. "Poland, 1956: Khrushchev, Gomułka and the 'Polish October.'" *Cold War International History Project Bulletin,* no. 5 (1995): 40–43.

Hajdu, Tibor, közread. "Az 1956. október 24-i moszkvai értekezlet." In *Évkönyv,* vol. 1, *1992,* edited by János M. Bak, Csaba Békés, András B. Hegedűs, and György Litván, 149–56. Budapest: 1956-os Intézet, 1992.

Halmosy, Dénes, ed. *Nemzetközi szerződések, 1945–1982.* Budapest: Közgazdasági és Jogi Könyvkiadó—Gondolat Könyvkiadó, 1985.

Haraszty-Taylor, Eva, ed. *The Hungarian Revolution of 1956: A Collection of Documents from the British Foreign Office.* Nottingham: Astra Press, 1995.

Az igazság a Nagy Imre ügyben. Budapest: Századvég Kiadó–Nyilvánosság Klub, 1989.

Izsák, Lajos, and Miklós Kun, eds. *Moszkvának jelentjük. Titkos dokumentumok, 1944–1948.* Budapest: Századvég Kiadó, 1994.

Jain, Jagdish P., ed. *Documentary Study of the Warsaw Pact.* New York: Asia, 1973.

Juhász, Gyula, ed. *Magyar–brit titkos tárgyalások 1943-ban.* Budapest: Kossuth, 1978.

Kalinovsky, Artemy M., Sergey Radchenko, eds. *The End of the Cold War and the Third World. New Perspectives on Regional Conflict.* London: Routledge, 2013.

Kalmár, Melinda, and Béla Révész, eds. *A rendszerváltás forgatókönyve.* Vol. 6. Budapest: Új Mandátum Kiadó, 2000.

Kecskés, Gusztáv D., ed. *Brüsszelből tekintve. Titkos NATO-jelentések az átalakuló Kelet-Európáról, 1988–1991.* Budapest, MTA BTK–RETÖRKI, 2018.

———, ed. *Magyar–francia kapcsolatok, 1945–1990. Források.* Budapest: MTA Bölcsészettudományi Kutatóközpont, Történettudományi Intézet, 2013.

Keefer, Edward C., David C. Geyer, and Douglas E. Selvage, eds. *Soviet–American Relations: The Détente Years, 1969–1972.* Washington, D.C.: Government Printing Office, 2007.

Kiss, József, Zoltán Ripp, and István Vida. "Források a Nagy Imre-kormány külpolitikájának történetéhez." In *Társadalmi Szemle* 48, no. 5 (1993): 78–94.

———, ed. *Top Secret. Magyar–jugoszláv kapcsolatok 1956. Dokumentumok.* Vol. 1. Budapest: MTA Jelenkorkutató Bizottsága, 1995.

———, ed. *Top Secret. Magyar–jugoszláv kapcsolatok 1956–1959. Dokumentumok..* Vol. 2. Budapest: MTA Jelenkorkutató Bizottsága, 1997.

Kosztricz, Anna S., János Lakos, Karola Vágyi Némethné, László Soós, and György T. Varga, eds. *A Magyar Szocialista Munkáspárt Központi Bizottságának 1989. évi jegyzőkönyvei.* Vols. 1–2. Budapest: Magyar Országos Levéltár, 1993.

Kramer, Mark, ed. "The 'Malin Notes' on the Crises in Hungary and Poland, 1956." *Cold War International History Project Bulletin,* no. 8–9 (Winter 1996/1997): 385–410.

Locher, Anna, ed. *Records of the Committee of the Ministers of Foreign Affairs.* Washington, D.C.: PHP, 2002. www.files.ethz.ch/isn/108633/03_WP_Foreign _Ministers.pdf.

Magyar Távirati Iroda Magyar Közvéleménykutató Szolgálat, Budapest:1946

Mastny, Vojtech. "Third Meeting of the PCC: 4 February 1960, Moscow: Editorial Note." Parallel History Project on NATO and the Warsaw Pact, 2002. www.isn.ethz.ch/php.

Mastny, Vojtech, and Malcom Byrne, eds. *A Cardboard Castle? An Inside History of the Warsaw Pact, 1955–1991.* Budapest: Central European University Press, 2005.

Mastny, Vojtech, Christian Nuenlist, Anna Locher, and Douglas Selvage, eds. *Records of the Warsaw Pact Political Consultative Committee, 1955–1990.* Washington, D.C.: PHP, 2001. www.php.isn.ethz.ch/lory1.ethz.ch/collections/coll_pcc/ednote_56.html.

Mitrovits, Miklós, ed. *Lengyel–magyar "két jóbarát." A magyar–lengyel kapcsolatok dokumentumai, 1957–1987.* Budapest: Napviág Kiadó, 2014.

Munteanu, Mircea, ed. *Romania and the Warsaw Pact, 1955–1989.* Vols. 1–2. Bucharest: 2002.

Navrátil, Jaromil, Antonin Bencik, Václav Kural, Marie Michálková, and Jitka Vondrova, eds. *The Prague Spring, 1968.* Budapest: Central European University Press, 1998.

Némethné Vágyi, Karola, and Levente Sipos, ed. *A Magyar Szocialista Munkáspárt ideiglenes vezető testületeinek jegyzőkönyvei, I. kötet. 1956. november 11.–1957. január 14.* Budapest: Intera RT, 1993.

"Notes on the Conversation of Comrade N. S. Khrushchev with Comrade W. Ulbricht on 1 August 1961." History and Public Policy Program Digital Archive, Russian State Archive on Contemporary History (RGANI). Obtained and translated for CWIHP by Hope M. Harrison and included in CWIHP e-dossier No. 23.

Nuenlist, Christian, ed. *Records of the Warsaw Pact Committee of the Ministers of Defense, 1969–1990*. Washington, D.C.: PHP, 2001. www.php.isn.ethz.ch/lory1.ethz.ch /collections/colltopicb049.html?lng=en&id=14565&nav1=1&nav2=1&nav3=3.

Ólmosi, Zoltán, ed. *Mindszenty és a hatalom. Tizenöt év az USA-követségen*. Budapest: Lex Kft, 1991.

———, ed. *Uprising in East Germany 1953: The Cold War, the German Question and the First Major Upheaval behind the Iron Curtain*. Budapest: Central European University Press, 2001.

"Poland, 1986–1989: The End of the System; A Compendium of Declassified Documents and Chronology of Events." Institute of Political Studies of the Polish Academy of Sciences, National Security Archive, George Washington University, Warsaw, October 20–24, 1999.

"Posetiteli kremlevskava kabineta J.V. Stalina 1944–1946." *Istoricheskij Archiv* 4 (1996).

Procacci, Giovanni, ed. *The Cominform: Minutes of the Three Conferences, 1947/1948/1949*. Milan: Fondazione Feltrinelli, 1994.

Rainer, János M. "Távirat 'Filippov' elvtársnak." In *Évkönyv*, vol. 6, *1998*, edited by György Litván, 103–18. Budapest: 1956-os Intézet, 1998.

———. "The Yeltsin Dossier: Soviet Documents on Hungary, 1956." *Cold War International History Project Bulletin*, no. 5 (Spring 1995): 22–27.

Rainer, János M., and Károly Urbán. "'Konzultációk.' Dokumentumok a magyar és szovjet pártvezetők két moszkvai találkozójáról 1954–1955-ben." *Múltunk* 37 (1992): 124–48.

Rákosi, Mátyás. *Visszaemlékezések 1940–1956*. 2 vols. Budapest: Napvilág Kiadó, 1997.

Report of the Special Committee on the Problem of Hungary. New York: United Nations, 1957.

Savranskaya, Svetlana, and Thomas S. Blanton, eds. *The Last Superpower Summits. Gorbachev, Reagan, and Bush Conversations That Ended the Cold War*. Budapest: Central European University Press, 2016.

Savranskaya, Svetlana, Thomas Blanton, and Vladislav Zubok, eds. *Masterpieces of History: The Peaceful End of the Cold War in Europe, 1989*. Budapest: Central European University Press, 2010.

Snitar, Corina, ed. "Echoes of the 1956 Hungarian Revolt in Romania, 60 Years After." Briefing Book No. 566, National Security Archives, Washington D.C., November 18, 2016.

Sontag, Raymond J., and James Stuart Beddie, eds. *Nazi–Soviet Relations, 1939–1941: Documents from the Archives of the German Foreign Office*. Washington D.C.: Department of State, 1948.

Soós, László, ed. *A Magyar Szocialista Munkáspárt Központi Bizottságának 1957–1958. évi jegyzőkönyvei*. Budapest: Magyar Országos Levéltár, 1997.

———, ed. *A Magyar Szocialista Munkáspárt Központi Bizottságának 1959–1960. évi jegyzőkönyvei*. Budapest: Magyar Országos Levéltár, 1999.

Szereda, Vjacseszlav, and Aleksandr Sztikalin, ed. *Hiányzó lapok 1956 történetéből. Dokumentumok a volt SZKP KB Levéltárából*. Budapest: Móra, 1993.

Szereda, Vjacseszlav, and János M. Rainer, ed. *Döntés a Kremlben, 1956. A szovjet pártelnökség vitái Magyarországról*. Budapest: 1956-os Intézet, 1996.

Szobolevszki, Sándor, and István Vida, ed. *Magyar–kínai kapcsolatok, 1956–1959*. Budapest: MTA Jelenkorkutató Bizottsága, 2001.

A szocializmus útján: A népi demokratikus átalakulás és a szocializmus építésének kronológiája, 1944. szeptember–1980. április. 2nd ed. Budapest: Akadémiai Kiadó, 1982.

UN General Assembly. Eleventh Session (1956–57). Plenary Meetings. Vol. 1 (12 Nov. 1956–8 March 1957, 574th–617th Meetings).

———. First and Second Emergency Special Sessions, 1–10 November 1956. Plenary Meetings and Annexes. 1956.

———. "Report of the Special Committee on the Problem of Hungary." Eleventh Session. Supplement No. 18 (A/3592). 1957.

UN Security Council. Eleventh Year, 734th–755th Meetings Inclusive. 1956.

Urbán, Károly, and István Vida, ed. "Jegyzőkönyv a Politikai Bizottság 1956. június 28-i üléséről." *Társadalmi Szemle* 48, no. 2 (1993): 83–94.

Vámos, György, ed. *A Szabad Európa Rádió és a magyar forradalom—Műsortükör 1956. október 23–november 5.* Budapest: História Alapítvány, 2010.

Vámos, Péter, ed. *Chinese Foreign Ministry Documents on Hungary, 1956.* E-dossier No. 50, Cold War International History Project, Woodrow Wilson International Center for Scholars, Washington D.C., May 19, 2004.

———. *Kína mellettünk? Kínai külügyi iratok Magyarországról, 1956.* Budapest: História–MTA Történettudományi Intézete, 2008.

Varga, László, ed. *A forradalom hangja.* Budapest: Századvég Kiadó–Nyilvánosság Klub, 1989.

Vida, István, ed. *Iratok a magyar–szovjet kapcsolatok történetéhez, 1944. október–1948. június (Dokumentumok).* Budapest: Gondolat Kiadó, 2005.

Volokitina, T. V., Islamov, T. M., Murashko, G. P., Noskova, A. F., Rogovaya, L. A. eds. *Vostochnaja Evropa v dokumentah russiskij archivov, 1944–1953.* Vols. 1–2. Moscow–Novosibirsk: Siberian Chronograph, 1997–1998.

Volokitina, T. V., G. P. Murasko, O. V. Naumov, A. F. Noskova, and T. V. Tsarevskaya, eds. *Sovietskij faktor v Vostochnoj Evrope, 1944–1953.* 2 vols. Moskva, Rosspen, 1998–2002.

"We Were Truly on the Verge of War—a Conversation with Nikita Khrushchev, 30 October 1962 (Obtained by Oldřich Tůma). *Cold War International History Project Bulletin,* no. 17–18 (Fall 2012): 400.

Westad, Odd Arne. "Concerning the Situation in 'A': New Russian Evidence on the Soviet Intervention in Afghanistan." *Cold War International History Project Bulletin,* no. 8–9 (Winter 1996/1997): 128–32.

Zinner, Paul E., ed. *National Communism and Popular Revolt in East-Central Europe: A Selection of Documents on Events in Poland and Hungary, February–November 1956.* New York: Columbia University Press, 1956.

Zubok, Vladislav. "The Khrushchev–Mao Conversations, 31 July–3 August 1958 and 2 October 1959." *Cold War International History Project Bulletin,* no. 12/13 (Fall/Winter 2001): 243–72.

Books and Articles

Adair, Bianca L. "The Austrian State Treaty and Austro–Hungarian relations, 1955–1956." In *The Ungarnkrise 1956 und Österreich,* edited by Ervin Schmidl, 201–13. Wien: Böhlau Verlag, 2003.

Adiibekov, G. M. *Kominform i poslevoennaya Evropa, 1947–1956 gg.* Moscow: Associacia issledovatelej rossiyskovo obscsesztva XX veka, 1994.

Applebaum, Anne. *Iron Curtain: The Crushing of East-Central Europe, 1944–1956.* New York: Anchor Books, 2012.

Asselin, Pierre, *Vietnam's American War. A history.* New York: Cambridge University Press, 2018.

Aunesluoma, Juhana, "Finlandisation in Reverse: The CSCE and the Rise and Fall of Economic Détente, 1968–1975." In *Helsinki 1975 and the Transformation of Europe*, edited by Gottfried Niedhart and Oliver Bange, 98–112. New York: Berghahn Books.

Autio-Sarasmo, Sari, and Katalin Miklóssy, eds. *Reassessing Cold War Europe.* London: Routledge, 2011.

Baev, Jordan. "The Establishment of Bulgarian–West German Diplomatic Relations within the Coordinating Framework of the Warsaw Pact." *Journal of Cold War Studies* 18, no. 3 (Summer 2016): 158–80.

———. "The Organizational and Doctrinal Evolution of the Warsaw Pact, 1955–1969." Paper presented at the International Conference, Spitzbergen Island, Norway, June 2003. www.coldwar.hu/publications/organizational.html.

Balogh, Sándor. *Magyarország külpolitikája 1945–1950, Második bővített, átdolgozott kiadás.* Budapest: Kossuth Kiadó, 1988.

———. *Parlamenti és pártharcok 1945–1947.* Budapest: Kossuth Kiadó, 1975.

Bange, Oliver. "Onto the Slippery Slope: East Germany and East–West Détente under Ulbricht and Honecker, 1965–1975." *Journal of Cold War Studies* 18, no. 3 (Summer 2016): 60–94.

Bange, Oliver, and Gottfried Niedhart. *Helsinki 1975 and the Transformation of Europe.* New York: Berghahn Books, 2008.

Bange, Oliver, and Poul Villaume, eds. *The Long Détente: Changing Concepts of Security and Cooperation in Europe, 1950s–1980s.* Budapest: Central European University Press, 2017.

Baráth, Magdolna. "Kis októberi forradalom. Hruscsov leváltása és a magyar pártvezetés." *Múltunk* 52, no. 4 (2008): 170–212.

———. "Magyarország a szovjet diplomáciai iratokban 1957–1964." In *Múlt századi hétköznapok*, edited by János N. Rainer, 55–89. Budapest: 1956-os Intézet, 2003.

Bar-oon, Mordechai. *Etgar Ve'tigra (Challenge and Quarrel).* Be'er Sheva: Be'er Sheva University Press, 1991.

Békés, Csaba. *Az 1956-os magyar forradalom a világpolitikában.* Második, bővített, átdolgozott kiadás. Budapest: 1956-os Intézet, 2006.

———. "Back to Europe. The International Context of the Political Transition in Hungary, 1988–1990." In *The Roundtable Talks of 1989: The Genesis of Hungarian Democracy,* edited by András Bozóki, 237–72. Budapest: CEU Press, 2002.

———. "A brit kormány és az 1956-os magyar forradalom." In *Évkönyv,* vol. 1, *1992,* edited by János M. Bak, Csaba Békés, András B. Hegedűs, and György Litván, 19–38. Budapest: 1956-os Intézet, 1992.

———. "Cold War, Détente and the 1956 Hungarian Revolution." In *The Cold War after Stalin's Death: A Missed Opportunity for Peace?,* edited by Klaus Larres and Kenneth Osgood, 213–33. Lanham, Md.: Rowman and Littlefield, 2006.

———. "Cold War, Détente and the Soviet Bloc: The Evolution of Intra-bloc Foreign Policy Coordination, 1953–1975." In *Imposing, Maintaining and Tearing Open the Iron Curtain: The Cold War and East-Central Europe, 1945–1989*, edited by Mark Kramer and Vit Smetana, 247–78. Lanham, Md.: Lexington Books, 2014.

———. "The Communist Parties and the National Issue in Central and Eastern Europe, 1945–1947: An Important Factor Facilitating Communist Takeover in the Region." In *6 Martie 1945: Incepturile communizarii Romaniei*, 245–53. Bucuresti: Editure Enciclopedia, 1995.

———. "Détente and the Soviet Bloc, 1975–1991." In *The "Long 1970s": Human Rights, East–West Détente, and Transnational Relations*, edited by Rasmus Mariager, Helle Porsdam, and Poul Villaume, 165–83. London: Routledge, 2016.

———. "East Central Europe, 1953–1956." In *Origins*, edited by Melvyn Leffler and Odd Arne Westad, 334–52. Vol. 1 of *The Cambridge History of the Cold War*. Cambridge: Cambridge University Press, 2010.

———. *Enyhülés és emancipáció. Magyarország, a szovjet blokk és a nemzetközi politika, 1944–1991*. Budapest: Osiris kiadó—MTA TK, 2019.

———. *Európából Európába. Magyarország konfliktusok kereszttüzében, 1945–1990*. Budapest: Gondolat, 2004.

———, ed. *Evolúció és revolúció. Magyarország és a nemzetközi politika 1956-ban*. Budapest: Gondolat Kiadó–1956-os Intézet, 2007.

———. "Hidegháború, enyhülés és az 1956-os magyar forradalom." In *Évkönyv*, vol. 5, *1996–1997*, edited by András B. Hegedűs, Péter Kende, Gyula Kozák, György Litván, and János M. Rainer, 201–13. Budapest: 1956-os Intézet, 1997.

———. "Hidegháború—enyhülés—új megközelítésben." *Külügyi Szemle* 23, no. 4 (2014): 3–18.

———, ed. *The History of the Soviet Bloc, 1945–1991: A Chronology*. Pt. 1, *1945–1952*. Budapest: Cold War History Research Center, 2012. www.coldwar.hu/main_pubs /Chronology1.pdf.

———, ed. *The History of the Soviet Bloc, 1945–1991: A Chronology*. Pt. 2, *1953–1968*. Budapest: Cold War History Research Center, 2013. www.coldwar.hu/main_pubs /Chronology2.pdf.

———, ed. *The History of the Soviet Bloc, 1945–1991: A Chronology*. Pt. 3, *1969–1980*. 2nd enlarged edition. Budapest: Cold War History Research Center, 2018. www .coldwar.hu/main_pubs/Chronology3.pdf.

———, ed. *The History of the Soviet Bloc, 1945–1991: A Chronology*. Pt. 4, *1981–1987*. 2nd enlarged edition. Budapest: Cold War History Research Center, 2018. www .coldwar.hu/main_pubs/Chronology4.pdf.

———, ed. *The History of the Soviet Bloc, 1945–1991: A Chronology*. Pt. 5, *1988–1991*. Budapest: Cold War History Research Center, 2017. www.coldwar.hu/main_pubs /Chronology5.pdf.

———. "Hungarian Foreign Policy in the Bipolar World, 1945–1991." *Foreign Policy Review* (Budapest]) 8, no. 1 (2011): 65–97. www.coldwar.hu/publications/csaba_bekes _-_Hungarian_foreign_policy_in_the_bipolar_world_1945%E2%80%931991.pdf.

———. "Hungarian Foreign Policy in the Soviet Alliance System, 1968–1989." *Foreign Policy Review* (Budapest) 3, no. 1 (2004): 87–127. www.rev.hu/portal/page/portal/rev /tanulmanyok/kadarrendszer/foreign_policy.

———. "The Hungarian Question in the U.N. Security Council: The Secret Negotiations of the Western Great Powers during the 1956 Hungarian Revolution." In *Cold War Eastern Europe*. Routledge, London: 2017. www.coldwareasterneurope.com.

———. "Hungary and the Prague Spring." In *The Prague Spring and the Warsaw Pact Invasion of Czechoslovakia in 1968*, edited by Günter Bischof, Stefan Karner, and Peter Ruggenthaler, 371–95. Lanham, Md.: Lexington Books, 2010.

———. "Hungary 1968: Reform and the Challenge of the Prague Spring." In *East-Central Europe in 1968: Responses to the Prague Spring and Warsaw Pact Invasion*, edited by Kevin McDermott and Matthew Stibbe, 147–67. London: Palgrave Macmillan, 2018.

———. "Hungary, the Soviet Bloc, the German Question and the CSCE Process, 1965–1975." *Journal of Cold War Studies* 18 (Summer 2016): 95–138.

———. Introduction to *Hungary and the Warsaw Pact, 1954–1989: Documents on the Impact of a Small State within the Eastern Bloc*, 4–5. Washington, D.C.–Zurich: 2003.

———. "A kádári külpolitika 1956–1968." *Rubicon* 8 (1997): 19–22.

———. "The Long Détente and the Soviet Bloc, 1953–1983." In *The Long Détente: Changing Concepts of Security and Cooperation in Europe, 1950s–1980s*, edited by Oliver Bange and Poul Villaume, 31–49. Budapest: Central European University Press, 2017.

———. "A lopakodó forradalom." *Rubicon* 9 (2015): 68.

———. "Mad'arsk politick krize na jare 1946." *Suodobé Dejiny* (Praha) 4–5 (1994): 509–13.

———. "Magyarország, a szovjet blokk, a német kérdés és az európai biztonság, 1967–1975." In *Évkönyv*, vol. 16, *2009*, edited by János Tischler, 315–52. Budapest: 1956-os Intézet, 2009.

———. "Magyarország és a nemzetközi politika az ötvenes évek közepén." In *Evolúció és revolúció. Magyarország és a nemzetközi politika 1956-ban*, edited by Csaba Békés, 9–27. Budapest: Gondolat Kiadó–1956-os Intézet, 2007.

———. "Magyarország és az európai biztonsági konferencia előkészítése, 1965–1970." In *Évkönyv*, vol. 12, *2004*, edited by János M. Rainer and Éva Standeisky, 291–309. Budapest: 1956-os Intézet, 2004.

———. "Nagy-Britannia." In *Evolúció és revolúció. Magyarország és a nemzetközi politika 1956-ban*, edited by Csaba Békés, 260–79. Budapest: Gondolat Kiadó–1956-os Intézet, 2007.

———. "The 1956 Hungarian Revolution and the Declaration of Neutrality." *Cold War History* 6, no. 4 (November 2006): 477–500.

———. "The 1956 Hungarian Revolution and World Politics." Working Paper No. 16, Cold War International History Project, Woodrow Wilson International Center for Scholars, Washington, D.C., 1996.

———. "Soviet Plans to Establish Cominform in Early 1946: New Evidence from Hungarian Archives." *Cold War International History Project Bulletin*, no. 10 (March 1998): 135–36.

———. "Titkos válságkezeléstől a politikai koordinációig. Politikai egyeztetési mechanizmus a Varsói Szerződésben, 1954–1967." In *Múlt századi hétköznapok. Tanulmányok a Kádár korszak kialakulásának időszakából*, edited by János M. Rainer, 9–54. Budapest: 1956-os Intézet, 2003.

———. "The Warsaw Pact and the Helsinki Process, 1965–1970." In *The Making of Détente: Eastern and Western Europe in the Cold War, 1965–75*, edited by Wilfried Loth and Georges-Henri Soutou, 201–20. London: Routledge, 2008.

———. "The Warsaw Pact, the German Question and the Making of the CSCE Process, 1961–1970." In *Helsinki 1975 and the Transformation of Europe*, edited by Gottfried Niedhart and Oliver Bange, 113–28. New York: Berghahn Books, 2008.

———. "Why Was There No 'Second Cold War' in Europe? Hungary and the East–West Crisis Following the Soviet Invasion of Afghanistan." In *NATO and the Warsaw Pact: Intrabloc Conflicts*, edited by Mary Ann Heiss and S. Victor Papacosma, 219–32. Kent, Ohio: Kent State University Press, 2008.

Békés, Csaba, László Borhi, Peter Ruggenthaler, and Ottmar Trasca, eds. *Soviet Occupation of Romania, Hungary, and Austria, 1944/45–1948/49*. Budapest: Central European University Press, 2015.

Békés, Csaba, and Melinda Kalmár. "Hruscsov és Kádár. Az elhalasztott lehetőség: a szovjet csapatok kivonásának terve 1958-ban." In *Magyarország Európában, Európa a világban: Tanulmánykötet Gazdag Ferenc 70. születésnapjára*. Koller Boglárka, Marsai Vikor, ed. 85–93. Budapest: Dialóg Campus Kiadó, 2016.

Békés, Csaba, and Gusztáv D. Kecskés, eds. *Az Egyesült Nemzetek Szervezete és a magyar forradalom, 1956–1963. Tanulmányok, dokumentumok és kronológia*. Budapest: Magyar ENSZ Társaság, 2006.

Bencsik, Péter, and György Nagy. *A magyar úti okmányok története, 1945–1989*. Budapest: Tipico Design Kft, 2005.

Berend, Iván T. *Central and East-Central Europe, 1944–1993: Detour from the Periphery to the Periphery*. Cambridge: Cambridge University Press, 1996.

———. *Gazdasági útkeresés. 1956–1965*. Budapest: Magvető Kiadó, 1983.

———. *The Hungarian Economic Reforms, 1953–1988*. Cambridge: Cambridge University Press, 1990.

Beschloss, M. R., and S. Talbott. *At the Highest Levels*. Boston: Little, Brown, 1993.

Bílý, Matěj, *The Warsaw Pact, 1969–1985: The Pinnacle and Path to Dissolution*. Washington D.C.: Academica Press, 2020.

Bischof, Günter. *Austria in the first Cold War: The Leverage of the Weak, 1945–1955*. London: MacMillan, 1999.

Bischof, Günter, and Saki Dockrill, eds. *Cold War Respite: The Geneva Summit of 1955*. Baton Rouge: Louisiana State University Press, 2000.

Bischof, Günter, Stefan Karner, and Peter Ruggenthaler, eds. *The Prague Spring and the Warsaw Pact Invasion of Czechoslovakia in 1968*. Lanham, Md.: Lexington Books, 2010.

Blanton, Thomas. "US Policy and the Revolutions of 1989." In *Masterpieces of History: The Peaceful End of the Cold War in Europe, 1989*, edited by Svetlana Savranskaya, Thomas Blanton, and Vladislav Zubok, 49–98. Budapest: CEU Press, 2010.

Borhi, László. *Dealing with Dictators: The United States, Hungary, and East Central Europe, 1942–1989*. Bloomington: Indiana University Press, 2016.

———. *Hungary in the Cold War, 1945–1956: Between the United States and the Soviet Union*. Budapest: Central European University Press, 2004.

———. *Magyarország a hidegháborúban. A Szovjetunió és az Egyesült Államok között, 1945–1956*. Budapest: Corvina Kiadó, 2005.

———. "'Magyarország kötelessége a Varsói Szerződésben maradni'—az 1989-es átmenet nemzetközi összefüggései magyar források tükrében." *Külügyi Szemle* 6, no. 2–3 (2007): 255–72.

———. "Rollback, Liberation, Containment or Inaction? U.S. Policy and East-Central Europe in the 1950s." *Journal of Cold War Studies* 1, no. 3 (Fall 1999): 67–110.

Bottoni, Stefano. "Kényszerből stratégia: a román állambiztonság válaszlépései a magyar forradalomra 1956–1958." In *Folyamatok a változásban*, edited by Fedinec Csilla and Ablonczy Balázs, 221–54. Budapest: Teleki László Alapítvány, 2005.

———. *Long Awaited West: East-Central Europe since 1944*. Bloomington: Indiana University Press, 2017.

———. "Románia." In *Evolúció és revolúció. Magyarország és a nemzetközi politika 1956-ban*, edited by Csaba Békés, 155–77. Budapest: Gondolat Kiadó–1956-os Intézet, 2007.

Brzezinski, Zbigniew. *The Soviet Bloc, Unity and Conflict*. Cambridge, Mass.: Harvard University Press, 1967.

Brown, Archie. "The Gorbachev Revolution and the End of the Cold War." In *Origins*, edited by Melvyn Leffler and Odd Arne Westad, 244–66. Vol. 1 of *The Cambridge History of the Cold War*. Cambridge: Cambridge University Press, 2010.

———. *The Rise and Fall of Communism*. New York: Ecco, 2009.

Bush, George, and Brent Scowcroft. *A World Transformed*. New York: Alfred A. Knopf, 1998.

Byrne, Malcom. "The Warsaw Pact and the Euromissile Crisis, 1977–1983." In *The Euromissile crisis and the end of the Cold War*, edited by Leopoldo Nuti, Frédéric Bozo, Marie-Pierre Rey, Bernd Rother, 104–120. Washington D.C.: Woodrow Wilson Center Press, 2015.

Campbell, John C. *American Policy toward Communist Eastern Europe: The Choices Ahead*. Minneapolis: University of Minnesota Press, 1965.

Carnesale, Albert, Paul Doty, Stanley Hoffmann, Samuel P. Huntington, Joseph S. Nye Jr., and Scott D. Sagan. *Living with Nuclear Weapons*. Cambridge, Mass.: Harvard University Press, 1983.

Catudal, Honoré. *Kennedy and the Berlin Wall Crisis*. Berlin: Berlin Verlag, 1980.

Chubarian, A. O., ed. *Sovjetskaja vesnaja politika v retrospective, 1917–1991*. Moskva: Nauka, 1993.

Creuzberger, Stefan, and Görtemaker Manfred, eds. *Gleichschaltung unter Stalin? Die Entwicklung der Parteien in östlichen Europa, 1944–1949*. Paderborn: Ferdinand Schöning, 2002.

Cristescu, C. "Ianuarie 1951: Stalin decide înarmarea Romaniei." *Magazin Istoric* 25, no. 10 (1995): 15–23.

Crump, Laurien. *The Warsaw Pact Reconsidered: International Relations in East-Central Europe, 1955–1969*. London: Routledge, 2015.

Crump, Laurien, and Erlandsson, Susanna, eds. *Margins for Manoeuvre in Cold War Europe. The influence of smaller powers*. London: Routledge, 2020.

Csaba, László. "Változó erőtérben—változó egyensúlyozás. Adalék Magyarország háború utáni gazdaságtörténetéhez." In *Távolodás és közelítések. Rendszerváltás és Kádár-korszak*, edited by Majtényi György and Szabó Csaba, 199–217. Budapest: Állambiztonsági Szolgálatok Történeti Levéltára, Kossuth Kiadó, 2008.

Cseh, Gergő Bendegúz, ed. "Documents of the Meetings of the Allied Control Commission in Hungary, 1945–1947." E-dossier Series No. 5, Cold War History Research Center, Budapest, 2018. www.coldwar.hu/main_pubs/documents_meetings_ACC_hungary.pdf.

Deletant, Dennis, and Mihail Ionescu. "Romania and the Warsaw Pact, 1955–1989." Working Paper No. 43. Translations by Viorel Buda, Cornel Ban, and Mircea Munteanu. Cold War International History Project, Woodrow Wilson International Center for Scholars, Washington, D.C., 2011.

Dessewffy, Gyula. "A békekötés előkészítése." Kis Újság, 2 December 1945.

"The Diary of Ben Gurion." In The Suez–Sinai Crisis 1956: Retrospective and Reappraisal, edited by Selwyn. I. Troen and Moshe Shemesh. 289–332, London: Frank Cass, 1990.

Djilas, Milovan. Conversations with Stalin. New York: Harcourt, Brace & World, 1962.

Dobrynin, Anatoly. In Confidence: Moscow's Ambassador to America's Six Cold War Presidents (1962–1986). New York: Random House, 1995.

Dockrill, Saki. "The Eden Plan." In Cold War Respite: The Geneva Summit of 1955, edited by Günter Bischof and Saki Dockrill, 117–54. Baton Rouge: Louisiana State University Press, 2000.

Dunay, Pál, Gazdag, Ferenc, ed. A Helsinki folyamat: az első húsz év. Tanulmányok és dokumentumok. Budapest: Stratégiai és Védelmi Kutató Intézet–Magyar Külügyi Intézet–Zrínyi, 1995.

Eisenberg, Carolyn. Drawing the Line: The American Decision to Divide Germany, 1946–1949. Cambridge: Cambridge University Press, 1996.

Engerman, David C. "Ideology and the Origins of the Cold War." In The Cambridge History of the Cold War. Vol. 1, edited by Melvyn Leffler and Odd Arne Westad, 20–43. Cambridge: Cambridge University Press. 2010.

Esterházy, Péter. Javított kiadás. Budapest: Magvető Kiadó, 2001.

Evangelista, Matthew. "'Why Keep Such an Army?' Khrushchev's Troop Reductions." Working Paper No. 19. Cold War International History Project, Woodrow Wilson International Center for Scholars, Washington D.C., 1997.

Even, Yair. "Two Squadrons and Their Pilots: The First Syrian Request for the Deployment of Soviet Military Forces on its Territory, 1956." Working Paper No. 77, Cold War International History Project, Woodrow Wilson International Center for Scholars, Washington, D.C., 2016.

Fehér, Ferenc. "A hruscsovista mintaállam." In Magyar Füzetek: A stabilitás vége, 27–44. Paris, Dialogues Européens, 1981.

Feitl, István. A bukott Rákosi. Rákosi Mátyás 1956–1971 között. Budapest: Politikatörténeti Alapítvány, 1993.

———. Talányos játszmák. Magyarország a KGST erőterében, 1949–1974. Budapest: Napvilág Kiadó, 2016.

Fejtő, Francois. History of the Peoples Democracies. New York: Praeger, 1971.

Felkay, Andrew. Hungary and the USSR, 1956–1988: Kádár's Political Leadership. New York: Greenwood Press, 1989.

Fischer, Beth A. "US Foreign Policy under Reagan and Bush." In Endings, edited by Melvyn Leffler and Odd Arne Westad, 267–88. Vol. 3 of The Cambridge History of the Cold War. Cambridge: Cambridge University Press, 2010.

Fischer, Ferenc. A kétpólusú világ. A Kelet-Nyugat, 1945–1989. Tankönyv és atlasz. Budapest: Dialóg Campus Kiadó, 2005.

Földes, György. Kádár János külpolitikája és nemzetközi tárgyalásai. 2 vols. Budapest: Napvilág Kiadó, 2015.

———. "Kötélhúzás felsőfokon. Kádár és Brezsnyev." In *Ki volt Kádár? Harag és elfogultság nélkül a Kádár életútról*, edited by Árpád Rácz, 103–13. Budapest: Rubin-Aquila könyvek, 2001.

———. *Magyarország, Románia és a nemzeti kérdés 1956–1989*. Budapest: Napvilág, 2007.

Frankel, Joseph. *British Foreign Policy 1945–1973*. Oxford: Oxford University Press: 1975.

Fülöp, Mihály, ed. *Az elfelejtett béke: Tanulmánykötet a párizsi magyar békeszerződés életbelépésének 70. évfordulójára*. Budapest: Dialóg Campus Kiadó, 2018.

———. "A Sebestyén-misszó." Pts. 1 and 2. *Világpolitika* 10, no. 2 (1987): 141–76.

———. *The Unfinished Peace: The Council of Foreign Ministers and the Hungarian Peace Treaty of 1947*. Boulder, Colo.: Social Science Monographs, 2011.

Für, Lajos. *A Varsói Szerződés végnapjai—magyar szemmel*. Budapest: Kairosz Kiadó, 2003.

Fursenko, Aleksandr, and Timothy Naftali. *Khrushchev's Cold War: The Inside Story of an American Adversary*. New York: W. W. Norton, 2006.

———. *"One Hell of a Gamble": Khrushchev, Castro and Kennedy, 1958–1964*. New York: W. W. Norton, 1997.

Fürst, Juliane, Silvio Pons, and Mark Selden, eds. *Endgames? Late Communism in Global Perspective, 1968 to the Present*. Vol. 3 of *The Cambridge History of Communism*. New York: Cambridge University Press, 2017.

Gaddis, John Lewis. *Strategies of Containment: A Critical Appraisal of Postwar American National Security Policy*. Oxford: Oxford University Press, 1982.

———. *We Now Know: Rethinking Cold War History*. Oxford: Clarendon Press, 1998.

Gaiduk, Ilya V. *The Soviet Union and the Vietnam War*. Chicago: I. R. Dee, 1996.

Garthoff, Raymond. *Détente and Confrontation: American–Soviet Relations from Nixon to Reagan*. Washington D.C.: Brookings Institution, 1985.

———. *The Great Transition: American–Soviet Relations and the End of the Cold War*. Washington D.C.: Brookings Institution, 1994.

———. "When and Why Romania Distanced Itself from the Warsaw Pact." *Cold War International History Project Bulletin*, no. 4 (Spring 1995): 111.

Gati, Charles. *The Bloc That Failed: Soviet–East European Relations in Transition*. Bloomington: Indiana University Press, 1990.

———, ed. *Caging the Bear: Containment and the Cold War*. New York: Bobbs–Merrill, 1974.

———. *Failed Illusions: Moscow, Washington, Budapest, and the 1956 Hungarian Revolt*. Washington, D.C.: Woodrow Wilson Center Press; Stanford, Calif.: Stanford University Press, 2006.

———. *Hungary and the Soviet Bloc*. Durham, N.C.: Duke University Press, 1986.

Gazdag, Ferenc. "Szövetségtől szövetségig: Magyarország útja a Varsói Szerződéstől a NATO-ig." In *Magyar külpolitika a 20. században*, edited by Ferenc Gazdag and László J. Kiss, 195–220. Budapest: Zrínyi Kiadó, 2004.

Gazdag, Ferenc, and László J. Kiss, eds. *Magyar külpolitika a 20. században*. Budapest: Zrínyi Kiadó, 2004.

Gecsényi, Lajos. "Ausztria." In *Evolúció és revolúció. Magyarország és a nemzetközi politika 1956-ban*, edited by Csaba Békés, 207–25. Budapest: Gondolat Kiadó–1956-os Intézet, 2007.

Gémes, Andreas. *Austria and the 1956 Hungarian Revolution: Between Solidarity and Neutrality*. Pisa: PLUS-Pisa University Press, 2008.

Germuska, Pál. "A magyar hadiipar a hatvanas évek elején." In *Múlt századi hétköznapok. Tanulmányok a Kádár rendszer kialakulásának időszakáról*, edited by János M. Rainer, 90–128. Budapest: 1956-os Intézet, 2003.

———. *Unified Military Industries of the Soviet Bloc: Hungary and the Division of Labor in Military Production*. Lanham, Md.: Lexington Books, 2015.

Gibiansky, Leonid. "Kak voznik Kominfom: Po novym arkhivnum materialam." *Novaia i noveishaia istoriia* 4 (1993): 135–36.

———. "The Last Conference of the Cominform." In *The Cominform: Minutes of the Three Conferences: 1947, 1948, 1949*, edited by Giovanni Procacci, 645–67. Milan: Fondazione Feltrinelli, 1994.

———. "Soviet–Yugoslav Relations and the Hungarian Revolution of 1956." *Cold War International History Project Bulletin*, no. 10 (March 1998): 139–48.

Glant, Tibor. *A Szent Korona amerikai kalandja, 1945–1978*. Debrecen: Kossuth Egyetemi kiadó, 1997.

Godard, Simon. "Shaping the Eastern Bloc through the Economy: The Difficult Genesis of a Socialist International Solidarity in COMECON." *Vingtième Siècle. Revue d'histoire* 109, no. 1 (2011): 45–58.

Gori, Francesca, and Silvio Pons, eds. *The Soviet Union and Europe in the Cold War, 1943–53*. London: Palgrave Macmillan, 1997.

Grozev, Kostadin, and Jordan Baev. "Bulgaria: Balkan Diplomacy and the Road to Helsinki." In *Helsinki 1975 and the Transformation of Europe*, edited by Gottfried Niedhart and Oliver Bange, 160–174. New York: Berghahn Books, 2008.

Gyarmati, György. "A Mindszenty–ügy 'diplomáciai' rendezésének kudarca. *Történelmi Szemle* 42 no. 1–2 (2000): 69–90.

Hajdu, Tibor. "Szovjet diplomácia Magyarországon Sztálin halála előtt és után." In *Magyarország és a nagyhatalmak a 20. században. Tanulmányok*, edited by Ignác Romsics, with contributions from András D. Bán, 195–201. Budapest: Teleki László Alapítvány, 1995.

Hanhimäki, Jussi M. *The Rise and Fall of Détente: American Foreign Policy and the Transformation of the Cold War*. Washington, D.C.: Potomac Books, 2013.

Hanrieder, Wolfram F., and Graeme P. Auton. *The Foreign Policies of West Germany, France and Britain*. Englewood Cliffs, N.J.: Prentice-Hall, 1980.

Harrison, Hope. *Driving the Soviets Up the Wall: Soviet–East German Relations, 1953–1961*. Princeton, N.J.: Princeton University Press, 2003.

Hershberg, James G. *Marigold: The Lost Chance for Peace in Vietnam*. Washington, D.C.: Woodrow Wilson Center Press, 2012.

———. "Peace Probes and the Bombing Pause: Hungarian and Polish Diplomacy during the Vietnam War, December 1965–January 1966." *Journal of Cold War Studies* 5 (Spring 2003): 32–67.

Holloway, David. "Nuclear Weapons and the Escalation of the Cold War." In *Origins*, edited by Melvyn Leffler and Odd Arne Westad, 376–97. Vol. 1 of *The Cambridge History of the Cold War*. Cambridge: Cambridge University Press, 2010.

———. *Stalin and the Bomb. The Soviet Union and Atomic Energy, 1939–1954*. New Haven, Conn.: Yale University Press, 1994.

Hook, Stephen W., and John W. Spanier. *American Foreign Policy since World War II*. 21st ed. Thousand Oaks, Calif.: CQ Press, 2019.

Hopkins, Michael F. "The United States and Eastern Europe, 1943–1948." In *Imposing, Maintaining and Tearing Open the Iron Curtain: The Cold War and East-Central Europe, 1945–1989*, edited by Mark Kramer and Vit Smetana, 39–54. Lanham, Md.: Lexington Books, 2014.

Horváth, István, and István Németh. . . . *És a falak leomlanak. Magyarország és a német egység, 1945–1990: Legenda és valóság.* Budapest: Magvető, 1999.

Horváth, Julianna, Éva Szabó, László Szűcs, and Katalin Zalai, ed. *Pártközi értekezletek 1944–1948. Politikai érdekegyeztetés, politikai konfrontáció.* Budapest: Napvilág, 2003.

Horváth, Miklós, and Jenő Györkei, eds. *Soviet Military Intervention in Hungary, 1956.* Budapest: Central European University Press, 1999.

Huszár, Tibor. *1968: Prága, Budapest, Moszkva. Kádár János és a csehszlovákiai intervenció.* Budapest: Szabad Tér, 1998.

Hutchings, Robert L. *American Diplomacy and the End of the Cold War: An Insider's Account of U.S. Policy in Europe, 1989–1992.* Washington D.C.: Woodrow Wilson Center Press; Baltimore: Johns Hopkins University Press, 1997.

Immerman, Richard H., ed. *John Foster Dulles and the Diplomacy of the Cold War.* Princeton, N. J.: Princeton University Press, 1990.

Ionescu, Mihail E. "Romania, *Ostpolitik* and the CSCE, 1967–1975." In *Helsinki 1975 and the Transformation of Europe*, edited by Gottfried Niedhart and Oliver Bange, 129–43. New York: Berghahn Books, 2008.

Jarzabek, Wanda. "Hope and Reality: Poland and the CSCE, 1964–1989. Working Paper No. 56, Cold War International History Project, Woodrow Wilson International Center for Scholars, Washington, D.C., 2008.

———. Impact of the German Question on Polish Attitudes toward CSCE, 1964–1975." *Journal of Cold War Studies* 18 (Summer 2016): 139–57.

Jervis, Robert. *Perceptions and Misperceptions in International Politics.* Princeton, N.J.: Princeton University Press, 1976.

Jian, Chen. *Mao's China and the Cold War.* Chapel Hill: University of North Carolina Press, 2001.

Johnson, Ross A. *Radio Free Europe and Radio Liberty: The CIA Years and Beyond.* Washington, D.C.: Woodrow Wilson Center Press, 2010.

Judt, Tony. *Postwar: A History of Europe since 1945.* London: Penguin Books, 2005.

Kádár, Béla. "Magyarország gazdasági kapcsolatai az NDK-val és az NSZK-val." *Külpolitika* 13, no. 1 (1986): 18–33.

Kalmár, Melinda. *Ennivaló és hozomány. A kora-kádárizmus ideológiája.* Budapest: Magvető Kiadó, 1998.

———. "From 'Model Change' to Regime Change: The Metamorphosis of the MSZMP's Tactics in the Democratic Transition." In *The Roundtable Talks of 1989: The Genesis of Hungarian Democracy*, edited by András Bozóki, 41–69. Budapest: Central European University Press, 2002.

———. "A politika poétikája. Irodalomideológia az ötvenes évek első felében." *Holmi* 5, no. 5 (1993): 715–30.

———. "Socialist or Realist: The Poetics of Politics in Soviet Hungary." In *Socialist Realism in Central and East-Central European Literatures under Stalin: Institutions, Dynamics, Discourses*, edited by Evgeny Dobrenko and Natalia Jonsson-Skradol, 217–34. Cambridge: Anthem Press, 2018.

———. "A sztálinizmus kelet-közép-európai esélyei: A népi demokratikus elkanyarodás."
In *Metszetek bolsevizmusról, sztálinizmusról* Gyarmati György, Pihurik Judit, ed,
133–62. Budapest: Magyar Történelmi Társulat, Állambiztonsági Szolgálatok Történeti
Levéltára, Kronosz Kiadó, 2018.

———. *Történelmi galaxisok vonzásában. Magyarország és szovjetrendszer, 1945–1990.*
Budapest: Osiris, 2014.

Kansikas, Suvi. *Socialist Countries Face the European Community: Soviet-Bloc Controversies
over East–West Trade.* Frankfurt: Peter Lang, 2014.

Kecskés, Gusztáv D. *Franciaország és a magyar forradalom, 1956.* Budapest: MTA
Történettudományi Intézet—História, 2007.

———. "French Foreign Policy and the 1956 Hungarian Revolution." *COJOURN* 1, no. 3
(2016): 98–110. http://real.mtak.hu/42438/1/COJOURN_Vol1_No3_08_Gusztav_D
_Kecskes_1_u.pdf.

———. "The North Atlantic Treaty Organization and the Hungarian Revolution of 1956."
In *The Ideas of the Hungarian Revolution, Suppressed and Victorious 1956–1999*, edited by
Lee W. Congdon and Béla K. Király, 112–41. Colorado: Social Science Monographs, 2002.

———. "The Suez Crisis and the 1956 Hungarian Revolution." *East European Quarterly* 35,
no. 1 (Spring 2001): 47–58.

Keleti, György. "Szovjet csapatkivonások. Magyarország katonai függetlenségének
története—a jugoszláviai konfliktus." In *Magyarország politikai évkönyve* Vass László,
Sándor Péter, Kurtán Sándor ed., 381–409. Budapest: Demokrácia Kutatások Magyar
Központja, 1992.

Kenez, Peter. *Hungary from the Nazis to the Soviets: The Establishment of the Communist
Regime in Hungary, 1944–1948.* Cambridge: Cambridge University Press, 2009.

Kertesz, Stephen D., ed. *The Fate of East Central Europe. Hopes and Failures of American
Foreign Policy.* Notre Dame, Ind.: University of Notre Dame Press, 1956.

———. *The Last European Peace Conference, Paris 1946: Conflict of Values.* Lanham, Md.:
University Press of America, 1985.

Kieninger, Stephan. *Dynamic Détente: The United States and Europe, 1964–1975.* Lanham,
Md.: Lexington Books, 2016.

Király, Béla. *Honvédségből néphadsereg. Személyes visszaemlékezések, 1944–1956.* Paris:
Magyar Füzetek, 1986.

Kiss, László J. "Az első államközi megállapodástól a diplomáciai kapcsolatok felvételéig.
A magyar–NSZK kapcsolatok egy évtizede (1963–1973)." *Külpolitika* 3, no. 3 (1976): 3–18.

———. "A kádárizmustól az EU-tagságig: A magyar külpolitika metamorfózisa." In
Magyar külpolitika a 20. században: tanulmányok, edited by Ferenc Gazdag and
László J. Kiss, 45–78. Budapest: Zrínyi Kiadó, 2004.

Kocsis, Piroska. "Magyar orvosok Koreában, 1950–1957." *Archivnet* 5, no. 6 (2005). www
.archivnet.hu/politika/magyar_orvosok_koreaban_19501957.html.

Kovrig, Bennett. *The Myth of Liberation: East Central Europe in U.S. Diplomacy and
Politics Since 1941.* Baltimore: Johns Hopkins University Press, 1973.

———. *Of Walls and Bridges: The United States and East-Central Europe.* New York:
New York University Press, 1991.

Kramer, Mark. "The Collapse of East European Communism and the Repercussions
within the Soviet Union." Pts. 1, 2, and 3. *Journal of Cold War Studies* 5, no. 4 (Fall
2003): 178–256; 6, no. 4 (Fall 2004): 3–64; 7, no. 1 (Winter 2005): 3–96.

———. "The Early Post-Stalin Succession Struggle and Upheavals in East-Central Europe: Internal-External Linkages in Soviet Policy Making." Pts. 1, 2, and 3. *Journal of Cold War Studies* 1, no. 1 (Winter 1999): 3–55; 1, no. 2 (Spring 1999): 3–38; 1, no. 3 (Fall 1999): 3–66.

Kramer, Mark. "The Kuklinski Files and the Polish Crisis of 1980–1981. An analysis of the newly released CIA documents on Ryszard Kuklinski." Working Paper No. 59, Cold War International History Project, Woodrow Wilson International Center for Scholars, Washington, D.C., 2009.

———. "New Evidence on Soviet Decision-Making and the 1956 Polish and Hungarian Crises." *Cold War International History Project Bulletin*, no. 6 (Winter 1996–1997): 358–84.

———. "Stalin, Soviet Policy and the Establishment of a Communist Bloc, 1941–1949." In *Imposing, Maintaining, and Tearing Open the Iron Curtain: The Cold War and East-Central Europe, 1945–1989*, edited by Mark Kramer and Vit Smetana, 3–37. Lanham, Md.: Lexington Books, 2014.

Kramer, Mark, and Vit Smetana, eds. *Imposing, Maintaining, and Tearing Open the Iron Curtain: The Cold War and East-Central Europe, 1945–1989*. Lanham, Md.: Lexington Books, 2014.

Kyle, Keith. *Suez*. London: Weidenfeld and Nicholson, 1991.

Lamb, Richard. *The Failure of the Eden Government*. London: Sidgwick and Jackson, 1987.

Larres, Klaus, and Kenneth Osgood, eds. *The Cold War after Stalin's Death: A Missed Opportunity for Peace?* Lanham, Md.: Rowman and Littlefield, 2006.

Leffler, Melvyn P. "The Cold War: What Do 'We Now Know'"? *American Historical Review* 104, no. 2 (April 1999): 501–24.

———. *For the Soul of Mankind: The United States, the Soviet Union, and the Cold War.* New York: Hill and Wang, 2008.

Leffler, Melvyn P., and David S. Painter, eds. *Origins of the Cold War: An International History*. London: Routledge, 1994.

Leffler, Melvyn P., and Odd Arne Westad, eds. *The Cambridge History of the Cold War*. 3 vols. Cambridge: Cambridge University Press, 2010.

Lévesque, Jacques. *The Enigma of 1989: The USSR and the Liberation of East-Central Europe*. Berkeley: University of California Press, 1997.

Lidegaard, Bo. *A legmagasabb ár: Povl Bang-Jensen és az ENSZ, 1955–1959*. Budapest: Magyar Könyvklub, 2000.

Lipkin, Mikhail. "Soviet Snowdrops in the Ice Age? The Surprising Attempt of an Early Economic Détente in 1952." In *The Long Détente: Changing Concepts of Security and Cooperation in Europe, 1950s–1980s*, edited by Oliver Bange and Poul Villaume, 53–75. Budapest: Central European University Press, 2017.

Litván, György. "A Nagy Imre-per politika háttere." *Világosság* 33, no. 10 (1992): 743–57.

Locher, Anna. "Shaping the Policies of the Alliance: The Committee of Ministers of Foreign Affairs of the Warsaw Pact, 1976–1990." In *Records of the Warsaw Pact Committee of the Ministers of Foreign Affairs, 1976–1990*, edited by Anna Locher. Washington, D.C.: PHP, 2002.

Loth, Wilfried. *Overcoming the Cold War: A History of Détente, 1950–1991*. New York: Palgrave, 2002.

Loth, Wilfried, and Georges-Henri Soutou, eds. *The Making of Détente: Eastern and Western Europe in the Cold War, 1965–75.* London: Routledge, 2008.

Louis, W. M., and R. Owen, eds. *Suez 1956: The Crisis and Its Consequences.* Oxford: Clarendon Press, 1989.

Lundestad, Geir. *The American Non-policy toward East-Central Europe, 1943–1947.* New York: Humanities Press, 1975.

Machcewicz, Pawel. *Rebellious Satellite: Poland, 1956.* Washington D.C.: Woodrow Wilson Center Press, 2009.

———. "Social Protest and Political Crisis in 1956." In *Stalinism in Poland, 1944–1956: Selected Papers from the Fifth World Congress of Central and East European Studies, Warsaw, 1995,* edited by A. Kemp-Welch, 102–4. London: Macmillan Press LTD, 1999.

Magyarics, Tamás. "Az Egyesült Államok és Magyarország, 1957–1967." *Századok* 130, no. 3 (1996): 571–612.

Mariager, Rasmus, Helle Porsdam, and Poul Villaume, eds. *The "Long 1970s": Human Rights, East-West Détente, and Transnational Relations.* London: Routledge, 2016.

Mark, Eduard. "American Policy toward Eastern Europe and the Origins of the Cold War." *Journal of American History* 68, no. 2 (1981).

———. "Revolution by Degrees: Stalin's National-Front Strategy for Europe, 1941–1947." Working Paper No. 31, Cold War International History Project, Woodrow Wilson International Center for Scholars, Washington, D.C., 2011.

Marton, Kati. *Enemies of the People: My Family's Journey to America.* New York: Simon & Schuster, 2009.

Mastny, Vojtech. *The Cold War and Soviet Insecurity: The Stalin Years.* New York: Oxford University Press, 1996.

———. "Eighth Meeting of the PCC: 4–6 July 1966, Bucharest: Editorial Note." Parallel History Project on NATO and the Warsaw Pact. 2003, www.isn.ethz.ch/php.

———. "Learning from the Enemy: NATO as a Model for the Warsaw Pact." In *A History of NATO: The First Fifty Years,* vol. 2, edited by Gustav Schmidt, 157–78. London: Palgrave, 2001.

———. "Seventh Meeting of the PCC: 19–20 January 1965, Warsaw: Editorial Note." Parallel History Project on NATO and the Warsaw Pact. 2003, www.isn.ethz.ch/php.

———. "The Soviet Non-invasion of Poland in 1980–81 and the End of the Cold War." Working Paper No. 23, Cold War International History Project, Woodrow Wilson International Center for Scholars, Washington, D.C., 1998.

———. "The Soviet Union and the Origins of the Warsaw Pact in 1955." In *Mechanisms of Power in the Soviet Union,* edited by Niels Erik Rosenfeldt, Bent Jensen, and Erik Kulavig, 241–66. New York: St. Martin's Press, 2000.

———. "Tenth Meeting of the PCC: 17 March 1969, Budapest: Editorial Note." Parallel History Project on NATO and the Warsaw Pact. 2001, www.isn.ethz.ch/php.

———. "The Warsaw Pact as History." In *A Cardboard Castle? An inside History of the Warsaw Pact, 1955–1991,* edited by Vojtech Mastny and Malcolm Byrne, 1–73. Budapest: Central European University Press, 2005.

Maurer, Pierre. *La réconciliation soviéto–yougoslave 1954–1958: Illusions et désillusions de Tito.* Cousset, Fribourg: Delval, 1991.

McCauley, Brian. "Hungary and Suez 1956: Limits of Soviet and American Power." *Journal of Contemporary History* 16, no. 4 (October 1981): 777–800.

McDermott, Kevin, and Matthew Stibbe, eds. *East-Central Europe in 1968: Responses to the Prague Spring and Warsaw Pact Invasion.* London: Palgrave Macmillan, 2018.

Mićunović, Veljko. *Moscow Diary, 1956–1958.* Translated by David Floyd. Garden City, N.Y.: Doubleday, 1980.

Mikoyan, Sergo, and Svetlana Savranskaya. *The Soviet Cuban Missile Crisis: Castro, Mikoyan, Kennedy, Khrushchev, and the Missiles of November.* Washington, D.C.: Woodrow Wilson Center Press; Stanford, Calif.: Stanford University Press, 2012.

Miles, Simon. *Engaging the Evil Empire: Washington, Moscow, and the Beginning of the End of the Cold War.* Ithaca, N.Y.: Cornell University Press, 2020.

Miller, Chris. *The Struggle to Save the Soviet Economy: Mikhail Gorbachev and the Collapse of the USSR.* Chapel Hill: University of North Carolina Press, 2017.

Mitrovits, Miklós. *A remény hónapjai . . . : A lengyel Szolidaritás és a szovjet politika, 1980–1981.* Budapest: Napvilág Kiadó, 2010.

Molnár, Miklós. *Budapest 1956: A History of the Hungarian Revolution.* London: Allen and Unwin, 1971.

Mong, Attila. *Kádár hitele—A magyar államadósság története 1956–1990.* Budapest: Libri, 2012.

Munteanu, Mircea. "Over the Hills and Far Away: Romania's Attempts to Mediate the Start of U.S.–North Vietnamese Negotiations, 1967–68." *Journal of Cold War Studies* 14, no. 3 (2012): 64–96.

Murányi, Gábor. "A Konduktorov-ügy." *Magyar Nemzet,* August 21, 1991.

Murashko, Galina P., and Albina F. Noskova. "Stalin and the National-Territorial Controversies in Eastern Europe, 1945–47." Pt. 1. *Cold War History* 1, no. 3 (2001): 161–72.

Nagy, András. *A Bang-Jensen Ügy: '56 Nyugati Ellenszélben.* Budapest: Magvető, 2005.

Nagy, Ferenc. *The Struggle behind the Iron Curtain.* New York: Macmillan, 1948.

Nagy, Imre. *On Communism: In Defense of the New Course.* London: Thames and Hudson, 1957.

Nagy, Miklós, ed. *A magyar külpolitika, 1956–1989. Történeti kronológia.* Budapest: MTA Jelenkorkutató Bizottság, 1993.

Naimark, Norman. "The Sovietization of Eastern Europe, 1944–1953." In *Origins,* edited by Melvyn P. Leffler and Odd Arne Westad, 175–97. Vol. 1 of *The Cambridge History of the Cold War.* Cambridge: Cambridge: University Press, 2010.

———. *Stalin and the Fate of Europe: The Postwar Struggle for Sovereignty.* Cambridge, Mass.: Harvard University Press, 2019.

Naimark, Norman, Silvio Pons, and Sophie Quinn-Judge, eds. *The Socialist Camp and World Power, 1941–1960s.* Vol. 2 of *The Cambridge History of Communism.* New York: Cambridge University Press, 2017.

Nezhinsky, L. N., ed. *Sovjetskaja vesnaja politika v godi holodnoj vojni, 1945–1985.* Moscow: Mezdunarodnaja Otnashenia, 1995.

Niedhart, Gottfried. "Introduction: CSCE, the German Question, and the Eastern Bloc." *Journal of Cold War Studies* 18 (Summer 2016): 3–13.

———. "Ostpolitik: Transformation through Communication." *Journal of Cold War Studies* 18 (Summer 2016): 14–59.

Nielsen, Catherine C. "Neutrality vs. Neutralism: Austrian Neutrality and the 1956 Hungarian Crisis." In *The Ungarnkrise 1956 und Österreich,* edited by Ervin A. Schmidl. Wien: Böhlau Verlag, 2003.

Okváth, Imre. *Bástya a béke frontján. Magyar haderő és katonapolitika, 1945–1956.* Budapest: Aquila, 1998.

———. "The Initial Phase of Hungary's Integration into the Unified Armed Forces of the Warsaw Pact, 1957–1971." Parallel History Project on NATO and the Warsaw Pact, 2001.

Oplatka, András. *Egy döntés története. Magyar határnyitás—1989. szeptember 11. nulla óra.* Wien: Paul Zsolnay Verlag, 2008.

———. *Der erste Riss in der Mauer: September 1989. Ungarn öffnet die Grenze.* Wien: Zsolnay, 2009.

Ostermann, Christian F. *Between Containment and Rollback: The United States and the Cold War in Germany.* Stanford, Ca.: Stanford University Press, 2021.

Oudenaren, John Van. *Deténte in Europe: The Soviet Union and the West since 1953.* Durham, N.C.: Duke University Press, 1991.

Pach, Chester J., Jr., and Elmo Richardson, eds. *The Presidency of Dwight D. Eisenhower.* Rev. ed. Kansas City: University Press of Kansas, 1991.

Paczkowski, Andrzej. *The Spring Will Be Ours: Poland and the Poles from Occupation to Freedom.* Translated by Jane Cave. University Park: Pennsylvania State University Press, 2003.

Paczkowski, Andrzej, and Andrzej Werblan. "'On the Decision to Introduce Martial Law in Poland in 1981': Two Historians Report to the Commission on Constitutional Oversight of the SEJM of the Republic of Poland." Working Paper No. 21, Cold War International History Project, Woodrow Wilson International Center for Scholars, Washington, D.C., 1997.

Parrish, Scott D., and Mikhail M. Narinsky. "New Evidence on the Soviet Rejection of the Marshall Plan, 1947: Two Reports." Working Paper No. 9, Cold War International History Project, Woodrow Wilson International Center for Scholars, Washington, D.C., 2011.

Pataky, Iván. *A vonakodó szövetséges. A Magyar Népköztársaság és a Magyar Néphadsereg közreműködése Csehszlovákia 1968. évi megszállásában.* Budapest: Rastafari, 2008.

Pechatnov, Vladimir O. "The Big Three after World War II: New Documents on Soviet Thinking about Post War Relations with the United States and Great Britain." Working Paper No. 13, Cold War International History Project, Woodrow Wilson International Center for Scholars, Washington, D.C., 1995.

———. "The Soviet Union and the World, 1944–1953." In *Origins*, edited by Melvyn P. Leffler and Odd Arne Westad, 90–111. Vol. 1 of *The Cambridge History of the Cold War.* Cambridge: Cambridge University Press, 2010.

Pető, Iván. "A. J. Visinszkij: A magyar–csehszlovák lakosságcseréről." *Századvég*, no. 6–7 (1988): 142–49.

Pető, Iván, and Sándor Szakács. *A hazai gazdaság négy évtizedének története, 1945–1985.* Budapest: Közgazdasági és Jogi Könyvkiadó, 1985.

Plokhy, Serhii. *Yalta: The Price of Peace.* London: Penguin, 2011.

Politicheskie konflikty 50–60.h godov v "Vostochnoj Evrope." Moscow: 1993.

Pons, Silvio, and Federico Romero, eds. *Reinterpreting the End of the Cold War: Issues, Interpretations, Periodizations.* London: Frank Cass, 2005.

Poznanski, Kazimierz Z. *Poland's Protracted Transition: Institutional Change and Economic Growth, 1970–1994.* Cambridge: Cambridge University Press, 1997.

Pritz, Pál, ed. *Magyar külpolitikai gondolkodás a 20. században.* Budapest: Magyar Történeti Társulat, 2006.

Pula, Besnik. *Globalization under and after Socialism: The Evolution of Transnational Capital in Central and East Europe.* Palo Alto, Calif.: Stanford University Press, 2018.

Quimet, Matthew J. *The Rise and Fall of the Brezhnev Doctrine in Soviet Foreign Policy.* Chapel Hill: University of North Carolina Press, 2003.

Radványi, János. *Delusion and Reality: Gambits, Hoaxes, and Diplomatic One-Upmanship in Vietnam.* Southbend, Ind.: Gateway, 1978.

———. *Hungary and the Superpowers: The 1956 Hungarian Revolution and Realpolitik.* Stanford, Calif.: Hoover Institution Press, 1972.

Rainer, János, M. "Hruscsov Budapesten, 1958. április." *Budapesti Negyed* 4 (1994): 159–90.

———. *Nagy Imre 1953–1958. Politikai életrajz.* Vol. 2. Budapest: 1956-os Intézet, 1999.

———. "Szovjet döntéshozatal Magyarországról." In *Évkönyv*, vol. 2, *1993*, edited by András B. Hegedűs, Péter Kende, György Litván, János M. Rainer, and Katalin S. Varga, 19–38. Budapest: 1956-os Intézet, 1993.

———. "Sztálin és Rákosi, Sztálin és Magyarország, 1949–1953." In *Évkönyv*, vol. 6, *1998*, edited by György Litván, 91–100. Budapest, 1956-os Intézet, 1998.

Rainer, János M., and Katalin Somlai, eds. *The 1956 Hungarian Revolution and the Soviet Bloc Countries: Reactions and Repercussions.* Budapest: Institute for the History of the 1956 Hungarian Revolution, 2007.

Rajak, Svetozar. "The Cold War in the Balkans, 1945–1956." In *Origins*, edited by Melvyn Leffler and Odd Arne Westad, 198–220. Vol. 1 of *The Cambridge History of the Cold War.* Cambridge: Cambridge University Press, 2010.

———. *Yugoslavia and the Soviet Union in the Early Cold War: Reconciliation, Comradeship, Confrontation, 1953–1957.* London: Routledge, 2011.

Rákosi, Mátyás. *Visszaemlékezések, 1940–1956.* Edited by Feitl István, Gellériné Lázár Márta, and Sipos Levente. 2 vols. Budapest: Napvilág Kiadó, 1997.

Resis, Albert. "The Churchill-Stalin 'Percentages' Agreement on the Balkans, Moscow, October 1944." *American Historical Review* 83 (April 1978): 368–87.

Révai, József. "Nemzetrontó sovinizmus." *Szabad Nép*, 25 December 1945.

Rey, Marie Pierre. "Europe Is Our Common Home: A Study of Gorbachev's Diplomatic Concept." *Cold War History* 4, no. 2 (2004): 33–65.

Rieber, Alfred J. *Salami Tactics Revisited: The Hungarian Communists on the Road to Power.* Trondheim: Trondheim Studies on East European Cultures and Societies, 2013.

———. *Stalin and the Struggle for Supremacy in Eurasia.* Cambridge: Cambridge University Press, 2015.

Ripp, Zoltán. *Belgrád és Moszkva között. A jugoszláv kapcsolat és a Nagy Imre-kérdés: 1956. november–1959. február.* Budapest: Politikatörténeti Alapítvány, 1994.

———. "Jugoszlávia." In *Evolúció és revolúció. Magyarország és a nemzetközi politika 1956-ban*, edited by Békés Csaba, 55–82. Budapest: Gondolat Kiadó–1956-os Intézet, 2007.

———. *A pártvezetés végnapjai 1956. október 23–31.* In *Ötvenhat októbere és a hatalom. A Magyar Dolgozók Pártja vezető testületeinek dokumentumai 1956. október 24–28*, edited by Julianna Horváth and Zoltán Ripp, 288–95. Budapest: Napvilág Kiadó, 1997.

Ritter, László, Christian Nuenlist, and Anna Locher, eds. *War on Tito's Yugoslavia? The Hungarian Army in Early Cold War Soviet Strategies.* Parallel History Project on Cooperative Security, 2005. www.php.isn.ethz.ch/lory1.ethz.ch/collections /colltopicaccb.html?lng=en&id=15463.

Roberts, Geoffrey. "A Chance for Peace? The Soviet Campaign to End the Cold War, 1953–1955." Working Paper No. 57, Cold War International History Project, Woodrow Wilson International Center for Scholars, Washington, D.C., 2008.

———. "Stalin at the Tehran, Yalta, and Potsdam Conferences." *Journal of Cold War Studies* 9 (Fall 2007): 6–40.

Romano, Angela. "Untying Cold War Knots: The EEC and Eastern Europe in the Long 1970s." *Cold War History* 14, no. 2 (2014): 153–73.

Romano, Angela, and Federico Romero. "European Socialist Regimes Facing Globalization and European Co-operation: Dilemmas and Responses—Introduction." *European Review of History* 21, no. 2 (2014): 157–64.

Romsics, Ignác. *Az 1947-es párizsi békeszerződés.* Budapest: Osiris, 2006.

Rubleczky, Géza. "Készüljünk a békére." *Kis Újság,* 28 December 1945.

Ruff, Mihály. "A hivatalos Magyarország nyugatnémet politikai kapcsolatairól, 1956–1958." *Századok* 132, no. 5 (1998): 1113–32.

———. "A magyar–NSZK kapcsolatok, 1960–1963. Útkeresés a doktrínák útvesztőjében." *Múltunk* 44, no. 3 (1999): 3–40.

Ruggenthaler, Peter. *The Concept of Neutrality in Stalin's Foreign Policy, 1945–1953.* Lanham, Md.: Lexington Books, 2015.

———. "On the Significance of Austrian Neutrality for Soviet Foreign Policy under Nikita S. Khrushchev." In *The Vienna Summit and Its Importance in International History,* edited by Günter Bischof, Stefan Karner, and Barbara Stelzl-Marx, 329–48. Lanham, Md.: Lexington Books, 2014.

Sarotte, M. E. *Dealing with the Devil: East Germany, Détente, and Ostpolitik, 1969–1973.* Chapel Hill: University of North Carolina Press, 2001.

———. *1989: The Struggle to Create Post-Cold War Europe.* Princeton, N.J.: Princeton University Press, 2009.

Savranskaya, Svetlana. "The Logic of 1989: The Soviet Peaceful Withdrawal from East-Central Europe." In *Masterpieces of History: The Peaceful End of the Cold War in Europe, 1989,* edited by Svetlana Savranskaya, Thomas Blanton, and Vladislav Zubok, 1–47. Budapest: CEU Press, 2010.

Savranskaya, Svetlana, and William Taubman. "Soviet Foreign Policy, 1962–1975." In *Crises and Détente,* edited by Melvyn P. Leffler and Odd Arne Westad, 134–57. Vol. 2 of *The Cambridge History of the Cold War.* Cambridge: Cambridge University Press 2010.

Schwartz, Hans-Peter. "The Division of Germany, 1945–1949." In *Origins,* edited by Melvyn P. Leffler and Odd Arne Westad, 133–53. Vol. 1 of *The Cambridge History of the Cold War.* Cambridge: Cambridge University Press, 2010.

Selvage, Douglas. "The Treaty of Warsaw: The Warsaw Pact Context." In *American Détente and German Ostpolitik, 1969–1972,* edited by David C. Geyer, 67–79. Washington, D.C.: German Historical Institute, 2004.

———. "The Warsaw Pact and the German Question, 1955–1970." In *NATO and the Warsaw Pact: Intrabloc Conflicts,* edited by Mary Heiss and S. Victor Papacosma, 178–92. Kent, Ohio: Kent State University Press, 2008.

———. "The Warsaw Pact and Nuclear Nonproliferation, 1963–1965." Working Paper No. 32, Cold War International History Project, Woodrow Wilson International Center for Scholars, Washington, D.C., 2001.

Service, Robert. *The End of the Cold War, 1985–1991.* New York: Public Affairs, 2015.

Shakhnazarov, G. Kh. *Tsena svobodi.* Moszkva: Rossika–Zeus, 1993.

Sipos, Levente. "Miért ragaszkodott Kádár a szovjet csapatokhoz?" *Ring,* 4 July 1990.

Smetana, Vit. "Concessions or Conviction? Czechoslovakia's Road to the Cold War and the Soviet Bloc." In *Imposing, Maintaining and Tearing Open the Iron Curtain,* edited by Mark Kramer and Vit Smetana, 55–85. Lanham, Md.: Lexington Books, 2014.

Snyder, Sarah B. *Human Rights, Activism and the End of the Cold War: A Transnational History of the Helsinki Network.* New York: Cambridge University Press, 2011.

"Speech by József Révai on the 'Hungarian Peace' at the Conference of Intellectuals Held at the Musical Academy, April 26, 1946." *Szabad Nép,* April 28, 1946.

Steiner, André. *The Plans That Failed: An Economic History of the GDR.* New York: Berghahn, 2013.

Stolarik, Mark M. *The Prague Spring and the Warsaw Pact Invasion of Czechoslovakia, 1968: Forty Years Later.* Mundelein, Ill.: Bolchazy-Carducci, 2010.

Stone, Randall W. *Satellites and Commissars: Strategy and Conflict in the Politics of Soviet-Bloc Trade.* Princeton, N.J.: Princeton University Press, 1996.

Symser, W. R. *Kennedy and the Berlin Wall: "A Hell of a Lot Better Than a War."* Lanham, Md.: Rowman & Littlefield, 2009.

Szabó, Miklós. "From Big Elephant to Paper Tiger: Soviet–Hungarian Relations, 1988–1991." In *Lawful Revolution in Hungary, 1989–1994,* edited by Béla Király and András Bozóki, 395–411. Boulder, Colo.: Atlantic Research, 1995.

Szakolczai, Attila. "A forradalmat követő megtorlás során kivégzettekről." In *Évkönyv,* vol. 3, *1994,* edited by János Bak, András B. Hegedűs, György Litván, János M. Rainer, and Katalin S. Varga, 237–57. Budapest: 1956-os Intézet, 1994.

———. "Győr-Sopron megye." In *A vidék forradalma, 1956,* vol. 2, edited by Atilla Szakolczai, 141–210. Budapest: 1956-os Intézet–Budapest Főváros Levéltára, 2006.

Szerencsés, Károly. *A kékcédulás hadművelet. Választások Magyarországon 1947.* Budapest: IKVA Kiadó, 1992.

Szőke, Zoltán. "Delusion or Reality? Secret Hungarian Diplomacy during the Vietnam War." *Journal of Cold War Studies* 12 (Fall 2010): 119–80.

———. "Magyar békefenntartók Vietnamban." *Külpolitika* 5, no. 3–4 (1999): 149–75.

Szörényi, Attila. "Adalékok a Vogeler-ügy diplomáciatörténetéhez, 1949–1951." *Külügyi Szemle* 12, no. 1 (2013): 141–71.

———. "A brit–magyar diplomáciai kapcsolatok és a Sanders-ügy, 1949–1953." *Valóság* 49, no. (2006): 74–92.

Taubmann, William. *Khrushchev: The Man and His Era.* New York: W. W. Norton, 2003.

Thomas, Daniel C. *The Helsinki Effect: International Norms, Human Rights, and the Demise of Communism.* Princeton, N.J.: Princeton University Press, 2001.

Tischler, János. *"Hogy megcsendüljön minden gyáva fül." Lengyel–magyar közelmúlt.* Budapest: Jelenkor Kiadó–1956-os Intézet, 2003.

Tismaneanu, Vladimir. *Stalinism for All Seasons: A Political History of Romanian Communism.* Berkeley: University of California Press, 2003.

———, ed. *Stalinism Revisited: The Establishment of Communist Regimes in East Central Europe.* Budapest: Central European University Press, 2009.

Tőkés, Rudolf, *Hungary's Negotiated Revolution: Economic Reform, Social Change and Political Succession, 1956–1990.* Cambridge: Cambridge University Press, 1996.

"Történelmi utunk. A Munkabizottság állásfoglalása a jelen helyzet kialakulásának okairól." Special issue, *Társadalmi Szemle*, 1989.

Trachtenberg, Marc. *A Constructed Peace: The Making of the European Settlement, 1945–1963*. Princeton, N.J.: Princeton University Press, 1999.

Troen, S. I., and M. Shemesh, eds. *The Suez–Sinai Crisis 1956: Retrospective and Reappraisal*. London: Frank Cass, 1990.

Tucker, Robert C. "The Cold War in Stalin's Time." *Diplomatic History* 21 (Spring 1997): 273–82.

Tudda, Christopher. *The Truth Is Our Weapon: The Rhetorical Diplomacy of Dwight D. Eisenhower and John Foster Dulles*. Baton Rouge: Louisiana State University Press, 2006.

Ulam, Adam B. *Expansion and Coexistenc:; Soviet Foreign Policy, 1917–1973*. New York: Praeger, 1974.

Urbán, Károly. "Magyarország és a Varsói Szerződés létrejötte." *Társadalmi Szemle* 50, no. 11 (1995): 69–82.

Vámos, Péter. "Sino–Hungarian Relations and the 1956 Revolution." Working Paper No. 45, Cold War International History Project, Woodrow Wilson International Center for Scholars, Washington, D.C., 2006.

Varga, László. "Az ENSZ és a magyar forradalom." *História* 14, no. 8 (1992): 30–36.

Vida, István. *A Független Kisgazdapárt politikája 1944–1947*. Budapest: Akadémiai Kiadó, 1976.

Villaume, Poul, and Odd Arne Westad, eds. *Perforating the Iron Curtain: European Détente, Transatlantic Relations, and the Cold War, 1965–1985*. Copenhagen: Museum Tusculum Press, 2010.

Watts, Larry L. "Mediating the Vietnam War: Romania and the First Trinh Signal, 1965–1966." Working Paper No. 81, Cold War International History Project, Woodrow Wilson International Center for Scholars, Washington, D.C., 2016.

Wenger, Andreas, Vojtech Mastny, and Christian Nuenlist, eds. *Origins of the European Security System: The Helsinki Process Revisited, 1965–75*. London: Routledge, 2008.

Wentzke, Rüdiger. "The Role and Activities of the SED, the East German State and Its Military during the 'Prague Spring' of 1968." In *The Prague Spring and the Warsaw Pact Invasion of Czechoslovakia, 1968: Forty Years Later*, edited by M. Mark Stolarik, 137–64. Mundelein, Ill.: Bolchazy-Carducci, 2010.

Westad, Odd Arne, ed. *Brothers in Arms. The Rise and Fall of the Sino–Soviet Alliance, 1945–1963*. Washington, D.C.: Woodrow Wilson Center Press; Stanford, Calif.: Stanford University Press, 1998.

———. *The Cold War: A World History*. London: Allen Lane, 2017.

———. *The Global Cold War: Third World Interventions and the Making of Our Times*. Cambridge: Cambridge University Press, 2005.

———. "The Sino–Soviet Alliance and the United States." In *Brothers in Arms: The Rise and Fall of the Sino–Soviet Alliance, 1945–1963*, edited by Odd Arne Westad, 165–88. Washington, D.C.: Woodrow Wilson Center Press; Stanford, Calif.: Stanford University Press, 1998.

Westad, Odd Arne, Sven Holtsmark, and Ivor B. Neumann, eds. *The Soviet Union in East-Central Europe, 1945–1989*. New York: Palgrave Macmillan, 1994.

White, Brian. *Britain, Détente and Changing East–West Relations*. London: Routledge, 1992.

Williams, Kieran. *The Prague Spring and Its Aftermath: Czechoslovak Politics, 1968–1970.* Cambridge: Cambridge University Press, 1997.

Wintermantel, Péter. "A magyar–japán diplomáciai kapcsolatok felújításának története, 1945–1959." *Külügyi Szemle* 8, no. 2 (2009): 117–49.

Wynne, Greville Maynard. *The Man from Moscow: The Story of Wynne and Penkovsky.* London: Hutchinson, 1967.

Zhai, Qiang. "Beijing and the Vietnam Peace Talks, 1965–1968: New Evidence from Chinese Sources." Working Paper No. 18, Cold War International History Project, Woodrow Wilson International Center for Scholars, Washington, D.C., 1997.

Zubok, Vladislav M. *The Collapse. The fall of the Soviet Union.* New Haven: Yale University Press, 2021.

———. *Failed Empire: The Soviet Union in the Cold War from Stalin to Gorbachev.* Chapel Hill: University of North Carolina Press, 2007.

———. "Khrushchev and the Berlin Crisis, 1958–1962." Working Paper No. 6, Cold War International History Project, Woodrow Wilson International Center for Scholars, Washington, D.C., 1993.

———. "Soviet Foreign Policy from Détente to Gorbachev, 1975–1985." In *Endings*, edited by Melvyn Leffler and Odd Arne Westad, 89–111. Vol. 3 of *The Cambridge History of the Cold War.* Cambridge: Cambridge University Press. 2010.

———. "Soviet Policy Aims at the Geneva Conference of 1955." In *Cold War Respite: The Geneva Summit of 1955*, edited by Günter Bischof and Saki Dockrill, 55–74. Baton Rouge: Louisiana State University Press, 2000.

Zubok, Vladislav, and Constantine Pleshakov. *Inside the Kremlin's Cold War: From Stalin to Khrushchev.* Cambridge, Mass.: Harvard University Press, 1996.

Unpublished Dissertations and Manuscripts

Bange, Oliver. "Ostpolitik und Détente: Die Anfänge 1966–1969." Habil. thesis, University of Mannheim, 2004.

Baráth, Magdolna. "A 'csúcsról' szemlélve: a Szovjetunió és a magyarországi átmenet." Paper presented at the international conference "Political Transition in Hungary, 1989–1990." Budapest, 10–12 June, 1999.

Békés, Csaba. "Kísérletek a külföld felvilágosítására a párizsi béketárgyalások előtt." Doctoral diss., Szeged: József Attila Tudományegyetem, 1988.

Hegedüs, Gyula. "Magyar–angol kapcsolatok, 1944–1956." PhD diss., ELTE, Budapest, 2011.

Kiss, László J. "A Magyar Népköztársaság és a Német Szövetségi Köztársaság kapcsolatainak fejlődése, 1963–1975." Unpublished manuscript, 1976.

Marchio, David James. "Rhetoric and Reality: The Eisenhower Administration and Unrest in East-Central Europe, 1953–1959." PhD diss., University Microfilms International, 1992.

Park, Jungwon. "Conformity and Relative Autonomy in the Soviet Bloc: Hungary's Westward Policy since the 1956 Revolution." Diss., Budapest, 1994.

Urbán, Károly. "Sztálin haláltól a forradalom kitöréséig. A magyar–szovjet kapcsolatok története (1953–1956)." Unpublished manuscript, 1996.

Index

Bulganin, Nikolai: as chair of committee for military development, 62; Eisenhower's message to, 146; and Suez, 153, 157, 193; attempts to conciliate Tito, 78; official visit to Britain, 90

Bulgaria: 1944 capitulation, 19; approach to reform, 295, 306; bilateral agreement with Hungary, 63; Communist takeover, 39, 41, 42, 46, 64; and the FRG, 93, 184, 215, 238, 245; Joins the UN, 81; as less developed country, 215; and Paris Peace Conference, 33, 59; political stability, 279; as quasi-Sovietized, 34; share of Soviet influence, 20, 21; size of army, 61, 62; Soviet influence on removal of Chervenkov, 126; Soviet territorial interest, 26; troop withdrawals, 149, 175, 269

Bush, George, 273, 286, 287, 313

Canada, 210, 231, 252, 254, 263, 296
Carter, Jimmy, 259, 261, 270
Castro, Fidel, 185, 226
CCP, 195, 203
CDU/CSU, 302
Ceaușescu, Nicolae, 223, 226, 228, 229, 246, 293, 296, 310
CENTO, 85
Chamberlain, Neville, 22
Chervenkov, Valko, 61, 64, 125
China, 28, 61, 102, 244–46; Chinese offshore islands, 193; civil war, 27, 30; and the Hungarian Revolution, 132, 133, 135, 136, 163; Soviet relations, 191, 195, 203, 204, 208, 242, 243; Soviet territorial ambitions, 26; Vietnam, 222–24
Churchill, Winston, 18, 19, 20, 21, 44, 88, 200, 201
CIA, 141
COCOM, 67, 69, 214
Cold War: 1953–56 reduction of tension, 69, 71, 72, 89; and Afghanistan, 270; arms reduction, 276, 277, 285; atom bomb, 28, 77; and Berlin, 178, 182, 193; characteristics of, 24, 60, 69, 74, 75, 215, 269; crises, 192, 193; and Cuba, 185; and détente, 73, 268; early Cold War, 18, 21, 23, 44, 89; end

of, 313; and European security, 230; and Finland, 54; and the FRG, 260, 268; and Hungary, 68, 107, 137, 147; and NATO, 59; responsibility, 23–25, 27, 34; second phase, 82, 89, 110, 126; and Suez, 153; two-zones theory, 96

collective leadership, 75, 79, 197

Comecon, 176; bloc coordination, 182, 208, 213, 215, 292; end, 310, 313, 314; formation, 59, 60, 82; revival, 81, 85, 93, 96; summits217; trade with the West, 214; transformation, 292, 305, 306, 311

Cominform, 82, 85, 208; antecedents, 35, 44, 46; consolidating communist power, 47–49, 59; and Yugoslavia, 60, 66, 67

Comintern, 40, 41, 48, 64, 164, 199

compelled coexistence, 73, 75, 171, 172

conferences and summits: Belgrade (1977–78), 272; Bucharest (1948), 60; Bucharest (1966), 231, 232; Bucharest (1989), 296, 297; Budapest (1957), 166, 168; Budapest (1970), 254; Budapest (1989), 308; Budapest (1991), 313; Galyatető (1949), 60; Geneva Paris (1954), 86; Helsinki (1975), 235, 255, 256, 261; Karlovy Vary (1967), 233, 241; Madrid (1980–83), 272; Malta (1989), 286, 287, 313; Moscow (1944), 21; Moscow (1951), 60–63; Moscow (1952), 68, 69; Moscow (1954), 93; Moscow (1955), 73, 83, 88, 90, 99; Moscow (1958), 175; Moscow (1961), 181, 182; Moscow (1969), 253; Moscow (1990), 311, 312; Moscow (January 1956), 82, 92, 96, 97, 216; Moscow (October 1956), 125, 133; Paris, (1946), 33, 56, 57, 184; Potsdam (1945), 19, 31, 32, 33, 83, 84, 172; Prague (1956), 87; Prague (1969), 251; Prague (1972), 255; Prague (1991), 313; Rekyavik (1986), 286; Szklarska Poreba (1947), 49, 69; Tehran (1943), 18, 34; Vienna (1961), 178, 179; Warsaw (1965), 231; Warsaw (1967), 239; Yalta (1945), 18, 19, 21, 22. See also European security

constructive loyalty, 213, 256, 263

CPCz. See Czechoslovakia

floating the Brezhnev doctrine, 283, 294

Fock, Jenő, 237, 244

France, 18, 22, 48, 302; Hungarian relations, 99, 236, 302; local communists, 37, 47, 169; Soviet policy toward, 77; and Suez, 78, 138, 141–44, 146, 150, 152

FRG: border non-recognition, 83, 84, 233; contribution to Helsinki Agreement, 232; diplomatic relations with Soviet bloc, 238–47, 253; economic cooperation with satellite states, 108, 184, 185, 235; NATO membership, 83, 84, 300; relations with Hungary, 211, 215; target for better Soviet relations, 94; two-state acceptance, 232. *See also* Berlin; GDR

Garthoff, Raymond, 74

Gati, Charles, 147

GDR, 63, 64, 211, 234; 1958–61 crisis, 177–82, 187; border non-recognition, 83, 84, 230; as an economically developed state, 215, 235; and Hallstein Doctrine, 94; and Hungarian Revolution, 163; influence on Soviet policies, 184, 206; non-participation in Soviet-led invasion in 1968, 228; and Polish October, 132; presence of Soviet troops, 172, 188; relations with Hungary, 216; relations with the FRG, 230; as a security-concerned state, 184, 215; Warsaw Pact, 221

general staff (Warsaw Pact), 220

Genscher, Hans-Dietrich, 265, 313

Gerő, Ernő, 162, 226; "Gerő interregnum," 101, 102, 106, 125–27, 133; Soviet troops, 87; Translyvania, 57

Gheorghiu-Dej, Gheorghe, 57, 64, 124, 133

Gibiansky, Leonid, 47

Gomułka, Władisław, 64, 195, 226, 229, 238; and the Hungarian Revolution, 125, 128, 134; and the Polish October, 104–6, 133, 162; and the Warsaw Pact, 191, 246

Gorbachev, Mikhail, 194, 226, 273, 285; arms reduction, 278, 303; and Bush, 287; and Comecon, 305; and East Central Europe, 279, 280–84; end of the Cold War, 268,

285; foreign policy, 276, 299, 308, 310; and Hungary, 292–94, 300, 304, 305; and Reagan, 286, 289; and Soviet economic crisis, 260, 275; superpower rapprochement, 75, 268, 281, 291; troop withdrawals, 277, 303; and Warsaw Pact, 302, 308–13; and Western European leaders, 290

Gottwald, Klement, 40, 66

Great Britain, 51, 56, 65, 80, 210; Greville Wynne case, 190; improved relations with Hungary, 98, 154; lack of reaction to Hungarian revolution, 150; meeting between Thatcher and Gorbachev, 290; opposition to electoral fraud, 39, 50; Sanders case, 68–70, 98; Soviet rapprochement, 77; Soviet control expectations, 20, 21, 22; 50; Suez crisis, 78, 88, 138, 141–45, 151; Trieste, 33; visit by Khrushchev and Bulganin, 90

Grechko, Andrei, 183, 187, 188

Greece, 21, 27, 29, 30, 47, 84, 148, 188, 210

Gromyko, Andrei, 253, 267

Grósz, Károly: compared with Gyula Horn, 294; disputes with Romania, 292, 293, 296; intervention in FRG-Soviet talks, 281, 308; lectured by Gorbachev, 283, 308; and Soviet troops withdrawal, 305

Groza, Petru, 46, 52, 56

Guatemala, 153

Gyöngyösi, János, 56

Hallstein Doctrine, 94, 238

Hammarskjöld, Dag, 122

hard communists, 226

Harmel Report, 233

Havel, Václav, 313

HCP, HWP. *See* Hungary

Heinemann, Gustav, 243

Helsinki: Agreement, 88; Conference, 235, 255, 256; human rights campaign, 261; process, 260, 262, 288; "second Helsinki," 308

Helsinki Final Act, 71, 76, 83, 172, 222, 232, 241, 256–59, 261, 308

Ho Chi Minh, 224, 225

Honecker, Erich, 265

Horn, Gyula, 263, 264, 267, 294, 296, 297, 299, 304, 308

Horthy, Miklós, 19

Horváth, Imre, 102

human rights, 259, 261, 286, 305; and Helsinki Final Act, 255, 261, 272, 296; violations, 272, 296

Hungary: 1945 election, 39, 40; with Austria, 95, 99, 210, 250, 252; border issues and treatment of ethnic Hungarians, 25, 33, 51–57, 161; with Britain, 68–70, 98, 99, 108, 145; capitulation, 18–20; Communist takeover, 38–43, 45, 46, 48–59, 63; Council of Europe, 308; and CSCE, 251–55, 274, 308; Cuban crisis, 187–89, 191; foreign relations with Soviet Union, 56, 71, 80, 119, 123, 195, 264–67, 292–95; and the FRG, 94, 183–85, 211, 215, 235, 238, 241, 249, 256, 259, 267, 273, 290, 307, 308; Hungarian Revolution, 71, 80, 95, 104, 106–39, 142, 148, 156, 160, 161, 170, 192; and impact on western public opinion, 149–51, 151, 154, 155, 157–60; multilateralism and Soviet bloc, 162, 163, 167; multi-party system, 165–67, 286, 301; Prague Spring and Soviet-led invasion, 225–29, 297–98; size of army, 62, 183; Smallholders' Party, 38, 42, 51, 53, 54; Soviet troops, 78, 85, 87, 109, 115, 116, 118, 125, 129, 173, 303–05, 310; on third world, 152, 155; tripartite determinism, 212–15; troop withdrawals, 172–75; and the UN, 81, 108, 109, 114, 115, 120, 122–24, 142–46, 151, 154, 210; with United States, 67, 68, 70, 98, 99–101, 138, 139, 141, 146, 152, 153, 156, 210, 211, 261, 263, 287; and Warsaw Pact, 78–82, 85–87, 91, 92, 94, 95, 97–104, 106–39, 141–70, 172–76, 180–85, 187, 202, 204–18, 220, 222–36, 240, 250, 268, 295–97, 301, 311–14; World Bank/IMF, 273, 308; and Yugoslavia, 66, 67, 98

HWP. See Hungary

Iceland, 210

IMF, 28, 110

Indochina, 71, 77, 81, 223, 269. See also Vietnam

interdependence, 71, 72, 262, 268

Iran, 24, 25, 29, 269

Israel, 143, 144, 153, 244, 245, 321, 322

Italy, 24, 25, 27, 34, 274, 288; CSCE consultations, 252; Hungarian diplomacy, 210, 304; local communist party, 32, 37, 47, 49, 169. See also Trieste

Jannuzzi, Giovanni, 302

Japan, 18, 19, 24–26, 28, 29, 32, 33, 176; Hungarian involvement in Soviet rapprochement, 101, 102; opening of Hungarian embassy, 210

Jaruzelski, Wojciech, 126, 226, 313

Johnson, Lyndon B., 125, 147, 210, 211, 222

Kádár, János, 154, 291; and 1957 Soviet bloc "tribunal," 164, 167; and China, 203–4, 209, 223, 246; and Cuban crisis, 188–91, 217; Euromissile crisis, 274; European security, 243–45; foreign policy, 205, 207, 209, 211–15, 217, 226, 250; and the FRG, 183, 241, 256, 267, 268, 273; Helsinki Final Act, 258; and Hungarian Revolution, 109, 117, 119, 122, 134, 151; and Khrushchev, 127, 174; mediation between Prague and Moscow in 1968, 226–29; mediation in the Vietnam war, 224; and military expenditure, 173; Polish crisis, 273, 274; post-revolution policies, 154, 155, 157; as prime minister again, 183, 184; promoting foreign travel, 257; quarrel with the Soviets, 265–67; and Rákosi, 202–3; removal, 293; and removal of Khrushchev, 193–95, 197, 199–202, 204, 209; selected as PM in Moscow, 131; Soviet troop withdrawals, 174, 175; and Tito, 158, 165; on Trianon, 257; Warsaw Pact, 176, 196, 218–22, 242, 253, 256

Kádár doctrine, 193, 199, 267

Kállai, Gyula, 189, 222

Kalmár, Melinda, 167, 209, 285

Kania, Stanisław, 226, 229

Kardelj, Edvard, 135

Rankovic, Alexandar, 135
Ravndal, Christian, 100
Reagan, Ronald, 270, 285, 286, 288, 289
Red Army, 19–21, 34, 35, 153
Révai, József, 52, 57, 71
Rogers, William P., 261
Rokossovsky, Konstantin, 61
Romania, 44, 191, 279, 285, 303; absence
    from Warsaw Pact meetings, 227, 274;
    armed forces, 62; bypassing parliament,
    37; capitulation, 19, 20; conservatism, 283,
    295; deviant policy, 190, 192, 206, 218, 221,
    229, 276; easing intra-bloc travel, 97, 102;
    in East-West relations, 237, 238; as an
    economy-oriented state, 184, 215, 235;
    election-rigging, 40, 48; and European
    security, 243–46, 248–53, 255, 256; and
    the FRG, 94, 184, 190, 215, 232, 238, 239;
    friendship and cooperation agreements
    with bloc states, 59, 63; and the GDR,
    239; and the Hungarian Revolution, 124,
    132, 133, 158, 161, 163–66; Hungarian
    territorial demands, 33, 51–57; involve-
    ment in Ferenc Nagy's arrest, 58; loss of
    foreign prestige, 272; nationalism, 41; and
    Polish crisis, 273; Prague Spring and
    Soviet-led invasion, 228, 242; quasi-
    Sovietized state, 34; relations with
    Hungary, 216, 292, 293, 295–97, 299;
    relations with the Soviet Union, 212, 213,
    215; Soviet aid to local communists, 42;
    Soviet occupation, 21; Soviet perceptions
    of Georghiu-Dej, 64; Soviet troop
    withdrawal, 85, 87, 118, 148, 161, 172–75;
    suppression of opposition parties and
    leaders, 45, 46; territorial adjustments
    with the Soviet Union, 22, 26, 33, 34; and
    the UN, 84; and Warsaw Pact bloc
    cooperation, 78, 87, 206, 217–22, 301;
    western allies' influence, 20
Roosevelt, Franklin Delano, 18, 19, 21
Rostow, Walt, 180
Rühe, Volker, 302
Rusk, Dean, 225
Rykov, Alexei, 80
Ryzhkov, Nikolai, 260

Sanders, Edgar, 68–70, 98
Schmidt, Helmut, 261, 263, 265, 267, 273
SDI, 278, 285, 286, 288
SEATO, 85
Serov, Ivan, 128, 134, 135, 137
Shepilov, Dmitry, 130
Shevardnadze, Eduard, 276, 281
show trials, 65, 66, 68, 107
SIOP, 170
Široký, Villiam, 134
Sobolev, Arkady, 124
soft Communists, 226
Soviet foreign policy, 24, 83; Active Foreign
    Policy, 92; bilateralism, 81; changes after
    Stalin's death, 76–78; collapse, 71, 151, 259,
    260, 278, 289, 311; comintern, 44;
    Hungarian miscalculation, 56; invasion
    of Afghanistan, 193, 262, 267, 270–73;
    military intervention in Hungary, 80, 115,
    125, 127, 170, 187, 283; nuclear arms, 185,
    186, 302, 305; overreach, 275, 278; postwar
    policy, 27; relations with Japan, 101; two
    zones theory, 96; with satellites, 54.
    See also Andropov, Yuri; Brezhnev,
    Leonid; Gorbachev, Mikhail; Khrush-
    chev, Nikita; Stalin, Joseph
Sputnik, 150, 153, 209
Stalin, Joseph, 80, 82; atomic bomb, 28;
    Comecon, 60; Cominform, 46–49;
    death, 72, 75, 76, 82, 89–92; on East-
    West relations, 61–63, 69; and Ferenc
    Nagy cabinet, 49, 54, 56, 58; and
    Germany, 31, 32; motivations, 25–27,
    60; mutual suspicion, 28–30, 35; and
    NATO, 59; and Rákosi, 62, 64–67;
    Sovietization, 33–36; at Tehran, 18–21;
    territorial gains, 22–24; undermining
    democracy, 38–46, 58, 59
Standard Electric, 68
Stassen, Harold E., 139, 140
stealthy revolution, 36, 40, 43
Stevenson, Adlai, 15
Šubašić, Ivan, 46
Suez crisis, 71; absence of Soviet military
    military involvement, 78; boost to Soviet
    propaganda in the third world, 78, 83,

USSR: and Berlin crisis, 177–81; cooperation with Hungary in the European
security process (1964–75), 213–58; and
Cuban missile crisis, 185–88, 190–92; and
De-Stalinization in East Central Europe
(1953–56), 78–85, 92–98; and East-West
crisis in 1980, 264–68; and the Euromissile crisis, 274; and Hungarian peace
treaty, 53–57; and Polish revolt (1956),
105–6; and political transition in East
Central Europe (1981–91), 275–85; and
revolution in Hungary (1956), 94–98,
113–37; and Sovietization in East Central
Europe (1945–49), 33–46; and Stalinism
in East Central Europe (1949–53), 60–66;
troop withdrawals, 172–76, 276. *See also*
Andropov, Yuri; Brezhnev, Leonid;
Gorbachev, Mikhail; Khrushchev, Nikita;
Stalin, Joseph
Soviet foreign policy
U Thant, 189, 210

Vásárhelyi, Miklós, 57
Vasilyevsky, Alexander, 61
Vass, Zoltán, 65
Vatican, 210
Vietnam, 147, 193, 211, 222–25, 243, 269
Vishinsky, Andrei, 56
Vogeler, Robert, 68, 69
Voroshilov, Kliment, 38, 39, 50

Ward, Sir John, 142
Warsaw Pact, and Afghanistan, 262, 263;
Berlin crisis, 179, 190–91; debate on
Czechoslovak intervention, 163, 167;
disarmament, 298, 304; dissolution, 310,
311, 313, 314; economic crisis, 276;
establishment according to NATO's
organizational framework, 85; European
security, 230–32, 241, 246, 252, 255, 310;
foreign policy coordination, 216–18, 233,
243; German question, 238; Hungary's
attempted withdrawal, 116–123; internal
conflicts, 94, 192, 213, 221, 222, 238, 240,

253, 295, 350; military reform, 220, 292,
300–304; as NATO's lethal enemy, 74,
271, 273; October 1956 summit, 33–135;
Polish crisis, 271; Prague Spring, 167, 227,
228; rationale, 78, 81–86, 93
Weinstock, Louis, 65
Willman, Adam, 119
World Bank, 28, 273, 308
World War I, 24, 25, 51, 257, 275
World War II, 18, 22, 24, 25, 47, 50, 51, 59, 74,
76–78, 82, 88, 90, 94, 99, 101, 108, 153, 170,
178, 188, 192, 211, 223, 230, 233, 234, 237,
240, 243, 269, 275, 288
Wynne, Greville, 190

Yakovlev, Alexander, 292
Yugoslavia: attempts at Soviet reconciliation,
79, 97, 129; briefing on plans for dealing
with Hungary, 132, 133; Council of Europe
special observer, 298; communist political
strengths, 39; 41; Danube Valley cooperation, 256; defense pact with Soviet Union,
59; émigrés in postwar politics, 38; end
of closed border with Hungary, 275;
expulsion from Soviet bloc, 60; fears
of Poland and Hungary as "Second
Yugoslavias," 105, 106, 109, 113, 116, 119,
121; Hungarian cooperation agreement,
63; indecision on position over Hungary,
158; proposed invitee to communist
summit, 159; quasi-Sovietized state, 34;
relations with Hungary, 163; renewed
deterioration in Soviet relations, 159;
Soviet-Western share in influence, 20;
territorial claims by Hungary, 51;
territorial claims on Italy and Austria,
27; Trieste dispute; Yugoslav socialist
road, 86, 90, 91. *See also* Tito, Josip
Broz

Zagladin, Vadim, 267
Zhdanov doctrine, 49, 96
Zhukov, Georgy, 140, 154
Zinoviev, Gregory, 80

CPSIA information can be obtained
at www.ICGtesting.com
Printed in the USA
LVHW100005180522
719011LV00018B/127